Flower of the Soul

Selected Writings of a Rosicrucian Mystic

Raymund Andrea, FRC

Published by: The Rosicrucian Collection®
               Greenwood Gate, Blackhill
               Crowborough TN6 1XE
               United Kingdom.

               Tel: +44-(0)1892-653197
               Fax: +44-(0)1892-667432
               Email: sales@amorc.org.uk
               UK Website: www.amorc.org.uk
               International Website: www.amorc.org

Copyright: The Supreme Grand Lodge of AMORC, Inc.
               © 2009, All Rights Reserved

ISBN-13:   978-0952642-06-0

All rights reserved. No part of this publication may be reproduced, stored in any retrieval system or transmitted in any form or by any means, electronic, mechanical, photocopying, recording or otherwise, without the permission of the copyright holder.

Printed and bound in Great Britain by Athenaeum Press Ltd

Dedicated in memory of

ELLEN TURNBULL

Whose tireless dissemination of the writings of

RAYMUND ANDREA

was an inspiration to the compilers of this book.

Raymund Andrea (1882-1975)

Contents

Foreword 11

Raymund Andrea (21 July 1882 - 22 July 1975) 13

Section 1: Early Writings of Herbert Adams
          The Occult Review (1919-1928)
          The Theosophist (1921-1922)

      Introduction 21
1. The Occult Life 21
2. Wagner and Occultism 25
3. The Future of Occultism 28
4. The Pain of Development 30
5. The Occultist and His Critics 32
6. Theosophy and Anti-Christianity 36
7. The Novitiate 39
8. The Tibetan Messenger 42
9. Self-Knowledge 46
10. The Science of Death 50
11. The Light of the Soul 54

Section 2: The Mystic Triangle (1927)

      Introduction 59
1. The Rosicrucian Order in Great Britain 59
2. The Theosophical World Teacher 62
3. Spiritualism, the Church and Ourselves 65
4. The Comte de Gabalis 70
5. The Technique of the Master (1927) 77
6. The Rosicrucian Manual: An Appreciation 84
7. Reflections on the Third Temple
    (Postulant) Grade: Article 1 85

Flower of the Soul - Selected Writings of a Rosicrucian Mystic

Section 3: The Mystic Triangle (1928)

1. Reflections on the Third Temple (Postulant) Grade: Article 2............93
2. Reflections on the Third Temple (Postulant) Grade: Article 3............96
3. Reflections on the Third Temple (Postulant) Grade: Article 4..........100
4. Yone Noguchi, Poet and Mystic..105
5. The Rosicrucian Order, Past and Present 111
6. The Comte de St Germain 115
7. Three Years in Tibet..121
8. Raymund Lully..., Eminent Rosicrucian Master.............................129
9. The Rosicrucian Order and Cooperation 136

Section 4: The Mystic Triangle (1929)

1. Bulwer-Lytton 141
2. The Technique of the Master (1929) 150
3. Waiting for the Master..156
4. Lafcadio Hearn's "Karma" 161
5. Occult Initiative 168
6. Roger Bacon, The Rosicrucian 172
7. The White Brother...178

Section 5: The Rosicrucian Digest (1929 - 1935)

Introduction..189
1. To Me, Jesus is All in All 189
2. Paracelsus, the Rosicrucian 193
3. Love's Apotheosis 200
4. Are We Abnormal? 202
5. The Dark Night of the Soul 208
6. The Science of Seership..213
7. Lodge Masters and Activities 216
8. The Rosicrucian Technique: A Word to the Critics........................219
9. The Technique of the Disciple 223

Section 6: The Modern Mystic and Monthly Science Review (1937 - 1947)

Introduction..229
1. The Guiding Hand 229
2. The Mystical Novitiate..232

    3. On The Mystic Path 237
    4. The Three Wise Men 240
    5. Crises In Development 246

Section 7: Messages to Members (1931 - 1945)

    Introduction 253
    1. Letter to Members (Christmas 1931) 253
    2. Letter to Members (28 August 1940) 254
    3. Letter to Members (18 December 1940) 256
    4. Letter to Members (3 April 1941) 258
    5. Letter to Members (4 August 1941) 260
    6. Letter to Members (18 December 1941) 262
    7. Letter to Members (10 June 1942) 265
    8. Letter to Members (December 1942) 266
    9. Letter to Members (20 April 1943) 271
    10. Letter to Members (December 1943) 273
    11. Letter to Members (December 1944) 277
    12. Letter to Members (December 1945) 283

Section 8: The Rosicrucian Digest (1939 - 1945)

    1. Rosicrucians and World Affairs 289
    2. A Task for Rosicrucians 293
    3. A Message from the Grand Master of Great Britain 298
    4. Ambition or Stagnation 300
    5. World Catastrophe and Responsibility 306
    6. The Hour of Trial 313

Section 9: Selected Correspondence (1932 - 1964)

    Introduction 319
    1. Address to the Francis Bacon Chapter by Jessie Kenney (July 1960).319
    2. Letter to Jessie Kenney (24 March 1933) 320
    3. Letter to Jessie Kenney (11 July 1934) 321
    4. Letter to Jessie Kenney (17 October 1935) 321
    5. Letter to Jessie Kenney (22 June 1936) 322
    6. Letter to Jessie Kenney (26 September 1938) 323
    7. Letter to Jessie Kenney (25 May 1959) 324

8. Letter to Ellen Kirkpatrick (9 December 1939) 325
9. Letter to Ellen Kirkpatrick (5 June 1950) 325
10. Letter to Ellen Kirkpatrick (10 March 1955) 326
11. Extract from letter to Ellen Kirkpatrick (27 January 1962) 328
12. Extract from letter to Ellen Kirkpatrick (24 July 1962) 328
13. Extract from letter to Ellen Kirkpatrick (9 January 1964) 329
14. Extracts from various letters to Ellen Kirkpatrick 330

Section 10: The Rosicrucian Digest (1946-1957)

Introduction 335
1. The Atomic Bomb and Ourselves 335
2. The Sanctity of Work 341
3. The Rejected Gift 350
4. The Divine Experiment 354
5. The World Shadow 361
6. Thus Spake Zarathustra 367
7. Idealism in Practice 371
8. The Irredeemable Moment 375
9. Facing the Truth 380
10. A Prophet of the Times 385

Section 11: The London Rosicrucian (1952 - 1961)

Introduction 397
1. Recorded Message to the first Rosicrucian Rally in Great Britain - 3 August 1952 397
2. From the Grand Master's Sanctum 399
3. Our Need to Cultivate the Art of Reflection 401
4. The Magical Power of Thought 402
5. Discipleship on Trial 404
6. Perspectives of Progress 406
7. That Frustration is a Good 408
8. The Tibetan Tragedy 410
9. Men Learn Most by the Negative Way 411
10. Minds: Ancient and Modern 413
11. The Cult of the Average 416
12. Anxious Aspirants 419
13. Advance or Retreat? 421
14. Birthday Message to Francis Bacon Chapter 423

Contents

    15. Brains: East and West 424
    16. Impersonality 427

Section 12: Writings of Unspecified Date

Introduction 433
1. A Word of Encouragement 433
2. Human Identification 434
3. A Word to the Neophyte 436
4. The Unseen Influences of our Rosicrucian Studies 437

Section 13: Francis Bacon Chapter Bulletin (1963 - 1973)

Introduction 443
1. Seeking Ourselves 443
2. Towards the Ideal 444
3. Loneliness 446
4. Mind Quest and Soul Vision 447
5. The Critical Decision 449
6. The Word of the Prophet 451
7. Master and Members 452
8. The Potency of the Word 453
9. Mystical Neophytism 454
10. Mystical Ascension 459
11. The Problem of the Neophyte 463
12. The Time for Decision 464
13. Reading and Being 465

In Memoriam 467

Alphabetical List of Selected Writings and Letters 471

Index 477

The Rosicrucian Order 487

Rosicrucians and Mysticism 490

FOREWORD

This book brings together many of the reflections of Raymund Andrea (1882-1975) on aspects of the mystical life, of which he said: "*The mystical life perfects itself in the deep silences of our nature. It is the flower of the soul.*"[1] This quote epitomises the central message of his life's work, the flowering and maturing within the human breast of the personality of soul itself. It is also the source of the title of this book.

The author is remembered for his comprehensive works on mysticism such as *The Technique of the Master*, *The Technique of the Disciple*, and *The Mystic Way*.[2] But he also wrote many shorter pieces of which nearly 100, originally published in various periodicals between 1919 and 1973, are contained in this book. Also included are samples of his letters to members of the Rosicrucian Order, in which he served as the Grand Master of Great Britain for 26 years.

Sixteen lectures which were published in 1996 have been excluded as they are available under the title of *The Way of the Heart*.[3] Another collection of Raymund Andrea's writings, *Waiting For The Master*, was issued to mark the centenary of his birth. This is out of print but its contents are included here, except for three chapters which are contained in *The Way of the Heart*.

The author was clearly a man of compassion who felt that true mysticism should embrace a deepening of the *"life of the heart"* and include acts of service to one's fellow human beings. But in contrast to these gentle qualities, he adopted, perhaps surprisingly, a trenchant tone of writing when the circumstances warranted it. He explained this in a message to a group of Rosicrucians in 1961:[4]

> "My mission, if I may call it that, was to challenge and agitate and cut across some of the old-time accepted thinking about our studies and the path. In that sense, I have been directly critical and an intentional destroyer of many accepted and complacent views which I knew meant stagnation instead of advancement, and therefore could only prove unhelpful."

Andrea wrote in the style and manner of his day, which in 21st Century terms may seem old-fashioned. But his writings are truly timeless, motivated as they are by a deep concern for humanity and the quest for greater spiritual self-realisation. With the advent in recent decades of many new paths of spirituality, some of the terms he used are either out of favour, not understood, or have been assigned new meanings. Foremost amongst these is the word "occult," which he uses frequently. During the time of his most prolific writing in the 1920s and 30s, the word "occult" referred to matters of a purely spiritual

---

1. See Section 3, Chapter 4: *Reflections on the Third Temple (Postulant) Grade*.
2. *The Mystic Way*, *The Technique of the Master* and *The Technique of the Disciple* are available from the publisher.
3. *The Way of the Heart* is available from the publisher.
4. See *Birthday Message* in Section 11.

nature and of high moral integrity, things that in today's world we would happily refer to respectfully with the simpler term: "spirituality." When writing of the occult, the author used the word reverentially, always with its earlier meaning of sanctity and self-realisation, and never with even a hint of the interpretation that has been placed on it in more recent times, namely, as something strange, dangerous, a bit unbalanced or even malevolent. Read through his words and absorb the feelings of a man who was deeply attuned to the spiritual pulse of the ages and left us with this wonderful legacy.

As a Rosicrucian, Andrea used terminology which continues to be used in Rosicrucian circles today. Foremost among these are the terms "fratres and sorores" meaning simply "brothers and sisters" [of the Rosicrucian Order]. In other places you will encounter names such as "benefactor," "divinitrix," and others, most of which are pseudonyms for certain Rosicrucians who assisted in his work, though annonymously and under the cloak of secrecy.

As the compilers of this book, we would like to thank Julie Sanchez-Parodi, the librarian of the English Grand Lodge for the Americas of the Rosicrucian Order, for bringing to light many articles from old editions of the *Rosicrucian Digest*. We are also indebted to the Library of the Theosophical Society, and Geraldine Beskin of Atlantis Bookshop [London], for their help in researching various publications in which Andrea published his earlier articles. Several members of the Rosicrucian Order also provided material for this edition and their contributions are gratefully acknowledged. Special thanks go to Ed Davies and Ken Alexander for their valuable advice and assistance.

But there was as well a small group of dedicated Rosicrucians who worked under tight deadlines to proofread and perfect the various manuscripts that went into this compilation, and formost among them were two people without whom the book would never have been compiled. In the spirit of humility and anonymity expressed by Raymund Andrea on so many occasions, these silent workers have expresssed their wishes to remain anonymous.

Biography

RAYMUND ANDREA
(21 July 1882 - 22 July 1975)

Edited from the Francis Bacon Lodge *publication* "Waiting For The Master" *(1982), published on the centenary of the birth of Raymund Andrea.*

There is little to say about the life of Raymund Andrea, but much to be said about his work. Little is known about his earlier life, for he seldom spoke about himself. From the beginning of his stewardship of the Rosicrucian Order in Great Britain in 1921, he shunned any kind of ostentation or publicity, regarding both as completely unnecessary. When asked to talk about himself, he would say: *"You will find me in my books; what do outward appearances matter?"* However, one can piece together certain aspects and details of his life, both from the occasional article in the *Rosicrucian Forum*[1] and from remarks dropped by himself during recorded conversations and in his frequent letters.

He was born as Herbert Adams in Bristol, England on 21 July 1882, a little over a year before the birth of his mentor and Imperator of the Rosicrucian Order of later years, Dr Harvey Spencer Lewis. Bristol remained his home throughout his life, but his early years were ones of struggle and hardship, and upon leaving school he was compelled by circumstances to work for long hours on low wages. It was only some time later that he secured a post as a clerk in a solicitor's office and as a consequence, in the course of his duties he came into contact with people in the higher walks of life..., literary and professional men and women who by their bearing and savoir-faire made a profound impression on the youth. The environment in which he found himself was therefore favourable for the early development of his hitherto latent talents, which quickly began to make themselves felt. He read assiduously, particularly the biographies of the famous, and drew inspiration from the descriptions of their lives and ideals.

His retiring and reticent nature was dropped once in a fiery defence of the Rosicrucian Order against its critics who, being content wholly with spiritual abstractions, accused it of being too practical. In *The Rosicrucian Digest* of July 1932 he emphasised the particular value of "The Rosicrucian Technique"[2] when applied to daily life and illustrated his argument as follows:

> "One of the reasons why the declaration [by the Imperator[3]] on Rosicrucianism as an art and a science, not a religious philosophy, struck a deep chord of sympathy within me, was because it took me back in mind some 12 years, when I commenced active work for the Order in Great Britain. I had from youth been an ardent student of philosophy, Theosophy and the occult, and the time had arrived when a large body of mystical truth and

---

1. The *Rosicrucian Forum* is a private magazine for members of the Rosicrucian Order which began in 1930 and is still [2009] published quarterly by the publisher.
2. This article appears in Section 5.
3. The Imperator (chief executive officer) of the Rosicrucian Order in North America at the time was Dr Harvey Spencer Lewis.

awakening past experience demanded expression in a truly active sphere of service. I was equipped, far more than I knew, for active service over a wide field in other lives. I sought this above all things. I had made many sacrifices to fit myself for this service during a period of nearly 20 years. My case was analogous, to some small degree, to that of Roger Bacon. I had knowledge, but not a single door would open to a sphere where it could be applied to practical and useful ends. I remember the keen disappointment I felt as I approached one Theosophical leader after another in the hope that in their wide contacts and personal influence I might find some opportunity of giving back that which the Masters had given me. Every effort I made failed.

"There are those it seems, who decry the fact that the Rosicrucian Order should condescend to advertise itself. Well, I am a notorious example..., whatever its value may be..., of one who contacted the Order through an advertisement and found a sphere of labour for which I have ever been grateful. When I first wrote to the Imperator he immediately recognised the applicant through profound psychic prescience. He recognised my associations with the Order and its work in past cycles. He bridged the chasm of lives for me, formed a link between the two, and brought me into active cooperation with students, old and new, who are recognised pioneers in many countries. This man had the prescience to see and the generosity to act immediately."

In his letter to Dr Lewis, Mr Adams had asked for further details and offered his help in any way possible. Dr Lewis had replied immediately saying, rather surprisingly, that he had been waiting for him *"to make his appearance,"* charged him with the task of re-opening the Order in the United Kingdom and enclosed the Grand Seal of the Order for his use. He was also told that henceforth his name in the Order would be *Raymund Andrea*. To quote Andrea:

"His [Dr Lewis'] letter presented to me the broad, firm outline of what the inauguration meant and what it would entail; the only condition being that I should become a servant of the Order and leave everything else to find its proper place. That is how my real life started."

In 1921 Dr Lewis granted an official charter appointing Andrea Grand Master and Deputy Inspector General of Great Britain. Some years later Dr Lewis wrote in a discourse on the subject of the Masters that *"probably the greatest living Rosicrucian is the Grand Master of England, Raymund Andrea."* But from the beginning, Andrea remained always in the background, yet found many willing and earnest helpers to carry out his wishes.

Raymund Andrea married in 1926 and his wife Clara assisted him in his chosen life's work, ever being a source of solace to him and giving her unstinting support until her death in 1966. Andrea's love and specialised knowledge of music gave added richness and profound pleasure to his leisure moments. His superlative mental gifts found expression in the numerous works on mysticism and philosophy which are acknowledged masterpieces in their genre. He was deeply versed in both Eastern and Western philosophies as a result of his wide and intensive study of various systems of mystical and religious belief and practice, and was therefore able to pronounce authoritatively and with acute vision on these subjects in all their aspects.

His perennial interest in the nature of genius resulted in a thorough study of what he called the "mastermind." From thence *"...it was but a short step to a belief in the perfected, spiritual genius,"* the servant of the supreme Master.

> "I endeavoured to apply, although perhaps imperfectly, the laws of the technique observable in the master minds to the technique of the Masters..., as both derive from the plane of divine inspiration."

This may account for the originality of Andrea's works, particularly in view of his keen insight into his personal experiences. He began writing his books almost by accident. When attending a banquet, Dr Lewis casually said to him..., *"you should write a book."* And he did! First came *The Technique of the Master,* followed by *The Technique of the Disciple* three years later. And in response to requests for yet more enlightenment on the path, he wrote *The Mystic Way*.[4]

During World War II Raymund Andrea found it impossible to continue the regular activities of the Rosicrucian Order in his jurisdiction. As a consequence, the recently installed Imperator of the Order for North and South America, Ralph Maxwell Lewis, decreed that the Grand Lodge, based in San Jose, California, would assume the responsibility of extending all study services to members throughout the United Kingdom, the costs being covered by donations from American members. However, Andrea sustained members with his writings and private letters, including an annual letter he sent to all members each Christmas. In the last of these, written in 1945, he writes, *"The war of arms is ended, now begins the war of minds."*[5] And of his opinion of the postwar world he left no doubt, calling it an *"...age of lost values and spiritual decadence."*

In 1946 Imperator Ralph Lewis undertook a 'mission to Europe' (see *Rosicrucian Digest* October 1946 to May 1947) to encourage and revitalise the surviving members of various Rosicrucian jurisdictions in Europe. He met Raymund Andrea in London where they discussed the future of the Order in Britain. Due to a common language, heritage and ideals, it was felt that the two jurisdictions should exemplify the Order's principles by working in unity. The American jurisdiction would continue to distribute written study material directly to members in the United Kingdom while Andrea would supervise the formation of new member groups [in the form of Lodges and Chapters] drawn from

---

4. *The Technique of the Master, The Technique of the Disciple* and *The Mystic Way* are available from the publisher.
5. This Message appears in Section 7.

previous groups of individual Rosicrucians who had met informally for years. Now, some 65 years later, we can look back and see the great progress that has been achieved as a result of this momentous decision.

Raymund Andrea's postwar books ventured into new ground. *Discipleship on Trial* and its sequel, *The Disciple and Shamballa* consider the heightened life of a disciple who has been accepted by and is cooperating with the higher spiritual forces [referred to as 'Masters' by Andrea] which guide and encourage humanity to ever greater forms of spirituality and self-realisation. In addition, six sketches of the lives of distinguished mystics of the past were published under the title *Six Biographical Sketches*.[6]

Raymund Andrea has a peculiar style of writing that to some appears pompous, to others unintelligible, but to many is a source of deep inspiration. For many, it is precisely his style of writing that inspires them so deeply and when reading his works for the first time, it is best to adjust oneself inwardly from the start and try and move one's mind into the mindset and times of the writer. And above all, it is important to read his writings in the tone and at the pace at which they were meant to be read, namely, deliberately and thoughtfully. A respected Rosicrucian once remarked to Andrea that his books are difficult to read at times because of their long sentences. He replied, "*I had no choice, they are Master books and must follow the rhythm. Let the rhythm into your inner self and you will get the true vibration.*"

In 1958 by special request of Imperator Ralph Lewis, all recognised Rosicrucian groups in Britain[7] were asked to honour retired Grand Master Andrea on the occasion of his birthday each year.[8] This special ceremony was held until Andrea passed away on 22 July 1975, the day after his 93rd birthday! During the later years of his life, the work done by Raymund Andrea was accomplished primarily on the inner planes, though he still carried on a prolific correspondence with his many friends in the Order, wrote many articles, and recorded many of his discourses.

A special memorial ceremony in honour of Andrea was held by Francis Bacon Lodge of the Rosicrucian Order on 14 August 1975. It was led by Imperator Ralph Lewis and tributes were paid in person by the Grand Masters of France [Raymond Bernard] and of the Netherlands [Van Drenthem Soesman]. One of his students from pre-war days, Ellen Turnbull, shared with members some of the letters which he had written to her throughout that period of nearly 50 years and a few of these are reproduced in this book. She said that of himself, Raymund Andrea once wrote:

> "I have been a close student of the best and often the most difficult in all kinds of literature.
> In fact, I have lived almost entirely within the influence of these masters of the past, for there is nothing in the present to approach them. Today these inner things are pushed

---

6. *Discipleship On Trial, The Disciple and Shamballa* and *Six Biographical Sketches* (now published as *Six Eminent Mystics*) are available from the publisher.
7. At the time, these member groups were organised into what were called *Chapters* and *Pronaoi*.
8. Raymund Andrea retired as Grand Master of Great Britain in 1947.

into the background. People are just not ready for them and cannot stand them. Perhaps the political and general chaos of the national life is partly responsible for it. But there will be a striking reaction to all this, not in my day, but probably before the end of the century."

The 20th century has passed and many seekers of greater spiritual realisation would concur with the view that the world, despite the many brutal conflicts it has endured in recent years, is still a better place, and at the very least, a place where untold millions of people yearn for deeper values in life, and are seeking broader and more inclusive forms of religious worship. The world of human affairs speeds on towards an unknown destiny, sometimes at almost breakneck speed, and one can be forgiven at times for despairing about where it may all be heading. What will become of humanity we cannot tell…, but we can certainly surmise that a happy future is not at all guaranteed if mankind does not move more boldly in the direction of greater personal freedoms, greater compassion for all forms of life, greater consideration for the well-being of the planet, higher forms of justice…, and a universal movement towards greater spiritual awareness and self-realisation.

The future is within our means to change and mould into something better than it is today, if we would but make the effort to become involved. In our spare moments and moments when we have silence and solitude, we could hardly do better than to pause for an hour or two every so often to consider the deep spiritual and humanitarian principles embodied in the writings of the eminent Rosicrucian mystic…, Raymund Andrea.

Section 1:

Early Writings of Herbert Adams

    The Occult Review   (1919-1928)
    The Theosophist   (1921-1922)

APRIL 1919   NINEPENCE NET

THE OCCULT REVIEW

EDITED BY RALPH SHIRLEY

Contents

NOTES OF THE MONTH   By the Editor
     The "Orthodoxy" of Gilbert K. Chesterton

TO INDIA   By Ralph Younghusband

ON PASSING OVER: And Our Welcome Home
     By May Crommelin

THE FAKIR AND THE CARPET: An Indian Story
     By Gerda M. Calmady-Hamlyn

A PSYCHIC FAMILY   By "F"

LUX BENIGNA   By Frederick Nicholls

THE OCCULT LIFE
     By Herbert Adams

CORRESPONDENCE

PERIODICAL LITERATURE

REVIEWS

LONDON: WILLIAM RIDER AND SON, LTD.
CATHEDRAL HOUSE, PATERNOSTER ROW, E.C.

UNITED STATES: THE INTERNATIONAL NEWS COMPANY, 85 DUANE STREET, NEW YORK
NEW ENGLAND NEWS COMPANY, BOSTON; WESTERN NEWS COMPANY, CHICAGO.
AUSTRALASIA AND SOUTH AFRICA: GORDON AND GOTCH.
CAPE TOWN: DAWSON AND SONS, LTD.
INDIA: A. H. WHEELER & CO. AND "THEOSOPHIST" OFFICE, ADYAR, MADRAS.

Introduction

Raymund Andrea wrote for *The Occult Review (1919-1928)* and *The Theosophist (1921-1922)* under his natal name of Herbert Adams. The earliest of these writings precedes the date of his joining the Rosicrucian Order.

The Occult Review was an illustrated monthly journal, published between 1905 and 1951, containing articles and correspondence by notable occultists and authors of the day, including Arthur Edward Waite, Franz Hartmann and Paul Brunton. It was published in London by *William Rider and Son Ltd.*[1] Six of these articles were later reprinted in the *Rosicrucian Beacon* between 1994 and 1996.

The Theosophist was, and remains, the monthly magazine of the Theosophical Society. It was established in 1879. This magazine published four articles by Herbert Adams. Three of them are included in this Section and the remaining article, *The Apotheosis of Love* was published in the October 1925 issue of *The Theosophist*. This was subsequently revised and included in the December 1929 issue of the *Rosicrucian Digest* under the title of *Love's Apotheosis*. See Section 5.

1. The Occult Life

Reprinted from the April 1919 edition of The Occult Review. *Also published in the Spring 1994 issue of the* Rosicrucian Beacon.

A truth which the occult student must early lay to heart is, that mystical teachings cannot be read in the same way as the literature of other departments of knowledge. The teachings of the mystic are always shrouded in mystery; and there is no greater mistake than to believe that all who run may read them.

It is not the deliberate intention of the mystic that his writings should have a double meaning; he cannot help himself in the matter. He speaks from a higher plane of experience and the truths of that plane demand their own peculiar mode of expression, or must remain unexpressed. This is why mystical teachings are riddles and bundles of contradictions to the majority; they descend from another world; they breathe of another existence; and human ears are too dull to catch the strains of their diviner meaning.

This is why the Bible, which every so-called Christian reads and knows so much about, is only understood, I suppose, by one Christian in a thousand. I believe the Bible is the most deeply occult book extant, it is profoundly mystical and is the offspring of inspiration; and only the inspired mind can interpret it. The man Jesus was such a Master of Science that I despair of interpreting His utterances until I behold those lofty intellectual and spiritual eminences from which He delivered them. It is always so. Before

---

1. Later *Rider and Company*, and now an imprint of *Century Publishing Ltd* which is part of *Random House UK Ltd*)

you can understand a thing you must be it.

You shall not know the power of devotion until you have been wrapped about with the presence of the Infinite and been struck dumb with inspiration. You shall not conceive the majestic power of love until you have felt its revolutionising and transfiguring glory in the temple of your own being. And it shall not be given you to interpret the wisdom of souls until you have long knelt down to the good, the true and the beautiful and desired the spiritual above all things. For these great souls are the Masters of Compassion, who have suffered all and know all.

The eyes are the windows of the soul. All poets know that: and that is why the eyes of beautiful women made music in their souls. They bowed down in ecstasy before that shrine and worshipped beauty and through that the living soul. Nor does the poet reject the eyes that are capable of tears; nay, rather, they awaken his soul to greater activity and bring to pass an intenser communion.

The soft tears that bedim and fall like pearls from the eyes of a noble woman, whose great heart is overflowing with the pain of life, are like the bewitching accents of angels' voices sweetly echoing through the corridors of heaven and that tremble on the ear of the mystic in the deep silence of the night. The poet rejects nothing; all are his, whether it be joy or sorrow, love or hate, pleasure or pain. Blessed be his most sacred heart, for he is the son of God!

But there is a difference, a great difference, between the poet and the mystic. The poet is the man of quick sympathies, vivid feelings and keen sensibilities, united with a marvellous imagination; with a soul that identifies itself almost magically with the phenomena of objective existence. He draws to himself the blood of life from every object along the wayside which awakens response in his hungry soul. As he drinks, a divine madness comes upon him and he must drink again and yet again. He is a spiritual vampire that preys upon the forms of Mother Nature but to them his influence is sanctified and holy. There is a divinity in his touch; and in responding to his love-song they magnify their own glory.

The mystic, on the contrary, seeks dissociation from the phenomenal world; he retreats ever inward to the source of all. Yet it is also true, that while the mystic is often a poet, the poet, too, is sometimes a mystic. Tennyson had experienced the cosmic consciousness, or he could not have written of the mystic:

> "Angels have talked with him and showed him thrones;
> Ye knew him not; he was not one of ye,
> Ye scorned him with an undiscerning scorn;
> Ye could not read the marvel in his eye;
> The still, serene abstraction."

How marvellously beautiful! *"The still, serene abstraction!"* This comes of the discipline of life and the steeping of the soul in reverie upon God. This is the bitter way of the mystic: through the pain of life and communion with the Infinite unto perfect abstraction of the soul. Then vision lends marvel to the eye; the fire of the heart kindles on the tongue a living eloquence; the whole personality is actuated with new power and purpose; and at a single bound the mind attains that sublime altitude wherefrom it looks down upon vast multitudes of men.

Vision has rendered his eyes incapable of tears; the pain of existence has given him the *"Still, serene abstraction;"* the sorrows of humanity have purified his sight. His mind, like a becalmed and boundless ocean, spreads out in shoreless space and he becomes the interpreter of all things. He dwells with universes and solar systems and the music of the spheres makes unending harmony in his soul. He is the God-intoxicated man, who has gazed upon the ineffable mystery of his own heart and by virtue thereof has obtained the power to read the hearts of others; who has renounced all that he might gain all; and who, while his body is serving in the world of men, is in holy communion with the Spirit of God.

Before the eyes may discern things spiritual they must become incapable of the tears of wounded pride, undeserved abuse, harsh criticisms and unfriendly statements, the irritations, annoyances, failures and disappointments of daily life. This does not mean that the student should harden his soul against these things; there must be no hardening on the higher path. On the material plane one is constantly open to the influences of others on the same plane and the more finely organised he may be, the more keenly does he feel the pain from all manner of persons and things.

If his attitude toward these influences is antagonistic, then such an attitude tends only the more to entangle him in the meshes of material existence. There is only one way of escape and that is in aspiring upward to an altitude where these things have no power over him. Not in isolation must he seek it; for he who runs away from the world before he has learned the lessons it has to teach him, will be thrust back into it again and again by the great law of life, until he settles down and performs the tasks set for him. And when the student realises that this world is but a school of discipline, a temporary existence and not the real life at all, he ceases to weep over hard and bitter experiences.

It is not physical tears that are referred to; it is the feeling that there is anything whatever to weep for; it is the thought we entertain which accompanies the manifestation, rather than the manifestation itself. The lesson which this truth teaches is, that the student must endeavour to rise above the incidents of personality and realise his individuality; that he should learn to function upon a plane which is beyond the agitations of the personal life.

This is really a stupendous achievement! So stupendous in fact that it has been said that man while embodied is incapable of apprehending this condition. He is even now passing through a vale of tears; he is subject to pain; he cannot live without causing pain; and it is through the power of his own heart that he attains the mystical experience and becomes united with the whole. Again and again and ever more frequently, must arise within the student that sweet tenderness which is tears and which by degrees dissolves the bonds of separateness. For the enlightened soul is known by his infinite pity, his capacity for the deepest sorrow and compassion; which attributes are of the essence of the nature of the Masters of Life.

Moreover, it is also said that the ethereal self within the physical body sheds tears of far too subtle a character to be shed by the physical eyes; and the spirit weeps as it stands on the threshold of matter and is attracted into its density and darkness by the unalterable laws of life and affection and the bonds of kinship and association. In this way does the whole being of man become softened and suffused with the dew of its own tenderness. So must the occult student become softened and suffused before he may enter into that condition in which he is incapable of tears.

Now what is the practical way to this wonderful realisation? Years of study and application in this realm of knowledge, in this Art of all arts, this Science of all sciences, reveals one sure and safe path. It is by living life to the full where we stand; nothing more or less than accepting with as much grace as we can summon and as much prayer as we can find in ourselves to offer, the cross of present circumstances and using them in every possible way in which an alert and inventive mind can discover, for the building of faculty and the extension of experience.

There is one thing which is worth all the pain, grief, sorrow and disappointment of human life and that is the augmentation of personality. The augmentation of personality! Do you realise this? I recently insisted upon this point to a successful man of the world. He replied, *"I judge a man by his wage-earning capacity."* You see the logical outcome of that statement? It means this: Select any master of art, literature, music, or science, and, no matter in what degree the production of either has blessed humanity, place beside him a man of wealth, no matter to what extent he has ground the faces of the poor to amass his riches; and my business man will prefer the latter and reject the former. He would reject even the Light of the World Himself, for He had no salary at all!

The augmentation of personality! I insist upon it. There is nothing grander on God's earth. The very Spirits before the Throne are there by virtue of the same augmentation in past evolution, not because of their wage-earning capacity. Whoever worships material things before faculty is a materialist and an outcast from the world of the great, the sublime and the true. He will pass into the Beyond naked, destitute and covered with shame; the mighty glittering edifice which he has built and worshipped for long years will vanish before the first breath of the spiritual and he will seek in agony and despair to recover it. But, he will not recover it, for it never had a real existence. It is the great, the sublime and the true that have real existence.

To endeavour to express through this body of flesh the powers of an awakened mind, the amazing inspirations of a great soul; only to endeavour to do this, even though the world never knows of it, this is the Eternal Life.

O, the beatitude of divine contemplation! O, the bliss of solitude and reverie upon God! O, the passion to behold the naked human heart, to know its mysteries and minister to it. O, to be inspired from within, to be illuminated, glorified and transfigured by the Light Invisible and to unfold serenely, spontaneously, triumphantly, from glory to glory, like mighty Nature around us!

This makes life worth living in spite of it all. And surely in the fullness of time the eyes of the mortal body shall be touched with the mystic radiance; the rising sun of glory of the Christ within shall inscribe upon those precious orbs the marvel of secret revelations; and men shall bow down in silent adoration and lift their outstretched hands to welcome the New Dawn.

2. Wagner and Occultism

Reprinted from the July 1919 edition of The Occult Review. *Also published in the March 1995 issue of the* Rosicrucian Beacon.

The greatest of all themes for the contemplation of those who are ardently seeking the Inner Light, is undoubtedly the life of renunciation. This is the fundamental tone in the grand harmony of all the great religions of men. In the East and in the West, on the lips of prophet, poet, mystic and sage, it finds unending expression. Is it then surprising that this divine chord sounding through the centuries from the highest heaven should awaken a sympathetic response in the lofty soul of the illustrious tone poet, Wagner?

I have been reading his letters to Mathilde Wesendonck and while so doing I have been a silent but not unmoved spectator of the struggles of a great soul passing beyond the boundaries of art and entering the greater world of occultism. I have come to the conclusion that Wagner, whether he knew it or not, was a candidate for initiation. Inner suffering and sacrificial love inspired this remarkable book of confessions and the sublime doctrine of renunciation expounded in it gives it an occult value. The supreme aim of the student on the occult path is to give light..., Wagner does that and pre-eminently. The minor personal aims which absorb the minds of the majority must be completely laid aside by him who aspires to become a teacher of men. Such a condition, however, is only possible for those who have arrived at a certain maturity of soul. Wagner had attained to that condition.

I intend to quote from these letters certain passages which clearly show that, master artist in music as Wagner was, art alone could not satisfy him; that he was conscious of a great antagonism between art and that calm, spiritual, contemplative state which, through deep study of the Eastern teachings, he knew was the secret of the greatness of Buddha.

> "Surely," he writes, "the glorious Buddha was right when he sternly prohibited art. Who can feel more distinctly than I, that it is this abominable art which forever gives me back to the torment of life and all the contradictions of existence? Were this strange gift not within me, this strange predominance of plastic phantasy, clear insight might make me obey my heart's dictate and turn into a saint.... Oh, if ye foolish men of learning but understood the great love-brimming Buddha, ye would marvel at the depth of insight which showed him the exercise of art as the most certain of all pathways from salvation!"

It will surely come as a revelation to many that Wagner was a disciple of Buddha! Yet here, in his own words, is the notable confession. He is seeking the light, desiring that spiritual peace which "abominable art" cannot give; in a moment of vision he is conscious of the life of ineffable love for which his heart craves: and then, overflowing with the ecstatic joyousness, his vision finds rapturous expression as it blends with the marvellous "depth of insight" of the "love-brimming Buddha."

For Wagner there existed an antagonism between art and occultism. Is there in reality any antagonism? Art ransacks the whole world with quickened pulse and gleaming eyes and claims all the living wealth of nature as its own. The silent stars, growing faint at the dawn of day, the still trees reflected by evening light in a woodland mirror, the joyous melodies of God's assembled choristers at the grand festival of spring, the everlasting thunder of gigantic breakers on the solitary seashore; these and every other marvel in nature, it clasps in its burning grip and, remodelling them all with a magical skill, echoes them back to an astonished world in painting, poem and symphony. Occultism confronts the world with calm, steady eyes but its gaze is beyond. Its hands are not cold but the fever has left them. It has glimpsed a light beyond the hills and felt a joy from within the veil which beggar description. It loves nature with a most holy love but during its quest of ages it has come face to face with the "love-brimming Buddha" and the compassionate Christ, and henceforth the face of nature and the face of man have a new significance. Wagner, looking long and adoringly at the glorious Buddha, had, perhaps unconsciously, stepped across the sacred border which divides the two worlds, then art became "abominable."

In Wagner's soul, at the time he wrote these lines on Buddha and art, a drama was proceeding which no art could adequately express. Every advanced occult student has experienced that awful transitional stage of evolution, when he is passing from the sight of man into the still presence of God. That ordeal is a test for the strongest soul. Wagner passed through it; constituted as he was, for him there was no alternative. He had reached that degree of inner unfoldment where this supreme trial of the soul became the very next step of advancement; and he took it. It was a struggle well-nigh unto death. He told something of it in these words:

> "Last night, when I drew my hand back from the rail of the balcony, it was not my art that withheld me! In that terrible instant there showed itself to me with well-nigh visual

distinctness my life's true axis, round which my resolution whirled from death to new existence."

Here was a man too excellent and noble to be lost to the world. In that moment of agony the vision of the very heart of divine love opened to him; it revealed him to himself in the clear light of divinity and he returned to finish his work. The significance of the conception expressed in the following citation will only be fully appreciated by those who are familiar with the processes of interior unfoldment.

> "There must be some indescribable inner sense, which is altogether clear and active only when the outward-facing senses are as if in a dream. When I strictly neither see nor hear distinctly any longer, this sense is at its keenest and shows its function as creative calm; I can call it by no other name. Whether this calm is all one with that plastic repose which you mean, I cannot say; merely I know that this calm of mine works from within to without; with it I am at the world's centre."

And with what affecting pathos he writes of fellow-suffering. He confesses to an instinctive dislike of the rich and proceeds:

> "With studied aim they hold at arm's length whatever might betray to their dormant fellow-feeling that misery whereon all their wished-for ease is based; and that alone divides me from them by a whole world. I have searched my heart and found that I am drawn with sympathetic urgency towards that other side and nothing seriously touches me save in so far as it awakens my fellow-feeling..., that is, fellow-suffering. This compassion I recognise as the strongest feature in my moral being and presumably it also is the wellspring of my art."

Wagner here touches the very summit of the spiritual life. Humanity's pain is his pain. He had diligently searched too for a knowledge which would give a satisfactory reason for, and ultimately reconcile him to, the manifest and disturbing inequalities among men. He found the solution in the doctrine of reincarnation.

> "Only the profound hypothesis of reincarnation has been able to show me the consoling point where all converge in the end to an equal height of redemption, after their divers life-careers, running severed but side by side in Time, have met in full intelligence beyond it."

Surely we must recognise at last that Wagner is our brother! My last citation is one which a man of Wagner's temperament would only write to his dearest friend, to one whom he knew really understood him.

"So I pour my heart out much less freely, also, reflecting that I'm not the man for understanding through my actions, and hoping that something at least of my works will meet with understanding some fine day. Yet I may tell you this much: my sense of purity alone confers on me this power. I feel myself pure of heart: in my inmost depth I know that I have ever wrought for others only, never for myself; and my perpetual sorrows are my witness."

Wagner had studied well at the feet of Buddha. So deeply engrossed have I been in watching his ascent into the "region of white flame," that I have almost forgotten he was a master musician and wrote out a fragment of the universal harmony. To me, he is the devoted disciple of the Compassionate One: I leave it to others to speak of his monumental creations. The spirit of God possessed him, wrote through him and made the frail mortal tremble at his own productions. Some day, when we have suffered enough, no doubt we shall understand the language of them. But after having witnessed the passing of this great soul through the cruel tempests of personality into perfect calm at the world's centre, I know that, in the case of Wagner at least, occultism made art sublime and the master of art a revealer of truth.

3. The Future of Occultism

Reprinted from the March 1920 edition of The Occult Review. *Also published in the June 1995 issue of the* Rosicrucian Beacon.

The science of the soul will be the study of the immediate future. Once again, after long ages, the tides of living thought are returning inward to the spiritual source of all; and Occultism, the ancient divine science, is destined to illumine with its transcendent radiance the Western world. The time has come for humanity to take the most important step in its evolution: it is passing swiftly onward to cosmic vision. From the struggles and pains and manifold experiences to which a complex civilisation has inevitably called it, the soul of man emerges chastened and calm but not satisfied. In the silence which ever follows the storm it has paused and listened: the voice of the masters has been heard and obeyed. Deep as the foundations of the universe, glorious as the destiny of man. Occultism, yesterday ridiculed and rejected, is today with power coming into its own.

The study of Occultism will give us spiritual men. It should have been the special prerogative of the Church to teach the science of the soul and furnish us with spiritual giants; but she has, in the main, mistaken her mission and misinterpreted the teachings of Christ. However, the hour of spiritual revealing is at hand and all things will be changed. So long as man continues to ally himself with false and decaying systems of theology, so long will he remain unvisited by the fire from heaven and lack divine strength and initiative. It is time for him to regard himself with the keen eye of a critic and peremptorily refuse to follow blind teachers any longer. The ascending sun of the twentieth century is disclosing stupendous possibilities for man. He should arise, shake off the hypnotic sleep of centuries, push boldly on one side professional and private prejudice and come out into the electric atmosphere of spiritual thought.

The reason for the spiritual sterility of the Church is briefly this: her pulpit still waits for men of vision. The power of the Church is passing because men of today are thinking. They are sitting upon the hilltops, dreaming with Nature and asking deep questions which the Church cannot answer. Into their own hands they are taking the Bibles of humanity and interpreting in the light of their own awakening souls the illuminating philosophy of the seers of the ages. Of little importance, indeed, is religious chaos among the temples made with hands, when the power of the Spirit is leading man to worship the Infinite in the temple of the soul.

Neither the theology of the Church, nor the science of the schools can satisfy the craving of the heart which is crucifying humanity today. It is blasphemy to offer lifeless theological dogma and the frigid theories of materialistic science to a humanity stretched in agony upon a cross of pain. It needs the divine voice of inspiration and the strong hand of healing; and those of us who, through study and long-suffering are privileged to be conscious helpers in the present evolution, should constitute ourselves the blessed mediums of that healing and inspiration. It is for us to lay tremendous emphasis upon the life of vision and revelation and by the holy beauty of that revealing vision to help others to loose their hold on blind belief and reach up to the mystic light. Once again must be reiterated the treading of the ancient path as the true way to profound self-knowledge and consequent effective action; that within man is the deep mirror of God and by withdrawing from the senseless confusion of tongues and looking therein he may behold the glories and immensities of his own infinite life.

The great day of the recognition of the masters of science is at hand. It will not be true of this century, as of preceding centuries it has been, that the voice of inspiration and prophesy shall fall upon deaf ears. The history of many of the inspired ones, the prophets, the pioneers of the race is, we well know, a history of persecution, yet nevertheless, oracular as the Apocalypse. The vision of God was in their hearts; the glory of it shone in their eyes; and on their tongues the wisdom of the Spirit found a solemn utterance. By their own efforts they raised themselves to spiritual eminence that they might bear witness of the Divine and assist in the grand work of the redemption of humanity. The choicest spirits of the times in which they lived and taught, possessing a knowledge and exercising powers which exalted them immeasurably above their contemporaries, they were misunderstood and wrongly judged, yet shed abroad an irresistible influence which will outlive the evolution of man. They achieved this immortality by laying upon the altar of the spiritual with pitiless resolution everything which savoured of mortality. They were the mighty seers whose names we revere today and the study of whose philosophy is helping us to mould the humanity of tomorrow.

Occultism will achieve some of its greatest triumphs in the immediate future. On every hand are unmistakable signs of spiritual awakening. The investigation of supernormal phenomenon and the realities of spiritual vision is active throughout the world. The law of evolution is the Spirit of God in action, and whoever attempts to arrest the onward sweep of spiritual forces will behold every endeavour wonderfully instrumental in completing his own ruin.

In this great day of awakening of the soul, no man in authority, whether monarch or otherwise, will be permitted to exile the man of vision. Humanity awaits him with yearning heart and will welcome him as an elder brother. When he appears he will not stand alone; others will emerge on the same path to accompany and assist him in radiating the light and knowledge which will prove a sure panacea for all ills. Those who have the eyes to see may bear witness to the initial steps in the fulfilment of this prophecy.

4. The Pain of Development

Reprinted from the September 1920 edition of The Occult Review. *Also published in the September 1995 issue of the* Rosicrucian Beacon.

During recent years, when the path of life was saturated with blood, the subject of human suffering furnished matter for countless themes. Humanity, passing collectively through the vale of tears, drunk deeply as one from a common cup of sorrow. An unparalleled and poignant grief inundated the human heart, stirring up from unknown depths, emotions, thoughts and yearnings of a character and potency hitherto unsuspected and beyond belief. Pain cultured the soul to a clearer vision, a profounder life, an unusual experience. Pain, the celestial messenger which accompanies every soul into the world, opened a secret way of communion with God.

It is long before we recognise the mission of pain and willingly suffer it to accomplish its beneficent purpose in our lives. To many the fear of pain is greater than the fear of death. They tremble and shrink at its mere approach. They have not the strength to question it, subject it to patient analysis, divine the meaning of it. Like a terrible apparition, it confuses the senses, disorganises the faculties and enthrones darkness in the inner sanctuary. In innumerable instances the pain of bereavement has done this. The pain of loss has rendered insignificant every other pain of mortal existence.

The acceptance of pain and the understanding of it are simultaneous. If loss on the physical plane means possession on the spiritual, then there is compensation even in death. The physical eyes grow dim with tears while the eye of the spirit becomes radiant with love. Every seer has testified to this truth; and that testimony inspires us to set our feet to tread the path of research, not of despair.

We may observe the metamorphosis of pain through all the planes of existence. There are some who know nothing of pain beyond that experienced in the physical body. But pain becomes increasingly acute as consciousness passes upward and functions upon the mental and spiritual planes. As the troubles of childhood are not the troubles of youth, nor those of youth, the troubles of manhood, so is it with pain operating on the three planes of consciousness in man. We experience pain through disharmony on the physical plane, maladjustment on the mental plane and cosmic cognition acquaints us with the collective pain of humanity.

Pain is a factor in all real development. The stage of development with which I am immediately concerned is the transitional stage, when consciousness is seeking to raise itself from the purely mental plane to function on the level of cosmic cognition. This is the most difficult step in the evolution of consciousness; and many are engaged upon it at the present time. In the empire of purely mental achievement they are supreme, and yet unsatisfied. Pain has attended every step of the journey up to this point: at every step of advancement a promise of final contentment has lured the seeker on. But there is no abiding peace in the realms of the mind. The greatest struggle of all awaits him.

The stresses of thought through which man passes on the way to selfhood constitute the path of development. They continually change him in his own eyes and in the eyes of others. The perpetual reaching up to larger life is actually breaking his bonds asunder and drawing him nearer to the goal. In his soul is hidden the genius of his life. The holy thing is born with his flesh and by thoughtful recognition he comes to feel its magic life quick within him, fresh and divine as the dawn of creation. It is this ideal self that can make him ten times a man; and it is because, for various reasons, it is not permitted adequate expression that the pain of development is intensified. No joy exceeds that which accompanies the effort towards the expression of the ideal self: every bandage torn from its glorious countenance reveals a deeper and more entrancing beauty which breathes of greater possibilities in the glory to be revealed. The pursuit of lofty ideals belongs to the transitional stage; it is the link between the mental and the spiritual. Not however, until he comes to realise that only the spiritual really matters, does man take any decisive steps to enter spiritual conditions.

The life of the spiritual man is lived in the shadow of the Cross. It is how much a man has felt, how far he has gone down into the abysses of life, that determines the stature of the soul. The body may be young, yet within itself the soul may bear the record of ages. It has been said that the poet feels the burden of souls. So does the spiritual man carry in his heart the collective pain of humanity. This is an inestimable privilege, the greatest which earth life has to offer. Only the few recognise this privilege. The many who travel together in pain until now wait for the knowledge of the truth of the meaning of pain in their lives. And it is the sacred work of the mystic to carry to those who suffer the divine message that all pain is gain and leads ultimately to spiritual beatitude.

The mystic is the apostle of pain. It is he who knows that the carrying of the Cross gives perfect strength. He is the suffering servant of God. Gentleness and wisdom are two of his loftiest attributes. For him all ideals have been merged into the supreme passion for holiness. Utter consecration is for him alone. It is he who has come out of great tribulation, who has washed the robes of his inner life and made them white through the operation of the Spirit within him; who dwells in the light and the knowledge of the masters of life; who, while with body and mind performing his allotted task in the world of men, is spiritually free from the limitations of material existence.

Such is the ideal of the spiritual aspirant. It is the destiny of every suffering soul in the great fellowship of men upon earth. People talk of conversion, as if by the performance of a simple ceremony the soul could enter into the peace of God. There is no truth in it. The path of the spiritual is difficult. The mental experiences which the aspirant encounters, the phases of consciousness through which he must pass, test his strength and endurance to the uttermost. It often seems as if the soul were on the road to the darkness of hell, rather than stepping upward to the light and peace of the Christ life. The loneliness of the way is sometimes almost maddening. The embraces of earth are cold: no voice speaks to the bewildered soul as it stands out there isolated in the very midst of the crowd. It is the awful, silent, unwitnessed travail of the soul, and none knows but those who have passed that way. But, as the soul presses on to the mysteries which *"abide in the dark avenue amid the bitterness of things occult,"* it is something to remember that this is the way of *development* and that pain is perfecting it to stand with clear vision in the presence of the highest.

5. The Occultist and His Critics

Reprinted from the May 1921 edition of The Theosophist.

HP Blavatsky once said that *"if a man would follow in the steps of Hermetic philosophers, he must prepare himself beforehand for martyrdom."* No zealous student of the occult can progress far in his studies without realising the truth of that statement. He quickly finds, too, that he must, in the words of the same writer, *"be ready for everlasting encounters with friends and foes."*

When the student first meets with these experiences on his path, he is liable to waver and examine very seriously the grounds of his belief. He has, even at that early stage of his endeavours, found new strength and deeper insight; yet, in the conscientious expression of the new life which has come to him, he encounters blunt opposition from the most unexpected sources, and then he really begins to count the cost. It is at this critical point that many have turned back and made peace with their tempters. They were not strong enough for martyrdom.

There are others, comparatively few, who set their faces to the task from the very beginning and never look back. For them the call of the soul has been so emphatic that they yield to it heart and life, and are totally reckless of the future. They scarcely needed to count the cost; they entered the arena fully prepared to pay any price. In one clear vision they glimpsed the goal and are conscious of a perfect assurance that all obstacles on the way thereto will be met and overcome. These are the strong ones who elect to follow in the steps of their great predecessors. Such as these the world needs above all others at the present time.

The prevailing opinion in the world concerning the occultist is that he is a dreamer and unpractical. They who best know the world are the least disturbed by the world's opinion. No intelligent man, I suppose, will deny that the best in the world, whether of literature, art or science in all their manifold expressions, originated in the minds of men of genius. Well, the genius is a dreamer; he is the medium through which operate powers and influences which he neither understands nor can adequately control. Such as he receives he gives, and is very often an irresponsible agent. But his gifts are always a blessing to humanity; although that is generally realised after he is dead.

If this is the common lot of genius, what must be the fate of the man of vision, who is the super-dreamer? Most people dream, chaotically enough; more organised are the dreams of genius, beautifying life and civilising men; but the sculptured dreams of the occultist surpass these and build a cosmos.

Let us obtain a glimpse of the work and character of the super-dreamer. He is a master-builder engaged in the monumental work of building the soul of man. And if there is any person in whose presence the little intellectual men of our day feel uncomfortable, it is the spiritual enthusiast, the man who believes divinely in the human soul. His simple dignity and authoritative speech have a magic of their own which is not to be overcome. There is something eminently disconcerting in that quiet impressiveness and unusual influence, born of vision and certitude, which threatens to set floating every cherished idea of the unspiritual. It argues a great deal, and should teach the latter many lessons, that in the face of all opposition the power of that august personality remains unhurt.

The occultist is completely dedicated to the lofty work of the spiritual evolution of mankind. He has perfect knowledge of the spiritual forces in man and of the method of their discipline and manifestation. For him, direct inspiration and spiritual communication are daily experiences. He brings a new interpretation of life from super-physical levels of consciousness, making existence infinitely grand and significant.

He does not deny that man must stand with both feet firmly upon the earth, handle material things, and adjust himself in all the relations of life. In this respect he is, in fact, the most practical of men. But if that were the whole of his philosophy, he would undoubtedly be as foolish as those of his contemporaries who deem this phase of it sufficient. No, he bears witness also to the divine light which, emanating from the shrine of his own inner being, sheds its radiance upon the whole panorama of human life and reveals its purpose in the cosmic scheme.

The occultist is the revealer of truth. His mission is to give light and open up the sources of spiritual knowledge in man. He stands far ahead of humanity as a whole. He sees it struggling blindly along the weary path of life behind him. From that vision compassion is born, and that compassion is the secret of all his power. When perfect love acts, it has nothing to fear from malignant men or spirits of hell.

Let the critics of the world's Saviour bear that in mind. If, after many endeavours, they find the terms of his royal mission above their comprehension and antagonistic to the accepted rule of the academy and the market place, let them at least show their better nature by accepting in silence the proffered gift. Time will surely prove that the gift is a priceless one.

What a pathetic spectacle is the man who refuses enlightenment in a world like this? He is virtually dead, and little remains but to bury him with his forefathers. I once gave to a minister of the gospel an accepted occult work, sincerely believing that it might illumine his world of facts and raise his message to the level of spiritual enthusiasm. He returned it with the remark: *"I am too rational."*

How many so-called spiritual teachers are too rational to remove the veil and look into the face of Truth! That is why they are a menace to the spiritual life of the nation. By what authority does that man consider himself the messenger of Truth who is content to study the laws of nature and refuses, either through bigotry, or fear, or self-satisfied indolence, to investigate the laws of the supernatural, which alone can give true spiritual knowledge? What right has he to teach in the name of Jesus, who does not understand the Master because he fears to follow him? What right has he to condemn the occultist who does understand the Master, because he has followed him even to the Cross, and speaks a wisdom which only dawns upon the darkness of that last hour?

On every hand one meets with persons who pride themselves upon their religious status in society, yet the first breath of genuine spiritual truth upsets them; consistent men who fear, for personal considerations, to revise the musty ideas thrust upon them in their youth by ignorance and prejudice. On referring to the world-wide work of a remarkable occultist, I was asked whether that teacher was consistent! But what has revelation to do with consistency? Consistency is the everlasting enemy of progress: what has a great soul to do with it? Was Jesus consistent? No, he was a perpetual surprise, and did the most unaccountable things. Was St. Paul consistent? No man wrote a bolder confession of his inconsistency. These teachers followed the Spirit that liberates, not the letter that binds. I wonder how many more centuries will elapse before Christians will realise this and follow their example.

The occultist is giving to the world the complete history of man. Science has done its best to prove conclusively that man is primarily of the earth and cannot exist apart from it. Now we know that its conclusions are childish. Theology, too, stands arraigned before the world and will have to be rewritten, or suffer the fate of an exploded myth. It shuts its eyes to the irreproachable light which accredited psychic investigation is flashing full in its face, choosing to call that which it cannot understand, because it is too bigoted to investigate it, the work of the devil.

I have little to say here about Spiritualism; I know its value and its dangers. If, however, it is one of the avenues which lead to the Great Light, students of the laboratory and the Church may profitably join hands and take a few steps in that direction. They would then at least show some signs of life and initiative, be in a position to verify the knowledge we already possess, and perhaps add more to it of an interesting and inspiring character. It is certainly better that the explorers along this avenue should be thought a little mad, as pioneers usually are, and even lose sight of a companion now and then during the strange adventure, than that they should sit with the critics on the banks of Lethe, loving darkness and stagnation, fearing light and revelation, and become a byword to future generations.

But I am concerned with the occultist who lives in the Great Light and is conscious of an indisputable mission to men. Every man with a Mission is entitled to respectful consideration, and receives it..., unless his mission be a spiritual one. Yet the life of the occultist is a sacrifice to the world; and the reason that he so willingly suffers the derision of his enemies is because they most need the sacrifice. It is to the materialist he first speaks of an invisible world and the means of cognising it. He knows that without a spiritual interpretation life must ever remain an amazing and grievous enigma.

The profound ignorance of otherwise sensible men in the matter of their own soul-life and spiritual possibilities is truly astounding. It is difficult to know how to begin to direct their thought to the inaugural truth of spiritual science..., their own identity. Their manifest astonishment is almost disconcerting; one has said too much, and would willingly retreat to silence and neutrality, but it cannot be. And these are the men who, rejoicing in their sordid ineptitude for spiritual truth, and shouting an unmodified denial of all beyond their own infantile vision, endeavour to silence the oracle of divinity and with profane hands to crucify afresh the Son of Man.

It may be asked whether I include in this sweeping denunciation those ministers of religion who ridicule the occult sciences and psychic research. Certainly I do; there is no alternative. Professing a more sacred calling in the world than their brethren, the spiritual exaltation of the people, they are the more culpable. I do not know a more pathetic, yet surpassingly ludicrous spectacle than that of the ministers of God denying the grand fundamental of their apostolical mission, and choosing to walk in darkness rather than in the light. They appear to labour under the influence of a hideous obsession in standing before the world as the acknowledged exponents of the inspired Word, and at the same time vehemently impugning those forces and instrumentalities by which that Word was recorded.

The Bible is an impressive spiritual and psychic phenomenon, the production of spiritual seers and mediums, for which the occultist has a reverential regard. And the judgement awaiting those who preach this Word, yet deny its secret doctrine, will be this:

instead of from pulpits, wisdom and prophecy will cry with inspired voice in the market place; Pentecostal fires will fall upon those sitting by the common hearth; and the learned priest will descend from his eminence to receive grace and illumination from the tongues of the unlettered.

The occultist is writing the true history of man. That is one of the many duties imposed upon him which do not exist for other men. He will execute that duty in spite of anything his contemporaries may say or do. He knows that it is futile to expect complete justification from the men of his own time, and therefore he is unmoved in the face of all opposition. It is enough for him to remember that his teaching has the corroboration of every great soul before and since the advent of Jesus, and of Jesus himself, who also was an occultist.

Never are the critics more flagrantly mistaken than when they write down the occultist as a mere visionary, and an enemy to reason and religion. *"God geometrises,"* Plato said; so does the occultist, and in a way which has staggered many a mathematician. Nothing could be more illogical and presumptuous than the attitude of these critics who would have us believe that the last word of Infinite Wisdom has been spoken to man; that all the heavens of revelation were finally sealed when Jesus ascended to a greater ministry invisible. They do not realise that by refusing the enlightenment handed on by the chosen messengers of the great Brotherhood of Masters, they are impeding the predestined spiritual evolution of humanity.

But sublime is the patience, ineffable the peace and certainty, of the illumined seer. With Spirit attuned to the mighty rhythms of the unseen universe, and compassion his guide, he passes swiftly onward through the incarnations, ever bearing humanity's cross until suffering love shall have transformed it into a glorious Crown.

6. Theosophy and Anti-Christianity

Reprinted from the September 1921 edition of The Theosophist.

There recently appeared in a London newspaper an article containing certain malevolent statements about the Theosophical Society and its founder, Madame Blavatsky. I do not imagine that it much disturbed any member of the Society, inasmuch as it is to be expected that a powerful organisation which threatens the strongholds of ignorance and prejudice should constantly meet with fierce opposition.

The Theosophical Society has passed through many storms since its formation, yet it stands immovable upon the same foundations; and it will stand. But there is one reason why the article referred to should not be entirely ignored and allowed to pass in silence: in it the Theosophical Society is grossly misrepresented, and a sinister attempt is made to damage the fair reputation of the Society in the eyes of the public.

The writer of the article, when he sat down to blast the reputation of the Theosophical Society and its founder, dipped his pen in the poison of asps and wrote, knowingly or unknowingly, a tissue of unvarnished lies. The history of the Society from the beginning has been written, the facts are accessible to all; and a person who writes without a knowledge of the facts, or who deliberately rejects the facts and casts forth foul aspersions, merely to satisfy the morbid craving of a vitiated mind, may make an excellent newspaper vendor, but is in no sense qualified to build public opinion.

He tells us with some gravity that the Inner Circle of the Society is engaged in revolutionary work, and that it is antagonistic to Christianity and to the orderly government of Western Civilisation. Not being a member of the Inner Circle, he is not in a position to speak with authority as to its aims and work. As to the government in the West which he describes as orderly, the less any of us say about it the better!

The article teems with probabilities: the only certainty in it is the writer's determination to paint the Society and its founder as black as possible in the face of all facts and conscience. *"Whether Madame Blavatsky started the Theosophical Society as a revolutionary organisation one cannot say."* I repeat, the chronicles are extant, and honourable research will convince him.

"Certainly it was an anti-Christian organisation," he proceeds. His certainty here would evoke a smile were we not upon serious ground. Again: *"It is probable that Madame Blavatsky was a revolutionary."* If she was, so am I, and I sincerely hope every Theosophist is. Other foolish and unfounded statements follow which it would be a waste of time to comment upon. We have but to look back to 1879 to find Madame Blavatsky replying to almost identical charges, and concluding with these memorable words:

> "Out of all this pother of opinions, one fact stands conspicuous…, the Society, its members, and their views, are deemed of enough importance to be discussed and denounced: Men slander only those whom they hate…, or fear."

Now I leave the atmosphere of men who slander to think of Madame Blavatsky. I confess to an absorbing passion for great characters. I have studied them from my youth. And when Madame Blavatsky stood in my path, like the lioness she was, I acknowledged her immediately as one of my teachers. The history of her extraordinary career awakened in me less wonder than reverence and love. Few are able yet to follow her earthly pilgrimage, and believe. Hers was a life which would make more sceptics than converts, even in our time. But I knew that she belonged to me; my deepest intuition told me that. And I have often thought that I would give a world of wealth to have shared her days and nights of battle. Yet, though we cannot share her personality, her knowledge we can; and with her example before us we can use that knowledge with dynamic effect against the materialistic spirit of the age.

Her devotion to the Masters, who prepared her and sent her forth as their messenger to accomplish her colossal task, impresses me as one of the most remarkable passages in the biography of personalities. Undoubtedly it was this devotion alone which enabled her to stand firm in the face of a world of persecution. And the same drama, with some modifications, will yet be enacted in the lives of more than one of us.

Truly, some advancement has been made since the great days when Madame Blavatsky roused the nations with her battle cry; even so, only a very small minority is prepared to accept the reality and teaching of the Masters as compared with a huge majority which is not. When one calmly places side by side for consideration the attitude of the Press, the Church and the general public toward the lofty aims of the Theosophical Society as proclaimed forty years ago, and the attitude of the Press, Church and public of today, is there very much difference? The selfish, clutching hand of materialism is still heavy upon the Western nations, and the work of the pioneers is vast.

There is only one way in which the reformation will come, and that is through the individual. I lay tremendous stress upon individual progress. I do not need to be reminded at this late hour of the virtue of self-forgetfulness and the working for others: that is included in my programme. The first item on that programme is knowledge and power in self. That will give conviction, and conviction in a great soul always breeds enthusiasm.

Be an occult enthusiast! Dig deeply, and so steep your soul in the occult life, that your personality will publish it and your speech be a mighty affirmation of it. I find all this in Mme Blavatsky. Wherever she was there existed a rarified atmosphere in which knowledge and power were spontaneously born. But she made herself a vehicle first of all. It is the only way to leave footprints upon the sands of time: it is the only way to make a Movement strong, consolidated and overwhelmingly influential.

Little can be achieved without enthusiasm. The fire should be hot about every student who is desirous of reaching the feet of the Masters. I find this also in the language of the Masters themselves. *"Young friend! Study and prepare." "Our cause needs missionaries, devotees, agents, even martyrs, perhaps." "Child of your race and of your age, seize the diamond pen and inscribe the innumerable pages of your life-record with the history of noble deeds, days well-spent, years of holy striving."* There speaks a voice unhampered by the illusions of mortality. It is a clear call from the sublime heights of the Manvantara to devotional study and the onward march to divine adventure.

Some one to whom I had given a few glimpses of my faith said to me: *"Yes, but suppose it turns out to be a will-o'-the-wisp?"* You will meet with the same suggestion, and your enthusiasm alone will save you. The oftener my faith is called into the witness box, the stronger it becomes.

Criticism always has one effect upon me: I return to my studies with increased fervour and make sure, doubly sure. Why should you allow others, whether they be friends or otherwise, who possess neither knowledge nor experience of that to which you have dedicated your life and effort, to make you falter? Their victory will cause you incalculable remorse. Their defeat means that you stand firm as a rock upon your chosen ground, thereby rendering firmer the footing of every other student. That is the best answer to those who either hate the Society, or fear it.

Enthusiasm brought the Theosophical Society into existence: enthusiasm has carried it to its present triumphant position; enthusiasm will make its principles universal. There is no more anti-Christianity in the ranks of the Society than there is in the ranks of the declared exponents of Christianity: there is less. There is no influence operative in the Society from which any man or woman entering therein would receive incentive to become anti-Christian. On the contrary, he or she often realises for the first time the true and beautiful significance of the Christ-life.

7. The Novitiate

Reprinted from the September 1922 edition of The Theosophist.

The most prominent feature of intellectual life today is criticism. So deeply engrained in the Western mind is this habit, that one can expect little thanks for decrying any section of it. It may be urged that it is a time-honoured national trait; but a national trait may be also a national evil; and with us, to a great extent, the habit of criticism *is* an evil.

Unquestionably, through every department of culture there runs a strain of noble and helpful criticism which opens the mind to a real appreciation of the highest in human production; there is, too, an accompanying strain, as strong as it is pernicious, steadily and deliberately bent upon a sinister campaign of damnation, the sole object of which is to arrest the propagation and influence of unfamiliar truth and attain for itself a cheap notoriety at the expense of those who will not think for themselves. This latter class of criticism it is which, with a counterfeit air of omniscience, robustly applies its narrow canons to the revelations of occult science, and in so doing becomes the object of well-merited contempt.

I have always thought it a truism that the criterion of just criticism is a knowledge of the principles and practice of the subject under consideration. Clearly this criterion is acceptable only to the few; for the main stream of criticism provoked by occult disclosures has its source in a most profound ignorance of even first principles. We have grown so accustomed to this purblind treatment of advanced research that, for ourselves, we are not disquieted: we recognise its impotence to stay the upward progress of the human soul.

But there are students who are peculiarly susceptible to the imperious onslaughts of ignorance, and who experience no inconsiderable anxiety and doubt when exposed to cross-questioning and ridicule in their immediate circle on account of their belief. The foothold of these students is not sure; the period of their probationary study is not far advanced; they have taken but a few steps on the path to self-knowledge. Doubt and questionings spring up at every step, and time must elapse before the mind can thoroughly assimilate the deeper truth. This is the critical period for the novitiate in Occultism, and a word from a fellow student may establish an occult career.

If you mean to progress, you must cultivate a certain indifference to this crass criticism. You must not fear in the least being proclaimed a fool for your ideas. Not having yet penetrated deeply enough, the edifice of occult knowledge does not stand foursquare in your vision; and, because of that lack of growth, your thought is infirm and you cannot give a satisfactory account of yourself. Your opponents will feel your uncertainty and take advantage of it, and you will half believe at times that you are resting your soul on a chimera.

There is only one thing, however, about which you need be solicitous…, your inner unfoldment. Wrestle silently with the divine facts until your thought grows strong. Many defeats will conspire against you, but you will get used to them and draw strength from them. When at length you realise just where you stand in the vast evolutionary scheme, the word of power will be born in you and you will be anxious to enter the arena.

Occult growth is different from any other kind of growth: you cannot register your progress day by day, like a student in art. It has nothing to do with that culture which is often only a synonym for arrogance; neither brilliant accomplishments nor social prestige will provide you with a passport. Occultism is no respecter of persons. Buddha was a prince; Jesus was a carpenter; both became Adepts. The only thing that avails is a fervent soul; that will open the door to everything in time.

The crucifying struggle of life around you, inscribing the sign of the Cross indelibly on the brow of humanity…, is it anything to you? These *"faces of the world's deliberate refusal,"* the pariahs of society, are they anything to you? Is the sombre panorama of the human soul, passing and repassing between the two eternities, and feeling blindly and unknowingly after the Great Secret, anything to you? Because here is the basis of all your growth. The human soul must draw you irresistibly. To be, to know…, these are the angels of aspiration which must stir the waters of life within and urge you to activity.

A man who had been stung by circumstances said to me that it was a mockery to utter the name of Jesus; and I felt sad because I had not the power to rend the veil of the temple in twain and show him the living Christ. The suffering of the human soul must become *personal to you*. And the initial step lies in the cultivation of the fullness of power of a broad humanity.

A head full of theories will make you a tinkling cymbal and known of men; but only from a real depth of nature proceeds an understanding sympathy. Your development may cost you an incarnation, nevertheless the true aspirant forgets utterly the price of achievement. He accustoms himself to think in terms of incarnations, not years; the magnitude of that contemplation sets its ineffaceable seal upon his thought; and those who do not bless him for his opinions will yet be unable to forget them.

If you demand swift progress, the path will present greater difficulties. Undoubtedly there are difficulties, but they will never deter a mind of the right calibre. Some there are who mildly depict the path of occult progress as one of sweet pleasantness and undisturbed peace. It is a view which experience does not justify. You are called to a long inward struggle with many conflicting forces, and a will of steel is requisite to carry it through. How can it be otherwise, when you have to look your accumulated past straight in the face? But out of the very darkest moments of this season of trial, and from the deepest heart of pain, you may draw a keen ecstasy of mastery which surpasses infinitely the joy of easy conquest.

This probationary work will be succeeded by a psycho-spiritual culture of an advanced nature at a certain stage of your development. You need to be somewhat of a spiritual artist, possessed of an exquisite intuitional awareness of inner processes, if you would successfully mould the constitution to respond to keener and unusual vibrations. A reorganisation of the subtler forces takes place, a gradual transformation, necessitating a series of readjustments extending over a considerable period, during which you will become receptive to an ever widening area of psychic influences. And inasmuch as important changes in any sphere are usually attended with a certain amount of disturbance, so the concentration of forces for advanced evolution meets with more or less temporary resistance in the personality.

One of the most immediate results of the new development is the pronounced occult tone of the personality. Responding now to a higher vibrational ratio, the breath of life circulates as a peculiar power; however faintly perceived externally, an actual spiritualisation of self ensues. Sensitiveness is increased to a remarkable degree; and while it is not to be implied that your aim is to become so etherealised as to preclude the enjoyment of a natural and healthy existence, it is clearly necessary to take thought for much which formerly did not concern you.

Whatever the objections raised, by those who understand nothing of the goal in view, against the ultimate issue of this process of refinement, one of the chief aims must be the growth of sensitiveness. And in the pursuit of this, any discomforts incidental to the alchemical process will be regarded as inevitable, and not in any sense as deterrents. You will know that you are deliberately fitting yourself for the reception of a greater power of human helpfulness, to be used in a career of sublime service.

This transformation of your inner life, silent and unperceived by others, will affect in many ways your relationship to the world at large. You will mark the change in yourself, and, whether you speak of it or not, others will mark and question it.

This is where you will meet with criticism. Your right to grow will be severely questioned. By whose authority do you aspire to spiritual things? In the opinion of some this departure from the plain path of conformity will be a rank heresy, calculated to call down upon you the wrath of heaven. Even so have greater heretics preceded you; and you must not hesitate to deal with these critics peremptorily, if need be, once and for all. *Be a heretic and stand out.*

You will be tempted to argue pro and con, but it will be of little use..., you have gone on before, and they have resolved to stand still, and reconciliation on these terms is impossible. You have elected to be a light in the world, whatever the darkness you may have to pass through; and most unwise it would be to turn back to the open arms for the sake of a merely ephemeral popularity and peace.

There is one thing which should steel you mightily to break with the false gods of tradition, and that is the appalling ignorance and consequent stagnation of hosts of your fellow beings who daily kneel to them. Those gods, from whose brazen cups these hosts drink the most stupefying abominations, tremble on their thrones at the entrance of every new aspirant on the path of spiritual attainment. They know that when spiritual zeal possesses a man, nothing is safe in any of their kingdoms. The weakest among them are even now falling into irretrievable ruin, riven by the keen eye of the Spirit which flames in the forehead of the twentieth century. But many yet stand firmly upon the old foundations and will not easily be moved.

Man, with the pride of intellect more deeply rooted than ever within him, will not willingly turn an ear to spiritual truth. With closed eyes and in perfect faith he worships the great god of intellect; only when he knows that you possess a more precious gift will he pause and receive the first hint of his own blindness. Only when you become in all simplicity an oracle of the Spirit, and reveal to him a new scale of values, will he realise that all accumulations of worldly knowledge are indeed a very little thing as compared with an insight which is divine.

No higher service can you render your brother than that. No other reward is greater than the reward of that service. Before the contemplation of that august ideal of adept service, the glories of all the lesser ideals of men will suffer for you a peaceful eclipse; the voice of criticism will have lost the power to wound; and your thought will blend silently with the cosmic purpose, in which is no variableness, neither shadow of turning.

8. The Tibetan Messenger

Reprinted from the October 1924 edition of The Occult Review. *Also published in the December 1995 issue of the* Rosicrucian Beacon *where the editor appended the following comments.*

"On the title page of this article the following apology was printed by Ralph Shirley, *the Editor of* The Occult Review:

> 'It will, of course, be understood that I am in no way responsible for the opinions expressed in this article, or for the author's criticisms of the Theosophical attitude towards Mrs. Bailey's works. As a matter of fact, Mrs. Bailey's books are sold by the Theosophical Publishing House, as well as by my own publishers, William Rider & Son, Ltd., and I would suggest that the

attitude referred to is therefore probably rather that of certain individual Theosophists than of the Society generally. The fact that these communications have been received through some entirely independent channel would hardly, I think, militate against their being read and appreciated by Theosophists. As a matter of fact, The Occult Review itself, as is well known, is entirely independent in its outlook and yet is widely read in Theosophical circles. I understand that Mrs. Bailey is a very remarkable woman and the teaching given through her is certainly calculated to arouse interest amongst Theosophists, whatever view may be adopted as to its origin. For the benefit of inquirers I may mention that Mrs. Bailey's books on sale by my publishers and also by the Theosophical Publishing House are Letters on Occult Meditation; Initiation, Human and Solar; and The Consciousness of the Atom."

"As Editor of the Rosicrucian Beacon and knowing, from the many letters received from its readers, how popular the writings of Raymund Andrea (Herbert Adams) are, I have no hesitation in publishing this article written by him seventy-one years ago. In my opinion it says much for both the author and the editor of The Occult Review that this particular article was ever written and published. The author, a regular contributor to the magazine, was prepared to write in his very forthright way the truth as he saw it and the editor was prepared to publish the article, albeit with apologetic comments, bearing in mind its controversial nature. It is interesting that the author continued to contribute articles to The Occult Review for several years after this and was evidently as popular a writer with its readership as he is today with that of the Beacon."

Beyond a brief review I do not recollect the appearance in the Theosophical magazines regarding the remarkable books recently published by Mrs Bailey in America. This has seemed to me a curious omission. It is not that the work of Mrs Bailey needs the special form of advertisement which an eloquent eulogy in the journals would furnish; occult students are very well aware of it. But I cannot help thinking that Theosophists should have been the first to recognise and acknowledge freely and openly in their magazines the exceptional gift passed on to them. I do not hesitate to say that the teaching referred to exceeds in value anything published by the Theosophical Society since the foundation work of H P Blavatsky [HPB]; nor is there anything, I believe, of such directly practical value in that work of instruction given in the Letters on Occult Meditation.

Perhaps one reason for the silence of these magazines is the fact that this teaching was not entrusted to any recognised leader of the Theosophical movement and published by its Society, and therefore it is not to be considered an authentic work, having the personal sanction of those Masters to whom Theosophists look up to with reverence. Such an attitude would be a capital mistake. I know there exist diverse opinions as to the actual source of the teaching which Mrs Bailey is giving to the world. For my part, I believe that, if not directly given by the Masters of the second ray with whose names we are familiar, it is nevertheless being imparted with the express sanction of those Masters. I have heard it remarked by a well-known Theosophist that the teaching is probably only the work of a chela, the implication being that it is therefore not reliable. This is nothing to the point. Do not the Masters use chelas? Do not the letters of the Masters show clearly enough that through the instrumentality of chelas some of their best work has been accomplished? This is not sound Theosophical judgement. Theosophists should be competent to recognise an occult classic when it appears.

I express my opinion that the Tibetan Teacher who is imparting this instruction to Mrs Bailey, whether he be a chela or a super-chela, is imparting it with the full knowledge and the express sanction of the Masters of the second ray. I can give no objective proof of this; it is merely my opinion. But my opinion matters little. The intrinsic value of the teaching will be recognised by those who have reached a certain point of occult evolution and the question of who is the author will not in the least disturb them. For the first time in the history of the Theosophical movement this teaching supplies its members with a lucid and scientific method of attainment on the path. It does not appear that Mrs Bailey is a member of that movement. That she has the high sanction to publish independently I consider of much significance..., especially for Theosophists. Every Theosophical student must revere the foundation work of HPB; even so, hundreds have been bewildered by the technical complications of it. It is safe to say that from that work only a mere handful of students have been spiritually discerning enough to deduce a practical way of attainment.

This statement may be resented by some but no one acquainted with the private opinions of Theosophical students can conclude otherwise. *The Secret Doctrine* of HPB, grand, impressive and revealing, baffles and perplexes the average student. As he reads he feels that he has set foot in one of Nature's untrodden wildernesses. Trees of giant growth rise on every hand. Around him is a great silence. He glimpses here and there secret paths along which a few strong and skilful feet have passed and in moments of unusual enthusiasm he attempts these paths, but unexpected boulders loom ahead and he is compelled to return. He is sure there is a way; he sees the footprints of the great Companions; but they appear to terminate abruptly and he is left in greater perplexity. He has courage, his heart is true, his desire keen; yet he can make little progress. He is helpless without a competent and communicative guide.

This is not an imaginary or an exaggerated picture. It is permissible to write from experience. And in so doing, my last thought is to attempt to disparage the noble work of a pioneer whom I revere. That which was given to her she gave out; and through her man became aware of the existence of the vast unexplored territory of the sages. She fulfilled precisely the purpose of the Masters in drawing a map of this territory, which was to be surveyed from every point of view possible to us. We were to measure the distances in the mind's eye, endeavour to appreciate the difficulties and count the cost of the journey across it, and then raise a petition of such intensity for a detailed chart of the path as would justify the Masters in sending a messenger to furnish it.

There is no doubt in my mind that the Tibetan Teacher who is using Mrs Bailey to transmit his valuable instruction is an authorised messenger; and it is vastly significant that it is not being transmitted in the name of Theosophy, but in the name of the Masters to the occult students of the world. I am not greatly concerned who the Tibetan Teacher is; I only know that those who are desirous of following the Eastern path can trust his guidance. The information contained in the Letters throws a wonderful light along the whole path which HPB took to the feet of the Adepts. Since her day, the books written on meditation have been legion.

Nearly all of them profess to teach what is vaguely called the Yogi method of attainment. The barest outline of the science has been published, for the simple reason that the majority of those who persistently multiplied these instructions had little else to give. Yet up to the present time Theosophical students have had to be content with this bare outline in the pursuit of the meditative life; nothing in the form of a scientific method has been presented to them. On their part it has been mainly a matter of faith and the solemn worship of a few outstanding characters several incarnations ahead of them. Again and again I have encountered students who have given the best years of their life to meditation on the real and the unreal, the Self and the not-Self, who express dissatisfaction with their attainment and who acknowledge that they are still unable to say just where they stand on the occult path, or whether indeed they have made any considerable inner headway at all.

I believe the work in general of the Tibetan messenger is what might be termed an esoteric supplement or key to the foundation work of HPB. At least, there are many indications therein which would incline the analytical and intuitive student to so consider it. As in her day, so in ours, few are the really practical Theosophists, and I am far from thinking that the majority of students who read the treatise on meditation will be either willing or ready to test out practically the strong Master vibration in it. Here again, it is chiefly a matter of past evolution. It is easy enough to talk Theosophy: the question is, what can you do with it?

However, Theosophical students are not wholly to blame for not being practical mystics. They could only use such methods of attainment, insufficient as they were, as were given them. With the advent of the Tibetan messenger a new epoch opens and if he cannot assist them to make good they are poor Theosophists indeed. But let it not be thought that they have here a short cut to adeptship. Far from it; it is still the same old path, steep and difficult, demanding a clear brain and strong hands from the very beginning. The lukewarm Theosophist and the omniscient one will alike go empty away. For it is characteristic of the Teacher that he plunges immediately into the depths of his science, without preamble or explanation, with masterly skill, assuming that his reader comes thoroughly prepared and dedicated to the task and is willing to be taught what he really does not know.

9. Self-Knowledge

Reprinted from the May 1927 edition of The Occult Review. *Also published in the March 1996 issue of the* Rosicrucian Beacon.

The formula "Know thyself" has been paraphrased into countless other formulae, all of which are familiar to the student in his reading of occult literature and most of which throw more or less light and meaning upon the primary one. These formulae have a deeply cosmic import and prove somewhat disconcerting when analysed reflectively. To know oneself from the occult point of view is a comprehensive matter and one with which most of us will be well occupied for at least the term of our present incarnation.

We should know, for instance, that true self-knowledge cannot begin until some degree of egoic response has been attained: up to that point in evolution we are nothing but speculators, however remarkably clever from a personal and worldly standpoint. That in itself is a humiliating conception; but it is well that we realise it at the outset because it is a true one. The assurance some students have by reason of a little occult reading is at once amusing and alarming. It is common enough and to be expected among those who have no occult reading and live soundly in the intellect; it is just as common among those who have the occult classics by heart.

The first thing for us is to realise thoroughly the difficulty of the task we are engaged upon. We are enthusiasts and too often possess the cardinal failing of the class. We expect to complete a life task in a few weeks; but it cannot be done; and I draw no pessimistic picture in saying so. The Gita just as plainly says: *"Of the successful strivers scarce one knoweth me in essence."* Upon serious reflection it appears more and more to me that the attainment of self-knowledge is mainly the demonstration of an increasing measure of impersonality. This is the central thought of the Gita and every theme in that classic is grounded upon it. Impersonality is its secret doctrine and no matter how great is the appeal of its beauty and desirableness to the intellect or the aesthetic sense, we remain but in the outer court until impersonality becomes a factor in practical life. Impersonality is usually preceded by a long cycle of development and experience of the most varied, and often perplexing, character. There is a world of inner experience to be garnered before we can become living exponents of the fact; and only a genuine occult discipline compels that experience and leads naturally and lawfully to a safe and proper demonstration.

Impersonality has many degrees. They range from the minor detachments exercised by an aspirant to that extreme spiritual poise so striking and natural to the adept; but in whatever degree manifested, there is in it something exceedingly arresting and influential to those who witness it. Its nature is so comparatively unique, so apparently contrary to the well-known laws of personal expression in the world, that the person engaged in its culture is quickly, though tacitly, distinguished from his fellows. It is a departure from the rule of common life. It originates from a plane outside that of everyday thought and observation and its manifestations are such as the ordinary consciousness almost refuses to sanction; it makes us aware of the divinity overshadowing human consciousness and invites us to make a heart surrender to its beneficent promptings; it upsets our preconceived ideas of thought and action, rejects the limitations and pride of the intellectual self and falsifies well-grounded maxims of a liberal education. And herein is the reason that so few are able or willing to enter seriously upon a culture the nature of which has a more or less forbidding aspect and is opposed to so much that is firmly established and prized in the personal life.

Yet we are dealing here with a condition, a force, which is of supreme value in the evolution of consciousness. Nothing so co-ordinates the powers and enhances the true prestige of man as this unfolding sense of higher perception and values. A multitude of anxieties and perturbations which hitherto held undisputed sway within the soul lose their tyranny and pass away. Not that we forsake the arena of personality and deny the constant interplay of forces therein but that we stand at a remove and survey them from a point of ascension, with a new power of self-direction and insight and have the ability to harmonise opposing vibrations. The consciousness of this descending harmony and peace has a wonderful effect upon the disposition of the mental faculties and its increasing momentum enables us to achieve swiftly and one-pointedly the tasks allotted to them. Indeed, it is only at the stage of development that we come to realise the true strength and beauty of mental action and create after the law of the spiritual man. Hitherto, we were very much at the mercy of the mind; it reigned over us with the authority of a tyrant; we were marshalled hither and thither at the behest of thought and often involved by it in pitiful uncertainty and confusion. But the dawn of the sense of impersonality reverses this condition of affairs. We consciously and deliberately impose the will of the ego upon the activities of the various faculties with marked results. The immense possibilities therefore which open before the man who has entered upon this personal conquest are obvious.

While one has no wish to magnify the many difficulties that have to be surmounted on the way to the attainment of impersonality, such difficulties cannot be discounted and claim attention. The prolonged and conscientious labour necessary for the development of a faculty for any art or science is no less requisite here. We shall feel little relish for this struggle with the secret forces ruling our personal life until we have suffered all too long under their stern domination. There is a definite point in evolution when we become acutely conscious that we must come to judgement within, investigate and understand the opposing factors in our constitution and devote ourselves seriously to the task of self-discipline. Even this preliminary self-cognition brings reflections of not the happiest kind. We have travelled along the path of least resistance and taken life much as it came; we have not felt it incumbent upon us to regard too critically the swift stream of thought and emotion, the action and reaction of these upon self and others. But with this awakening the sense of security vanishes. The stable centre of consciousness around which our life hitherto revolved and to which all our activities were related, becomes decentralised.

Conscientious study and meditation have produced their inevitable consequences: the ego has responded to persistent aspiration and made us aware of its existence and supremacy.

This first clear sounding of the note of the ego in the personal life is of tremendous importance. We become conscious of a division, of a painful discord between the two. The new and stronger vibration causes a certain disruption, a disorganisation among the mental faculties, which pass for the first time under the acute observation of a spiritual critic. And, conformably to the maxim of occult science that expansion of consciousness induced by the advent of spiritual truth produces pain and unrest, we realise the great responsibility devolving upon us to take up the task of self-conquest and establish the power of the ego as the dominant factor in our life in the interest of evolution.

This initial trial of the occult life requires an act of discrimination of a very extraordinary character. It is not a simple matter to put aside the physical, emotional and mental bodies, to remain apart and unaffected by their vibration, poised in the clear and undivided consciousness of I AM THAT. Perhaps the difficulty of the task is a wise provision. It is to be doubted whether an immediate recognition of the immortal Self would prove altogether desirable without a mature development of the three bodies as a preliminary thereto. The way of the Gita seems to enforce this thought: it shows the peculiar method used in preparation. It was not a single lesson easily taught, at once received and understood, which imparted the qualifications for recognition. The teaching was many-sided, each presentation lifting one veil after another and causing to pass from the pupil one vice and weakness after another, until we have his final words at the moment of complete realisation: *"Destroyed is my delusion. I have gained knowledge through thy grace."*

It may be helpful to note that during the series of presentations of different aspects of the Wisdom the whole nature of Arjuna passed under review and discipline, resulting in the acquirement of all the necessary qualifications for initiation. Suppose that some magical act, and this is a point for some impatient students to remember, had been substituted for that gradual unfoldment to him of all the powers and weaknesses of his nature, whereby he had momentarily realised his immortality apart from the perishable bodies, would that have proved sufficient for the arduous work of the path? I think not. He is shown at the outset a goal to be worked for. *"The man, balanced in pain and pleasure, steadfast, he is fitted for immortality."* But that is not the achievement of a moment, nor does it arise from an incantation. It is an organic process of unfoldment in and through the life and texture of the bodies over a long period of time. It really means growth of a singular order. In a recent book dealing with the occult path there is a simple and unpretentious statement which arrests attention because of its deep and far-reaching truth and application. It is this: If many students were subjected to clairvoyant investigation they would be seen to be not *"big enough"* to grasp the attitude and handle the work of the Masters. Precisely; and it is in the three bodies that the student must grow big, permeated and enriched throughout by the strong vibration of the ego, before he is in any wise fit to make that conscious dissociation of personality and stand, recollected and able, in his immortal part.

It is only upon completion of this cycle of growth, where the bodies have, as it were, taken the depth of human experience and been raised to a new power, that it is possible to *"perform action, dwelling in union with the divine, renouncing attachment and balanced evenly in success and failure."* This *"skill in action"* of yoga has a significance which many students little dream of. It takes every phase of personal power into its province and marshals it up to the main event. A magic life has to touch the heart and brain even lightly to comprehend it; and only the constantly accelerated pulse of that inner life can meet the demands of it. It evolves naturally in the bodies of the aspirant who insists upon steady and ordered progress, with a willingness to accept unreservedly all that progress entails. Arjuna had difficulty here. The lesson had to be presented to him again and again and from many different aspects, before he reached that point of entire submission to the truth of the divine within. The difficulty is not an imaginary one. Very real and persistent are the attachments of the three bodies in spite of their relative unreality. It is scarcely a matter for the surgeon's knife; only the student who is skilled in action can safely use that. His instrument must be a patient and loving comprehension; yes, a willingness to be in bondage to the contacts of matter for the time being, with all the failings of Arjuna written upon him. For a wise willingness to endure defeat is a mark of progress. *"Endure them bravely, O Bharata."*

The *"slaying of the self"* is a distinctly personal matter. I believe no two students will deal with it in precisely the same way. One finds success through a complete expression of the personal powers; another adopts the method of withdrawal in a total denial of the self. Many fail here in a wise discrimination. They assume that they are not and cease to be natural; whereas the true disciple, with the touch of the Master within him, should be as simple, natural and expressive as Nature herself. There should be something so intensely human and spontaneously affectionate in him that wherever he goes there is immediate recognition and understanding on his part of every contact and a certain response from all to him. But whatever the method the student chooses, the problem remains the same; the initial trial is the same; the same qualifications are essential to meet it. And every method has its price.

For the disciplined self to move among sense objects with senses free from attraction and repulsion; to be mastered by the Self and enter into spiritual peace wherein is the extinction of all pain; this is not a light task or the effort of a day.

10. The Science of Death

Reprinted from the January 1928 edition of The Occult Review.

The Western occult student, after perusing the *Tibetan Book of the Dead*, will feel that he has been treated to a very liberal amount of instruction on the science of death. Perhaps [Francis] Bacon's dictum: *"Some books are to be tasted, others to be swallowed, and some few to be chewed and digested,"* will appropriately come to mind. Some will certainly only taste, a few will swallow, but only one in thousands will chew and digest and attempt to apply seriously the detailed instruction of this remarkable book.

That enthusiast will probably be a Theosophist, who is prone to believe that every occult doctrine from the land of the Buddha has profound significance for him, whether or not it has for anyone else, and who therefore may feel quite equal to the task of truly orientalising himself by memorising, and prevailing upon his relatives to memorise, the storied progress of his consciousness principle from the dying moments to that state of complete liberation, or some lesser condition of felicity, commensurate with his Karmic merit.

The average occult student will regard this book with mixed feelings. Even in the light of a life's study in his chosen field he will find it difficult to give offhand a clear unbiased opinion. In spite of his reading of Oriental literature and many years of practical application of its esoteric instruction, he yet has a Western mind; he likes the concise and practical; and even in dealing with Oriental philosophy and practices he will, in his swift and discriminating manner, put aside a vast amount of the ritualistic and the tortuous and lay hold of the main fact and apply it. This is a national trait, and with all his superimposed Oriental thinking, he will be strongly influenced by it when he comes to put any instruction to the test. Nothing will so much nettle him as a fine-spun philosophy, no matter what its credentials may be, which he cannot reduce to working formulae that bear every evidence of utility and guarantee adequate results for his pains.

It is true that the comprehensive knowledge offered by the textbooks on such subjects, for instance, as the world periods and similar abstruse studies, is accepted on the word of qualified initiates: the student is assured of the immediate and remote value of accustoming the mind to conceptions of this nature; but for the most part he has to accept this cosmic knowledge on faith, in the hope that some form of enlightenment will at length be vouchsafed to him, and everyday life become the grander for the vision. So it is concerning the practical work of occultism.

The philosophy of yoga and the remarkable powers attributed to the yogi have an immense fascination for the Western student, and many have taken as their ideal the developed yogi and endeavour to follow the severe outline of the yoga practices. It is not sufficiently observed, however, that the yogi is a master mind with a far different objective in life than that of the Western student. Moreover, the long novitiate required of the latter is practically impossible of achievement without the direct assistance of a personal teacher.

These reflections are not irrelevant to our subject. The mental constitution of the Western student, his inborn dislike, even though he be an occultist, of the deeply involved or abstract, and the fact that what is immediately possible to the yogi or master mind is painfully intricate or practically insurmountable for himself, come forcibly to mind when considering a book of the class before us. The book is undoubtedly of great interest to the occultist, the spiritualist, and to psychic researchers generally. Nor is its intrinsic helpfulness to be for a moment doubted to those who may be in a position or who have the inclination to apply its teaching as it is no doubt applied by many in the East. But like other works of a deeply esoteric character requiring exceptional conditions of usage and exceptional advancement for the right use, it will serve in the main to emphasise once again how vast is the difference between simple occult belief in the West regarding the preparation for transition, and the elaborate ritual adopted at that important moment by some of the highly evolved initiates in the East.

The introduction to the translation of "The Bardo Experiences" is a lengthy one and is a necessary commentary on the text. The miscellaneous knowledge of Eastern beliefs and customs contained in it will be chiefly interesting to the historical student.

In the introductory section of Book One, instructions are given for the application of the science to the departing entity under the three headings of: *The Transference of the Consciousness Principle*; the *Reading of the Thodol*; and the *Practical Application of the Thodol by the Officiant*.

In the first, the devotee is enjoined to examine the symptoms of death as they gradually appear in his dying body, after which he is to apply the transference by merely remembering the process..., a process not absolutely impossible, perhaps, if the death hour is not troubled by any of the pains and perturbations to which flesh is commonly heir; but, as is pointed out in the valuable notes accompanying the text, the process being essentially yogic, the transference can be employed only by a person highly proficient in mental concentration. The Western student is therefore confronted with a major difficulty at the very threshold of the Bardo, namely, making, as a conscious fact, the necessary discrimination between the ego and its vehicles, the realisation of the Self as a centre of spiritual force and activity entirely apart from the transitory bodies. Such a degree of realisation enables one to apply the transference effectually and attain liberation through a simple remembrance of the process. The reading of the Thodol will be unnecessary for such a person.

But for the majority who are not able to make the transference as above, the reading of the Thodol is prescribed. Should the corpse be absent, the reader should occupy the seat or bed which the deceased has been accustomed to use; he is then to summon the spirit of the deceased..., in other words, he is to indulge in a little necromancy..., imagine it present and listening, and recite the Thodol. If the body is present, at the moment of expiration, the Guru or a trusted friend must place his lips close to the ear of the corpse and recite the Thodol.

Again, we are confronted with a particular difficulty. For the success of this simple and unpretentious piece of instruction the presence of one skilled in necromancy appears to be necessary; nor presumably can he be assured of the effectiveness of his effort unless he has developed vision of the Bardo Plane. Neither is it an easy matter, in this hemisphere, for a qualified person, or even a trusted friend, to ensure such congenial conditions at the time of transition, what with the likely presence of relatives and possibly of medical practitioners and others, for the carrying out of an elaborate ritual. For the Great Thodol is to be read either seven times or three, according to the occasion: this, with certain other preliminaries, is the practical application of the Thodol by the officiant.

Part One of the First Book concerns *The Bardo of the Moments of Death*, and deals with two stages of experience: "Instructions on the symptoms of death..., the primary Clear Light seen at the moment of death;" and "Instructions on the secondary Clear Light seen immediately after death." These instructions consist of considerable detail, and the detail ramifies into so many possible conditions of application that the student will begin to realise that he must become an expert in the diagnosis of the symptoms of death before he can hope to make the right application. I will quote one or two of these conditions that the student may judge for himself.

> "When the expiration hath ceased, the vital force will have sunk into the nerve centre of Wisdom, and the Knower will be experiencing the Clear Light of the natural condition. Then, the vital force, being thrown backwards and flying downwards through the right and left nerves, the Intermediate State momentarily dawns. The above directions should be applied before the vital force hath rushed into the left nerve after first having traversed the navel nerve centre."

Again:

> "If the expiration is about to cease, turn the dying one over on the right side, which posture is called the 'Lying Posture of a Lion.' The throbbing of the arteries on the right and the left side of the throat is to be pressed. If the person dying be disposed to sleep, or if the sleeping state advances, that should be arrested, and the arteries pressed gently but firmly."

A variety of instructions follow for the different applications of the process, the object of which is to set the departing spirit face to face with the Clear Light. All which is profoundly interesting but, as is pointed out in the notes to the text, the departing entity must have attained to unusual proficiency in yoga and much Karmic merit in order to benefit by the process.

In the instructions of the second stage dealing with the secondary Clear Light, provision is made for the person who is unable to attain the primary Clear Light on transition, and further elements of the ritual are given for assisting him to recognise the lesser Light. In the appended note, the precise condition of the entity at this point is very clearly and ably expounded. It is indicated how rarely is the normal mental condition of the dying person equal to retaining the state in which the Clear Light is manifested. His mentality remains momentarily balanced in perfect equilibrium, in a condition of oneness, but owing to unfamiliarity with this exalted state of non-ego, the consciousness principle of the average person lacks the power to function in it; Karmic propensities interfere, and the consciousness principle falls away from the Clear Light.

Part Two deals with *The Bardo of the Experiencing of Reality*, and covers a wealth of instruction concerning the third stage of the Bardo. This is the stage in which the Karmic illusions reveal themselves: there is much to prepare for and much to overcome. A lengthy ritual is given for seven successive days during the "Dawning of the Peaceful Deities;" a further ritual for seven successive days during the "Dawning of the Wrathful Deities."

This phase of the ritual takes up fifty pages of the book; and when it is said in the conclusion of the section that *"the training in this Bardo being of particular importance even while living, hold to it, read it, commit it to memory, bear it in mind properly, read it regularly thrice; let the words and the meanings be very clear; it should be so that the words and the meanings will not be forgotten even though a hundred executioners were pursuing thee...,"* one might readily be pardoned for asking where, in this workaday Western world of ours, may we expect to find even among serious occult students any, except possibly one extraordinary enthusiast, who will feel disposed to put this process to a practical test?

Book Two also consists of two parts: the first, concerning *The After-Death World*, the second, concerning *The Process of Re-birth*. In the first a further recital to the spirit resting in the intermediate state takes place, again with many possible conditions of application differing according to the status of the departed one. The various experiences he may expect to encounter in this state are to be voiced to him for his immediate guidance. In Part Two, *The Process of Re-birth*, instruction is given for assisting the spirit to liberation, and thus preventing entry into a womb. In the words of the text: *"This is a very profound art; in virtue of it, a womb is not entered."* Thereupon follow five methods of closing the womb door.

All these different aspects of the ritual are known as so many *"settings-to-face,"* and if the entity is not liberated at one setting-to-face, at another liberation should be achieved. *"Therefore, the perseverance in the reading of the Great Bardo Thodol for forty-nine days is of the utmost importance."* It is possible, however, that owing to the great force of Karmic obscurations and previous unspirituality, the entity may not be liberated; in which case, instruction is given for the selection of a womb door.

There is a short appendix to the text followed by an addenda in which such subjects as Yoga, Mantras, the Guru and chela, and others, are touched upon.

I have given but a few glimpses of what is certainly a remarkably interesting and thought-provoking book. For reasons above given, its nature is such as not to incite to practical demonstration among ourselves. Rituals of this character, valuable as they may be in themselves and suitable in usage among initiates in the land of their origin, will be regarded but curiously by the many, and searched diligently by the few, chiefly for additions to technical knowledge, in the West. To quote from the introduction:

> "Although it is remarkably scientific in its essentials, there is no need to consider it as being accurate in all its details; for, undoubtedly, considerable corruption has crept into the text. In its broad outlines, however, it seems to convey a sublime truth."

Just so, and it is the broad outline that the student will seize and retain; and observing in the notes to the text the reiterated emphasis on the necessity for egoic development to ensure success in the ritual of the Bardo, he will perhaps receive a new incentive to achieve the cosmic state here and now. He need have no anxiety about the future.

11. The Light of the Soul

Reprinted from the May 1928 edition of The Occult Review.

As occult students are aware, within the last 50 years several little occult classics of unquestioned value and authority have proved of untold assistance to them in their endeavours on the path. I refer to the Patanjali *Sutras*, the *Gita*, the *Voice of the Silence*, and *Light on the Path*. The latter treatise, as we know, is a comparatively recent one and was communicated to the world through a disciple of the Masters within the present century.

To HPB we are indebted for the translation of the ancient fragments in *The Voice of the Silence*; whilst the *Sutras* and the *Gita* have been accessible to students for centuries back. Perhaps the two most illuminating treatises students could have for use in practical occult training are the *Sutras* and *Light on the Path*. In fact, the *Sutras* will help them to understand and master the sententious and luminous rules of the latter work. There are many editions of the *Sutras*. That of Vivekananda was for years considered a highly authoritative one. An edition more suited to the Western student was published a few years ago by Charles Johnston; but while simple in character and helpful to many who had hitherto been unable to enter thoroughly into the practical significance of the *Sutras*, the treatment was of the nature of a personal interpretation only.

A new book has, however, just been published from the pen of Mrs Bailey, the author of several remarkable occult works comprising the cycle of teaching above-mentioned. It is called the *Light of the Soul: its Science and Effect*, and is a paraphrase of the Yoga *Sutras* of Patanjali with commentary by Mrs Bailey. The *Sutras* were dictated and paraphrased by the Tibetan Brother who is responsible for the impartation of Mrs Bailey's previous works, and the commentary upon the *Sutras* was subject to revision and comment by the Tibetan.

It may be interesting to relate that the system of teaching, first compiled by Patanjali some 10,000 years BC, has been in use since the beginning of the Aryan race, and that the Yoga *Sutras* constitute the basic teaching of the Trans-Himalayan School, to which many of the Masters belong. It is also held that many of the schools of mystical thought and discipline connected with the founder of Christianity are based upon the same system and that their teachers were trained in the Trans-Himalayan School.

We are also informed that the various Yogas have been instrumental in the different races in the unfoldment of the human being. In the Lemurian race the Yoga of the physical body, Hatha Yoga, was imposed upon infant humanity. In the Atlantean race two Yogas were given, Laya Yoga, the Yoga for the development of the etheric body and astral body; and later, Bhakti Yoga was incorporated with the Laya Yoga for the purpose of laying the foundation of mysticism and devotion. In the present Aryan race control of the mind is the objective, and Raja Yoga is the Yoga for the student on the Eastern path.

An interesting point is made by Mrs Bailey in her introduction to the effect that the coming spiritual impulse is a second Ray impulse and will reach its zenith towards the close of the present century, but it has no relation to the first Ray impulse which produced the work of HPB. First Ray impulses rise in the first quarter of each century and reach their climax on the physical plane during the last quarter. The great interest now manifested in the science of Raja Yoga indicates the trend of the rising second Ray impulse. This authoritative statement is of considerable interest, especially in view of the acrimonious controversies which have raged in theosophical circles regarding certain *"probable appearances."*

The paramount value of the present edition of the *Sutras* lies chiefly in the fact that it emanates virtually from the Brotherhood, in that it has been produced by the express authority and under the personal supervision of the Brother specially appointed to communicate the new cycle of teaching necessary at this point of evolution in connection with the second Ray impulse. It is not possible in a short article to indicate in any adequate degree the remarkable scope of this commentary on the *Sutras*; nor is it desirable to quote from a treatise which contains more than 400 pages of masterly instruction for the serious student of Yoga.

It must suffice to say that nothing in the direction of searching analysis and detailed information on the kingly science such as this book contains has hitherto been published. As in the case of the previous works of the Brother issued by Mrs Bailey, it comes to the student without any label attached to it. It is offered to the sincere seeker, but chiefly to those who are attracted to the Eastern path and have some acquaintance with Eastern philosophy and its nomenclature.

And surely it comes at a propitious time. In the midst of religious controversies on every hand emptying the churches and filling sincere and seeking souls with disquiet and eager questioning; and our friends the Theosophists divided into half a dozen societies and pathetically asking one another what is truth; surely it is a great solace and matter for thankfulness that the ever watchful Brotherhood of Masters, ignoring all the petty issues, or, rather, answering them most effectively by the voice of an accredited messenger, declares once again in clear and solid English the Science of the Spirit hidden in the *Sutras*.

Section 2:

The Mystic Triangle (1927)

MAY, 1927

The
MYSTIC
TRIANGLE

A Modern Magazine of
ROSICRUCIAN PHILOSOPHY

ISSUED PRIVATELY TO THE MEMBERS OF
A M O R C

Our Visit to Europe
Doctrines of Reincarnation
Brother of the Rosy Cross
Interesting Facts for Our Members
AMORC in Great Britain
Membership Activities
Radio Department
Questions and Answers
Rosicrucian Dictionary

Introduction

The Mystic Triangle magazine, published by the Supreme Grand Lodge of the Rosicrucian Order, from 1925 to 1929, was the successor of *The American Rosae Crucis* and the forerunner of the *Rosicrucian Digest*. All issues of the magazine have recently been reprinted in their entirety. The 23 articles penned by Raymund Andrea for *The Mystic Triangle* comprise this Section and Sections 3 and 4.

1. The Rosicrucian Order in Great Britain

Reprinted from the May 1927 edition of The Mystic Triangle.

On every hand we discern a rapidly increasing interest in occult and mystical philosophy. There is also observable a great effort on the part of many to achieve the stages of discipline inculcated in the various schools of this philosophy, for the attainment of illumination in the personal life and contact with the personalities who initiate them.

Yet long before this contact is possible we may arrive at some understanding of the methods of these invisible agents from an unbiased scrutiny of the movements initiated by them. We who are students of the Ancient Wisdom are familiar with the idea of the existence of a spiritual Brotherhood which is responsible for the dissemination through definite channels of the occult philosophy we know. The teachers selected by this Brotherhood, and the schools inaugurated by these teachers through which to accomplish its work, are here in the midst of the strenuous life of the world; and anyone sufficiently interested may obtain information of the schools and the teachers.

Springing up alongside of these we find, of course, spurious movements making claims to high occult authority which cannot be substantiated. They enlist the attention of the curious, flourish for a day, and disappear. The teaching they impart borrows its lustre from the original doctrine given to the world and is passed off as the inspired utterance of many a bold innovator.

We are not deceived by such. The right student never is. There is an influence so vital and commanding, so powerful for immediate good and enlightenment, in every direct effort of the Brotherhood for the evolution of mankind, that the man who is ready knows unmistakably in the depths of his soul that the truth is there for his guidance. There is no need for him to run to and fro asking the opinion of others; as little need is there for him to be much concerned about the vehicle of the efforts of the Brotherhood. The teaching itself bears witnesses; and the opinion of the whole world cannot abate one jot the vibratory response set up in his own heart.

Such an appeal as this, it is, that the Rosicrucian Brotherhood and its work is making to its students of the Wisdom. This work stands before the world on its own intrinsic merits, not on the claims of some infallible personality. In that respect it is almost unique in these days of frantic occult publicity.

Its aim is precisely that of the original Fraternity; its method adapted to the needs of the present day. It has no self-appointed leaders making pompous claims. It does not ask of those who participate in it that they shall subscribe to this doctrine or that dogma. It does not assume to monopolise the main interest of the Brotherhood. Of stage effects there are none. It is the voice of the Brotherhood itself speaking to the occult students of the world. The Cosmic Masters who initiated it are well known in our ranks, therefore no greater guarantee of its authenticity is necessary.

The present work of the Brotherhood has been launched with definite and far-sighted intention. It constitutes a well-directed clearance of the field for personal action under occult laws such as has not been hitherto known in the history of the Fraternity. The lectures issued by it are the basis for this action; and the graded teachings compiled for the various grades of students are in a high degree illuminating, and are precisely adapted to the needs of all occult students, but especially for those who follow the elect path of the Rosicrucian initiation.

It is sane and practical and is fundamentally based upon the system pursued by the Rosicrucian Adepts. It is not a professed shortcut path to adeptship, simply because no such path exists. On the contrary, the intricacies and difficulties of the true path are set before the student in all their detail, and the way to deal with them is skilfully elucidated step by step in a scientific manner.

This is a point that requires emphasis. Long has it been customary among students to regard occult attainment with considerable bias. The idea is prevalent that the heights and glories of Rosicrucianism can be attained with little effort and sacrifice. This is a misconception that can lead to greater disappointment than perhaps in any other field of endeavour. It reveals at once the great necessity for a thorough examination of the grounds and principles upon which we are basing our effort.

Careful investigation will show that too many place all their hopes of attainment upon isolated fragments of instruction, with no solid substructions of essential doctrine to which all practical endeavour to be successful must ever be referable. One of the most valuable aims of the teaching of the Rosicrucian Brotherhood is to dissipate this misconception and indicate the true path. Its keynote is personal effort scientifically conducted under well-known laws, with every step productive according to faith and endeavour. A rare opportunity is thus afforded to the earnest student to qualify for mastership.

Of the many qualifications demanded for mastership the most important is sound mental equipment for occult service. This is the main objective of the Brotherhood, and all its methods are directed to this end. No student can serve wisely without drastic discipline for the mind. There must be a sound comprehension of the fundamentals of the Wisdom. The mind must be trained in analysis and synthesis, must be clear and logical in definition and judgement. These terms, I know, are not new; yet only those who have closely observed the development of students of occult literature know how great is the need among them for systematic training along these lines.

The training of the Brotherhood is both original and universal in character, as is amply proved by its membership, which comprises advanced students of every kind of occult persuasion. The mystic is led sympathetically along the path of devotion: the occultist is grounded in all the essentials of his science. Both are taught to scientifically blend the two paths to the end of taking up specific work under a Master. The Christian student is shown the depth and beauty of the Christian life and initiated into the esoteric significance of the basic principles and truths of the Christian doctrine. All this is achieved in a manner so methodical and illuminating that almost insensibly the student realises that he has gained new accessions of knowledge and power of the greatest value in his work and influence in the world.

In other schools we find instruction imparted in solid form. No special attempt is made to stimulate the creative activities of the student: there is no call for specified experiments in the different departments with a view to assisting him to synthesise related information. In the Rosicrucian Brotherhood he is greatly encouraged in this direction. He is taught to classify and arrange his occult acquisitions, to transmute them into personal power, instead of permitting them to remain in the mind incoherent and unassimilated, of little use to himself and of no value to others. He learns to build consciously a comprehensive and discriminative mentality. This means work..., but it is absolutely essential if the student sincerely desires to handle the work of the Cosmic Masters.

It is scarcely necessary to emphasise that an effort of this scope is for the serious student only. His occult persuasion is of little moment: his wholehearted devotion is everything. The Brotherhood is not an open door to the medium and spiritualist. The methods of spiritualism it discountenances. It has the power of the Cosmic Forces behind it, and its work is imparted to those who approach it in the right spirit and desire to participate in it. It is gratifying to know that it has a splendid body of advanced and selfless workers throughout the world who recognise that the time is now that a forward movement should be made in the interests of their fellowmen.

If the Brotherhood has its critics I ask them, what can they do in the face of the increasing momentum produced by this cycle of teaching? The impersonality of the undertaking renders them impotent. They become weaker for every attempt to turn back the tide of evolution.

Let them rather show their wisdom by either assisting it or standing back and allowing the strong ones to progress and bear in silence a little of the Karma of the world. Let them remember that there are those who, like the early pioneers, resolve to make the great Renunciation and who, like them, deliberately seek the shadow of the Cross that they may be found worthy to shed abroad the Light of the World.

2. The Theosophical World Teacher

Reprinted from the July 1927 edition of The Mystic Triangle.

In a recent issue of the *Herald of the Star* there appeared an article entitled, "The Happy Valley Foundation." This article may possibly be accepted by a few, but it will certainly be challenged by the many. It will be repudiated by occultists of every class and persuasion.

The subject of the World Teacher is by no means a fresh one. The public Press in England has already dismissed it with the most scathing comment, so that it is quite understandable that a happy nook is sought for it in the solitudes of California rather than among the Welsh mountains. And the Theosophists in England are not far behind the Press. They are bitterly divided among themselves on the question and many of their best workers have deserted their leaders in view of the extravagant claims put forward by them.

In confirmation of the above I need only refer to a letter published in the *Morning Post* by Mr A T Barker, the transcriber and compiler of the *Mahatma and Blavatsky Letters*. This letter appeared as a protest against certain articles of an irresponsible writer in that paper who set out to deny the authenticity of the said Letters.

Mr Barker, who is a well known Theosophist, referring to the *"Besant and Leadbeater prophecies and apostolical announcements"* appearing in the *Herald of the Star,* proceeds to state that any serious and impartial student who has read the two volumes of the Letters is aware that they are full of philosophic teaching which is the direct antithesis both in principle and application of the whole of the Messianic and sacerdotal insanity which is exposed in the *Herald of the Star*. And further, *"if Mrs Besant and Leadbeater are right in their claims and teaching, then HPB (Helen P Blavatsky, founder of Theosophy) was wrong."*

I have quoted this much to show how true it is that these announcements in the *Herald of the Star* have shocked some of the best Theosophical workers and spread uneasiness throughout the Society. It does not follow that such workers have, in every instance, left the Society. Many have felt it their duty to continue firmly in the footsteps of their honoured founder with the hope that some fortunate turn of events will ultimately restore to the Society its original healthy tone. However, I am not to speculate upon that aspect of the matter here.

According to the article first mentioned you are to have in America a New Civilisation, and Krishnamurti is to be the founder of it. With due submission, I suggest that the New Civilisation is well under way and that the occultists of the world will no more recognise Krishnamurti as its founder than myself. Any advanced soul who has a message for humanity has a right to form a group of workers with the object of disseminating it; but it is sheer egotism to place that group on a vantage point with a self-appointed World Teacher in its midst and claim for its objective the proclamation of a World Religion.

America can boast of some of the most enlightened groups of students in the world. From these sources have emanated classics of occultism which have raised aspirants to disciples and brought disciples to the feet of their Masters without the sound of voice or trumpet.

Our Rosicrucian brother Steiner, taught us what Theosophy really is as a practical science. Compared with the life and initiated knowledge of that man, other leaders and teachers of Theosophy stand remote. He was a lofty and humble soul who refused to testify of himself or point to any personality, but was so filled with the light of Christ that his students everywhere have received a profound incentive to find the Christ in their own hearts. M Heindel, another Rosicrucian brother, following the same light of Rosicrucia, established another group of your New Civilisation in California and shed the same influence across the world through countless students.

Our own Order, a vital part of the same great New Civilisation, established many years ago in your America, is in the front rank of all your groups, and numbers among its workers men and women of light and leading, notable for their intellectual and occult attainments, in both professional and private life. Internationally it is a tremendous organisation, but is it to be excluded in this New Civilisation?

But what of all this? A New Civilisation is to be founded, and the Theosophists have chosen Krishnamurti to found it. That is what it amounts to. He has been recognised by a large number of people as the one chosen by an invisible World Teacher to be the visible Vehicle when He again visits His world.

It appears then a simple matter to recognise a World Teacher. We have always understood, and it is a firm maxim of occult tradition, that Adepts move among the sons of men, unsuspected and unknown. The Adepts themselves have so taught us. Nevertheless, in the case of so lofty a Being as a World Teacher there has been no difficulty in establishing identity. A well-selected group of Theosophists have put their heads together, made this momentous discovery, proclaimed it with considerable personal authority, and the recognition grows apace.

Indeed this is a far too serious matter to treat with a jest, or with the inimitable ridicule launched against it by the English Press. It is a matter of such moment, with such far-reaching results, that the occultists of America, if not of the world, should be as active in its repudiation as the Press, only from a different standpoint.

Is it nothing to sincere Theosophists, for instance, to name them only, that with the teachings of the Masters in their hands and the recently published Letters before them, this extravagant claim should be offered for their passive acceptance on the mere assertion of a few leaders of their group? Is it not in flagrant opposition to the unalterable laws of occult secrecy which are a tradition of the Eastern Brotherhood and which are again and again insisted upon by the Masters in their communications?

Did HPB, towering head and shoulders above any subsequent leader in the movement in the secret and initiated knowledge of the Hierarchy, as the direct agent of the Masters in formulating and imparting the Theosophical teachings, ever so much as mention her own occult status, whether for personal aggrandisement, to satisfy public curiosity, or in response to serious inquiry?

Or have we ever read any such claim by our own great leader, Dr H Spencer Lewis? And are we to believe that the immutable laws of the Hierarchy have been abrogated and to a handful of Theosophists a concession has been made in imparting to them in objectively recognisable detail perhaps the most important hierarchical information bearing upon the future enlightenment of humanity through a well known member of their group?

Is the long established and reiterated prophecy that another World Teacher would come toward the close of the present century a miscalculation on the part of the Masters and they have taken a group of Theosophical students into their confidence on the matter? I will not say the whole proceeding is contrary to occult law. In view of the above, it must be so; for the power claimed to create a World Teacher cannot, by any possibility, be a rightful power in a notoriously limited group, much less in a single member of it.

Far too long have Theosophists remained passive under the influence of Theosophical teachers. The worship of personalities has been their bane. And the inevitable and pernicious effect of this proclamation will be twofold.

Firstly, a number of Theosophists will be so misguided as to veritably kneel down and worship Krishnamurti as their new Saviour, thus taking the easy path of passive devotion to a personality setup, rather than the more difficult but appointed one of *"grasping their whole individuality firmly"* and *"plunging into the mysterious and glorious depths of their own inmost being"* wherein only is to be found *"the way, the truth, and the life."* Thus will they set at naught their own scripture; for bound as they are to the voice of personal leaders, they will follow that voice anywhere, with implicit faith, when in truth they should be seeking the Christ by *"making the profound obeisance of the soul to the dim star that burns within."*

Secondly, the divisions in the Society will grow more marked daily. This is a pathetic point and can only be referred to with regret. Everyone is aware of the painful cleavages which have already occurred in the Society on points of doctrine, latter-day communications of Theosophical writers that are directly opposed to the authentic adeptic statements, and the dogmatic assertions and departures of others resulting from exalted ego.

This is surely enough to perplex and agonise sincere and spiritually minded aspirants, but the recent proclamations have filled the cup of many to the brim. They have been exceedingly patient, they have endeavoured to the utmost to remain loyal to leaders who in their day have done much for humanity, but the test has proved too great. The crucial point with them has been at length reached when they had to decide between the voice of their deepest intuition and some external authority, and their decision has brought them to a total severance from Theosophical groups.

I know whereof I speak, for letters before me from our own members, themselves with past or present Theosophical connections, reveal the position only too plainly. It is that of conscientious men and women who have given some of their best years to

Theosophical service, who had pledged themselves to a Society they formerly were proud to belong to and to leaders in whom they had placed a perfect trust. But suddenly their ears were assailed with a language they could not comprehend, they were confronted with issues they could scarcely understand, angry controversies raged around them which took away their peace, and had they remained they would have lost their faith. It is not in the least surprising. It is to be expected, and the schisms will increase.

And what have we to say about Krishnamurti? Have we any hard words for him? Most assuredly not! He needs, and has, our sympathy. We believe him to be a young disciple desiring to serve the Masters and do good; one of a growing number of similar young disciples throughout the world who are doing their Masters' work and spreading the New Civilisation wherever men congregate. It has been many times said that he himself disapproves of the grand role staged for him; and well might he, for he will need much strength and humility to keep him steady upon so lofty a pinnacle.

It is clear that his group proposes for him a unique measure of liberty, the effect of which will be that he may do what he pleases. We shall observe what he pleases to do. Liberty means power; and the power which his group will bestow upon him is also unique and will prove a trying possession. We shall observe what use he makes of it.

The world has a peculiar regard for a strong man displaying unique power in any chosen field of endeavour, if it be used for its advancement, legitimately and honourably, without vain pretensions or self-seeking. But it has little regard for power and prestige not self-derived, but conferred. And what it thinks of the present election we know. For never before in the history of the saviours of men have we known of one being deliberately taken and *"swaddled, and rocked, and dandled into a Christ."*

England has given its opinion of this classic example. It remains to see what America thinks of it.

3. Spiritualism, the Church and Ourselves

Reprinted from the August 1927 edition of The Mystic Triangle.

The growth of Spiritualism in England during the past few years has been such as to induce a prominent section of the Press to impartially discuss it, and chiefly in its relation to the Church.

I propose to relate some of the facts put forward in this discussion because I think they will prove of particular interest to our members, and for this reason: Spiritualism, as generally understood, is an enemy to sound logical thought and true spiritual culture. To have this brought home freshly to our minds from a different point of observation should prove a strong incentive to critically regard the insidious influences of this enemy among those we contact and be alert to point the new convert and unwary experimenter to the true path of the science of the soul.

This alone can lead to an orderly evolution of the faculties within us and in good time to a safe demonstration of all our powers. I am no advocate for antagonising the views of one's fellow men. It is precisely this ignorant habit rife in the various religious sects which has so often filled the world with strife; but, whenever opportunity permits, we shall never be wrong in uttering a word of warning.

It is estimated that in England there exist some 600 Spiritualist Churches. Of these about 100 are unattached, while the remainder are affiliated with the Spiritualists' National Union. The attendances at the unattached churches cannot be computed, but it is calculated that every Sunday at least 100,000 persons attend the services of the affiliated churches. This number represents, of course, only a small proportion of those who are interested in Spiritualism and is really insignificant in comparison with the representative figures of other religious bodies.

But that which so deeply impressed our Press correspondent on visiting some of these churches was the rapt and breathless interest of the packed audiences. These audiences were composed of almost every type, from the professional man to the labourer, and the atmosphere was tense with the eager, almost pathetic, hunger after knowledge of the things invisible. While professional "mediums" abound, real Spiritualism is largely independent of them. They are sought mainly by those who desire a shortcut to information without personal trouble. The value of the information is always problematical. Yet so popular are these "mediums" that they are usually booked up with engagements months ahead; so that of one thing we can at least be sure..., mediumship pays.

However, the professionals are not so indispensable to the average Spiritualist as is usually imagined. In the north of England, for instance, which is the real stronghold of Spiritualism, these ladies and gentlemen can scarcely exist. The law deals most drastically with them. If they are caught exercising their lucrative art they merit three months' imprisonment with hard labour. Spiritualism flourishes in the north because it is founded upon the home circle. A typical instance of this intimate Spiritualism is cited, which is worthy of particular note, as just here emerges our responsibility as Rosicrucians.

A bereaved mother meets a Spiritualist, also bereaved. The former is overcome with grief but the latter confidently affirms, *"I had a talk with Bill in the spirit world last night!"* What are the chances of the first mother refraining from Spiritualism? What controlling influences are there to guide her enquiries into wise channels? I know of none that are authorised by her spiritual advisers in the orthodox sense. This is a bare recital of facts as they presented themselves to our correspondent. From these facts he draws four conclusions:

That Spiritualism is bound to make ever increasing progress. That the Churches cannot afford to ignore Spiritualism. That, as a religion, it presents a situation which is unique in history, and not to be dealt with in the way in which new faiths have been dealt with in the past. That, at present, this situation is manageable from the point of view of the Churches, but that when Spiritualism becomes more coordinated, less diffuse, and stripped of numerous side issues and charlatanry, progress will become more rapid and it will be far harder for the Churches to cope with it.

Now a word from the viewpoint of a well known divine, a doctor of divinity, who contributed in conjunction with our correspondent to this discussion, but in regard to the relationship of Spiritualism to the Church.

His experience was that large numbers of Church people were content with a vague idea that there is something queer, mistaken and wrong, called Spiritualism, in existence. On the other hand, the Spiritualists consider they have evidence enough to justify them in going ahead. This large body he considers an honest, wholesome folk who have practised Spiritualism, to his knowledge, for 80 years, yet the Church has not had a word for these sincere souls who, in their own crude way, are seeking the truths of immortal life.

The great fault on the side of the Church has been the want of any serious attempt to understand and guide true seekers. So it is that the many separate movements along religious lines are the Church's penalties, says this doctor, for ignoring in the past some important aspect of truth. And the Spiritualistic movement has arisen because the Church has ignored the ever widening field of psychic research. The Church is, in fact, psychologically dead. The study of modern developments of psychology has been openly discouraged; and the handful of men who have had the courage to speak within her precincts have lost their chances of professional advancement. The Church has been guilty of a deliberate conspiracy of silence.

I need not carry these citations further. The editorial comment upon them points to the desirability of churchmen investigating psychic phenomena, and of Spiritualists studying history and philosophy. That the Church of Rome has always recognised the existence of such phenomena, and has consistently forbidden its members to have any dealings with Spiritualism. That the Church of England has remained silent, but should issue an authoritative pronouncement. That her own members look to her for guidance, obviously so, in a matter which is indissolubly associated with that religion which it is her duty to teach. And that, finally, if she continues to postpone her decision, not only will she be faced with a formidable rift but much irreparable harm will be done.

In our Order there is a fair percentage of members who, before they united with us, gave much attention to Spiritualism. They came in for various reasons. Many were what we should term mental types, and the emotional tendencies so pronounced in the Spiritualistic practice could not long either appeal to or satisfy them. Some were full of complaint regarding questionable influences at work in the Circles they frequented and rightly felt they could no longer participate in them. Others were vaguely conscious of the deep stirrings in their natures of genuine psychic and occult forces, and the passive surrender of their ripening individuality to extraneous entities of whose genuine identity they could obtain no assurance compelled them to an active search for a Path of true scientific investigation which would lead to a clear knowledge and wise manipulation of the forces in and around them.

When these members have passed up through our higher grades they will find their patience and perseverance amply rewarded and their grave doubts about the Spiritualistic procedure fully justified. For doubt in one aspect or another of this procedure will be found to be the burden of nearly all the seceders from Spiritualism. There has probably never existed a cult so prolific in the propagation of doubt and uncertainty as Spiritualism. This will of course be vehemently denied by its firm adherents, simply because they fail to exercise a keen discrimination in a connection in which it is of the first importance..., where their emotions and sympathies are strongly concerned.

What are the chances, indeed, of the bereaved mother, above referred to, not falling a ready victim before the dogmatic assertion of her Spiritualist friend of holding converse with her son? The majority of those who rush headlong into Spiritualism are bereaved people, and under the stress of the sense of overwhelming loss, reason has the greatest difficulty in holding its own. In innumerable cases the reason is abruptly dethroned by the overmastering desire for resumed intercourse with those who have passed at any price.

The price is this. The average Spiritualist is a passive tool in the hands of incarnate or discarnate entities, or both. And precious years are spent, thinking backward instead of forward, brooding over a periodically ejaculated sentimental jargon which adds nothing to morality, is practically destitute of intellectual worth, and is but a caricature of religion even in its most conventional forms.

I would not take away the faith of anyone who feels he has received real and genuine help and information from the cult. There are no doubt such cases, but I believe they are precisely those where the receiver is, probably quite unconsciously, indebted to his own evolving psychic nature. And when this is so it is somewhat of a misfortune that he has been led to participate in the Spiritualistic practice instead of allying himself with an occult body in which his development will be safely and scientifically carried forward.

Many of these have come to us and they will quickly realise how vastly different it is to work upon a sound scientific basis of knowledge, building faculty for the future and demonstrating the truths of immortal consciousness in world service, from the retrogressive habit of surrendering their sacred individuality and placing their hopes of spiritual culture and divine inspiration upon the airy abstractions and fuming vanities that float across the séance rooms from the lips of unconscious media.

Do I then, it may be asked, relegate men like Sir A Conan Doyle and Sir Oliver Lodge to the category of unconscious media? I do not, but I have no wish to shirk the issue. Sir O Lodge is a scientific investigator, and Sir Arthur has been engaged upon the psychic question for 40 years. Yet, so far as I am aware, both rest their case upon mediumistic revelation. It is also to be remembered that both gentlemen have been bereaved of a son and have resorted to mediumship as a means of intercommunion, and the communications received are apparently the only basis upon which they rest their present belief.

Sir Arthur's latest book, *Pheneas Speaks,* is a record of communications received in his family circle through the agency of mediumship, and I have not the slightest doubt but that qualified occult investigators would ground those communications upon an entirely different basis from that upon which Sir Arthur is, under the circumstances, naturally disposed to ground them. Sir Arthur accepts the word of mediumship that Pheneas is a great spirit with considerable knowledge of world affairs, and believes implicitly in the general information imparted about his son and family and the predictions put forth by Pheneas. But has not Sir Arthur's long course of psychic reading any possible bearing upon these communications?

Indeed, there is something analogous here to certain statements in Sir Oliver Lodge's book of communications from his son, Raymond, regarding which Dr Steiner, having evidently been specially questioned on this matter at a course of lectures, showed how easy it is for so eminent a scientist as Sir Oliver to found belief upon false inferences. In a word, certain facts imparted by the medium and which, for Sir Oliver, were conclusive, Rudolf Steiner ascribed to pre-vision on the part of the medium, and having no necessary connection with the soul of the dead.

The teachings of our higher grades are emphatic and conclusive on this subject of Spiritualistic communications. They are corroborated by other eminent Rosicrucian initiates. The work of Steiner, for instance, is known throughout our Order and to the world at large, and it is sufficient to quote a concise statement of his on true and false paths in spiritual investigation.

> "True paths lead right into the Spiritual world, and thence to the knowledge of birth and death, etc.... On the other hand, all experimenting with other paths which do not lead through the ordinary consciousness, as in mediumship, etc..., all these are false paths, for they do not lead into the true Spiritual world."

Again and again, in the personal letters of the Master K H we meet with the most definite denunciations of the Spiritualistic procedure. On every hand there stands for our enlightenment and guidance in this matter the authoritative statements of illuminated and master minds; men far ahead of the normal evolution of humanity who have firsthand knowledge of the underlying causes in the realms of the psychic and spiritual, and they are unanimous as to the dangers and unfruitfulness of mediumship.

Where, then, is the commonsense in ignoring all these authorities? They are expressly given us for our guidance. An incarnation is all too short to achieve certain stages of the occult path; why waste it hunting the mocking chimeras of the séance room and listening to the counterfeited voices of the dead? Instead of her ministers and interpreters, we become but the fools of nature.

Many perhaps turn to Spiritualism who have long been conversant with better things for the very reason that they realise time is short. We have known of such cases. Possessing much occult knowledge and with every promise of future achievement, they have succumbed to the temptation which so strongly besets us upon this path; they imagined they would find a short cut and become the recipients of divine inspiration without paying the inevitable price of effort and sacrifice. Never did they make a greater mistake or labour under a darker delusion. But Karma is patient and long suffering and will repay them in kind, and not otherwise.

There remains one unforgettable truth in connection with this subject which I wish to focus on. Upon us, as Rosicrucians, rests a great responsibility. It is our duty, on every possible occasion, to point out to every person we contact who is resting his hopes of spiritual culture on the Spiritualistic procedure, the dangers and unfruitfulness of that procedure and apprise him of the greater possibilities of the sure and safe path of development it is our privilege to know.

The citation of facts with which I set out to emphasise once again what most of us already know, are from an entirely independent and shrewdly observant quarter. The intense yearning abroad for higher knowledge; the increasing numbers who are taking the easiest way, the only one known to them, to satisfy that yearning. And the attitude of the Church which, with full knowledge of the facts, preserves its ancient dignity and decorum, and silently looks on.

A more severe arraignment of this attitude could not be made than was made by the correspondent quoted: *"What controlling influences are there to guide her enquiries into wise channels? I know of none that are authorised by her spiritual advisers in the orthodox sense."* That applies to the Church, but it must never apply to us. We have a knowledge of the facts. Let us take care to use it, each in his own sphere as opportunity permits, with strong intent and courageously and with unprecedented vigour. Let us, too, preserve the ancient dignity and decorum of the famous Brotherhood to which we belong, but let us also see to it that we follow steadily and fearlessly the ancient path to True Seership which the Masters have taught us, and project a potent and unchallengeable message for the revolutionary times.

4. The Comte de Gabalis
Some interesting facts about a character mentioned in Lord Lytton's "Zanoni."

Reprinted from the September 1927 edition of The Mystic Triangle. *Also published in* "Waiting for the Master" *by* Francis Bacon Lodge *(1982).*

There is something immensely satisfying to the mind when, after a certain lapse of time, a rare occult authority is re-perused in the light of the extended reading and experience of years.

It is not merely that the subjective mind has been ruminating the material of the first perusal, although a perceptible clarification results from this; but rather that the subsequent study and reflection of related matter illuminate and amplify basic principles and reveal the esoteric wisdom and practical issues of the document to an enlarged consciousness.

A secret commentary upon its hidden lore has been silently unfolded in the heart, and thereafter that document becomes a truly personal possession. It has a significance which is individual and peculiar; and the intervening studies which have made it so acquire also a new import and value in our eyes.

At least, such was my own experience when reading once again that remarkable series of discourses and commentaries published by the Brothers under the mysterious title, Comte de Gabalis.

Great advances have been made in the occult world since this book first appeared in 1670. It was then understood but of the few; its appeal now is to the many. Readers of *Zanoni* will remember the author's citation of the Comte and, although a deep chord of sympathy may have been awakened in some by it, the original work may still be unknown to them. But the Brothers, as ever in their great work, issued this document with far-sighted intention; they knew its time would come. For us it was sent forth. It should be known to every aspiring Rosicrucian and is worthy of close and reverent study.

When the voice of Wisdom sounds over the world at rare intervals in the years from the invisible Temple of the Brotherhood, it is to us, the children of aspiration, that it speaks; for the divine promise has gone forth from ancient times that we should not come down among the sons of men, mature in soul and filled with the spirit of service and sacrifice, and fail to find the precious truth needed to perfect us that we might more truly serve. For service, and yet greater service, is the incommunicable burden of the Rosicrucian heart from incarnation to incarnation.

The very first words that meet the eye on opening the book of the Comte are these: *"We seek to serve, that mayest illumine thy Torch at its Source."* This is followed by a beautiful "Invocation to the Flame," so well known to many of us and which is responsive in letter and spirit to the elevating ritual of our temple service:

> I call upon Thee, O living God, radiant with illuminating fire!
>
> > O unseen parent of the sun!
>
> Pour forth thy light-giving power and energise thy divine spark.
> Enter into this flame and let it be agitated by the breaths of thy Holy Spirit.
> Manifest thy power and open for me the Temple of Almighty God
>
> > which is within this fire!
>
> Manifest thy light for my regeneration, and let the breadth,
>
> > height, fullness and crown of the solar radiance appear.
>
> And may the God within shine forth!

It would be a great task to take up the thread of these discourses of the Comte and unfold their symbolism; a wisdom equally great would be necessary to translate their precise meaning that every student may understand.

Fortunately, the Abbe de Villars has appended a commentary in the course of which much that is veiled in the discourses is there made plain; and it is in this commentary that our higher grade members will find so much that is intensely interesting and significant for them. They will meet with the most luminous statements regarding the Solar Force, another name for that Living Vital Force or Cosmic Energy which they are taught to direct and manipulate in their advanced work, and its various modes of manifestation.

I only propose to reproduce here a few of the many most arresting references, which will prove peculiarly illuminating to those in our higher grades. These references will serve to show how much has been given them in their lecture studies in the way of practical experiments to enable them to translate basic principles into works of power and service. They will realise that those studies are a practical key to the references themselves which are so luminous to the understanding.

First, the discourses, enigmatical and infolded; then the commentary, unfolding somewhat the mystic word; and finally the lucid explanations and practical demonstrations of the revealed word in their own lectures.

At the close of the first discourse which took place on the mysterious appearance of the Comte in the study of the Abbe Villars, the latter expresses astonishment at the calm and authoritative display of wisdom and the concluding instruction given him, and regrets that the Comte should so soon leave him after having shown him a "Spark of his Light." He comments upon this Light thus:

> "In the Master this light, developed, is visible as an elongated cleft flame extending upward from the centre of the forehead. This flame is ever the distinctive mark of all highly evolved beings who are able to manifest and to keep in touch with their divine consciousness while in the physical body."

We shall soon realise from his comments that the Abbe was already no mean member of the Order to the society of which the Comte had promised to introduce him, and was fairly competent to rate the instruction imparted to him at its true value.

After passing the night in prayer, as requested by the Comte, the Master visits him again early the next morning and they prepare for an "excursion" together. The "excursion" was the well-known...

> "experience in a disciple's training which is made the occasion of teaching him through observation many truths regarding super-physical beings and states of consciousness. Henceforth he is able to leave and to enter his body at will and with an ever increasing freedom, until gradually the experiences while out of the body become as real and continuous as those in the flesh."

Let us take a few fragments of the conversation which transpired during this excursion. Some of us may find ourselves in the same position as the Abbe in our journey on the path, when a momentous decision has to be made.

> "My son," says the Comte, "do you feel within yourself that heroic ambition which is the infallible characteristic of the Children of Wisdom? Do you dare seek to serve God alone, and to master all that is not of God? Do you understand what it means to be a Man? And are you not weary of being a slave when you were born to be a Sovereign? And if you have these noble thoughts which the map of your horoscope does not permit me to doubt, consider seriously whether you have the courage and strength to renounce everything which might prove an obstacle to your attaining that eminence for which you were born."

Let us remember that a master does not put that alternative to a man until he sees within him that enlargement of consciousness which is capable of appreciating it, and also every possibility of the man making a wise decision. It is not to the worldly and unheeding that the Master appears, but to those who have suffered and sacrificed much and who stand at the portals of the Temple although they may not know it. The Comte continues:

> "When your eyes have been strengthened by the use of the very Holy Medicine you will straightaway discover that the elements are inhabited by the most perfect beings.
>
> "...through the use of the Holy Catholic Medicine (government of Solar Force) the pineal gland is regenerated and endows man with super-physical or seer vision."

And of the people of the element we read:

> "Man's consciousness is limited in direct proportion to the development of his senses of perception. Man has within himself, in the sympathetic and cerebro-spinal nervous system, minor brain centres. When by purity of life and thought, and the right use of Solar Force, man awakens and energises these centres, he is able to penetrate into other states of being and discovers himself to be living in a world teeming with intelligences and entities existing in certain well-defined realms of consciousness hitherto unknown and unperceived by him."

Referring to the secret alliance which exists between the true philosopher and the People of the Elements, the comment is carried out to a practical issue which we shall fully appreciate.

> "As on the physical plane, so on the super-physical planes, when two centres, each vibrating at a different rate, meet, a balance is struck and a mean vibration results. The

true Philosopher or Initiate is a highly dynamic centre of divine consciousness and all less evolved entities and souls contacting this centre have their own level of consciousness raised in consequence."

What a world of meaning and responsibility that statement contains! This intensified aura of ours is transmitting incessantly its rhythmic impulses and on every hand silent and invisible contacts are taking place. Its accelerated vibration can crush and degrade and destroy as easily and potently as it can elevate and expand and raise to God. The greater its power the more crucial is the responsibility, the more searching the temptations from the powers of the Shadow; and the solemn exhortation of the Comte to watch, pray, hope and be silent, is of profound import and must ever be our talisman. The Comte refers enigmatically to this intensification of the aura:

"We have only to concentrate the Fire of the World in a globe of crystal, by means of concave mirrors."

The commentary says:

"To the seer, man appears surrounded by an oviform luminous mist or globe of crystal. This luminosity of the finer bodies is the manifestation of the emotions and thoughts of the individual. It is termed the aura and interpenetrates the physical body, being present during life and withdrawn at death. . . Constant aspiration and desire to know God's Law liberates in man that Force which is a Living Flame, and which acts under the direction of God in man, and with or without the conscious effort of the finite mind.

"This Fire, once liberated, begins immediately to displace the sluggish nervous force, and to open and perfect those nerve centres or minor brains, atrophied from disuse, and which when regenerated reveal to man super-physical states of consciousness and knowledge of his lost Sovereignty over Nature. . . The Solar Force manifests on the physical plane by passing through the ganglia of the sympathetic nervous system and thence up the spine to the brain where its currents unite to build up the deathless Solar or Spiritual Body. In its passage from one ganglion to another its voltage is raised, and it awakens and is augmented by the power peculiar to each ganglion which it dominates. The ganglia or centres are the 'concave mirrors' whose property it is to concentrate the Fire of the World or Solar Force. In the cerebro-spinal system there are many centres awaiting regeneration. Hence the spinal cord is the relaxed string whose pitch must be raised by the exaltation of the Element of Fire which is in us."

I feel justified in quoting at length these intensely interesting passages in this truly remarkable occult commentary. They serve to show what a wealth of secret lore is often concealed within a single statement of the Master.

Little wonder is it that the half informed and merely curious mystery hunter is so often misled and resorts to all kinds of dangerous practices in the vain hope of seizing the power of the gods at once for selfish aggrandisement. But our members will realise that they are indeed working scientifically with the philosopher's stone and treading the ancient Rosicrucian path.

"You have," says the Comte, *"the infinitely more glorious and more desirable advantages, true Philosophic Procedures..."* These are explained thus:

> "By concentration in meditation upon a given subject, and by the effort of regular breathing, the inhalation and exhalation occupying the same space of time, the mind may be held so that it is not subject to other thought than symbol that pertaining to the object or symbol of expression about which man desires knowledge. And if man will persist in this practice he can enter into a harmonious relationship with the Divinity within and from that source can gain knowledge which is the result of the soul's own experience while passing through the higher and lower states of matter... At the same time, if man will concentrate upon the highest he can evoke from within self that Solar Force and Power which if directed upward will awaken and revitalise those ganglia or organs of perception hitherto withheld from his use."

Let us hear the Abbe on the subject of prayer.

> "When you pray, think! Shut out all lower thoughts. Approach God as you would the entrance to the Holy Place. Ask if it be well to demand to be given wisdom according to Law. Be strong in purpose and firm in demand, for as you seek and demand power of a spiritual nature you will balance that power in self on the lower planes. It is to penetrate beyond these lower planes or spheres of illusion that Jesus said, 'When you pray, SAY' these things.

> "You have by a direct and positive effort to reach the higher sphere of consciousness, therefore let your thought be clear and concise; for a sincere, positive and well defined prayer harmonises man with God. On the other hand an idle or unthinking prayer without definite expression becomes an affliction to the mind and destroys its receptivity to the Light. A fervent prayer to the Deity crystallises the mind so that other forms of thought cannot enter, and prepares it to receive a response from the God within."

In connection with which we may add a pertinent quotation on the power of sacred words and names:

> "These sacred words have not their power in magical operations, from themselves, as they are words, but from the occult divine powers working by them in the minds of those who by faith adhere to them; by which words the secret power of God as it were through conduit pipes, is transmitted into them, who have ears purged by faith, and by most pure conversation and invocation of the divine names are made the habitation of God, and capable of these divine influences; whosoever therefore useth rightly these words or names of God with that purity of mind in that manner and order, as they were delivered, shall both obtain and do many wonderful things."

All which brings to mind the words of power in our own work and the many mysterious responses accruing from their use. Commenting upon the "Angel of the Grand Council" referred to by the Master, the Abbe tells us:

> "When a group of souls is sent forth from the Infinite Mind to perform a desired work and to gain a definite range of experience, these souls descend into matter and lose consciousness for a time of their own true estate. A chosen member remains on the loftiest plain of consciousness in which it is possible to function while maintaining constant communication with the most highly evolved soul of the group now immersed in matter.

> "This chosen member is the Angel of the Grand Council, whose office it is to be the channel of that Source which sent them forth in the beginning. This exalted being retains and makes known to those of his own Order, working in the lower states of consciousness, a knowledge of the divine plan and purpose for which they incarnated."

It is fitting to conclude these quotations with that solemn strain of eloquence of the Comte which passed so deeply into the heart of Lytton and is unforgettable. It is the oracular voice of the Master who has attained, who has sounded the vast depths of all experience and stands poised and calm, illuminated and compassionate, beholding his yet aspiring pupil with many imperfections of the incarnations still upon him, but yearning to make him worthy of the greatest wisdom.

> "How true it is that God loves to withdraw into His cloud-enveloped throne, and deepening the darkness which encompasses His Most Awful Majesty, He dwells in an inaccessible Light, and reveals His Truths only to the humble in heart.

> "Learn to be humble, my Son, if you would penetrate that sacred night which environs Truth. Learn from the Sages to concede to the devils no power in Nature since the fatal stone has shut them up in the depths of the abyss. Learn of the Philosophers to seek always for natural causes in all extraordinary events; and when natural causes are lacking have recourse to God and to His Holy Angels, and never to evil spirits who can no longer do

aught but suffer, else you would often be guilty of unintentional blasphemy and would ascribe to the Devil the honour of the most wonderful works of nature."

There is strength and peace to the soul in that voice; and if we turn to the beautiful portrait of the Master given in the book, the words live again and vibrate in the silence of the heart. Such is the power of the word eternal and of the consecrated personality which is the chosen vehicle of it.

5. The Technique of the Master (1927)

Reprinted from the November 1927 edition of The Mystic Triangle.

I neither propose to ask permission of, nor to render any apology to, our friends the Theosophists for writing intimately in our Rosicrucian magazine of the Master Kut-Hu-Mi.

The publication in our magazine a few months ago of the Master's photograph, with a list declaring his very prominent position in the hierarchy of the Masters and the extent of his great authority in world activities, no doubt came as a considerable surprise to a large number of our friends; who had hitherto regarded the Master as exclusively concerned in the affairs of their Society and themselves as the main objective of his personal interest.

I write in all seriousness, for there have existed the strongest reasons for the creation of this impression. However, the illusion on this head has passed, and it is now practically demonstrated that the Master is far too universal a character, and too versatile in activity, to confine his unique influence to any group of aspirants of a single name. Indeed, it is surprising how such an idea of limitation and exclusive interest should ever have been entertained by any well-informed occult student.

The most simple application of the law of analogy should dissipate this error. The objective of the aspirant in his studies is to transcend the personal attitude, to observe life and his fellow men from a Cosmic standpoint, and to offer his hand in help wherever the cry of man reaches his ear.

What then would he expect to be the invariable attitude of the Master whom he aspires to meet and be assisted by on the path to liberation? Is not the Master the Compassionate One who has given all for the world, and can perfect compassion exclude, or be bound by a name? Does not the scripture say, *"When the pupil is ready, the Master appears?"*

I am firmly of the opinion that when we become fully initiated into the super-physical and enter, in full consciousness, into the secret assemblies and councils of the Masters, we shall be not a little surprised at the diverse nationalities, and the manifold types and the independent status of the pupils there contacted and engaged unitedly in world service under that august supervision.

Perhaps no other experience will so quickly and effectually divest us of this mean bondage to locality and name, nor so readily enable us to attain that comprehensive and catholic view which is the note of the truly occult mind. In the light of the increasing information vouchsafed us in our day of the Masters and their work, we may take a bold and decisive step toward an entirely fresh adjustment of outlook regarding their personality and procedure.

The old…, yes, ridiculous and conceited…, idea of a great world worker, such as a Master of Occultism, devoting his transcendent powers and wisdom to fostering exclusively the dreams of a small group of aspirants gathered around the one or two accredited pupils to whom, at that time, he embraced an opportunity, under the law of Karma, of making known his activities to the Western world, must go. It no doubt served a good purpose, in as much as it gave a considerable importance to those who entertained the new knowledge, imparted a consciousness of exclusive adoption and of individual worth, and urged them to unusual activity in disseminating it.

We today recognise the importance of our mission. We need the consciousness of individual worth and, the incentive to unusual activity, but we know nothing of exclusive adoption. The voice of the Masters is an impersonal one: that is the cardinal fact for us; and he who can respond to that voice is known and accepted, whoever and wherever he may be.

The swift movement of events during recent years, the increasing complexity of human life and relationships, the resolute pioneer work in the realms of mind, the amazing progress in the great fields of scientific discovery, and the emergence of the psychic on every hand, are all strong indications, for those who have the eyes to see, of hierarchical response to the demands of the growing soul.

The old dividing lines have vanished. The cry is: Onward in the name of the soul! The man with that irrepressible passion deep in the heart is known, whether he hide himself in the solitudes or among men. He is known to the Master who is a world focus of the same constraining passion. The two are one under the Occult law…, the law which is perfected in the technique of the Master.

Few subjects are so profound and fascinating as that of the technique of the Master. It is with certain phases of the technique of the Master Kut-Hu-Mi that I propose to deal. He has been well named *"The Illustrious."* He is presented to us as of singular and majestic mien, with a lustre and dignity of personality edifying to behold. In the clear and tranquil light of the mesmeric eyes we discern the concentration and completion of human experience.

It is a blessed thought that the Higher Powers have given such men to humanity, comparatively unknown but ever watchful, to guide and inspire it, through the agency of their disciples, along the difficult path of evolution. With all its trials and sufferings, life affords no greater privilege to man than to be consciously active in some aspect of this endeavour.

But the technique of the Master is not easy to understand or to translate into life. He knows too well the extreme rigour of his laws to demand from any soul what it has not yet found the power and insight to give. For the first step is an entirely spontaneous one and the offspring of a high order of vibration which is the culmination of a mature experience in the knowledge of the planes. This experience is often not an acquirement of the present incarnation, but exists as subjective memory.

The history of its direct attainment is hidden in the past and is now chiefly shown in swift and versatile response to occult truth in any form, accompanied with exceptional ability of some nature for the expression of that truth. Wherever this response exists, and is of a pure and powerful character, there we may discern the silent influence of the Master's realm upon an awakening soul in the far time. He is now ready for the technique of the Master.

There will be for him, in the scripture of wisdom, a geometry of the Spirit which he will delight to ponder and apply to the infinite intricacies of life and character. Humanity, passing and re-passing between the two eternities, will no longer appear to him as an uninteresting pageant and unrelated to himself. The power and passion of its living blood will create a mighty music in his soul, often very hard to be borne.

Vibrant harmonies will arise within and sweep to celestial heights, strange chords of sombre pitch will mingle with his song of life, and the keen breath of a superhuman strength must have touched both heart and brain to enable him to stand before the knowledge that this symphony of a thousand voices of joy and sorrow is indeed his own collective Karma, in martial array, opening the gates of self-cognition.

It is the Master's response to the soul's endeavour; it is the Master's technique demonstrating within him, whose inexorable law is: That every latent germ of good and bad in his temperament shall be awakened and declare itself. Many are the misgivings of an aspirant when that law begins to operate in his personal sphere. Well may he think that far from making the smooth progress expected, he is on the path of retrogression.

Says the Master…,

> "It is not enough to know thoroughly what the chela is capable of doing or not doing at the time and under the circumstance during probation. We have to know of what he may be capable under different and every kind of opportunities."

A stern and exacting law of which the world knows nothing! Therefore the aspirant must be perfectly ready and willing to withstand its criticism. There is nothing intentionally mystifying in the procedure; it is simply a procedure which runs counter to all other procedures he is conversant with and for which he has to develop a rare discrimination. It cannot reasonably be expected that he will be entrusted with new and altogether higher responsibilities in a totally different realm of mentation and action, unless he has been drastically probed and tested by the searching influences proceeding from that superior realm.

New faculties emerge under stress; not in the unexercised nature of him who fears the consequences of self-discovery. There is no smooth and easy path of ascent here; and with that assurance the aspirant must be prepared to find the confidence which the Master will certainly demand in him for the initial trials.

A member recently wrote to me in these words:

> "Sometimes I feel further than ever from this attunement. I wonder why it is. I have an idea, probably gathered from my reading, that while one does not make any effort in this direction consciously there are influences at work which keep things balanced for you. You have your ups and downs. But once you begin making conscious effort these forces are upset and you may have all ups, or you may have all downs. You might easily make a great mess of the whole affair. I know at the moment my mind feels just in that state with regard to everything."

How exactly, though quite unconsciously, does this member shadow forth the fact of the initial experience referred to! In her case it has not been delayed; her work in the occult field has been of short duration, and in the work of our Order she has only advanced to the third National grade.

But there is no time in this realm. We are dealing with the intangible self, pregnant with undelivered Karma. And the word of knowledge of the right vibrational value may be all-sufficient to precipitate a phase of circumstance, perplexing and painful, but written largely in Nature's great law, and which must be met and understood.

It is the conscious effort made to progress on the path which is the determining factor. Until that moment life moves slowly onward at its accustomed pace. There is an established rhythm in the vehicles which imparts a relative sense of ease and adjustment in the various contacts of life. The furniture of the mind is well-known and thoroughly catalogued, the selection considered excellent and becoming, nothing eccentric, nothing revolutionary, nothing at variance with the preconceived scheme, nothing to disturb the aesthetic taste of its possessor.

But alas! The counterfeit peace of stagnation and conformity is not for the pioneer; the tidal wave of evolution will surely agitate the still waters in good time and compel advancement. And if, through fervent aspiration to the divine, the aspirant deliberately seeks the feet of the Master, sooner or later the trial comes to the soul. And well for him who, even through disappointment and tears, recognises the guiding hand and clasps it in perfect faith.

For the Master has said:

> "The mass of human sin and frailty is distributed throughout the life of man who is content to remain an average mortal. It is gathered in and concentrated, so to say, within one period of the life of a chela…, the period of probation."

A large percentage of our members are wrestling with the difficulties incident to the period of probation. It is the period paramount, wherein the technique of the Master is so unexpected and penetrating that the aspirant's intention must be at once steadfast, pure and spiritual, to intuitionally grasp and personalise it. One has constantly to confront the lamentations of aspirants who do not appear to realise that occult progress must be slow, and that trials met and overcome are of the very essence of advancement.

Says the Master…,

> "The iron rule is that what powers one gets he must himself acquire. He must not even desire too earnestly or too passionately the object he would reach; else the very wish will prevent the possibility of its fulfilment."

The aspirant is working upon himself, upon the texture of his vehicles of expression, not upon external matter, as an artist fashioning material after his own conception. He has been so accustomed, in the physical world, to impose his will, objectively upon men and things and receive an immediate response, that it is long before he comprehends that the deeper laws of the psychic and spiritual are alien to this.

There is no time in occultism. The liquidation of Karma transpires in accordance with an inner law which is not in our will to hasten or delay. That is why the voice of the Masters, though often foreboding and tinged with warning, is ever a voice of encouragement; he knows that the persistent and courageous spirit will ultimately triumph over all. Has he not, as mortal man, himself triumphed? In every aspirant there is that which is akin to the Master's own immortal nature; the vital, dominant, irresistible, seed of immortality which is destined to blossom into adeptship.

But adeptship is a starry altitude supremely difficult of attainment. At every step of the way the Master has progressed scientifically and spiritually under the stern imposition of iron rule. Obviously, then, no one better equipped than he to involve and guide the aspirant through the manifold intricacies of that rule, imperative for his complete knowledge and mastery of personal forces. Only through ceaseless application and after pains incredible do the masters of the arts and sciences attain their superb insight and mastery, and inspire and redeem humanity from the commonplace and trivial, and entrance the dreaming idealist into ecstatic yearning for the Infinite.

Only through steadfast service and never-failing aspiration, through love and compassion and sacrifice, through success and failure, through lonely vigil and impassioned admonition, through all the heights and depths of thought and emotion of which the eager heart and the awakened mind are capable, shall we gain a true perspective of the sure and perfect action, and become worthy exponents of the Master's technique.

We may expect a very marked characteristic in the aspirant as the result of consciously passing through such an eventful inner discipline: he will be spiritually positive. A passive character can never hope to handle the work of the Master. It is not in the nature of things. The master of art uses his vehicle or material of expression with power. He will undoubtedly be receptive to superior influences and often appear to be a tool in the hands of the genius of his art: but there is a world of difference between a highly cultured receptivity and a passivity without strength and poise.

The Master is very direct on this matter:

> "It is not enough that you should set the example of a pure, virtuous life and a tolerant spirit; this is but negative goodness, and for chelaship will never do. You should…, even as a simple member…, learn that you may teach, acquire spiritual knowledge and strength that the weak may lean upon you, and the sorrowing victims of ignorance learn from you the cause and remedy of their pain."

That is one of the hard sayings of occultism, but it must stand. Conventional goodness, and all the qualities which constitute a well tempered character, are to be prized; but the aspirant who intends to take the stages of the occult path must possess, or must resolutely cultivate, a certain aggressiveness of spirit which compels every difficulty to yield its secret and grows stronger for the struggle.

I speak to the aspirant who aspires to be a light and guide to others, who feels this deep call in his nature, who can take defeat in the arena of life and yet pass on, that thereby the qualifications for higher service may be born and raised to power within him. And one of the reasons for this insistence upon interior assertiveness is that we have to deal subjectively with powers and influences on planes other than the visible, which work actively into the personal life. The aspirant is now assailed entirely upon the psychological side of his nature.

"*The direct hostility of the Brothers of the Shadow always on the watch to perplex and haze the neophyte's brain*" is not an imaginary menace. It is a Karmic heritage ranged along the path for opportune attack, before which the strong survive and the weak fall back. However keenly the sensitive nature may suffer and recoil before the inimical and unsuspected vibrations which impinge upon it, the inner self must have reached that measure of strength which can do and dare and be silent.

Through conscientious study of himself in the light of such reflections as these the aspirant comes to realise the full significance of the outworking of Karma in his life. On this matter he cannot be too rightly introspective and discriminative.

The Master's comment is:

> "To unlock the gates of the mystery you must not only lead a life of the strictest probity, but learn to discriminate truth from falsehood. You have talked a great deal about Karma but have hardly realised the true significance of that doctrine. The time has come when you must lay the foundation of that strict conduct..., in the individual as well as in the collective body..., which, ever wakeful, guards against conscious as well as unconscious deception."

His endeavour on the path will develop this discrimination and so clarify his vision that the truth of things will respond to his right-mindedness. For the Master is truth; he has no pleasure in the error of the aspirant: nor will he be subject to error if he persistently tries to identify his thinking with the thought of the Master. There is a pregnant admonition of the Master which he will profitably ponder:

> "My chelas must never doubt, nor suspect, nor injure our agents by foul thoughts. Our modes of action are strange and unusual, and but too often liable to create suspicion. The latter is a snare and a temptation. Happy is he whose spiritual perceptions ever whisper truth to him! Judge those directly concerned with us by that perception, not according to your worldly notions of things."

That spiritual perception is the basis of everything. It will contradict much that the aspirant has always believed to be true, and he will experience pain in renouncing that which is so firmly woven into his world of facts. But his greatest help will be dogmatic faith, although his world crumble around him. There will be many a secret struggle, but the right aspirant scarcely troubles to count the cost.

And from this new strength indifference to opinion will arise. The aspirant must let appearances go. What his inmost heart dictates is the law, not the urgent voices of external authorities. The Master's word is:

> "He who damns himself in his own estimation and agreeably to the recognised and current code of honour to save a worthy cause may some day find out that he has reached thereby his loftiest aspirations. Selfishness and the want of self-sacrifice are the greatest impediments on the path of adeptship."

Cannot we rest our case implicitly on adept assurance? There can be no half measures in occultism. We either want the Master life or we do not. If we do, there is but one law of conformity for us, and the technique of that law embraces every circumstance of life. It does not complicate, it simplifies life..., if the necessary preparation has been taken.

> "What better cause for reward, what better discipline, than the daily and hourly performance of duty?"

The technique of the Master ramifies every phase of experience past and to come. It touches the inmost secret of his own supreme altitude and passes back to the common task of the present hour. Nothing is veiled to the eye of occult omniscience: no circumstance that cannot be divinely adjusted in the evolutionary scheme. We have to make the adjustment, whether in sorrow or in joy, and emerge more purified from the fire.

> "It is with armed hand, and ready to either conquer or perish, that the modern mystic can hope to achieve his object."

6. The Rosicrucian Manual: An Appreciation

Reprinted from the December 1927 edition of The Mystic Triangle.

The Rosicrucian Manual *is no longer in print but a revised edition of the* Rosicrucian Code of Life *is available from the publisher.*

The advent of the *Rosicrucian Manual* marks an epoch in the history of our Order. It is of such general and particular interest to every member that I feel I must say a word about it. The comprehensive range of subjects and the extent of the information comprised in it have already been noticed in the advertisement in the magazine, and that should be sufficient to convince our members that the *Rosicrucian Manual* has a personal message for them.

It is not my intention to comment upon the many valuable sections of the book. I just select one of special interest, part ten, which deals with the work of the Great White Lodge, the attainment of illumination and the *Rosicrucian Code of Life*. It is characteristic of the Rosicrucian Order that it expounds truth from a unique standpoint. No matter what information we already possess, when we approach the temple of Rosicrucian science and practice we are sure to encounter a stream of knowledge which places the particular subject dealt with in a distinctive setting, reflects a new light and reveals peculiar applications of many aspects of truth of which we were more or less ignorant.

Such is the case regarding the matter before us in this section, hence its great value. It may be considered indispensable to every member entering upon our work; for he is shown here just what his objective is and what is the true method of procedure; what Cosmic initiation really is and what is the Cosmic awakening which follows.

The material on psychic awakening and development is direct and pertinent, and if the new member will take to heart the facts given he will probably be saved some future discouragement. These facts are precisely those which one is so often called upon to embody in correspondence with members who do not realise the laws involved in development. The question of progress and delay is naturally one of the commonest themes in this correspondence, therefore the information given on this question cannot fail to be of much interest and practical assistance.

The topic of special service rendered to members in the course of their studies is treated and should be instrumental in increasing their confidence in the work of the Order and in themselves. The value of consistent contact with the Order is outlined and the possible consequences of negligence in permitting lapse of membership.

Special opportunities to progress are discussed and the points given cannot be too carefully observed. Members receive hints from the inner side which may lead to important objective results. Other topics bearing directly upon the work and progress follow.

The *Rosicrucian Code of Life* which appears in this section is of real value. It reveals in a singular manner the distinctive cast of Rosicrucian thought and teaching. The Code consists of thirty rules concerning the daily life of the Rosicrucian and are remarkably penetrating; they search every chamber of consciousness and quicken the desire for nobler living. Merely to read this Code is an inspiration: to live it will impart that strength, dignity and grace which are fundamental to the principles of the Order and influential in the personal sphere.

I have alluded to one section only; but the *Rosicrucian Manual* is replete with general information of value. I would like to refer to the Sixth Grade Temple References. Under this heading is given a series of valuable charts hitherto only passed on to members who have reached the Sixth Grade. This is a privilege to all members below the Sixth Grade. They have before them now for study in advance these charts and the accompanying explanations, and the opportunity of assimilating this knowledge beforehand will prove of great assistance when they reach the Sixth Grade.

It only remains to say that the format of the *Rosicrucian Manual* is all that could be desired and reflects considerable credit on the compilers and on the Brother who has performed this exceptional act of service to the Order in publishing it.

7. Reflections on the Third Temple (Postulant) Grade: Article 1

Reprinted from the December 1927 edition of The Mystic Triangle.

Members in the advanced grades are often reminded, in the course of their lectures, that it will be necessary for them to revert again and again to the early grades and dwell upon the principles and suggestions therein, as these constitute the indispensable foundation of the subsequent studies and demonstrations.

This admonition is inclined to be overlooked, or its full import is not grasped, by many who are solely intent upon the works of practical occultism. Sometimes a member who has passed into the sixth or seventh expresses disappointment because the unique vistas of knowledge and the wonderful possibilities opened out in these grades are not at once demonstrable factors in his hands.

It is a simple matter, indeed, to read and intellectually understand what the master mind has written; but it must inevitably prove disappointing to overlook the esoteric character and development of that mind. We need a true perspective regarding the question of preparedness for the accomplishment of master works.

The Rosicrucian Mystery flames silently at the heart of life, not on the surface; and only the deeply initiated soul passes within the precincts of the temple. And when this Mystery is actually embodied before us in a master personality, and a transcendent knowledge flows from it as a special revelation illuminating the material and immaterial worlds alike with a Cosmic comprehension which is supremely arresting and convincing, a sense of proportion is requisite to place that personality in the exceptional category which Karma has decreed for it, and ourselves in the category to which we, too, rightfully belong.

In a word, the category of the master mind is one; that of the pupil is another. I do not wish to impress an idea that an impassable gulf exists between the two. That would prove a sad and depressing conviction; but· in the early progress through the grades this idea of the two distinct categories should be recognised, and the recognition should give a true perspective and mitigate any feeling of temporary disappointment experienced through the inability to perform offhand master works.

The teaching in the Third Temple Grade is of great suggestiveness and value and indicates a wide field for study and reflection on the expansion of consciousness. The eager aspirant who has reached the seventh or eighth may conceivably be highly gratified at the masterly exposition of esoteric knowledge continuously passing into his hands and the brilliant prospect of achievement possible through its application: and justly so. But has he grasped the real significance of the Third, with all it suggests of a wide preparedness indispensable for subsequent demonstration? Does he realise what this extension of consciousness implies?

When we survey the work of the expert in any other realm our first thought is of the prolonged attention and assiduous toil of years he must have given to expound and demonstrate with ease and facility the deep arcana of his science. We know he has had to wrestle with nature at every step. At many a point he has been thrown back by what appeared overwhelming odds..., a little progress, a seeming retrogression, an abrupt halt..., but through it all the proud beat of the dedicated heart steadily advancing along the undiscovered path to firm conquest.

It is the history of all conquest. And the same novitiate awaits us. We are entering upon what is, for us, the undiscovered country. The footprints of the elder brothers are before us making straight for the goal; in our hands are their charts for our guidance; over us silently broods their sacred influence. They cannot do more: the law of life forbids. It is we who err in that in our enthusiasm we glimpse the heights of occult mastery in the master mind and, lacking experience, we would attain those heights ourselves..., now!

But nature soon undeceives us. Have we the perfected organism necessary to exist on the heights? What though enthusiasm like an incantation should suddenly raise us, if the fearful loneliness of the heights prove too much and we fall back through want of the sustaining vigour of the ripened powers of the inner man?

For the master personality must stand alone. The reward of his attainment is a tremendous responsibility in teaching others the way and in sharing their burden. The great soul stands apart, and alone. *"And he went up into the mountain to pray, himself, alone;"* that he might receive power, not of men, but from God, and do greater works for their sakes that they should likewise do after him.

We read that the path of preparation must precede the path of initiation. But we do not take this matter of preparation with sufficient seriousness. It implies far more than a brief period of daily meditation. A prevalent idea among aspirants is that their exclusive concern must be with the things of the Spirit; that the personal life matters nothing; that their whole attention is to be focused upon the Self that is real over against the personality which has no life in itself and must therefore be excluded from consciousness.

The teaching of the Third is diametrically opposed to this idea. The genius of man is fourfold; and it is pointed out that the perfection of the master mind consists in the fourfold realisation of the dream of beauty in the physical order, of love in the moral, of poetry in the intellectual, and in the spiritual of the mystics. Here are indicated the four lines of personal culture which is to culminate in that extension of consciousness which is the mark of the full orbed Rosicrucian life in all its strength and beauty.

The Rosicrucian life is a Cosmic life, an enlargement of consciousness which is susceptible of and responsive to the manifold appeal of the entire gamut of vibrations which reach it along these four avenues of expression of the genius of man. I venture to affirm that however far on in the grades an aspirant may be, the work suggested in the Third must never be lost sight of, must indeed form the essential basis of all the later work.

I would not be misunderstood in saying that we cannot build upon the spiritual alone. The attitude of many aspirants seems to suggest that we can. They possess an enthusiasm which is laudable enough and declare emphatically that they wish only to realise God and perform the miracles of the divine life. It is well: they are the richer for such an ideal. But their novitiate has hardly commenced. There is a long series of readjustments to be made throughout the whole economy of their lives, a rearing of faculties and discipline of powers, a resurrection of the soul in its many aspects of beauty and expression, and a firm welding together and a concentrated and wise direction of all these masterful forces, before the Master can use them for responsible world service.

A member once wrote to me to ask whether I thought a pair of blue eyes, which she discerned in the psychic distance, were those of a certain great Master. The obvious reply was that while there was no reason why the Master should not be as personally concerned in her welfare as in that of anyone else, provided she were ready, yet it was reasonable to think that if such were indeed the case she would have no doubt whatever on the matter. The fact was, this good soul was prone to overestimate her evolutionary status, and perhaps her personal value in this particular direction.

There is a great lesson here involved. We need but study impartially the biography and works of the master mind to gain a vivid conception of the vast range of vibrational response which is the keynote of his unique influence. Let us think for a moment of the comprehensive genius of Bacon. We cannot but regard with profound admiration the almost unsearchable riches of knowledge and wisdom of this great Rosicrucian. It is a far cry from the humble aspirant in the grades, breaking new ground in the elementary principles of our science, to the intellectual grasp and amplitude of thought which unfolded and systemised with consummate mastery the volume of universal knowledge.

Yet that is our objective. The fourfold genius of man, latent in every one of us, has to be resurrected through the incarnations and compel the attention and arouse the sleeping ambition of the multitudes that walk in darkness. It is the central aim of the work of the grades to awaken to vital consciousness the manifold nature of the aspirant, to bring into the field of acute conscious realisation every power and possibility that slumbers in human personality.

With full knowledge of the responsibility of the assertion, I say, it is of little avail for us, possessed with a simple desire for the mystical life, to spend our time in affirming the Self and denying the human self through which alone the Self can express its powers. Yet innumerable cults are founded mainly upon this magic process of affirmation and denial. It is not surprising that many of our members have based their faith upon it, by reason of their former association with these cults.

I say not a word to belittle sincere effort. On the contrary, their original spiritual intention has opened the way for well-directed and scientific work. Neither is it surprising that they did not make the progress they anticipated. Many of them took to heart the science of Yoga in its severest outline: their ideal was the Eastern yogi resting peacefully in his Samadhi. Here, too, the ideal is a noble one; but it must receive certain modifications when transferred to Western life. The aspirant has a far different objective in daily life than the Eastern yogi. Moreover, the yogi is a master mind whatever works he chooses to do or leave undone; and the master mind belongs to one category and the aspirant to another, with a severe novitiate separating them.

The aspirant in the Third must take his work seriously. He must take his personal self just as it has been fashioned by him in the past, recognise its strength and weakness, assess the value of the faculties he has, and resolve to build those he will surely need. The curriculum of the university is not necessary for a knowledge of self. Some of the best occultists have not had the opportunity of academic training; others have disdained and refused it as a probable menace to their native and aspiring genius. But they have always been tutors to themselves and submitted to an arduous personal discipline.

Neither did they deny themselves the beholding of the beauty of the world, lest the glory of it should blind them to the greater glory of God. They held it to be the part of wisdom to increase, not diminish, their power of response. And if we learn to live solidly and humanly in the natural man and understand what a wholesome creation he is, we shall not have the heart to deny his existence.

Let us survey the living face of nature as freshly as a child and absorb the wisdom of the sages through our cultured senses from the eloquent earth and sky and human countenance divine, before we acquiesce with the gospel of a textbook that these are but illusions to lure us to sin and corruption. If nature is the art of God, is it not an insult to the Artist to neglect the cultivation of those senses through whose instrumentality we are to interpret it? There is not a mood of the Great Mother which has not a beauty of its own, and the aspirant with cultured senses will learn to appropriate its secret essence and thereby enrich his soul's expressiveness. There is a beauty of voice, gesture and motion which should never pass unheeded, but should awaken some sleeping harmony and incite to nobler living.

He should never weary of reading and interpreting the infinite shades of expressive beauty that flash from the countenances of his fellow men and women. In them he will read the history of the world. He will see Christ saving the world, communing alone with the Father, going up to Calvary with never a glance behind Him. He will see Him suffering on the Cross and forgiving even those who crucified Him. In them he will see the struggling soul in every phase of its eventful evolution, advancing passionately in joy, stricken cold by the hand of fate, eagerly questioning all experience, indifferent through grief of the pain of life. All divine fragments that went forth in the morning of their creation, curious and wondering and beautiful to look upon, for the author of all beauty created them; and returning at the setting sun, bearing each one the indelible traces of the long search of the incarnation.

O aspirant, this is the very beginning of your novitiate; for unless you have learned to see and to understand, how will you serve even the least of these? It is the fullness, the completion of life experience we need, not the denial of it. It is undoubtedly true that he who is somewhat derogatively referred to as a man of the world is often in many respects far nearer the Rosicrucian life than the student who has deliberately refused the contacts of personality and banks upon his own sweet conviction of self-righteousness and spiritual aloofness.

But nature has not so instructed him. Her law is that of swift response to the primal urge. She knows nothing of the doctrine of denial: she lives and expresses. So does the master mind; and thus in him the realisation of the dream of beauty is perfected and the Cosmic law fulfilled.

Section 3:

The Mystic Triangle (1928)

January 1928   25 cents

The MYSTIC TRIANGLE

A Modern Magazine of
Rosicrucian Philosophy

OFFICIAL MONTHLY PUBLICATION OF

AMORC
TRADE   MARK

Mystic Illumination,
    Reflections on the Third Temple Grade,
        Authentic History of the Order
            AMORC Will Not Colonize on the Nile,
                Introduction to the Master Amatu,
                    Membership Comments,
                        Other Interesting Articles.

1. Reflections on the Third Temple (Postulant) Grade: Article 2

Reprinted from the January 1928 edition of The Mystic Triangle.

At this time, perhaps it would be as well to mention that in these articles I address myself, not to those who have made considerable progress in the grades..., or in occultism generally, but chiefly to young aspirants who have comparatively recently entered upon this study: whose interest is keen and whose enthusiasm is high, but who, in many instances, have not made a proper survey of the path to their objective.

I hope I shall be pardoned if I say that this undue haste to achieve the goal without having first taken careful measure of the various stages of progress thereto, is more characteristic of the American than of the European student; although it is more or less in evidence in groups of every nationality. However, it is a fault which always brings disquieting thoughts and doubts in its train. But it can be avoided if the aspirant will give sufficient thought to the basic work outlined in the Third Grade and thoroughly realise that there is no dramatic short cut to mastery within some insignificant time limit he chooses to set for himself.

I recall the case of a member in my jurisdiction who recently took up our work. He was keen, enthusiastic and studious, but he had little knowledge of occultism. Only a few weeks had passed when letter after letter reached me in feverish succession, expressing the utmost anxiety because certain objectives had not been met almost immediately, and urgently requesting special assistance in these matters. Now, the instruction he had received was entirely new to him. It had opened up a distinct and original line of reflection, and he confessed that it had proved a tremendous help to him and brought fresh interest into his life! Well, what more could be expected, what more was necessary in his case, in the early stages of the National (correspondence) work? Surely nothing: for the new knowledge had entered like a flood of light and created a veritable happy chaos among his established philosophy of life. He found he would have to rearrange his whole mental programme and lay an entirely new foundation of thought. Surely the first steps had proved very productive ones.

Several similar cases could be mentioned, and one is prompted to say to young aspirants: do not try to push on the lines, but take time to develop. Enthusiasm alone can never achieve; it must be accompanied by calm and sustained thinking and reflection. In these early stages we are but clearing the ground for action; and when the Third Grade is reached a further large field opens and demands thinking and reflection of a far more comprehensive nature, some aspects of which I am endeavouring to suggest in these articles.

We are to deal here with the realisation of the dream of love. And the burden of my theme is: the aspirant must be a lover of souls.

No man can become a Rosicrucian who does not widely serve. No man is worthy of that sacred name who does not feel a pure and spontaneous joy in the service of others. He may call himself a mystic or an occultist because of his much reading, but any other name will have just as little value if he has not so lived and wrought and sacrificed that the spirit of service dominates his life.

The aspirant often finds this a hard saying. He cannot conceive why the doctrine of service should be so strongly insisted upon when there is so much to do for himself. It is true; he has very much to do for himself. But on the occult path be comes within the working of a stern law whereby, no matter how much knowledge he has absorbed, he cannot realise the full value of it, nor truly profit by it, until in some form of service he distributes it.

The extent of the sacrificial service of a great soul is a revelation when one first becomes aware of it. It is so ready and painstaking, that the average person is astonished and doubts the pure intention of it..., which is quite understandable, for a rare virtue indeed is true disinterestedness. A man may devote himself to the study of an art or science and be perfectly happy in the facility gained in it and the diversion he derives from it; but soul unfoldment is of another order. The awakening soul must find its reactions in the world of men at every step of advancement.

It may be said that I am merely voicing what every aspirant knows. So much the better if he does; but experience shows that a large percentage of students of theosophy and occultism do not act upon what they know. Their interest cannot be disputed, but they are chiefly interested for themselves. They add volume to volume with tireless persistency; nay, they are little short of occult encyclopaedias; they have devoured more books than I shall probably see in a lifetime. Yet they are at a stand..., because they have occultism on the brain, but not in the heart. Occult truth, to be of any use, must become life experience. It must descend into the heart, pass through the fires of love and transfiguration, and rise again into the highest: a spiritual creation, to be shed abroad for the blessing of the world.

We are considering the very highest aspect of the realisation of the dream of love. I am overlooking other aspects of the expression of personal love in a more restricted sphere: these have their place in the aspirant's development and will be fulfilled according to temperament and in the ordinary course of life.

I have in mind here that form of service which is peculiar to the aspirant and which is imperative for his rapid advancement in spiritual knowledge and world response; and in bringing him within a sphere of occult observation in which he will receive an unusual access of higher influences and be gradually fitted for greater work and responsibility in the science he has adopted.

And let it be remembered that he is not to wait and be carefully selective as to the form of service he shall render. That is a common error. He is disposed to think that he is only ordained to some mysterious high-class occult service, that if it does not bear the dignified insignia of occultism, the opportunity is beneath him. That is a very narrow, orthodox error. Spiritual service has no selective channel for its operation; it is the attitude of an ever watchful soul which inspires hand and brain to act in any conceivable way that circumstances suggest to assist, uplift or alleviate. It is precisely the attitude of the Imperator, mentioned in the August magazine: *"The call comes; it is the call of opportunity to serve, and such a call is a command to the mystic."*

There can be no higher ideal than that; and the greater the master mind the more gloriously is it possessed with this ideal. I know of nothing so profoundly stimulating as adept service. The supremacy of the adept rests entirely upon the universality of his service.

Is it necessary to remind the aspirant that Christ was a servant? It is sometimes necessary; for he often fails to see any connection between his study and the way of the Cross. Indeed, there is no other way. The sign of the Cross is before him directly he enters the portals of our Order, and he must be prepared to see it dramatically change at any moment into personal experience. It is at this point that fear descends upon him and his persistence is put to severe trial. Every step he takes toward higher unfoldment calls for some fresh adjustment in his objective life.

H P Blavatsky once said that true occultism is altruism and it throws him who practises it out of the calculation of the ranks of the living altogether. That is wonderfully true. It is not in the nature of the unreclaimed human self to think and act for the good of others, to pour out its life for the world; it is far too intent upon self-appropriation, often at the expense of others. It is vehement in its pursuit of its personal rights and manifests the instincts of lower evolution.

The aspirant, on the other hand, is endeavouring to leave all this behind him. He is thinking earnestly of the higher possibilities of man, he is putting aside the worldly standard and becoming a force in the work of the evolution of the soul. That is what throws him out of the calculation of the ranks of the living. He will be misunderstood and criticised, his strength will be considered weakness, and the hell that lurks in the depths of human nature will rise to defeat him. But is it not a privilege that he should suffer because of the stronger manhood within him? Is it not a manifest sign to him that already some powerful law has wrought a change in his nature that the world puts it to the searching question?

If he is wise he will turn his eyes upon himself as never before, and in that deep scrutiny think upon the master mind who is his ideal. Now is he engaged in the first real battle in the arena of selfhood and he will need to study carefully the temper of his weapons. This experience will give him a clear insight of the great suffering which the master mind has known, who has advanced infinitely beyond him, and who has endured the world's frown and bitter opposition along the whole path of his sublime service. That has made the master mind intrinsically what he is. But now he is in peace.

Height, although it has its perils and is the more easily singled out as a target for the animosity of the world, has also its own inestimable privileges. The good law provides for that. The great soul must indeed suffer; but Cosmic susceptibility brings also the inward poise and force to detach himself from the ever present burden of souls, or inevitably he must falter. Thus is he able to dispense his power serenely and uninterruptedly within the sphere of a perpetual peace.

The aspirant would do well to ponder this point and deduce an analogy for himself. Every step of his upward progress brings him within range of a more refined working of the evolutionary law. He passes through a series of miniature rebirths of the soul; and the more steadfast he is in translating his increasing knowledge into forms of world service the more inwardly productive will these rebirths be. Service releases the soul: it creates peace and power in self; it enables him to know himself and others to a degree never deemed possible. The influence of his life upon others will be so instant and reactionary that it will not be long before he demonstrates for and in himself what the law does in the master mind: in perfecting in him the power and peace to persist through all circumstances until he, too, stands upon the heights.

The dream of the realisation of love is a very practical matter. It is not the expression of a sickly sentimentality enjoined upon its adherents by certain sections of the Christian community. It is the intelligent and well-timed expression of force which gradually reveals the true majesty of the soul. It calls for the steady assertion of real manhood, regardless of many probable consequences which render the average man actionless. The aspirant must clear his mind here and now of all illusions respecting it. Some of the difficulties which will confront him have been hinted at, but they should not deter him. It is a fact of experience that, *"the more his feet bleed, the whiter will he himself be washed."*

If he will try to grasp that fact now, in the Third Grade, he will build a sound basis for future ascent. It will enable him to crucify fear at the threshold, and make him inwardly and undeviatingly fixed upon his goal. For in the heart of the true server there is a resurrected power which is irresistible and equal to any foe.

2. Reflections on the Third Temple (Postulant) Grade: Article 3

Reprinted from the August 1928 edition of The Mystic Triangle.

The keynote of the present articles is realisation. Our work on the path consists of a series of realisations; an entering into, with complete understanding, one phase after another of life experience, through external contact, or inward cogitation, or the steady ascension of mental forces. Through external contact we realise the beauty of the world. We sense the ever changing panorama of form, colour and sound expressed with infinite prodigality in the face of nature and of humanity. Poor indeed are we if we have not passed a long novitiate within the suffusing embrace of this living dream!

Resting here, with clear senses and full appreciation, we clothe ourselves in the mystic garment of the ideal. We sense the immensity of God and feel within us the divine afflatus of the spirit of creation. Every man should be a creator after his kind, and in the temple of nature the aspirant must discover his first strength and learn his technique as an artist of the beautiful.

Through inward cogitation he interprets the dream of love as service. His reflection on the bountifulness and resourcefulness of nature teaches him the law of wise and timely expressiveness in the service of his fellowmen. He is to give himself royally in his chosen sphere of life and prove to the Powers that are ready to assist him that he is a reliable worker and not a mere theorist. No matter where his humble lot is cast, he is called to act a part that will shed a divine halo around it and be instrumental for good.

Civilisation, brilliant and culminating, yet proud and materialistic and ignorant of its goal, cries aloud for the sacrificial service of the humble aspirant. He must not fail it. He should know that occultism is not a soft religion for the attainment of a personal Elysium, but the relentless light of the devastating truth that makes men ashamed in the presence of the soul.

He must pass out of the conventional life and explore the lonely promontory of thought until he has that knowledge and conviction. He must not unwillingly suffer the peace derived from finite adjustment to be disturbed as he pushes forward to the higher peace of Cosmic attunement, intent upon radiating its assurance upon the turmoil of the world. He must realise that the soul is impregnated with creative power, and that power he must resurrect with dedicated purpose and total recklessness of the common and unenlightened opinion of those who fear for his sanity. He is on the road to Damascus, and when the full light comes all service will be sublime and he will give all and suffer all in the Master's name.

In all these realisations the conscious directing power of the soul is implied as the ever present and persistent motive. In the first realisation the soul inspires the senses to a higher and more cultured observation of the manifested beauty of the Author of nature.

In the second realisation, by virtue of an enlargement and enrichment of the soul's qualities, we minister understandingly to the common life of our fellowmen in the way of everyday service. We have now to consider the intellectual life as the realisation of the dream of poetry. The term is significant and admits of a wide application. The expression of life is rhythmical. From the vast and illimitable ocean of cosmic vibration issues with fervent appeal every inspired creation of the mind of man. And if we go at once to the fountainhead of the sublime and poetic, to the divinely inspired prophets, whose intellectual superiority and oracular utterances will never be eclipsed inasmuch as they were the august revelators of the truth of the things of time and eternity, who saw the things that were and foresaw those to come and whose rhythmic and prophetic speech has inspired and given an universal theme to many a prophet of the modern world, we shall do well.

It is related of Bossuet, the famous orator, that on first reading the book of Isaiah, he was so struck with the beauty and sublimity of it that he became a man of one book. A remarkable tribute to his intellectual appreciation and an example not unworthy of imitation! For Isaiah is the revealer of facts and his outstanding characteristic is his many-sidedness. He is the great anticipator of the Christ entering into human evolution. He has the triple sight of poetic genius: observation, imagination and intuition; from which arises that heavy burden of reproach and prophecy which descends with such majestic elocution upon the civilization of his time.

I am not proposing a sermon for the aspirant on the book of Isaiah. The churches have given him so many that he has probably overlooked the sterling value and culture of the prophet, and he lives in his memory but as a name. My aim is to suggest that he should put aside the ecclesiastical influence and permit these world poems to speak for themselves, to his own reverent and searching mind in all their naked majesty, until he gains something of the strength and nobility of their cosmic thinking. It is intimated by some that we Rosicrucians make little of the Bible; I suppose, because we are not always quoting it.

If the inference were true, the fact would be recorded to our shame. Nothing could be further from the truth. The fact is, the truth of the Bible is so deeply engraved in our hearts that we endeavour to live it, instead of filling our lectures with quotations from it. That is the point I seek to impress on the aspirant. If he cannot realise the dream of poetry in the mighty strophe of Isaiah, he will either not realise it anywhere else, or his realisation will be incomplete.

I remember a good soul who, every time we met, would ask me with much concern whether I believed in the atonement? My belief or unbelief apparently settled the whole question for her, whether or not I was entitled to the heaven she expected. Had she known how often I had repeated in my solitude, not without the deepest emotion, the poignant fifty-third chapter of our prophet, her interrogation would surely have been deemed unnecessary.

We must not be disturbed by such interrogation, or by the cutting assertions that we depart from the standard of faith. Our faith is made of sterner stuff. It has an esoteric foundation which only the initiated know. It is rooted in the life blood of the primitive thought and if we culture its passionate fervour in the rhythms of the heart we can forego the name in the conscious possession of the substance. That living substance is in the book of Isaiah. To imbibe its gorgeous rhetoric with full artistic appreciation is to ascend to one of the summits of the dream, far above the rude clamour and hideous babble of the world. But to endeavour to fashion his intellectual life after the lofty example of inward law and morality enjoined in it will raise the aspirant beyond this, to the plane of the epic mind where sublimity of thought and manly duty blend in lawful consent and reveal the granite laws of the ideal shining through the dream.

And in the other prophets he will find an unique field for the application of this special process of culture. They are the great primitive poets, men of profound vision, the

God-intoxicated clairvoyants, denouncers and transformers of civilisations, from whose inspired lips issues an amazing and apocalyptic poetry which carries the mind out into the infinitudes of Cosmic thought and expands and enlightens it in the measure of its inborn nobleness.

If it is asked, what has this to do with occult advancement, the answer must be that it has so much to do with it that nothing can take the place of it. Occult science demands in its disciples a large understanding: a small mind will do nothing with it. It is a science pre-eminently of grand and lofty conceptions, and unless the mind is gradually habituated to conceptions of this nature, how can it assimilate and expound the greatness and majesty of God as revealed in the living universe which this science teaches? By steeping himself in the works of these world writers he will contact their vibration, reflect the contagious fire and express the heavenly harmony of their lives. Insensibly will his entire nature be ennobled in vision and purpose for the fructifying of the soul life of his generation.

Here it cannot be too strongly insisted upon that the aspirant is not to be a man of a single idea, so to speak, even though it be an occult one. He must be able to touch life at many points. He must aim to become a full man; and only the assiduous culture of the intellectual life can make him that.

I remember reading a very illuminating remark by an occultist to the effect, that if many students were subjected to clairvoyant investigation they would be found to be not "big enough" to handle the work of the Masters. That is a great truth and pertinent to my theme. That "bigness" can only come through entering with heart and soul into the all-inclusive realisations referred to in the Third Grade. The Master requires the fourfold genius of man to be evolved and highly balanced before he may entrust him with any special phase of world service. The expectations of some aspirants, it must be said, transcend all the bounds of common sense in this matter. If the mere reading of occult literature and the passing technically through the grades were sufficient, how soon should we all be qualified initiates!

It is not my intention to outline a course of reading or propose a guide for the intellectual life. I only seek to impress upon the young aspirant the absolute necessity of gaining a broad mental outlook and of applying himself to this end in his own way. He will observe that in the Third Grade there is not a word regarding specialising in literature, not a single direction as to author or book.

The Rosicrucian is a thinker, and a hint is sufficient for him to expand a thought or suggestion into all its manifold possibilities. He is not asked to become a specialist in prose or prosody. A categorical statement is given of the content of the fourfold realisation which constitutes perfection and it is for him to work out that realisation in all its fullness and variety as perceived in the master mind.

To propose for himself as an ideal the encyclopaedic knowledge of the epic mind of a Bacon or Shakespeare, for instance, may end in his throwing up his hands in despair. Nevertheless, in the serious contemplation of epic minds lies a fertile source of inspiration and culture. In the realm of the dream he may approach the fountainhead of creation, whence issues that supreme psychic phenomenon, the inspiration or God-obsession which pervades the whole literature of great art.

These epic minds are the benefactors of the race. They emerge radiant with light from the core of the world. They rise from the earth and contact the fullness of God in the ether. In them human thought attains its greatest intensity. They compress the infinite into a word which reverberates through all the ages of man. And withal, so vibrant is it with vision and power that it contests the very ground of religion itself. The poet, the artist and the philosopher traverse equally the immensities of the dream and return weighted with archetypal thoughts from the deep profound and cast their priceless treasures at the feet of poor man.

And the Rosicrucian is a dreamer of the first magnitude, possessing the triple sight of the artist, the poet and the philosopher. But with the added power of divinity, he so interprets the laws of destiny that all the Bibles of humanity are revealed as one vast intonation of the Word of God, the same yesterday, today, and forever.

3. Reflections on the Third Temple (Postulant) Grade: Article 4

Reprinted from the March 1928 edition of The Mystic Triangle.

The dream of mysticism completes and perfects the realisation of the fourfold genius of man. Upon the basis of study and effort sketched in the former articles, the mystical life is to be reared. To express the beauty of life, to realise the fullness of love in service, and to be conversant with the noble creations of inspired minds, affords a sound preparation for entering upon the deeper life of spiritual attunement.

As Rosicrucians, we are concerned with the ascension of consciousness under law which is thoroughly sane and wholesome in character, impairs not the personal self, is eminently practical at every step and makes for efficiency in all departments of life. That is practical mysticism; and the Rosicrucian is a practical mystic.

So much should be clear to the aspirant who has reached the Third Grade; yet some have protested because their work, up to this point, has appeared to be mainly technical and foundational instead of experimental. I trust these articles will help them to see more clearly how much is involved in the early work, how basic and necessary it is if they wish to become vehicles of the Master's influence and be of real service in the world of men.

It is not difficult to become a visionary and be carried hither and thither by every wind of doctrine of ethereal nature, without chart or compass or any sure foothold upon lawful research. But the silent mystics who stand behind the thrones of kings, compel governments to act better than they know, infuse the breath of life into the arts and sciences and impress their influence upon the metropolises of men, are of another order. They are men of such a calibre that they have to conceal half their power to justify their existence; for the world is still unable to recognise its saviours and wilfully destroys what it cannot understand.

Visionaries indeed they are, but not hothouse visionaries. They are the ripe product of a cultured and storied evolution and hold their pre-eminence because they possess a working knowledge of every aspect of life experience over which they exert their influence.

The literature of Rosicrucian biography reveals this fact on every page. Every subject portrayed in those unique annals stands in the bold outline of a great character, a force to be reckoned with in his chosen sphere, and so supremely practical, so adaptive, so truly an expression of the life of his day, as to remain unknown in his mystical nature even to those nearest to him.

There are, and always have been, men of this stamp in the forefront of our Order. They are complete men, they stand in the light, they have met and overcome every obstacle of darkness that strikes terror into the hearts of the multitude. Their perfected realisation is a thing of rare beauty and power and singularly potent in its blessing. Practical to the fingertips, at heart they are great devotees and their closeness to the Cosmic is the only secret of their lives. We are to touch upon this attitude of devotion in this article.

In the former articles we dealt with three stages of practical effort: an active advance, purporting to awaken the aspirant to a strong sense of the necessity of training his vehicles of expression as a worker in the world. Of dissipating once and for all any too sanguine expectations he may foster of touching the master level without putting forth every ounce of emotional and mental strength to that end. Of making him realise that faith without works is dead, and of urging him to call forth the latent reserves of all his faculties and impressing his personality uniquely without the sphere of his daily activity.

All this he will discern in the master mind and in such a degree of excellence as will no doubt incline him to regard his own life value as very limited indeed in comparison. His encouragement lies in the thought that by working steadily and continuously, with patience and perseverance, at this all-round culture of his soul life, latent faculty may unexpectedly emerge into consciousness and enable him to cover many stages of the path in a very short time.

Many aspirants can bear witness to the demonstration of this law in their lives. The aspirant can determine just where he stands in evolution only after he has made prolonged and unfaltering effort to get right down to the foundations of his soul life and stimulate into activity the latent memories of former existences. It is for him to find out for himself how much of this concealed growth is waiting to emerge under the combined stimulus of healthy introspection and objective application. The growth he has made in the past is there. Nothing can obliterate it. It rests with him whether or not he has at this point the desire and strength, engendered through daily experience, to become his own preceptor and bring that Karma quickly to fruition.

The mystical life perfects itself in the deep silences of our nature. It is the flower of the soul. We intuitively know that its many-coloured petals are unfolding as we meditate and serve. No matter what the stress of thought, the agitation of circumstances, or the swift retribution of Karma which we have consciously or unconsciously demanded, the fragrance of the divine bloom will ascend and pervade the temple of being, and evoke the compassion of the Master.

Yone Noguchi, the Japanese poet and disciple of Buddha, in a beautiful description of a Japanese Temple of Silence in which he experienced his third spiritual awakening, relates that in this Temple there was a picture of Dharuma, the ancient Hindu monk who established Zen, the religion of silence. On this picture Yone wrote these words:

> He is a pseudonym of the universal consciousness,
> A person lonesome from concentration.
> He is possessed of Nature's instinct,
> And burns white as a flame;
> For him mortality and accident of life
> No longer exist,
> But only the silence and the soul of prayer.

For years those lines haunted my soul. It would be difficult to pen a more beautiful description of the mystical consciousness. In the silence and the soul of prayer we realise the dream of the mystics, adumbrated in the Third and consummated in the Ninth Grade. It is the stage of the sacred retreat into the Peace Profound of the soul.

We have lived the beauty of the world and understand it; we have learned to serve and service has become the breath of our life; we have communed with great and holy minds until their contagious fervour has possessed us and made us hunger and thirst after the sources of power and inspiration. Now we stand within the temple, if so be that in wordless prayer, we may evoke the mystic consciousness in the soul and know the divine will.

This day the outer man has done his work bravely and intensely. He has striven mightily to accomplish the greater things; he has fallen short of much he would have done, but what he has done is well and time will justify it. Now we put off the outer man and partake of the holy sacrament of the altar within us. In mystical communion with the eternal we kindle the sleeping fire that burns away the illusions of finite consciousness. Our pledge with the Cosmic is once again ratified, and its responsive vibration as the voice of the silence is perfect assurance that we have not sought its aid in vain.

At this point a pertinent question may arise in the mind of the young aspirant. It is this: To whom, or to what, should I direct my devotion? He has already received the clearest indication on this matter, but the question is important and may be profitably considered. Most of our members have been brought up in the nurture and admonition of some form of the Christian religion. So much is obvious from individual declarations on entering our Order, and not a few have earnestly stressed in their subsequent correspondence their profound acquiescence in the teachings of Christ and their wholehearted acceptance of the way of the Christ in their studies.

Their aim in uniting with us is to acquire that knowledge and understand that discipline which they behold so wonderfully expressed in their perfect exemplar. It is well: they have nothing to renounce on this head through their association with us. It is written in the Fama:

> "But that also every Christian may know of what religion and belief we are, we confess to have the knowledge of Jesus Christ."

That is a most expressive declaration. Note the content and force of it: We confess the knowledge. Now, we see in Christ the perfect expression of Cosmic illumination, the complete at-one-ment; and our work, from first to last, is to so prepare the soul, that the false wrappings of many incarnations may be put off and we may become attuned with this same Christ or Cosmic consciousness.

We are not content with a simple belief in Christ or in any other great teacher, or our lives would not be more mystical or spiritual than is the life of the average so-called Christian. We are not content with belief. Belief can make a man an orthodox Christian at any moment he chooses; it can never make him a Rosicrucian.

It is the knowledge of the interior way of the Christ or the Buddha that we teach, as revealed through the study and application of the cosmic laws by which alone that way can be trodden. That is the working faith we have, and it is strong enough to bear the most searching interrogation and to confront the boldest criticism, whether of those who believe or those who doubt. And it matters not whether the aspirant is a follower of Christ or of Buddha, or of any other great leader of the human race. We raise no issue with him on the matter; we simply point out that if he desires to know the secret of their knowledge and power and become himself, according to his capacity, a teacher of men, he must focus attention not upon the historical figure but upon the interior way which every one of these teachers epitomises in himself.

If the aspirant is accustomed to watch the trend of human thought and affairs in well-known organisations such as the Church and, for instance, the Theosophical Society, he may draw important conclusions for himself. At the present time he will observe that the Church is seething with controversies respecting the moral and scientific value of its articles of belief, and once again thousands within its pale are asking, *"What is the truth?"*

The reason is not far to seek. It is because their religious life is founded almost entirely upon theological canons relative to an historical personality which have given rise to endless contention in the past and will continue to do so as long as they exist.

He will observe something similar, but on a very small scale, in the Theosophical

Society. For years Theosophists knelt down before the shrine of H P Blavatsky, and bitter controversies raged around the fact of what she actually wrote, what she meant to write, and what her successors have kindly written for her. Just then, when every well-meaning Theosophist was at his wits' end as to what to believe or whom to worship, the heavens were opened and a new revelation was vouchsafed; a Christ-Buddha appeared in their midst and another phase of hero worship dawned.

In both cases personal salvation is made easy by adhering, in the one case, to narrow formulae of belief, with little or no emphasis on the urgency for individual effort toward the essential and mystical life. And, in the other case, in deliberately and apparently with fullest and highest authority offering a fictitious Christ for the allegiance of students of the Wisdom Religion, a substitution which is regarded by a large percentage of those students as a direct betrayal of the honoured founder of their society.

These facts are not irrelevant to our theme. They reveal the clearest possible answer to the question of the sincere seeker as to where he shall look for true progress and enlightenment. The mystical consciousness is to be sought within, and nowhere else. The Rosicrucian is the last person on earth to reject exalted characters; he is a seer and takes the measure of a personality at sight. His chief work in the world is to exalt human lives by inculcating that practical knowledge of inherent forces which unfolds the divinity in humanity and makes men saviours of the world by virtue of the superiority and versatility of their word and action.

If the aspirant looks deeply enough he will discern at the heart of all our teaching and all our work in the world, the rapt devotee. We preserve that inner attitude with most jealous care. The master mind who has trodden the interior way and recorded the scripture of his cosmic communion, we recognise; and we know the secret of his greatness. He has explored the infinite solitudes of the soul and beheld the mystery of his own divinity; he has gazed with fearless eyes upon the unsullied mirror of the power of God within and reflects the brightness of its everlasting light. That is the ritual of the Rosicrucian worship. In the Third Grade the suggestions and adumbrations of it pass in swift review, to be unfolded and lived and perfected according to the persistent research and experimentation of the aspirant.

All the glorious possibilities of imaginative absorption in the living beauty of the world, the nobility of ever extending and sublime service to humanity's need, the far cry of men of vision who have seen the light on the heights of literature and art, and the holy offering of every perfected power and faculty on the shrine of silence within the temple. Such is the fourfold realisation of the genius of man, the goal of all our endeavour.

4. Yone Noguchi, Poet and Mystic

Reprinted from the April 1928 edition of The Mystic Triangle.

It has occurred to me that the reference to Yone Noguchi in my last article on the Third Grade has probably awakened the interest of many who are unacquainted with anything from the pen of this adventurous and lovable character. I propose therefore to give a few glimpses of his life.

Between the years 1900 and 1914 Yone wrote several articles which appeared in various English journals; and in 1914 these articles were published by him in a volume under the title *The Story of Yone Noguchi*. They possess all the curious charm of a poet's narrative of his rude encounter with the rough and tumble of life in our hustling Western world, how it enabled him to find himself and his true mission, and how, disciple of Buddha at heart as he was, after running the full circle of experience he found emancipation of soul in the silent temple of his dreams.

In the opening article we learn how young Yone learned the English language. In his 10th year he was destined to begin this terrible task; and humour and pathos are happily blended when he relates how he slept every night with his first spelling book by his pillow, hoping to repeat the lesson whenever he awoke at midnight, and how he still recalls the smell of the first foreign book which troubled his nostrils and charmed, mystified and frightened his childish mind.

He was very ambitious to master his English, and when sent on an errand carried his reader in his sleeve and chalked his lesson on all the wooden fences as he went; but on confessing to his father the reason of his long absence he was sent out with a wet rag to rub off what he had written. The trials and pains of Yone's English novitiate are too many to record. I hasten on to the year 1893 when, in his 18th year, he left Tokyo for California on the Pacific liner Belgic. It was a bitter experience when his big brother came to Yokohama to bid him farewell and left him standing on deck, alone and friendless, and with less than a hundred dollars in his pocket.

"I immediately grew conscious of the fact that I had to face unknown America, a land of angels or devils, the darkness." We hope Yone found that his lot was cast among neither, but among average humans with the angelic and other quality in reasonable proportions. However, he had a very bad time on board, lost his appetite and was obliged to fasten himself to an iron pole to preserve his equilibrium; all of which resulted in making him a thorough sea-hater for life.

I cannot forbear a word on Yone's original conduct at the Cosmopolitan Hotel, to which he was taken on arrival in San Francisco. The fruits he had purchased he placed in a white bowl under the washing table..., only to be reminded that the bowl was for another purpose. At the dinner table he fared even worse; salt was taken for sugar and cheese declared unfit for consumption; which hand was to manipulate the knife was a problem; a table spoon was used for sipping his unsweetened coffee for he could not understand the lumps were sugar!

Stepping out into the crowded streets, all the poet in Yone came to his eyes. The lovely complexions and quick steps of the American women were a revelation of freedom and beauty; they were all young, beautiful and divine, stripped of all the forms of convention known in his native land. Months passed before he could venture to discriminate and criticise these *"perfectly raised Californian poppies."*

Yone's one letter of introduction brought him into contact with a political League, the activities of which first acquainted him with the excitements and consequences of political discussions. The League published a daily paper, the San Francisco News, and Yone was engaged as a carrier. Five or six carriers endeavoured to eke out a living from the circulation of two hundred copies of this paper. Fortunately, they were able to lodge together without regular payment of rent. Yone and his friends used to get up in turns and build a fire to prepare their big pancakes..., with water. A cup of coffee was all he had for breakfast. There was no bed in the house: they slept on a large table with newspapers as a mattress.

"O, such a life," cried Yone; but there was a great compensation in the circumstances. He had much time for reading and was becoming proud of his advancing taste in literature, especially poetry.

In a little while Yone began to entertain serious misgivings about his general appearance. His heelless shoes and dirty coat scarcely became a growing scholar. He decided to work at the Menlo Park Hotel as a dish washer until he could put himself into respectable shape. From four in the morning until ten at night he worked..., but not for long.

Japan had declared war with China, and the exciting battle news made him drop the dishes and hurry back to the San Francisco News. His old friends were still penniless, so he bought shoes and shirts for them, acted the philanthropist on his thirty dollars savings, and after a short round of extravagances found himself once again with little to boast of. But Yone had read to some purpose. The News needed someone to translate from the English papers, and Yone became the indispensable man.

Now the spirit of poetry was watching over Yone and had secretly claimed him for her own. He had heard of Joaquin Miller, a poet regarded with reverence by the Japanese as a sennin or *"hermit who lived on dews."*

This man ignored modern civilisation and had but one joy in life: to raise roses and carnations. Miller lived away up the hills behind Oakland at the "Heights," and Yone went up to see him. It was a case of love at first sight. Miller desired Yone to stay with him, and he did. No teaching was promised beyond that of understanding the full value of silence. So that night, when he retired to sleep at a neighbouring house, Yone decided that he would become a poet.

It was not long before Yone's name began to ring in American ears; but alas, he had committed an unpardonable sin in the eyes of the never-sleeping critics. His first poems in a Californian magazine, *The Lark*, elicited much praise from its editor; but one of his early poems was bitterly attacked and declared to be a plagiarism from Poe. Yone was a devout reader of Poe; it was the only book, in addition to the work of a native poet and a book on Zen Buddhism, that he had brought to the "Heights." He therefore published his defence as follows.

> "Let critics say what they please! Poetry is sacred to me. It is not art for me, but feeling. My poems are simply my own journal of feeling, the footmark of my experience. I can stand anything but deceiving myself. I am not sorry a bit if there be an exact correspondence in shape. I am thankful to God for giving me the moment when I felt the same thing with Poe. I cannot understand why you could not feel the same thing with Poe if you want to. It is not poetry at all if you must express yourself in some other fashion when you think of one thing."

That was a good start; and when later he was again attacked by the same critic for his poems "On the Heights," the appreciative editor of another journal very promptly came to the rescue. His defence of Yone is worth quoting:

> "The occurrence of the word 'window' in the first line of Noguchi's and the seventh line of the quoted section from Poe is, of course, a damaging affair for both; and when it is reinforced by the damning fact that 'beauty' is mentioned in the third verse of Noguchi and the fifth verse of the quotation from Poe, the candid reader must admit that the two writers spell according to the same dictionary. It is to be feared, however, that Poe's claims to originality are not on a much better foundation than those of Noguchi. Noah Webster had already published all the words of 'The Sleeper' before Poe, and Dr Johnson before Webster, and still others before Dr Johnson."

After a brilliant course of two years the "Lark" died and Yone was left alone at Miller's "Heights," "*...standing like a ghost in the smiling mysteries of the moon garden.*" But a poet is a restless creature and the passion for wandering blazed up again in him. The trees, mountains, waters and skies called to him from the far distance. He resolved on a *"poetic tramp life."*

With a book of poems instead of a holy staff he started off for the Yosemite Valley. Once he slept in a barn and at midnight felt a queer warmth and heard a prophetic nibbling sound near him. He was too tired to investigate, but in the morning found he had been sleeping between the four legs of a horse. The Valley reached, his imagination peopled it with wonderful spirits and weird voices, which were soon translated into many a haunting line.

After many ramblings and more dishwashing Yone made for Chicago. His racy description of life in Chicago is delightful reading, although not too complimentary to Chicagoans. But every American must love him for this:

> "One thing, however, that strikes me most forcibly in walking on the streets of Chicago is the total absence of stupid-looking faces..., there is not even one sleepy mortal, I tell you. How foolishly the Japanese look in brown skin and dreamy eyes! Brown itself is the colour of melancholy and stupidity: but it shows some sweetness and pleads guilty to contentment. Brown is like night. The white-skinned Americans are like the day; they are the people of hard working, as the daytime is the time of work. The Orientals are the people of rest and dreams."

His first London experience was also a great shock to our poet. He arrived in the month of December and found himself standing on Westminster Bridge *"perfectly sieged by the greyness of fog."* This was an unfortunate moment for Yone's muse, since he recalled just then that his friend Miller had often told him to *"avoid the word of fog in poetry;"* the old poet's beloved word was "mist!" However, by nearly midnight he reached his lodgings in Brixton Road which he shared with his friend, Yoshio Markino, a Japanese artist. He had many encounters with *"impossible fogs,"* but there was one place of popular resort to which he often found his way..., the National Gallery: and there, in the Turner's Rooms, he would often indulge in a critical soliloquy standing before the work of the master artists.

A second visit was made to London by Yone and an interval of ten years intervened between the two pilgrimages. His comments upon English life and manners are as various, searching and humorous as those on America. But I hasten on to the concluding chapter in his story "A Japanese Temple of Silence," for it is here that we shall feel most strongly a sense of mystical kinship.

The wandering poet has returned home with a mind richly stored with experiences of the Western world, its wonderful wealth of natural scenery, its multifarious and strenuous life, its peoples strange in custom but very human and lovable when truly known; yet withal, not quite the world for a childlike Japanese dreamer who loved the silence and the quiet stars and felt the Cosmic stirring in his heart. He is writing in a temple: *"the room is softened into a mellow silence, through which the lonely aspirant can enter into the real heart of Buddhism."*

> "Oh, magic of meditation, witchery of silence,
> Language for which secret has no power!
> Oh, vastness of the soul of night and death,
> Where time and pains cease to exist!"

He also wrote this:

"The silence is whole and perfect, and makes your wizard life powerless; your true friendship with the ghosts and the beautiful will soon be established. You have to abandon yourself to the beautiful only to create the absolute beauty and grandeur that makes this our human world look trifling, hardly worth troubling about; it is the magical house of Faith where the real echo of the oldest song still vibrates with the newest wonder and even a simple little thought, once under the touch of imagination, grows more splendorous than art, more beautiful than life."

That is better than America or England! Through the open doors of his room in the Tortoise Temple he could see facing him a great forest of Japanese cedars, by whose shadows the Zen monks young and old could be seen now and then as spirits moving on the road of mystery. In this Temple his third spiritual awakening began.

His first awakening was in San Francisco when, in the company of Joaquin Miller, he wrote his *Seen and Unseen: Monologues of a Homeless Snail* [1897], the first creation of *"his retreat into dream and poetry, the world of silence where is no breath or speech, but the aloneness that is the soul of Nature."*

His second awakening was in London, when he found that poetry and art were the great force of life and wrote *From the Eastern Sea* [pamphlet, 1903]. From his third awakening in the Temple came forth a third book of poems, *The Pilgrimage* [1909]. Yone's description of his first night in the Temple is very interesting. For a long time he had wished to attend a special ceremony called the "Great Meeting with Spirit." He was conducted by a young priest into the Assembly Chamber.

"It seemed to me that I was already led into a magic atmosphere, in whose world-old incense..., what a song of exclamation!..., I lost all sense of time and place. Here the silence-wrapped monks seemed to my eyes as if they had returned long since to those grey elements of nature which stand above Life and Death. And it is the very problem of Life and Death you have to solve with the Zen philosophy, if you like to call it philosophy.

"I was gracefully entering into dream, which is a path of retreat into the world of silence, when a priest brought into the chamber the lighted candles, announcing that the ceremony would soon begin. Straight before me was a candle whose yellow flame rose in the shape of bands folded in prayer to the Buddhist image, which I could observe behind the lattice door of the holy dais of the chamber. What a face of profundity, which is but mystery! And that mystery will become at once the soul of simplicity, which is nature. I was told that the Buddha was nobody but the right mind, to whom the perfect assimilation with great nature is emancipation. and that you and I can be Buddha right on the spot. It is the dignity of this Zen Buddhism to arise from devotion, pity, love, and the like; it is not a religion born in your understanding, perhaps, but the highest state of mind, before yourself was born, breaking the peace of the world. You have to leave your human knowledge before you may enter here. And so did I, to the best of my ability."

After the ceremony the priests rose and retired to their Meditation House, whilst Yone was taken to the guest room next to the Assembly Chamber. But he passed the night in meditation, not sleep.

"In truth, ZaZen, or sitting in abstraction, is the way to concentrate and intensify your mind so that it will never be alarmed, even amid the crash of thunder or at the sight of a mountain falling before your eyes."

He thus describes the Buddhist meditation:

"You have to bend your right leg and set it in the crotch of your left, which, too, must be put on your right. Then the back of your right hand must be placed on the left leg, and the back of your left hand within your right palm; and both of your thumbs must be raised to form a circle. You must not look up nor down; your ears and shoulders must be straight in line, and also your nose and navel. Open your eyes as usual, and breathe in and out slowly. Above all, you must find the place of imaginary existence of your soul right in your left palm. Then will your mind grow into silence, as Buddha on the lotus flower..., how pure the silence of that flower floating on the peaceful bosom of the universe, pure from all the sense of life and death, you and nature being perfectly at one. Silence is the power of nature; it is the true state in which to perfect one's existence. It is non-action..., which does not mean inactivity; it is the full urge of active actionlessness. It is the very completion of one's health and spirit."

It was here, in the Tortoise Temple, that Yone wrote on the picture of the monk:

"He is a pseudonym of the universal consciousness,
A person lonesome from concentration.
He is possessed of Nature's instinct,
And burns white as a flame;
For him mortality and accident of life
No longer exist.
But only the silence and the soul of prayer."

And here, in its deep silence, we must take our leave of him.

5. The Rosicrucian Order, Past and Present

Reprinted from the May 1928 edition of The Mystic Triangle.

The history of our Order published by the Imperator in several issues of the magazine of recent date met a very real need among members and will undoubtedly have had its effect upon students of advanced thought and research in the world at large.

Nothing is so calculated to increase confidence in the members of an organisation in the work in their hands as a clear statement of the historic past and prestige of that organisation and a roll call of the famous characters who have battled strenuously for it at different periods of world evolution in the face of much opposition from church, state and popular prejudice. From the perusal of this statement every member should rise with a feeling of legitimate pride in his connection with the Order and a deep sense of personal obligation and responsibility in preserving and extending its power and influence in the present phase of activity. For it is not a debating society to which we have given our allegiance, in which we have to wrestle for an opinion or a name; nor is it a religion whose formulae, having no true and scientific foundation, are liable to be questioned at any moment by an able adversary and proven false.

As Rosicrucians, we have a noble ancestry. We derive from men of an imposing and majestic culture. We inherit the accumulated wisdom of a line of royal souls who lived beyond their age and fought for a far-off future. Their deep research and superior enlightenment laid the foundations of a science of life the magnitude and value of which we are yet far from fully conscious, but which is destined in the present century to compel the attention and win the allegiance of progressive minds in every rank of life.

The resolute pioneer work of these illustrious men was so firmly grounded upon the divine laws and carried forward so steadily and effectively with supreme will and single intent, that the barest outline of their activities cannot fail to react upon us as an inspirational impetus to forward their great work.

These men were not members of the aristocracy; they were aristocrats of the mind. They were men of a peculiar nature and defied common classification. They were often of obscure abstraction, yet of profound and independent spirit and conscious of a mission. Most of them were men of letters: all were laborious students. They took the measure of their age with the sureness and facility of practised statesmen. They were solitary contemplators and accomplished actors and wielded their knowledge with deadly effect against the ignorance, prejudice and bigotry which held their fellowmen in bondage to fear and servile dependence. They bore in their hearts the insignia of the wisdom of the Order to which they secretly belonged and were pledged to stamp it indelibly upon the times. They were great devotees and in solitude drew back the mystic veil by intrinsic right which hides the supersensible and divine.

But when they came forth to declare their Art they were changed men. There was nothing of the visionary or the fanatic about them. They were cool and masterful, vitally poised and immovably fixed upon the task in hand. The light shone on their path, the goal was clearly defined, and with calm judgement and immutability of purpose they passed straight on. They cared nothing for the criticism and obloquy heaped upon them. The flame of their aura was of that temper that the opposition of the ignorant and the learned alike recoiled from it. The charms of pleasure could not undo them; the allurements of the world lay far behind them; death they feared not, for they passed at will beyond its frontiers and were assured of immortality.

Although beyond their age they were a part of it, and infused their Art into science and learning to be recognised and used chiefly by later generations. They were divine benefactors possessed of one overpowering passion directed to one great aim, the evolution of knowledge and advancement of the race. Surely there can be nothing nobler for us in this life than that we should share in their labour, having with us..., it is more than a conjecture..., some of these royal souls themselves to inspire and assist us.

The historical outline has therefore served a twofold purpose of much inspirational value. In the place of a good deal of conjecture and erroneous speculation we have an authentic, if necessarily concise, statement of the great workers who preceded us, much of which may be verified from writings accessible to us; and we know that our present studies and work in the Order follow the same venerable traditions and have the same objective, the attainment of Cosmic comprehension and illumination and the advancement of the race. But we have many singular advantages which those early workers had not. They were a voice crying in the wilderness and met with persecution from an unenlightened people.

Today, our voice is heard and recognised of men. Science has made swift and wonderful advances and is meeting us on the borderline; it is verifying daily the results of our researches. The mystic truth of the philosopher's stone is offered it without fear or favour; the vibration of the lost word of power which will transmute the very elements in their hands is increasing in rhythm and intensity over the world. Religion is on the eve of its great renaissance; its forms have fulfilled their purpose and are passing. It demands the knowledge of the way, and we point it to the one path the Brothers have trodden.

True, ignorance rises in its primitive boldness to obstruct us, but we are too strong to be driven into obscurity and silence; we have nothing to fear now from either state, science or religion. They need us. They voice intuitively, yet inarticulately, our highest ideals. But a little while and they will seek our cooperation.

We are also to recognise that the cycle of activity on which we are launched is perhaps the most momentous in the history of the Order. This is emphasised by the recent appearance of the *Rosicrucian Manual* which makes public for the first time the facts pertaining to the establishment of the Order for this cycle, and extensive information regarding its main lines of activity and study as pursued by ourselves. It is fitting that such a publication should be in our hands and that it can be produced authoritatively to those who are interested in our work and seek the Rosicrucian path. The time is propitious and demands that such a comprehensive declaration of our work and activities should be available.

I have heard it affirmed that the Rosicrucians do not exist in this age, and the belief is widely held. The reason that it is so held is because of a general ignorance, even among occult students, of the cycles of activity and of objective inactivity of the Order. However, the time has come to acquaint the growing body of occult and psychic researchers among us with the Rosicrucian name, to reiterate the magnificent accomplishments of our predecessors, the dignity and extent of their work, that it is pre-eminently practical world work, not a dream or a speculation but a vital dynamic force operating in human lives here and now on the physical plane. It is incumbent upon us, accompanied as we are with a cloud of Cosmic witnesses, to sound dominantly the note of the practicality and demonstrability of the work we are engaged in.

I have no wish to strain the point, but the one fact that strikes me most forcibly about these master minds is their labour in and for the world. There are so many cults around us in which students are infinitely absorbed to save their souls for themselves. I would not be a saint under this prime condition! It is not manly; neither can the soul come into its own through this craving to renounce the world by becoming too good to serve it.

Let us take an example from the present hour. A great soldier of world renown recently passed to his rest. We are all aware of his vast military achievement, but I do not refer to that. I am thinking of the great work to which he dedicated his soul in the name of his broken fellowmen through the last years of his life.

What is this but the Rosicrucian ideal? It is a classic example with the very virtue of the Masters in it. Moreover, it is the basic principle which gives life and stamina to our Order. Without this there is peace..., an ephemeral and insipid peace..., for us, but no glory, nothing to venerate, nothing to lift us beyond self. And every Brother who has gone before us has been a warrior engaged in a strenuous battle against ignorance in the name of his fellowmen; and whatever special interest his personal and peculiar occult qualifications may have for us, it is for his great humanitarian labour that we honour him.

I said how timely was the publication of the *Rosicrucian Manual* for authoritative production to inquirers. Doubt and hesitancy on the part of many arises through the observance of a traditional secrecy about our activities, but to a large and legitimate extent the *Rosicrucian Manual* is calculated to break through this secrecy in a manner consistent with the evolution of the Order and the present manifestation of interest in it on the part of students.

I might cite the case of a member in this jurisdiction. He had nearly completed the National grades and yet had a most nebulous idea of both the Order and its broad objectives. After reading the *Rosicrucian Manual* he found his doubts cleared away and his many questionings answered; nor until then did he have any clear idea of the existence of the Masters. Now he is proceeding with confidence in the higher grades and finding a sure basis for past experience. And if, as has been pointed out, advanced egos of the

Egypto-Chaldean period are at this time bringing into evolution their knowledge and guidance, we may expect an increasing interest shown by a large percentage of students who have had past association with the Order in that period and who will surely be led to unite with us. It is this ancient and fundamental Rosicrucian knowledge which the inquirer will find outlined in the section of the *Rosicrucian Manual* setting forth the various grades of the Temple Lectures, the methods of psychic attainment in connection with such knowledge being completely adapted to the present evolutionary standpoint.

Nor can it be overlooked that students of modern scientific research are in their studies literally waiting for the knowledge we possess to advance their researches to practical issues. Is it not then precisely in such an epoch as the present, an epoch of great mental and scientific achievements, that our work must make its great appeal? The opportunity is ours to voice this appeal and convince these students that we understand their need and that it can be fully met in the demonstrations of our deeper science.

There is another aspect which throws out in bold relief the duty we owe to others in bringing this work prominently to light. On every hand in the psychic world we hear the cry of the upstart and the innovator, making large promises which cannot be fulfilled and which are nauseating in the extreme to the scientific mind of the age. This, in itself, is scientific reason that if we have inherited the greater wisdom, we should declare it. We should be a living challenge to the specious and unworthy cults that flourish for the hour, and die.

If we are to be true to our profession as democrats of thought and liberators of the soul, now is the time to set our ideas in motion over a wider field. We have studied the use of the word of power; let us use it. We have studied how to dream; let the dream become a concrete thing. That which our higher grade members have demonstrated let them project into public life; that which they have found within the precincts of the temple and fashioned within the laboratory of the soul, let them carry out into the world of men.

Let us welcome criticism as an opportunity to speak the truth we know the more robustly. Why allow the truth we know to remain a dead weight in the heart when those who have it not gain proselytes merely by reason of a calculated effrontery?

I am of course not advocating a wild enthusiasm and a reckless dissemination of that which, under law, must yet be preserved in silence. My object is to stress one great point. Our Order is the repository of a noble science, the Divine Arcana, and those members in it who, after patient research, have reached that stage where the word of power becomes a vibrant reality in the soul should be good for something. In some individual and peculiar way they should be practitioners, and some portion of their resurrected inner life should be placed unreservedly at the service of humanity.

There should be no doubt whatever on this head. Upon them rests largely the responsibility of carrying the prestige of the Order to greater heights than ever before. If we glance back along the line of the splendid men who preceded us we observe their names carved indelibly in the history of the world. They stand there a challenge for all time.

Some of them were not known as Rosicrucians to their contemporaries, but their works proclaim them, and we know their responsibilities and their difficulties. Every one of them was a fervent doer in his chosen line; and the world was well aware of his presence whether or not it understood him. They trod no easy and perfumed path: they were called and submitted to the Cosmic urge, sometimes scarcely knowing how they wrought. The more they were baffled the stronger they became. Driven from one objective they commanded another. They neither retracted, nor apologised, nor cared aught for their detractors because the soul in them was awakened and would not be silenced. Once assured of their mission, either on the mountain top or within the temple, and everything else was settled..., or unsettled..., just as it came.

These reflections should fill us with a divine zeal and a genuine emulation. I know very well the individual difficulties at this stage in attempting to shape the whole man after the inner laws for original work. The fire of the Spirit that vitalises and refines is keen, and we must often pause and stand aside with great patience and endurance and watch the hand of nature wondrously mould us when we cannot help ourselves. And this is good, for it teaches a necessary humility and confidence in the wise architect within us.

But with the vision fixed in the heart of what our Order has achieved in the past under the dominating influence of master minds. and conscious of the heritage of knowledge which is ours as the price of their solid effort, I feel we should lay hold of the present opportunity of following firmly in their path and carry our lives to sound practical issues in the world of men.

6. The Comte de St Germain

Reprinted from the July 1928 edition of The Mystic Triangle.

Perhaps no subject is of such perennial interest to students of the occult as that dealing with the Great Masters and their lives and works. And I think it may be safely affirmed that this rapidly increasing interest will soon be met by a further response to sincere inquiry, and from many unexpected sources information regarding the secret history of the Masters, their work and methods will be vouchsafed to us.

Let the demand only be strong enough and made with the pure and sincere intent to know, that thereby our knowledge may be used legitimately for the one purpose of being of profound service to the race, and the response will come. Amid the clash of world affairs and innumerable disquieting controversies, there is little doubt in an awakened mind that within the sacred portals of the Brotherhood the Masters are initiating important events for the enlightenment of the West along the lines of higher unfoldment; hence it is that the voices of their disciples are heard with force and authority in many directions proclaiming fearlessly the truths of a new consciousness and stimulating aspirants to the life of the path and selfless endeavour.

The name of the Master Rakoczi is familiar to many of us. He is that member of the Brotherhood who was actively engaged in the affairs of the Western world for some time past, and is active today. A pupil of Indian and Egyptian hierophants, he has worked in the world under various names and in the eighteenth century passed under the well-known name of the Comte de St. Germain. H P Blavatsky, writing in 1881, and referring to a defamatory article on the Comte and his "adventures," said that there were highly important documents existing in Russia about the Comte and she hoped the long needed but missing links in the chain of his history would speedily be made public.

Her hope was soon fulfilled, for in 1897 a series of articles appeared from the pen of Mrs Cooper-Oakley who had travelled widely in Europe and visited many famous libraries for purposes of research, and for the first time fragments of the eventful life of the great occultist were published. These articles, with further subsequent material, were issued as a monograph in 1912, and in view of its rarity and prohibitive price this monograph has just been reissued. If the few outstanding characteristics of the famous adept and a brief allusion to one or two of the more extraordinary episodes of his appearance as the Comte which I propose to sketch in this article, lead readers to peruse the book for themselves, they will gain a striking conception of a supreme master mind in world action, of the master mystic who stands behind the thrones of kings and foretells and influences the destiny of nations.

The personality of Zanoni we know very well; but he is a character of fiction. We cannot quite conceive a Zanoni in real life. But the Comte de St. Germain lived; he was seen of many at courts and in royal houses, fragments of his prophetic and magisterial conversation have been preserved, even some of his musical compositions are extant; and everywhere the Master went his personality was stamped so signally and indelibly that he exists for us as truly and realistically as any figure in political history.

It is only at rare intervals and at decisive stages in history that an accredited adept such as was the Comte appears openly and seeks to influence objectively the trend of human affairs.

Within the past 20 years there have certainly existed such momentous world conditions as would seem to have justified, if ever conditions justified, the public appearance and interference or guidance of adepts of the Brotherhood, yet we have no record of such appearances or guidance. The absence of any record is of course no proof that necessary guidance was not given; only those on the inner side know. But the dramatic appearance of the Comte in the 18th century as fully testified by the records of men and women of high social, political and mystical rank, seems to be the only instance in modern times of the Brotherhood permitting a qualified adept of occultism to play an astonishing role on the stage of the world, surpassing in fact all the fiction of a Lytton.

But we must give credit to the Masters for knowing human nature better than ourselves. With all our knowledge of occultism we complain of their aloofness and silence and are unconvinced of the good reasons for it. Let us reflect: if the Masters were among us and accessible even to those only who have sincere interest in them, what would their lives be worth? How many of us are so dispassionate, so purged of worldly vanity and curiosity, so intent upon forms of real service and expression of the soul, as to renounce a personality intrusion upon them and remain confident in their wisdom to approach us when they will?

That is another hard saying of occultism: it is also one of its laws and cannot be annulled. It is demonstrated clearly enough in the life of the Comte. Often during his arduous mission he was compelled to hide from the hand of the assassin; just as often to refuse the society of those who would have prostituted the very gifts by which he confounded them. Will the great artist speak of his marvellous technique to a fool?

"A century will pass," said the Comte to Madame d'Adhemar, *"before I shall reappear there."* She burst out laughing..., and he did the same. The Comte, when he appeared, gained precisely the same kind of reputation he would be assured of were he to appear today. He was a romantic, a charlatan, an adventurer, a liar and a swindler. When a man receives a galaxy of titles of that description he is usually a character worth investigating.

Those who investigated the character of the Comte testified that he lived according to a strict regime; that he had a charming grace and courtliness of manner; that he was an excellent musician and demonstrated powers which were incomprehensible and amazing; that he painted beautifully, and spoke the languages of half a dozen countries so perfectly that he might have been a native of either. He adopted various names the better to execute his mission: a custom which we thoroughly understand, but which to his contemporaries was a most damning reflection on his character. He conversed with people when they were young and met them again when they were old, but appeared not a day older himself. They could assign a sinister reason for his numerous names; but when he appeared at the court of Louis XV and encountered those who had met him in Venice 50 years before, reason failed them. The Countess v Georgy called him, *"a most extra-ordinary man, a devil!"*

From hints in his conversations it is clear that he had travelled extensively and was familiar with India, China and other Eastern countries, where no doubt he gained his vast occult lore. He was deeply versed in physics and chemistry, and possessed a rare knowledge of secrets of nature, which astonished those who happened to witness some of his demonstrations. He applied a particular mysterious colour to his paintings in oil which produced a wonderful brilliancy; in historical pieces he introduced into the dress of the women sapphires, rubies and emeralds of so remarkable a hue as to incline the spectator to believe their beauty was borrowed from the original gems.

From 1737 to 1742, the Comte was at the Court of the Shah of Persia, and it was here that he learned many of the secrets of nature. During the Jacobite Revolution of 1745 we find him in England, suspected as a spy, and arrested. In one of Walpole's letters we have the account:

"The other day they seized an odd man who goes by the name of Count St. Germain. He has been here these two years, and will not tell who he is or whence, but professes that he does not go by his right name. He sings and plays on the violin wonderfully, is mad, and not very sensible."

Not long after he appeared in Vienna and lived as a prince; he was well received, and became an intimate friend of the Emperor, Francis I. We have it in his own words in a letter to a friend that he made a second journey to India in 1755!

"I am indebted for my knowledge of melting jewels to my second journey to India, in the year 1755, with General Clive, who was under Vice Admiral Watson. On my first journey I had only a very faint idea of the wonderful secret of which we are speaking; all the attempts that I made in Vienna, Paris and London are worthless as experiments; the great work was interrupted at the time I have mentioned."

The power of improving precious stones was but one of the many arts the Comte is commonly reported to have possessed. In the year 1757 he was introduced by the Minister of War to Louis XV, who assigned to him a suite of rooms at his royal Chateau of Chambord, where a laboratory was fitted up for the experiments of the Comte and a group of students. This glimpse of laboratory work with others reveals clearly one aspect of his mission.

Further details of his character and abilities are preserved in a letter from Graf Karl Cobenzl to the Prime Minister in Russia. The Graf said the Comte was the most singular man he ever saw in his life; possessing great wealth yet living in the greatest simplicity, knowing everything, and revealing an uprightness and goodness of soul worthy of admiration:

"Among a number of his accomplishments, he made under my own eyes, some experiments, of which the most important were the transmutation of iron into a metal as beautiful as gold, and at least as good for all goldsmith's work; the dyeing and preparation of skins, carried to a perfection which surpassed all the moroccos in the world, and the most perfect tanning; the dyeing of silks, carried to a perfection hitherto unknown, like dyeing of woollens; the dyeing of wood in the most brilliant colours penetrating through and through, and the whole without either indigo or cochineal, with the commonest ingredients, and consequently at a very moderate price...."

Another writer says:

"Sometimes he fell into a trance, and when he again recovered, he said he had passed the time while he lay unconscious in far-off lands; sometimes he disappeared for a

Section 3 - The Mystic Triangle (1928)

considerable time, then suddenly reappeared, and let it be understood that he had been in another world in communication with the dead. Moreover, he prided himself on being able to tame bees, and to make snakes listen to music."

It was during the few years that preceded the revolution in France in 1793 that the Comte gave the most daring and emphatic warnings to the queen, Marie-Antoinette, of the machinations of certain ministers against the king. Letters reached her from the *"mysterious visitor"* filled with tragic prophecies of the coming storm but, although she had already had ample proof of his foresight and wisdom, she was loath to believe the vision of blood and slaughter outlined in these communications and personally confirmed in an interview the Comte subsequently had with her.

Carlyle [Thomas] in his famous *History* wrote:

"To whom, indeed, can this poor queen speak! In need of wise counsel, if ever mortal was; yet beset here only by the hubbub of chaos! Her dwelling place is so bright to the eye, and confusion and black care darkens it all. Sorrows of the Sovereign, sorrows of the woman, thick-coming sorrows environ her more and more."

If to the vivid pages of the historian the secrets, efforts and negotiations of the Comte were truly intercalated in all their masterly progress, what an amazing record we should have! Wise counsel the queen did have..., but even nations have their Karma. *"We are walking on dangerous ground,"* she confessed; *"I begin to believe that your Comte de St. Germain was right. We were wrong not to listen to him."*

To Madame d'Adhemar she said, *"Here is another missive from the unknown. This time the oracle has used the language which becomes him, the epistle is in verse."* This prophetic verse contains a lurid picture of the Terror that shortly after carried away king, throne and altar and spread chaos throughout France. Subsequent warnings reached the queen, but she was too weak to act.

There are hints of numerous diplomatic missions in which the Comte was engaged but the details of them are, no doubt advisedly, missing; but from what is known it is clear that he was the trusted friend of kings, princes and statesmen, moved freely among all dispensing light, knowledge and rare instruction, then vanished from the scene as mysteriously as he appeared. He came to give peace to France, but the personal ambitions of the French ministers thwarted his mission.

Of the Comte's Masonic and mystical connections a good deal is known as the result of research in certain archives. Although modern Freemasonic literature attempts to eliminate his name and the assertion is made by some that he was regarded as a charlatan by leading Masons, it is known that the Comte was one of the selected representatives of the French Masons at their convention at Paris in 1785. To many assemblies in Paris the

---
1. Bear in mind these words are those of one who did not understand. The Master never claimed to talk with the "spirits" of the dead.

Comte taught his philosophy. Meetings were held in a Lodge of the "Philaletes" which according to records, had a strong Rosicrucian foundation from the true Rosicrucian tradition. Practical occultism and mysticism were their aim. They were however involved in the violent Karma of France and their studies terminated.

From a Masonic source comes the information that amongst the Freemasons invited to the great conference at Wilhelmsbad in 1785 the Comte and Louis Claude de St. Martin with many others were included. Further, the librarian of the Great Ambrosiana Library at Milan says…,

> "And when, in order to bring about a conciliation between the various sects of the Rosicrucians, the Cabalists, the Illuminati, the Humanitarians, there was held a great Congress at Wilhelmsbad, then in the Lodge of the 'Amici riuniti' there also was Cagliostro, with St. Martin, Mesmer and Sainte-Germain."

It is well known that the Comte and Mesmer were connected in the mystical work of the last century, and search among the records of the Lodge meetings mentioned above verifies this. Vienna was the great centre for the Rosicrucians and allied societies, and among these there was a group of the Comte's disciples.

> "One day the report was spread that the Comte de St. Germain, the most enigmatical of all incomprehensibles, was in Vienna. An electric shock passed through all who knew the name. Our Adept circle was thrilled through and through. St. Germain was in Vienna!"

So writes Franz Graffer, a Rosicrucian and friend of the Comte. There is a touch of the melodramatic in this writer's narrative of the memorable meeting with the Comte which followed. During the conversation the Comte became gradually abstracted, rigid as a statue, after which he launched forth into one of his remarkable sententious prophecies, concluding:

> "Towards the end of this century I shall disappear out of Europe, and betake myself to the region of the Himalayas. I will rest; I must rest. Exactly in eighty-five years will people again set eyes on me. Farewell, I love you."

Undoubtedly the Comte is one of our Great Brothers of the Great White Lodge. Last century literature affords evidence of his intimacy with the prominent Rosicrucians of Hungary and Austria. H P Blavatsky refers to a "Cypher Rosicrucian Manuscript" which was in his possession and which proved his high authority in the Lodge. He was connected with the *"Knights of St. John the Evangelist from the East in Europe,"* with the *"Knights of Light,"* and with the *"Martinists"* in Paris. Writes one…,

"It is a fact that the Count knows details which only contemporains could tell in the same way. It is fashion now in Cassel to listen respectfully to his stories and to be astonished about nothing. The Count does not praise himself, neither is he an importune talk-teller; he is a man of good society, whom everyone is glad to have. He can speak in different voices and from different distances, can copy any hand he sees once, perfectly. He is said to be in connection with spirits who obey him, he is physician and geognost and is reported to have means to lengthen life."

And as a concluding quotation we have this from an article of an Austrian writer:

"He was the 'Obermohr' of many mystic brotherhoods, where he was worshipped as a superior being and where everyone believed in his 'sudden' appearances and equally 'sudden' disappearances. He belongs to the picture of 'Old Vienna' with its social mysteriousness; where it was swarming with Rosicrucians, Illuminates, Alchemists, Magnetopaths, Thaumaturgs, Templars, who all of them had many and willing adherents."

What is the central truth to be gathered from these few scattered glimpses of the life of the Comte de St. Germain? That he was living the master life in all its fullness and power and demonstrating on a grand scale the identical philosophy and practice to which we are devoted, of the same Great Lodge to which we aspire today.

To the many, the Comte will appear but a fiction like *Zanoni*: to us, he is a lofty and present spirit appearing there for a brief moment of time in a perfected and deathless life. His hand is in our work. A little more culture, a little more persistent endeavour, a little more of that tense, absorbing, spiritual passion to become, and that hand will grip our own.

The Master's skill in action is a wonderful theme and transcends all the dreams of fiction; but the mere reading of it will accomplish nothing. It is for us to translate life to life until the virtue in us merits his approach and compels his guidance. When that attitude is as firmly established in us as breathing, we need have no anxiety about our progress or the future.

7. Three Years in Tibet

Reprinted from the October 1928 edition of The Mystic Triangle.

Lafcadio Hearn, the author and journalist, who went to Japan, adopted the Buddhist religion, became naturalised under the name of Yakumo Koizumi, and for several years held the post of English lecturer at the University of Tokyo, records that he once submitted to the graduating classes, for a composition theme, the question: *"What is eternal in literature?"*

The discussions proved very interesting and lofty in character, and revolved around ideas such as these: *"The great thoughts and ideas of our ancestors;" "Books which rightly explain the phenomena of the Universe;" "The holy books of China, and of the Buddhists."*

And becoming thoroughly immersed, as I read on, in the atmosphere of wonderful Japan and the reverence shown in its schools for the teachings of Buddhism, I fell to thinking of the first Japanese priest to explore Tibet for the purpose of making a reliable translation of a collection of Buddhist books, into Japanese in an easier style than the difficult and unintelligible Chinese.

Thereupon I took down to read once again *Three Years in Tibet* by Ekai Kawaguchi, the Rector of Gohyakurakan Monastery in Tokyo, who was the first Japanese priest to explore Tibet. Some of our members may have met with his book, so what I say about it they can corroborate; while the many who have not read it may be interested in this reference to it.

Kawaguchi says that he was reading the "Aphorisms of the White Lotus of the Wonderful or True Law" in a Sanskrit manuscript under a Bodhi tree in Benares, and whilst doing so was reminded of the time, some years previously, when he had read the same text in Chinese at a great Monastery in Kyoto, Japan, a reading which determined him to undertake a visit to Tibet. In 1891 he gave up the Rectorship of the Monastery of Gohyakurakan in Tokyo and left for Kyoto, where he remained living as a hermit for about three years, totally absorbed in the study of a large collection of Buddhist books in the Chinese language; his object being to fulfil a long-felt desire to translate the texts into his native language.

Subsequently, however, he came to the conclusion that it was not wise to rely upon the Chinese texts alone, without comparing them with Tibetan translations as well as with the original Sanskrit texts which were to be found in Tibet and Nepal. Many of them had been discovered by European orientalists in Nepal, and a few in other parts of India and Japan; but those texts which included the most important manuscripts of which Buddhist scholars were in want had not yet been found.

Moreover, the Tibetan texts were reputed to be more accurate translations than the Chinese; not that the Tibetan translations are considered superior to the Chinese, merely superior as literal translations; but for their general meaning, the Chinese are far better than the Tibetan translations. However, Kawaguchi's intention was to study the Tibetan language and Tibetan Buddhism, and then endeavour to discover manuscripts in Tibet.

He accordingly left Japan in June 1897, and returned in May 1903. In October 1904 he again left Japan for India and Nepal, with the object of studying Sanskrit and the hope of penetrating into Tibet in search of more manuscripts.

So great was the enthusiasm in Japan at this first exploration of Tibet by a Japanese that leading papers published Kawaguchi's articles every day during 156 issues. Later, the articles were collected and translated into English, and published under the above title.

The book therefore contains a highly interesting narrative, giving the point of view of an Asiatic having firsthand knowledge of the customs, manners and intimate life of the Tibetans. It is also thrilling in character because of the remarkable incidents and adventures, and the many dangers and difficulties the writer had to pass through during his journey.

What immediately strikes one on reading this narrative is the simplicity and the singleness of mind of the narrator, and the strong sense of personal detachment in everything he recounts. This is almost surprising at first sight, until we recollect that we are reading into a character of an exceptional cast, and a mind that had risen above the personal idea long before his arduous mission, and had experienced the strength, beauty and peace of inner illumination.

Not that there is any very direct reference to this in the book; we are left largely to conjecture this from the manner and action of the man. For there are some things done by men, whether at home or abroad, which can never be accounted for in the ordinary way, and which point unerringly to certain developments not enjoyed by the majority. And it is conclusive enough that no ordinary person would have had the soul to face and surmount the cruel hardships, for the sake of even the highest scholastic triumph, which fell to the lot of this singlehanded priest in his desire to bring the light of Asia to his fellowmen.

They thought he was mad to venture upon such a mission. A certain judge came expressly to tell him that he would become a laughing-stock of the world by meeting death out of foolhardiness, and would do far better by staying at home and engaging in his ecclesiastical work. *"Suppose you lose your life in the attempt? You will not be able to accomplish anything."* To which the priest replied: *"But it is just as uncertain whether I die, or I survive the venture. If I die, well and good; it will be like a soldier's death on the battlefield, and I shall be gratified to think that I fell in the cause of my religion."* Judges are not priests..., their laws differ.

The next day Kawaguchi left Japan, and we have a sketch of his solitary figure standing on deck clad in his robes, with hand uplifted above his bare and unshaven head bidding his friends farewell. The monotony of the voyage was relieved by religious controversies in which he engaged with an Englishman who was an enthusiastic Christian, to the edification of themselves and all on board; also in preaching much before the officers and men of the ship, the most willing and interested audience he had ever met.

The judge he had left behind was not the only authority he put to silence and reflection. Encountering the Japanese Consul at Singapore, who had heard about him from the captain, he was asked about his programme, as there were only two possible ways of accomplishing his purpose: either to force his way by sheer force of arms at the head of an expedition, or to go as a beggar. Kawaguchi replied that as he was a Buddhist priest the first course was out of the question, the latter the only possible way, and that he had no definite programme. Exit the Consul in deep meditation.

He remained a week at an hotel in Singapore and did much preaching whenever and wherever an opportunity presented itself, which greatly pleased the proprietor. Accordingly he was treated with special regard, but just before leaving Kawaguchi narrowly escaped a mortal accident.

Every day, when the bath was ready, he was the first to be asked to have the warm water ablution. On this particular day the usual invitation was extended, but just then he was engaged in reading the sacred Text and did not comply.

The invitation was repeated, but somehow or other he was not ready and remained in his room. Then he heard a great noise and a thud that shook the building. There had been a collapse and fall of the bathroom from the second floor to the ground, with bath, basin and all other contents, among which was a Japanese lady who had accepted the invitation to take her bath first. This lady was buried under the debris and later taken to hospital with little hope of recovery.

Arriving in Calcutta he placed himself under the care of the Mahabodhi Society, and was advised by the Secretary to become a pupil of Chandra Das in Darjeeling who was at the time compiling a Tibetan-English dictionary at his retreat, Lhasa Villa.

This scholar proved very hospitable to his visitor and took him to a temple called Ghoompahl, where Kawaguchi was introduced to an aged Mongolian priest, renowned for his scholarly attainments and as a teacher of the Tibetan language. Under the guidance of this old priest he studied the language, daily walking three miles from and back to the retreat.

A month had barely passed when the Mongolian proved to be the third authority to persuade the priest from his mission.

> "I would advise you to give up your intention of going to Tibet. It is a risky undertaking and chances are against you. You can acquire all the knowledge of the Tibetan language you want here, and you can go back to Japan, where you will be respected as a Tibetan scholar."

But it was of no use. Kawaguchi told his tutor that he was more anxious to teach him Tibetan Buddhism than the Tibetan language. With the aid of his kindly host he changed schools and was provided with a private teacher in addition to receiving a regular schooling. He became one of the household of a Lama in which he learned the vernacular, and at the same time matriculated into the Government School of Darjeeling where he received systematic lessons.

At the close of the year 1898, after 12 months' hard study, Kawaguchi was satisfied with his proficiency in the use of the Tibetan language in its literary and vernacular forms, and had to decide upon a route for entering Tibet. The most advantageous one appeared to him to be by way of Nepal, which abounded in the footsteps of the Buddha and in which were complete sets of the Buddhist Texts in Sanskrit.

These were strong inducements even in the event of failure to actually enter Tibet. Moreover, no Japanese had hitherto ever been in Nepal. To prevent betrayal it was given out that he was obliged to go home at once, and thereupon he left for Calcutta. In Calcutta he obtained letters introducing him to an influential gentleman in Nepal. On the 20th of January, 1899, the famous Buddhagaya, sacred to Buddha, was reached, and the night was spent in meditation on the Diamod Seat under the Bodhi tree.

Kawaguchi was a poet at heart and his language is often touched with beauty and vision. Many a poem is interspersed among his pages. The feeling he experienced during this night of meditation was indescribable:

"Whilst seated on the Diamond Seat, absorbed
In thoughtful meditation full and deep
The lunar orb, suspended o'er the tree -
The Sacred bodhi tree shines in the sky.
I wait with longing for the morning star
To rise, the witness of that moment high
When His Illumination gained the Lord
The Perfect Buddha, Perfect Teacher Great."

After a critical encounter with certain travellers who put to him the most searching interrogatories he discovered the gentleman to whom he bore letters of introduction, and was granted a pass to the Nepalese frontier as for a Chinaman living in Tibet. At this point of the narrative we find Kawaguchi well on his way.

His book, however, is a formidable one, consisting of over 700 pages, so that I can only hope in this article to convey some impression of the great interest of the narrative, the extreme difficulty of the quest and the character and temper of the man who made it. There is one point I would emphasise here: the reader is not to expect that he will find in this book accounts of interviews with Masters or any wonderful experiences of an occult character.

Kawaguchi wrote his narrative for the public and has not told all he might. I have no doubt that the conversations he had with the many remarkable characters he met would make a very different kind of book. These holy men were most likely well aware of his approach and his mission, and did much to assist him. A Buddhist knows his brother all the world over.

When bidding farewell to his friends in Japan on the 26th of June 1897, Kawaguchi had said that he would be able to enter Tibet in three years; on the 4th of July, 1900, he was on the frontier of Tibet. Three days previously, when nearing the frontier, he dismissed his guide and journeyed steadily on, a solitary traveller in one of the untrodden depths of the Himalayas, loaded with a weight of 65 pounds. The sketches in the book depicting him crossing these vast solitudes enhance the impression of profound loneliness and desolation which the narrative forces so vividly upon the imagination.

After tramping some five miles, often through snow 15 inches deep, he observed several tents pitched ahead. Here he was doubtful what route to take; whether to risk encountering the occupants of the tents which lay in his path, to follow a declivity in another direction, or to negotiate a succession of high mountains.

It is interesting to note his common practice of arriving at a decision when faced with imminent danger. He entered upon a meditative process which in Japanese-Buddhist terminology is called Danjikwan Sanmai, in which the self is abnegated and then a judgement formed, a method which borders upon divination or an assertion of instinctive powers.

He decided to go by way of the tents; he met a kind dame and her son from whom he received much hospitality, after which the son accompanied him to the abode, a day's journey onward, of a Lama, Gelong Rinpoche, the very holiest of all the priests in the western steppes. This holy man was held in great reverence by his followers, which included natives living within a 100 mile radius of his cave.

Approaching the white cave with the crowd of expectant devotees, who came every morning to receive instructive precepts and personal blessing, Kawaguchi made himself known to the venerable priest and in the course of a conversation said to him:

"You are saving the souls of the multitude, and I wish to learn the grand secret which serves so well for your purpose." To which the holy man replied, *"Friend, you know that well enough yourself. All Buddhism is within you, and you have nothing to learn from me."* Kawaguchi was loaned a sacred volume of Buddhist instruction to peruse before resuming his journey.

After leaving the Lama, many hardships were undergone, but these were softened a little at one juncture by a real romance; a young damsel, belonging to the party of pilgrims Kawaguchi had joined, conceived a passion for him. Kawaguchi treats this phase of his experience with rare modesty and inimitable delicacy. So perfectly did he conceive the workings of this child's heart, and so consecrated was his own heart to the spirit of Buddha, that in a little while…,

> "instead of an object of love, I had now become an awe-inspiring Lama to my little Dawa. As such, I counselled her with a good deal of earnestness, and finally succeeded in subduing her passion, and conquering the temptation."

Many sacred temples and holy places were visited in the region of Lake Manasarovara, most of which are described in detail; whilst the scenery here was so magnificent that Kawaguchi's pen again and again forgot to prose and, touched with poetic fervour, surrendered itself to the rhythm of nature.

> "Like to the Milky Way in heaven at night,
> With stars begemmed in countless numbers decked,
> The Brahmaputra flashes on the sight,

His banks, fit haunt for Gods, appear
In gorgeous splendours from the snowy height."

In the month of November, accompanied by other travellers, he was far within the interior of the forbidden country. They were on the outskirts of Lharche, the city which is third in importance in Tibet, only five days journey from Shigatze, the second Tibetan city, and soon reached the imposing monastery of Sakya. Later, the Nartang Temple was visited where valuable information was acquired on Buddhism.

Arriving in Shigatze, Kawaguchi stayed for a while at the famous Tashi Lhunpo Temple where over three thousand priests were in residence. To some of these he preached on the Buddhist virtues and aroused in them a real zeal for Buddhism..., a fact which he considered a sad commentary on the ignorance of the average Tibetan priests.

Then on to Lhasa where preparations were made to visit the palace of the Grand Lama. In the meanwhile he entered the Sera monastery. One day a young priest dislocated a bone in the upper arm and Kawaguchi, who possessed a good deal of medical knowledge, thereupon set it. Other healing ministrations which he performed soon made him famous in the locality, and shortly after he received an invitation to attend the Royal Palace..., not that the Dalai Lama was in reality ill, but wanted to see what the new doctor looked like. An interesting description follows of the interior of the palace as seen by Kawaguchi, of his audiences with the Dalai Lama, and of frequent subsequent interviews with him.

He was invited to the chief physician to talk of medicine, with the result that the latter wanted to recommend Kawaguchi as a Court physician. This was declined on the ground that his object was not medicine, but to study Buddhism; against which the physician plausibly argued that as it was the ultimate object of Buddhism to save men, Kawaguchi might as well stay in the city as a doctor and practise medicine.

> "I might heal them of their diseases," was the reply, "but I could not give peace to their souls, while a priest could free them from the most painful and durable of all diseases. It was more urgent to study how to heal this. Buddha was the greatest doctor, who had given eighty-four thousand religious medicines to eighty-four thousand mental diseases, and we, as His disciples, must study His ways of healing."

Here he met with many remarkable personages, one of whom was the highest priest in Tibet, who taught him Buddhism in its true form. While his close observation and study of Tibetan life in all its phases are demonstrated in the wealth of detail in some of his chapters; such as those on wedding ceremonies, punishments, Lamaism and the Tibetan Hierarchy, government, education and castes, trade and industry, printing, festivals, and Tibetan women and amusements.

Although some of the distinguished scholars Kawaguchi was in with knew him to be a Japanese priest, it appears that during the whole time he stayed at the Sera monastery studying Buddhism, and ministering to the sick, his secret was well preserved. There is every indication that had his identity been revealed and his purpose in entering Tibet known, he would have met with an untimely end.

On several occasions, just prior to his departure for home, matters nearly reached a climax as a result of the sharp interrogations he had to face from persons who shrewdly suspected him. An extended account of these incidents is given. At last the secret was out and return inevitable now or perhaps never.

> "Must I now leave," thought I, "this quiet land of Buddha to which I have become attached; must I steal out of this beautiful country without telling who I am, just as a spy would do? Are there no means to say that I am a Japanese, without causing harm to others? Death comes to all sooner or later. Why should I not run the risk of death, presenting the letter to the Pope? When I have made such a good composition, how sorry I am not to show it to him."

The letter to the Dalai Lama referred to came to be written in this way. When Kawaguchi found that it was known he was a Japanese priest and was doubtful what the outcome would be, he resolved to write a letter and make a clear statement of his mission. This epistle took three nights to complete, when his fellow priests were fast asleep within the monastery. Its contents he summarises thusly:

> "My original intention in coming to this country was to glorify Buddhism and thus to find the way of saving the people of the world from spiritual pain. Among the several countries where Buddhism prevails, the only places where the true features of the Great vehicle are preserved as the essence of Buddhism are Japan and Tibet.

> "The time has already come when the seed of pure Buddhism must be sown in every country of the world, for the people of the world are tired of bodily pleasures which can never satisfy, and are earnestly seeking for spiritual satisfaction. This demand can only be supplied from the fountain of genuine Buddhism. It is our duty as well as our honour to do this. Impelled by this motive, I have come to this country to investigate whether Tibetan Buddhism agrees with that of Japan.

> "Thanks be to the Buddha, the new Buddhism in Tibet quite agrees with the real Shingon sect of Japan, both having their founder in the person of the Bodhisattva Nagarjuna. Therefore these two countries must work together towards the propagation of the true Buddhism. This was the cause that has brought me to this country so far away and over mountains and rivers.

> "My faithful spirit has certainly wrought on the heart of Buddha, and I was admitted to the country which is closed from the world, to drink from the fountain of Truth; the Gods must therefore have accepted my ardent desire. If that be true, why should your Holiness not protect me who has already been protected by the Buddha and other Gods; and why not cooperate with me in glorifying the world with the light of true Buddhism?"

He yet hesitated whether to have this letter delivered or not. His friends who understood the posture of affairs better than he, were against the idea. He would surely be imprisoned and secretly poisoned. So in the Great Hall of the monastery before the image of Buddha he read his prayer of farewell and passed out into the Dharma garden, his favourite resort, where the peace and loveliness of nature inclined him to postpone his departure.

Suddenly a voice, *"Go back quickly,"* came to him from somewhere in the garden. He paused, investigated, but detected no one. It must be imagination! A few steps further and the same voice, louder and clearer, reached him. He interrogated the voice and searched again, with the same result. Again and again the same strange voice admonished him until, fully resolved to obey, it ceased.

With the kind and skilful assistance of friends Kawaguchi's return journey was rendered safe but not without many memorable events. The most important were the three audiences he had with the King of Nepal who presented him with a collection of rare books containing 41 parts of Sanskrit text, which he had specially desired of the King.

One's closing reflection is that Kawaguchi's mission was a wonderful achievement and his narrative a most fascinating record of it. It was possible and was a complete success because the man was so selfless, so perfectly attuned with the Divine life, that he was as one of nature's forces and encountered her on equal terms.

The very hardships and dangers, before which the strongest physical prowess would have succumbed, established him the more firmly in that spiritual consciousness which led him to renounce the peaceful precincts of temple life in Japan that he might bring greater peace to his fellowmen.

I confess to a peculiar affection for this intrepid priest.

8. Raymund Lully..., Eminent Rosicrucian Master

Reprinted from the November 1928 edition of The Mystic Triangle.

The monograph on Raymund Lully [1232-1316] from the pen of the prolific writer on freemasonry, A E Waite, which appeared a few years ago, may be known to some of our readers. If so, and their impression of it coincides with my own, they will not have been much inspired with it.

In the spirit of historical research the author ranges through a host of unrelated and often unauthentic materials in an endeavour to lay hands upon the real Lully, and produces a piece of patchwork which is neither stimulating nor very edifying. So elusive is the master mystic that again and again he vanishes within the cloud of his own raising, and leaves the historian gasping and perplexed, and driven to the shift of presenting three personalities instead of one for our acceptance. That is Mr Waite's view, but we may demur.

When he assures us that…,

> "…from beginning to end, the story of his life is embedded in devotional myth and the wonder-working element of his period, so that I cannot extricate it entirely. Its verifiable and probable facts have their setting in legend, and must be left therein."

That is sufficient reason for our not being much inspired with his monograph.

Perhaps after all this is not the last word about Lully. A member of the University of Liverpool, Mr E Allison Peers, has been engaged in extensive research work in this direction and has just produced a life of Ramon Lull, written by an unknown hand about 1311 and now first translated from the Catalan. The book is issued by the publishers to the Holy See, and it is probable that the Catholic Church, placing its own construction upon the life of Master Ramon, regards him as one of her own children. That, however, does not concern us. Lully was one of the master minds in the early history of the Order, and any hitherto untranslated text of his life dating from the period of his memorable activities is of value to us.

The translator points out that this contemporary life, written about the year 1311, is by far the most important source for our knowledge of Lully. We are not to expect to see here revealed the complete esoteric Lully, obviously. That is never disclosed in the biographies even of contemporaries, but we have a general connected account of his career down to some four years from his death, except for a few understandable "silences," and also a vivid description of two of his missionary expeditions to Africa.

Further, we have an unique phase from the spiritual history of the man unfaltering in his duty, willing to reveal his moments of human frailty that others might gather strength from them. The translation is literal, following exactly the original, with no thought or intention of avoiding the occasional crudity of the original; and a full length biographical study is promised by the translator, shortly, with the text satisfactorily annotated.

The unknown writer of this little Life, consisting of only 45 pages, prefaces his narrative as follows:

> "To honour, magnify, glorify and praise our Lord God, Jesus Christ, Ramon Lull of the kingdom of Mallorca, a master reverend and worthy of great remembrance, urged and solicited both once and many times by certain of his followers, related and recounted the

things that are written below wherein are contained his life, conversion and most lofty and marvellous penitence, according as will appear below in detail."

In giving some of the more intimate touches of the record this writer has left us, reflecting as they do a picture of beautiful simplicity and veracity. I am sure Lully will remain in the memory as a very real and human personality, pursuing an independent and arduous path to which he had been clearly called, and suffering the full measure of persecution which we know to have been the lot of our Brothers in former ages.

In his youth he gave himself to the composition of songs and lays concerning the follies of the world. And one night, when, in his chamber, seated upon his bed, he was composing a vain song for a woman of whom he was much enamoured at the time, he turned and beheld the figure of Jesus Christ hanging upon the Cross. In the great fear that came upon him through the apparition, he resolved to abandon the project he had in mind. On the following morning the vision had lost its power over him and he turned again to his composition; but at the same hour and in the same place when so engaged, the vision appeared to him a second time.

In spite of this he persisted in his purpose until after the fifth appearance of the apparition he felt fully assured that the interpretation of the vision was that he should wholly give himself to service. He prayed with great fervour that light should be given him how to devote himself, and after meditating upon the life of Christ and what he should do in the name of his Master, he resolved to make books against the errors of unbelievers.

This came to him by divine inspiration. Yet he was perplexed as to what would be the advantage of such books since he knew neither the Arabic nor the Moorish tongue; moreover, he knew that he was entirely alone in this great venture. But his illumination had given him strength, purpose, and initiative, and he resolved to go to the Holy Father and to the princes of Christian peoples to exhort them to establish monasteries wherein men of wisdom and letters should study and learn the Arabic tongue, and the languages of other unbelievers, that they might be able to preach and propagate the truth.

This is the threefold purpose that came to Lully upon receiving divine illumination: that he would lay down his life for Christ, that he would make books, and cause to be established monasteries that others should follow his example. Some time passed before he could determine what steps to take, but one day, which was the feast of St. Francis, he heard a bishop preaching upon the feast and recounting how St. Francis, leaving all worldly things behind him, devoted himself wholly to the service of the Cross.

Immediately Lully was decided, renounced his worldly business, sold his possessions, and after setting aside a certain part of his goods for the sustenance of his wife and children, visited divers holy places, seeking the way to fulfil his purpose. Returning to his home in Mallorca he cast off his superfluous clothing, dressed himself in the coarsest cloth, and set himself to learn grammar and other sciences to enable him to accomplish his mission.

After nine years of this preparation he went up onto a mountain[2] called Randa, which lies to the southeast of Palma, and gave himself up to contemplation, when, on the eighth day, a Divine illumination revealed to him the form and order wherein to write the books, he had in mind, against the infidels. Straightway he came down from the mountain and took up his abode in the monastery of La Real where he wrote the first of his books on his Art; and returning to the Hill of Randa where he had received his enlightenment, he caused a hermitage to be built thereon in which he remained for four months and continually prayed that his Art might prove of value in the service of truth.

At this point in the narrative appears a brief but significant allusion to the meeting of Lully with a singular character. I give the passage just as translated:

> "Now, while the said reverend master was living in this form and manner, it came to pass one day that he met a shepherd, a youth exceeding pleasant and comely of feature, who, in a single hour, related to him as many and as singular things concerning the Divine Essence and the Heavens, and especially concerning the angelic nature, as a great man of science could have expounded in two days. And when the said shepherd saw the books which the said reverend master had compiled, he kneeled upon the ground and kissed them, and said, with tears, that there would follow therefrom much good in the Church of God. Then he blessed the said reverend master, making over him the sign of the Cross, as though he were a great prophet. And he left him, and the said reverend master remained in a state of amazement, for it seemed to him that he had never before seen this shepherd, nor even so much as heard of him."

Now, whether this Life of Lully be accepted as authentic or not, that account of his meeting with one who stood to him in the relation of a Master is impressive, and in full accordance with many of the recorded encounters between the Brothers and those who aspire to serve them.

To me, it is one of the most arresting passages in the narrative. It is just one more instance, and many are known to us, of the necessary Teacher and the needed wisdom coming to the devoted servant who is ready for both and knows how to profit of them. It is to be observed that he had not waited for this Master to appear before he served him; he had given himself absolutely to the urge of the soul and wrestled with his problems in solitude and persistently endeavoured in every way within his power to be worthy of a high calling. Only after he had mastered the long and difficult initial steps as a servant of men, came the objective and personal recognition and acceptance at the hand of one who had doubtless been sent to set a seal upon his great work.

It is a fact for deep reflection, and one upon which much stress is laid on the esoteric side of our work in the Rosicrucian Order. It falls aptly into place in connection with the reflections in a former article dealing with our individual effort as workers for humanity.

---

2. The perceptive mystic will see the beautiful significance of nine years of preparation before *"going up onto a mountain."*

The Master does not want the theorists..., the world is full of them. But the Lullys are few; and the Master knows where to find them and uses them.

When the king of Mallorca heard that the reverend master had written certain books he invited him to come to Montpellier. On his arrival the king caused the books to be examined by a master in theology, especially the meditations, therein, for every day of the year, and great admiration and respect was entertained for them. In the city Lully wrote his book, the *Artis demonstrativae*, read it publicly, and wrote a commentary thereon, wherein was declared how the first form and the first matter constitute an elemental chaos, and how the ten universal predicaments descend and are contained therein.

Lully improved the occasion by obtaining the sanction of the king for the building of a monastery in the kingdom of Mallorca, well endowed, so that thirteen friars should live therein to study the Moorish tongue and convert unbelievers.

From thence he went to the Holy Father and the Cardinals to urge them to found monasteries throughout the world for a similar purpose. On arriving at the Papal Court he found that John XXI had just died, so he set off for Paris with the intention of publicly reading and expounding his Art. In Paris he lectured, publicly, in the school of the Chancellor of the University, then passed on to Montpelier where he compiled another book, the "Art of Finding Truth" [*Art Abreujada d 'Atrobar Veritat*].

Later, in Genoa, he translated this book into Arabic, after which he returned to the Roman Court to renew his request for the foundation of monasteries. There he met with great hindrances, but, refusing to be discouraged, he returned to Genoa resolved to do what he could; single-handed and alone. There he disputed with the unbelievers, according to his Art. He had conceived the purpose of passing over to Barbary [Coast]; but having taken passage and gathered his books for the journey, it was suddenly made clear to him that the Moors would neither hear him nor permit him to dispute or preach to them, but would either stone him or condemn him to perpetual imprisonment.

So he remained at Genoa, yet laboured so strongly inwardly, under deep misgivings that he had probably succumbed to the temptation of being diverted from the path of duty by the hardships revealed to him, that he fell grievously sick; but to none would he tell the reason thereof. Thus he continued until the feast of Quinquagesima when he suffered himself to be carried to the church of St. Dominic, where during the festival he prayed to be pardoned for his great defection.

Now, after he had been set in a room within the dormitory where, after beholding several mystical visions and receiving Divine instructions, he embarked, against the will of his friends, for Barbary. On reaching Tunis Lully sought out these who were most learned in the sect of Mahomet, declaring to them how he had studied the law of the Christians, whose faith and its foundations he knew well; and that now he desired to learn of their sect and belief; and if it were found to be better than that of the Christians and they could so prove it, he would become a Moor.

He then expounded his Art to them. But one of the Moors, observing the great influence of this lofty and marvellous teaching upon the countrymen and foreseeing the extermination of their sect, related all to the king and prayed him to put the Christian to death. The king convoked his council and it was resolved by a majority that the master should die. This decision was revoked, however, through the timely interposition of a great Moor, who spoke against the opinion and counsel of all the rest:

> "It befits not so lofty a prince and king as art thou to pronounce such judgement and sentence upon one who, in order to exalt his law, has put himself into this peril; for it would follow that, if one of our own countrymen went among the Christians to convert them to our law, they would slay him likewise after the selfsame manner, so that hereafter there would be found no Moors who would dare to go and convert them to our law and to the better way, the which thing would be an argument against our law and a derogation to it."

A very wise Moor! Thus was the king turned from his counsel and determination, and resolved that the Christian should be expelled from the kingdom of Tunis. They dragged him from prison to a Genoese ship, stoning him as he went.

Nevertheless, he was not prepared to renounce his mission, because of those in the city who desired his teaching; so he landed again, secretly, and waited for an opportunity to re-enter the city. While he waited a Christian, resembling himself in habit and gesture, was seized by the mob as he walked the city and would have been stoned to death had he not cried, *"I am not Master Ramon!"* And regarding this as a Divine ministry to show him that he could in nowise profit by remaining there, the master returned to Naples where he read his Art in public.

Lully did not easily surrender his project of obtaining the direct sanction of the Pope to introduce his Art into the Catholic domains. He besought Pope Boniface VIII many times concerning this project, but, as we may expect, he only suffered many trials and rebuffs for his enthusiasm. An infallible Church stands beyond the need of any Art.

The master returned to Mallorca and continued his disputations and sermons among the Moors; and so effectually did he confound the heretics that when, through his labours, he fell into a bodily sickness, the chaplain who attended him scrupled not to give him poison.

Discovering this, he took his leave with great humility and went to the city of Famagusta, where he was joyfully received by the Master of the Temple in the city of Limisso. Here he remained until he had recovered his health, then departed once again for the University of Paris.

Later, we find him, nothing daunted, in Barbary again, engaged in learned arguments with the Bishop, who so marvelled at his lofty reasoning that he had the master brought to the prison and detained for a long time with a heavy chain around his neck. The officers of the law called a council and it was resolved that the master should be brought before them, and if they found him to be a man of learning he should be slain, but if he was mad he should be allowed to go. But a Moor who had known him in Tunis showed a creditable wisdom when he said:

> "Beware ye! Make him not to come here before you all, for he will bring such arguments against our law that it will be impossible to answer them...."

So Lully was removed into another and a more horrible prison. For the space of six months he was confined, during which time the Moors came daily and prayed him to be converted to the law of Mahomet, offering him infinite treasures, honours and women. But, established on the immovable rock of fervent love, he answered them:

> "And if ye yourselves will renounce this your false sect, and will believe in the Holy Name of Jesus, I promise you eternal life and treasures that will never fail you."

At length it was agreed between them that each should make a book wherein he should prove his law to be true, and that the law should be held to be the better which was proved by the better arguments. This opportunity was denied him, for the king ordered him to be placed in a ship going to Pisa, the master of which was commanded, under grievous penalties, not to leave the Christian in any country of the Moors.

After suffering shipwreck, he reached Pisa, where he rewrote the account of his discussions with the Moors and compiled a further book on his Art. Subsequently, again in Paris he engaged in public declamation.

> "There came to hear him, not students alone, but also a great multitude of masters, who affirmed that the said holy science and doctrine was corroborated, not only by philosophical arguments, hut also by the principles and rules of sacred theology, albeit some averred that the holy Catholic faith could not be proved, against whose opinions the said reverend maser made divers books and treatises."

Hearing through Pope Clement [V] that a General Council was to meet in the city of Vienne [France] in 1311, Lully resolved to go to the said Council to propose three things for the honour, reverence, and increase of the holy Catholic faith. First, that there should be built certain places where certain persons devout and of lofty intelligence should study divers languages to the end that they might preach the holy Gospel to all nations; second, that of all Christian knights there should be made a certain order, which should strive continually for the conquest of the Holy Land; third, that in opposition to the opinion of Averroes, who in many things has endeavoured to oppose the Catholic faith, men of learning should compose works refuting these errors aforementioned and all those that hold the said opinion. And this, concludes the writer:

"He has indeed done in divers books, for the said reverend master, a servant of our Lord and an expounder of the truth, has made more than a hundred and twenty and three volumes of books in honour of the Holy Trinity."

The year 1313 saw Lully in Mallorca once again, where he founded a Lullian school. In 1313 he went to Sicily and in 1314, after another brief visit to Mallorca, left for Tunis. In Tunis, or in Bugia, according to the traditional chronology, he was martyred, in the summer of 1315. But it has now been established that the date of his death could not have been earlier than December 1315, and was most probably rather later.

So runs the main narrative of this little life of Ramon Lull by the unknown writer who was contemporary with the master. Some of the facts related are embodied in A E Waite's monograph, gathered apparently from other sources, but to these he appears to attach little credit and touches them lightly and humorously.

For ourselves, we are accustomed in dealing with biographies of the early Rosicrucians to read reverently and between the lines, and discern a weight of meaning and extract many a lesson of profound value from the intimate glimpses of personality that have come down to us.

From this simple account of one who evidently knew Lully in the flesh the true character of the man stands out clearly enough. Wherever he went he left his mark upon his contemporaries. He was greatly loved, and undoubtedly thoroughly hated; for he was just one of those inspired and original characters who go steadily along their own path, knowing very well what they are about, but exceedingly difficult to deal with by those who deliberately attempt to force them from it.

Indeed, this world would be decidedly "hum-drum" and non-progressive were it not periodically agitated and shaken out of its materialistic dreaming by such characters. Our Order in the past has furnished a goodly number of them, and it is refreshing and stimulating to meet with an old record at times which reveals to us one of these rare souls daring all things in the name of the Powers that sent him forth, and passing away into the silence, leaving behind a reputation for good works which today we regard with admiration and may well seek to emulate.

9. The Rosicrucian Order and Cooperation

Reprinted from the December 1928 edition of The Mystic Triangle.

I recently read, with much interest, an editorial which appeared in a contemporary journal entitled: *"Wanted, a Paul Revere!,"* in which it was intimated that a movement was imminent, the aim of which will be to segregate true occultism from false.

A pertinent question occurred to me: What will be considered the criterion of true occultism? Will it consist in names, or personalities, or the beliefs and practices of certain movements or societies suggested by a committee of persons who ought to know? Or will the selection be made with regard to the tendencies, underlying motives and form of expression of any particular type of occultism under consideration? Because, I venture to think, when the innumerable types of occultism are called to the bar of judgement, few of them will accept the death penalty without a severe struggle.

Presumably, for instance, certain types of spiritualism and mediumship which masquerade under the name of occultism will be arraigned; and when these are relegated to the death chamber, there will be assigned, along with them, a large percentage of very real seekers of truth, full of the spirit of sincere research and endeavouring to live the Christ life, for all their misguided association with questionable cults. I foresee a phase of violent controversy such as we in England have witnessed in progress in the Church, where bishop is ranged against bishop, layman against cleric, and both against Parliament, for refusing to sanction the use of an amended and popish prayer book.

We are as likely to kneel to the Chair of St. Peter as we are to Mr Krishnamurti; and I am sure America has as little stomach as ourselves for this of kind of allegiance. However, the ideal as expressed in the editorial in question appeared to be the amalgamation or cooperation of all types of occultism which are moving Christward. That is a matter of great significance. If it can be done, America will soon cease to be regarded as the realm of the dollar. She will quickly become the Light of the West. But how will it be done?

What appears to me to be the sure criterion of genuine occultism is whether or not it gives paramount emphasis to the spirit of service. I care nothing for its name, or its prestige, or for the hum of personalities in the journals. That form of occultism which is not founded upon the spirit of service falls short of the ideal here expressed. It may offer all the rewards in creation, promise to make millionaires of its students in a day, or rear yogis by magic through breathing and affirmation in a night; if it does not give, instead of grasp, it will perish.

Those of us who have intimate relationships with students of the occult have had this demonstrated to us over and over again. Some of these students have dabbled for long and in good faith with many varieties of cultism. They have been lured by specious promises into this and that school of magical practice, and upon leaving it have found themselves standing just where they were before, and seekers still.

Every student has a right to choose his own path and attach himself to any cult or body of seekers he thinks will meet his inner need; but obviously it is to his best interest to demand to see the credentials of those to whom he gives his allegiance. It is a curious fact that a person who is most fastidious in selecting a diet in every way suitable for his physical well-being will often lack the slightest discrimination in the matter of nourishment for his mind and soul.

I recall in this connection the case of a young lady to whom I was speaking recently concerning the higher culture. Whilst living a most exemplary life from the physical standpoint, she confessed that so far as higher things were concerned, she regarded one of Miss Corelli's novels as practically her Bible. She did not see why this highly coloured romance should not be absolutely possible for herself, why it should not apparently blossom forth in her own life without any definite discipline such, as in reality, was the basic factor in the novelist's own development and power. This was clearly a lack of perspective. There certainly was a substratum of truth in the chosen novel, but the aerial structure built upon it, and on which my young friend had religiously fed her imagination for years, had raised her into a world of dreams from which she was extremely loath to descend.

There are thousands of students engaged upon a similar quest of magic and wonder-working in following one cult or another, which has nothing to recommend to them beyond a cheap advertisement. In these too there may be a substratum of reality, but only a very discriminating mind can find it. And the pretentious structure built around it is often so highly glossed and sonorous, so promising and captivating in its pronouncements, that they become veritable esoteric bibles to credulous souls. It is not for me to name and arraign any questionable cults or their teachings; those who run after them must learn from hard experience. I only know that if they could be summoned to an occult assize and prevailed upon to declare themselves before a competent tribunal they would not survive the test of the criterion mentioned.

I do not propose to pronounce a panegyric on the science of Rosicrucianism as taught in our Order. It stands in no need of it. We know what it is, what it has done, and what it is doing in the world. We know that its principles can be traced in the lives of a long line of historic characters from a remote past to the present day, and that these principles have inspired some of the most valuable works in the world's literature.

Those principles are known to the world for what they are..., for their height, their basic soundness, and for their instant appeal to the best in human nature. Others may find their prestige in bombast and their truth in a lie. By a low criticism they may seek to diminish and crush the fair and sincere efforts of those who believe in truth. But we keep to our own path, because it points upward. We believe in combined and constructive endeavour, and have no interest in occult dissention which adds a hundredfold to the strife of the world.

So far as I see, cooperation on these principles is the only cooperation worthwhile. How it is to be brought about is not for me to say. I only know that it would prove to be one of the greatest achievements of the century, and that the present conditions in America imperatively demand it. It would have a tremendous influence upon world thought. It would furnish a masterly example even to the Christian churches; while the reaction upon every sincere student, and the confidence and leading given to the doubting and hesitant seeker would be incalculable.

Section 4:

The Mystic Triangle (1929)

The Mystic Triangle

Sept. 1929

25 cts.

Souvenir Edition

Rosicrucian Mysteries

AMORC

Entered as Second Class Matter at the San Jose, Calif., Postoffice

1. Bulwer-Lytton

Reprinted from the January 1929 edition of The Mystic Triangle.

The main biography used for the above article is "Life of Edward Bulwer" *by* T H S Escott. *The other little publication referred to is* "Bulwer-Lytton as Occultist" *by* C Nelson Stewart.

Lytton, in one of his essays, insists on the necessity of so much similarity between a writer and his works as almost to resolve authorship into autobiography. Not every author, however, has the ability or the inclination to be autobiographical in his work. Moreover, some classes of work absolutely prohibit anything in the nature of autobiography. True, an author's style may reveal much of personal character to the critical reader, but Lytton evidently referred to something more intimate and revealing than style.

A novelist of the first magnitude and a master of narrative, much of his own varied experience was portrayed to the letter and formed the basis and inspiration of his many works, so that his insistence on this canon of literature is understandable and justified, at least in works of a similar nature.

Most of us have long been familiar with Lytton's great Rosicrucian story, *Zanoni*, yet few perhaps know much about the life of the man.

There is often a great satisfaction in reading, for the first time, the biography of a notable character whose name or work has been familiar to one for years, either through quotation or in bulk. How often we have pondered, for instance, upon the quotation from the Comte de Gabalis which heads the seventh chapter of *Zanoni*. How singular the pleasure when we read that quotation, in its eloquent context in the fourth discourse of the Comte, for the first time![1]

The same may be said of the Comte de St. Germain, whose name is so often encountered in occult literature, but who stands forth a living and virile personality in the monograph recently referred to in this magazine.[2]

When we meet the living man in the pages of authentic biography and realise his many-sided humanity, his failures and successes, his onward progress through his allotted span; and weigh the opinions of those who beheld his labours and laboured with him; his name henceforth is a potent influence, his works in our hands acquire new meaning, force and dignity, and a relationship in spirit is immediately established, never failing in its inspiration.

We feel all this when reading the life of the author of *Zanoni*. On perusing that book we soon discover that here is the work of no ordinary novelist. Here are the luminous facts of real and uncommon experience; and we may be sure that the writer who insisted upon the above-mentioned canon of authority applied this rule in this as in his other works.

---

1. Raymund Andrea's article about the Comte de Gabalis appears in Section 2 of this volume
2. Raymund Andrea's article about the Comte de St Germain appears in Section 3 of this volume

One writer goes so far as to allege that *Zanoni*, more than any other book, provided a matrix for the building up of modern theosophical philosophy in the English tongue. Certainly it is much quoted in early theosophical literature, and regarded as an authority by theosophical writers. H P B spoke of it in the highest terms and said that no author in the world of literature ever gave a more truthful or more poetical description of elemental beings; whilst of Lytton she said he was still claimed by the mysterious Brotherhood in India as a member of their own body, although he never avowed his connection with them.

And the poet Tennyson said that no one did more in his day towards intellectually raising the public and piquing its interest in better things.

The biographies of Lytton lay particular stress upon his distinguished ancestry. He combined two remarkably vigorous family strains. One of his ancestors was a certain learned and eccentric Dr Bulwer who studied the black art, wrote a good deal about the influence of the heavenly bodies on human beings, and of character and destiny in the conformation and lines of the hand.

In virtue of paternal descent, Lytton was a born ruler of men and a mystic, while the gentle and more gracious tendencies of the maternal Lyttons fitted him for the position he was to fill in letters and society.

He was born on May 5th, 1803, and was the third son of William Bulwer and Elizabeth Lytton. He was yet in his infancy when his father died. The eldest son was sent to a preparatory school, the second placed with his maternal grandmother, Mrs Warburton Lytton, and Edward lived alone with his mother. He was her favourite child.

Warburton Lytton, a learned man, still survived, and Edward and his mother passed a portion of each year at his house. Lytton was practically born in a library, for his grandfather's house was literally inundated with books. In 1810 Warburton Lytton died and his library passed as a gift to Edward's mother.

Thus, on the threshold of life, young Lytton was introduced to the world's literary treasures. Histories and legends illustrated by artists and engravers of Eastern potentates, treatises on chivalry and knighthood, and German metaphysics in abundance. The latter no doubt inspired the blooming philosopher of 8 years one day to ask his mother whether she were not sometimes overwhelmed by the sense of her own identity. He was promptly told to go to bed.

He passed from one private school to another, and impressed his preceptors and school fellows alike with his intellectual power and easy superiority.

At the age of 16 he became a private pupil of an Ealing clergyman who prepared young gentlemen for the universities. The years at Ealing, however, witnessed such general progress in moral and intellectual development, in the knowledge of books and character, that this period of tuition was all that was necessary to improve Lytton into a full-fledged poet and philosopher, as well as an accomplished man about town.

In due course of time he was entered at Cambridge. The college routine proved irksome; he relished work provided he could do it at his own time and in his own way. He fixed upon English history as his object of intellectual interest, and made careful excursions into a vast mass of ancient documents and rare biographies. The great historical novelist was in process of formation.

Trinity, the much loved college of Lytton's famous contemporaries, was to him a solitary cell, endurable only through private reading in which the tutors could help him little. He was shy, self-conscious, and self-concentrated, and could get along far better alone.

It was at Cambridge that he first became acquainted with Chauncey Hare Townshend, one of the earliest enthusiasts in clairvoyance, mesmerism, and studies of the supernatural; a man of much personal charm, whose influence upon Lytton was considerable.

The biographies of Lytton with which we are acquainted are almost exclusively devoted to the man in his social, personal, or political aspects: there is very little information concerning his esoteric and Rosicrucian activities. There has been a number of miscellaneous articles written from time to time about him and these perhaps throw some light, gleaned from various sources, on some of those activities.

A recent little publication on Lytton as an occultist probably gathers the few glimpses contained in these articles, and therefore supplements the main biography before us. The main biography, however, makes but the briefest allusions to the man as mystic; yet these hints, of small significance to the general reader, give us pause and invite reflection. Here is one of them:

> "The acquaintances he had made at the Cambridge Union brought him many invitations to country houses, and after a fortnight spent with an old Whig family in the North of England, he performed something of the nature of a religious pilgrimage. In the Lake District was the grave of an early lover of Lytton, and coming upon it after much search, he spent a night beside it in prayer. A simple act of devotion and understanding enough. At dawn, it is said, he felt himself a new man, as one re-baptised, if not reborn; and all that he esteemed best in his spiritual or intellectual life, as in his work, was dated by him from the vows and inspiration of those dark and lonely hours in a Cumbrian churchyard."

On returning southwards for home on this occasion he was aroused from a reverie by the voice of a zingari girl asking if she should tell his fortune. He consented, and having crossed her palm with silver, he was told that in infancy he had lost his father, that he had brothers, but no sister, and that as a boy he had a sweetheart whose loss nearly killed him, and made it impossible for him ever to be gay again.

As destiny seemed to have marked him out for adventures, he stayed at the gypsy encampment for a week, thinking it an opportunity for learning astrology, chiromancy, and other phases of occultism. But he found no teacher there, for these subjects were a sealed book to the gypsies themselves. Unfortunately, the zingari girl fell in love with the handsome stranger. His subsequent comment on the affair was: "*Alas! I went further for a wife, and fared worse."*

His second term in the school of the world dates from 1825 when he went to France. There he soon became a well-known social figure, made many acquaintances, and passed a dual existence, as he indeed did throughout his life. His Parisian apartment kept him in touch with the excitements and revelries of the time: but in his quiet country lodgings at Versailles he was laying the foundation of his future fame.

To a young man, Paris offered every temptation to extravagance and indiscretions, but the allurements of folly Lytton turned into experience, and fashioned copy for the printers. Gibbon, the celebrated historian of the Roman Empire, once said that his history was all the better for his having at one time been in the militia and a member of the House of Commons.

It may likewise be said of Lytton that the brilliant portraiture in some of his novels owes not a little to his Parisian experiences. Whether in society or in solitude he was a perfect slave to toil.

His career however was not yet fully decided upon. Returning to England, a reaction set in..., his pen seemed to have lost its charm. His famous ancestors had been men of action, soldiers or statesmen, who played a prominent part in the affairs of their day; these he felt he must emulate. The noise and excitement of battle was just then around him. Napoleon had fallen, and with keen interest Lytton had watched the remoulding of the world after Waterloo. He decided on a military career, and for three years was nominally an officer in the British Army.

But of more consequence to Lytton than his soldiership was the sequel of the welcome given him by his mother on reaching England. She was engaged to attend a tea party and prevailed on her son to accompany her. Even a tea party was an occasion for printer's copy, and many of the guests became the originals of characters in a future novel. Here he met a young Irish lady, Rosina Wheeler, the lady destined to become his wife, and with whom he "fared worse."

It sometimes happens that a fond mother prefers to select a wife for her son rather than permit him to select for himself. It was so with Mrs Bulwer. Rosina Wheeler, writing to a friend about her relations with Lytton, refers to, *"the attentions of a young gentleman whose mother, a widowed lady, objects to his marrying me."*

All the trouble that followed arose through a dutiful son complying with his mother's request to show himself at a literary tea table. The ineligible attachment grew apace, much to the chagrin of Mrs Bulwer. The situation was delicate, for Lytton was practically dependent upon his mother for an expenditure of several thousand pounds a year. He promised his mother that, without her consent, he would never become Miss Wheeler's declared lover, much less her husband. He wished the lady goodbye, mounted his horse and made for the West of England. His last words to his mother were:

"God knows that, notwithstanding the dejection and despondency making me often so silent, sometimes so querulous, I am tenderly attached and grateful to my dearest mother. Hence my readiness, as now, to sacrifice so much that is nearest and dearest to my heart, if by so doing, as in all the great events of my life, I can secure her approbation, and prevent her regretting or being ashamed of the kindness and affection she has shown me."

At Bath, Cheltenham and Bristol he buried himself in literary work. But the brilliant young Irish lass, of fascinating presence and considerable literary ability, was not so easily exorcised.

He returned to his old quarters in Paris, and to his study in Versailles, and resumed the same systematic industry in the planning of works and hunting up authorities. The mornings found him absorbed in books and papers, the afternoons were passed in solitary rides through the forest.

He renewed his former acquaintances and figured actively behind the scenes of social and political life in Paris. But there was no peace for him. He was but experiencing in himself the truth of Goethe's dictum that the most universal effect of the highest genius is to unsettle.

In the meantime, matters between Mrs Bulwer and Miss Wheeler had assumed a serious aspect. In attempting to kill the attraction between the young lovers by separation, Mrs Bulwer had not counted upon the temper of Irish blood. She had vowed that the "Limerick girl" should never be the mistress of Knebworth, and the "Limerick girl" accepted the challenge.

The second absence abroad entirely failed to produce the result for which it was undertaken. The lady wrote no letters, although Lytton occasionally wrote to her; but she well knew that the temporary separation was strengthening the attachment and she could afford to wait. Her nationality and taste coloured his literary meditations and suggested new subjects for his pen..., she had become his inspiration. Suggested by the vivid word pictures of her own conversation, his new poem, "O'Neil" was dedicated to his love in glowing terms. In this poem he offered his homage to a people's patriotism and beauty in inscribing it to the concentrated loveliness of One.

At this point during the second season abroad, he first entertained the idea of living by his pen. His resolution to make Rosina Wheeler his wife was fixed. He was aware that there was a probability that his mother would either stop or reduce his allowance, in which case his own exertions must supply the deficiencies. His idea had always been to pass as a gentleman of intellectual tastes, devoted to literary study and capable of literary performance, but by circumstances of family and fortune set quite apart from the poor hacks who were compelled to barter for every line they wrote.

His experiences in France wrought a great change in his ideas about the future, and upon his second return to England in 1826 he showed himself as a clearheaded, shrewd man of business, resolved upon giving the public his very best, but equally keen upon finding the most advantageous market for his work. With a wealth of notes for literary treatment he settled down to a further period of study and preparation, with a view to working up all his material for the public journals and his novels.

Nor were politics to be excluded. From childhood he had lived among professional politicians and from an early age had cherished the ambition of taking a seat, some day, in the House of Commons. Thus Lytton's career was swiftly maturing.

In 1827, he married Miss Wheeler with the two-fold resolution that his pen as novelist and essayist should first win him fame and power; and then ability, not birth or fortune, should entitle him to take a part in ruling the state.

And now, entering upon married life, Lytton drew up a lofty programme for himself. There were to be three years of retirement at his country home, occupied in writing, which should bring him fame and enough to make both ends meet; then three years of foreign travel for the purpose of gathering more material. And after this, a parliamentary career which should carry his name down to posterity.

But affairs were not to run so smoothly as this. His financial responsibilities were in excess of his resources. The unlimited allowance from his mother had ceased; and at the outset of his literary life he was depressed in spirits, impaired in energy, and his capacity for good work lessened, because the mother he loved and honoured continued to embitter his existence by a refusal to acknowledge his wife.

The constant bickerings on both sides, together with overwork on his own part, seriously affected his health. The writing, with which he had formerly varied his reading, had been done for pleasure without thought of profit. He had chosen subjects to suit his taste. Now he could afford to read little, and write nothing that did not promise immediate returns. In the ears of Lytton and his wife still rung the kind anticipation of Mrs Bulwer on the eve of their marriage: "*If you marry this woman, you will be, in less than a year, the most miserable man in England.*" The mother-in-law's disfavour it was that laid upon Lytton the necessity of an industrious slavery which almost deprived his wife of his society.

The year 1829 found Lytton, his wife, and little daughter living in London. His mother had not failed to remind him of his inability to support without her assistance..., which only made him slave the more pitilessly at any commissions, in pen and ink journeymanship, offered him. His mother periodically showed that she could combine a taunting tongue with an open purse; but the effects of these acts of generosity upon a sensitive, irritable and overwrought aspirant, striving to ensure his own and his family's independence, may be conjectured.

To make matters worse, it was not long before he realised that his wife was far from a perfect helpmate for an overdone breadwinner. He soon had occasion to resent her improvidence. The lady, too, had her grievances. Absorbed in work that kept him to his study, and absences in London on literary or newspaper business, there was little time to spare for his wife.

Mrs Bulwer continued to help matters in the wrong direction. She irritated him, exasperated his wife, and openly lamented that the price paid by her son for his marriage was his own indefinite sentence to a penny-a-liner's lot. His constitutional irritability, aggravated by overwork, business anxieties and the complication of family feuds, often made him unapproachable.

In 1831 his second child, a son, was born. But the tranquillising agencies of home life were denied him, for even the children became an occasion of dispute in the household. The mother's health did not permit her to nurture her infants from the first, and they were consequently put out to nurse.

During his London residence, while his fame was rapidly mounting as a literary artist, he was far from well, either in body or mind. He suffered from a certain cutaneous trouble, from earache, and also from the personalities of the critics.

Regarding the latter, he had by long effort, schooled himself into concealing his feelings under the calm exterior of a well guarded reserve. His pen so far had lacked an organ in which he could deal in his own way with his critics; but the opportunity soon came. He was offered the editorship of the *News Monthly* magazine, and accepted this position as well for his literary usefulness as for the service he thought it might render him in his parliamentary course just about to begin.

This appointment increased the bitterness of the editors of contemporary magazines; yet it is worth recording that within a few months, on meeting the chief of his enemies, Lockhart of the "Quarterly," in a lady's drawing room, they advanced toward each other and cordially shook hands. These terrible literary critics are usually the mildest of creatures, and when they meet, common human nature is too much for them!

The early years of his London life witnessed Lytton's gradual promotion to the front rank of novelists and pamphleteers. But a more important event was at hand; he was returned as member for St. Ives, and took his seat in the House of Commons. It is said that he studied history and political economy for the House as systematically as if he had been preparing for a university examination. His knowledge of foreign affairs and international relationships was minute and authoritative. In one of his essays written before his parliamentary life we have this:

> "You English do not pay enough attention to foreign literature and foreign politics to understand your own. You ought to hear what the rest of the world says of you, and see how true are the views which, from a distance, foreigners, Frenchmen in particular, form of your successive political situations, and of the causes which have produced them."

Which is a good illustration of how Lytton qualified to become a teacher of his time. To teach his generation the principles of a sober and practical cosmopolitanism was his constant aim. In his parliamentary speeches and in his magazine, this idea appeared paramount.

It was during this period of his parliamentary life that the separation between Lytton and his wife transpired. It is abundantly clear that his course of love and marriage with Miss Wheeler, and the tactless procedure of his mother in connection therewith, brought great unhappiness to all the parties; and deflected him, during his early years, from the path of a gentleman of ease and affluence.

It is no less clear that through being forced into a line of original and independent action he attained to a vast influence in his day, and the unhappy details of his domestic life fade into insignificance when we contemplate the finished man and his splendid work. The cruel prophecy of his mother, Lytton could never forget. His deep affection for her and the confidence which he placed in her knowledge and understanding of life caused him again and again to recall her words when differences arose between himself and his wife regarding her wastefulness. The disreputable suggestion did its work; he came to feel that his mother must be right.

Prudent and self-denying in his personal outlay, Lytton was a stern domestic economist. Not so Mrs Lytton and the displays of ill temper which naturally resulted gave fresh occasion to her for posing as an unappreciated or injured woman. To this she readily added other grievances, some of which were quite imaginary.

We have to remember just here that we are considering the life of one who was an occult adventurer. Behind the veil of vigorous literary and political activities was the eccentric explorer of the unknown and supernatural. Throughout his life he had a habit of multiplying the houses he either rented or owned. Whether in some fashionable quarter of the city or in the obscurity of a suburb, if a particular dwelling attracted him, he at once bought or hired it. In these solitary retreats he would remain for weeks in lonely meditation upon the problems of the times, and engaged in many strange experiments of which glimpses are found in his writings. How could a vivacious, pleasure-loving Irish lady, fond of gay dinner parties and sparkling wit, accept such a lot as this!

Perhaps it was not an unnatural suspicion, which grew in her mind, that made her think of the different domiciles of her husband, although rarely visited by her, might be presided over by other ladies of more congenial quality. At all events, it was about the time of the separation when, hearing that Lytton was sick in his bachelor chambers in town, she hurried off with the medicine chest to his assistance, arriving just in time to see, through the half opened door, the flutter of a departing dress, and a tea table laid for two.

By what stages the separation was finally reached we do not know. We have to be satisfied with knowing that if Lytton was to continue his career, literary or political, it became necessary for him to deliver himself from the disabling society of an uncongenial wife.

This deliverance, in 1836, from a mistaken partnership entered upon ten years previously was followed by a period of intense work in several directions, but which culminated in a serious physical failure which had its inception in 1830 when compelled to pursue with little intermission the severe labours referred to. He was gifted with an iron will, and a powerful brain, united with a vigorous constitution, but the latter had not received sufficient attention.

"*We do not sufficiently*," he writes, "*reflect upon our outward selves.*" For 16 years he fought with ill health; and the remedies and regimen which helped him most and made life tolerable were chiefly of his own devising. He found the doctors at fault and studied medicine for himself. Mental science, physiology and psychology were his favourite studies; and when he needed expert advice he visited an unorthodox healer in a little side thoroughfare.

"*A visit to a quack*," he said, "*is a very pleasurable excitement.*" It was Lytton who familiarised the English public with the water cure. His article on the subject in his magazine was reprinted as a pamphlet and is still to be found at Hydropathic institutions, which owe their existence to him.

All along the way we discern in Lytton the fervent pioneer. The doctors failed him and he was driven to search for relief in the healing forces of the visible and invisible universe. His discoveries made material for many of his essays, of little permanent value perhaps, but all pointing to *Zanoni*, and his other mystical and occult works.

In 1842 appeared *Zanoni*. Asked in later years which of his novels he liked best, Lytton replied, "*I think, on the whole, Zanoni.*" It was the first of his books which received complimentary notices from associated admirers throughout Europe. In every capital critical groups and literary clubs discussed the inner meaning of the book. Was it simply an allegory, or merely a narrative in which typical meanings were concealed? I am afraid Lytton's biographer, writing in 1910, was as much in the dark as those who discussed the book in the literary clubs on its appearance.

He says, "*Into 'Zanoni' was condensed much fresh information about the men and incidents connected with the overthrow of the old regime.*" The preparation for "Zanoni" had partly begun in the study of French politics whose results appeared in the form of the "Quarterly Review" articles. It is much to be regretted that Bulwer should not have been encouraged by his successful treatment in *Zanoni* of the overthrow of the old regime to write a book in which French affairs should have been, not a casual episode, but the central and sustained theme.

There were two active political periods in Lytton's life. The first from 1831 to 1841, when he left the House of Commons a young man of 38 years; the other from 1852 to 1866. It does not appear that he ever greatly excelled as an orator, but his value as a statesman cannot be doubted. He impressed his contemporaries by a certain prescience in affairs which he had always possessed.

"*I have little repartee*," he says in 1841, "*my memory is slow and my presence of mind not great.*" This however his biographer will not allow; he says his presence of mind never failed him, and seemed in its calm collectedness a contradiction of his shy, nervous, and irritable temperament.

For ourselves, there is no mystery about this dual nature of Lytton; he was a psychic of the first order and consequently far more at home in his own inner world of vision and contemplation than among his fellow men who were solely immersed in worldly affairs.

In fact, it took some years before he became on friendly terms with his hearers, as well as less preoccupied with himself, and developed some measure of the art of the orator. There is another point to be noted: true to the type of character we are studying, his intellectual development continued throughout the whole course of his life and in his latest year showed greater power than in his prime.

In 1866 he was compelled to retire from political life on account of failing health, and in that year was raised to the Peerage. For some time deafness and difficulties of the voice had persistently increased, but his brain continued powerful and clear, and his other faculties unimpaired. His remaining years were spent in active literary work.

He died in 1873 and was buried in Westminster Abbey. From the funeral sermon delivered from the Abbey pulpit these appropriate words of encomium are preserved:

> "To have served his own generation in a higher or lower sphere is a glorious description of any man's life. Lord Lytton's life was a solid good to the world. Now that he has gone, there is one person less to carry out the will of God here below."

2. The Technique of the Master (1929)

Reprinted from the February 1929 edition of The Mystic Triangle. *Also published in* "Waiting for the Master" *by* Francis Bacon Lodge *(1982).*

Members of our Order who are acquainted with the Theosophical text books will not be unaware that the founders of the Theosophical movement were considerably indebted to a Rosicrucian Brother of the Eastern Brotherhood for instruction and personal guidance in connection with the problems associated with the carrying out of their mission.

I refer to the Brother Serapis, and I have felt prompted to base the matter of this article on a quotation from one of his letters. It leads us to the heart of the subject of the Master's technique, a subject of unfailing interest and value to all of us; and one, moreover, upon which some members have asked me to write further because so many of the deepest problems contingent upon their progress along the path are bound up with it.

Inevitably so, for the word of the Master is truth, and as we strenuously qualify through self-understanding to work skilfully upon and with the souls of our fellow men, we become more and more possessed with the desire to see as he sees, speak as he speaks, do as he does, that our influence may become at last a living light to kindle the ready soul to self-recognition and larger purpose.

There is one important and palpable fact about the personal communications of the

Masters, and that is their complete and unassailable expression of the phase of truth under consideration. This may appear a truism, yet it is one for reflection. For instance, if we take the majority of textbooks on occultism we find that the exposition is fragmentary, subsequent textbooks along the same lines, at a later date, even from the pen of the same writer will..., I do not say, annul the former ones..., but necessitate considerable mental readjustments on the part of readers.

I need not specify cases, but any student of Theosophy can verify this statement. Further, such textbooks dealing with the same subject matter but from the hands of different writers are often very contradictory, and these divergences in the exposition of occult truth are anything but satisfactory or helpful to the student. The positive assertions of these expositions, each so dogmatic and convincing in its way, appear equally to demand complete acceptance. If these different presentations were harmonious fragments, if they dovetailed into and corroborated each other, and formed one composite body of Cosmic truth, a very disturbing factor would be eliminated.

Upon that one basis of sound and tested doctrine, the offspring of many advanced investigators in direct contact with one unimpeachable source of illumination, the student might well feel that he could ground his soul life with a deep sense of inner security. However the case is otherwise.

But when the Master speaks for the guidance of the soul we feel and know at once, and for all time, the indubitable certainty of his word. There is no need to compare it with any other utterances; no textbook is required to corroborate it. It is a phrase from Cosmic experience, and true to the experience of the evolving soul. We may not be ready to accept it now, but the time will come when we must accept it if we wish to advance.

This indubitableness of the Master's word in its immediate or remote relationship to our human experience is a fact which always appeals to me as unique in literature. It is not difficult to see why it is never open to question or subject to qualification. There is no hidden depth of the soul which the Master has not sounded; no problem which he cannot instantly detach from every hampering consideration and observe it in the clear, cool light of illuminated intellect.

I use the term intellect intentionally. I see no reason for assuming, as many seem to assume, that the Master, because of his lofty spirituality, condescends not to use so poor a tool as intellect. Observe the vexations and perplexities that hedge round our problems because of the ever fluctuating and darkening shadows of the emotional and mental life, obstructing the clear light of the thinking principle, and raising a host of discordant vibrations which involve us in sore distress.

The Master is entirely free from that. When he surveys the problem of the soul he stands above, not within it; it is reflected comprehensively and alone upon the clear and illuminated mirror of the intellect. He knows just what it means to us; he sees the defect of knowledge or foresight which gives it birth, the keen struggle of the soul to find a solution, or the resultant reactions upon our future growth.

How often an aspirant questions the wisdom, justice, and compassion of the Master because the particular burden of life is not at once removed for the asking! But if the Master is a living example of adjusted Karmic forces every conceivable soul problem must be known to him, and he also knows the beneficient reactions of every Karmic problem which besets us.

Why, we cannot behold the Master's countenance, or those of any of his high initiates, without discerning deeply charactered there the blessed memorials of manhood perfected through ancient suffering. It is this immense world experience, this agedness of the soul in the Master which vibrates in his word of guidance with such sombre emphasis, and holds us true to him even in the darkest hour. I have known a trembling soul to hang upon the Master's word when nothing in life or circumstance seemed to justify it; but the soul knew even though it could not understand, and that link of imperishable force and sympathy was all sufficient.

The necessity for specialised culture of the will in occult work is a matter upon which all of us are in full agreement. In all world progress it is the great driving force; but the will to tread the path is of a higher nature. It is in reality the inner spiritual self acting steadily and unceasingly through the personality.

And when, through study and meditation, and one-pointed determination to achieve masterhood, this inner self or spiritual will is gradually released and begins to act powerfully in the vehicles of the student, only then do the real problems of the path emerge and call for the greatest strength to deal with them.

Then it is that many grow profoundly doubtful of their progress, and are ready to turn to the former relative security which was theirs. So long as we do not think too deeply or demand too much, the normal rhythm of life remains undisturbed; but to have thoroughly visualised the higher possibilities and sent forth a petition into the Master's realm to share in the responsibilities and blessings of a larger service, is a direct request of the soul to be subjected to that keener discipline which alone will make the greater service possible.

And the student who is not yet sure of himself, who has not realised fully the depth and reality of his pledge of allegiance to the Higher Powers, is often greatly perplexed at the definite changes occurring in his mental life, and the altered aspect of circumstances.

Yet this is but one of the tests which sooner or later confronts every student, and if the general trend of his life has not evolved a measure of strength and ripeness in his faculties he will be compelled to actively school himself in further world experience in order to successfully meet the test.

That life itself is the great initiator is a profound occult truth. It can be observed in the world of men every day. There are individuals around us who have no leaning toward the occult, yet so intense and varied are their labours, so strenuous and devoted are they in manifold works of ideal service for the race, that they have all the mental and inner equipment for rapidly passing the tests of the occult path.

We have known many remarkable examples of this in the case of such individuals contacting the Order; and it brings to mind a statement in one of the early issues of our magazine: that the potentialities of a new member cannot be fully foreseen, and every care should be taken and encouragement given him in the early stages of the work in view of his possible great value and influence in the Order.

In these men the will has reached its strength through long and versatile response in world experience; they stand at the point of mature mentality where they can receive the deeper knowledge of the soul; the sharp contacts and pain of life have rounded off a whole cycle of minor attachments and given them clear judgement, and a high degree of detachment from purely personal issues whereby they are able to bear the accelerated vibration which will eventuate when they take up the discipline of the path.

This is a factor for reflection. If the common experience of life has not been such as to initiate the student into the true value and force of the will in some of its higher aspects, his allegiance to and active work in the Order will surely demand this at no distant time. He will be thrown back upon his own inner strength in the very act of demanding that strength from the Master.

I will give a concrete example. A member in this jurisdiction had reached a certain stage of the Temple lectures. He had received much encouragement from others in his studies, but ultimately resigned, alleging as his reason that the work lacked what he called the human element. This is the first instance I have known of a member giving this reason for his inability to progress.

The facts of the case were these. The student was satisfied with what he termed "Rosicrucian principles" and admitted that he did not want any teaching beyond these..., whatever the "principles" might be. He simply was not ready to accept the inner consequences of taking practical knowledge. His will was not equal to an advance: he was content to remain stationary, resting in a limited theoretical acceptance of certain fundamentals.

This is not a case for criticism, but for clear understanding. It is an occasion for regret that a student who has expressed a strong wish for higher unfoldment should yet deliberately put aside the surest means for attainment. But just at the crucial point the law of elimination became operative and he was unable to proceed because of his unreadiness.

If a student fears to take the consequence of enlightenment, prefers to remain upon the little platform of knowledge he has carefully measured and erected for himself, and stifles the voice of the soul which is actually urging him to larger issues, the door of opportunity is automatically closed and he must wait until a further cycle of experience has reinforced the mental faculties with greater strength and purpose. The law demands that a student must help himself.

Now the Brother Serapis, of the Egyptian Brotherhood, refers very specifically to this matter of energetic direction of the will:

> "For he who hopes to solve in time the great problems of the Macrocosmal World and conquer face to face the Dweller, taking thus by violence the threshold on which lie buried nature's most mysterious secrets, must try, first, the energy of his Will Power, the indomitable resolution to succeed, and bringing out to light all the hidden mental faculties of his Atma and highest intelligence, get at the problem of Man's Nature and solve first the mysteries of the heart."

It is useless for us to attempt to shirk the issue by saying that the human element is lacking in phraseology of this kind. If we are still children and require our disciplinary instruction well sugared, nay, lived for us, the divine admonition of the Master will certainly prove too much for our human nature, and repel us.

It is to be hoped that the majority of our members are beyond that stage; that the exigencies of life have compelled the assertion of their manhood. That they are aware of their deepest need and the need of their fellow men, and are not likely to turn back from the path they have studied and the truth they know because of what may appear to be a strain of severity in the word of the Master, which foreshadows a higher discipline and consequent renunciation perhaps of certain common interests which have had their day and dissipate energy.

There may be many a secret struggle between these interests and the graver aspect of truth which silently beckons us on. It cannot be otherwise in view of the strong momentum of unspiritual mentation established during the long past in the subjective consciousness.

Those of us who have persistently fought our way along certain hard phases of the path know well enough the painful misgivings, the harassing doubts, the solitary questionings of the heart, which have beset us; yet I believe there is not one of us but would testify, on emerging from the shadow, that it is well. What matters the difficulty if we have comprehended the way, the truth and the life that the Master offers us?

Indeed, there is no other way by which the will can reach its strength, or the Master would certainly have told us. No matter to what Master we look for guidance, one admonition characterises them all in regard to passing from our world into his: the necessity for the dominant force of the spiritual will is ever insisted upon. The technique of the Master is pre-eminently active, not passive. Observe the leading thoughts of the above quotation: *"Conquer: take by violence: try: indomitable resolution: bring out: get out."*

The whole process is one of intense inner action. I venture to affirm there is not a great character in universal history in which this supreme motive power is not seen to be a compelling factor. At first sight it may not always appear to be so. According to the manifold types and careers this central force of the awakened will may be strongly objective or more or less underlying, but it is there, organised, concentrated and potent. Only, on occult levels, a different order of experience ensues.

The great character on the stage of world history does not necessarily enter consciously and with specific intent into the secret domain of the Spirit: his direction in life is technically unspiritual. Great as are his works in the manifold fields of human endeavour, strong as his ray of individual genius may be, he is not an occultist in the accepted sense of the term, nor is he subject to the laws of the occult.

The sovereign faculties of intuition and reason, developed to a rare degree, make him what he is. He is not engaged in a culture, the discipline of which would carry him beyond a certain exalted stage of human consciousness. The purely occult tests are withheld; from such he may as surely shrink as would the average human being.

Now, the Master exercises all the prerogative of genius, all the faculties of human consciousness in him are raised to their highest potency. And, in addition, the spiritual counterparts, so to speak, of these faculties, are operative and under perfect control, hence his vast authority, supreme value, and august ascendency over the higher manifestations of human genius.

It is to the development of these deeper faculties, the spiritual counterparts of the finest faculties of human consciousness, that our attention as occult students is given; hence the note of severity which characterises the discipline inculcated by the Master.

And in attempting to pass beyond the frontiers of common worldly experience, no matter to what height of experience in any of its varied forms natural genius may have carried us within this experience; in the deliberate, conscious attempt to take the word of the Master and occultly speculate into the silent and mysterious domain of the Super Experience, the will is subjected to the finer and superphysical tests which are the unalterable laws of that domain.

No man can offer himself sincerely as a candidate for his quest of the Spirit without setting up within certain powerful reactions of a peculiar and intimate character, which will surely try out what sort of man he is.

It is the initial stage of a process of readjustment of all his values. There is nothing to be feared in the experience; it is a great privilege that he feels the call in his nature to meet it. Conscientious study and meditation should give him the necessary strength to meet it. It is not that he has to prepare to lose that which is dear and valuable to him, or renounce any talent or prestige he possesses in the world of men, or throw off any business or domestic obligations to which he is committed..., not a word of this is written in the vocabulary of true occultism.

He has simply to cultivate strength of will to realise himself as he is..., which implies far more than we usually think, for when the force of concentrated will is focused steadily and over a long period upon the psychic and spiritual self, every motive and tendency buried in the heart of man is awakened to palpitating life and activity; all that Karma has written in his members arises and confronts him.

That is one phase of the great problem to which the admonition of the Master applies: and there it is, before that intimate personal disclosure of the man he is, that the student has to stand firm and undismayed in the face of much that he would hesitate to utter. Is there then any wisdom in averting the eyes from that which the Spirit demands that he should fearlessly confront and steadily overcome?

We have called upon the name of the Master and the answer comes in the form of the vital refining fire that descends within to purge and purify every one of us who aspires after the hidden mysteries. Shall we weakly decline what we have deliberately invoked and postpone the blessed work of personal redemption because of the imminent possibility of the mortal self, which we love so well, being stretched sacrificially upon the cross which rises mystically on the path before us?

Is there any tragedy in life like unto that in which a man, having taken knowledge of the way, retreats from the call of the Cosmic when the dark hour comes in which he must find his own light and press steadfastly on?

In my work in the Order it has been my privilege to have this problem again and again raised by students who have stood face to face with the shadow of the dark night of the soul, to which their strong and sincere effort on the path had brought them; and one of the greatest inspirations to me has been to note their firm grip on themselves, their philosophical stand in their trial, and the deep spiritual assurance they have had that all must be well and the goal would be reached.

They are right. The Master's word has not gone forth for naught; and we can prove this by taking the austere ritual of the conquering will uttered by the Brother, and working it out in the silence, until all that is hidden in the inmost recesses of the heart is brought to light, and understood, and the baser metals transmitted into the pure gold of inner illumination.

3. Waiting for the Master

Reprinted from the March 1929 edition of The Mystic Triangle. *Also published by* Francis Bacon Lodge *in a compilation of the same name (1982).*

In the Ninth Grade we stand at the threshold of a greater life. We await the Master who is to initiate us into divine cognition and knowledge of our true mission on the path. In this highly mystical grade there is significant pause and vast scope for contemplation. Looking back over the grades, it seems as if we had gradually ascended a great and narrowing stairway, step by step, and now stand on the last stair, far away from the voices of earth, before the portals of the unseen temple.

Many have fallen away as the ascent grew steeper. The reward was too remote and the goal intangible. They fell away because they had not faith, and their portion will be a still continuing and unappeased hunger for that life which lies beyond the threshold which is approached in the Ninth Grade.

The pause and silence in the Ninth Grade constitutes one of the greatest tests we have to meet on the path. We may have done all in our power, and the Master has not appeared. I know not why: I only know that in many lives the fact is so. Yet I feel convinced that there are certain conditions to be met, certain work to be accomplished, which we may dimly apprehend but which the Master knows, absolutely and in detail, are necessary for us to meet and to accomplish before we may share in his life.

At this point we retain a firm footing through the exercise of an indomitable faith. I doubt whether one of us has come so far without realising within, in one form or another, the strongest reason for this faith in those things which remain hidden to us just beyond the threshold.

Those of us who have given the best part of our lives to the study and contemplation of higher things are seldom troubled with anxious questionings as to the path we have chosen, the reward of our effort, or the ultimate goal. We live onward from day to day in confidence that such aspects of truth and revelations of the divine as we are ready to accept and fitted to receive will be lawfully unfolded to an aspiring consciousness, and that veil after veil will pass away as we live and serve in the world of men. And it is inconceivable that those who entered upon the study of the path for the first time when they contacted the Order, passed through the grades understandingly, and now stand with us in the mystical pause of the Ninth Grade, have not the inner assurance of a reward for their labour and a realisation of expanding consciousness.

Their ability to demonstrate objectively may still be negligible; they may feel that they have little to show as a result of their study and meditation. Yet experience warrants us in saying that such objective demonstration is by no means the only criterion of progress. It is just at this point in his studies that so much depends, in my opinion, on a student having a fairly clear idea of his inner status on the path.

If he were studying in a certain course at the university with the hope of graduating for a specific profession, a time would ultimately arrive when he would need to take thorough stock of himself before presentation for examination to that end. He would need to gauge his weakness and his strength. He would submit to a careful self-examination and exercise himself in every way for qualification.

Is not his position in the Ninth Grade somewhat analogous to this? But here he is largely his own instructor. He need entertain no fear of being "sent down" in the absence of certain qualifications. The period of waiting may be prolonged, but there is no failure.

This leads us to the important question of what is the outstanding qualification for passing beyond the threshold in the Ninth Grade. We are clearly confronted with no ordinary test. Upon entering each grade we have passed a threshold, at least symbolically. But at some stage of our progress through the Ninth Grade there is to be a definite translation of consciousness. During the interval of this grade we are engaged in a refining preparation which is to culminate in a complete change of polarity.

Personally, I do not think this is to be achieved by any specific occult experiment, although some members in the Ninth Grade appear to hold this idea.

I have often studied, with a good deal of interest, photographs depicting the remarkable throws of the proficient in ju-jitsu; but woe to the man who attempts these if he has not a sufficiently athletic body and the requisite flexibility and strength of muscle and mental resources. There may not be the element of danger in the occult experiment that resides in the simple looking throw, but a vast amount of conscientious preparation is necessary in both cases.

There was a time when I could not altogether understand the urgent admonition of advanced occultists to serve. On more than one occasion when I had almost implored these greater souls of one school or another of occult teaching to give me some exceptional soul knowledge or instruction to satisfy the fierce hunger for advancement, I was uniformly pointed to the path of service.

It was put to me most strongly that it was practically useless to engage in meditation and speculation about the soul unless the knowledge and force already possessed as the reward of past effort were communicated in some form for the assistance of others. Indeed, it was not until I contacted our Order that the significance of this admonition was fully realised and given effect.

It appears to be a condition of the threshold that the aspirant must retreat from the very point to which he has attained if he would go further. It seems that he is called upon to show in a very unique manner what sort of man he is; and this is not, as we are apt to think, by some remarkable demonstration of divine or occult power, but rather in what measure he can work upon the souls of lesser aspirants and raise them, too, to this level of renunciation.

And unless I am greatly mistaken, that is the keynote of the pause in the Ninth Grade. There must be some dominant characteristic in the nature of the aspirant which stamps him as a different man from his fellows..., or surely the reality of his position in this grade is lost to him!

That characteristic must be as the vital breath of the soul and radiate powerfully in the world of men. For, in a sense, no one has a right in the Ninth Grade unless he is willing to assume the responsibility of taking knowledge. That responsibility is, that he shall project the light he has into the darkness for the guidance of others.

Failure lies in considering too critically and nicely the quality of the light possessed. Such as we have we must use..., now, and be grateful that our earnest search for knowledge has kindled so much in the soul. The aspirant, in order to gain confidence in using the light he has need only reflect upon the multitudes around him, a good percentage of which would give nearly all they possess to have the knowledge and conviction about the deeper realities of life that he has.

We are far too prone to think, because we have not some extraordinary insight into supersensible truth, or lack the facility of some admired exponent of it, or cannot immediately unravel every problem that confronts us and read the soul of man as an opened volume, that we must wait and do nothing. This will never satisfy the soul, nor prepare us for that which we must handle with strength and mastery when we pass beyond the threshold.

Here, then, we come face to face with the one qualification which overshadows all others and which must be brought out in the Ninth Grade. We have almost to forget the goal in inspiring others on the way to it. We have to cool ourselves of this fever for advancement which constantly tempts us to leap away on to the heights and stand there, conscious of our celestial radiance and elevation beyond the masses, only to look down.

What use has a Master for a surveyor of human lives? This is one of the most prolific of the poisonous plants in the garden of modern occultism; it propagates serene and debonair souls, clothed in majestic repose and conscious meritoriousness, having a rosary of theories too sacred for utterance except among the elect, and far beyond the comprehension of this evil world, or any advanced soul in it who thinks not likewise.

If that is height, they have the right to it since they sought and attained it; but if in some incarnation they happen to contact a Master I think the first admonition they will receive will be, to come down. And this is a hint for us if so be any of us have misinterpreted the way. We must do something with might and main for those who want what we have. We have to come down now to the problem of any soul that confronts us and wrestle with it, even though it be formidable and apparently far beyond us.

We have no idea of the strength and range of our knowledge and power until we, with something akin to heroic passion, endeavour to use them. Surely, the past years of silent thought and meditation, and upward aspiring must be allowed to have fostered something in the soul worthy of use, or we have wasted precious time.

We might have mastered a language or studied a literature as a desirable acquisition and a proof of culture, and taken infinite delight in a skilful expression of it in the associations of every day life. Yet this is insignificant in comparison with the secret forces of light and leading of which every true aspirant should be conscious and desire to manifest.

If this seems a severe judgement, I can only say that I see no reason for speaking less unreservedly, since it touches the heart of our own particular problem of the threshold. Before we take serious knowledge of the way, our life may be as easygoing and indifferent as we choose to make it; others may have their problems and suffer under them, and there may be no inner compulsion on our part to trouble much about them. It is the note of the world; and since we have to build for ourselves there appears nothing illogical in making our own path sure.

On the occult path this is a crime. It will shut fast every avenue of approach to the life of the Masters. True, we must think for ourselves; a true knowledge of self and an endeavour to achieve a right adjustment to life must necessarily be a constant aim..., but only that we might work the more skilfully and effectively upon the souls of our fellowmen for their advancement.

A soul in pain..., I use the words deliberately..., will vibrate every living chord in the heart of a true Rosicrucian. He will forget conventions, rise beyond himself under the strong impulsion of the will to enlighten and ameliorate, and pass into another soul without let or hindrance by the divine right of an understanding compassion, and that mystic and vital contact will have wrought in secret and never be forgotten.

This capital qualification, then, or self-exploitation for the assistance of others, has either to appear spontaneously in the soul of the aspirant before the threshold or must be cultured for with a no less conscientious laboriousness than that of an artist seeking to reflect the light and truth of ethereal nature across his canvas, or that of a writer labouring to embody immortal truth in language that wrings tears from human hearts.

The personal self has to be laid upon the altar of service to living souls. Nothing less than this will suffice. Do we not plainly discern this stern, unrelenting, self-denying service in the Masters of men? That unearthly beauty and profound peace which they reflect are derived fundamentally from this one thing. If not, what else can give this majesty to mortal man? Nothing in the world; either in literature, art or science, or the path of life would be marshalled with angelic beings; whereas the flower of humanity is so rare that our life is one long yearning to encounter it.

Some of us, at least, are only too well aware of this; we know what it is to greatly serve and we know that it calls for the right kind of soul. We have seen many a path of lesser glory in the eyes of the Masters, but of great account in the eyes of the world, which we could have trodden and thereby seized just and coveted rewards; yet have renounced them until they now grow dim in the distance. It is well, and as it should be..., for us.

As surely as we await the Master, the Master waits for us, until the one decisive attitude is so firmly established as to preclude even the thought of sacrifice. Supreme dedication is the secret key in any great life. It is an extreme polarity which refuses to be biased by lesser things than the flaming ideal upon which the eyes are fixed. But on the occult path there is no violence, no forced development to this end. The service demanded by the Master is the full bloom of the soul, not the strained exertion of a disproportional development of any particular faculty.

This is obvious; for when confronted with the problem of a soul we shall be little more than helpless before it if our life and knowledge have moved simply to one point and the problem be viewed merely from thence. The problem must become our problem and be viewed from the precise angle and altitude of the soul whose problem it is. We translate ourselves by inner and sympathetic contact.

I said that the established attitude of service precludes even the thought of sacrifice. There may be something of the nature of a crucifixion of the personal self, but we cannot regard it as loss or deprivation. The increasing momentum of the outgoing force of the soul seems to overwhelm and obliterate or, shall we say, depolarise the personal factor. I should be more inclined to term it the way of loneliness than of crucifixion. One of the occult scriptures says:

> "When the disciple has conquered the hunger of the heart and refuses to live on the love of others, he finds himself more capable of inspiring love; when the heart no longer wishes to take, it is called upon to give abundantly."

That is high doctrine, and perhaps we have not touched its level yet: but the approach thereto is not crucifixion..., it is spiritual loneliness. And this particular stage of the path will be difficult to tread and its vibration hard to bear according to the native or acquired vigour of the soul for the quest.

Certainly there is immense possibility in it, and here in the Ninth Grade I believe we are dealing with it. There are many references to this fact of loneliness in occult literature; yet, for all our theoretical knowledge of it, we are more or less disquieted in experiencing the solitudes of the path. What we have aspired to has in part been attained, and then we question the rightness of the attainment.

But there is a never failing and tranquillising thought upon which the aspirant can rest in such an exigency. Whatever altered condition of mental aspect or conscious awareness of finding himself well out on a comparatively solitary path of investigation and remote from the common interests of men, whatever inner questionings may arise as to further pursuit of an uncommon enterprise which lesser souls are only too ready to pronounce unprofitable and discourage him from, he will know that a higher and subtler strength is of greater value in evolution than a lower one, and when he becomes fully adjusted to it he will be capable of the greater works of that higher strength.

Remember, it will be impossible to contact and hold the intense vibration of life beyond the threshold without this specific culture of the vibration within ourselves. To this end we labour. We seek to touch the super-levels of consciousness, and as the growing pains we have to experience and the intervals of loneliness that test us in the ascent are necessary and unavoidable, let us hold steadfastly on until the Master appears.

4. Lafcadio Hearn's "Karma"

Reprinted from the May 1929 edition of The Mystic Triangle.

Hearn is perhaps chiefly known through the recent publication of his sketches and stories of old Japan. He left New York for Japan in his fortieth year, after an eventful career and the most remarkable and multifarious literary and journalistic activities in America and other countries.

These activities I do not touch upon, intensely fascinating as they are to the student of literary biography, because I want to record a few reflections about the artist generally, and about a little art work or ethical study from his pen, in particular, called "Karma," which was published in *Lippincott's Magazine* in 1890 after Hearn had gone to Japan.

When the romantic and chequered career of Hearn in America was drawing near its close he formed a friendship with a certain Dr Gould. This good man exercised a far-reaching influence over Hearn, and the many conversations between them led up to the writing of "Karma." In the Doctor's own words:

> "I do not think there is exaggeration of the importance of the story, and what led up to its writing, in saying that it was the greatest of the turning points in his life, and that directly, because of it, the magnificent works of the Japanese period were profoundly influenced through the attitude of mind thereby gained."

To those who have studied Hearn's life it is fairly clear that the Doctor's influence upon him was a spiritual and abiding one, and instrumental to Hearn eventually adopting the Buddhist religion and becoming a great literary and spiritual force in Japan during his later years. As he himself wrote to a friend, referring to Dr Gould:

> "My friend is a much larger man than I had ever imagined from my first knowledge of him. He has taught me enough to make me over again in an ethical way..., though I fear it will be several years before I can show the result in a durable piece of work. How wonderfully a strong, well-trained mind can expand a feebler and undisciplined one, when the teacher has pleasure and time to teach!"

Here then is the reason for that sudden departure from an almost unique field of beautifully artistic and queer objective studies, concerning men, books, and life; into the deeper world of occult truth; which is not easily accounted for, in the absence of the above facts, to those who know Hearn only through his various writings.

He was a highly gifted but weird character, and resembled not a little that eccentric genius of American literature..., Poe. Both were passionate seekers of the beautiful in every phase of artistic expression. They lived aloof from the world of men, in an atmosphere of mystery and pathos, dreaming and misunderstood, yet turning every item of experience encountered into a bewitching phrase of surpassing loveliness and charm. But Hearn's work is the more enduring of the two.

During the first forty years of Hearn's life he was a soul struggling with adversity to find itself. A sensitive critic cannot follow the passionate hunger of those years unmoved, for all their eccentricity and waywardness; for beauty was his religion, and if it led him into manifold aberrations, we do not therefore lose our faith in the beautiful, but interrogate nature..., he was her child, and she taught him to love.

He lived so near to nature's heart that he felt it beating within his own bosom. He was ever feeling his way back to the great Soul of Beauty, even as he lingered among the lovely, blood-red, scent-laden blossoms of passion and love scattered along the wayside. It was the cosmic emotion which pulsates in every atom and floods the wide universe with colour and music, that eventually carried Hearn to the threshold of the golden gates; and there his fine ear caught those haunting strains which ascend like holy incense in the land of temples and dreams.

There was a time, it is said, when Hearn declared himself an agnostic and sneered at the mystic. Well, what then? His early life was hard, bitterly hard; the iron had entered into his soul and he did not know himself. And yet, I cannot but think that a man of his almost tragic insight, a true lover of nature, is religious, whether he has a religion or not. To him, nature is a literature of mystical symbolism which he translates in moments of vision into the meaner language we know. I do not speculate upon an artist's religion when his voice trembles with the oraculous music of God and inspires me to worship with him at the altar of divinity.

There is something terrific and worthy of all reverence in that unerring insight which sees and opens up the very soul of things, which transforms the common fact into an article of faith and adds a new scripture to the literature of man. Far be it from me to condone the errors of the artist who, in the enthusiasm and ecstasy of the excess of life, sets at naught the canon of righteousness.

There are such, whose self-identification with the spirit of nature is so complete, who so abandon themselves to the panoramic manifestations of that spirit, that they utterly forget at times the bounds of morality which the Author of nature has set for His children, and they trespass to their own undoing.

It is even so, and yet we dare not condemn. When we think sometimes of virtue and its narrowness, and of the selfishness of religion, of the Christianity which refuses to bear the Cross and knows nothing of the sin of the world..., how poor and empty is that which has "*none of the poetry of pain!*"

Yes; artist of passion, and artist of pain. In some of his heaven born lines the images appear only dimly through the falling tears of love's agony. He loved the plum and cherry blossoms; their fragrant breath is all around him. He dreams the long dream of nature and her resurrection; the melancholy tones of his golden harp float aloft and mingle with the music of all creation. Offspring of the apotheosis of love born out of suffering in the artist's heart, it has an immortal life.

It not merely satisfies the aesthetic taste..., it invokes the spirit in man. He is one of those in whom love must realise itself through every phase of expression until the dawn of the apotheosis; in whom all experiences are appointed ministers and constitute a necessary probation. The novitiate of an artist's soul like Hearn's is a world drama. From the inner plateau of imaginative insight he looks across the world and beholds all things transfigured; but the transfiguration is in himself. It is a sweet or awful surrender, as the case may be, and unconscious dedication to compelling and unknown Karma.

The turning point of Hearn's life came when he began to reflect seriously upon the working of Karma. Once possessed of an idea there came the inevitable result. He gave it unforgettable expression. One thing he could not do, at this period of his life, he could not give it the cold, scientific treatment of an occultist. It must come forth a fragment of living art from the concentrated fire of the soul, instinct with magical beauty and dramatic force, thrilling with passion and breathless charm, a revelation of his own abysmal experience.

So his study of Karma found expression in a little prose poem: a story of a wonderful love, of cruel suspense, of doubt, fear, and hope, moving swiftly to an unexpected climax where the law was fulfilled and he, the writer himself perhaps, passes abruptly into the realm of spiritual understanding, from which will blossom in good time the mature work of the soul.

The theme of Hearn's Karma can be given in a few lines; but no words of mine can suggest the beauty and originality of his treatment. It is not the common story of lovers; yet only a lover, and a great one, could have written it. It is the portrayal of the soul's awakening to the existence of law, the outworking in human experience of a deeper aspect of truth and the subsequent adjustment of life divinely wrought through the seership of a noble woman.

They had often walked alone in the silence and solitude of nature, and these but added to the loveliness, the ideal grace, and the strange power of the woman who had become the object of his idolatry. Yet, while in her presence he was helpless to declare his love for her. But one day, in greater embarrassment and confusion of mind, when even conversation had failed, she divined his thoughts and suddenly confronted him with the exclamation:

"Well, what is it? Tell me all about it."

He declared his love for her. She was not surprised, but grew more serious, and replied, "I do not yet know…, I am not sure you love me."

"Could you but try me? What I would not do!"

"But I do not approve of those words," she said. "If I thought you meant all that is in them, I might not like you."

"Why?" he queried.

"Because there are so many things one should not do for anybody…. Would you do what you suspected or knew to be wrong for the purpose of pleasing me?"

"I do not really know," she resumed, "whether I ought to allow myself to like you."

He feared this strange girl…, as much as he loved her.

"Let me tell you," she continued, "what to do. Go home now; then, as soon as you feel able to do it properly, write out for me a short history of your life. Just write down everything you feel you would not like me to know. Write it…, and send it."

"Everything you feel you would not like me to know". What a crucial test!

For weeks the task remained unfinished and he kept aloof. Again and again he wrote the cruel confession. The conflicting thoughts of losing this wonderful companion through a childlike avowal, of losing her through a cautious silence or half confession, lashed into burning remembrance every secret memory of the storied past.

Each day he would tear from the fateful manuscript a certain page which he could never permit her to read; each day the vindictive inner voice which denied him one palliating word, compelled him to re-write it….

Why had he always feared that slight girl even while loving her? Feared her unreasoningly, like a supernatural being, measuring his every thought in the strange restraint of her presence? How imperfect his love, if perfect love casteth out fear! Imperfect by so much as his own nature was imperfect; but he had loved less perfectly with never a thought of fear . . . By what occult power could she make him thus afraid? Perhaps it was less her simple beauty, her totally artless grace, which made her unlike all other women, than the quiet settled consciousness of this secret force. Assuredly those fine grey eyes were never lowered before living gaze; she seemed as one who might look God in the face.

Men would qualify such sense of power she had as "strength of character;" but that vague term signified nothing beyond the recognition of the power as a fact. Was the fact itself uninterpretable? A mystery like the mystery of life?

Write down everything. He wrote it, and sent it. Two days later he received the single word, "*Come.*"

"Do you wish me to burn this?" she asked, with the missive in her hand, and her eyes flashing to his face. Her voice had the ring of steel!

"Yes," he responded.

"You say the woman is dead?" she questioned at last, in a very quiet voice.

He knew at once to which page of his confession she referred. "It is almost five years since she died."

"And the child?"

"The boy is well."

"And…, your… friend?"

She uttered the words with a slow, strange emphasis, as of resolve to master some repulsion.

"He is still there…, in the same place."

Then turning to him suddenly, she exclaimed, with a change of tone cold and keen as a knife: "And when you wrote that, you had really forced yourself to believe I might condone the infamy of it!"

He attempted no response, so terribly he felt himself judged. He turned his face away.

"Assuredly you had some such hope," she resumed, "otherwise you could not have sent me that paper…. Then by what moral standard did you measure me? Was it by your own? Certainly your imagination must have placed me somewhere below the level of honest humanity, below the common moral watermark…! Conceive yourself judged by the world…, I mean the real world…, the world that works and suffers; the great moral mass of truthful, simple, earnest people making human society! Would you dare to ask their judgement of your sin? Try to imagine the result; for by so easy a test you can immediately make some estimate of the character of what you confessed to me as a proof of your affection…!"

"You think me cruel," she resumed, after a brief silence. "Oh, no! I am not cruel; I am not unjust. I have made allowances. I wished you to come and see me because in every line of your avowal I found evidence that you did not know the meaning of what you wrote, that even your shame was merely instinctive; you had no manly sense of the exceptional nature of your sin. And I do not intend to leave you in the belief that so deadly a wrong can be dismissed, least of all by yourself, as a mere folly; something to be thought about as little as possible. For the intrinsic vileness of it is in no manner diminished, either by your cheap remorse or by your incapacity to understand it except as a painful error. My friend, there are errors which Nature's God never fails to punish as crimes. Sometimes the criminal may escape the penalty, but someone else must bear it. Much that is classed as sin by the different codes of different creeds, may not be sin at all; but transcendent sin, sin that remains sin for ever in all human concepts of right and wrong, sin that is a denial of all the social wisdom gained by human experience; for such sin there is no pardon, but atonement only. That sin is yours; and God will surely exact an expiation…."

"You will go, my friend, to that man whom you wronged, that man who still lives and loves under the delusion of your undying lie, and you will tell him frankly, plainly, without reserve, what you have dared to confess to me. You will ask him for that child, that you may

Section 4 - The Mystic Triangle (1929)

devote yourself to your own duty; and you will also ask how you may best make reparation. Place your fortune, your abilities, your life, at that man's disposal. Even should he wish to kill you, you will have no right to resist. But I would rather, a thousand times rather, you should find death at his hands, than to know that the man I might have loved could perpetrate so black a crime, and lack the moral courage to make expiation...."

A year passed. Letters he wrote she never answered; until one day, when passing through the suburb where she lived, he wrote, praying that he might only be allowed to see her. His request was granted, but he did not go alone.

"I have brought him to you," he said. "I thought you might wish it."

She knelt to put her arms about the boy and kiss him. And to the father she said, "Suffering is strength, my beloved! Suffering is knowledge, illumination, the flame that purifies! Suffer and be strong. Never can you be happy; the evil you have wrought must always bring its pain. But that pain, dearest, I will help you to bear, and the burden that is atonement I will aid you to endure. I will shield your weakness; I will love your boy... "

So runs the theme of this little study of Hearn on Karma. Whether or not it was evolved from his own life experience is immaterial to us. It may simply be said that, comparing it with the work he had previously done, we observe in it a record of the birth of a new consciousness.

There is nothing to remind us of the calm advent of light on the problems of life to the expectant and spiritual devotee: just the opposite. True to the type of the eager, creative artist, the truth is approached violently, in a veritable psychic upheaval within the soul, through the remorseless rending of the veil which hides a dark and haunting past unatoned for, compelling recognition and demanding reparation through suffering and the knowledge that, "*the evil you have wrought must always bring its pain.*"

Nor is it surprising that to an artist of this character the truth should come in a way unique and unlooked for. His whole life was unique, reflecting all the incident, colour and movement of a soul in rapid evolution. And passing onwards to the rich output of the Japanese period, the particular turning point in Hearn's life which we have been considering is seen to be of peculiar importance and interest; for the time came when he wrote of Karma with the calm and measured diction, and with the philosophic insight of a priest of the science.

Indeed, the beauty, lucidity, and depth of this matured work would well repay consideration in a separate article.

NOTE: Some of Hearn's work is no doubt known to most American readers. This particular study on Karma is included with other stories in a volume of English Classics, produced in a style that would satisfy the most fastidious book lover, with a portrait of Hearn. It can be obtained from William Glaisher Ltd., 265 High Holborn, London. WC1.

5. Occult Initiative

Reprinted from the June 1929 edition of The Mystic Triangle. *Also published in the* Rosicrucian Forum, *Volume 52 Number 3 (December 1981).*

> *"Chelas, from a mistaken idea of our system, too often watch and wait for orders, wasting precious time which should be taken up with personal effort. Our cause needs teachers, devotees, agents, even martyrs, perhaps."*

These are the words of the Master K H and they should be taken to heart by every aspirant in our Order. It is the weighty admonition of one who, glancing through the rank and file of aspiring souls, discerned unerringly an outstanding failing which was clearly holding them back from a closer contact with his own divine sphere of influence.

As is ever the case, and as we have said before. the word of the Master stands for all time and has perhaps more significance today than when first written; if only for the reason that the ranks of the occult have grown tremendously during recent years and we cannot afford to lose any hint of adept instruction.

This admonition..., grave, temperate and appealing..., indicates the need in the aspirant of an indispensable and basic quality: initiative.

We hear a good deal about initiative in these days. It is demanded in every field of world work. Initiative is initiative wherever met with, but in the aspirant it should manifest as a very special, distinctive and forceful quality.

Those who have much to do with the work of members in the Order cannot help noting very quickly those who have this quality and those who have it not. It is often singularly lacking in some of the new members during the early grades of the work, while those who have progressed to the higher grades have almost unconsciously acquired it.

A young member is prone to bombard his Class Master with questions, relevant and irrelevant, as rapidly as they arise in his mind. He has little reliance upon himself and desires to be led at every step. To interrogate is good, but he has not the confidence to interrogate himself. If he cannot see the whole path at once he thinks he is entitled to demand that it should be immediately revealed: he should not be left in doubt, all should be clear and understandable, now.

I write chiefly for the young aspirant. Let us think about his problem and try to view it in the light of the words of the Master who does know the path as a whole. The grievance of the aspirant..., if it deserves the appellation, and it sometimes does..., is that he cannot grasp and assimilate occult truth as he would the most ordinary knowledge of everyday life, and induce at will that spiritual exaltation which gives peace and attunement.

Section 4 - The Mystic Triangle (1929)

He has read or heard of the Masters and of the great prerogatives they exercise, of their pupils who appear to possess extraordinary privileges of interior wisdom and of utilising force, and his imagination paints a picture true in outline but entirely lacking in any reasonable conception of the composition of it.

Now, in that simple sentence we have the whole matter in a nutshell. The task before him is to obtain a true and comprehensive conception of the complicated life activities which go to make the mature occult student what he is.

A true conception of the Master mind and its superhuman activities is a far vaster thing and must come later. He has quite enough to think about and do in getting a just idea of the outlook and the difficulties of those who seek to help him to that point of vantage on the path to which they have strenuously fought their way.

There is no wish, nor is it right, to destroy the glowing picture which his imagination so readily conjures of a Zanoni in all his brilliant capabilities and exploits. He needs all the encouragement that his imagination can give him; but it is necessary that he place his picture in a far perspective and then set to work and closely consider the details of the process of composition, if he ever hopes to give it actual existence..., in himself.

There is nothing more grand or more helpful to the aspirant than a glowing ideal set up in the heart and contemplated daily; but it is imperative that he should study himself conscientiously from every possible point of view, as an individual soul in the process of evolution and also his status as a mental being in relationship with other mentalities around him in their various grades of development.

It is the want of a true perspective that lies at the root of most of the doubts and perplexities of the beginner in our science. And there is only one way in which it can be gained: by reading and thinking about his subject.

It has been enjoined upon him that in taking up the extensive work of the Order, he should lay aside for a time his previous studies of philosophies and systems, and allow the work a fair and unbiased entrance to the mind. But this injunction obviously applies to those who are acquainted with philosophies and systems, not to the beginner who is newly entered upon the field of occultism.

I have heard it suggested that those will make greater progress with our teachings who have not previously taken knowledge, for instance, of Theosophy; but I can scarcely agree with this view. Much depends upon the particular mind and temperament of the theosophical student who later turns to Rosicrucianism. If he is resolved to fight and argue tenaciously for every theosophical idea, and refuses to lose sight of it because the truth of our science seemingly or in fact militates against it, then the above suggestion must hold good.

But my experience with students of theosophy is that, having long accustomed themselves to occult study and meditation, they are often able to grasp and apply the work of our grades far more readily and understandingly than those who have no previous knowledge. There are exceptions, of course, but in the main I think this is the case.

To some extent the words of Bacon apply here: "*Those things which are in themselves new can indeed be only understood from some knowledge of what is old;*" but with the qualification that our science is not new, but of great antiquity. But this axiom of Bacon clearly shows that previous knowledge in this field is good, and it is admitted that those who have it will more quickly advance in the science by virtue of the possession of this knowledge as a point of departure. That is of importance for the beginner to note, for he cannot apply the law of analogy to that which he does not possess.

On the other hand, we have this further axiom of Bacon which applies to those who have previous knowledge: "*We must bring men to particulars and their regular series and order, and they must for a while renounce their notions, and begin to form an acquaintance with things.*" The truth of these two aspects of the matter could not be more distinctly put than in the words of the famous Rosicrucian. The truth of his axioms is so finely balanced, his perspective so clear and just, so sane in its disposition and inclusive in its detail, that the mere acquisition of them is sufficient to dissipate any perplexity on this question.

This perspective, then, in the beginner is of primary importance and must be gained now, at the threshold, by well considered study of the teachers of occultism. It is not necessary to specify here what he shall study. He should be so much alive to his own needs and enlightenment in this matter through his contacts with the Order, as to furnish his mind with the basic facts of occultism and enable him to apply suitably the work of the grades to his own capacity and temperament.

Presumably, he may have read much in the literature of the day on cosmic illumination and of those of the past and present who have experienced it. In the grades, therefore, he will find the regular series and order of steps of progress to be pursued which will lead him gradually onward to a profound understanding of himself and a maturing of his faculties preparatory to attaining higher cognition.

He must get out of his mind the prevalent idea of the shortcut to understanding and accomplishment which precludes patience and perseverance. Neither in nature nor in the life of the soul will he find any sympathetic response to the feverish effort of the shortcut. For what is the shortcut but a form of insincerity? It is the path of superficial achievement, a process of forced development without the stability of fundamental experience. Nothing great or durable can be built upon it.

The pleasure derived from the illusion of things done in a hurry on the path is but short-lived; it passes as quickly as it came, leaving a painful consciousness of insufficiency and hesitancy, and of insecure foothold.

It is admitted that there are shortcuts, made possible through the long endeavours of painstaking investigators, in many fields of culture; but those who discovered them are the most indefatigable students and workers, and their discoveries are the mature results of long and self-denying toil.

The soul knows no haste; it unfolds after its own laws. Its infinite life will only yield up its vast knowledge through years of study and meditation devoted to this end. We have to build stone by stone the mystic bridge of reciprocal response with the Cosmic.

And the young aspirant must accept this fully verified truth and be willing to pay the price of soul culture, since there is nothing in the realm of man's achievement to be compared with the study of human personality and the gradual approach to knowledge of the master within us.

Now we see more clearly the significance of the Master's admonition that, from a mistaken idea of the work to be done, the pupil often watches and waits for orders, thus wasting time which should be given to personal effort.

If he ever hopes to become a devotee of the path, an agent of the Brotherhood, a teacher of its sacred truth, he must resolve here and now upon initiative and do things for himself. He will call in vain upon Masters, and it will not be of much use for him to call upon men unless he demonstrates a strong mental willingness to fight for himself.

This is not harsh doctrine; it is simply the working of the law of attraction. It is a law of the occult path that the aspirant must compel results for himself, not run to and fro asking for that which only his own soul can give him.

One can only write from one's own experience. How often in times of acute mental suffering have I questioned the apparent aloofness of the Masters, their deafness to appeal, their refusal to favour me when I have tried to serve them most! Alas, it is wasted energy. When the hour has passed the answer comes in peace, through difficulties overcome in our own way, under the guidance of the divine within us.

That is my word to you, my brother. Do not eternally ask for that which you have; call upon the soul and live through the silence with the difficulty which is the answer. Nothing will so surely yield the insight and strength to cope with the trials of the path as a daily retreat into the silence within. No study will adequately take the place of it.

The aspirant's personal effort on the path must be founded upon this periodical withdrawal. These are the two aspects of his progress: active participation in the vibration of life to the limit of his capacity, and the daily carrying inward to the chamber of meditation the results of world contact and receiving the impressions of the soul through assimilation and quietude. This will enable him to apply his studies correctly and make a constructive and advancing personal effort. He will gain the ability to deal with his own problems with confidence.

It is the way of the Masters themselves and they demand this same initiative in the aspirant. They cannot use that man for responsible world work who lacks self-reliance and individuality, and perpetually runs hither and thither seeking soul growth from others.

The fundamental fact for the aspirant is that he is to become a centre of spiritual force for the purpose of inspiring, awakening and uplifting others, in that particular way which his karma indicates, to set their feet upon the path; and his own soul is the only true guide in this matter.

He must study the work passed into his hands, brood over it in his moments of retreat, until his inner life is fructified and strengthened with the new ideas and reflects them into the objective self as assimilated truth for use in daily world contact.

All that can be safely and wisely imparted to him is given simply and faithfully by those Masters in the Order who have his interest at heart, but what he will build upon it must come entirely from himself.

If he will learn this vastly important truth now, at the threshold, he will quickly develop that initiative and confidence in the leading of the soul which the Master stresses in his admonition. He will not watch and wait for that which cannot under the law be thrust upon him, but which must be grown into and grasped by an intensely inspiring will.

I believe the Masters are aware of and love to see that strong personal effort in the aspirant and that he never strives in vain. It is the soundless voice which vibrates audibly in their realm and is sure of a response.

6. Roger Bacon, The Rosicrucian

Reprinted from the July 1929 edition of The Mystic Triangle.

It is gratifying to observe the steadily growing interest in the old Masters of our Order as shown by the various biographies and monographs appearing from time to time from the pens of scholars of different persuasions of thought.

That our predecessors will, during the present century, come into their own; that their lives will be rightly valued and their work thoroughly understood, may, I think, be safely augured. Through many generations mankind has profited of the advanced thought and discoveries of these pioneers; but in the immediate future the keener eye of the modern student will be fixed upon the personalities who disseminated the deeper science, and due honour will be accorded to them.

It seems a little cruel, yet it is the way of the world, that men of great intellectual acumen so often fail to realise the paramount value of a peculiar knowledge accessible to them in the world's greatest libraries; maybe in the very libraries and museums of the universities in which they were nurtured and trained for professional life: and that they should deem this knowledge so unorthodox, so opposed to accepted belief and demonstration, as to consider the exponents of it a set of imposters and worthy of contempt.

If they happen to live long enough to take a few steps, through some happy circumstance, beyond the hard and fast bounds of orthodoxy and undertake a little pioneer work themselves, they will perchance turn suddenly back with reverent thought to the despised authors they have violently impugned, and thank God that their eyes have been opened to appreciate them.

Indeed, this is somewhat the position at the present time. We have been inundated for the last quarter of a century with biographies and autobiographies of little men and statesmen, of the living and the dead. But the advancing scholars of our day, whose eyes are riveted upon the higher evolution of the race, are interrogating the past for authentic information about the elect few whose works are now seen as underlying and making possible our highest civilization; yet themselves have received scant recognition at the hands of their immediate successors.

I am not so uncharitable as to suggest that those men of science who are now giving us biographies and monographs of the early Rosicrucians were formerly denouncers of these same pioneers; but it is significant that they are fellows of colleges in which orthodoxy is rampant.

It is significant, for instance, that a statue of Roger Bacon was erected in the University Museum of Oxford in 1914, in commemoration of the seventh centenary of Bacon's birth. It is significant, too, that for the annual lecture on a master mind read in the British Academy, Bacon was the chosen subject for 1928.

It is immensely gratifying to read the able and sincere discourse just published by Dr Little, a Fellow of the Academy; and I believe it will do much in focussing the interest of his fellow members upon the life and work of the father of experimental science and of medieval occultism. From this lecture and the biographies available I propose to sketch a few of the main features and incidents..., I am not competent to do more..., of the personality and thought of the master which will bring him very near to us.

We shall realise that the thought of the Rosicrucian of yesterday is precisely that of the Rosicrucian of today..., profound and practical, revolutionary in application, intent upon enlightening, uplifting and ameliorating, and withal, from the point of view of the orthodoxy of the schools, disruptive in character.

Comparatively little appears to be known of the life of Bacon. The date and place of his birth cannot be stated with certainty, but was probably in 1214 in the county of Somersetshire. So scanty is the information available that in a standard biography some thirty pages alone suffice for it, while the greater space is given to speculation and discussion of his works.

His early education was received at Oxford University, where he gained considerable reputation for his knowledge; and later he removed to Paris to study theology.

No date or reason can be assigned to his joining the Franciscan Order. His forty years of study, to which he referred in 1267, fall into two periods of equal length: the time before his admission into the Order and the time afterward.

Twenty years were devoted to the study of languages and of science at Oxford and Paris. Subsequently he entered the Franciscan Order, presumably for the protection it offered as a powerful organisation, and the facilities for study that membership provided. It is conjectured therefore that he was over thirty years of age when he became a member, and entered the Order for very good reasons and after mature consideration.

A word about the Franciscan Order will not be out of place, since an interesting portion of Bacon's life centres within the period of his membership. He had evolved doctrines which contained "*certain suspicious novelties*" that put the brethren in a panic and which they were authorised to avoid as reprobated by the Order.

The Franciscans, Minorites, or Lesser Brethren, are an austere religious order working under the auspices of the Roman Church and founded in 1208 by St. Francis of Assisi.

At one time, owing to internal dissensions, the Order was split into three bodies. Today the Order consists of the Conventuals, Observants, and Capuchins. The Second Order consists of Nuns; and the Third Order consists of members who live in society, not taking the vow of celibacy, but are bound by the spirit of the rule of the Order.

The Franciscans have always been foremost in foreign missionary work, and throughout all their internal dissensions have faithfully continued St. Francis' work of ministering to the poor.

Most of the great Scottish theologians were Franciscans, as also were many popes of famous name; and in the world of letters Bacon was a prominent member of the Order.

The Franciscans reached England in 1220. At the reformation there were sixty-five monasteries in England, and after the dissolution of the monasteries the Order was restored by the foundation of an English convent in Douay in 1617. It is now reputed to have twelve houses in Great Britain and seventeen in Ireland, and is held in peculiar reverence by the Catholic community.

We can predict without difficulty what would happen were our Imperator to betake himself to the quiet retreat of a Franciscan monastery for reflection and literary activities; and in due course, feeling that the time were fully ripe, hand his Cosmic revelations to his brethren to peruse. His retreat would abruptly terminate in a chorus of anathemas and a probable communication from Rome.

This is what appears to have actually happened to Bacon. He had not long been a member of the Franciscan Order before he incurred the suspicion of his superiors. When Bonaventura, an aspiring character eager to revive the spirit of St. Francis and impatient of new and curious learning, became General of the Order in 1256, it is likely that he was responsible for Bacon's removal from Oxford to Paris, where he was placed under close supervision.

Dr Little, in the opening of his lecture says...,

> "Is there any other instance of a medieval thinker receiving a command from the reigning Pope to send him his works, not because their orthodoxy was suspected, but because they might suggest remedies for the evils from which the world was suffering?"

But, as one of Bacon's biographers points out, when Pope Clement IV wrote to Bacon in 1266, commanding him to send His Holiness his works with all speed, there is reason for thinking that the relations between Bacon and the Franciscans were far from normal.

How could it be otherwise when we are assured that his invective against the intellectual and moral vices of his time increased in severity? He was in a privileged position inside the Order and he made the most of it.

He took the measure of the whole system and found it corrupt in the sight of God. Never before had the moral corruption of the Church, including the court of Rome, been so fiercely arraigned.

> "The whole clergy is given up to pride, luxury, and avarice. Wherever clergymen are gathered together, as at Paris and Oxford, their quarrels their contentions, and their vices are a scandal to laymen."

He prophesied that unless sweeping reforms were instituted by the Pope, there was no prospect but the advent of Antichrist in the near future. No wonder that Pope Clement grew warm and wrote him a letter. I imagine he thought that the advent of Antichrist had come and that Bacon was he. More than once in the world's history has Antichrist proved to be a Rosicrucian.

Bacon, however, was hot on the trail; no Pope could stop him. He made a violent onslaught on the scholastic pedantry of his contemporaries, their false standards of wisdom, and their preference of metaphysical subtleties and verbal contention to the pursuit of real knowledge; until in 1278, Jerome, the new General of the Order, held a chapter in Paris.

Bacon was summoned for his "novelties," condemned and cast into prison. What precisely these "novelties" were we do not know; his works were full of them, but we know that the Church of Rome dislikes "novelties" and should not be molested with them.

He had been suspected of unsound views for twenty years. Who ever heard that valuable truths might sometimes be concealed beneath the jugglery of the magicians; that the history of Greek philosophy should be under the keeping and guidance of Providence no less than the history of Judaea; that the teaching of the Stoics on personal morality should be superior to that of any Christian teacher; or that there should be any ethical value in the works of Mohammedan writers?

In Paris he found everything within the Order calculated to arouse his fiery spirit to the limit. He was eager for the promotion and diffusion of science and the reform of the Church, and he found the university seething with dialectical controversy. The controverted questions were of momentous importance and Bacon was prepared for them; but they were prosecuted by men destitute of scientific training, unable to distinguish truth from error, verbal subtleties from fundamental realities, and who had never troubled to read Aristotle and the Bible in the original.

To these wooden disputants his wisdom was anathema, and they silenced him by incarceration. The General of the Order, Jerome, who was responsible for this, anticipated appeals to the Pope on Bacon's behalf and took care that his decision was confirmed. It is believed that he remained a prisoner for fourteen years.

After the death, in 1292, of Jerome, who had previously been raised to the papal chair, a chapter of the Franciscans was held in Paris, at which the then General of the

Order liberated some of those condemned in 1278. Bacon, it is thought, was one of those liberated; for in that year he was again at work on his last treatise.

The date of his death is uncertain, but transpired soon after. He was buried in the Franciscan Church in Oxford.

Dr Little refers to the legendary Bacon which grew up side by side with the real Bacon soon after his death, and quotes the following from a writer of 1385:

> "Friar Roger called Bachon, an Englishman, intent rather on practical philosophy than on writing it, performed wonderful experiments. For he was of such subtlety in natural philosophy that he was more intent on his wonderful experiments (the truest science) than on writing or teaching. By natural condensation of the air he sometimes made a bridge thirty miles long over the sea from the continent to England, and, after passing over it safely with all his retinue, destroyed it by rarefying the air by natural means.
>
> "He was so complete a master of optics that from love of experiments he neglected teaching and writing, and made two mirrors in the University of Oxford. By one of them you could light a candle at any hour, day or night; in the other you could see what people were doing in any part of the world. By experimenting with the first, students spent more time in lighting candles than in studying books; and seeing in the second their relations dying or ill or otherwise in trouble, they got into the habit of 'going down' to the ruin of the university; so by common counsel of the University both mirrors were broken."

Dr Little contends that Bacon was not speaking strictly original, that he always needed some external stimulus, that few of his ideas were his own, and that his originality lay in finding fresh applications and combinations of the ideas of others.

I am not disposed to confute this statement, since there may be an element of truth in it. Indeed, the Doctor gives one or two instances of the enunciation of principles for which Bacon has been given great credit, but points out that these principles had previously been enunciated by others.

His predecessors enunciated, and that is as far as they got. Bacon enunciated also, and then harnessed his principles to the forces of the sun, moon and stars and produced unheard-of results by his unique applications and combinations of these forces. Our modern men of science are none too happy when they have to deal with an "original;" they must prove him a plagiarist somehow, even though they perforce must kneel to him.

Bacon met the objection that experimentation in searching out the laws of nature did but limit or deny supernatural agencies, in this way:

> "We do not perceive the wonderful actions of nature which are done every day in us and in things before our eyes; but we think they are done either by special divine operation or by angels or devils or chance. But this is not so, except in so far as every operation of

the creature is in some sort from God. But this does not prevent operations being done according to natural laws or reason; for nature is the instrument of God's handiwork."

We may well smile, with the history of the Roman Church before us, at the onerous tasks and responsibilities which Bacon enjoined upon the Pope in his earnest efforts for reformation:

"It is the duty of Christian prelates and princes to encourage the investigation of the secret powers, of art and nature, not to forbid it because they might be used for bad purposes. And yet it is true that these magnificent sciences, through which great good can be wrought as well as great evil, should only be known by certain persons authorised by the Pope, who subject to the feet of the Roman Church should work for the public good under papal command, so that the Church in all its tribulations can have recourse to these powers, and at last Antichrist and his followers would be met and, as miracles like his were done by the faithful, it would be shown that he was not God and his persecution would be hindered and mitigated in many respects by measures of this kind.

"And therefore if the Church would arrange for the study of them, good and holy men might work at these magical sciences by special authority of the Pope."

In his advocacy of experimental science Bacon clearly defined the two kinds of experience for the attainment of knowledge.

"There are two kinds of experience: one is of the senses, and the other by illumination or divine inspirations. The simplest example of the first is the conviction one gets that fire burns, by putting one's hand in it; this is more efficacious than any amount of argument. Of the second there are seven degrees, culminating in the mystic's vision of God. These two kinds of experience are alike in this, that they proceed by immediate contact with reality, not by reasoning."

He held that all knowledge went to the writing of the Bible, but that all knowledge was necessary to the understanding of its words, in their literary and in their mystical sense.

The first aim of his contemporaries, he insisted, should be to restore the text of St. Jerome's translation, which could be done only by going back to the earliest manuscripts, many of which were still in monastic libraries.

In any case of doubt or obscurity the readings should be compared with the original Greek or Hebrew; corrections by irresponsible individuals do more harm than good and ought to be stopped. The revision should be undertaken by an authoritative papal commission consisting of competent scholars working on definite principles. In a letter to Pope Clement IV he says: "*I cry to you against this corruption of the Text, for you alone can remedy the evil."* He did not cry in vain. For many years the Vatican Commission has been working under the presidency of Cardinal Gasquet and Bacon's plan is being carried out.

A few weeks ago the famous historian of the Vatican, Cardinal Gasquet, passed to his rest and was buried at Downside Abbey in England of which Abbey he was at one time the Prior. No doubt this work of his last years will be continued by able successors and brought to completion.

Strange revolution in the centuries! In the 13th century the Church of Rome accepted Bacon; in the 13th century the Church of Rome threw him out; in the 20th century he rises from the dead within the precincts of the Vatican.

Bibliography

- *Life and Work of Roger Bacon,* John Henry Bridges, Williams & Norgate, London.
- *Roger Bacon,* H S Redgrove. Rider & Co., London.
- *Roger Bacon,* Dr A G Little. Annual master and mind lecture 1928 in the British Academy. Issued by the Oxford University Press.

7. The White Brother

Reprinted from the September 1929 edition of The Mystic Triangle.

There is a class of book which never fails to interest the occult student: that which speaks of the personal contact of a pupil with a Master. A kind member of our Order recently sent me a book called *"The White Brother,"* an occult autobiography; and since it belongs to the class above-mentioned, I believe our members will be particularly interested in some account of it and in references to certain items of oral teaching imparted by the Brother to his pupil.

In the first place, I think that, on reading a book of this nature, a wise discrimination should be made on certain points. The Brother therein referred to, for instance, is called M; and it is just possible that some may immediately jump to the conclusion that this individual is none other than the Master M known to many of us in occult literature.

This would be a profound mistake. Those of us who have any just conception of what a World Master must be, of the vast works under his supervision and his well-known traditional aloofness from physical contact in mundane affairs, would never identify the Brother M in this book with the Great Master Morya.

The correct view to take of this matter, it seems to me, is that an aspirant of occult promise, such as the writer of this autobiography, may contact a Brother, who to him, may undoubtedly occupy the position of Master to pupil; but that Master is not to be considered by the reader for one moment as one of the august Chiefs of the Brotherhood.

With all due respect to this particular writer, we cannot conceive, in the face of all our studies on the subject, of such a Master dwelling in London, taking part in the meetings of little groups of students, submitting to interrogation upon all kinds of topics, occult and otherwise, and taking his pupil for an occasional excursion on the astral or mental plane. Happily, the writer himself makes no such claim: but it is astonishing what claims some of his readers might make for him, and it is these credulous souls I am thinking of.

If they will bear in mind that the Great Masters have under their supervision initiates of various degrees operating all over the world, we shall place this particular case in its proper setting and profit by its publication. No doubt it was one of these initiates that made himself known to the writer of this book with the definite intent of personal instruction. As the Brother himself says: a man's Master may be waiting just around the corner, or living in the same house, but he will not make himself known to his prospective pupil until the right moment for contact and recognition.

And such Masters, as a general rule, are initiates, agents, or messengers of those higher, yet in the scale of occult evolution they are themselves under the superior supervision of a Great Master. And these initiates are prepared and sent forth to contact and instruct those who are ready to profit by the knowledge they can impart and equip them in turn for greater spheres of service.

The author says that his book is the chronicle of a student who sought and became the pupil of one deeply learned in the knowledge of the Divine Sciences. On that statement, therefore, we accept the authenticity of his book, and the various fragments of teaching given by the Brother to his pupil appear to leave no doubt that the narrative is authentic.

We shall be specially interested in the account of the author's eager mental pilgrimage from one persuasion of thought to another, each to be thrust aside in turn as unsatisfying to the hunger of the developing soul, until finally the unexpected meeting took place when he was given that personal inner assistance which enabled him to manipulate certain occult forces and take his own higher evolution consciously in hand, some hints of which are given in the book.

Members of the Ninth Grade of our teachings will be interested at this point in connection with the instruction therein which deals specifically with the preparation for meeting a personal Master. The author touches the matter very briefly, but it is clear that he was acquainted with some aspects of the Rosicrucian teachings and it is left to conjecture whether the Brother was not himself a member of the Order, since the meeting, we are told, took place in the room of an organisation which is unnamed.

And thinking of our own members in the Ninth Grade, I am led to refer to the case of one of these members whom I recently contacted for the first time. This man has been a close student of occult literature for many years; and his lament to me was, that in spite of all his eager research, he had not yet made the contact he desired. He felt that he had not been used in any definite way. His knowledge lay broad and deep in his mind, logically built up and duly assimilated, but he had not felt a particular call in any direction.

The case is not exceptional. There are others in a similar position. And I am thrown back upon this thought in considering it. That in such a life there is a cycle of Karma to be liquidated, that his long and sincere efforts can by no means have been in vain; that he is, perhaps quite unconsciously, steadily progressing to a point where all his knowledge and experience will be requisitioned. For it is needed, deeply needed, and any day the hindering conditions may pass and his mission be revealed.

For that member, and others like him, this book may have a message. From poverty, through doubt, and onward to increasing knowledge, the author pressed on, never despairing that at length he would find the true nurture for the soul. The Brother was there and knew him from afar, but waited until the hour for recognition came, until the accumulated knowledge and world experience of his prospective pupil had matured to the point of right use and could be safely utilised.

I can only touch briefly on the main points of the autobiography leading up to the time of the meeting, and then note one or two of the aspects of instruction given by the Brother. And first I wish to observe how often it is the fact that those who make some exceptional progress on the path and eventually contact an initiate in this way, have had an arduous struggle with circumstances and have been severely schooled in various adverse conditions before coming into their own.

This is the very opposite of what the average student expects to find. He imagines that the privileged one must have had every assistance and convenience that circumstances could afford and been sheltered from anything in the nature of the inimical restrictions and oppositions that have fallen to his lot. Yet he is entirely wrong in this assumption. Those who have gone up the mountain have had to do their own climbing, but in the majority of cases we know nothing of the difficulties they have had to encounter. In this book the writer takes us unreservedly into his confidence. Perhaps it is well for him that he writes, as I think, under a pseudonym.

He was born in a poverty-stricken quarter of a great city, probably London, and was a *"wanderer burdened with the cross of poverty,"* among a populace of souls made weak through suffering and of low and undeveloped character. Once he lived in a court, surrounded with all that was foul, drunken, and sordid and which, to a sensitive and imaginative child, was a heavy and continual horror.

His education was of the meanest, provided by the authorities for the children of parents who were considered the scum of society, where any sign of personality in a child was immediately attacked and suppressed, and the views and doctrines of the Education Board reigned omnipotent.

He sat at his desk, *"like a fool,"* uninspired. And passing from school into many trades in none of which he excelled, he looked back at the age of eighteen to realise that only one ideal had ever possessed him..., to write a book.

Then he began to take notice and soon reached a point where he became a conscious and determined rebel against circumstances and grew apace in egotism and cynicism. In this favourable mood he fell in with an atheist, and atheism was championed for a while with sounding rhetoric and youthful virility. But the way was hard and progress slow and he passed as suddenly into the promised land of socialism.

In this enchanted realm great hopes sprung up and he eagerly sought to gather material for three vast volumes on *Egotism..., Past, Present, and Future*. A step further, blindly, and he entered the dark valleys of anarchism, and joined the noble army of anarchists pledged to destroy all tyrants and revolutionise society. This task was harder still. Enthusiasm cooled and, in a peaceful interlude, he reposed for a while in the nourishing bosom of philosophy.

But this proved a disquieting resting place for a onetime atheist, for spiritualism and theosophy were already threatening his repose. He studied the theosophical literature, joined the library, and entered the society. There he found friends but got on ill with them. They lived in a serene air of unthinking faith and his interrogations upset them. The *"Secret Doctrine"* he read, but understood little of. Some of the characters in the group he was allied with are described and classified with keen discrimination. They were a strange people and provoked his curiosity.

With one or two of his mystical intimates he visited in the evenings the cafes of Soho, the resort of every type of artist, and there observed life in many of its most unedifying aspects. Yet this period was marked by their great devotion to theosophy. But theosophy was one thing: the Theosophical Society another.

> "Yet we stayed on in the society," he writes, "because we were enchanted by the shadows and emotional fountains that played upon our senses, becoming more and more somnolent. And it was a long time after that we were forced to admit that all we could learn was of an intellectual nature, which could only lead us into a perpetual mirage. For, above all, what we really desired were realisations that would enable us to comprehend the meanings of life, to understand why humanity suffered, and the cure. For we no longer believed that life woke from the unconscious passions of the elements to snarl and tear its way up a staircase built from the bones of lesser lives."

For three years he had studied theosophy and grown weary, not of its doctrines, but of the lack of spiritual incident, when, unexpectedly, he met the Brother. It was in the room of an organisation which, he says, has long since passed away. A few students had met for discussion and were awaiting the arrival of him whose identity was evidently not suspected.

As soon as he entered the writer says he felt an immediate difference in the mental atmosphere. This meeting led to a personal invitation from the Brother to visit him. From that time onward he received various fragments of teaching and instruction from the Brother, some of which I will refer to.

Having on one occasion heard him speak of the Masters, the author asked the Brother if he would define their state of consciousness. In answer to this, the Brother brought him a book which was none other than that known as the *Comte de Gabalis*, about which an article appeared in this magazine not long since, introducing it to members, and in which is given a definition of the Master.[3]

The Brother pointed out that this book contained much truth and that the commentaries had been written by one who had experienced certain illuminations. We are told that the Brother did not confine himself solely to occult matters but was also conversational on many unrelated topics. He indicated the talents of his pupil, and encouraged him to continue his early efforts in verse writing. He was told many things about himself which nobody else could possibly have known, and given clear descriptions of people personally unknown to the Brother but well known to the writer; their habits, talents, and so forth.

On questioning the Brother about the elementals, the book mentioned above was indicated as a source of reliable and firsthand information.

It is interesting to note the remarks of the Brother on marriage. He pointed out that the student was perfectly free to do what he would, though it would be inadvisable to marry a person who was below him in caste and development, for then he would be more often hindered than helped, particularly if he married when young. Though, of course, marriage sometimes could also help, for the student seeks balance, and if the student arrives at that stage there is little to fear. He then mentioned a case of a married Master with a family, whose wife was completely ignorant of the fact that her husband was different from the ordinary type of mankind, save for the exception that he possessed a vast knowledge that surprised his family.

I am reminded, on this topic, how that once, in conversation with a theosophical leader, a book came up for discussion in which it was stated that certain of the Masters marry. This statement was strongly repudiated and the book was completely discounted because of it.

Now, what particularly commends itself to me in the Brother's conversation with his pupil is the breadth and tolerance of his views upon vexed questions of this nature, and the entire absence of assertiveness and bigotry which so strongly characterise some of those who would hold us in bondage to their narrow and preconceived opinions.

Speaking of failures, the Brother said that many of his pupils had failed through sex, egotism, and jealousy,

> "…but though they had failed they were not forgotten, and a time would come when the fallen pupil would be given another opportunity. For the Teachers are very patient and can understand the weaknesses of mankind because they had also suffered in the past before succeeding. Treading the path is a case of constant effort and though years may pass, persistence in carrying out the various exercises will ultimately be rewarded with success, for not the smallest effort is wasted. And the moment comes when something

---

3. Raymund Andrea's article about the Comte de Gabalis appears in Section 2 of this volume.

is opened, some sleeping force awakened, and the seeker has a new realisation of life, an extension of the senses that makes one more sensitive of things passed unnoticed before."

And let us particularly note this:

"There is no autocrat among a group of pupils, for each teacher is somewhat of a specialist along certain given lines. Also it can happen sometimes that the apparently lesser evolved members may become the teacher to the rest of the group, though even then he would not attempt to command or force obedience from the rest. For the freedom of each student is considered sacred, though all are supposed to work in perfect harmony for the good of all and for the good of mankind.

"One of the saddest moments in a teacher's life is when he is challenged by his pupil for knowledge, for the pupil's soul must be given freedom of expression, and anything that tends to limit the soul's expression brings upon the teacher the Karmic responsibility. Above all, let people alone with freedom for their soul's expression. The true student asks the other man's soul how he can help it, and the student's own soul will transmit the message. Keep the mind calm, for this is the higher form of clairvoyance, and the confessional, if done impersonally, is a spiritual thing."

The chapter devoted to various occult teachings contains many instructive fragments. That on initiation is enlightening:

"Within the soul of each mortal dwells a watcher, one who waits patiently for the time when his charge will cry out for a consciousness of the divine realities, and when that occurs, the inner watcher guides the seeker into a series of experiences that will perfect and make him fit to enter the temples of Truth. Wherever the seeker dwells, whether he be white, yellow, or black, whether he dwells in a hovel or a palace, directly he desires to become a helper for humanity and work in unity with the laws of the spirit, directly he listens to the compelling voice of intuition that bids him seek beyond the glamour of events, and he obeys it, then the watcher within takes him upon a voyage that can only end when the seeker has found his own. But when guiding him, the watcher also gives to him various keys, keys that will open each of the seven doors that lead into ancient chambers, wherein can be found books written by the other selves of the past, works wherein are inscribed the symbols of divine powers.

"Only by perseverance and relentless pursuit can the seeker attain his desires. For in his aspiration for initiation, he must not permit his energies to be frittered away in the mental clamour and voices of parasitic and vague interests, that are shaped from mist and bring only temporary nourishment. For initiation consists of discovering one's own limitations, though one also discovers an affinity to the elements of nature and the universe. And a time comes in his occult studies when he enters through the curtains of air, and he discovers new regions, new laws, and truths, which he endeavours to build into his character, and possess powers that can demonstrate to humanity the existence of higher kingdoms and forces."

Other fragments on art, consciousness, and symbolism are of absorbing interest but are too long to give here. To abbreviate them would be to lose their import, since the Brother is economical in the use of language; every sentence tells and is necessary to the evolution of the main idea.

The concluding chapter on travel on the mental plane merits attention. For over two years the pupil practised various exercises prescribed by the Brother and eventually certain higher faculties were awakened. He was soon after to have his first experience of journeying out of the body into the mental world. On this occasion, he says, though travelling was vague he was not entranced; his senses were more acute and sensitive to the slightest sound than ever before, and the Brother's voice sounded louder although he spoke in low tones.

This journey was a prelude to many more, until his mental sight became clear and reliable. I select the following from several experiences. It is very arresting.

"One evening M took me upon a mental trip, wherein I travelled with great difficulty. Something seemed to pull me downward and it was only with M's help that I managed to arrive at the place he desired to show me. It was a small room in which a young child was writing, while through a nearby window a great shaft of silver light came flowing. I looked at the child and seemed to recognise him as somebody I had known long ago.

"I asked M if he could tell me who the child was and heard with astonishment that it was myself upon this mental plane. I noticed that as the child gazed up into the stream of light, the face grew younger; but when he bent down, the face grew very old. M told me I was writing a book that would appear in the future, which did not surprise me, for I had often seen complete new poems in my dreams. For in sleep the soul journeys to its realm of true being, with clear metrical forms and subjects, which were ultimately written, though many were also unwritten, as I could not recollect the words."

A prologue to one of the chapters in the book may suitably conclude this article. It is entitled *"Human Spectra."*

"Ponderers peering through the mist, builders of minarets of sand, ghosts who walk and laugh and work. You are bewitched by the shadows, the thoughts, the dreams of the hidden people. They are in your room, holding in their hands the secrets that would make you as gods. They overshadow you with their shekinahs; invisible, they whisper to you, and you become inspired.

"They call themselves the humble servants of God, and you call yourselves masters of Earth. And yet you are as spectrums, reflecting their thoughts, their emotions, but diverting their shafts of power, often for evil motives, and flooding the earth with stained beams of thought that return to the instrument, bringing with them destruction. Yet in the aegis of their love and their divine patience they still guide you into fresh realms of experience."

Section 5:

The Rosicrucian Digest (1929 - 1935)

The Rosicrucian Digest
"The Mystic Triangle"

Covers the World

The Official, International Rosicrucian Magazine of the World-Wide Rosicrucian Order

VOL. VII	OCTOBER, 1929	No. 9

Contents

The Thought of the Month................By the Imperator

"To Me Jesus Is All in All"....................By Ramund Andrea

In the Shadows of the Pyramids................By Frater Hatchuep

Why Are We?................By Eugene Cassidy

Report of the Convention............By the Convention Secretary

Report of the Egyption Tour (Installment Eight)............
................By the Trip Secretary

Pinning Your Faith to a Star........................By Frater Deigne

Thoughts, Words, Acts......................................By Puritia

---

Subscription to the *Rosicrucian Digest*, Three Dollars per year. Single copies, twenty-five cents each.

Entered as Second Class Matter at the Post Office at San Jose, California, under Act of August 24th, 1912.

Changes of address must reach us by the tenth of the month preceding date of issue.

PUBLISHED MONTHLY BY THE SUPREME COUNCIL OF
AMORC, THE ROSICRUCIAN ORDER
ROSICRUCIAN PARK   SAN JOSE, CALIFORNIA

Section 5 - The Rosicrucian Digest (1929 - 1935)

Introduction

The *Mystic Triangle* was renamed the *Rosicrucian Digest* with effect from October 1929. See Sections 8 and 10 for articles by Raymund Andrea which were published in the *Rosicrucian Digest* in later years. The *Rosicrucian Digest* is still published today as the magazine of the English Grand Lodge of the Rosicrucian Order for the Americas. The magazine of the English Grand Lodge for Europe, the Middle East and Africa of the Rosicrucian Order is published as the *Rosicrucian Beacon*. The magazine of the English Grand Lodge of the Rosicrucian Order for Australia, Asia and New Zealand is published as *The Rosicrucian*.

1. To Me, Jesus is All in All

Reprinted from the October 1929 edition of the Rosicrucian Digest.

As the days shorten and the year draws near to its close, and the spiritual vibrations increase in momentum to reach their culmination in the birth hour of the Christ, the mind becomes introspective and inclined to meditation upon divine things.

During the long bright days of summer many confess to a disinclination, some experience a disability, to make the necessary detachment from objective attractions and interests at regular intervals required for spiritual progress. This is largely due to the fact that they are not yet sufficiently polarised in the spiritual life. But for those who are well along the path this hindrance has passed away. The mystical impulses are so strong and persistent within them that the varying rhythms of the year have lost their power to disturb the greater rhythm of aspiring consciousness.

There is no rest for the awakening spirit; nothing in nature has the power to diminish or to satisfy the unquenchable thirst for the knowledge of God. Nothing in the objective world can take the place of holy communion or deflect the will from the passion for service. If it were in the power of man to take from these souls the divine ardour, they would perish utterly. But this is the one thing which the world can neither give nor take away from those who have found a peace beyond the oscillations of personal existence.

In a series of miscellaneous articles during the past months we have considered various aspects of truth relating to our studies. We have reflected upon different phases of soul life and endeavoured to give concrete expression to experiences almost too subtle sometimes for words. In moments of inner brooding, with the earnest desire of sensing the present problems of other souls on the path, the fire of the immortal self has awakened, a vibration has been contacted, and that which appeared to elude all expression has taken form and found utterance.

We have found pleasure and received new impetus in our lives in tracing the hallowed footsteps as well as we could of some of the greater souls who have trodden the path and left glorious memorials of exalted living and works that we might be inspired to follow them. Many have written beautiful appreciations of what we have striven to do. It is well, and it is good to know that we go onward together, striving to understand and express the deeper truth.

It is a solemn and responsible task; and the further we go the more the soul demands of us. And the note of my present article is this: do we individually realise the solemnity and responsibility of this mission we are engaged upon? It is one thing to intellectually appreciate; it is quite another to seize the spiritual vibration of that which is appreciated and so permit it to work in the life of the soul as to bring about a higher order of culture and growth.

We students of the divine science should take ourselves with real seriousness. Our lives in thought should be a continual metamorphosis into higher and higher values. We should have such a conception of the Christ to be born within us that every day should be counted as lost in which we do not deliberately and consciously take some definite step in preparing the way for the holy birth in our own souls. Every transcript we read of the soul's earnest experience in those who travail towards this birth should have a pregnant message for us. Our reading should be translated living upward to Christ.

I write in this way because I am possessed with one dominant thought: we cannot fulfil our mission in life as students of the divine science unless we set our hearts steadfastly upon the goal of personal sanctity. No matter what our professional or commercial ambitions may be; if we wish to give a worthy example to our fellowmen, if we elect to be a light and leading in an age of materialism bent mainly upon worldly success and personal prestige, we need to lay primary emphasis upon the spiritual.

Worldly success and personal prestige are not wrong in themselves; but if we are resolved upon living the life of Christ, then the things of Christ must come first. There is tremendous opposition in the world against us, but for this ideal we must stand if we mean what we profess. We may suffer for our profession, we may want many things which we feel we ought to have; yet every soul who has attained Christhood has suffered and wanted, and we must choose the one path or the other.

Every great soul whose life we have considered in these pages has been clearly seen to have made this choice. Every one of them has given himself in the name of Christ active in soul. Let us resolve now, as one composite soul organism, in one great aspiration to redeem the time and forestall the Karma that so easily besets us.

There are certain formulae or statements of esoteric experience which have fallen from the lips of holy men through the ages, and which are destined to survive and inspire throughout the whole duration of the evolution of man. Such are many of the profound utterances of Christ, of the Masters and their elect, of the philosophers and sages of every nation.

They shine forth from the sacred pages of history and biography and repossess the mind after long intervals of ripening experience with a power and significance unbelievably great. In the Fama we meet with one of these magical utterances: *"To me Jesus is all in all."*[1]

I remember being deeply moved on first reading it many years ago; and in thinking over it recently the cosmic import of the statement came upon me in all its fullness and divinity. The realisation came to me that if indeed Jesus to me is all in all, then nothing else matters. Why should I strive for anything else? What matters it whether I realise this little ideal or that if in the attainment of Christ I find the consummation of all things?

But the full strength of this realisation did not come to me simply from a riper process of logical thinking; it came after an interval of acute experience. I will not hesitate to refer to it, since upon it I base my theme.

I had been sitting by the bedside of a precious mother, a soul I deeply revered. She was passing calmly and with entire resignation to her rest in Christ. The clinging mortal self would have held her back, but peace profound was there with us and I knew its wise decree. Then it was that Jesus to her and to me became all in all. And I remembered that this mother it was who first read the sacred text to me in childhood, and that that early influence had bound us together to the end.

I am not writing emotionally to assure myself of a sympathetic response. I write simply of a common experience which means little or nothing to one man, but which in another becomes the occasion of a further ascent of consciousness in which the purpose of life is more clearly revealed.

"To me Jesus is all in all." If that were really and in fact so with us, we should know in truth the illumination and blessedness of the Christ light. Since this is a goal to which we yet aspire, the veils of mortality still prevent the holy consummation. And it is plainly obvious that only by the long and arduous road of experience encountered and transmuted within do we make advance to that which is above and beyond and includes all.

It is a wonderful fact of the path that when one speaks intuitionally, sometimes prophetically, of that which is essential to personal advancement, the moment is often not far distant when that which has been prophetically intimated transpires in the life as a fact of experience. It is as if the Christ within had voiced a phase of the soul's evolution for the blessing of others, which nevertheless must be thereafter lived in joy or in sorrow in the soul that uttered it.

It is as if the Christ within in the process of reaching its full stature, cannot attain to full expressiveness even upon the basis of truth uttered as intuition or prophecy, but that the soul must know it in concrete vital experience. I have always felt this, but never perhaps so fully as now.

I venture to affirm that strongly as some lay emphasis on the fact that true religion is joy, no man wilt have progressed far along the path of the Christ life without realising acutely that pain is one of the most pronounced factors in the culture of the soul. It is

---

1. The Latin quotation from the *Fama Fraternitatis* is "Jesu Mihi Omnia" which tranlates to "Jesus is my all."

long indeed before we recognise the mission of pain and willingly suffer it to accomplish its beneficent purposes in our lives.

To many the fear of pain is greater than the fear of death. They tremble and shrink at its mere approach. They have not the strength to question it, subject it to patient analysis and divine the meaning of it. Like a terrible apparition, it confuses the senses, disorganises the faculties, and enthrones darkness in the inner sanctuary.

In innumerable cases the pain of bereavement has done this. The pain of loss has rendered insignificant every other pain of mortal existence. Yet how often has it cultured the soul to cleaner vision, a profounder life, unusual experience, and opened a secret door of communion with God?

The acceptance of pain and the understanding of it are often simultaneous. If loss on the physical plane means possession on the spiritual then there is compensation even in death. The physical eyes grow dim with tears while the eyes of the spirit become radiant with love. And the ample testimony we have of this inspires us to set our feet to tread the path of research, not of despair.

We can observe the metamorphosis of pain through all the planes of existence. There are some who know nothing of pain beyond that experienced in the physical body. But pain becomes increasingly acute as consciousness passes upward and functions upon the mental and spiritual planes. We experience pain through disharmony on the physical plane, maladjustment on the mental plane, and cosmic cognition on the spiritual plane.

Cosmic cognition acquaints us with the collective pain of humanity. Thus pain is a factor in all real development. And no man so truly realises this as he who can understandingly project into the Cosmic the divine fiat: *"To me Jesus is all in all."*

If this is the goal we really seek, let us never again fear when the Christ within compels us to suffer with him in the shadow of the Cross. In the first moments of loneliness and anguish we may ask that the cup be taken away; but if we can accept it in perfect trust and resignation, knowing deep in the heart that it contains the essence of immortal life, we shall find a divine strength unknown before.

The mystic is ever the apostle of pain. He knows that the carrying of the Cross gives perfect strength, and therefore is he willing to be the suffering servant of God. And I do not hesitate to say, that one of the greatest blessings in his development is his personal acquaintance with the manifold experiences of pain which the indwelling Christ will have him suffer; that he may say with complete understanding, *"To me Jesus is all in all."*

2. Paracelsus, the Rosicrucian

Reprinted from the November 1929 edition of the Rosicrucian Digest.

It has been said that the mystic has the faults of his type..., he is visionary, emotional, and impractical, and entirely lacking in that quality of mind called discrimination. I think I have never been so impressed with the underlying truth of this statement as when I first met with Evelyn Underhill's textbook on "Mysticism." In her chapter on mysticism and magic she indulges in a hearty sneer at Rosicrucians of the past and occultists of the present and evinces herself one of the most visionary and impractical writers that ever disgraced the annals of modern mystical literature. One or two brief quotations will be quite sufficient for us:

> "Hence in every period of mystical activity we find an outbreak of occultism, illuminism, or other perverted spirituality.... During the middle ages and the Renaissance there is the spurious mysticism of the Brethren of the Free Spirit, the occult propaganda of Paracelsus, the Rosicrucians, the Christian Kabalists...."

So lofty and penetrating is the "mystical" presumptuousness of this writer that she does not hesitate to treat with contemptuous sarcasm Rudolf Steiner, one of the greatest of modern mystics and occultists, and accuses him of *"the usual exaggeration of the professional occultist."*

When a writer on mysticism treats eminent mystics in this strain of emotional rant she depreciates the value of her whole work and declares herself an impertinent commentator and an incompetent authority. Underhill's book was published in 1911; the tenth edition appeared in 1923. In this last edition the above statements appear.

The writer is still alive: short reviews by her of books on mysticism appear at times in the journals. Therefore, she has had ample time between the dates of the first and last editions of her book to study the lives and teachings of those she wildly arraigns and effect an honourable revision. As this has not been done, conscientious students of mysticism and the occult will regard her textbook as conspicuously biased and unreliable.

An English edition of the life of Paracelsus by Miss A M Stoddart appeared in 1911. For some years she had devoted her life and energies to the preparation of this work. She died within a few hours of the passing for press of the last sheets of her book.

Her wide study and well balanced learning, and her knowledge of languages specially fitted her for her task, and she spent some time in Germany and Italy in order to investigate on the spot the career of her remarkable subject. Let us then glance through her work and obtain just an idea of the kind of *"occult propaganda"* this *"professional occultist"* was guilty of.

The period of the Renaissance is one of engrossing interest to the student in many departments of life: in religion, in art, in letters, and in natural science. It was a period prolific with great personalities who were destined to move the world. As one writer says:

> "It was the new birth to liberty…, the spirit of mankind recovering consciousness, and the power of self-determination; recognising the beauty of the outer world, and of the body through art, liberating the reason in science, and the conscience in religion, restoring culture to the intelligence, and establishing the principle of political freedom."

In the year 1493, in which Paracelsus was born, Savonarola, the Italian preacher and reformer, was inveighing against princes and clergy, in discourses denunciatory and prophetical, at St. Mark in Florence. Luther was just ten years old and at school in Magdeburg, unconsciously preparing himself for his war against the pope and the doctrines of the Church of Rome. And Pico Della Mirandola, born in the year 1463 and passing away prematurely in 1494, had yet in those few years of feverish research penetrated into the secrets of ancient philosophies and many Eastern languages and at length, coming to Rome, had offered to defend nine hundred bold paradoxes, drawn from opposite sources, against all who would meet him.

These and many others were the inspired voices that gave a new expression to religion, science, and art in the face of every kind of opposition, derision, contumely, and cruel persecution. And Paracelsus fared as badly and perhaps a good deal worse than most of them.

We need not concern ourselves with details of his birth and the progress of his youth. We are informed that he was a pupil of the Abbott Trithemius, a man of great renown in occult research and learned in the knowledge of his time, a lover of art and poetry, alchemist, historian, and physician. There is extant a reproduction of a rare classic in alchemical literature called *Splendour Solis,* containing the alchemical treatises of one Solomon Trismosin, who is therein said to have been an adept and teacher of Paracelsus.

However, there is no reason to think that his biographer is mistaken in this particular point, since a man like Paracelsus may have been the pupil at different stages of his development of more than one great teacher. At all events, he appears scarcely to have attained to manhood when he made a journey to Trithemius, after having read a manuscript by this teacher, and with him he studied occultism.

This man was versed in the secrets of magnetism and telepathy, and in his mystical experiments could read the thoughts of others at a distance. But above all he insisted on the study of the Bible, and in this he influenced Paracelsus for life. His pupilage with Trithemius determined his career. He renounced all things that led to worldly preferment and gave up his life to the search after wisdom.

He was about 22 years old when he set off to work in the silver mines and laboratories of Schwatz. Probably curiosity took him thither, for he had read much of the transmutation of the baser metals into gold. There he found two groups of workers, the miners and the chemists. The latter were still alchemists, and their analyses and combinations were allied to occult experiment.

Paracelsus worked with both groups, for he was bent upon firsthand experience at the fountainhead. He learned the risks and hardships of mining and studied the veins of precious ore! He frequented the laboratories of the alchemists and soon after left them, convinced of the futility of "gold-cooking." The outcome of his researches at Schwatz is summed up in the axiom:

> "Alchemy is to make neither gold nor silver: its use is to make the supreme essences and to direct them against diseases."

Ten months in Schwatz had driven him to the decision that his experience in a university had been barren of results and that he would study in the university of the world. He spent about nine years in travel.

> "A doctor," he said, "cannot become efficient in the university. How is it possible in three or four years to understand nature, astronomy, alchemistry, or physics? A doctor must be a traveller, because he must inquire of the world. Experment is not sufficient. Experience must verify what can be accepted or not accepted. Knowledge is experience."

Disgusted with one university, he did not, therefore, avoid others. He tried them in every country which he visited, hoping to find a kindred spirit. Vienna and Cologne, Paris and Montpellier, thence to Bologna, Padua, and Ferrara. All the great centres of learning figure in his program: but neither in Germany, France, nor Italy could he find the truth he was seeking. He would not submit himself to the teachings and writings of the universities, and travelled on to Spain and eventually to England, where he spent some time at the lead and tin mines in Cumberland and Cornwall.

While in England he received news of fighting in the Netherlands, and applied for and obtained the post of barber-surgeon to the Dutch army. This was not an erratic move but definitely a part of a settled plan for enlarging his knowledge of wound surgery, which he had previously practised with his father who was a surgeon. He eagerly sought employment in a series of campaigns and pursued his study of the healing art among the soldiers with indefatigable industry.

Later, he is traced among the Turks and Tartars, steadily augmenting his stores of positive knowledge. When wandering with eastern nomads he learned from Saracens and Turks the lore of their saints, from Jewish physicians and astrologers the secrets of the Kabala, and became convinced of the reality of that occult power which amongst the nations of antiquity was the highest endowment of the priesthood.

At the age of 32 years he was an experienced surgeon and a distinguished physician and had taken his degree in both arts. Wherever he went he was renowned as a healer, and was often sent for by men of high rank whom he successfully treated for diseases which the doctors considered hopeless. Students gathered around him to watch his analyses or listen to his teachings.

He was already too great for his professional contemporaries and had to flee from Prussia, Lithuania, and Poland. He pleased no one but the sick whom he healed. He preferred the university towns because students assembled in them. From them he could obtain a hearing, but his remarkable teachings and cures only aroused the jealousy of the professors and doctors, who felt it their duty to crush him.

He was summoned to attend the Markgrave of Baden who was ill with dysentery and his life despaired of. Paracelsus stopped the dysentery, and so quickly that the household doctors insisted that they had performed the cure and that he was not worthy of his fee. The fee was refused on their advice.

He had not long returned to western Europe when he received a request to travel to Basel (Switzerland) to heal the famous publisher Froben who had disabled a foot through falling.

Froben enjoyed considerable reputation in Basel. He was educated at its university, founded a printing office in that city and issued some three hundred books, including the New Testament in Greek, subsequently used by Luther, and editions of the Fathers of the Church. It was largely owing to Froben that Basel was the leading centre of the German book trade in the Sixteenth century. Paracelsus resided with this man and within a few weeks effected his cure.

Through Froben, Paracelsus became acquainted with Erasmus, the eminent scholar and theologian, who had formerly lived for some years with Froben. Erasmus consulted Paracelsus about his own declining health and was astonished at the insight of his diagnosis. His admiration for Paracelsus influenced the magistrates shortly after in their decision in the appointment of a town physician, which post was then vacant.

In 1526 he was duly appointed to the lectureship of the university of Basel. He had lectured only a few weeks when the academic authorities interfered and prohibited his continuance.

> "They note," he writes, "that I explain my art of medicine in a manner not yet usual and so as to instruct every one."

What disturbed the authorities was his departure from old methods and the substitution of his own experience and his own experiments. He also dared to lecture in German instead of Latin, so that all might understand, and that the new teachings might be liberated from the fetters of the old. Dr Franz Hartmann (another Rosicrucian, and personal physician to Mme Blavatsky) says:

> "The glory of being the first man who taught in the German language in a German university belongs to that true German, Theophrastus von Hohenheim (Paracelsus) to all time."

Some said it was because he knew no Latin, and insinuated that he had never taken his degree. They tried to anger him that they might have something against him. He was forced to put his case to the magistrates, at whose bidding he had left his work at Strasburg to comply with their appointment, to preserve to him certain rights connected with his office. The petition was granted and the immediate persecution ceased. Night and day he worked at his lectures with unabating vigour. Even during the Basel holidays he determined to retrieve the time which academic opposition had wasted, and the lecture hall was crowded with eager students.

Experience was better than anatomy lessons, so he supplemented his lectures with practical demonstrations in true Rosicrucian style. He took his students into the surrounding country to study the herbal medicines *"where God had placed them."* He led them on to the study of alchemy, to chemistry, and to experiment, that they might be their own apothecaries. He took the poorer students to his own house, clothed and fed them, and taught them everything. And among these were those who betrayed him.

From the wealth of his material extant on the art of healing, the biographer of Paracelsus has given a brief précis of one or two lectures to indicate what manner of teaching the students of Basel received from this inspired master. After perusing these we cannot wonder that he had difficulties when at the university. The condition of the medical profession and the character and conduct of its practitioners in the first half of the sixteenth century were deplorable and merited the sharp invectives he directed against them. A characteristic sentence or two from the *"Three qualifications which a good and perfect surgeon should possess in himself,"* will give a just idea of the trend of his criticism:

> "The doctors who have got themselves made doctors with money or after length of time, read their books over in a hurry, and retain but little in their heads. But the asses go about the town just as if it were a crime for the sick to contradict a doctor."

But his constructive, axiomatic teaching in these lectures is precious and stands for all time. Although little understood by the Germans of his time, the best thinkers of today acknowledge his great importance to the German renaissance. Says Dr Franz Strunz:

> "Paracelsus was a pioneer as doctor, as student of nature, as theologian; for he beheld nature and the world as they are, and saw all things in the light of nature, so that he roused to new life, orderly induction, and comparison."

Ten years after his death, the doctrines of Paracelsus were taught at Basel. Warned by friends of his impending seizure and imprisonment in Basel by an order of the judges, he was compelled to an ignominious flight during the night. Once outside of their jurisdiction he was free and lingered a short while at Colmar, healing others and busied with researches. Later he was found housed in Esslingen, where he fitted up a laboratory and worked at alchemical and astrological problems.

His occult occupations soon attracted a collection of so-called disciples, some of whom were his servants, some his secretaries, and some his pupils. He was already prematurely aged at thirty-five years. He worked most of the night and allowed himself but four hours of sleep. Here there were no wealthy patients to help him. Many of his followers were rogues who probably did not scruple to rob him. He was forced to relinquish his house and take to the road again.

At length he came to the famous city of Nuremberg [Nürnberg]. He carried with him his book, *"Prognostications,"* and another volume just completed, on the French Malady. These he hoped to see published in Nuremberg. But the Medical Faculty in Leipzig had read his work and addressed themselves to the Council of Nuremberg with a request that the books should not be published.

Paracelsus had been lavish of epithets concerning the doctors of the old school: they did not appreciate the title of "imposters." He addressed a courteous letter to the magistrates on ·the matter, but received no acknowledgment.

He left Nuremberg for Beratzhausen, and here he wrote some of his most valuable works. The prohibition to print in Nuremberg was a discouragement, but did not check him. He knew his books would be published somewhere; if not then, later. Basel, which rejected him, was the first city to print the volumes he was now writing at Beratzhausen.

Other cities were visited, in which he stayed for a time, all the while intensely active, healing the rich and the poor and writing his books. Then came a period when he rested from writing on medicine for some months and gave himself up to evangelistic work, and to the teaching and distribution of the Bible.

He wandered through Appenzell and its mountains, seeking the poor and sick, healing and teaching them. This occupation with the spiritual as well as the corporeal needs of men was the cause of further persecution at the hands of the priests. So fierce was their resentment that they persecuted those who showed him hospitality. Lodging, food, and clothing failed him. He was reduced to poverty and compelled to flee.

It is as well to note that Paracelsus was impelled towards his researches as much by his spiritual as by his intellectual powers. The views of Cornelius Agrippa, the neo-platonist, who was contemporary with Paracelsus, the latter developed and presented in a more perfected form.

> "He strives everywhere," says Steiner, "to go back himself to the deepest foundations of natural knowledge, in order to rise by his own strength to the loftiest regions of cognition."

From his early acquaintance with neo-platonism and the Kabala, Paracelsus developed his spiritual philosophy. A mystic he certainly was, in the true sense of the term. His occultism too, was derived from the same source as were the doctrines of Cornelius Agrippa, and later, those of Van Helmont and Boehme, who were his disciples. It is interesting to note just here that of Boehme, Evelyn Underhill writes:

> "He is one of the best recorded all-round examples of mystical illumination; exhibiting, along with an acute consciousness of divine companionship, all those phenomena of visual lucidity, automatism, and enhanced intellectual powers which properly belong to it."

We might ask, what less than this was Paracelsus and what less than this did he exhibit? Professor Strunz, writing of the personality of Paracelsus, says:

> "His was a mind of mighty features whose rare maturity converted the stating of scientific problems into warm human terms, and we owe to him the realisation of a cultured human community based upon Christian and humanitarian piety and faith, which things we may well regard as the bases of his teaching concerning both the actual and the spiritual . . . Paracelsus felt like an artist and thought like a mathematician, just as he combined the laws of nature with the laws of the microcosm; that is of man with his consciousness, his feelings, and his desires. It was this delicate artistic sense which proved to be the daring bridge from the man Paracelsus to the keen-visioned observer of reality, a wonderful viaduct resting upon the traverse of the new humanity, the Renaissance."

Little is recorded of his last days. He was suffering from an insidious disease, no doubt contracted from the many poisonous substances with which he experimented, and he was paying the inevitable penalty of an excessively strenuous life. The whole chronicle before us is one of intense and unselfish labour, of wanderings and persecutions, of bigotry, insult, and contumely, of a sublime soul despised and rejected of men.

"*Rest is better than restlessness,*" he wrote, "*but restlessness is more profitable than rest.*" He died in 1541 at Salzburg and his body was interred in the churchyard of St. Sebastian's.

> If I stoop into a dark tremendous sea of cloud,
>   it is but for a time.
> I press God's lamp close to my breast;
>   its splendour soon or late
>   will pierce the gloom;
> I shall emerge one day.

3. Love's Apotheosis

Reprinted from the December 1929 edition of the Rosicrucian Digest. *Also published in the September 2002 issue of the* Rosicrucian Beacon.

In rare moments of clear vision, we are able to observe ourselves dispassionately from an altitude of spiritual contemplation. We desire truth fervently, and in good time it dawns with the clearness of light upon the mental vision. Truth in these calm retrospects of the mind, the truth about ourselves and life, the growth and meaning of the years become focused in the present hour that we may make a right assessment and a wise determination for the future.

And one of the first things we realise is that the Spirit within is the only true guide, and that under its influence, life is a process of revelation and reconstruction. Truth comes, and all the past is transfigured by its coming. We too, are changed. The significance and relationship of that which before remained detached and meaningless is discerned and understood, because thought and emotion ascend to superior levels and acquire new power and dignity. In a word, we see the wonderful blending of the human with the divine.

It is by virtue of these revelations of truth to the unfolding soul that love attains to its apotheosis. Love is a divine mystery; its apotheosis appears to be the object of all our incarnation. Little is this suspected in the earlier stages of the soul's growth; we only realise it through the manifold transformations of love as the soul reaches maturity.

How wonderful, for instance, it is that the sweet, silent, understanding communion between souls is gradually transformed by the power of the Spirit within into a deep, solemnising all-inclusive humanity that blesses wherever it touches. It is only at that stage that the glory and purpose of love begin to reveal themselves and the soul visions somewhat of the deific nature of the Masters who guide it. It is only then that the soul sees the possibility of the renunciation of its personal life and the blending of itself with the Cosmic life and love divine.

The denial of love is love's crucifixion; and to crucify love is to abrogate the law of life, which decrees the growth of love. You cannot discount the law of life, and live. Love is the divine fire in the heart of man and must be recognised and nurtured. It is true that only a spiritual love can reach the apotheosis; but that dawns only after long probation.

To become perfect, love must realise itself in every phase of its manifestation. Not by denial, but by complete realisation comes the apotheosis. The experiences of the relations of love in its personal aspect are appointed ministers and constitute a necessary probation.

These experiences humanise, enrich and sanctify the lover as he passes on to the higher recognition and relationship. No outpouring of the heart's immortal treasure is unfruitful, however trivial and unsatisfying it may be, and regardless of whatever pain may accompany it. All are instrumental in effecting that conscious detachment of the soul from love's limitations and the ultimate establishment of its full-orbed cosmic expression.

The dawn of spiritual love works a revolution in the life of man. Glancing back along the eventful path he has trodden, he surveys the change wrought in his constitution with tranquility and quiet joy, nay with humiliation. He has lost much, but the gain is infinite. The child heart which knows no fear, is finally his. He has passed, if only for an interval, within the sacred precincts of ineffable peace and experienced the true rest of the soul.

Harmless and void of all offence, he receives the power to read the hearts of others and minister to them. For him, this is the only true life and he desires none other. His one prayer is that the old self may be utterly transcended and forgotten, with all its conscious pride, its feverish ambitions and restless antagonisms. May the will of love be done in and through him. What is there in the world that can be compared with this sanctifying resurrection? How often is it mistaken and misconstrued, and taken for weakness when only it is strength. Truly has it been said that the power of the disciple appears as nothing in the eyes of men.

When the apotheosis is reached, the compassion of the Masters ceases to be merely a name on the tongue of the aspirant; he knows it as a living force actuating his own personality. He is automatically freed from many laws that hitherto circumscribed his life and comes to recognise but one, the law of sacrifice. He gives himself.

That statement looks simple enough, but it means nothing less than the birth of Christ in man. How rarely do we meet, even among occult students, with the divine, active quality of true self-effacement? Yet no man can become a real saviour of men without it; and a true aspirant will conceive it to be the highest goal of his aspiration.

Think what it means to the great host of encompassing souls upon Earth, bound fast by the bonds of the manifold limitations of love, with all their consequent fluctuations of tumultuous passions, their bewildering psychic complications, and the eternal hunger of bleeding hearts continually broken. Think what it means to be the aspirant, with the light of the apotheosis upon his brow and its deep peace in his heart. Glancing across the sea of human life and gathering all sorrow and chaos into his own ardent bosom, he dedicates his soul to the service of man!

That love has supernal power. It is the only key to the human soul, invested as it is with a divine magnetism that nothing in the personal life can resist. Moreover, it is the far-off dream of every soul. The love that has been tried in all the furnaces of life and become radiant, is the one priceless treasure which all souls are instinctively feeling after. And nothing but a true self-effacement will give you this vision of the world's need, or enable you to a right dedication to it, or provide you with a panacea for it.

As the aspirant unfolds in spiritual knowledge, finer adjustments to truth and to his fellow men become ever necessary, and far-reaching responsibilities devolve upon him. His one passion is to give himself, whether it signifies gain or loss. The apotheosis attained, his one and inestimable privilege is that of shedding its glory continually around him.

It becomes wondrously potent and fulfils its purpose without let or hindrance in countless ways in the common lives of men. There is no ostentatious announcement of its benign influence. It passes silently into the human heart as strength, calm and lofty aspiration. It is an atmosphere of prayer; and where it rests a sweet resignation possesses the soul and the burden of life is mysteriously lightened.

In the Masters of life, the grand alchemical process of transmutation is seen in its perfection. How familiar in our ears is the everlasting praise of the compassion of the Buddha and the Christ. We are apt to think that examples of divine blessedness are for some reason incompatible with our time.

This is a mistake. Not every glorious soul stands before the world as a teacher of men. There are with us those who perform such holy works of the fullness of the apotheosis as would stagger the credibility of the uninitiated. Few were they who were able to recognise the Masters in the olden time. It is precisely the same today. Again and again the Master passes by; but not a sign of recognition will be manifested, unless as his devoted disciple you have sought him unconditionally through years of silence of the heart.

4. Are We Abnormal?

Reprinted from the June 1930 edition of the Rosicrucian Digest.

The "friends" of the Master said, "He is beside Himself;"
Saint Paul was declared "mad" by the highest tribunal.

On perusing recently a record by an eminent medical scientist and alienist of causes of abnormal personalities, men and women distinguished in the arts and sciences whose works and deeds have left an indelible impress in world history, an arresting speculation offered itself: Is abnormality a necessary concomitant of the evolution of consciousness?

Since we are particularly and practically applying ourselves to the science of the evolution of consciousness it will be interesting to pursue this speculation. The question as to whether or not there are certain abnormalities attendant upon this evolution has been a subject of controversy among many and ridiculed by not a few, so that our reflections may incidentally produce some frank expressions of opinion and personal experience which will lead to valuable data.

The days have gone, we hope, when persecution was meted out to individuals who professed what were considered peculiar views, incautiously proclaimed the possession of unusual vision and exercised supernatural powers before a sceptical and intolerant public. Yet these days have barely gone. Observe what this eminent writer says:

"We are at present so shackled by traditions pertaining to religion, law, science, and work, that an artificial code of restriction and prohibition has become imposed upon our individualities to such an extent that, in order to remain free, we must perforce not only refrain from Self-expression, but adopt, advisedly, an artificial attitude of hypocrisy which, instead of leading to light, is manifestly sham and subversive."

That is a grave indictment of presiding authorities and its severity is well merited. It is not long since that I received a letter in which the writer, referring to his experience of Cosmic Consciousness and his reluctance to speak of it, says he knew a man who had experienced Samadhi and narrowly escaped being confined in an asylum because he told his friends. A pitiful state of affairs, and the warning is worth noting. The world in general is little less tolerant in these matters today than it was fifty years ago. That needs no qualification; it is amply corroborated by this same writer, one of the foremost physicians and psychologists in the kingdom.

> "At this stage of our evolution the trend of humanity must be for tradition to give way to knowledge, and for knowledge to give way to moderation and a more complete toleration. To live and let live, to know and let know, to have and let have, to do and let do, are all excellent guides, although the real charter for the evolution of humanity is to be and let be."

The attitude of the public press has somewhat changed, it is true, during the past ten years, and now condescends to relate without criticism what are considered authentic cases of psychic happenings and personal experiences of a psychic character. Certain newspapers now offer prizes to their readers for the most striking narrative of personal experiences of this nature, whilst others solicit personal testimonies to the truth of reincarnation. Even a scientist here and there is becoming unusually bold and charitable withal.

An article recently appeared in a popular news sheet from the pen of an English professor, in which he wrote:

> "The old alchemists tried to turn lead into gold, and for generations they were a laughing-stock of scientists. But now we are beginning to think that although their methods may have been crude, their idea was sensible."

Whether this professor has been automatically relegated by his fellows to the category of the abnormal is a matter for conjecture. Permit me to quote at length before passing on.

> "The main difference between the sane and many of the insane is that in the latter there is loss of control over the hypocritical and artificial bonds of convention, which loss places them out of harmony with their advisedly more secretive brethren. Thus we have the curious fact that when an individual believes the word of his pastor, and frankly states he believes his soul to be lost, or that he is in danger of eternal damnation, he is certified as insane and relegated to an asylum. If he soars into the region of philosophy, science,

aesthetics, or conjecture, he is regarded as a crank; and if he be eccentric, unconventional, or abnormal in his behaviour, he is treated with ridicule by the community, irrespective of the fact that he may be a God-fearing, law-abiding, self-supporting, and responsible human being.

"These are but some of the shackles of so-called civilisation, and, needless to say, this trend is in itself not only subversive but also explanatory of the fact that many of the world's geniuses have had to seek asylums for protection against the intolerance displayed by their fellow beings. That such havens of refuge exist for those who receive inspirations denied to the majority is, without doubt, beneficial so long as the public continues to treat them with ridicule. It would, however, be better advised were it to take more cognisance of the Toms o' Bedlam who subvert those inspirations, and gull the public with their own spurious imitations. Were religion, science, art and industry to become more tolerant of the inspirations and aspirations of others, there would result a considerable reduction in the numbers of those who have to seek protection from their interferences, restrictions, and prohibitions."

If these are facts..., and who can question them?..., they show indubitably the strongest justification for the active work in many departments of research to which we, as Rosicrucians, have set our hands. They justify us in the fearless prosecution of our studies and in direct action in world service with unabated vigour, with total indifference to and defiance of the attitude and opinion of dignitaries in whatsoever seat of authority.

What has particularly led me to treat this subject in relation to ourselves was the remark of a member in charge of a group. It had been put to him that our studies probably had a tendency to mark one as queer or eccentric, or, in a word, abnormal. The rejoinder was, that nothing of the kind should transpire, but, on the contrary, in giving attention also to the evolution of the inner personality instead of exclusively, as hitherto, to the individual self, a man should become in every way more normal and be able to function sanely and effectively upon both the objective and the Divine psychic planes.

Certainly, his normality consists in, and is only fully assured by, this parallel and equal development. The questioning that arises in this matter only too clearly proves how comparatively few among us are concerned with this dual development; and our increasing normality through devotion to the culture of the soul is considered by the majority as a want of balance, a perilous condition which merits the derisive aspect and the opprobrious epithet.

Now the member to whom I have referred is himself one of the many examples of increasing normality through culture of the soul. On many occasions he has told me that he never could have done this or that piece of good and exacting work had the individual self alone been in requisition; that it has been the new knowledge and the strength arising therefrom, as a result of deeper acquaintance with the inner personality, which has insured the cohesion and balance of somewhat opposing forces and enabled him to serve his fellowmen to a degree impossible before he entered upon this culture.

We require no stronger assurance of increasing normality than that we can more understandingly and efficiently be of service in the world through the study and practice of Rosicrucian principles, than in electing to remain ignorant, and conventionally normal, of the depth and essentiality of our Divine nature.

It is demonstrable that the more intimate we become with the working and inspiration of this inner personality, the more remarkable is the facility observable in the members of the objective organism along all lines of adjustment and use on the material plane. If in any case this is not so, the cause is to be looked for either in the fact that one has not yet gone far enough in his study and realisation of the science he has adopted, or he has, so to speak, overreached himself; he has endeavoured beyond what his particular point of evolution justifies and there is strain or tension resulting in temporary maladjustment and consequent slightly erratic emergence. In both instances the causes are but temporary.

In the one instance, further progress in the science will evolve a sure and valuable facility; and in the other, a curbing of the impatience for specific development and a calm reliance upon nature's method of steady and orderly advance will duly regulate the processes of expression and eradicate any tendencies liable to criticism.

Obviously, I speak more to the novitiate than to the advanced student on the path. The latter has long since settled this question for himself and is not disturbed by the derision or the innuendoes of the ignorant. He knows that whoever runs counter to the tide of general opinion will have his sanity questioned at one point or another. He knows, too, from experience that there is in the awakening soul something of so puissant and urgent a nature that even his critics find it difficult to believe their own lie. As well might they criticise the unexpected glory flooding the evening sky and accuse nature of abnormal extravagance.

The divinity of the soul, through the benign and liberating influences of spiritual culture, has the unexpectedness of that unique and glorious expressiveness which belongs to nature; and when those moments come in which a new word is communicated and a bold action done, it is time for men of really abnormal scientific and theological reputation and other lesser conventionalists to stand back.

The soul will no more heed them than nature does the dead leaves of autumn. They will tap their foreheads and consult the textbooks to no purpose. The word has been uttered and the deed done. Inspiration has sped across the earth and passed like light into aspiring souls who await it and need a fresh impetus to their faith. The advanced man knows this and is indifferent to the cries of the "sane" majority.

But the matter is not so easy for the novitiate. It is not easy for him to feel quite sure of himself when, in his immediate circle at home or abroad, he is the subject of sympathetic scrutiny and a target for the envenomed tongue. I have known cases where aspirants have been compelled to creep away to their communion with God as if they were avoiding detection for the commission of a crime. Is it any wonder they run the risk of being considered abnormal?

I have known of wives being subjected to the bitter invective and persecution of their husbands because they had found at length in soul culture the one thing that made life tolerable to them. Judge between the two where the abnormality lies. This is one of the grossest indignities that can be inflicted upon defenceless human nature.

The criticism which many novitiates experience in this way from those around them is traceable to that profound axiom which has often been voiced in occult literature: when concentrated attention is directed upon the soul and a higher course of action insisted on, something in the nature of a psychic revolution in the personality of the man transpires which reacts, more or less powerfully according to his innate force and ability, upon the entire concatenation of circumstances and relationships which are his. If he is fervent and resolved the soul life works out with drastic pressure upon his settled thinking and acting, and a speedy readjustment becomes imperative.

This is so natural and insistent that he scarcely realises how marked the change in him appears to others. But the parting of the ways has been reached and a choice has to be made. The problem now does not lie simply in the mental acceptance of a new departure in life which concerns him privately, as a man might entertain an adverse opinion to his friends on a question of art or politics and say nothing of it: no, the soul under spiritual culture affects the whole living, acting personification of the man in his relation to others, and if they are not broadminded enough to place a right construction upon his altered values they will obviously place a wrong one.

And in the general contacts of everyday life the latter construction will be the usual one. For however effectually the novitiate may shroud in silence his colloquy with the divine, the effects of that colloquy will publish themselves in him to be read by all men. And the fear that besets him is, that he will, if he persists upon his new path, have to forfeit friendships and sympathies which have hitherto meant much to him.

I speak understandingly of these things because I have experienced them; and I know there is no opening whatever for compromise regarding them. I remember when, on the threshold of manhood, I embraced the occult life with complete acceptance and experienced all the untoward consequences in my environment through so doing. All the life currents turned upward as if through predestined inspiration, and the reactions outwardly were as critical and disquieting as the inward reconstruction was definite and unalterable.

And I put it to the young aspirant facing similar contingencies: I find it difficult to conceive how he who has experienced the decisive call of the spirit within him can temporise or hark back to the dead level of the purely mental self through any temporary criticism or discomforts he may encounter in prospect of following it. It would mean deliberately to forfeit the richest gain which an incarnation can afford, whatever value he may place upon the things he fears to lose.

The call of the awakening soul never comes by chance; it comes when the man is really ready and able to take a step forward in evolution, a normal and necessary step decreed by Karma. He may half doubt his readiness and ability at times when outward things are inimical and threatening; but the call is an unmistakable intimation that a critical juncture has been reached in the individual life, and without appearing to strain the point, I ask the aspirant to consider the gravity of the long run loss to himself if, for any personal considerations of the opinions of others, he refuses to countenance, and with the fullest liberty possible in the circumstances to follow, the intuitional prompting that urges him to tread the path.

It will be helpful for him to remember that the spiritual evolutionists are in a comparatively small minority, and they are likely to be for some time to come. He has not only the personal differences consequent upon educating his powers for higher purposes to contend with; there are opposing world forces around him and he will not, therefore, be surprised or easily deterred by the antagonistic currents which often, he can scarcely say how, seem to set against him.

This fact has often been stressed by members at the early stages of the path, but proper encouragement and the lapse of time carries them on to deeper assurance and greater strength to withstand the environmental opposition. Some of these members will agree with me when I suggest that one of the hardest trials they have had to meet is the consciousness of loneliness in their studies in their respective circumstances. They are conscious of growing radically different from those they contact, in many respects, and there is no one at hand to whom they may express themselves.

This is so; and in some circumstances it is inevitable, but only for a time. As knowledge increases and the aspirant reacts to it, opportunities for service present themselves, and what he may not communicate in speech will be powerfully expressed in action. It is right action, no matter how unusual in character, that will discountenance all the little appearances of abnormality or peculiarity which the unenlightened love to mark.

Lastly, it might be mentioned that we do not need advancing medical and scientific investigators to assure us that after all we are not abnormal in endeavouring to follow understandingly and scientifically the Master and to do the works that He did. We have long since set them an example which, however reluctantly, they are beginning to emulate. Nor is there any Egomania implied in the assertion. As the author says:

> "We note how humanity is gradually scaling the ladder of an emergent evolution to a self-realisation..., a realisation of self as but an integral part of a greater whole. Egomania implies belief in self as being 'the one and only,' whereas self-realisation means evolution."

Obviously, the Egomania has been on the other side, not with us. And we are deeply grateful for the liberal concession made to us that *"a philosophy of the infinite is, however, far from being a source of aberration of thought amounting to actual insanity."* So much for the question of abnormality. I have not, however, finished with the subject of criticism in relation to the novitiate, and propose to deal specifically with it in a subsequent article.

5. The Dark Night of the Soul

Reprinted from the August 1930 edition of the Rosicrucian Digest.

In a previous article on "Waiting for the Master,"[2] we considered certain aspects of the mystical pause in the ninth grade. We stood, so to speak, individually alone, at the close of a long cycle of study and experiment, within the silent chamber of meditation. The hour for entering upon the divine assumption had arrived, and putting all lesser things aside, even ourselves, we stood, individually alone, in the holy place of stillness, expectant, according to our fitness, of some breath of inspiration and guidance from within the veil.

We considered one very essential qualification in the aspirant at this stage..., the power for service. This, however, is but one aspect of the mystical pause. It is necessary to approach the subject from the standpoint of the reactions in the personal life subsequent upon our work in the ninth.

I do this the more readily because members have written to me very earnestly on the matter of the above-mentioned article; and it is clear that the suggestions which were given awakened a decided response in many aspirants who are working steadfastly through the grades and are looking forward with confidence to the supreme tests of the ninth.

Another thing which particularly impressed me was, that some members, who are still in only the earlier grades, responded swiftly to the vibration prompted by the specific work of the ninth. Some of them, indeed, had passed through certain phases of inner experience, the rationale of which they will only meet with in that grade, which fact indicates that there are no hard and fast boundaries regarding growth on the Path, and that if some phase of truth, spoken or written, answers to experience, there is the pointing hand, the open door to deeper understanding, and a strong incentive to renewed effort.

In mystical literature we meet with many references to what is called the dark night of the soul, of a temporary suspension of that peace, joy, and assurance which the soul enjoys as the reward of long communion and dedication to things spiritual. The term, the dark night, refers primarily to a specific and culminating experience in the mystical life when the soul has to survive in its own strength for a period, the illusionary sense of spiritual loss and desolation, the sense that all it has striven for and attained has been taken away and the soul passes through a dark inward abyss of hopelessness and despair. The experience cannot be antedated, but it is amply recorded that every soul on the mystical Path at some time passes through it. But the fact which strongly impresses me on this subject is, that while the dark night of the soul may be regarded as a major experience,

---

[2] See Section 4, Chapter 3.

there are many minor experiences of a similar character which are encountered by us during our work in the higher grades, and chiefly during that stage, long or short as the case may be, which I have called the mystical pause, in the ninth.

Nor is this a mere speculation on my part. Again and again have members voluntarily attested the fact. Neither does it apply to those members only, who might be considered as not specially enthusiastic in their studies and who become more easily discouraged at the little ups and downs of circumstance, or the inability to quickly achieve their aims on the Path. No, the cry comes from those who have fought long and hard for the higher things, who are intense and vital in their interest and have much creditable work behind them. They have made vigorous ascents, blessed human souls, given and given again; they have felt the touch of the Master in their lives although they have not seen his face; they have forgotten themselves and their interests for his sake. It has been natural with them to do so: they know of no higher ideal than this; and blessed forever is the sacred spirit among us which gives them this holy bias to the life of service!

Now, these are worthy that the light which shone upon them should darken for certain seasons, that they might grow stronger in their own strength and be able to bear the greater light which shall surely shine upon them. Lesser souls, lukewarm individuals who are neither one thing nor the other, have little to record of interior seasons of trial of this nature. Indeed, they are inclined to think that there is something radically wrong with your philosophy that you should be subjected to them. And, if one were writing entirely from his own experience, he would wonder how far right they were. But the experience is very far from being an isolated one; it is a well attested fact of certain stages of the Path.

Perhaps some of the most poignant letters bearing upon this subject that I have read came to me recently from a lady in America, outside our Order, who had been a seeker for years. While staying with a friend, who is a member, she met with our magazine. She read several issues, and certain articles awakened her interest. Embittered by hard experiences, she wrote me a somewhat skeptical letter, which might easily have been put to one side and ignored. But I have learned during a long experience with correspondents..., and I say this impersonally and for the reason that it might prove a hint of advice and warning to others..., that behind a flippant or skeptical letter may stand a writer profoundly suffering; nay, one who is too proud for the moment in the circumstances, even on the gravest subject, to be serious. and who needs and really craves for all the compassion and understanding a man has to offer.

In any event, we who endeavour to serve can never ignore an opportunity for service: and in the case of my correspondent, I was more conscious of what had not than what had been written. To that I responded, and the letters referred to were the result. The burden of these letters was this: the lady had apparently almost completed the circle of worldly experience, and her knowledge was full and valuable. She had studied with teachers of theosophy, received tuition in philosophy and psychology, and had experience with various cults. She had suffered acutely at the hands of friends for deserting causes which brought her neither peace nor hope. Through poverty, illness, and cruel estrangement, she had fought her way; and at this point, having thrown all her books and beliefs to one side, a voice in our magazine made her pause and impelled her once again to interrogate. I will note a passage from one of the letters:

> "If Christ and His Masters are today living in the White Brotherhood, surely out of mere human, if not divine compassion, they would have reached unto me with one tiny ray of their infinite power to endure, if not enlighten... Surely the incense of my prayers in agony would have dimmed their eyes with tears of pity, often and over. I am always so utterly..., alone. The weight of God's silence is very great."

That is sufficient. I can only say that when a cry of this nature is wrung from a sincere soul struggling upward to the light, craving to be understood and to know the reality of life, the very silence of God is filled with a divine music for it and the Master only awaits the propitious hour. And the point of this narrative for the aspirant is this: when the dark night descends in this form upon a noble and aspiring soul, the voice it needs will speak for it, even across far flung seas.

The dark night of the soul is just that, sometimes extreme, as in this case, sometimes of brief duration, a temporary veiling of the light and joy which have filled the chalice of life to the brim. Yet what is it but a clear call from the heights that we should stand firmly by the soul and refuse to relinquish what we have attained? That which we need above all things to meet successfully these temporary eclipses of our finest activity is an unswerving allegiance to the highest we have experienced, a perfect confidence in the inner self to reassert itself the more vigorously and understandingly by reason of a deeper comprehension of the law of evolution.

The most heartening thought we can entertain at such times is, that it is our own strong efforts on the Path which cause these variations in consciousness, and that they are a part of the technique of advancement. In the ascension of the mountain of illumination there are many dead levels which must be trodden: the soul has its breathing spaces like the natural man, during which its forces must be recollected and adjusted for further ascent. The periods of waiting and silence are often tedious, but if we are observant we shall quickly realise how necessary they are and how richly productive when rightly utilised.

If we consider the lives of the famous mystics of the past, we shall find the most striking confessions regarding these oscillations of consciousness tabulated as the dark night of the soul. The ardent mystic, forgetful of all but the inflamed aspiration for contact with reality, touches some high vibrational altitude and rests awhile in the peace and ecstasy of a larger dimension, but the mundane world still exists and demands the daily toil of his hands and feet. He needs must descend, perhaps unwillingly, and think again in terms of mortality. The wise rhythms of nature prevail; the vision passes, and so completely that he often wonders whether it were vision or illusion. He has disturbed the old equilibrium, and the new is not yet established; but he knows the law and allows it to work for good and seeming ill in all his members.

Here, too, is the psychological explanation of that which we observe in the lives of men of genius in many spheres, the creative artists who live on the borderline of the mystic state. They rise triumphantly to accomplishments of superb beauty and power and pass as suddenly into the depths of negation and despair, believing they will never achieve again.

Those who have read the intimate letters of the illustrious tone poet, Wagner, will see there a classic example of this experience. Indeed, he is an example of peculiar interest to the occult student; for while Wagner is known to the world generally as a musician only, a study of the man reveals him as an aspiring disciple of Buddha. Art alone could not satisfy the soul of this great master. He was conscious of a great antagonism between art and that calm, spiritual, contemplative state which, through deep study of the Eastern teachings, he knew was the secret of the greatness of Buddha.

> "Surely," he writes, "the glorious Buddha was right when he sternly prohibited art. Who can feel more distinctly than I, that it is this abominable art which forever gives me back to the torment of life and all the contradictions of existence? Were this strange gift not within me, this strong predominance of plastic phantasy, clear insight might make me obey my heart's dictate, and…, turn into a saint. Oh, if ye foolish men of learning but understood the great love-brimming Buddha, ye would marvel at the depth of insight which showed him the exercise of art as the most certain of all pathways from salvation!"

In Wagner's soul, at the time he wrote these lines on Buddha and art, a drama was proceeding which no art could adequately express. Every advanced student of the occult has experienced that transitional stage of evolution, when he is passing from the sight of man into the still presence of God. That ordeal is a test for the strongest soul. Wagner passed through it; constituted as he was, for him there was no alternative. He had reached that degree of inner unfoldment where this supreme trial of the soul became the very next step of advancement; and he took it. It was a struggle well-nigh unto death. He has told us something of it in these words:

> "Last night when I drew my hand back from the rail of the balcony, it was not my art that withheld me! In that terrible instant there showed itself to me with well-nigh visual distinctness my life's true axis, round which my resolution whirled from death to new existence…."[3]

I have referred to Wagner advisedly, because in him we have the instance of a master musician who was also a rare thinker about the mysteries of life and a devotee of Buddhism, whose mighty poems of orchestration fill our opera houses today with a Cosmic harmony

---
3. The reader may note the repetition of some text from "Wagner and Occultism" in Section 1 of this volume.

which lifts the soul beyond the things of sense and time and acquaints us with the vast rhythms of the Master Artist. Moreover, the dark night of the soul shrouded this man in some of his rarest hours. Only a soul which had passed sympathetically through the heart of the world could have drawn from the Cosmic keyboard those gigantic phrases of super-harmony which chasten the soul and inspire it to lofty exercise and service.

The same laws of the eternal rhythms prevail in the soul of the artist and in the disciple on the Path. We can never rise to the heights without passing through the depths. *"I have trodden the wine press alone."* The disciple who can say that without bitterness and with a consciousness of inward strength has the inestimable privilege of having passed a severe test. Trials must come; failures, relative failures, must come; but there is a power in the real man to use the one and build upon the other. In the ninth grade we have to strongly stand prepared for both.

Life is a mystic symphony, and harmony and discord mingle forever to give it meaning and purpose. Now it rises clear and inspiring to the highest heaven, anon it descends to the deepest chord of mortal existence. Only those who have known both extremes and are able to blend the highest with the lowest and act consciously and freely at the central point of equilibrium, can discern the purpose and meaning of the seeming chaotic and conflicting.

It is admitted that on the surface of life there is stress and confusion arising from the babel of worldly tongues and circumstance. It is admitted that sometimes, at particular stages of our progress, difficulties seem to thicken upon us as we advance, and there is a tension in the vehicles of expression which is inclined to defeat the very aim of the new forces which they invite. In fact, there are so many unlooked for and surprising contingencies attendant upon the slow and painful birth of the new consciousness, that the cry of the travailing soul is a common factor of the Path and is ever heard attentively and compassionately by those who have had experience with it. For the danger at this point is, that a period of almost overwhelming stress of circumstances may so baffle and disappoint a powerful organisation of a specific type that it turns back in discouragement and disgust and declares the whole search after reality a vain illusion.

The case of the lady I have mentioned above is precisely such an instance. In spite of many advantages of personal contact with those of considerable knowledge and advancement, the swift reactions of a Karma, deeply enfolded and awaiting propitious emergence for her trial and ultimate conquest, threw her violently back upon the strength of that knowledge she had acquired; but this, being insufficient to sustain her in the crucial hour, she doubted the value and reality of it and cast it behind her in hot denial.

"Henceforth I walk by faith alone.... The only comfort I have at present is that in eternity there is quite time enough to teach me *if* there shall be anything."

It may be, proud, noble woman! But only in love, not in bitterness and unbelief.

It is easy to pass on defiantly and affirm the non-existence of that which we have not attained. It is so easy for reason to slay the Divine intuition and leave it lying like a cherub with broken wings on the Path to God. But the Masters are yet compassionate, because they understand and have infinite patience. If it were not so, then God help us in all our weaknesses and trials and manifold sufferings, both our own and those of others who trust in our sincerity and desire to assist, as we press on through whatever ominous doubt and conjecture to a fuller comprehension of the Christ within.

Indeed, if it were not so, my correspondent would have remained unanswered. I should have found no voice to respond to the cry of the dark night of her soul: and whether or not the response shall fail in its purpose, I at least should have been the poorer for not making it.

6. The Science of Seership

Reprinted from the October 1930 edition of the Rosicrucian Digest. "Science of Seership" *by Geoffrey Hodson is published by Rider, London.*

So prolific is the output of books on spiritualism in our day, and so questionable in character and void of any helpful instruction is the majority of them, that one may be pardoned for regarding askance a volume that recently appeared under the above title by Mr Geoffrey Hodson. On perusing this book, however, we find ourselves in an entirely different field of investigation. The matter is exceedingly interesting and merits close attention.

In the first place, the author's method of procedure is thoroughly scientific and his record of results from personal investigation is corroborated by many independent witnesses in the Theosophical and scientific world. There is nothing here of a spiritualistic or mediumistic type. The author is an advocate of exact clairvoyance, and the information he gives of a superphysical nature is derived from careful research through the exercise of that faculty.

In his introductory chapter he states that his purpose is to make a critical examination of the subject of supernormal cognition. Such a purpose can obviously only be adequately fulfilled by one who has personal experience arising from the exercise of supernormal faculties. With these faculties he has made crucial tests along the lines of scientific research and the diagnosis of disease.

As a matter of fact, research of this character has been in progress for a considerable period in our Order, and many of us who are intimate with the procedure therein are aware how far advanced are some of the proficients in it and the work they have accomplished. To these the book will make a definite appeal; they will note the researches with complete understanding, and be in a position to compare his explanations and conclusions with their systematised grade instruction and experimental practice.

The records of clairvoyant investigation in the fields of scientific research and the diagnosis of diseases submitted by the author in two memorable chapters on these subjects indicate only too plainly how necessary to the better welfare of humanity is the introduction into professional spheres of a supernormal method of cognition. Every day testifies to the inadequacy of ordinary objective methods of research and application in science and healing, and not in these alone.

Many of the author's clairvoyant investigations were carried out in conjunction with the scientific section of the Theosophical Society, when several members of the section were always present and his observations recorded verbatim. The tests perhaps were all the more valuable and convincing because he himself had no knowledge either of occult chemistry or physics, and his descriptions were often recognised by the scientific members as applicable to occult and physical chemistry.

Of a scientific character his investigations embraced such subjects as the Astronomical, Bacteriology, the Electron, Radio-active Substances and the Electric Current. He considers that the value of this research lies in two things: in the actual confirmation, or otherwise, of existing chemical and physical conceptions, and in the proof, which is gradually accumulating, of the value and usefulness of clairvoyance in the observations of physical as well as superphysical matter.

In his chapter on the diagnosis of disease the author points out that the faculty of positive clairvoyance enables its possessor to respond to rates of vibrations which are beyond the normal human range. This is, of course, one of the fundamental tenets of occult science. Vibrational response is the key to the entire progress of the student on the path. The author tabulates five specific powers of cognition which the ascension of vibration in his own experience has opened to him, and which are of special interest in connection with medical research.

They are: (1) X-ray vision; (2) The power of magnification and of television; (3) The power to see the feelings and the thoughts of others as well as the vehicles or "bodies" in which those aspects of consciousness normally function; (4) To observe the vital or etheric body; (5) To transcend, in varying degrees, the limitations of matter, time and space, as far as vision is concerned.

These added capacities are the direct result of the active functioning of the force centres or Chakras. The supernormal cognition arising from the activity of these centres the author has applied with much success to the diagnosis of disease. Six cases are dealt with. Professors of medical science may scoff, then may pause and consider; the fact remains that here once again they have something of first importance for them.

They can scarcely be expected just yet to accept the author's assertion, for instance, that certain conditions investigated by him are due to a Karmic heritage from the past, that cancer is an elemental disease, and that its cure lies primarily in the exorcism and destruction of the elemental. Moreover, he considers that the most effective method of treatment in all cases of cancer to be that of the use of radio-active substances internally and externally, the direction of electrons, and the application of electric-magnetic forces.

Extensive experiments in the field of psychometry were also made by the author and his information and speculations on this subject are more reasonable than those usually met with in the works of less scientific investigators. The speculative aspect of this chapter centres around the two questions: whether the object used serves as a medium for transmitting vibrations which are conducted from it along the hand and arms of the psychometrist and to his consciousness; or does the object merely serve as a link to place the seer en rapport with the Akashic records, which he then reads without reference to the object itself? The author does not offer a final explanation but proposes the subject as one worthy of study and elucidation.

In the chapter on experimental explorations are given clairvoyant observations of what are called in Theosophical terminology the ego, mental and emotional consciousness. In these brief studies are presented graphic visualisations which are very illuminating and helpful. There is a living reality in these pictures which makes for personal unfolding.

The same high level of investigation is maintained in the study of discarnate life. The claims and methods of the spiritualist are placed in sharp contrast with those of the occultist, and we find ourselves in agreement with the author. The information here is refreshing and stimulating and in frank opposition to the wealth of material published on this subject which is the offspring of automatic writing and other spiritualistic communications. One is bound to affirm that a large percentage of this material is of a nature to nauseate any advanced student of occult research.

The author is well aware of this when he warns the student seriously against any methods which demand cessation of full consciousness and intellectual awareness in order to obtain contact with the unseen. The medium, as he truly asserts, is entirely at the mercy of such intelligences as he permits to make use of his body, and is quite unable to scrutinise his unseen visitors, or to apply the reasoning mind to the communications which he receives whilst in a state of trance. *"Complete understanding of any plane of Nature cannot be gained from the level of that plane."*

There is a hint of Baconian sagacity and conciseness in this statement, and it is typical of the author's method. He has made certain clairvoyant investigations of discarnate life and the examples given of communication with discarnate egos are transcripts of postmortem existence, instructive in character and entirely free from the sentimental outpourings of the passive and untutored communicant.

In the chapter on "Clairvoyance in time" the author would appear to have transcribed from the Akashic Records: one section is biographical, the other historical. He presents *"The Story of Simon the Essene..., an account of a clairvoyant vision of Palestine at the time of the coming of the Lord Christ;"* and *"Early British Races."* We have no means at hand to corroborate these descriptions, but may conjecture whether they are readings from the Records, or possibly phases of the past existence of the author.

The chapters on the psychic powers and the psychic sense organs are enlightening. Forms of meditation are indicated for their awakening and use which are general and Theosophical in character and no doubt constitute a hint in the right direction for development; but, as is usually the case with textbooks on the subject, the student will regret the absence of any system of practical methods of discipline for the evolution of the higher faculties.

These chapters on the psychic organs and powers are, of course, the culminating and arresting points of the author's documents, since it is a special development of these powers in his case which has made his investigations possible. But the persistent question of the aspirant is, how to proceed in a definitely practical and systematic way towards this development. In this matter the author does not enlighten us; but concludes with general information regarding the position and functioning of the various psychic centres, with illustrative diagrams, in a truly Theosophical style and in corroboration of its many textbooks.

The book, however, is of much interest and is in many ways so clearly in line with important investigations and experimental work which have long been maturing in our hands in the Order and have been brought to considerable proficiency by members of our lodges, that the author's efforts deserve recognition.

7. Lodge Masters and Activities

Reprinted from the February 1931 edition of the Rosicrucian Digest

The responsibilities of those who "supervise and direct in lodge or group work" in the Rosicrucian Order have changed considerably since this article was written. The Order is administrated by different methods today, although these thoughts of Raymund Andrea are still helpful from a broader perspective.

I propose to give here a few reflections upon the responsible status of those who supervise and direct in lodge or group work in our Order, on their adjustment to the diverse temperaments and capacities contacted therein, and on some of the individual problems constantly presented and which demand considerate handling.

In this work, which is undoubtedly highly responsible and technical, we are looking upward and forward and calling upon the best that is in us to take part in a task in which we confer real and enduring benefit upon others in the matter of their soul evolution. Therefore it is not demanding too much of those who assume the responsible control in lodge activities, that whatever their practical ability may be for the discharge of their duties, they should possess some commendable degree of qualification, in the occult sense, in order to fill that capacity.

The object of the appointment of responsible heads in lodges under the supervision of the Council of the Order is obviously the extension of the influence and a sharing of the responsibility of the Head of the Order in carrying out its work. It is not within the province of the Order to equip lodge masters with the necessary ability to discharge secretarial duties. They are presumed to have in some measure this ability and also the qualifications for instructing others, apart from the fact that they are students of occultism.

I discriminate here, because even a considerable knowledge of the science would not necessarily equip one for the specific task of working upon the lives of other students. A master is indeed entrusted with a very special kind of authority; and as I am writing impersonally, I do so freely and without bias.

I regard it as essential in a lodge master in dealing with a student that he have a knowledge of the general mental status of the student, together with such incidental information as would be supplied to him with regard to age, occupation, studies or leisure, even personal idiosyncrasies perhaps, upon the student coming under his supervision. The personal life of a student will naturally have a direct and powerful influence upon his life as a spiritual aspirant. The fullest general information is therefore desirable; and most students will be willing to supply particular information if they have the assurance that those who are to supervise their work and development are actuated with a sincere desire to understand and adjust to their present outlook.

The aspirations of a student in any field of endeavour, apart from his occult studies, constitute a factor for the careful consideration of the master, since they will work out, influence, and be applied almost unconsciously in his lodge work. His personal studies and aspirations will, for one thing, be something of a guide to a student's possibilities on the path, indicate the quality and calibre of his thought and reveal tendencies liable to accelerate or retard his spiritual evolution. The extent of his reading in occultism should especially be known, the schools of thought to which he inclines, and his progress in the science of meditation, before entering the lodge.

Upon this data the master will base his method of adjustment to the student..., a more or less objective adjustment. But he should also have a measure of soul responsiveness which will enable him to read subjectively and fairly accurately the soul atmosphere of the student. Not much can be said on this point: no precise rule can be given. If the master has been working long with others, he will automatically register through the written or spoken word the soul vibration of the student.

He should be able to discern very quickly how much the latter is capable of at any particular point, what aspects of truth he is able to respond to, whether he requires sympathetic handling and encouragement, or the strong assertion of will impulse to inspire and carry him forward. It is here that the master will meet with testing conditions for himself. A lodge will presumably consist of many diverse types of students, some of whom will require special attention and treatment, and for that kind of work special qualifications are requisite in the master.

It should be his aim to arrive at that measure of balanced development which will enable him to adjust to and handle successfully every type of student that comes under his supervision. He will insist in himself upon a careful blending of the mystic aspect of devotion and contemplation and the occult aspect of will and sound thinking, thereby demonstrating an ability of responsiveness to types in nature either mystical or occult, or manifesting both in the process of evolution.

A student should receive a powerful impression of adequacy in a master; not that of imperious authority, but a sound and solid sensibleness which imparts a feeling of reliable strength, assurance of understanding and instant response. This feeling of implicit confidence will perhaps only be present in its fullness where the master is in advance of the student in evolution.

It is not desired to demand too much of those who feel the call to this particular service and who feel difficulty and responsibility in assuming the task, in addition to the exigencies of their own development. The question of relative development and reciprocal response, however, stands upon an entirely different footing from that of teacher and pupil in a school or university.

Authority there in the majority of branches of learning rests almost exclusively upon superiority of mental content derived from the accumulation of facts well digested and memorised, and clearness and facility of statement. The preceptor himself may not, often does not, count for much; his personal influence may be negligible if he is no larger than his reading.

But in the case of a master, the authority should be almost the reverse of this. It is soul capacity that will have true and lasting influence upon the soul aspect of the student. This admits of neither argument nor requires demonstration. I believe it to be true that very few of those who supervise in any school of occultism possess the distinctive capacity of soul responsiveness, the height and the breadth, and the fine and penetrative understanding to deal at will with practically any type of student, even with students of various degrees below their own range of response.

This is a statement not calculated to deter, but rather to inspire a master to take the largest possible view of his calling and make every effort to equip himself for his office through specialised study and research.

It may be objected that ideal men cannot be waited for, the material at hand must be used. This is so. It is practical common sense and true in any line of endeavour, yet must receive some modification in connection with the highly responsible task of working with others. And while it rests with the Council of the Order in deputing responsible officers as supervisors at a distance, the main burden of the responsibility in this matter lies with the students themselves assembled in any particular locality in making an unanimous choice of one among them who has manifest qualifications for the position of authority.

It is then that the Council ratifies the choice made both on the ground of the proclaimed approval and from its personal knowledge of the one proposed. Hence the importance in a lodge of making a careful selection on the basis of adequate and intrinsic merit. That only should justify the choice of a master, not in any case zeal for personal advancement, or to be considered of value and prestige in the Order.

A choice made under any such consideration would be likely to maintain a master in a position of authority in which he would be naturally indisposed to disburden himself of any really too exacting task entrusted to him, with the inevitable result that there would be inadequate dealing with present problems of the students under his charge.

Moreover, in this connection a matter of considerable importance emerges. A student breaking new ground can be very exacting in his demands, according to type. Some of an inquisitive and ingenious nature have the ability of presenting a particular problem that searches the depths of experience. That is not to be trifled with, neither ignored, nor yet does it call for lengthy examination from the master. But the indispensable requirement is, that deep should answer deep, or the opportunity has passed.

In submitting these remarks I have in mind the highest interest of the student, the creditable discharge of lodge activities, and the allocation of responsible authority to those only who have given undoubted proof of capacity for leadership and disinterested devotion to the august ideals of the Order.

8. The Rosicrucian Technique: A Word to the Critics

Reprinted from the July 1932 edition of the Rosicrucian Digest.

I was deeply interested in the recent declaration by the Imperator on Rosicrucianism as an art and a science, not a religious philosophy. This declaration was very timely and appropriate, with all the point and emphasis and corroborative evidence to enforce it, not only for the proper information of members but for the enlightenment of certain blundering critics and defamers who appear to have nothing better to do than to seek for some new weapon of offence against the Rosicrucian Order and its work.

One of the reasons why this declaration struck a deep chord of sympathy within me was because it took me back in mind some 12 years, when I commenced active work for the Order in Great Britain. I had from youth been an ardent student of philosophy, Theosophy and the occult, and the time had arrived when a large body of mystical truth and awakening past experience demanded expression in a truly active sphere of service.

I was equipped, far more than I knew, for active service over a wide field in other lives. I sought this above all things. I had made many sacrifices to fit myself for this service during a period of nearly 20 years. My case was analogous, to some small degree, to that of Roger Bacon. I had knowledge, but not a single door would open to a sphere where it could be applied to practical and useful ends. I remember the keen disappointment felt as I approached one Theosophical leader after another in the hope that in their wide contacts and personal influence I might find some opportunity of giving back that which the Masters had given me. Every effort I made failed of success.

There are those, it seems, who decry the fact that the Rosicrucian Order should condescend to advertise itself. Well, I am a notorious example..., whatever its value may be..., of one who contacted the Order through an advertisement and found a sphere of labour for which I have ever been grateful. When I first wrote to the Imperator, he immediately recognised the applicant through profound psychic prescience. He recognised my associations with the Order and its work in past cycles. He bridged the chasm of lives for me, formed a link between the two, and brought me into active cooperation with students, old and new, who are recognised pioneers in many countries. This man had the prescience to see and the generosity to act immediately; whereas every influential Theosophist I approached had the prescience to offer me a few well-worn Theosophical platitudes and a recommendation to the kindness of a far-off future.

I find myself, then, a concrete example of what is set forth in the declaration, that Rosicrucianism is a field of action, in art, science, profession and business, and not merely another religious philosophy which inclines a man to dream the years away and do nothing of value in the world for his fellowmen. There are instances enough within my experience to point the manifest difference.

Some of the staunchest members of the Order, I might say the majority of them, in Great Britain, are men and women engaged in business and professional life, who have made their lives stronger and more productive through the practical application of Rosicrucian science and art in their various spheres. Many of them are old students of philosophy, Theosophy and the Christian religion; and so far from considering that Rosicrucianism should be a replica of either of these fields of thought, or that it annuls or antagonises fundamental tenets of either, they find it enables them to put their philosophy and other studies on a practical basis and be of use and inspiration in other lives. They have found in it the link which enables them to reduce philosophy to practice, add works to faith, and live a progressive life.

The critics, therefore, who accuse us of having too practical aims to please them, not only do us a great injustice but are flagrantly guilty of attempting to hinder to the best of their poor ability the onward march of evolution. They have not observed the signs of the times. They stand where they stood half a century ago. Have we not entered upon a new age in which science and art are destined to make even more momentous discoveries than have already been made? Is it not obvious to every student who is keenly alive to the trend of the times and the meaning of evolution, that on every hand men are pressing forward in every department of world activity, eagerly seeking some method, some technique, which promises them better personality equipment and extended power for the amelioration of the people?

The Theosophists should know this, if anybody does. They have talked enough about evolution for several generations; they have still to learn its practical application in everyday life. Yet they have gone out of their way to favour, in some localities, attacks upon the Rosicrucians of this cycle because they choose to be practitioners instead of theorists. They are hurt because we are a practical and progressive section of the community applying science to life and healing bodily disease, and believe in using the faculties we possess to increase our personal influence and be of some little use, unostentatiously and humbly, in the world of men. They would have us, it seems, desist from doing good and be content with weaving spiritual abstractions for our own soul inebriation. They would deny us even the right to acknowledge any relationship with their Masters..., those Masters whom they have sought to keep in Theosophical isolation in their lodges and libraries like rare first editions collected at great expense.

Evolution and Masters do not wait even for Theosophists. Their Masters have disciples safely housed in personalities often the least suspected..., and their work is well known.

No, the Rosicrucians are not here for soul inebriation. They have put their hands in the most practical way to the task of being of real use in human lives. Their lodges are merely an incident; the real work is being done outside in every quarter of the globe. They are on the side of evolution and will not accept the neutral role, which the critics feel competent to dictate to them. They will not take instructions from petty, libelling scribblers, revilers of the servants of Masters, unbalanced with envy and chagrin, impotent of tongue, and with sinister intent throwing abroad a trail of poisonous vituperation in the hope of causing disaffection to keep their own wrangling selves in countenance.

Now, to pass to a more important phase of the subject, there exists, and always has existed, within the Rosicrucian Order, a technique of peculiar value when applied to everyday life; and there are men in every department of life who need nothing more than this technique in order to make their lives eminently productive, and conclusive in investigation and demonstration. In principle and aim they are potentially Rosicrucian. They possess all the characteristics of the pioneer in the mystical and progressive quality of their minds. They are actors, not theorists; but their sphere of action is greatly curtailed because they lack an organised technique which will bring them to a profound understanding of their constitution, enable them to establish a ready response between the psychic and physical organisations, and look to Cosmic sources at once for inspiration and the working power to actualise it immediately and locally. It is these men, who are capable of great work in this cycle, whom we seek to contact, that they may have the opportunity of participating in a technique which will bring them to conscious knowledge and strength, the resurrection of latent faculty, and a soul consciousness and personality equipment truly Rosicrucian in character.

Those members who feel disposed to read a little book entitled, *The Technique of the Master*,[4] which is being issued forthwith by the Order, will find that I have endeavoured to approach this subject of the technique from several related angles and

---

[4] *The Technique of the Master* is available from the publisher.

give a comprehensive idea of the use of personality, from the inner and technical point of view, in its progress on the path while qualifying for initiation into Cosmic contact and pupilage under a Master.

I have no two opinions about this one fact; that the Masters will use any man who can efficiently use their technique. That proposition is basic to all I have written. What he is by profession, whether he be highborn or humble, of this race or that, as well as practically every other consideration these factors are incidental. If he can prove himself in the eyes of the Masters as a sound technician on the cardinal lines set out in my book, he may be sure that he has reached a point in evolution where important disclosures await him from their sphere. I am not dogmatic in this matter. I am merely suggestive. I express an opinion.

If it is considered of value it can be used; if not, it can be rejected. But my aim has been to offset the idea so prevalent among students that they can attain to high evolution on the path mainly through abstract meditation, and postponing action until they receive a mandate from a Master, ill equipped as they are, to carry out some momentous campaign. Not by meditation on the Self, but by using the self, is the burden of my theme. I do not emphasise the latter to the exclusion of the former. The Rosicrucian technique recognises completely the dual aspects of development. But whilst philosophical meditation has been the main feature of countless cults, the path of action, in the most varied and practical sense, has ever been distinctly Rosicrucian.

We have only to glance back over the history of the Order to realise how profoundly true this is. The discoveries and practical works of the Rosicrucians of the past stand as a challenge and an example for all time. It is for us to keep this fact ever in mind and endeavour to apply this technique with all possible urgency and with complete dedication of all our powers in the place where we are. That is what the Masters demand first of all from us. When we have proved our efficiency and attuned our lives to the Cosmic forces, sympathetic response and contact will result and our sphere of service will be correspondingly enlarged.

The aspects of the subject I have sketched in my book are all related to the technique: its fundamentals, the preparation for it, common delusions about it, its impersonality and magic, the Masters on the technique, vocation in relation to the technique, personal adjustments, the neophyte and his critics, and in conclusion, the vexed question of probation. My hope is that the book will be an inspiration and companion to every member.

9. The Technique of the Disciple

Reprinted from the February 1935 edition of the Rosicrucian Digest.

In my book, *The Technique of the Master*,[5] published two years ago, certain basic principles of thought and action were outlined, and methods of esoteric discipline were suggested, which appeared to me to characterise the Master in the training of a disciple. These principles and this discipline constitute the necessary foundation upon which a disciple has to build through graduated development, a comprehensive structure of technical equipment in order to attain to high initiation.

I endeavoured to sketch the subject from the Master's point of view. I took it for fact that readers would accept the act of the existence of the Masters as living personalities, actually operative on this material plane as well as on the Cosmic plane, having full knowledge of the activities of the Order to which we as members are attached, and inspiring certain advanced initiates in carrying on those activities.

The response from members to the teaching of this book was highly gratifying. It proved beyond question that within the Order a large body of appreciative understanding existed of the subject under consideration. Not only so, but that a very real hunger was present to grasp all the related aspects of truth discussed and work them out in the individual life.

What was especially significant to me was the appreciative comment that came from young members in the Order, of an age at which one scarcely expects to find subjects of this nature to be of interest, much less of being grasped with any real understanding.

Surely this fact is a sign of the times in the occult world. In a world still full of unrest, with superficiality and light-mindedness manifest on every hand to a painful degree, to find young people seeking the wisdom of the Masters with an earnestness of thought and aspiration worthy of their elders, is the most promising sign of the onward march of evolution and an inspiration, to us who endeavour to teach and guide, beyond any other incentive.

It is in compliance with the request of these and many members of all ages in the Order that I have been prompted to prepare another book, as a companion volume to the first, dealing with the technique.

In this book I have had the neophyte in mind. I have gone back to my own early days of study and effort on the path and placed myself side by side with the neophyte as he sets forth on his journey of self-development. I have endeavoured to treat the subject from the point of view of the neophyte as he seeks to qualify from the outset of his studies, knowing little of the path before him, or how his new departure in life will react upon himself and his environment.

It is not an easy task to embark upon, but I have written from my own experience

---

5. *The Technique of the Disciple* is available from the publisher.

of the path and taken the young aspirant along with me, until light and knowledge dispel doubt and hesitancy and he finds the technique unfolding in his mind and soul and expressing skilfully in his hands in the one great service to which we have dedicated ourselves, the service of the Master.

In these books on the technique I am not, I need scarcely say, proposing to offer a teaching which shall be in any way a substitute for the actual studies of the aspirant within the Order. I seek rather to throw a light upon definite phases of inner experience which will transpire as he proceeds in his unfoldment through the various grades.

As he works on through his studies ever new problems arise of a deeply personal and intimate nature; yet experience has shown how uniform in character are many of these problems, and again and again one finds that the same difficulties, the same searching questions and perplexities in one's own experience, beset others, though in different circumstances, and the solutions which one has found in his own researches into the soul become an inspirational guidance in other lives.

Take, for instance, the Obscure Night, which is specifically dealt with in the teachings of the Order. It comes to all at some time or other: all must pass through it. It is fraught with temporary doubts and difficulties: some almost lose their faith and their hold upon life in it.

To each it comes in a peculiar and individual form, contingent upon circumstances and temperament and evolutionary status. But those who have passed through it know the actual experiences of it; they know the nature of its trial and the necessary requirements for passing on in spite of all illusionary aspects which suggest defeat. And here it is that an individual exposition of this and other related phases of development can be an added inspiration to the aspirant to face his task with courage and qualify for a worthy mission in life.

An advanced member of the Order recently proffered the opinion that the book, *The Technique of the Master,* was really for ninth grade students. Perhaps this is so, although it had not before occurred to me. I dealt in that book with intricate points of the technique which had long burdened my mind in connection with some of the deepest problems of our experience on the path.

Inevitably, therefore, I was speaking therein mainly to the student of experience, faced with some of the hardest problems that may beset him. For it is just here, when the student has made considerable progress and is awaiting the decisive touch and influence of the Master in his life, that his greatest strength and perseverance are in requisition.

It is to be expected that before this great privilege is his, he should be subjected to the keenest possible trial of his powers to ensure his proper use of that privilege. And these considerations had my earnest attention in the first book.

But in the second book to be published, I have reviewed the earlier stages up to this point of attainment. The neophyte and the advanced student will find in it an interpretation of personal experience and, I trust, an inspiration to attainment. One cannot do more in a book of this nature.

One would like, when face to face with acutely perplexing problems and circumstances of students, to live the life for them and translate them secretly into a larger consciousness. But the wish is vain; and were it possible, it would not be true growth, but a forced development, unable to stand the strong reactions which must come from day to day in the fulfilment of Karmic obligations.

We must proceed on our own, not on the borrowed strength of others. Indeed, that is the underlying truth of the technique in all its phases, and the way of it is precisely the many-sided and purposeful use of self in the largest sense.

I feel that these books will have served a good purpose if they emphasise to the student in the various grades of the Order that they must work their studies into the fabric of daily life, that reading and discussion have their place in accumulating facts and clarifying the mind, but that upon their own persistent and conscientious efforts alone can any real progress be achieved.

The advanced student knows this; but the neophyte is slow in realising it. His eagerness is laudable, his enthusiasm inspiring, but his anxiety and impatience hamper him at every step, and increase the responsibility of those who guide him.

Nothing that one can say to him can fully satisfy. There is a wisdom which comes of old experience which cannot be imparted; yet he will not believe that this experience is necessary. He is prone to believe that because he has read a certain corpus of literature and has by heart a reasonable amount of information regarding development, that therefore he is ready for the gift of deep insight and singular demonstration.

But the fact is, that this knowledge has not yet been worked out in experience: the circumstances of daily living have not yet brought him to the test of his knowledge, and nothing but the passage of time and the application of his life to those circumstances can bridge the gulf and open his inner vision to the adjustments to be made between the objective brain consciousness and that of the soul.

A young student of science may read the recorded researches and discoveries of the master scientists and feel himself very well versed in the subject; but these men have often wrestled with nature in the laboratory for a lifetime before they put pen to paper.

The living of life must precede the revealing of its technique. Let the neophyte be thankful that there are those who have trodden a few hard stages of the path and have been constrained by the Masters to record in the fire of their souls some fragments of their hard-won wisdom.

This is my message to him. If he has trust and devotion, and the patience of the true seeker, he will not have to wait long before the fire of his soul is kindled; and once launched upon the path of individual discovery, the successive steps of advancement will open to him as quickly as he is ready to ascend them.

Section 6:

The Modern Mystic and Monthly Science Review (1937 - 1947)

The Modern Mystic

VOL. 1. No. 2.   FEBRUARY 1937   2/-

Contents

	PAGE
Eleanor C. Merry — SOME SECRETS OF THE EGYPTIAN-DRUID AGE OF CULTURE	4
Cyril Scott — OCCULTISM, YOGA AND HEALTH	8
René Lagier — LA FRANCE MYSTIQUE	11
Raymund Andrea — THE GUIDING HAND	12
William Gerhardi — MY GREATEST EXPERIENCE	14
W. J. Turner — MUSIC AND DIALECTICAL MATERIALISM	16
Robert E. Dean — KABBALAH—THE TRADITIONAL LORE	18
Claire Cameron — POEMS	14–16–18
Shaw Desmond — WHAT WE REALLY KNOW ABOUT THE NEXT WORLD	23
Norman Adcock — THE MYSTERY OF ATLANTIS	26
The Editor — MAN AND HIS FAITHS	30
"Justifica" — EGYPTIAN MAGIC	32
René Pontoise — SCIENCE — A LAYMAN'S OBJECTIONS	34
W. J. Tucker — ASTROLOGICAL SUPPLEMENT	42

BOOK REVIEWS

TITLE	PUBLISHER	PAGE
THY KINGDOM COME	Ivor Nicholson & Watson, Ltd.	39
SHILOH	G. P. Putnam's Sons	39
SEVEN SYMBOLS OF LIFE	The Buddhist Lodge, London, 1936	39
VIENT DE PARAITRE	Edition Gallimard	39
LA BOURSE SUBIT-ELLE LES INFLUENCES PLANETAIRES ?	Editions J. Oliven, Paris	39
THE ASTROLOGY OF PERSONALITY	Lucis Publishing Co., New York	40
THE MEASURE OF LIFE	Stanley Nott, Ltd.	40
LES LOURDS SECRETS DE 1937	Denoel et Steele, Paris	40
LA SPHERE SENSITIVE	Editions "Sous le Ciel," Paris	Cover iii

OUR POINT OF VIEW

Introduction

Raymund Andrea wrote 23 articles for *The Modern Mystic and Monthly Science Review* (1937-1938) which was published by King, Littlewood and King. This Section consists of five of these articles. Other pieces not included here are the entire 12 chapters of *The Mystic Way* (King, Littlewood and King 1937) and a series of six biographical sketches of Bacon, Pascal, Rousseau, Saint-Martin, Goethe and Poe.[1] *The Mystic Way* was reprinted by Francis Bacon Lodge in 1982 and published under the title *The Mystic Path* by the English Grand Lodge for the Americas of the Rosicrucian Order a few years later.[2]

1. The Guiding Hand

Reprinted from the February 1937 edition of The Modern Mystic and Monthly Science Review

"There is a mystic guiding hand in the life of man."

There may be hard journeying through many eventful years before he realises it, yet even in youth this hand is laid softly upon the soul to keep it true to the compass of its destiny. But the ambitions of youth are many and strong, the hunger of the heart keen and insistent, and only after active search and eager essays along many paths..., which invite to achievement but end in disillusionment..., is the guiding hand recognised that points to the mystic quest.

Is there something sombre and suggestively unreal in this thought? If so, a man must wait until the force of ambition in the material realms has done its work. Because I am thinking of those who have run the gamut of emotion, taken the full measure of mental action and reaction, and returned with empty hands..., yet with full heart and mind..., to the same door whence they entered in. There is something unreal and discouraging about things when one so returns. He wonders what all the struggle has been for: the use and lesson, and the justice of it. He laments the time spent, if not wasted, which might have gone to something more enduring and peace giving. It is a fortunate awakening, and none other than the guiding hand laid softly upon the soul.

Those who have travelled far in this way and returned with empty hands and a burdened heart ask the same anxious question: *"Why should this be? If there is a guiding hand, why did it not hold me back from this or that long cycle of cruel experience, of disappointed hopes and frustrated aims, of misdirected efforts and false beliefs?"*

---

1. Revised editions of *The Mystic Way* and the six biographical sketches were released in 2009 and are available from the publisher.
2. *The Mystic Path* is currently [2009] out of print.

I think this is to mistake the meaning and purpose of the guiding hand. If life is a meaningless jumble of uncoordinated events, with no underlying purpose and no promise of the ultimate achievement of the soul's noblest vision, then we may question..., and in vain. But the guiding hand is in all: in conquest and in failure, in what we have done and in what we cannot do, in the years that have passed like a troubled sleep..., giving neither rest nor hope..., as in those in which trophies of victory mark our progress along life's highway.

We cannot mark off the good from the ill, victory from defeat, the firm step onward from the perplexing pause where no glimpse of a path is seen to choose. We cannot mark off the gift of incarnated life in this way, as if one part were God and the other part devil, and infer that the latter should not have been. The history of the whole journey is with us from the beginning, and the mystery of the guiding hand is with us to the end.

The questioning aspirant may take comfort from the fact that the lives of practically all who have trodden the mystic path have the same story to tell. Those who have gone far on that path are now in peace and certitude of soul because they have paid the price of attainment and entered into the fruition of their labours. They have vision, and the knowledge which comes of it; a faith which nothing can disturb or break, and a spiritual strength and magnetism which carry a blessing to all.

It was not so before their novitiate. They have, every one of them, passed over the troubled waters of life, explored with unresting heart every avenue that seemed to promise satisfaction and fulfilment, made inquisition with tireless persistence into religion, science and art: accepting, rejecting, ever accumulating along the way. The depths were sounded but the eternal hunger persisted. Everything failed them. Of only one thing were they certain amid the flux of desires and ambitions, manifold ideals and changing goals; and that was the unappeased soul, and an incentive to ceaseless search and enquiry. At length, weary of it all, the soul turned back upon itself. Experience in the three worlds had done its work and they stood, with empty hands, before the path of the mystic quest.

The strong soul, when it reaches this point, does not regret the past or question its value. It may not understand, or be able to reconcile the inconsistencies and contradictions of the journey, but it instinctively knows it has been well. It accepts the whole train of events as a necessary preparation for the mystical novitiate which lies before it. It recognises the laying of the foundation for future conquest. Everything on the way has been the subject of deep scrutiny and investigation. The thought of injustice has sometimes crept in. The mind has rebelled at its self-imposed confines and retreated many times from mistaken paths with hard names for its own blindness. But the cycle of self-discipline has been accomplished. Experience has built a structure of knowledge which will now be requisitioned for the mystic quest.

There have never been so many as today who are standing before the path of the mystic quest, or entering upon its novitiate. A large percentage of these students is of Christian persuasion and principles, but the Church has failed them. This is their own confession.

Section 6 - The Modern Mystic and Monthly Science Review (1937 - 1947)

Again and again one encounters seekers who enquire anxiously whether the following of the mystic path will diminish or take away their faith in the Christ life. It is a pathetic enquiry and reveals only too clearly how little orthodox religion has done or can do for them. If the teaching of the Church provided a self-discipline and a way of practical training for them, they would never feel this hunger of the soul for the reality of the spiritual life and be urged to enquire outside for it.

The fact is that it is not to the churches we look for the illuminated mystic and the spiritual man. These are found outside in the common ways of life, teaching..., by example and service and inspiration of the enlightened soul, the ancient way of divine development and attainment taught by Christ and by every other great teacher before and since His advent.

The controversies within the Church and the frantic efforts of its leaders to coordinate forces to meet what is called the "modern problem...," the irreligiousness of the people..., is sufficient proof that the tide of individual evolution has passed far beyond both: that the advance of the spirit within man is asserting itself and discarding the lifeless forms of orthodoxy. It is forcing man into the wilderness and to the mountain top to pray, alone, and divest himself of the narrowness and bigotry begot of creed and dogma. The Church has lost its hold upon the mind of the age, but instead of looking for the reason within itself it impugns the right of independent search of that advancing mind.

Nearly a century ago, a celebrated historian wrote:

> "The professional theologians alone are loud and confident, but they speak in the old angry tone which rarely accompanies deep and wise convictions. They do not meet the real difficulties; they mistake them; misrepresent them, claim victories over adversaries with whom they have never even crossed swords, and leap to conclusions with a precipitancy at which we can only smile. It has been the unhappy manner of their class from immemorial time; they call it zeal for the Lord, as if it were beyond all doubt that they were on God's side – as if serious inquiry after truth was something which they were entitled to resent."

It is for these students of life, who are seeking under the urge of the guiding hand, that the mystic quest opens a path of spiritual adventure. *"For,"* says a mystic classic, *"man creates his own life, and 'adventures are to the adventurous' is one of those wise proverbs which are drawn from actual fact, and cover the whole area of human life."* But adventures are for the strong soul which has something to build upon. That is why I refer to those who have taken the measure of life, sounded the depths of emotion and explored the far reaches of thought, and have the fullness of experience which can stand them in good stead in this adventure of the soul.

Fear of the unknown holds back thousands of otherwise ready aspirants from it. They will go as far as the general mind has gone, but no further. They must have the majority with them. They dare not push thought beyond the confines of the world they know: they tremble at an emotion that would carry them one step into the supersensible. If they would but forget themselves for one brief moment and relax their grasp upon the obvious and real!

This is what the adventure of the soul demands. Something must go that something else may take its place. The same man cannot be a changed one. That which he has known must become in his eyes relatively futile if he would welcome the opening portals of the mystical novitiate. For entering upon the novitiate means..., in the simplest terms..., a changed mental attitude, a looking within to the leading and impressions of the indwelling soul; instead of everlasting occupation with and immersion in, as hitherto, the life of the objective mind and sense life.

It means periodical withdrawal to the wilderness and the solitary place for the purpose of meditation and reassessment of life's values as seen in the quiet of the soul. The aspirant has to fall out of step with the self-seeking multitude and set up a new life rhythm within himself.

The initial colloquy with the soul, if undertaken under proper guidance, often proves to be contingent upon the type of aspirant..., the most momentous and decisive experience in his personal history. It is akin to the stillness in nature after the storm has spent itself. "*Such a calm will come to the harassed spirit, and in the deep silence the mysterious event will occur which will prove that the way has been found.*" Many, young and old, have testified to it; and from that moment the rhythm of life has been changed and they have gone forward to deeper assurance and insight.

Others have to wait longer at the portals, until the old rhythm they brought with them has fully spent itself and confidence in the new way is established. But it will not be long. How could it be, when at last they have recognised the presence of the mystical guiding hand which has brought them safely, if battle-scarred, through the pilgrimage of tribulation and sorrow to the quietude of the soul whose great hour has come?

There is now only the certainty of the sure guidance and the unfolding of intimate touches of the genius of the spirit within. And if, with perfect abandon, they will invocate that ever present genius of their life, the initial steps of the novitiate will have been taken.

2. The Mystical Novitiate

Reprinted from the March 1937 edition of The Modern Mystic and Monthly Science Review.

One whose province it is to contact many students entering upon the mystical novitiate and assist them with their various problems of advancement is faced with a personal problem of paramount importance. It is this: students approach and view their studies and development from very different and often unexpected angles of vision, and to fail in meeting this great diversity in types is to miss the finest opportunity of all that personal service affords.

Nothing therefore can replace the competent teacher who can so infuse his own soul content into the individual problems that arise, that new factors will emerge under the deep passion of full life experience which he brings to bear upon them. No formal procedure can be advocated for him to work upon, no stereotyped chart of the human soul which will apply to one and all, since nothing would prove so fatal to the swift responsiveness it is desired to evoke in the student.

The whole matter rests upon the ability to assume intuitively the viewpoint of the student, of subjective contact through the written or spoken word with his mental level and soul capacity, and of discerning just where the student is held by certain limitations of thought, or of particular development or its absence.

Among the diversity of students some outstanding types may be noted. One type may be very literal and appear only to need for his understanding and advancement that facts which he already knows should be rearranged and tabulated in a different sequence, or further explained under the impetus of a wider experience. He sees the truth of that which is presented to him, but it must be fashioned anew after the law of his own mental constitution. He must have these facts re-coined, so to speak, from the teacher's point of view and with further amplification by him.

If this is adequately done, with apt illustrations drawn from diversified reading to focus and enforce the main propositions even with unrelated material from remote and recondite sources, this type will not only accept the basic truth with complete mental acquiescence and with added understanding of the truth revealed, but the amplification will play an important part in that the imagination will be intrigued and stimulated, and that literalness in the type which is of great value in the cultivation of clarity of thinking will be offset and balanced by a more discursive habit which is the forerunner of mental inventiveness.

The second type is continually influenced and often hampered by his early religious and orthodox views, and should be treated with great tolerance. Those views no longer satisfy him, or he would not be seeking beyond them. But it is to be remembered that they constitute practically the whole content of the religious basis of his soul life, and those concepts of righteousness and daily conformity have made him the man he is and have brought him ultimately to realise their inadequacy to inspire and guide him in the larger sphere of spiritual culture and truth which he has now contacted.

It is here that the possibility arises of failing a student who is wholly ready to take the novitiate. No matter how narrow and hindering those concepts may appear, and known to be, in the eyes of the advanced soul, it is no less unwise than intolerant to attempt to brush them aside and belittle the very foundation upon which the student must build.

Those concepts should never be deliberately antagonised because they are foreign to the requirements and extended knowledge of the mystical path. There should rather be an endeavour to give them a non-theological application and set them in a larger relationship of thought and significance.

Moreover, such concepts will be seen to possess in themselves a real and conservative strength of distinct value in the life, and it is not desirable to attempt to demolish abruptly a groundwork of personal evolution upon which a more comprehensive edifice can be safely erected. There are cardinal virtues in the orthodox religionist which are stable, rational and immensely productive in their own sphere, and that which is built upon them will be the stronger and more permanent for their continuance.

The third type may be the recipient of certain psychic contacts and loves to introduce and emphasise these intimate experiences of personal vision either of symbol, dream, or mediumistic tendency. Their value may be negligible in the present connection and the undue prominence given to them may bias the student and prompt him to question the need of systematic instruction as the necessary basis to which these emergencies should be related. As in the case of the previous type, the attitude of one who guides such a student, so far from dismissing these intimations as of no value and beneath notice, would observe in their emergence the key to a specific phase of personal unfoldment which would be valuable in directing to a deeper causal understanding of them and relating them to future development.

Moreover, in the true mystical life of the novitiate symbol and dream are often indications of a phase of psychic awakening, and are to be welcomed when properly related to the basic soul culture in process. I have known a student to say that his great wish was to sit at the feet of the Masters of Wisdom and learn from them, but that he should consider the price too high if this meant giving up certain psychic work pursued by him at seances and thereby prove in any way disloyal to those whom God had seen fit to send into his life.

This case comes under the present type, and it need only be pointed out that no disloyalty to what has already been vouchsafed is required or necessary, but simply a diligent application to that teaching which he is offered during the novitiate. This will provide him with a rational and esoteric foundation to which he may relate those experiences he specially values. Experiences of this nature are often indications of the awakening and activity of psychic centres and therefore should not be discountenanced, but their relative value recognised. Nevertheless, this must be said: the mystical novitiate stands in no need of, nor does it countenance, spiritualistic procedure.

The fourth type is of a truly mental class. It is tenacious and logical and demands the how, why and wherefore of things. It is a valuable type, at the present point of evolution, and requires in the teacher a high degree of mental analysis to deal with his problems fully and firmly. Inadequacy and vacillation are apt to disgust or disappoint him.

This type learns rapidly in his own way. All the elements of the instruction are immediately seized, related and adjusted to a progressive mentality. It is basically occult rather than mystical in character, hence with a view to balanced development it will be from the subjective and intuitional aspect that he will need to be prompted to initiate new effort. This type, which is capable of so much on the path, often defeats himself through the very logic which marks his mastery.

For the mind, which is ever a most potent instrument in the mystic, yet stands attentive and obedient to the finer touches of the soul's intuition. The soul does not weaken logic, never annuls it, but clarifies and leads it beyond the frontiers of the circumscribed mental realm. And it is during the stages of the novitiate that this repolarisation has to be accomplished.

As a final type, which however by no means exhausts the list, one may be indicated beautiful as it is rare, which stands beyond all the others. He is a spiritual soul demonstrating balance and proportion in vision and statement, both dreamer and thinker, and in his work and service manifests the strength and pathos of poetry and truth.

This is the type which has, in the fullest sense, a rich past. He has really advanced far along the path; his vibration is high and stable; his fullness of experience and sense of attunement with cosmic forces render him at once ready for the novitiate in its true form. He can quickly become a helper of the little ones, for his influence is comprehensive and penetrating. In him the divine life is in rapid evolution, and every opportunity should be afforded him to extend his knowledge and increase his responsibility in the work of the path.

One should never fail this type through want of spiritual sensitivity and discernment. Deep should answer deep with complete understanding and love, for the Master sends this man to do his own work.

Having considered some of the types of aspirants, it will be useful to consider what may be expected to be the attitude of one to whom they look for suggestion and guidance in their specific problems of advancement. And first, regarding his attitude towards the mystical life to which he commits himself for strength and inspiration.

His knowledge of the relationship between the soul and the Cosmic will give an attitude which is peculiar and distinctive, yet simple and direct, unencumbered and unbiased by creed and dogma, and making no appeal to the realm of controversial theology. He will be satisfied with the pure experience of feeling experimentally that he is accessible within to the periodical inflow of a power greater than he knows, and which makes the personal life vital and purposeful in the way of service.

His attitude to this power will not be one of passivity; it will be more of the nature of an instinctive blending and cooperating with that which comes to him spontaneously and unexpectedly; although this spontaneous visitation will probably only be experienced as the culmination of a series of aspirational invitations self-initiated over a considerable period of time.

If he has reached that point in spiritual evolution where he realises that he is in the very texture of his nature a devotee, he will find that this reciprocal response between the soul and the Cosmic is a normal feature and function of his constitution. He may be incapable of giving any very significant demonstration to others of the existence of this response, for the reason that, being an entirely spiritual condition, it is not susceptible of intellectual proof, or perhaps even of ordinary artistic expression. Yet, so potent is this contact within its own sphere, that the whole life of the devotee, even though discountenancing or little regarding accepted religious observances, will unconsciously demonstrate all the essential qualities of the mystical union, and will the more effectively do so because it is unconfined and in no way straitened or deflected by denominational adherence.

This inward attitude will determine very materially his attitude towards those he contacts in service. For this mystical union, so deep and real, much resembles nature herself in its simplicity and expressiveness and must prove highly inspirational in the realm of human contact.

Men can only recognise what their evolution permits, and they will interpret in accordance with that evolutionary standard. Yet it is true that the tone of the devotee can awaken a measure of response in all. This is to be expected, seeing that all souls are one and subjectively in contact with the Cosmic life.

Men often desire the mystical life fervently even when they seek it least; and for this reason they feel the blessedness of union in another though incapable themselves of the merest utterance of it. Herein is an incentive to high endeavour on the part of those whose evolutionary development indicates a special and personal responsibility in exerting the mystical processes in their immediate vicinity and influencing others, perhaps unconsciously, to take the first steps in spiritual culture. It may be added that their special work may sometimes consist mainly in this exertion of the soul's blessing which the peace of the union diffuses in the consecrated heart, thus making him in truth a redeemer of men.

It will be understood that the above-mentioned attitude, that of the soul towards the Cosmic life and the complementary one of efficient expression towards his fellow students, is sought with fervent intention to evolve within himself the Christ consciousness. It is a great attainment to have become stabilised in this consciousness and be able to exercise its spiritual attributes. It is genius of the first magnitude, and gives purpose and persistence and the influence of the highest attributes decreed in this earthly pilgrimage.

Long may we have to travel before we dwell in the Christ in its threefold expression. Some have the Christ will to do, some demonstrate to a degree the Christ love, others have somewhat the directing mind of Christ. And the greater the unfolding of these three attributes of the mystical consciousness, the more potent will be our influence in the way of service.

We seek the mind that can intuit truth under every aspect, the love that can respond to the heart of all, the will that can execute what that mind and love dictate. The gradual perfecting of this threefold development of the essential life has a twofold result of much significance. So intimate is the connection between the three aspects of the overshadowing Cosmic life that, by a steady dwelling in the Christ nature through meditation, aspiration and service as taught in the Great Work, a process of transmutation takes place in the objective life on the one side, and a sympathetic response of the Cosmic life to the vibration of the Christ consciousness within may be assumed on the other.

This response may have to be taken for granted for some time. By analogy we can be sure of its existence. Through profound inwardness of life we shall feel and impart its influence without any special consciousness of it. I believe that the most sacred peace and suffusing compassion that withdraw the devotee at rare intervals apart from everything mundane and sensuous is in its intrinsic nature divine, of the Christ consciousness itself, and is a promise of that blessed overshadowing and guidance of the Cosmic Spirit, when the Son has sacrificed his threefold life that He and the Father might be one.

3. On The Mystic Path

Reprinted from the April-May 1937 edition of The Modern Mystic and Monthly Science Review

The mystical novitiate has for its objective the awakening in good time of the Christ nature in the aspirant. This experience lies at the heart of the mystical life. We can only expect to know the Christ in spirit and in truth when this awakening becomes a fact of experience.

The master mystics are unanimous in their declaration of the reality and importance of this experience. Whatever the symbols in which they express the fact, the realisation and wonder of it shines forth unmistakably and reveals possibilities for our common humanity which will dignify every activity and bless untellably.

Every recorded instance of the awakening has a long history of preparation behind it, a preparation sometimes unconscious, but usually directed to this end through years of inward struggle and aspiration, intense unrest and varied discipline. Nature reveals not her treasures to the indolent, and the mystic glory broods hidden and silent within the veils of mortality, awaiting the insistent passion of the Christ love to set it free.

The main feature of the approach to this stage is that of inward unrest, continuous readjustment, and the longing after a precious possession which is instinctively known to belong to us by right as aspirants on the path. We become as children on this path, in many ways as helpless as they, and Nature often seems to conspire against us.

We knew nothing of the sorrow of the soul until the spirit quickened in the recesses of the heart. Had we continued of the world as well as in it, we had been spared the keen opposition of forces that range themselves unseen against the awakening sons of God. Yet we would not return. We cannot return. We have passed beyond the strong rampart of the mental selfhood; we have felt the subtle influences of an undiscovered country; and we travail together until the Master appears.

Let us not turn from this thought as recondite or remote. It is a fact of the path.

Every great literature confirms it. It is written large in every scripture of the way. It is an unalterable condition, a law of the inner life, a covenant between the Christ of the soul and the Cosmic. Search as we will, there is no other way in which we can know the height and depth of love and life but in passing the mortal selfhood through the fires of mystical suffering and death. Nor can we become a real spiritual help to others until we know *"the divine sorrow at the heart of things."* The whole mystical Hierarchy is a living testimony to the fact.

At the beginning of the quest some of us think only of the bliss of awakening to divinity; but that thought is speedily changed as we draw nearer to the divine. We desire passionately to understand. We crave for the right conception of the human heart, the unfailing healing touch, the potent word of power that shall unerringly accomplish its purpose. Long the struggle lasts, for a will greater than our own compels, but eventually the prayer is answered, a clearer vision of the way is given; and the novitiate is passed.

At this point of unfoldment, when the Christ impulse is active in the soul, the mystic feels the necessity of moulding his life after the pattern of the Ideal Man. Much has already been accomplished. The probation which lies behind has forced into prominence all the characteristics which are now required and which he will work upon and develop on the way to union.

This is an encouraging fact. For years the aspirant has been struggling upwards, and amid all the conflicts of life the divine seed has been planted and has silently come to fruition, until he realises that the probationary stage has been covered and the base metals of his nature transmuted. He has gained strength through obedience, insight from darkness and perplexity, and now accepts willingly and unreservedly the life of the Cross. It is this attitude alone which enables him to *"withdraw from everything, even himself."*

"Deny thyself and take up the Cross." So wrote the author of the *Imitation of Christ* in his chapter on "The highway of the holy cross." The words are familiar enough from earliest days, but in the devotional setting of St. Thomas they come back to us with a new meaning. Yet it is not St. Thomas who gives the deeper significance. It is the experience the years have wrought in us that reveals in the words the law of the soul's evolution, and the note of that experience blends with that of the admonition of the mystic as he unfolds all the implications of the pregnant injunction of the Master.[3]

And in the famous Rosicrucian document known as the *Fama Fraternitatis* we meet with the fervent avowal: *"To me Jesus is all things."* Could there be more conclusive assurance for the enquirer who asks whether the mystical life would take away the simple faith he has in Christ? Well is it with him if he realises the Christ as these early mystics did. There is a beauty, simplicity and other-worldliness in their utterances which captures the heart and makes the mind introspective toward the divine.

"Withdraw from everything, even thyself." *"Deny thyself and take up the Cross."* These

---

[3]. *"The Imitation of Christ"* is included in a collection of lectures by the author entitled *The Way Of The Heart* which is available from the publisher.

are the old challenges and there is no escape from them. They have to be met in the mystical experience. How much they imply! I anticipate the backward, reflective glance of some who have taken a few steps on the way, to whose memory return strains of the music and discord of the past, but who pause before these challenges which seem to demand so much.

This is understandable. But the path does not demand what we are unable to give. Through constant withdrawal into the soul a new life is awakened which neither breaks nor destroys that which has been sedulously built into the personality. It is, we may say, discriminative and selective in its influence, accentuating and increasing the virtue and magnitude of all that would truly minister to the inner life, and weakening the force and hold of all that would hinder its growth.

It is here that some aspirants make trouble for themselves. Instead of trusting to the law of growth innate in the soul, they wilfully force the pace of evolution beyond what they can really bear and suffer for it mentally or physically, accordingly. Moreover, they overlook the operation of the law of cycles in life, the ebb and flow of activity, the oscillations of progress and retrogression, which condition all advancement.

They fully recognise these conditions in ordinary life, whether they can explain them or not. They know only too well that life does not run smoothly along a straight line, that the days and weeks often show painful contrasts; and by the time they reach manhood they take this as a matter of course and with a degree of indifference. Yet when these alternations and contrasts in mind and emotion come upon them with added and peculiar emphasis on the path, as they inevitably must, they lose their indifference, and faith and perseverance have something against which to measure themselves. It is the pull of the opposites. One is losing ground and endeavouring to hold it. The other, in the ascendant, is gathering strength and is resolved to maintain it. It is just there that the aspirant is put on trial, and for a long time.

The path does not demand what we are unable to give, but it does demand that the soul shall give what it can. And it is because we live so much in the personality that we have so poor a conception of how much the soul can give, surrender and do.

"*Look for the Warrior,*" says the scripture, "*and let him fight in thee.... Obey him, as though he were thyself, and his spoken words were the utterance of thy secret desires, for he is thyself, yet infinitely wiser and stronger than thyself.*"[4] The condition we are examining could not be more aptly portrayed. The Warrior is the soul now in the ascendant, and on the path it must become more and more dominant. It becomes so, not by ascetical practice or fanatical procedure, but by assuming constantly the vantage point of the soul and by viewing life and living it from that altitude until the personal life falls into line and looks to its mentor for leading and direction.

Wherever the emphasis of life is placed, there will be its strength. If upon the personal self, the voice of the soul will be lost in dictate and direction and life proceed on

---

4. From *Light on the Path* (1888) by Mabel Collins.

its customary level. If upon the soundless voice within, that waits to move us by hint and intuition to larger and finer issues, then withdrawal and denial will soon become facts of experience and give new strength and peace.

That is the retreat into the life of the soul. It is the life of contemplation, so very satisfying that many make it their goal. But it is not enough in these crucial days. We are called to take up the Cross of life. There is no escaping the Cross on the mystical path. This is a fact not easily accepted by many students. They take knowledge and comply with the conditions leading to larger life and experience: henceforth they feel that everything should go well with them.

They forget that every phase of life and unfoldment has its difficulties and tests. They would be the first to acknowledge how soundly they have been tested and what difficulties they have had to encounter, and how necessary all this was in the past to bring them to clearer mental vision and stability and of value in their chosen spheres. Why should the unfoldment of the soul be less painful and perplexing than that of the mind? It is the law of all growth.

Can a man reverse the momentum of his life, pass from the life of personality to that of the soul, without knowing from experience what it means to renounce the one that he might live in the other? The personality is separate, self-interested and self-seeking, possessive and drawing ceaselessly to itself to augment its importance and prestige on the material plane. The soul is one with all souls and demands that the incommunicable burden of all souls shall be shared by it. The hard demands made upon the personal life are many and may well justify to the aspirant his inability to recognise the equally hard demands of the soul.

He will excuse himself in the name of the former, but the time comes when the choice must be made, consciously, wilfully, with open eyes and full understanding of all it implies. Then the Cross is for him no longer merely a symbol of what once was, but a fact of storied experience within the heart. It is that experience which makes the mystical path what it is, different in character for each aspirant, but resulting in all in a willing surrender of the personal attitude that the soul may be dominant and direct the whole life.

4. The Three Wise Men

Reprinted from the December 1938 edition of The Modern Mystic and Monthly Science Review. *Also published in the Winter 1993 issue of the* Rosicrucian Beacon.

With the coming of Christmas the mind of the mystical student turns reverently to the thought of the advent of Christ to the world. He will cast his mind in retrospect across the years and particularly the present year and ask himself what signs there are that the Christ Spirit is coming again to the world in its guidance and influence.

Section 6 - The Modern Mystic and Monthly Science Review (1937 - 1947)

His hopes had been raised as he progressed along the mystic way, that soon some sign would be manifested of a special outpouring of divine illumination, a kind of fruition of the consecrated efforts of all aspirants and disciples. Indeed, from many sources he had been taught to expect this second coming of Christ in His members. The call had gone forth from the inner place of the Hierarchy to combine forces for this event.

What is he now to think? His hopes have been dashed because the prophecy has failed to materialise. And now, at this season, when the heart turns more strongly to peace and good will and would demonstrate with renewed dedication the mind of Christ, the world without carries upon its face all the signs of the crucifixion hour. Stern trial, disappointment and humiliation, strife of tongues, the cross-purposes of men and nations, crimination and recrimination, threat and retaliation..., what gifts are these that men are bringing to celebrate the birth hour of Christ!

Whatever the misgivings the aspirant may have as he surveys the path of humanity and the present hour, one thought will refuse to be silenced and will grip him with its living and potent strength: no matter what the chaotic and warring elements that make the people rage and imagine a vain thing, the Christ Spirit cannot fail.

Many times during the past year I have asked myself what was the intention of the Higher Powers in their plan for stricken humanity. How many have asked the same question, most of all those who have given their all in service to those Powers but no answer has been vouchsafed.

Perhaps we have no right, in our humble standing, to expect an answer in any way satisfactory to the objective interrogating consciousness which questions, demands and ultimately receives its solutions through concentrated act of will in the ordinary ways of life. For we, however relatively advanced some of us may be, are but humble servants in the hands of the mighty Cosmic process of evolution.

If we had access to the Councils of the Higher Powers we should no doubt glimpse the plan as it is there unfolded to the minds of the Masters of life. Even so, it is doubtful how much of that plan we should be permitted to express and how far that expression would atone to a humanity in the throes of a new birth of consciousness through the pain and turmoil, anxiety and uncertainty and the haunting shadow of fear which hold millions in thrall.

Some have said that they could not believe the Cosmic Powers would ever permit such a catastrophe as threatens to materialise. But can we place the burden of responsibility on the Higher Powers? The thought of man is potent for life or death. We know there is no escape from the undeviating law of cause and effect. We know that as we think, forepicture and plan, so will it be unto us.

"The mind," says the great poet, *"is its own place and in itself can make a heaven of hell, a hell of heaven."* And if the minds of men, with a full knowledge of the law, deliberately and wilfully plot and scheme and build a devilish dweller of the threshold which hides the light of Christ from His own, can we lay the responsibility at the door of the Higher

Powers? It is the mind of man which has brought the nations to the gates of hell. Only the mind of man can prevent a descent into the abyss.

What the Higher Powers might presumably do, in the name of pity and compassion, is, at some point of climax, to work a calculated intervention by a reversal of law, in order to avert a doom which perverted thinking has rendered almost inevitable and demonstrate the power of Christ to the world by a divine miracle. Can we expect or hope for this? It would not remove the guilt of man which made such an intervention necessary. It would prove his utter responsibility for it.

This responsibility is man's and it is rooted in the hatred, distrust and suspicion of men. This threefold cord of evil is rampant in the modern world and it has well nigh submerged the mind of Christ which good men have persistently shown forth in it. At times it has been so appalling in its intensity, that the threefold good of love, kindness and goodwill as it was and is in the Christ Spirit seemed to have failed those who had staked all upon it.

I asked in these pages not so long since, feeling the despair of those who thought with me, where is the man so like Christ and man to so align and project the forces of good as to oppose and abolish forever the rule of tyranny and inhumanity? There was no answer and the evil progressed and conquered. And now, millions of good men and the aspirants and disciples of the world, raise one hand in entreaty to the Christ of peace and are compelled in the cause of justice to lower the other to grasp the sword.

I pity in my soul the devout mystic in these days. In his soul peaceful, harmless and Christlike in his service, the oppression of insolent tyrants strikes upon that sensitive organism like a cruel blow to the flesh and demands that he shall not remain neutral and voiceless but that the law of retribution shall be fulfilled. He is faced with stern alternatives. He may share in the cry for justice which echoes around him from righteous men who bear the stamp of universal right and goodness in their hearts; or he may bank upon the thought of goodwill and love of the Christ mind, believing in its ultimate rule and thereby foster and ostensibly encourage that very oppression in the world which he is ashamed to think of.

He is driven..., I cannot put it otherwise..., either to condone the wilful persecution and suffering of his fellowmen and at one and the same time to show forth the mind of Christ and also be a participator in building the preventive means and instrumentalities, the tools of destruction and suffering, to arrest the swift progress of organised tyranny and oppression.

These are the hard facts which face the mystic. Nor does he face them alone. They confront right-thinking men everywhere. The many recent broadcasts from men in various stations of life and responsibility attest the presence of this same tormenting perplexity. They have done good and it seems to have failed, completely. They would do good but cannot. They look for a superhuman leadership which is not forthcoming. They stand at a parting of the ways as crucial, if not more so, as that which faces the disciple in his inner ascent on the mystic way.

They are ready to pay any price if only the right thing be done. What is the absolutely right thing they cannot decide. Good men of the world, spiritually-minded men of the church, aspirants and disciples who have believed that at last the mystical influence abroad would triumph and carry all to higher levels of divine living and doing, stand undecided between two opinions and confess it. In countless cases their very faith in the goodness of providence is on trial and none more severely on trial than those who have travelled the mystic way and taught the truth of it. Never was a time when the truth that the disciple's Karma is inextricably bound up with the world Karma so forcibly driven home.

A thought prominent in the minds of aspirants in the face of present events is, that because they are upon some stage of the mystic way, they are in a somewhat privileged position of exemption from implication in national and international Karma; that their peculiar faith and belief, much in advance as these are of general faith and belief, justify them in expecting that what they stand for must prevail and at least modify the operation of that Karma insofar as themselves are concerned.

But is there ground for this opinion? It is fully granted that the aspirant, by virtue of his sanely directed thought life and his spiritual aspiration and communion, opens himself to a guidance and protection which the average individual can scarcely claim. The more fully he lives and acts from the vantage point of the soul, the more will he become a focal point for the reception of forces for good in his life. But he is not an isolated person living within a charmed circle of divine and favourable influence unrelated to and unmodified by the world of form in which he must participate. He is part and parcel, physically, emotionally and mentally, of the world form striving for adjustment amid innumerable conflicting ideals and whether he will or no he is drawn into the tide of world evolution.

Moreover, it is estimated that the projection of evil, or shall we say, of ill trained thought, is vastly in excess of the projected good in the world. How far true this estimate is, I am not prepared to say. The world conditions of the past year might provide something of the nature of a commentary.

The idea of exemption from participation is really a vain one for the aspirant on the way. He becomes, as I have often said, through his soul development, a participator in the soul atmosphere of all and there is no escape from that atmosphere. It is the registration of it by the sensitive soul that is the cause of his present perplexity and distress. He is sensitive on the one side to the beauty, peace and strength of the Christ mind; and on the other no less to the suffering of his fellowmen and he cannot remain indifferent to it. Inclusion and participation are the key factors in his development; and to expect exemption from those influences which these must inevitably bring to him is illogical and unworthy.

The plea comes to him from the Masters' own world to *"give your aid to the few strong hands that hold back the powers of darkness from obtaining complete victory. Then do you enter into a partnership of joy, which brings indeed terrible toil and profound sadness but also a great and ever increasing delight."* It is a plea to him to accept the toil and sadness which are his through the sensitivity he has invoked by his aspiration to divine service and to live and fight constructively in his own place for the ideal of the Christ life in which he believes implicitly and which he trusts shall triumph over the powers of darkness.

I have turned in retrospect to the events of the year because its shadow has been deep and impenetrable and the effects of it are still with us. But we look forward with a kindling hope, as we are wont to do at this season, remembering that the tide of thought will be with us as we reaffirm our dedication to the greatest of Masters, knowing that the most sacred gifts we can offer to Him and the world at this time are those same gifts which the three Magi brought and laid before the feet of the newborn Christ.

The selection of these three wise men by the Great White Brotherhood and gift offering they were to make, has a beautiful significance for us. Kaspar was chosen because he had overcome lust, which is symbolised by his gift of refined gold; Melchior had overcome pride and his gift was frankincense; and Balthazar, because of his conquest of hate, brought myrrh. The Magi had an enlightened knowledge of their secret mission and their gifts signified their consciousness of Christ's greatness and were symbolic of His divine nature. As one of the church Fathers has said:

> "They offer gold as to the great King; they offer up incense as to God, because it is used in the Divine Sacrifice; and myrrh, which is used in embalming the bodies of the dead, is offered as to Him who is to die for the salvation of all. And hereby we are taught to offer gold, which symbolises wisdom, to the new born King, by the lustre of our wisdom in His sight; incense, which signifies fervour in prayer if our constant praise mounts up to God with an odour of sweetness; and myrrh, which signifies mortification of the flesh."

Can we paraphrase and apply this regal symbolism for our immediate need and comfort and for the helping of the world? By the overcoming of the lust of life of the personal self, the wisdom of the soul shines forth as refined gold; by the dethronement of pride through the fervour of inner communion with the Christ Spirit, we show forth the gentleness and humility of the sacred heart of Jesus; and in conquering hate by the martyrdom of evil thought, we show forth the mind of Christ in pity and compassion for the suffering world. Is there any greater thing we can do, after all our reading and discussion and many tossings of troubled thoughts? I know of none.

This is our one responsibility to the Higher Powers and our fellowmen. It lies heavily upon good men and especially so upon those of us who take the mystic way. We are called to put away from us all conflicting issues, much as they intrude upon us, over which we have no control and to which heated opinion can but add renewed perplexity and consider the kind gifts we are offering to the Christ coming to birth in humanity. For the hope of the world is when men, wise and enlightened, with transmuted natures, come from the four quarters of the earth to pay tribute to the Christ Spirit born within their own redeemed hearts and give themselves as a willing sacrifice for the redemption of all.

The supereminence and incomprehensibility of the power of Christ are shown by the indomitable faith which nothing in the world or of the world can erase from the hearts of good men. It is the one divine miracle amid the chaos of nations. I wonder if that is the answer to the question we have asked. We have asked whether the Higher Powers, through their far-seeing vision of the plan of humanity's evolution and through their unquestionable knowledge of its tragic impasse, might sanction an intervention of special power and guidance to carry it safely through its hour of rebirth. But has not the key to the situation been long since given to us in the coming of the Magi to honour the advent of the Prince of Peace and in the three cardinal virtues symbolised by the gifts they brought to Him?

The three Magi were in themselves representative of the three virtues which signified a perfect manifestation of divinity, the only gift which was worthy of offering to One who was the perfection of creation. And search as we may through the whole range of our culture of knowledge and wisdom, we shall find no other key to the solution of our world problem, than in the acceptance and practice of the Magian rite which the coming of Christmas once again forces upon our minds.

In our status of aspirants and disciples on the path, it is incumbent upon us to set a peculiar example in this respect. We have taken our stand for the higher values of life. We are pledged in the name of the soul to the Higher Powers. We cannot be as those who have not taken knowledge. We have sought the Christ Spirit in the inner place and we know there has been response according to our capacity of reception of its influence. We have read much of the divine plan of evolution but even though we know nothing experimentally of it nor can prophesy one day of what it has in store for us, the compass of faith must not vary a hair's breadth from the point at which we have set it.

That may be dogmatic faith; it is also the voice of the soul. In our work on the path we have sought to renounce step by step the personal self and live from the soul; and to the degree we are able to do this shall we present to Christ the gift of the refined gold of wisdom for the building of the temple of the new age. Through the gift of ascending incense of deeper communion with the Christ Spirit will the manifold forms of pride and intellect be dissipated and the harmlessness which cannot give offence will be born in us. And by steadily disengaging ourselves from the glamour of the world atmosphere and mortifying the evil thought which it seeks to raise in us, the gift of myrrh to the Christ, who travails with us until now, will be the redeemed love which can never fail.

5. Crises In Development

Reprinted from the April 1947 edition of The Modern Mystic and Monthly Science Review, *and from the October 1946 edition of the* Rosicrucian Digest.

> "For the radical and permanent transformation of personality only one effective method has been discovered..., that of the mystics. It is a difficult method, demanding from those who undertake it a great deal more patience, resolution, self-abnegation and awareness than most people are prepared to give; except perhaps in times of crisis, when they are ready for a short while to make the most enormous sacrifices.
>
> "But unfortunately the amelioration of the world cannot be achieved by sacrifices in moments of crisis. It depends on the efforts made and constantly repeated during the humdrum, uninspiring periods, which separate one crisis from another, and of which normal lives mainly consist."[5]

I have quoted this passage from Aldous Huxley, the biographer and novelist, not because he is a professed teacher of mysticism, or, so far as I know, himself a mystic, but because he intimates in it a fundamental truth about mystical development. In his sketch of the life of Father Joseph, the Catholic priest, and a power politician and collaborator of Cardinal Richelieu, Huxley expatiates on the mystical aspect as well as the political aspect of his subject, and very efficiently.

In fact, if he is not himself a mystic, he has certainly taken pains to inform himself, through the guidance of acknowledged mystical writings, of the method of discipline followed by the mystics of the early schools of thought, a discipline which the world is sadly in need of today.

During recent years the professional novelist, in an endeavour to appear thoroughly up to date and in line with the progressive thought of the time, has often given us the so-called mystical or psychological novel, as being calculated to seize the imagination of many who are attracted by the mysterious or uncanny, presented in a simple and arresting terminology. This type of literary work is not new.

Many such stories have come down to us from the past, but with this important difference: they have usually been enlightening records of personal mystical experience..., serious, authentic, and non-fictitious; whereas the modern counterfeits drag into their service the doctrine of reincarnation, astonishing feats of clairvoyance, and diabolic excursions into the realm of black magic.

They may divert the mind for a moment from the prosaic routine of everyday life like the latest detective story; but they pass with the reading and are forgotten. For if this is indeed reincarnation, what a fearsome business it must be. If this is clairvoyance, what a

---

5. *Grey Eminence* by Aldous Huxley, published in London, 1941.

Section 6 - The Modern Mystic and Monthly Science Review (1937 - 1947)

curse it must be to humanity. If these tricks of black magic are true, how eternally vigilant we must be to escape the effects of them.

This is the stuff of the modern writer of the occult novel, and sorry stuff most of it is. Hence the pleasure in reading a passage like that which I have quoted above, by a professional novelist, from a biographical sketch which, if admitting of some fictional touches, is mainly based upon facts; historical facts. For rarely has a mystical character been so truly placed in its native setting, or the conflicting elements in so powerful a character been presented with so much understanding and propriety.

However, I am interested here in the sober conclusion at which Huxley arrives after his survey of the life of Father Joseph and the mystical discipline which made him an outstanding character of his time. It is true that the holy monk fell from grace in the eyes of his biographer because, almost unconsciously, he carried his mysticism over the forbidden frontier into the realm of power politics and became involved in affairs of state and war which it is not easy to reconcile with a professed contemplative and disciple of Christ. But that does not diminish his tremendous influence as a mystic of high degree and a man of exemplary self-abnegation and achievement.

Huxley is fully sensible of this, and looking back over this richly coloured life and the mysticism which had fashioned it, he concludes that there is but one effective method by which the transformation of personality can be attained, and that is the method of the mystics.

The term mystic is a general and inclusive one. The Rosicrucians are mystics; and the aspirants of many cults and schools of thought claim to be mystics. Some schools distinguish between the mystic and occultist, as if the path of the one were diametrically opposite to that of the other, although the goal of both is fundamentally the same. Both seek supersensible knowledge through the unfoldment of higher faculties of cognition, the extension of consciousness and culture of sensitivity and increasing responsiveness to unusual vibrational rhythms and impulses.

However a technique of procedure may differ in subsequent detail, contingent upon temperament, education and Karmic propensity, the same basic method underlies both of them: study, discipline, meditation, demonstration, and contact with the indwelling divine consciousness and the application of the fruits of inspiration to the enlightenment of man.

As Rosicrucians, we teach that what constitutes the mystic is a conscious attunement with divinity and the Cosmic, which comes from knowledge and the ability to apply and use the laws of God and nature constructively. If the mystic is said to follow more specifically the way of the heart, and the occultist the way of the head, we accept that discrimination and as Rosicrucians endorse it; for we combine union with Christ with the scientific procedure of the same Great Master who in Himself set the perfect example of compassion and love and the demonstration of the laws of God and nature before the eyes of men.

No matter what name we choose to give it, the mystical procedure demands, as Huxley states, a great deal more than the majority are prepared to give, *"except perhaps in times of crisis, when they are ready for a short while to make the most enormous sacrifices."* This was written before the enormous sacrifices made by countless people under the demand of the world war. Indeed, so great have been those sacrifices made by so many that it might have been thought that a wave of mysticism had swept over the nations instead of that of the spirit of conquest.

I am no optimist about the wave of mysticism; I was about the spirit of conquest. I discerned little of the former; the latter was overwhelming and sure. People prepared to make enormous sacrifices under the demand of a perilous war are not necessarily mystics; nor do such sacrifices make a mystic, although they may prove to be something of a preparation for advancement into a larger life. But, as Huxley truly says, *"amelioration of the world cannot be achieved by sacrifices in moments of crisis."*

Not in these days, but a few years ago we often beheld the entertaining spectacle of a fervent revivalist proclaiming to millions and threatening all and sundry with damnation if they did not straightway repent of their abominable sins and follow the leader. This is neither mysticism nor sanity. What happened to the repentants a year later, nobody knows. The "moments of crisis" passed, as they always do, and more sober thoughts ensue.

I do remember some periods of crisis in mysticism within the past thirty years, revivalistic in nature, when humanity seemed to be on the verge of a great illumination. They also passed, as did the others. Whether another wave will come now the war is over, and as a result of it, I cannot say. I see no sign of it.

Undoubtedly, many have turned their minds to the deeper issues of life, because crises of suffering and loss have driven them to it; and these will presumably show an interest in higher development and take the first steps on the path. But, the fundamental tension being over, the majority, even most of those who have sacrificed most, will revert very nearly to the former plane of living.

I have little faith in religious revivalistic waves, or in waves of mysticism. What may appear to some to indicate a mystical revival, I believe to be to a large extent a reaction to the fear of imminent death. To some that may not sound very complimentary, but I am a psychologist and prefer the truth. I am not interested in soothing statements or occult platitudes.

Nightly, for months, I have stood and waited, with countless others, under the bombing of the enemy, faced with the prospect, if not the expectation, of imminent death; and I know the kind of reaction that condition is calculated to produce upon serious-minded and religious people. It made them wonder and question about the possibilities of life beyond the flesh; and it is only natural that many of them, now the trial is passed, should wish to follow up that dire questioning and seek for more light.

But that is no indication of a wave of mysticism, or of the attainment of a higher level of consciousness. It is the attitude of thinking persons having become conscious

Section 6 - The Modern Mystic and Monthly Science Review (1937 - 1947)

under the pressure of events of their ignorance of a department of culture which would bring fuller life and understanding and a peace and sense of security regarding the future which they had neglected and now feel prompted to take action to remedy. Now that the crisis has passed which stirred them deeply, it remains to be seen what efforts they will make for themselves during the humdrum, uninspiring period which ensues and precedes the next crisis.

There is another aspect of this matter of periods of crisis which is of considerable interest to those on the path. This applies to us who are making our way along the definite stages of it. We are acquainted only too well with the humdrum uninspiring periods when nothing seems to happen to distinguish us with all our good intention and effort, from those who make no effort at all but take life as it comes.

The fault is largely in ourselves, not in our circumstances, that the pattern of our lives remains fixed and uninspiring and inwardly uneventful. We are pledged too rigidly to the word of mysticism, instead of living in the spirit of it. Sometimes a really live and progressive student writes to me of a series of crises in his life which of course had not been foreseen and the possibility of which he could never have anticipated. The whole programme of his life pattern has been altered as by a swift blow of relentless fate, and he finds the extreme difficulty of adjusting to it, and greater still the difficulty of assigning a meaning for it. But I have seen the good arising from this apparent evil at the first mention of it. This is the very law of the ascension of the soul.

Evolution in nature is usually so silent and imperceptible that we are unaware of it. But the awakening soul, with the Karma of a hidden past pulsating within it and insisting upon expression and completion, can thunder and lighten throughout the personal domain of the man who has strongly evoked it, and create such a turmoil of thought and emotion as to threaten the foundations of a well-balanced life. And the reaction of the aspirant to this kind of crisis will be according to his formal adherence to the word of the path or his ability of flexible adjustment to the puissant and moving spirit of it.

In the former case, he will be shocked and disappointed and perhaps regard askance the word in his hands and his faith in it, because life has not run true to the form of it; in the latter case he will stand back, alert, poised and obedient to the leading of the soul that announces itself so peremptorily through its cultured instrument.

It is not for nothing that these crises come to the advancing soul. They are a condition of that advancement. So true is this in the history of mysticism that I regard with some misgiving an aspirant who congratulates himself on the smoothness and uneventfulness of the path.

Mastery never comes of this. The very word mastery rejects such an idea. I have never known an aspirant to attain to any degree of mastery on the path without having had a hard struggle for it. I would disillusion any who think otherwise, whatever their present experience may be.

A man cannot evoke the living soul in all sincerity without having, sooner or later, to meet the response to that challenge. And it is well that it should be so; for if his word of service is ever to carry the inspirational force of the Spirit of God to men, he must descend into the hell of mortal and wounded human nature with Christ and rise again in his own renewed strength before he may accomplish any works the least comparable to His.

It is therefore for the aspirant who seeks degrees of mastery on the path, to prepare himself by the discipline of the path to meet an opening of the doors of the soul. To know that in the periods of crisis when the waters of life are troubled and clouds lower over the horizon, the hour of opportunity has arrived; and to know not to turn back in doubt but to meet this discipline with humility because he is considered worthy to bear it in the name of suffering humanity. To gather new strength and experience from it, and give it back in due time in the helping and enlightening of his fellow men.

Section 7:

Messages to Members (1931 - 1945)

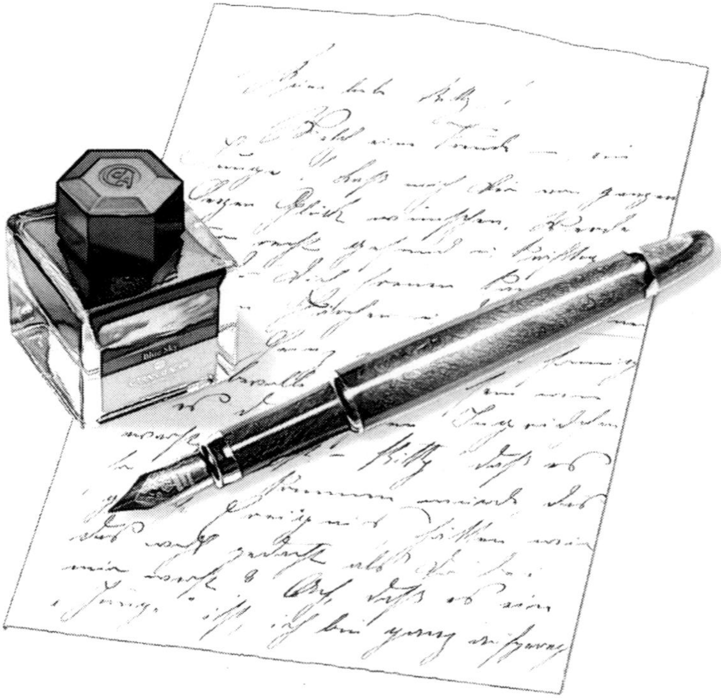

Section 7 - Messages to Members (1931 - 1945)

Introduction

In her address to the *Francis Bacon Chapter* in 1960 (see Section 9), Jessie Kenney said that Raymund Andrea sent circular letters to the members of the British Jurisdiction of the Rosicrucian Order when he felt there was a need for a special message or guidance. Eleven out of the following 12 messages were written during the stressful times of World War II.

1. Letter to Members (Christmas 1931)

Dear Fellow Member:

I felt that I would like to send you, in addition to the greetings expressed through the medium of the magazine, a personal message this Christmas and to express my gratitude for the privilege of cooperation with you in the work of development and service.

There is one thought of profound value to us at this time, which rises strongly in mind beyond the anxious thoughts pressing upon us through present world conditions, and that is, we are steadily working upon ourselves in the way of higher culture through and in spite of opposing conditions. Not for ourselves alone, far from it. We know that every effort on our part to perfect character and advance in knowledge, means that we are contributing our share, in common with other aspirants throughout the world, towards building up an efficient international vehicle of service for the use of the Masters.

But to this end we must hold in mind more than ever before the ideal of practical service in any form possible to us. This is the basic factor of all our development. The Masters themselves are perfected in service, and no aspirant can hope to share intimately in their life until the spirit of service becomes the ruling principle of life. I grant it is possible to make some occult progress without any special consideration of service to others. But the time comes when this kind of exclusive progress proves to be a most unsatisfactory affair. Psychic development is compatible with a selfish attitude towards life. Spiritual development is impossible on these terms. And the time does come when the soul asserts its deeper nature and seeks something consistent with its intrinsic nobility.

I want that assertion to manifest now, this Christmastide, and to be the strong motive power in all our future work. Let us work together in this spirit during the coming year and compel a larger response from the Cosmic, which needs our cooperation as much as we need it. The response will surely come to each one according to sincere effort and need.

253

> "The man or woman who is placed by Karma in the midst of small plain duties and sacrifices and loving kindness, will through these..., faithfully fulfilled..., rise to the larger measure of duty, sacrifice and charity to all humanity."

With my kindest personal wishes to you for a very happy Christmas and much progress and prosperity in the coming year.

Sincerely and fraternally,
    Raymund Andrea

2. Letter to Members (28 August 1940)

Dear Fellow Member of the Rose Cross:

I was deeply grateful for the kind of response my letter of June 28 evoked from members. There were no discussions proffered upon this or that aspect of truth or sentiment expressed, but a simple and sincere note of appreciation of what members were themselves feeling and living, unuttered, in their own minds and hearts.

When strong men and women, struggling with the difficulties of an unparalleled time of crisis, choose to reveal for a moment the battle of life within them, it is the soul that speaks, not the personality, and there is perfect attunement. I thank God that there are such men and women, and that together we go forward through the hours of trial and battle and are experiencing together the initiatory fire of circumstance which, more than all else, will bring us to greater vision and certitude.

It is not for nothing that we have been called to share this trial of humanity. We on the path share it perhaps in a far keener sense than the majority. It is not difficult to understand why. We have assiduously cultivated the arts of peace, service and sensitivity of soul; and consequently the universal suffering impinges upon the sensitive organism and compels our participation, dissipates our attention, and even menaces the very fabric of our spiritual life.

Some have rebelled and demanded why this should be. It is so cruel, appears so unmerited, penalises the kind and innocent, and seeks to lay violent hands upon all the good we know. But we cannot question infinite wisdom. Nor can the mind alone give us any answer. Ever the pathetic and compassionate words come back to us in the dark hours of waiting: *"Ye believe in God, believe also in Me."* We cannot go beyond that plea; and we dare not fall short of it. If we did, then our faith in the immortal life of the soul would perish.

Two very significant things are happening to us during this period of trial, almost unknown to ourselves. Firstly, we are probing into the truth of things and interrogating ourselves as never before. That silent demand to the Cosmic will be heard and surely bring its response. We shall come to see more clearly the meaning of life and understand better our own hearts. We are really passing through the hour of self-revelation, and we shall find in good time that startling discoveries have been made which will place life upon a new level of consciousness.

Secondly, and most important, a process of depersonalisation is taking place within us. We are being forced out of ourselves and through sheer force of circumstances are participating in the lives of others, nationally and internationally.

I want you to note the bearing of your present studies in the Order upon this fact. I want you to reflect upon how imperatively, through the medium of broadcasts and otherwise, we have been brought to share in and take upon ourselves the sufferings, privations and losses of our fellow men in other nations.

The reactions to this are great and far reaching, in understanding and development. We seek the life and spirit underlying all personality and circumstance. We have studied this as theory for years; but now, through the cumulative pain of international Karma the barriers have been broken down, and we stand united as one with the Forces of Light ranged against the domination of evil astral forces.

This participation in international calamity, which lies as a heavy weight upon us, has another aspect directly related to development. It is a call to us to take a more vital interest in world affairs. No aspirant in such a day as this should live to himself. We should seek to cultivate the art of telepathic contact with serious intent, for in this lies an instrument of extended service. Many of us know a good deal of this art. We have had many instances of its reality and use among ourselves. We should now develop it to larger uses by cultivating a mental sensitivity in world affairs and using our thought forces over larger areas.

I recently heard of a lady abroad who did not know that a war was in progress, and who studiously avoided the news of events in order that she might not be enlightened and have her peace of mind disturbed. This lady was a responsible leader of a group of students. What an appalling confession! I do not recollect meeting with so extreme an instance of personal insularity. I hope never to meet with such an instance in the Rosicrucian Order. This lady would no doubt deny any accusation of insularity brought against her. She might point to the number of meetings and functions she attends, to show how interested she is in her fellow men.

But real non-insularity is proven by an aspirant's ability to enter into situations and circumstances and personalities near and remote, and to lay open, to some extent, the minds and intentions of those acting in those situations and circumstances, even though he himself has no specific technical or professional knowledge of the matters under consideration. That geographical position has little to do with it, nor peace, nor war, but that it is an enablement in the man to cross the frontiers of the human mind in any sphere and to know something of the prevailing atmosphere beyond those frontiers. Only thus can we bring our thought forces to their true usefulness in inspiring and encouraging those who have little else to assist them.

That is the thought I wish to leave with you now. Not simply to read, to meditate, to accumulate knowledge; but to lay all these things upon the altar of sacrifice in thinking, feeling and willing into other lives. For this is the hour when all we have learned of the reality of the soul and the laws of thought must be brought into direct action wherever possible and so strengthen the hands of the Masters who watch, wait, and silently work for the hour of universal deliverance.

With my kindest regards and all good wishes for Peace Profound.
>Yours sincerely and fraternally,
>R. Andrea

3.   Letter to Members (18 December 1940)

Dear Fellow Member of the Rose Cross:

Much has happened since my letter to members in September last. Some of them are now on active service in the forces, and in many cases they have been able to continue their studies and use them as best they can in their various circumstances. Others have moved from the more dangerous areas and, in spite of restricted conditions, maintain their active membership. A few have suffered more directly from the raids, yet they have maintained unbroken contact with us. While the bulk of our members, amid the many difficulties and perplexities to be met by all of us, continue with the same firm faith and unyielding spirit and hope which have always characterised them.

I am grateful for this fine example of the collective spirit of loyalty to the Order and of members to themselves and their attained knowledge. When the confusion and din of the battlefield have passed, their reward will come in a deeper peace and renewed confidence in the leading of the light within them.

From time to time a member asks with eager sincerity, what he or she can do to help others, near or far, who are in dire need of strength, inspiration and comfort. It is a question which we all ask ourselves again and again as the tide of appeal and suffering unceasingly flows in upon us. I want to quote the words of a Teacher to a pupil, which seem to me apposite and illuminating.

> "It is not that you must rush madly or boldly out to do. Do what you find to do. Desire ardently to do it, and even when you shall not have succeeded in carrying out but some small duties, some words of warning, your strong desire will strike like Vulcan upon other hearts in the world, and suddenly you will find that done which you had longed to be the

doer of. Then rejoice that another had been so fortunate as to make such a meritorious Karma. Thus, like the rivers running into the unswelling, passive ocean, will your desires enter into your heart."

And to help us more specifically to put that admonition into practice, I am reminded of the words of a disciple of Confucius:

"Every day I examine myself on those three points: in acting on behalf of others, have I always been loyal to their interests? In intercourse with my friends, have I always been true to my word? Have I failed to keep in memory the precepts that have been handed down to me?"

There is nothing occult or magical in these words of those who have trodden the Way. Indeed, the Way is always like that, simple, direct, and applicable to the circumstances of everyday life. The truth as expressed by the Master of Masters is precisely the same; and all who have spoken before or after Him of the truth of the Way, no matter what their height of advancement or their depth of insight, no matter what their race, religion or philosophy, point in the end to acceptance by the pupil of the Karma of his life, of his duty to others in his own place and circumstances, and of doing that duty to the best of his ability.

Sometimes a member is overzealous for knowledge and power. If he were only master of this or that corpus of literature, if he but had this or that power, what might he not do! But neither learning nor power will advance him on the Way. On the contrary, I have known cases where they have proved a snare and a deterrent.

As to power, few are big enough to use it wisely. How often it leads to pride, self-aggrandisement, and ultimately to disillusionment. I never think of Christ as a learned man. He was a supremely wise man, and His word could touch the entire compass of the inner life. He was also a man of power; but he never used it except to a good end.

The careful application of our minds and hands to the task nearest us, with the humble conviction in ourselves that we are doing good, should be more to us, and will be infinitely more to others, than all the learning of the scholastic or the power to do spectacular things. Knowledge of every kind abounds on every hand. In fact, people have too much knowledge, unassimilated, unrelated to and dissociated from the deeper things of the heart, and it is a burden and a temptation to them.

More than ever we need to cultivate the art of reflection, yes, even with the noise of battle in our ears. There is the test for us..., and those who have stood this test will one day realise its tremendous value to them. We must still continue to stand for the soul and cherish its values above all that the personality can offer us.

Many of our members have found this secret for themselves and their lives show the dignity and grace, the calm and resolution of it. Let us all endeavour for this, taking the quotations I have given above as a guide, and put the knowledge and strength we have derived from our studies into daily contact with others. No matter how small the deed or apparently trivial the circumstance, no matter how unknown or unacknowledged, for the seeds of wisdom and real power are there, and later will be recognised as the foundation stones of the master character.

The Christmas season is at hand and I take this opportunity of sending you my kindest wishes for your welfare and happiness, and for that peace which the world can neither give nor take away, and for guidance and prosperity in the coming year.

In Peace Profound,
    Yours sincerely and fraternally,
    R. Andrea

4. Letter to Members (3 April 1941)

Dear Fellow Member of the Rose Cross:

I am sometimes particularly impressed by letters from members who, under the stress of circumstances, especially at this time, write to me straight from the heart the word of inner truth which hard experience has taught them.

The storm of trial has come upon them, and passed over them, but it has not left them where they were. They see more clearly; they stand in their own place with greater confidence; and through reflection they distil the essence of wisdom from personal, concrete experience. This is the one thing, above all others, which makes me realise how much their studies and work in the Order have done for them, how much these mean in their lives, and how much they can be relied upon for wise and well-directed service in the world.

One such letter I recently received from a lady member who has for years been one of our most steadfast workers. She has a wide knowledge of men and women, has contacted students of many cults and religions, and long since found a home of spiritual retreat and a way of service within our Order. I quote from her letter because it is so sincere and true to the experience of many of us.

> "I often say to myself, 'Well I can't help now. Life alone will teach, and some day in some incarnation they will know and understand the truth.' In fact I no longer try to press or hurry anyone. I offer my ideas, and in real trouble help with my physical hands and body, but no longer do I feel impelled to carry their Karma on my own shoulders. For I see it cannot be done, nor is it the Master's way. A forced plant is often the least able to survive

a tempest. The hardiest are those that continually stand up to climatic changes, conditions and difficulties."

The lessons conveyed in those words are aptly expressed. It will be well to note to what extent we comply with them in our contacts with others; because as soon as the war is over and our studies again take first place in our lives after a period of unprecedented distractions, we shall need to extend our influence and carry our knowledge and understanding of the higher truths of life to others who will much need them.

We hear many voices today promising a new world and greater opportunities in it. It will not prove an easy matter to fashion that new world, When the strain of battle has passed there will be seekers casting about in every direction in the endeavour to make new adjustments and aid in the work of reconstruction.

Then will come the greater opportunities for the older ones in the Order to speak the word of wisdom and guidance for the young students as they come in. The task of the latter will be to build up a structure of self-knowledge and try out powers of service and leadership to others. When the strain has passed there will be a new freedom of thought and action, aspirations will blossom forth afresh, and the Masters will look eagerly for those who can respond to the inspirations of the soul to help on the never ending work of evolution in the new age.

It will then be, even more than now, that the words of my correspondent will have a true message for us. We must ever do our utmost to lift a little the heavy Karma of the world, but cannot force the law of growth in ourselves or in others. We often try to do both. We shall be more tempted to do so when the time for reconstruction comes. We shall note this tendency more in the younger students than in the older ones. The long cruel days and nights of war will have taught the latter a tolerance and patience and a far truer perspective than all the previous years of peaceful experience.

Many of the older students already possess these attributes of mind and soul. The exigencies of war were not needed to teach them. They need no admonition to hold their hands and allow the younger ones to grow in their own way and learn the lessons they inevitably must learn in the evolving circumstances of their own Karma. They have faced the battle of life through the years with steady eyes and clear understanding and know when to speak and when to remain silent. In that sentence is practically the whole issue of true helpfulness and guidance. We need this, every one of us, and never shall we so much need it as in the immediate future on the path.

Referring to one of her studies, the same correspondent wrote:

"It is one that lifted me up in consciousness and swept all mundane worries and anxieties aside for the time. That I could hold the Christ Spirit all the time! This period of stress and strain is indeed teaching us all to know of what we are capable under all circumstances and of what we are not capable. It's a hard school we are now in, but out of it I feel certain will come many refined and strong souls moulded from the crucible of world agony."

That is indeed the truth. And the lesson for us is, never to intrude our ideas upon others, never to seek to hurry development. Yet ever to be ready to offer advice if asked, never to insist that something is right for others because it has served ourselves, but to be kindly and quietly helpful when occasion offers, and to leave the young students to make their own way under the guidance of their own studies and in the light of their own souls.

This is the simple and the true way of service. It is the Masters' own way..., wisely suggestive, never compelling, leaving the soul in absolute freedom to make its own choice and decision, and to find in true creative unfoldment the measure and strength of its own indwelling powers.

With my kindest regards and
    all good wishes for Peace Profound.
    Yours sincerely and fraternally,
    R. Andrea

5. Letter to Members (4 August 1941)

Dear Fellow Member of the Rose Cross:

Every year I am asked to transmit a special message of greetings from our members here to the Supreme Lodge, to be read at the Annual Convention there. This Convention took place two weeks ago and the usual report of it will no doubt appear in the Digest.

It would be expected that my message this year would be somewhat of a different character than on former occasions and that it would bear directly upon the serious issues confronting America and ourselves and upon the attitude of our members in both jurisdictions. I therefore propose to give below the substance of this message, since I believe it has a note of encouragement for ourselves and will also help our members in America to more vitally ally their thoughts, petitions and efforts with our own. I have no doubt it will: for our fellow members in America, I need scarcely say, are now fully alive to the meaning and magnitude of the ordeal in which we are engaged, and in the fullest sense we can be assured that they are with us.

"You know only too well the stress and difficulties which members in Great Britain and in the continental countries have had to face during the past year. They have been unbelievably severe and testing; and while at times we may have deeply questioned why we should have been thrown so unwillingly into the midst of the field of battle and been compelled

Section 7 - Messages to Members (1931 - 1945)

to witness so much of its desolation and suffering, it has been given to us not to forget ourselves, but to remember that an example was to be expected from us to our fellowmen. Our members have shown that example in full measure in the darkest hour, and others have been inspired and strengthened by it.

"We have tried to remember that, in spite of all appearances, love lies at the heart of all, and will prevail. We have endeavoured that national suffering and loss, instead of hardening and embittering character, shall deepen and sweeten it in human helpfulness and sympathy. We have remembered that Cosmic law fulfils and has offered us a great opportunity of spiritual evolution through pain. We have tried to see that behind the veil of events, so harsh and devastating, the fire of God has been working, swiftly and surely, with magical power, to release human souls from the bondage of form and carry us forward to a new estate of the things of the Spirit.

"I have seen this larger conception abroad in the lives of our members during the past year, and it is the most inspiring message I can send you of them. I know that we have your cooperation in thought and petition, and in action, that together we may all enter into greater fields of understanding service in the immediate future.

"There has no doubt been much questioning in the minds of our fellow members in America at the critical trend of world events. I am sure they will not forget what a unique opportunity is theirs to prove afresh their sincerity in their studies and to dedicate anew their thought and service to their fellowmen. They will recall that so many of our members in the war-ridden countries are passing through the dark night and can only cooperate in silence and in hope for the future. They will remember that our Order has passed through perilous times in the past; times of war, persecution and social upheaval; and while in some countries it was forced from public view by tyranny and oppression, nevertheless, devotion to the Great Work could never be eradicated from the hearts of its members, but shone forth with greater brightness and determination when the evil hour had passed.

"So it is, and will be, today. Whereas in other countries, and Great Britain and America are foremost among them, where freedom of thought and action is a priceless heritage which will never be surrendered, our members have the great privilege of following and disseminating the teachings of the Order for the benefit of true seekers, and their example continues to be a powerful and enriching influence in public and private life.

"Never so strongly have the word and deed of service to others been manifest in Britain as now. It is as if the sufferings of its people have brought thousands to the portal of the mystic way and are preparing them to take the first steps upon it. The Masters of life will use this opportunity. And as you in the American jurisdiction more and more inevitably participate in these sufferings in one way or another with us, I pray you may not miss the challenge of the hour to put aside the lesser issues and look to the larger consciousness and service of the new world to be. It is a challenge to every member of the Order and can only be declined at a loss in evolutionary status.

"Let us rise to the occasion, assert with fresh vigour our aspirations and make our influence felt for good around us wherever we are. To every organisation and institution working for the upliftment and betterment of humanity comes this challenge for new action and wider service, and upon every member rests a peculiar responsibility that all his mental and spiritual assets shall be used to the fullest on the side of Cosmic law and evolution."

With my kindest regards and
> all good wishes for Peace Profound.
> Yours sincerely and fraternally,
> R. Andrea

6. Letter to Members (18 December 1941)

Dear Fellow Member of the Rose Cross:

In these days of rapidly changing attitudes and values on all planes of life, I have been wondering what changes in thought and action our members will demonstrate in a desperately needy world after the war tension has passed.

During the long period of trial they have shown, as I am grateful to realise, and I feel sure they will continue to show as long as it lasts, a strength, purpose and kindness in their respective spheres comparable with the sterling qualities of those in many walks of life and in the services, of which we have heard so much. This is as it should be, for our studies are not merely a philosophy for the mind, but a vision in the heart and a power of service in the hands to strengthen and inspire wherever the Karma of life has placed us. And, in common with all other esotericists of whatever persuasion, we have a special mission to perform in just this humble way, of strengthening and inspiring now and in the difficult days to come after the war.

In fact, whatever mission our individual faculties may call us to in the future through an application of these studies, I think world conditions resulting from the war will demand of all of us to direct that mission into avenues of service to our fellowmen. For as the swift pace of evolution has compelled us to think nationally and internationally as never before, that impetus is not, in my opinion, a brief and temporary one; it will have to possess us until our work in this cycle is ended. A change in attitudes and values has been forced upon us. We have been compelled to grow under the sheer impetus of evolution, more perhaps in a few months or years than otherwise might have been possible in a lifetime.

That is a point I would like members to ponder when they feel a sense of frustration in their lives and studies, under present circumstances. We grow, not simply by reading and experiments, but by living; and life during recent years has been a most drastic discipline and of an inward nature which we could never have imposed upon ourselves. Will you carry that thought to others whenever you tactfully can and lift a little of the heavy burden of Karma resting upon them? It can be a prelude to a greater mission to which the Master will inspire you.

> "The Master places his person behind, yet it is found in the foremost place. He lives not for himself, yet his person is preserved. Being the most unselfish of all, he endures and fulfils his prime purpose."

In that threefold truth there is strength and inspiration. It is an ideal to which we are pledged.

A sense of frustration has indeed been upon many of our members in the matter of progress in their studies. Many have voiced it: I feel it more or less in all. But they should remember that all who are bent upon attainment have shared this frustration with them. Yet it is but a moment in the long story of evolution. It will soon be passed and swallowed up in the stream of time. That is for our hope and encouragement. In the meantime it is our duty, nay our mission, to suffer with those who suffer and be worthy of this mystic participation. The world trial is teaching us how to renounce and to give. This is the fundamental of all religions; and those who were not strong enough to teach themselves, it has by Cosmic law been brought to them, peremptorily and inescapably.

If there are those who dislike or cannot share that sentiment, there is something amiss with them. They may be students, but not servants of the Master. For the Master knows his own, and what is taken away for the common good will be given back, by his own strong hands, in the fullness of time. If we avert our eyes, or refuse the pain of the heart when the crucifixion of humanity stands out clearly before us, all is not well.

Recall how completely the prophets of olden time identified themselves with the sufferings of their generation, how ruthlessly they diagnosed the wickedness and blood-guiltiness of their day, how they wrote in letters of fire and pronounced a divine censure upon the misdeeds and cruelties of ungodly peoples; but above all, how profoundly they participated in and bore within themselves the pain and suffering of the downtrodden and innocent. It verily seems as if they wrote for our own day; even to set an example for us in calling down the wrath of God upon tyrannical and godless peoples in unmatchable utterance.

> "Also in thy skirts is found the blood of the poor innocents: I have not found it by secret search, but upon all these."

I have no wish to sermonise; but I do want to be sure that our identification with the sorrow of the world is deep and productive in the silence of the heart and carrying a blessing to multitudes who need that unseen visitation to strengthen and inspire them. I do not want to feel that because we are aspirants we therefore can stand secure and unruffled within the esoteric knowledge we have and feel that we have no part in the crucifixion of humanity. It is our mission to feel that we are a part of it and must bear some of the burden of it.

The true aspirant should be a sensitive organism, able to receive from near and far all the variations of consciousness, and able to transmit the thought and emotion which will strengthen and inspire others both near and far to bear the pain of unparalleled trial. The time is crucial and is not one in which we should be overconcerned about our own development. We have had ample time for that in the past: now is the time to use what we are and have. This is but to do in a small measure what the Christ did so potently and with complete self-abnegation, and who travails even now with a suffering world groping towards the light.

You know, as well as I do, the various opinions of present-day thinkers on the cause and meaning of the world crisis we are facing. A very prevalent opinion is, that humanity stands at the crossroads in evolution and is deciding for itself, because it is of age to do so, whether it shall go forward and through the portals of a larger consciousness, or fail the adjustments possible to it to achieve a higher spiral of life through the suffering consequent upon initiation. In spite of the intense resentment and imperative demand throughout the world for retribution focussed against those who have unleashed the forces of evil as well as against those who have abetted them, there sounds in increasing intensity the voice of justice, compassion and unlimited service to a world in peril and need from all the allied nations. Is this not a sign that the Christ is coming to birth in the consciousness of many peoples? It may not be too much to say that he is coming through the dedicated personalities of Masters and disciples.

If this is so, then our mission is very plain. Whatever our perplexities, we know too much to ignore the issue. We should stand ready in mind and heart, even in the midst of a multitude of tasks and duties, to receive the strength and inspiration which is surely descending upon us and to focus and distribute the gift to a world in direst travail and pain. It may be only in silent and humble ways that many of us can do this; but if the channel is clear, from the high secret places of the soul to mind and heart dedicated and pledged to service, all doubt will soon vanish as to where we are called and what we must do. The call is sounding and the service is waiting; and if we do not hear and see, there is no condemnation, but the rarest opportunity of approval in the sight of the Master and of proving our worthiness of recognition will have passed.

At this Christmastide it is my sincere hope that we may seek anew the Christ Light in the soul and that a fuller expression of it may radiate abroad to strengthen and inspire, to heal and bless.

I send you my kindest wishes for your welfare and happiness, and for that peace which the world can neither give nor take away, and for guidance and prosperity in the coming year.

In Peace Profound,
> Yours sincerely and fraternally,
> R. Andrea

7. Letter to Members (10 June 1942)

Dear Fellow Member of the Rosicrucian Order:

Most members will have realised, if only from reiterated statements over the wireless almost every day, the difficulties encountered by those who are dependent upon supplies in their profession or business from overseas. These difficulties apply most emphatically to the work of our Order in this country; for all our monographs, books and journals come to us from headquarters in California.

But some members do not appear to have foreseen these difficulties and are rather at a loss to understand why they have received monographs at times out of their proper and consecutive order, or grade.

The fact simply is, that some of our supplies have miscarried and been lost in transit; while others, for which we have been waiting several weeks, although actually now at the port of Liverpool, have been detained by Customs pending the grant of a licence for release by the Board of Trade. Some of these supplies are just now being released to us. We hope others will be released in due course. But one cannot expedite these matters. They have to take their course. The inconvenience to us is a secondary matter.

Moreover, I have just heard from headquarters in America that export regulations now forbid anything but very small packages to be sent here at any one time, so that, where some thousands of monographs reached us in a shipment hitherto for our members, only a few dozen will be permitted in a packet periodically. This will inevitably mean that as supplies on hand here diminish, there is little hope of replacing them fully for the present and until the ban is lifted.

This shortage will affect some members almost at once, in some of the grades; while others will not be much affected for a little while to come. The procedure I must therefore adopt is, to carry on certain members for the present, even though some monographs are missing here and there from a grade, until it becomes necessary to notify them that studies are temporarily suspended, to be resumed at the earliest possible date.

In such cases, when suspension becomes necessary, I propose to send the member a slip stating Studies Temporarily Suspended and this will indicate the position. Dues which have been paid in advance will stand to the credit of the member in our records and will take effect on resumption of the studies. Members under suspension will not be asked to continue their subscriptions, but if they wish to do so in support of the Order and its work, it will be appreciated.

I need not say how much I regret to have to send you this notification, when our work has gone forward for more than 20 years without a break. It has been a long and exacting task, especially under recent conditions, and my great hope was that we might bridge the war period; but in this matter we are subject to the decisions of government departments and can only acquiesce.

We must regard it as another hardship of the war, exercise good sense, patience and steadfastness, and hope the break will only prove a partial one and not be of long duration.

I shall be glad if members would forward their membership cards when writing so that dues already paid, or being paid, may be recorded. This will not only be for their own satisfaction, but will also save additional correspondence in acknowledgment.

With my kindest regards and
    all good wishes for Peace Profound.
    Yours sincerely and fraternally,
    R. Andrea

8. Letter to Members (December 1942)

Dear Fellow Member of the Rosicrucian Order:

Since the war has been in progress I have written each Christmastide a personal letter to members, and it will no doubt be expected that I should do so this year. This letter will however differ somewhat from the former ones. In the latter I sought to encourage members to reaffirm their faith in the Cosmic law and to persist in their studies, in spite of the cruel world events which must inevitably cast a shadow over the festival of Christmas and its customary expression of happiness and goodwill to all. I would encourage them even more to do so now. But in this letter I am responding to the requests of many members who at different times have asked for my views on Germany and the war. What I have to write therefore is personal comment, and I give it because members have asked for it.

I have sometimes thought that these members were of the opinion that I was so much of an idealist that I had no realistic views or comment to make on world affairs. If so,

Section 7 - Messages to Members (1931 - 1945)

I can only say they were much mistaken. I am an Englishman: I have the mind and heart of an Englishman. That means, that in face of what we have seen happening in Europe during these recent years, and in our own country, my views coincide entirely with those of my fellow countrymen.

I have studied the work of many schools of thought; I have written much from my own experience as a student on the path; but I have never considered myself therefore immune from sharing wholeheartedly in the common detestation and utter contempt for the barbarous Germany we have had to contend with for five years: lying, murdering, desolating and trampling upon all we, you and I, have striven all our lives to promote for the good of our fellowmen and the world.

I should not consider myself worthy of the name of an occultist, mystic, or Rosicrucian, or even a man, if I shrank back to a little heaven of my own and closed my eyes and ears to the sordid drama of unprecedented bestiality ever crying to them to participate in the worldwide declaration of opinion for a just and severe retribution of the inhuman actors in it.

There was little likelihood that such would be the case with me. I am a lover of liberty, and demand it for my fellowmen. For no reward within Christendom or outside of it would I thwart the liberty of the human soul. So, for the benefit of those members who have desired my views, and for others who may also be interested in them, I am quoting below the substance of a letter written in March 1941 to a group of students in America, but not connected with our Order.

We as a nation had been praised by these students for our resolute stand during the raid period, and I thought it a good opportunity to give my correspondents a plain idea of my own sentiments at that time, the sentiments which I also knew to be prevalent among our people, and how I believed those sentiments would mature into international opinion in due course. Nearly two years have elapsed since I expressed those sentiments, and I submit that there is little doubt now whether they are the sentiments of decent citizens throughout the world. Here then is the quotation.

> "In writing to you I have to remember that, because of your geographical position, you must inevitably view the present gigantic struggle on this side largely from an American standpoint. Further, you will also naturally view it very much from a Theosophical angle too. That is inevitable and natural, and of course there is nothing to be said against it. But from my vantage point, while with the Theosophical standpoint before my eyes also, I must view the present crisis from what I might call, a more realistic angle.

> "A fundamental difference comes to mind, and it is not unimportant, because it has a strong bearing upon the attitude entertained towards Germany here now and what it may expect to be at the close of the war when Germany will have to face some very grim facts. I refer to the point stressed by you that the present war is a singular one and the outworking of

particular forces hitherto unknown in history, and therefore apparently rather condoning the role of Germany as an exceptional one in her history and calling rather for forgiveness than rigorous punishment. My opinion is, that the British do not, and I hope never will, accept that view in Germany's favour. It is not in accordance with facts and is therefore unjust.

"You may have read the little booklet recently issued called *Black Record* by Sir Robert Vansittart, which contains the complete text of the seven broadcasts given by him to overseas listeners. Extracts published here were so much appreciated and commented upon that the talks were printed in full. In case you have not read it I have sent you a copy under separate cover. I doubt whether anyone has so concisely and truthfully set forth the facts for anyone to understand. What does this record show? That the present war is but one of a whole series of wars by Germany through the centuries, with the same aim of aggression, brutality and domination.

"You will observe that the writer quotes the historian Tacitus, and was criticised by some of the sentimentalists for so doing. On what grounds it is difficult to see..., except that these people, like many idealists, cultivate a perversion of mind which is always a danger to the national life. If we cannot believe historical facts, what can we believe? Because we believe in evolution, is that sufficient reason for shutting our eyes to historical facts? Is not evolution comprised of historical facts? If not, what is it comprised of? Fables, myths, lies? But if historical facts are the very texture of evolution, otherwise the whole universal system is a tissue of lies and ourselves the biggest liars in it, what do they prove about Germany? They prove conclusively that she has been an incarnate curse to her neighbours for centuries, an aggressor, a deceiver, a liar, and an invader of other nations right from the beginning.

"That is the fundamental difference I cite, between the idealistic view of the singular cause suggested to us as opposed to what history proves to be factually and indubitably true: that so far from Germany being urged somewhat helplessly by forces beyond her control to a barbaric onslaught upon unoffending nations for world domination, it has been her common role and purpose throughout many centuries. Historical facts prove, I suppose without question, that the barbarians have attempted the same thing twice even within my lifetime. This is the English point of view, realistic and founded upon facts, against which there is no hope of any other attitude prevailing.

"Tacitus, as you may know, wrote his Germany in AD 98, and in that masterly little record, known to every classical scholar, you will see Germany depicted to the life. If you have not read it, your first reading will give you many a pause, and in spite of centuries of advancing civilisation among nations since that time, you will, even if reluctantly, recognise only too well the sinister likeness.

"'Nay,' writes the great historian, 'they actually think it tame and stupid to acquire by the sweat of toil what they might win by their blood.' That is the phrase Vansittart quotes. But the truth is an ugly intruder, only too often, to the idealist and the sentimentalist. Happily, the latter have dwindled to an insignificant minority both here and abroad, and their voice no longer commands respect.

"You will not mistakenly conclude that I seek to make you a convert to realism, to anything like that I am, and a recusant from such idealism as you possess. Our ideals in the occult field are one thing: our outlook upon world affairs and the common rights of poor humanity is another. Nor are my remarks an indictment of such esoteric ideals as we have. On that we are in agreement..., at least to some extent. But in this matter of world affairs we in Britain have our feet firmly planted upon the bedrock of adamantine realism. We have been forced by the common and inhuman enemy of humanity to meet him in the gate with the one weapon of his age-long belief and use: force. There is no place for idealism there.

"The most abhorrent and hellish cruelty of the barbarians during the past three years stagger credibility. It has been such, and you are acquainted with the record of it, as to wipe clean out of the vocabulary of man the very suggestion of idealism in dealing with it. That is why our statesmen of note have swept aside, almost with contemptuous impatience, the premature and ill-advised plaints of a few to define peace aims in the face of an enemy dedicated heart and mind to the destruction of democratic life.

"I say, heart and mind, not soul. We cannot think here of Germany in terms of soul, because we see no expression of it. Great peoples of tradition and culture do not hate the soul when they see it manifest. But throughout Europe today a hatred descends upon Germany of inconceivable force and charged with devastating consequences, in the near future; but it is focused upon the dedicated heart and mind of Germany. Her soul has been long since bartered to the father of lies, and the price she will pay will be abject humiliation and unparalleled shame.

"Germany is the outcast of the nations of the earth. She has disciplined herself to this grand climax through twenty centuries of evil intention and evil-doing; and even though, as a subject people, she is brought at some far-off future time into a federation of nations, never again in Britain will the German name be trusted, never again will the oppressed nations trust her. The hand she extends in friendship or commerce will revolt every lover of humanity, for a spectre will ever hover over it. It will be a treacherous and a bloodstained hand. She will be encircled, watched, guarded against by superior force, until such time as suffering and penitence have bled the ingrained curse from heart and mind, and a soul comes to birth within her.

"You have said that Germany needs forgiveness. She undoubtedly will need it, badly; but I know of none who will give it. Forgiveness is a strange word in the present issue, so strange a word that it is never mentioned here.

"'Whoso sheddeth man's blood, by man shall his blood be shed.' That is both realistic and Scriptural. There are more damaging and fateful words Scriptural. 'The revolters are profound to make slaughter, that I have been a rebuker of them all.' 'Also in thy skirts is found the blood of the souls of the poor innocents: I have not found it by secret search, but upon all these.'

"The blood of the souls of the poor innocents! In the name of Christ, how true, and how damnable! And it is still being done with a diabolical cunningness and intent which marks Germany as the most deeply dyed criminal that Providence has ever permitted to disgrace human evolution. But at long last the scale has turned and her own soil is destined to bear witness that her own corrupt blood shall darken it.

"Mercy may be shown, as Churchill has said, to the people of Germany, to those who sue for it. None will be shown to those in power, or to those who have abetted and followed them. Forgiveness there will be none. She will pay the hard price of a nation devastated and a ruined national life. I scarcely expect even the idealists of Britain to utter the word forgiveness. The national voice would hurl it into the abyss.

"No: this war is a realistic one, and its denouement will be realistic. There is a law for nations as for individuals. When a murderer is brought to trial, arraigned, and sentenced to the capital penalty, no idealistic voice is allowed to intervene with the flimsy pretext that the criminal needs forgiveness. The law, based upon Scriptural authority and established through tried experience, takes its just course. A nation, with the record of Germany, cannot be sent to execution, but that she should be brought peremptorily to the bar of international justice and be condemned in the severest terms and subjected to the most stringent penalties within international law, is right and proper. I trust that Britain will see to it."

There is only one point of regret, if any, which I feel in writing this letter, and that is in making this topic the subject of a Christmastide message. But seasons are almost forgotten as we all stand in the midst of a world catastrophe and are all affected in one way or another by it.

It is scarcely for us to feel peace and joy in the midst of universal perplexity, disappointment and suffering. It is for us to share fully in the stern resolve to which the nations have pledged themselves: that by our thought force, and any other means in our power, we will steel our fellows in the combat wherever they are to the best of our ability for the complete overthrow of barbaric Germany and all it stands for, and insist upon the severest retribution in the name of common justice for every criminal who has raised a bloodstained hand against innocent and defenceless peoples.

I make no apology for this message at Christmastide; for the appalling cruelty which has been let loose upon the world by the German leaders, with the consent and consistent support of the German people, should determine us every day and every hour to throw every ounce of influence we have into the scale for the downfall and annihilation of an institution which is not worthy even in name to form part of an alliance of civilised and cultured nations.

I send to every member my sincere thoughts and kindest wishes for new enlightenment, new courage, and greater progress now and during the coming year.

Yours sincerely and fraternally,
    R. Andrea

9. Letter to Members (20 April 1943)

Dear Fellow Member of the Rosicrucian Order:

In June last I wrote to members on the matter of supplies of the monographs to us from headquarters in America and pointed out that under the regulations of the Board of Trade here, and the import and export regulations in force both here and in America, only a very small proportion of the usual monographs shipped to us periodically would be permitted during the war, owing to shipping difficulties.

Obviously, as the months passed supplies of the monographs in hand steadily diminished, and some of the grades are now quite used up. The periodical small parcels received do enable me to fill in some of the missing numbers of grades to some members, but in the main, there is little hope of filling in completely, or of continuing the work of the members already suspended during recent months, until after the war and supplies are moving normally again.

I put this matter to members again now, and to any new members since June last, to assure them that where monographs from some of the grades they have had are missing, or when, at times, the monographs cease to reach them, it is not a case of oversight or neglect, but arises entirely from war conditions, and I can only hope to resume the studies to them when the supply restrictions are removed.

Most members affected as above understand the position and are waiting patiently for normal times. A few however still cannot understand why they should be held up in this way. But we have had many official broadcasts regarding shipping difficulties and these should make the position quite clear, seeing that we depend upon material sent to us from overseas. But as a whole, those members affected by this shortage of material have taken the temporary suspension, or lapses in the grades, with the understanding and perspective expected of them.

Turning to another aspect of the war influence upon members, I have met in some with a note of disappointment because they feel that war conditions are against them in their studies. This is to be expected. One of the chief causes of hindrance to them is sheer physical and mental fatigue due to excessive working hours or duties. With the best will in the world, and in spite of undiminished interest in their studies, through one cause or another they feel their progress is retarded.

Most of us will feel this at times. But I think this sense of frustration should be accepted with patience and resolution. We are sharing in the Karma of the nations, and the Cosmic law which works through and with us can be relied upon to adjust the balance in due time in the life of every right-minded and earnest aspirant. In our view, precious hours have been taken from us which we could have used to good and noble purpose.

Yet I am sure they have not been lost, but used to even nobler purpose; and in serving that purpose we shall find that much more has been done for us than we could have done in solitude for ourselves. Action and experience have taken the place of meditation; but when the task is done we shall bring a new understanding and knowledge into the hour of silence and find an enrichment of personality and technique which only comes from active service.

Whatever the hindrances therefore, or the disappointments, or the fatigue of war conditions, let us keep the goal quietly in mind until the pressure of circumstances is removed, and we shall look back with a singular calmness and assurance of soul in having done our part in a most searching phase of evolution.

I know it has not been easy for many of us to accept gracefully all that has been imposed upon us and which is included under that simple phrase "pressure of circumstances;" but as I understand fully just what this has meant in the student's life, I understand too his reactions to it. Nor are the reactions, whatever they may be, anything to be ashamed of.

I know that these years of the cruellest of wars have been a severe trial to the high-minded and sensitive and those who had set their minds to the keynote of lofty attainment; and it is not in human nature to witness the frustration of so many hopes and purposes and remain unmoved by it. Indeed, the reactions do but show how strong and purposeful the ideals in view were. It is the strong soul which reacts, not the weak. And this is an augury of a more determined attitude towards the goal when the inhibitory conditions have passed.

I voice this as a note of encouragement to members who have revealed to me how difficult their lives have become of late and whose disappointments and sufferings have been hard to face and reconcile with much they have studied on the path. But as surely as we are known on the inner side by our light and work in the world, so I am convinced that no single aspirant is overlooked by the Masters, who themselves have to wait for the hour of human deliverance under law, and that we may be certain that, no matter what the turmoil within or without, their benign influence is ever with us.

"The Master dwells in the world with patience, adjusting his heart to the hearts of mankind."

With my kindest regards and
    all good wishes for Peace Profound.
    Yours sincerely and fraternally,
    R. Andrea

10. Letter to Members (December 1943)

Dear Fellow Member of the Rosicrucian Order:

This is the fourth Christmas letter I have written to members during the war. There is not a member, I am sure, who had not hoped, with me, that this letter might have been written in a time of peace. But it is otherwise. The same stress, strain and difficulty of war are still with us. We hope that the coming year may see the end of them.

    I do not intend to write here about the war. We all hear more of it than is good for us. But I must refer to some of the effects of it upon members, as shown only too clearly in their correspondence. Not only are they extremely disappointed because at last their monographs have ceased to reach them, owing to lack of supplies to us; there is also a note of disappointment in many because, in spite of all good intentions and what effort they are able to make, they seem to make so little headway in their studies.

    The heavens appear to have closed down upon them in this respect; or they stand as it were before a closed door; or their interest and energy do not seem to be equal to the will they have to advance; or, it may be, their sincere prayer for greater light and clearer guidance appears not to be heard, for there is no manifest response in the way they wish. All these, and more, disappointments and frustrations which tear at the heart and confuse the mind, are the lot often of the best, kindest and sincerest aspirants, of many who would make almost any sacrifice in service if called upon to do so.

    Of course, all these things are really born of the senses and the mind, not of the soul. But it is difficult to hold aloof from the former and dwell serenely in the latter. The times are against it. We are thrust, even against our will, into full contact with and immersion in the objective life of the day; and when we turn to think of the greater things of the soul at the close of day, energy is low and the time of opportunity has passed. So it seems.

    Yet perhaps our sense of values is wrong and we see things in the reverse order through the insistence of world events. Perhaps, too, all that we would do in the clear and bright atmosphere of peace is done for us during the hours of sleep. I think this must be so, or we should not have the strength and inspiration to continue unfalteringly day by day, in spite of all we may feel. The Cosmic is the realm of miracle, and it can do for us far more than we dare imagine in our objective selves.

I have known this to happen so often in the lives of members. They have placed their petition trustingly in the hands of the Cosmic Powers with confidence that they would do for them what they could not do for themselves; and in silent, unexpected and mysterious ways, the path has opened, the problem has been solved, and difficulty removed. Thereafter, nothing can shake the confidence of these aspirants in an overseeing Wisdom which guides better than they know.

I wonder how many members know that beautiful little book, *Gitanjali*, written by the Indian poet and saint, Tagore. It was published in England in the first year of the last war and received wide appreciation among students of Eastern literature and readers generally. Many of the poems in it, once read, are unforgettable, not only because of the haunting beauty and pathos of the style and sentiment, but because of the rich spiritual significance and life experience revealed in them. No. 14 in the book might be quoted as an example of this.

> "My desires are many and my cry is pitiful, but ever didst thou save me by hard refusals; and this strong mercy has been wrought into my life through and through.
>
> "Day by day thou art making me worthy of the simple, great gifts that thou gavest to me unasked..., this sky and the light, this body and the life of the mind – saving me from perils of overmuch desire.
>
> "There are times when I languidly linger and times when I awaken and hurry in search of my goal; but cruelly thou hidest thyself from before me.
>
> "Day by day thou art making me worthy of thy full acceptance by refusing me ever and anon, saving me from perils of weak, uncertain desire."

I select this number because there are sentiments and truths in it which seem to speak directly and so understandingly to the thoughts and feelings of all of us. Note how *"strong mercy"* is placed in the balance against *"hard refusals;"* how these same *"hard refusals"* save from *"perils of overmuch desire;"* that in seeking, sometimes languidly, sometimes hurriedly, the goal, it still eludes. Yet, nevertheless, through all the ups and downs of experience we are being made *"worthy of full acceptance"* by being held back to hard experience, from which alone will ultimately come the detachment from *"weak, uncertain desire."*

The value of this book lies not in its poetical quality, distinguished and appealing as this is, but in the unfolding and delineating of the personal experience of the poet in his contact with life and arising from contemplation and vision of the Reality beneath and expressing in all nature around him.

It is the voice of the mystic communing with his Master. He addresses himself at times directly to "my Master;" and the above poem is none other than a mystical prayer to the Master whom he glimpses at times and learns wonderful lessons of experience and adjustment through the contact, and then is left alone to find his own way through difficult paths with only the voices of nature to comfort him.

"Day by day thou art making me worthy of thy full acceptance." That is the faith of the mystic, not easy to be held or expressed during the cold hours of hard experience when no help seems to be at hand. But the faith of the mystic must be equal to that, or of what use is it?

I know that the faith of man has been severely tested during these latter years, perhaps as never before; but it is surprising how that faith, if only the ordinary faith that there must be in spite of all appearances a purpose in life and a wise government of it, has held millions upright and dedicated to duty, not only because their own life and security have been closely threatened, but because of a common sympathy they have felt with the sufferings of others throughout the world.

But the faith of the mystic is of a far deeper kind. It is the faith that, through his study, meditation and dedication to higher service, he is known to the Masters of life to whom he has constantly aspired, and no matter how *"cruelly thou hidest thyself from before me,"* he has experienced in the past too many instances of secret guidance in his life to doubt for a moment that what he is and does can never be hidden from the Master who knows all and is drawing him onward through widening paths of uncertainty and difficulty into larger consciousness of the truth indwelling the soul.

When Tagore visited London, I think about the time of the last war, and was interviewed, it was said by those who met him that they felt almost ashamed in his presence. About his venerable figure was an atmosphere of profound peace and serenity, so utterly alien to our busy and perturbed city life. The mystic carried with him the intangible results of long years of spiritual communion and ecstasy, an aroma of other-worldliness so foreign to our own. Well might they feel ill at ease, and yet wonderfully refreshed and inspired, by the Master's presence.

His countrymen revered him, for he was the flower of their spiritual culture of many centuries. *"Every morning at three,"* said one, *"he sits immoveable in contemplation, and for two hours does not awake from his revery upon the nature of God."* This is a far cry from our feverish life in the West. It is mystical faith passing into direct vision of Reality. But it shows us the goal; and in lesser degree we can make the same approach.

We know the way, but the times have not come quite right for us; yet I am certain we are learning priceless lessons through *"hard refusals"* which life is still imposing upon us. If we doubt that, we question our mystical faith and the guiding hand. And it is the object of our studies ever to increase and fortify the one and to make us more sure of the other.

While I was writing this I received a letter from a member containing a most pleasing confession of what the work of Tagore had done for her. She wrote...,

> "It was Tagore who finally led me to the path, and all that I learned to love in his words comes home to me more and more in the teachings of the Rosicrucians."

It so happens that this member recently passed through a keen personal grief in bereavement and many difficult experiences leading up to it, and I have no doubt that the words of the master poet taught her to bear both bravely; for she is the stronger for all that has passed.

The reason that the words *"come home to her more and more in the teachings of the Rosicrucians,"* is because the latter lead step by step into the real mystical life from which the poet drew his inspiration. And once our feet are firmly on this path and our eyes open to the underlying meaning of all experience and how it is shaping us and fitting us for larger life and service, we shall find sympathetic points of contact and understanding in the words of experience of writers like Tagore and others seeking the same goal of Cosmic union.

You note that I say *"words of experience,"* not particular or curious exercises; for some students are only satisfied when they meet with the latter, and the more the better, because they have an abnormal curiosity for something new or different to experiment with and stimulate their interest.

Mystical and other exercises are good and right in their place and needful; but it should never be overlooked that the words of inner experience of a mystical writer have a potent vibrational value, and the sensitive aspirant by brooding over and assimilating these expressive phases of a soul's high development and realisation, imperceptibly makes the steady ascent to higher consciousness and prepares himself to live through precisely those same aspects of mystical experience.

It is by no means only through a new exercise or experiment that progress on the path is assured, but also through a living into the actual experience of a teaching as mystically worded by a teacher who has passed along the way. Here is an example of this in poem No. 19.

> "If thou speakest not I will fill my heart with thy silence and endure it. I will keep still and wait like the night with starry vigil and its head bent low with patience.
>
> "The morning will surely come, the darkness will vanish, and thy voice pour down in golden streams breaking through the sky.

"Then thy words will take wing in songs from every one of my birds' nests, and thy melodies will break forth in flowers in all my forest groves."

There is more than a hint in these words of patience and serenity, of inward stillness and willingness to wait for the hour of revelation, which eludes us in our anxious striving and endeavour to compel response. In fact, it gives us the real key to the profound peace and spiritual magnetism of the poet himself as his presence impressed others.

We cannot do better; for half the battle of the path is, after all, in deep inner quietness and confidence, which alone give abiding strength.

It was at Christmastide 29 years ago that I first read "Gitanjali." How many times since then I have read these imperishable strains of pathos, yearning and spiritual communion, I cannot say. Time cannot diminish their value, for they were born in the realm of the timeless and eternal peace of the presence of the Master Singer.

"I know not how thou singest, my Master! I ever listen in silent amazement."

I pray that at this Christmastide we may sense something of this peace profound which is ever present and awaiting our recognition.

With sincere good wishes for Christmas and for the coming year.
Yours sincerely and fraternally,
R. Andrea

11. Letter to Members (December 1944)

Dear Fellow Member of the Rosicrucian Order:

There is one fact which we aspirants on the path should have deeply recognised during the past four years: the pace of evolution has quickened. I put this fact to members somewhat in the form of a challenge; because if we are not thoroughly awake to it we are neither commendably inwardly aware of ourselves, nor have we intelligently and critically followed the trend of events in the world around us; the unfoldment of new techniques on every hand has been unmarked; and the power of thought materialising with amazing rapidity the patterns of a new world structure, and the response of enlightened individuals everywhere to new possibilities of human achievement have been overlooked.

I go further and say that if, under the exigencies and sufferings of this greatest of wars, we have not caught the spirit of the accelerated tempo in evolution, we have missed a great opportunity and failed in the application of our chosen studies. *"How so?"* it may be objected. *"What have our teachings to do with war, or with the increased tempo of evolution caused by it, or which precipitated it?"* Such a question would clearly show that our minds are not awake to the issues of the evolutionary trend and that we are still living in a pre-war rut and immersed in the idea of self-development instead of thinking onwards and in terms of world service.

If that is the case we have missed an opportunity of sharing in the tidal wave of Cosmic forces which has carried human consciousness almost at a bound to higher levels of recognition and understanding and opened the door to at least a minor initiation. For life, and the experience of life, is the great teacher and initiator. You may say, if that is so, then all of us alike must have participated in this evolutionary wave and attained a new level of consciousness.

True, we are all subject to the general influence of it: and if we do not cooperate we shall be pushed. But it makes a great deal of difference whether we pass through a critical period with a keen sense of its meaning and importance and intelligently adjust to and cooperate with it, or whether we merely acknowledge with a fair sized majority that it is indeed a critical period, regret very much the disturbance and inconvenience it has caused us, and wait patiently to resume our peaceful posture of 1939.

But if it is true that there has been an unprecedented evolutionary advance during the recent years of Cosmic urgency, is it not obvious that the old patterns of life we have known and loved so well must already be out of date and will prove to be useless in the immediate future? Pain and sorrow, loss and bereavement, even the acute strain of everyday existence, have changed countless individuals almost beyond recognition in their conception of themselves and their attitude towards life. For them the former patterns of life have completely vanished, and new ones must take their place.

It has been stressed again and again publicly that the old world is crumbling and a new world forming. This has been said by statesmen and other public men who are not known as occultists or as particularly advanced persons on the path; but they are awake to the evolutionary tempo and what it portends, and they are far more ready and able to render expert service to the world than many of us who are supposed to be far ahead of them by virtue of our special studies and our pledge to the path.

This is not a happy thought, but it cannot be dismissed. If we have special privileges of knowledge we should be good for something and justify our worthiness of it. To add precept to precept and line to line through years of peaceful study and meditation may seem very commendable and make us appear, at least to ourselves, very good, virtuous and wise. But if that pattern of life is brought forward to the momentous year of 1945, with the full emphasis as hitherto upon development of self, the goodness, virtue and wisdom will not be so apparent or commendable. The real pioneers around us will see self-absorption, selfishness and stagnation in it.

The tidal wave may have passed by and left us high and dry, secure and unmoved, and satisfied with what we are in ourselves. If so, we may be grateful for our immunity and our satisfaction. Whether so or not, I would like to believe that there is not one of us who, amid the welter of these portentous years, has not been lashed and racked in soul at the spectacle of an expiring world and an unspeakable martyrdom of man.

Members sometimes express their longing for the days of peace. This is understandable in view of the tumultuous years of war. But I rather feel they wish to revert to the former pattern referred to, in which case I have some misgivings about it. It has been said that peace as the antithesis of war is not to be looked for at this crisis in evolution, but action. That is what I am thinking of in this letter; because, while peace, calm, serenity and self-contemplativeness, may be the ideal of the Buddhist and some other near neighbours of his, it is not the role of a Rosicrucian. I should be the last to decry these mental attitudes, so valuable in themselves; but they exemplify the life of aloofness, self-involvement and inaction; and this is not the ideal of a Rosicrucian. Moreover, it is the very antithesis of what the world will demand of us in the immediate future.

The history of the Rosicrucians of the past furnish the best example of the life of action, of self-expression, of the most versatile human achievement. The secret of their own development lay mainly in world service. They developed and rose to eminence not merely by what they thought, but largely by what they did.

They were always at war with the times or for the times and increasing the tempo of human advancement. And this should apply no less to the present cycle of the Order. Therefore, to rest back upon the teachings we have had in this cycle as just another means of intellectual satisfaction, or a morbid desire to lay eager hands upon secrets of development which would place us in a privileged position in advance of others, is a poor acknowledgment to the great souls down the centuries who made supreme sacrifices, sometimes even unto surrender of life itself, under the persecution and tyranny of state and church, that the living flame of inner truth might not die out but be handed on to us as worthy custodians of it. For we have no exclusive right to this truth. It derives from the soul of man and belongs to the souls of men. It underlies the souls of all men, and all are unconsciously seeking it.

I said that the Rosicrucians of the past were always at war with the times or for the times. They went into robust action against the national and social evils of the day, and fought for the liberty and advancement of human thought. They were divine revolutionaries, forgetful of themselves and heedless of public opinion, and pledged one and all to lift by any means some of the heavy Karma of the world. It may be the lot only of a few in a particular cycle to play a leading part in the affairs of the time. They will be called to it and realise their mission. They will need no prompting from outside. The awakened mind and dedicated heart open the door of opportunity and they will pass through it on their own initiative.

Some members wish to be told what their mission in life is. They must look within and interrogate the soul. Light and leading must come from within. A person with a great love for music, literature or art has no need to ask others whether or not he will excel in either or has a call in that direction. Music, literature or art possesses him, dominates his mind and heart, urges him to master and express it and dedicate his life to it. It should be so with the aspirant on the path. He has a body of teaching in his hands which, under suitable application to his entire constitution, should awaken every department of his nature and bring him to a realisation that he has a purpose in life far beyond the ordinary level of existence, a purpose which should be an inspirational incentive to assure him of direct influence and value in other lives.

It matters not what the service is, whether great or small, but some form of service there must be. The great souls of the world have always been those who have greatly served; and we little dream how humble was their service in the beginning. There is no appeal from this and no other way. Some aspirants lay the whole emphasis upon self-development, perfecting the self, and regard service as alien or something to come at a later period when perfection is attained. A miserable and antiquated doctrine! Whatever may be the methods of the East, in the West we are called to action.

It is not expected that we should render the perfect service of a Master. Few of us have any idea of the extent and value of that service of infinite pains and constant watchfulness which characterise, for instance, a Master during the period of the novitiate of a pupil. Unique psychic diagnosis is accompanied with the most skilful adaptation of instruction consistent with safe development and for the end in view; and, contingent upon the pupil's capability and cooperativeness are the intended results achieved.

But while a far more humble service remains for us, it has no limits, can be infinite in variety, and can be self-educative as it assists others. A sphere of useful service should be deliberately sought by the aspirant. Too many aspirants are concerned because they have not reached certain stages of demonstration in their studies. This seems to occupy their main attention. They need to reverse this attitude and ask themselves what they already possess of knowledge or practical ability to give.

I know this does not appear very inviting to ambitious students intent upon high development; but they must sooner or later realise one stable fact: a Master is only interested in a disciple as he is a server. It matters not how clever or informed he may be. This will not kindle the specific light in his aura which a Master desires to see; and until that light is seen he cannot expect the individual inspiration of a Master for specialised work. Therefore, the time must come when the aspirant pledges himself not merely to the path, as he did when entering upon his studies, but to service in other lives.

It has been said that *"life always gets harder towards the summit..., the cold increases, responsibility increases."* It is true that, for obvious reasons, life gets harder towards the summit. For one thing, increased knowledge and advancement on the path, creates new obligations towards those near and Karmically related to us, and our responsibility in life certainly increases. But while the cold increases towards the mountain summit, it should not increase in our advancement on the path. We may have to part company with some of our friends and with certain things on the way simply because we are advancing upon a higher spiral of evolution; but, on the other hand, we should make new friends and more

Section 7 - Messages to Members (1931 - 1945)

valuable contacts in the ascent, even though the friends are fewer and the contacts rarer; and that should mean sympathetic understanding and companionship, not the coldness of isolation.

There are warm, urgent, living sympathies upon all levels of life. They should be more so on the higher levels than upon the lower, because the range is wider, more inclusive and more spiritually magnetic; and during a normal development what is lost on a lower spiral of evolution is given back with added values upon a higher one. The law of compensation works here. If our aim is larger service, whatever we appear to lose in the endeavour to attain it will be restored sooner or later, if not precisely in the form we anticipated, then in unexpected forms of knowledge, power or love, perhaps all these, which will demonstrate that the law is not unmindful of us and is working for our highest good.

But our aim must be dedicated and sincere and selfless. We must not attempt to make terms with Karma, as if seeking some kind of business bargain, giving so much and expecting an appropriate return. What return does a Master receive for the care, compassion and unseen assistance given to a pupil? Very little, I think, sometimes, judging by the lives of some pupils. Nevertheless, it is given unstintingly and perfectly, in the hope that the seed sown may bear fruit.

I referred to the patterns of prewar years being now out of date. That is being voiced everywhere. We are being constantly reminded that the conditions of life in the new world will be radically different from those we have known. This should be obvious to any intelligent person: only the ignorant and thoughtless need to be reminded of it. But I apply it more specifically here to ourselves as aspirants, and especially to the older ones.

In the Order are men and women of mature age who have given many years to our studies, and to other studies of the path before them. Some of these members have 20 or 30 years of study and meditation to their credit; and unless they are flexible and versatile students the danger is that they will have built up a set pattern of what progress should mean for themselves and become firmly set and liable to crystallise within that pattern. It is these members particularly who need to turn round and make a reassessment of themselves and the values in their lives with a view to ascertaining how they can apply these values in new ways for extending their influence and usefulness in the world.

I think it a mistake to set limits to what might be achieved in any one cycle. Some students when they reach the later years of a cycle are inclined to sit back and let life run to its close without further effort on the path. There may be times when this is necessary owing to physical unfitness. But otherwise there is little justification for it. And those who are tempted to it should recall how much has been and is being done in the world by men and women who in normal times might be enjoying well-earned retirement and leisure. But the knowledge that the soul knows no age and the accumulated experience of a long life's endeavour to explore its possibilities and express them, should inspire new confidence and courage and assure us that we have much to give in a world which as never before needs our example and experience.

Nothing has so much inspired me as the biography of remarkable characters who have been unexpectedly called to position and authority after long years of unknown and strenuous preparation in the hope of rendering some kind of master service to the world. They were led in silent and difficult ways, whither sometimes they scarcely knew, but ever with a deep conviction of a guiding hand to a goal where all their maturing powers would be requisitioned. The lesson to be drawn from this is, that no effort is in vain if well directed and focused to a definite purpose. And if this is true of worldly success, it is even more true in the case of the dedicated aspirant with the purpose of world service in view.

The soul will respond if the demand upon it is powerful and continuous enough; for the Cosmic Powers are behind it, and they will inspire it and liberate its forces in accordance with the strength and persistency of the demand it makes upon them in the effort to adjust itself to the new pace in evolution and the fulfilment of its purpose.

Criticism of members is not the object of this letter. That scarcely needs to be said. Its object is encouragement, and I hope, new incentive. I know that many have served to the limit of present possibility and endurance. Many have had forms of service thrust upon them which they never anticipated nor thought they could ever fulfil. Others look for relief from service imposed because of its exhausting burdensomeness and responsibility. All these may well protest that they need no exhortation to serve. But I do not refer so much to these particular impositions of wartime service, but rather to a self-imposed service which as aspirants they might be expected to assume when time and leisure in postwar conditions are restored to them.

It is a new departure, in the name of aspirants pledged to the path, of higher personality advancement I hint at, which is expected from those so pledged. Not that there is any compulsion in this. But it is one of the obligations incurred by taking steps towards the summit. Indeed, some authorities have maintained that there is an element of danger in accelerating personal evolution through study and meditation and allowing the accumulated results to remain unused within the personality. The idea no doubt is, that upon every successive spiral of advancement new forces are released on the psychic and mental levels which should not be turned back upon themselves, but find adequate channels of expression.

I think there are few really progressive aspirants who do not instinctively feel this truth; and that is why they often voice a strong desire to find an appropriate field of service in which their abilities may be exercised. When that point of inward development and tension is reached and a persistent silent demand is made for it, I do not think it will be long before a door of opportunity opens for the aspirant in response to it.

If we enter upon the new year with such a demand in the forefront of consciousness and a settled resolution to follow any leading that is given to us, we may be sure that the Cosmic guidance will be good and productive, and that which at first may be done as a duty or obligation will soon become a daily habit of thought and action, and possibly later a definite goal and mission in life.

I suggest therefore that if, instead of making peace our watchword for the new year, we substitute for it the will to service. We shall align mind and heart with the Cosmic will and purpose, and the strength of our influence in the world will be greatly extended.

With sincere good wishes for Christmas and for the New Year,
> Yours sincerely and fraternally,
> R. Andrea

12. Letter to Members (December 1945)

Dear Fellow Member of the Rosicrucian Order:

This Christmastide we can say the war of arms is ended. Now we have the war of minds contending for peace. The latter is far more preferable than the former; but it has many unedifying aspects which we wish were absent. We have all looked forward to the ending of the war, not a few expecting immediate and handsome conditions to result from it; but the storm of war has left behind it world wreckage, confusion and bitterness, and a goodly heritage of disillusionment, which should cause surprise to no serious student of history.

The mistake many students make is in thinking that because they are peace loving individuals, and always have been, with an avowed ideal of a harmonious and progressive life, therefore others around them should naturally have a similar outlook, and abandon contention, disputation and self-interested motives and "study to be quiet" and selfless.

I do not share this view. I have shared the ideal and worked hard for it; but I have not read history or studied humanity so poorly as to expect to see it realised in my generation. In fact, I am not optimistic about the next generation: but that can wait. Much of our uneasiness and disappointment arises from expecting the impossible in a brief cycle of life.

Nature should teach us much. She is never in a hurry. She rises and declines, blossoms and fades, in the course of each year, under law. And races and civilisations have their high points and their low; but we only live long enough to catch a glimpse of the whole picture. The glimpse we have at present is a pretty wintry one, and the spring is remote. The long range view of the Masters, who regard an incarnation as but a brief moment in the far flung reaches of cycles, if accepted in theory, is not easy to act upon. Nor can we censure anyone for being disgruntled at the depressing spectacle of a world in ruins.

We do our best to take a long-range view because our ideal demands this of us. But I am not one of those fanatical idealists who say in effect: *"This is merely a passing phase and unreal. We have an ideal and all will be well. We are laying the foundation of a good future incarnation and shall come out on top. Let the fight go on so long as we remain at peace."* I am rather inclined to view the world as it is, now, wreck as it is, and study what little I can do to inspire any single worthwhile individual to do the best he can in it.

In my opinion, what we need most at this juncture, if we are really aspirants on the path of higher evolution, is to make as it were a new start, come back to ourselves, not to be too much involved in mind with the present world picture, and see in what way we can make ourselves count for more than in the past. For taking into account all aspirants of whatsoever persuasion, it does not look as if we have counted for very much in the past. At least, many so argue. But I have had more to say on these points in the Digest and elsewhere, so need not elaborate them here.

I know that many members are disappointed and disgruntled because the cessation of the war has not brought about, in some magical way, a feeling of new liberation and progress in their own lives. But when we remember that disorganisation and perplexity are universal in these first days of peace, and that there is little prospect of anything otherwise for some time to come, I think we should realise that the well-known statement that *"our Karma is inextricably interwoven with the great Karma"* is a very real fact today. There is literally no way of escape, whatever our views or persuasions are. We are a part of the world picture, this present phase of evolution, and nothing can alter the fact.

We may feel very tired of it and the prospect just ahead; but there is only one of two things we can do. We can either let go and allow the remainder of this cycle to carry us on as smoothly as we can contrive to the end of it and pick up the thread later on in another cycle at exactly this point in our evolution; for we cannot hope to inherit in a future cycle what we have not striven for and earned in this one: or we can, through our much increased experience of the recent years, set another definite standard for ourselves to reach. It does not matter so much whether we do reach it or not in this cycle, it is the definite, clear-cut and resolute intention which we impress upon our whole constitution, heart, mind and soul, which is the primary, important and always the main thing.

Remember, I am not suggesting the ideal of the fanatical idealist who *"yearns for Nirvana."* There is very much to be done before we reach that, in this cycle, or any other. I mean directing the personality, under mind and soul direction, to some worthwhile creative activity, in whatever sphere it may be, which will raise the vibration and tone of the individual life and react for good and inspiration upon the vibration and tone of the world at large and have even the smallest share in its reconstruction.

It is not for me or others to advise a member what to do. His aim, in his studies, is to find himself in this matter and use himself in the best possible manner as nature directs and his increasing knowledge suggests. I have never heeded to ask others what I should do, or what end I should serve. My problem has always been in not having enough time to do what I would, or the means to do it. If that is your problem too, you may feel some regret and have many a difficult hour with yourself, but you will have nothing to apologise for and you will have a quiet conscience.

I think some aspirants make difficulty for themselves in expecting to accomplish too much at this point where they stand in evolution. They are exhorted to endeavour to find their mission in life. That is well: there is a task for everyone. But a special or outstanding mission is not for all, irrespective of their mental attainments and spiritual status. This is a matter for reflection. If a student takes up the studies of the path, that is no guarantee that within a few years he will receive a "call" or a "mission" to be a teacher of men. Very much depends upon the innate gifts of a man in this or that direction in life. Whatever he is now engaged in as his active calling in life, the acquisitions he makes to his mental and spiritual nature through his studies should lead to greater achievement in that calling and add some additional means of service to it for his fellowmen. That is what we should expect and what he should seek.

The expectation of some aspirants seems to be that, because they are led to the path and preparatory study towards higher evolution, therefore some unique mission should open to them by virtue thereof. This view cannot logically be maintained, it is certainly not true to fact, as anyone acquainted with groups of aspirants of any school of thought can verify.

I know of many students who are mentally proficient, and successful in their profession or employment and who manifest some of the best qualities of discipleship. They are adjusted in life and doing good work, but they do not seek or expect any special "mission" outside of the sphere in which they live and act. They show increasing influence within that sphere and are recognised by others as having that influence, and are sought for because of their inspiring and sure guidance.

It is true, that some few of such come to feel a strong urge to renounce a more limited sphere and recommend themselves by their outstanding quality to a responsible position here and there in specific occult or other work of service. That is good. But in the majority of cases, and there are probably few exceptions, students qualifying for the path today, will find their means of progress within the limits of the work they are doing, for the preparatory steps of the path may well demand that particular kind of experience. Some of the exceptions may be in the case of young disciples in incarnation now who will find themselves led into educational careers of various kinds because they have a special part to play there in the immediate future.

We must remember that we each have a Karmic pattern in life, and the place and calling in which we find ourselves have a real significance for us. It is often said that most people want to be other than they are or do something other than they are doing. I believe this is peculiarly so in the case of many aspirants, because memories of previous cycles impinge upon the consciousness and awaken the ambition to pursue again lines of activity in which they formerly excelled.

This is often the source of much mental conflict. The past appeals strongly to the present and seeks to live its storied life over again: the present is dedicating itself to a new and higher spiral in evolution where service is the keynote and the lesser things of personal ambition have to take a secondary place and ultimately pass away altogether.

It is not for us to slay ambition. I am no advocate of surgery on the path. It is only that we need to discriminate between the tendencies and purposes of ambition. The fuller the life of the aspirant the more valuable will his service be. The criterion is: does that which calls us to be and do promise to further the purposes of the soul, or keep us down upon the concrete level of life? Obviously, the purpose of our studies on the path is to ascend, however painfully and slowly, but ascension must be the aim; and whatever our calling is, or whatever calling we aspire to, it should minister to that end.

This Christmas we shall do well to make another assessment and refuse to be discouraged by the fragment of the world picture which claims our attention. It will also claim our interest, but we shall do well to refuse to let it dominate us and drag us down to its own sordid level. It must have our attention and interest, for we have to live with it and through it; but it is for us to refuse to allow it to tyrannise over us and render us unfit for living usefully in it while we remain attuned above it.

We can keep our outlook sane and balanced and our inner life in poise and receptive to the good, which is ever ready to possess and lift us to greater achievement. However much alone we may feel in this work, we shall remember that this is but one of the illusions of the way. We may belong to a minority, but it is a potent and influential minority, striving in the same direction as ourselves, and it is our own lack of inner sensitiveness and proper receptivity if we do not feel and know this.

All real disciples know they belong to a noble brotherhood of souls having the same goal in view. There is a soul link which gives them spiritual access to the whole community of aspiring spirits near and far; and if they ask they will receive from the unseen reservoir of wisdom, strength and guidance.

They know, too, that they must let this gracious influence flow through them to inspire and strengthen those they contact and infuse peace into troubled and grieving hearts and minds. That may not seem much in view of our high ambitions; but I have known the Master to do just that for his anxious disciple and it has been enough and made the next step on the path possible.

So can it be for all of us. It is the pledge of all the great Masters to earnest disciples; and the pledge is redeemed in unexpected ways and at times when we never look for it. It is the paramount pledge of the greatest Master of all, the Christ. Indeed, if this were not so most of us would have failed long since in the stress of the storm.

With sincere good wishes for Christmas and for the New Year,
    Yours sincerely and fraternally,
    R. Andrea

Section 8:

The Rosicrucian Digest (1939 - 1945)

ROSICRUCIAN DIGEST

COVERS THE WORLD

THE OFFICIAL INTERNATIONAL ROSICRUCIAN MAGAZINE OF THE WORLD-WIDE ROSICRUCIAN ORDER

Vol. XVII	JULY, 1939	No. 6

New Rosicrucian Research Building (Frontispiece)	201
Thought of the Month: A Glass House Existence	204
Are We Civilized?	206
Questions of the Times: Are Large Families Advisable?	209
A Task for Rosicrucians	210
Unity in Diversity	214
Cathedral Contacts: Building a Reserve	216
The Feeling of Inferiority	218
Pages from the Past: Whitman, The Mystic	220
Religious Magic	223
Making Up the Mind	229
Sanctum Musings: Preparedness for Transition	233
Self-Preservation, Is It a Natural Instinct?	235
Rosicrucian Library Interior (Illustration)	237

Subscription to The Rosicrucian Digest, Three Dollars per year. Single copies twenty-five cents each.

Entered as Second Class Matter at the Post Office at San Jose, California, under the Act of August 24th, 1912.

Changes of address must reach us by the tenth of the month preceding date of issue.

Statements made in this publication are not the official expressions of the organization or its officers unless stated to be official communications.

Published Monthly by the Supreme Council of
THE ROSICRUCIAN ORDER—AMORC
ROSICRUCIAN PARK   SAN JOSE, CALIFORNIA

1. Rosicrucians and World Affairs

Reprinted from the January 1939 edition of the Rosicrucian Digest.

The Imperator's timely and courageous article on "Is America neutral?" in the October issue, struck a deep note of response in me. It was an article which could only emanate from a fearless mind, for it was a scathing rebuke of American big business and a placement of guilt upon the heads of those who deserve no concealment. And if big business in America, or elsewhere, has a conscience, it must have felt very guilty upon reading the article.

It also deeply impressed me because it was in accordance with the Rosicrucian tradition of fearless public utterance. There are not many men living in America who would have had the temerity to face up to a national stronghold and point to the rottenness of its glittering superstructure.

I say it was in accordance with Rosicrucian tradition because some of the most fearless and revolutionary pronouncements upon nations, men and society have come from the pens of Rosicrucians. The pronouncements have not been the professional diatribes of common politicians; they have been destructive and constructive in their influence, at one and the same time exposing corruption and misdemeanour and enforcing upon attention the antidote to these.

That is because the men who made them have been bound by no creed or party, church or platform of political thought, but have turned the clear light of intellectual and spiritual truth upon the matter at issue and, without bias or prejudice, have spoken the plain and unvarnished truth about it. And the Imperator's plain words to America on the subject of its boasted and one-sided neutrality, are in line with the Rosicrucian tradition and what we who follow it stand for.

If there is anything that we on the path of higher culture must be jealous of, and resolve that nothing and no one shall deprive us of, it is the fearless declaration of the truth of things as we see them, no matter how powerful the institution it antagonises or how influential the individuals who oppose that truth.

And it is pre-eminently for us Rosicrucians to set a resounding example in this respect; the more so because on looking around us at one cult and another we observe how little is accomplished by them in the name of world truth. They may consist of devoted students, good and blameless in their lives, but for any practical application of what they believe in to world advancement or amelioration, they might as well be safe and saved within the four walls of a monastery.

The trouble with most of these cults is, that their followers are spiritually inebriated and completely out of hearing of their fellowmen. They would be scared beyond reason to indulge in a little plain speaking upon world affairs as they are and the maladjustment of most of us in them. They have got it into their heads that even wholesome and constructive criticism is a sin and the highest they can do is to preserve a dignified silence and pray for their own salvation and trust God to save the rest.

My opinion is, that God waits for messengers and truth speakers, virile opponents of governments, authorities and business magnates, if need be, to expose the questionable methods, the dishonest legislation and the materialistic thinking to be found in all of them, which foster the very evil which we are in trust to curtail and stamp out and which has made the world almost a hell to live in.

In Great Britain we are tired to the soul of the sound of armaments and the oppression of the people to pay for them. This Christian country is obsessed with the thought of war and the preparation for war. And when we have read of the so-called neutrality of America, we have thought much but said little, because we love America. It is our blood brother, and we respect it.

The Imperator, in his article, has said all that needed saying; and well it would be if it were read from every pulpit in the land. It is true. America is arming the world for warfare because it is a paying proposition. If war materialises, it will share the guilt of war.

That is the objective aspect of neutrality. What of the esoteric aspect? A member in this country wrote to me recently that he could not believe the Cosmic powers would permit the precipitation of such a frightful catastrophe as then threatened the nations.

I asked, is the responsibility that of the Cosmic powers, or ours? Our minds are at cross-purposes. We pray for peace, and arm for war. What we plan for and work towards will materialise. And at the moment the tide of armaments runs stronger and stronger. The major portion of our thought and the money we need are concentrated upon it, and unless the course of it is altered, what can the law of cause and effect do?

Why is it not altered, members ask: why do not the Masters exert their supreme authority in world affairs and destroy this evil of national and international hatred and suspicion once for all?

The Masters inspire, but do not compel. Their voices have been sounding in this old world through their teachings from east and west for a long time now. How much have we profited of it! Increasing numbers profess allegiance to these teachings, for their own good. How many are using them for their fellowmen? How many voices, in the rank and file of aspirants, are raised in inspired utterance and direct challenge against the menacing forces of modern life?

I am ashamed to confess it: they are as rare as the voice of genius. One would think that the labourers in these enlightened days would be many. They are so few that they have not a present hope of making their influence felt in dominating and directing public opinion. That is how much our higher sciences have done for us, or how little we have done with them. Doubtful as we stand, I think we must say that the Cosmic powers have done their part: it is for us to do ours.

There was a time when men, and they were of the Rosicrucian ideal, wholly possessed with a passion for the Christ life, declared themselves in the written or spoken word before the world, with imminent peril to their lives, and arraigned error and ungodliness in tones that stirred multitudes to action. It is for us to resurrect that noble fire and direct it against those powers and dominations which are a present curse to culture and Christendom and which only maintain their boasted supremacy through intrigue and traitorous design in subjugating the individuality and liberty of their peoples.

If we have evolved thought forces of unusual influence, it is time we used them to some purpose. I verily believe that if the united thought forces of the aspirants of the world had been directed, with full intent and purpose, against the malignant excrescence of dictatorship and its damnable influence, the inhuman perverts that gave birth to it would have been ostracised long since and for the remainder of their wretched lives. But this zeal is too much to expect of aspirants today. They have not the spirit of their predecessors, but have become sentimentalists and effeminate.

Politicians cannot save the world. They are far too interested and time-serving. They are party men and cannot see things whole. They are controversial experimenters at the expense of the people. The true leaders of nations are among the people of the nations, without portfolio or office. They are spiritual men, not yet recognised for what they are or can do. I prophesy that events of the immediate future will compel their recognition and put the reins of leadership in their hands.

It is to this end that we in the Rosicrucian Order are working, or should be working. It is not enough to be loyal members of the Great Brotherhood of the centuries: there should be a deep and earnest purpose in membership.

There is a tendency in aspirants to keep apart in an eclectic circle of refined self-occupation for their own good. They stand aloof from world affairs and regard them as something alien to themselves and for which they should have no voice. That attitude may be quite compatible with some cults and societies: it is not in accordance with the tradition of the Rosicrucian Order.

We only need look back through its history to note the sterling characters that stand out all along the line and who have played a prominent part in the affairs of men and nations. They were men who had raised themselves to notability and power by the same august teachings which are in our hands. But they applied them. Directly they entered into a realisation of the truth of life and the soul, they demanded and found a place in the circumstances of their time in which they resolved that their influence should be felt.

They not only taught what they knew: they were not merely concerned to defend what they knew: they took the offensive against the abuses and errors and malpractices of their day, in church, state and society, and if they suffered for so doing, they did leave their mark and make the way easier for good men and very hard for those who oppressed them.

We have the example of the Imperator, in his article, arraigning the flourishing neutral culprits of America and exposing their guilt to the whole world. Not every member in the Order, far from it, has a voice for public appeal and challenge; but many have, and they are holding back. Let them remember that Christ spoke the truth in plain terms.

Many good things have come out of America. The united voices of enlightened Rosicrucians in it could achieve much, but it will not be on the side of neutrality. It can be by uniting their thought forces with the aspirants of Europe through a profound feeling of responsibility for cooperating with them in an unremitting esoteric attack upon the enemies of free and democratic states and their avowed hatred of those states and their traditions, and their secret machinations to overthrow them.

If to some this sounds a revolutionary doctrine, let them remember that we are facing an unprecedented emergency which calls for decisive action. The liberty of the individual which we Rosicrucians cherish above all things else in our daily life, is at stake. There is a gigantic shadow lowering upon it, and we shall prove false to our trust if we spare any pains towards dissipating it.

The statement of "Secret pacts" made by the Imperator in the booklet *1938 and Fate* has proved true to the letter. An optimistic minority in Great Britain regard the recent Munich agreement as a prelude to world peace. The majority think otherwise. Those who have flouted agreements and torn up treaties with scorn and levity in the past, none but fools would trust in the present or the future.

If we in Great Britain really believed in the sincerity of the present agreement and regarded it as a pledge for the future, would the government have secured an overwhelming vote to proceed to the most drastic measures of further armament? The fact is, that the crisis of the Munich agreement and the aftermath of it have brought an increased sense of insecurity and greater fear for the future.

And what has been the effect of it all upon students of the path in this country? They have had before their eyes the spectacle of thousands of fellow human beings being blown to pieces, or lying in agony, or waiting for a merciful oblivion from starvation and exile, of tyrannical persecution and barefaced robbery committed upon good and harmless citizens who are driven like cattle into the lands of strangers on the flimsy pretext of alien blood and hostile belief, and their indignation is full and their resolution inflexible against these monstrous crimes. It is a satanic blow to the lofty ideals they have cherished in mind and heart through years of study and aspiration and unselfish service.

Not only this: they are part of a national system dedicated to the construction of a war implement of vaster and more deadly proportions than ever dreamed of in the history of the world; and if not their hands, then the proceeds of their hands under a cruel taxation, are requisitioned for the purpose. They are compelled to be participators in building for destruction and suffering in flagrant breach of the ideal of peace and goodwill to which they have pledged themselves.

The aspirant in Great Britain today, is raising one hand in entreaty to the Christ of peace, and lowering the other, under the compulsion of the law, to grasp, or contribute to the shaping of, the sword of war. It is a grievous thing. It is an unparalleled sin which cuts to the very heart of all culture, civilization and righteousness.

Dare we say that the responsibility lies with the Cosmic powers who should never permit such a tragic impasse in this enlightened twentieth century? We hesitate to say so. If we had no knowledge of the law of cause and effect, we might say so. But civilized man, not enlightened man, is responsible. With all his civilization he still has an animal and bloody mind. He thinks, fore-pictures and plans bloodshed and devastation. His culture includes hatred, suspicion and ignoble pride.

A Master once said: *"As for human nature in general, it is the same now as it was a million years ago."* I never realised how true that was until these latter years. Human nature is still in the ascendant, not the soul. And where the soul is ascendant in the aspirants of our time, the world atmosphere drags it back to share in its own sordid bent.

And I say to the Rosicrucians and aspirants of America, they cannot be neutral in their attitude towards their brother aspirants in Europe. They should feel the same righteous indignation and the same inflexible resolution to stand for truth and right against this evil thing. They should cooperate in thought and will, in love and sympathy, with those who like themselves have pledged themselves to the noblest and best. Let them assemble themselves in one united influence of compelling thought force against all that would weaken the structure of the Rosicrucian ideal in the world.

The odds are great: so much the stronger shall be our will; and the Cosmic powers are with us. It is for us to give utterance to the Cosmic will. Not in thought alone, but in voiced indignation and concerted action through every avenue open to us, should we register our abhorrence of this violent usurpation of the rights of man and its growing menace to our democratic life.

2. A Task for Rosicrucians

Reprinted from the July 1939 edition of the Rosicrucian Digest.

I have been much interested in the swift and spontaneous response to my recent article in the Digest on world affairs. It revealed to me how strongly students within the Rosicrucian Order, and outside of it, were thinking about the incontrovertible facts set forth in the article.

To be quite frank, I expected this reaction. If I had not believed I was feeling the pulse of students on this subject, and a very strong pulse it is, I should not have appealed to them. But I found, from appreciative letters received from several countries, that I had taken the temperature of thinking minds on matters of profound import to them, and they welcomed a statement in plain language of plain facts which they had not voiced for themselves.

There is a point of special interest to Rosicrucians about the article in question. I make no apology for the reference. The article was, in some measure, prophetic. It was written prior to the days of the Jewish persecution in Germany and out of my hands; and by the time it had reached the editor America had been swept by a wave of indignation and disgust at the outrage, and the cooperation against the modern tyrants I urged was already on foot before the article appeared.

Do not mistake me. I did not expect my article would work an international miracle. The point is, that I anticipated an urgent need for cooperation and sensed approaching conditions which would precipitate it.

Those advanced in the Rosicrucian studies will recall that the faculty of prophecy is one which is fostered and becomes of unusual power and use under the training given in those studies. It is not a faculty to be lightly used: on the contrary, there is a great responsibility in its use. But I refer to this instance as one of a concrete nature which suggests that if we are alive to the work in our hands, we shall know not only what is happening within our immediate circle, but around us and a long way from us in matters pertaining to the trend of world affairs. We must place our thought upon the pulse of things where our fellowmen and their destiny are concerned, and take the offensive.

Now, since the article in question, I need scarcely remind readers that the offensive has been taken. In fact, it has been taken in America far more strongly and swiftly than I anticipated. I doubt whether the world has ever witnessed such a heady current of cooperative interest and alignment of aim as has been seen between our two countries within the past few months. And what pleases me is, the focussed interest and will of our members has had its part in it.

I have felt the increasing coalescence of thought force set solidly, at whatever cost, against the detestable crimes which have disturbed the peace of our day, and a gathering stress of world opinion against the depraved instigators of them.

This world stress is beating unrelentingly against the seats of iniquity, and those who sit on them are feeling the baffling insecurity of their tenure. The forces of social rightness, justice and humanity are of tremendous and irresistible strength. Every one of us has proved that in his own life. When great nations align themselves with those forces, something is bound to happen. It is now on the verge of happening; and we are taking a responsible part in its happening.

Some of my correspondents have asked me earnestly what special thing they could do to help offset these evils which have so distressed them. I have been asked for some kind of formula which might be used concertedly. This has its uses, but I doubt whether it is necessary in view of the stable and persistent basic thought tendency in our lives and the direction in which our quickened thought forces are now focussed and operating.

I have even been asked for some formula of peace to be used in concert. Yet there is not a religious community in this country which has not set this ideal daily before it; week in and out it has been the public theme of practically all statesmen; groups of all kinds and denominations of every description have voiced it persistently: and the press of the democracies has reiterated it untiringly. There cannot be an intelligent person in the democracies whose mind has not been impressed by it.

And for ourselves, in our Cathedral of the Soul contacts, there are special sessions for every day towards this ideal. Nor is the latter an emergency experiment: it has been an established institution within the Rosicrucian Order since 1930.

Every member of our Order should know beyond doubt or question, and I wish everyone outside of it knew as well, that the Order has nothing new to add to its traditional policy and aim in this respect. If that policy and aim were written in the hearts of whole nations of men, the present "international complex" would not exist.

The real Rosicrucian ever was, and I am persuaded is now, an individual with peace and kindness and compassionate helpfulness in his heart, one to whom the distressed and perplexed come in perfect confidence and trust and assured of understanding and upright treatment. That is what I read in the great souls of the past. It is what I see in the great souls of the present. There is nothing, fundamentally, they can add to that. But ostensibly, they can bring that goodness to a focus and not be afraid to take the offensive against any evil that menaces their fellowmen.

Emerson once said that our goodness must have some edge to it, or it is none. I believe that. It is not enough to sit down and pray for peace and goodwill and think we have wrought a miracle. We must assert ourselves, in any way in which we are able, to bring that goodness into active opposition against those circumstances, men and governments which threaten to curtail human freedom and crucify in soul the sons of men.

I said we were *"in trust to curtail and stamp out"* the evil that militates against our ideal. I repeat it, emphatically. I will never be a party to that quiescent frame of mind which takes comfort to itself in the placid thought that because we are at a crucial point in the evolution of the races, therefore it is inevitable that injustice and cruelty and all their attendant vices must prevail for the term of our natural lives and we can rest comfortably in our own assurance and knowledge and allow the blackguards of creation to run their course in triumph.

To me, that is the cardinal iniquity. It is an acquiescence in suffering and demoralisation and in flagrant opposition to our ideal. I may not be able to save my fellowman from the despoliation of vulturine men, but I will speak with plain and uncurbed frankness the word of justice for the one and against the other. And I am heartened that those who have written to me, are, to a man and woman, of the same mind. It often takes a great crisis to reveal the real soul of man. We know little of it while life runs smoothly and all is well. But let the devil raise his head on this planet and sneer at the goodness we have bled our hearts to attain, and the lightning of God will flash forth with terrible vengeance.

The scriptures have told us this from infancy. It was so in olden times: it is so today. And much as I deplore the cause, I, for one, am not sorry to have lived to witness the truth of it.

Rosicrucian members are distressed because their lot has been cast upon evil days. Let it be remembered that many notable Rosicrucians appeared and worked through very difficult historical phases. It was precisely in such cycles that they unexpectedly shed abroad their peculiar and dominant influence and gave hope to multitudes by their fearless works and raised their spirit to combat ignorance and oppression.

We resent incursions upon our peace of mind: we grieve that the world ideal of culture can be so ignominiously lowered under the authority of brazen usurpers before our eyes; we recoil at the abuse, lying and intrigue directed with malicious intent against verified and unshakable truth: and a feeling of inevitability creeps over the soul.

That should not be. It is a confession, not of the weakness of our ideal, but that it does not yet master us. The spirit of mental and spiritual conquest should become, under our profession and practice, so strong and sublimated, that we should not only accept any challenge against it, but take the offensive against any encroachment upon it.

One correspondent in America wrote to me in sorrow that she could do so little regarding the matters I wrote of. Yet she was awake and progressive enough to send the Imperator's article and my own to the governor of her state. That single act of devotion in a great cause may well have far-reaching consequences; far more, in fact, than that of a group of devotees who read the articles, prayed for peace, and slept soundly.

I am not incriminating any member, or group of students, but what nauseates me in a critical hour, or in any other hour, is a reading, meditating, lethargic, self-possessed and self-satisfied mystic who believes that policy fulfils his mission in life. I am convinced that far too many are primarily intent upon their own development and goodness, and far too little concerned to put any pressure upon themselves to bring their faculties and energies into requisition in this great day of opportunity.

For mistake it not, there is no such day of opportunity for the real mystic as when the floodgates of high crimes and misdemeanours in states are open and he has to fight for the highest he knows, or lose it. The contemplative mind may find its joy, inward satisfaction and ecstasy in the quiet days of repose and tranquillity. Even so, it is all too prone to become a contemplation of selfish personal abstraction and completely non-productive of any great work.

The present is far from such a period. If we could but see it, the greatest call today, blindly inarticulate as it may be, is for those who have the mystical power in their right hand and can use it. From the ranks of our high grade members should come forth those who have in silence through the years taken the measure of their abilities, equipped themselves to sound the note of mystical supremacy, and can make their influence felt in the affairs of their time.

It would be a sorry confession for us to have to make, that in these days, when under an urgent demand upon science and industry to perfect a war implement of unbelievable proportion, cleverness and destructive power to meet a material emergency, the response to that demand is met with incredible rapidity and completely; while we, who have given long years to the study of mind and the forces of thought, steeped our minds in the literature of men who have given a new trend to world history through their manipulation and use, and even fed our indulgent imaginations with the possibilities of doing ourselves likewise, should not play our part in adding something to the determination and strength of the democratic ideal and pledge that the aims of the aspiring Machiavellis of our day shall be rendered abortive.

Our task is to steel the will and hold it like a drill to the one point of higher and nobler achievement for specific purpose. That purpose is a broader, freer and more useful and expressive life, not only for ourselves, but for others.

If I am reminded that there is also love, I am not unmindful of that. Love can never operate in its true estate, efficiently, wisely, impersonally and with Christ-like compassionateness, unless the mind is developed, exalted, and knows the technical possibilities of the love force directed into other lives.

Jesus was a master of mind, and a very practical man: in fact, it is impressive to note how little suggestion is to be gained, from the scripture records, that he was in any sense a contemplative. He was an active, progressive, fighting mystic. Had He not been so He would never have been so astute in His action, so unerringly correct and direct in His speech, or so loved in the depth of His heart creatures whom we should find it very difficult not to justly condemn. How often did he warn His disciples and bid them beware of the hypocrites who were watching every opportunity to thwart Him and destroy His ideal?

That warning still sounds in our ears and is justification sufficient in urging that the understanding mind should be opposed with all its force against the threatening dominations in the world today.

This is our task: to put the mind, trained to the Rosicrucian ideal, on active service in the realm of world affairs. That applies, primarily, I grant, to the comparatively few who are ready. If they feel no call to that, they have a lesser call, and it is an imperative call which cannot be shirked. It is that they resolve to fit themselves for the morrow, and today throw the light and inspiration they have into other minds in preparation.

We know that is being done within the Order, continuously and unselfishly. I regard it as one of the greatest things being done. I have seen kindness, generosity and great personal pains expended in instilling into others knowledge and guidance which even those of early days in the Order possess. They have needed no encouragement; they have taken the initiative; and by taking upon themselves something of the burden of other lives, they have received added impetus to their own powers.

In conclusion, I would strike a note of encouragement. I believe the Rosicrucian Order has a greater standing and influence today than in any previous century.

That is probably due to the fact that in former cycles it worked under great difficulty. Political domination and religious bigotry made it very precarious for the early worker to do anything but in the closest secrecy. Yet in spite of restrictions, threats and penalties, the few real mystics wrote and published, and suffered for it. We owe them much. And in some countries of Europe today the same crass ignorance prevails, and the mystic has to work within the veil of obscurity.

But it is not so with us. We have a clear field for speech and action, and we mean to keep it. There is our opportunity and our bounden duty. Let us see to it that we leave a good record of our passing through this cycle.

3. A Message from the Grand Master of Great Britain

Reprinted from the July 1941 edition of the Rosicrucian Digest.

> *The following is a letter sent by Frater Raymund Andrea, Grand Master of Great Britain, to all Rosicrucian members in affiliation with his jurisdiction. Faced with tremendous obstacles in his nation, he expends great energy of mind and body in furthering, not alone the esoteric ideals of the Rosicrucian Order, but its physical aspects as well. He is a ceaseless worker, and as practical in his activities as he is idealistic in his thinking. Year after year, by accomplishment, he has proven his faithfulness to his sacred trust. He did not intend that his letter be published in the* Rosicrucian Digest, *but the determination which it virtually radiates, as well as its appeal to the members to stand firm upon the Rosicrucian principles in their ordeal, is worthy, in our opinion, of being read by Rosicrucians in every land. The exhortations contained in Frater Andrea's letter are not empty or pretty-sounding phrases. They have been exemplified by his modest and retiring life and what he has actually brought forth during the years of his service. Let Rosicrucians everywhere take new encouragement from his words. — Imperator (Ralph M Lewis).*

Dear Fellow Member of the Rose Cross:

I do not often send a circular letter to members, such as the present one. I have two reasons for not doing so more often.

One is, that members are in close contact with the work and influence of the Order through the regular weekly Monograph which reaches them, and that is in itself a personal message and assurance of being a part of that work and influence. Moreover, a personal letter from the Lodge sometimes accompanies a Monograph and is a medium of special help and inspiration.

The second reason is, that members are under my personal supervision and there is a constant stream of correspondence between them and myself throughout the year, much of which deals with intimate personal problems and has first claim upon my time and interest. Time very often forbids the writing of lengthy letters; nevertheless, those problems have first claim upon my time, interest and energy, and if dealt with concisely, it is to the best of my ability.

But today is one of deep gravity and concern to us all. Suffering and anxiety, disappointment and loss, have come to all in one form or another. And although we are facing this dark night of the soul with courage and steadfast faith in the truth we know, and believe in the relatively important part we are playing, each in his or her own sphere, in assisting to build the new world which is even now shaping itself behind the world chaos, we are grieved and perplexed because of the voice of suffering and despair which reaches us on every hand.

For our thought cannot remain at home, intent upon ourselves. It leaps out across the frontiers and tries to bless and shield those who are bereaved, broken, maimed and hopeless in the mournful wastes of the world's Gethsemane.

A letter recently received from a lady member, moved me to send this message to you at this moment of greatest crisis. The letter is the voice of deepest suffering and appeal, and I quote from it.

> "We millions of mothers are not able to carry on alone. My beloved son is missing. By God's loving mercy I received a message while asleep, and see him wounded, lying enclosed in a building. I have asked…, 'If it pleases the Masters, it is done,' holding this in the Cosmic Mind. He has a pure soul and body, 23 years of giving and gathering love, and blessed with a gift of music and a fine mind. I ask that you take him a message of love and comfort."

That letter, written in anguish of soul, is but one of many, many similar ones. But that fact does not diminish the individual suffering; it probably increases it. Yet this understanding and sharing of the suffering of others is a most potent help. It strengthens the kinship of souls and fits us for more extended service in the world.

This is the message I wish to send you at this hour. We hear much on the radio of sharing the common perils of today and of facing them bravely and with undiminished faith in the ultimate triumph of good. And that is well. But we in the Order, with a firm faith in the knowledge in our hands and in the Masters of life, must more than ever seek to be a living example of what we believe, and do our utmost in simple and common ways…, for that is the highway of great service…, to bring our influence to bear upon others wherever we are.

We must do our utmost to break down the glamour of fear which so insidiously endeavours to undermine our hope in the new age for which we have so long striven. We must refuse to doubt that there is a deep, if unrevealed, purpose behind the veil of events. Just as in the arena of warfare of every kind the watchword is, to doggedly hold out, so must it be with ourselves who are on a path from which there can be no retreat.

I have written elsewhere that the mystic must be militant. It applies today as never before. He must fight, often silently and unknown, against odds without and within. Only thus does he prove his strength and prove that his faith has an immortal foundation. No matter what his mistakes may be, or what the fogs of doubt may suggest, no matter how tired in body or anxious in mind, his one clear-cut duty and privilege is, to hold out. That attitude is of incalculable effect for good upon others. His thought cannot be hidden. It strikes upon the world atmosphere and encourages and inspires in ways he will never know, and attracts to himself the unseen agencies of good which wait upon his petition.

The pathetic letter from which I have quoted should emphasise in a deeply personal way our responsibility as members of our Order. We should share this suffering in thought, and take our part in alleviating it by cultivating a greater compassion of heart and a dedicated force of mind.

We know the law and should use it to the full, according to our ability. It cannot fail. It will work in miraculous ways and bring peace, comfort and fortitude to those who have nearly surrendered all in despair. It will restore faith which has all but vanished. And our reward will be larger vision, clearer insight, and a power of service which we looked not for.

With my kindest regards and
    all good wishes for Peace Profound.
    Yours sincerely and fraternally,
    R. Andrea

4. Ambition or Stagnation

Reprinted from the October 1943 edition of the Rosicrucian Digest.

That most illustrious Rosicrucian, Bacon, wrote of ambition:

> "He that seeketh to be eminent amongst able men, hath a great task; but that is ever for the public good; but he that plots to be the only figure amongst ciphers is the decay of a whole age."

According to Bacon, therefore, ambition to excel is worthy and commendable and ever of a public advantage. But he decries the selfish, dominating ambition that schemes to be the one and only authority amongst those without weight, worth or influence, the kind of ambition that promotes pride and leads to tyranny.

We cannot respect too highly the wisdom and sagacity of Bacon. He had an unparalleled insight into the nature of man and the conditions and circumstances of everyday life, and was a supreme master of the common sense approach and adjustment necessary for rising to eminence in all fields of human advancement.

Now, if we turn to the little occult classic known as *Light on the Path*, we shall find therein written something very different from Bacon's idea of ambition. There is a sententious admonition to *"Kill out ambition. Ambition is the first curse; the great tempter of the man who is rising above his fellows."*

Personally, I am strongly opposed to the idea of *"killing out"* human faculties or tendencies, whether in the physical or mental life, in the interest of *"self-development."* I can conceive of nothing so utterly destructive of human progress or so calculated to bring cultural evolution to a dead stop and reduce human life to a purely animalistic existence, as to teach our children that ambition is a curse and a devil in the path of the man who is rising above his fellows.

Every great man in world history has become such under the incentive of ambition: every achievement on the path of human progress has had behind it the driving force of ambition; and nothing of value has been or ever will be achieved without it. Obviously, therefore, such an admonition, at face value, is either ridiculous, or is applicable under exceptional and rare conditions, and only in the case of a very few. Consequently, such teachings should be accepted with very definite reservations; otherwise, they retard far more than they advance a student.

There is no branch of literature, no way of life, which so much requires a sane perspective in approach and use, as does that dealing with the science of soul development. Incredible as it may appear, it often costs a student ten or twenty years, and sometimes the best part of a lifetime to gain that perspective. This is not because he lacks mental ability or steady application, but because, accepting literally some occult canon early in his studies, he believes that such a Master condition as is depicted possible for himself through drastic measures of curtailment or denial, discounting entirely an extended vista of evolutionary experience which must intervene before he can even see the possibility of a right adjustment.

Light on the Path, for instance, contains undoubtedly a Master teaching of the highest tone and quality; it is also one of the most enigmatical. I wonder how many aspirants, pondering upon the opening sentences, which epitomise the whole teaching of the book, have laid violent hands upon their crying human nature and refused to shed a tear, deliberately closed their ears to all but what they wanted to hear, stifled the holy motion of their souls to utter a word of righteous indignation against the influence of a public evil or a private wrong, and left the idea of washing the feet in the blood of the heart to take care of itself.

Of the many in this predicament, we may find one who is fulfilling one or other of the injunctions orthodoxly and quite inadequately and giving the unhandsome impression of a forced development and not in the least inviting as an example of adjustment in life. As to the possible one who fulfils them all with the perspective required and in harmony with the Master intention and the natural law of growth, if we met him we should scarcely recognise him and possibly take him for a fool.

It is common to observe how, not only average aspirants but mature students of some advancement, with a good deal of study and meditation to their credit, pin themselves down to the actual word of occult scripture in thought and action with the questionable confidence that Mastership will follow upon there by simple obedience thereto. This orthodox approach to the science of the soul is a plain insult to their natural intelligence, to the spirit of life and the laws of living.

It is puzzling and perplexing, because these same students would be the first to recognise that in the sciences, arts and professions, many arduous years have to be devoted to progressive discipline and a multiplicity of related interests for the one purpose of gaining facility and experience in the use of mind and limb, of the whole man, before there is any prospect of a call to any notable field of service.

Of the most exacting science of all they make an exception. Adeptship, it seems, will flower suddenly. Worldly experience does not count and has no place therein. Let the man but obey the letter of the law by slaying three parts of the human element within him and supernal rewards must follow.

It is a vulgar belief and savours of self-murder. Emasculation is no passport to Mastership. It is a passport to nothing worthy in life. The law of success and development demands the fullest utilisation of the personality of man, the completest self-expression. Recognition, acceptance and use constitute the threefold key of attainment.

Read Bacon and Whitman, two of the most contrasted personalities, original, demonstrative and prolific, both classic exponents of the gospel of the fullness of life, and two of the richest examples of mastery living we may expect to see among men even in the world of tomorrow. They were men who brought life to full circle in themselves before they finished with it, by living it, not by denying it.

It has been said that it had been better if the elaborate breathing technique used in the East had never been brought to the attention of students in the West, because of its unfitness for the latter and the threat to health and sanity arising from the incautious use of it. I think it would also have been well if some of the occult classics on development had never reached many aspirants until after the meridian of life, when experience may have taught them better how to read and apply them.

The inflated ideas some of these books have given to students are astonishing. I was much influenced early in life this way. Fortunately, through a varied experience in the everyday world, and a dispassionate experience of the others, my ideas were quickly modified. I know that supermen are not born overnight, although my first ideas gave me that happy infatuation.

A statesman once said that *"we are capable of conceiving what we are incapable of attaining."* That may be true in politics and in many other things; and as the statement came from a statesman who was driven into exile, the significance and truth of it are apparent. But we have a maxim that anything we are capable of conceiving is possible of attainment. Yet that maxim is as false as the other, in the particular circumstances, may be true, if we place a time limit on the attainment.

This is where many aspirants go hopelessly wrong. An authoritative occult scripture which articulates smoothly, sounds magnificently and promises devoutly, appeals so subtly to their vanity, that they risk a wholly unnatural disciplinary self-slaughter to compass their end. But time is a painful and indifferent teacher; and at length, fatigued in body and disgruntled in mind, they count up the years which have cheated them of the great discovery, and begin to seek the reason for it.

They come to us in the Order with a life history of research behind them, and are brought the first time to face the laws and principles of adjustment here and now on the material plane where, whether they like it or not, they are going to spend all their days and take one step at a time. The difficulty is, that they are so often possessed with inflated ideas of what they were meant to be and ought to be, that it is a long time before they can accept themselves as they really are.

Sometimes a golden idol has to be smashed if only to release their gaze from it; or an ideal has to be exploded or the vision of it transplanted from heaven to earth in their own best interest. They constitute a difficult problem, for you cannot impart your own experience to others; but you can give your point of view, even if it shocks them.

Yet when I come to think of it, Jesus said a few shocking things to the aspirants of His day, so shocking in fact that some became secret enemies instead of open-minded disciples. Knowing the aspirants to whom He spoke, it was possible to enjoin some of them to deny themselves and follow; but for the majority, they were directed to living, action and experience.

I think He would do exactly the same today. I do not think He would say indiscriminately to an assembly of aspirants: *"Kill out ambition;"* for I doubt whether any aspirant is ready to deny himself, give up all, and follow Christ until he has known and taken the measure of ambition in the fullest sense.

Indeed, it has been said on good authority that a man is not ready to advance to high spiritual development until he has demonstrated his ability to command success on the material and intellectual planes, thereby gaining an understanding of the manipulation of the laws of those planes, as a necessary basis for their application upon a higher spiral of evolution. There is much to be said for this viewpoint; and nothing so strongly confirms it as those aspirants we meet sometimes who are so entirely hypnotised by a word of scripture that they regard normal humanness as an enemy of man.

I confess that I have met very few aspirants on the path, if any, whom I would conscientiously advise to kill ambition. The fact is, they are not ready for any such doctrine. The admonition is only a safe one to put to a disciple of high standing and very exceptional qualifications, and he would scarcely need it. For long before a disciple reaches the higher spirals of the path he will have sounded ambition to the depths and be fully aware of the necessity for transformation of desire both intellectually and spiritually. For the purpose of the aspirant the statement of Bacon is plainly and concisely informative.

It falls simply in two parts. In the first, ambition is shown to be laudable, but what is of greater importance, ever of public utility. That is the true criterion of ambition; and if the ambition of the aspirant passes that criterion, he need never fear it. The second part contains a warning against that sinister type of ambition which *"plots to be the only figure."* Therein lies the *"curse of ambition;"* but fortunately society is so constituted that, when that kind of insanity takes hold of an aspirant, he soon meets with his desert in loss of friendship, status and the respect of his fellows. We have no need to be on the path to learn that.

I must be frank on this subject, however much of a renegade I may appear to be. From the day I entered upon my work in the Order I have been an unceasing promoter and inspirer of the ambitions of students on the path. I know well the implications of the higher teachings of the path; but I have never had to deal with angels on it, but with men and women like myself who have desired to make their lives of some value in this world.

Nothing has given me more satisfaction than to hear of a student overcoming long-standing difficulties in life, passing to place, power or authority, achieving what hitherto had been deemed impossible, and throwing a powerful influence into other lives and leading them to a greater perspective and action. It is a *"hard task,"* as Bacon said, but if it is *"ever good for the public,"* as it undoubtedly is, there is nothing for which to apologise.

Looking through the rank and file of aspirants of all kinds, what higher service can one render them than to encourage and lead them on to a larger expression of the faculties and powers within them? We have no mission, nor any moral right, to regard all aspirants as if they had a special call to straightaway renounce material and intellectual life and assume the responsibilities of the highest stages of evolution approximating Mastership, because a comparatively few are of mature evolutionary status and are ready to dedicate themselves in mind and circumstance to such responsibilities.

We have no right to admonish aspirants to commit sacrilege in the temple of body and mind by slaying those wholesome desires and aspiring faculties necessary for success in the many worlds of human endeavour existing lawfully for none other than our utilisation and conquest, because certain Masters and disciples may have, in the order of evolution, attained to a superlative degree of attachment from and indifferency to the ordinary activities of men and are called to hierarchical duty which is concerned solely with spiritual issues.

To say that these ambitions of the majority of men should be slain at the very threshold of life and experience or in the early days of their fruition, is to perfectly misunderstand a refined and advanced occult teaching which can apply only to an isolated and negligible few among the disciples of our time in the West.

It is not wise to fight against the evolutionary urge at any period of history. Let us take a hint from the present urge. At no time so much as during the present world catastrophe have the ambitions of young and old, literate and illiterate, in every rank of life high and low, been called forth to assert themselves in all fields of thought and action for national and international well-being.

Admittedly, many of the personal and cherished ambitions of men have had to temporarily give place to those of more immediate national importance; but the force of ambition remains, and it is worldly ambition still. True, the main force of ambition today is directed against the overthrow of barbaric races who threaten not only the eclipse of all worldly ambition, but of civilisation and life itself. But it is the same force in man striving for achievement and mastery and superb technique wherever attention is directed and duty demands.

Would you slay that primitive force in human life? If so, you may aim directly at the destruction of the prime moving spirit of initiative in man and of all cultural survival. Never so forcibly as today has the personality of man been demanded and coerced into action by the choicest spirits of the time in every walk of life, and the response has been magical. Never before has the personality of man been so insistently urged to prepare itself for the expression of the fullest ambition in the world to follow after the war. Nor will anything less than the strongest ambition suffice to initiate even a fraction of what the idealists and preachers of utopia hope then to achieve.

There will be no place in the postwar world for the deniers of personality and slayers of ambition, whatever the doctrine upon which they stake their aloofness and salvation. The keen battle of life will go on, with ambition actuating and impelling every right-minded aspirant to fulfil the decrees of Karma which have brought him into the field.

Foreseeing somewhat the hard fight ahead which this will entail, he may turn to some high doctrine of the path which appears to offer him a safe conscience in sidetracking the issue and seeking a promised spiritual ascendancy which will eclipse or render unnecessary any lower or mundane adjustments and achievements. For him, this way of escape will bring neither satisfaction nor progress: he will waste valuable time and have to return later to the path of the development of personality.

There is no escape in aloofness from the daily battles in the fields of personality: the inevitable lessons which he must learn for self-conquest are to be found there and nowhere else. I do not minimise the value or authority of the high doctrine of the path; obviously not, for I have written much about it: but I have seen so many instances of aspirants, young and old, who have been inclined to evade the obligations and responsibilities of life for the sake of some nebulous spiritual supremacy which they thought would follow quickly upon a retreat, and I never feel happy about them. Not one of them will find it by so doing. They will but wrench asunder the chain of Karmic commitment and introduce into it, by their action, causes of future disaster and bondage which will bring them back relentlessly in the fullness of time to live a natural life and fulfil their plain duty. What they have sown, they must reap.

The fact that they feel tempted to evade the decrees of Karma by the assumed spiritual superiority of taking refuge in a high doctrine which appears to sanction flight from the actual and a premature detachment from worldly commitments, is a plain indication of surrender to personal weakness, rather than a consciousness of fulfilled destiny which would come to them without seeking at the right time.

If, as is taught by many, the present world tragedy has behind it a profound occult significance and the Karma of nations is being inexorably adjusted, then we cannot escape the fact that the individual Karma is inextricably interwoven with it; and if no nation can escape this adjustment, neither can any individual.

The aspirant is no exception, although he sometimes has the vanity to think he is. Inasmuch as the responsibility resting upon the aspirant, in view of his knowledge of occult law, is greater than that of the average individual who knows nothing of it, the more accountable is he in the eyes of that law to see to it that he fulfils his part in the common destiny of mankind; and that means, that no matter what doctrine of immortal felicity he cherishes and to which he would attain, a present faithfulness to all the calls of his personal life, on whatever plane of action which Karma has written in his constitution, is the only way of reaching it and should be heeded and fulfilled.

Having to resort to so violent a procedure as to *"kill ambition,"* can mean only one thing to the aspirant: that it is exceedingly strong and unfulfilled and a Karmic inheritance which will demand fulfilment; whereas its fostering and fulfilment in the service of the world is the one and only felicity the Masters are said to know.

5. World Catastrophe and Responsibility

Reprinted from the October 1944 edition of the Rosicrucian Digest.

In Britain we approach the sixth year of war; and while there is no doubt whatever that the aggressor nations will be overthrown, the end is not yet in sight. Direct action to that end is the keynote of the allied nations; so much so that there appears to be little time to reflect or trouble ourselves now about the causes of the world catastrophe. Yet there must be few intelligent persons who do not again and again, especially in times of crucial experience, ask themselves what is the cause of so far-reaching an effect.

Some esotericists assure us that we are witnessing a crisis in the evolution of humanity when the forces of good must declare their supremacy over the forces of evil, and that the untold suffering of millions is merited. The minds of many, seeking a cause at any price to rest upon and relieve themselves of further questioning or doubt, accept this statement as sufficient and satisfactory. It accords with their philosophical turn of mind to accept without question an abstruse, authoritative statement, even though it be incapable of proof and they themselves could not maintain an argument for it under the interrogation of the most just, open-minded questioner sincerely seeking enlightenment.

But experience shows that persons of this mental trend are troubled little about the fact that they have no *"reason for their belief,"* so long as they are in quiet enjoyment of the belief themselves and all doubt is allayed in consequence. I sometimes wonder whether their belief would have stood the fire of circumstances had they been subjected to it in Russia or Poland, or some other occupied country. Geographical position in a world catastrophe is apt to have a decided influence upon one's personal belief.

I am not suggesting that this particular philosophical view is untrue. I only think that few accept it who are really inwardly convinced of it. For instance, a note of fatalism is at once introduced by an assertion of this view, for the innocents have suffered with the guilty. We do not like the idea of fatalism. It implies a helplessness in the face of the circumstances of life; whereas the more liberal doctrine of cause and effect, as we know it, promises some control and personal shaping of those circumstances.

But if the present clash between good and evil forces is inevitable at this point of evolution, and if the allied nations have been compelled to take their stand against worldwide evil domination, then there has been no choice in the matter. We have been pitched, good and bad alike, into the maelstrom together. The very good we would have done has been struck out of our hands; and we became the humble, or resentful, observers of an indifferent stroke of fate.

In any case, the fact remains that the allied nations have been forced to take a stand, or perish; and we cannot be surprised if not a few, of all shades of culture and belief, should call it fate. Nor is it easy to dispossess them of this belief. Neither should it be met with anything less than understanding and tolerance.

Can it surprise us that it is not only considered a hard saying, but cool and incompassionate to counter the universal suffering of innocents, through every gradation of personal privation and desolation up to wilful, calculated and brutal murder; with an esoteric conception that the whole hideous masquerade is but a case of cause and effect, even of personal blameworthiness in a forgotten past, and that every suffering unit has received a just and merited reward?

It may be so, from the theoretical calculations of a recondite and philosophical point of view, and the abstruse interweaving technique of it may be visible to some very unusual minds, but who else has, or can be expected to have, experimental and exact cognisance of it? I know of none.

Some ambitious writers appear to have sought to elucidate, or, to speak more humbly, desired to comment upon this most abstruse of problems; but it requires little penetration to perceive that the position they adopt is an assumptive one, and that their deductions are made from certain well-worn Theosophical postulates introduced to buttress their views and give them an atmosphere of authority. These philosophical theories, or fundamental postulates, whichever they happen to be, appeal to such writers. They make them the basis of explanation of a universal catastrophe as completely beyond their own mental grasp or insight to fathom and justify, as those of their readers.

That a negligible minority of the latter accept these attempts to read the inscrutable as indisputably true, is not to be denied; but even these, I suggest, find it difficult to reconcile the idea of compassion and justice with the indiscriminate penalising and murder of countless innocents. For it is roundly affirmed that the innocents have suffered as the guilty. If therefore even one innocent has so suffered, the law of compassion and justice has been violated.

This is the kind of argument we have to face on this subject, and it is a well-grounded one. Among aspirants, and those who are not aspirants, we meet with many who turn away from it, much as they are affected by it. They see the logical conclusion but are afraid of it. No matter what the extent of their reading or their culture, they refuse to venture an opinion upon it.

Others can find no satisfying answer in heart, mind or soul. Keen thinkers, those of decided opinions in all other matters of life, here are silent and have neither solution or suggestion. It would appear almost better to say to them emphatically that every person, even those they know to be of most blameless character and fruitful service, must have suffered or have been slain because of past guiltiness; if thereby they could be given some inward satisfaction of reason and justice for the slaughter of innocents and not left numbed with the pain of a wounded heart for the rest of their lives.

But we cannot assert anything of the kind. We have no right to make an assertion of this nature, for we do not know; and if we did, what right have we to insult the maimed and desolated living, and, far worse, the silent dead?

A member from Canada, prominent and respected in one of our lodges there, came to Britain to attach himself to the air force. After training he was drafted into a bomber squadron. He came to see me several times during his training; and the last time he came he told me that, before an interview with his commanding officer who was to assign him to specific bombing operations over Germany, he had decided to ask to be relieved of this particular duty in view of his aversion to killing.

While preparing himself for the interview he happened to speak with a young woman who related to him the sufferings of her own family in a recent raid. He was so moved by the account that all scruples were swept at once from his mind and he thereupon accepted duty without question. He wished to have my confirmation of his decision, which I unhesitatingly gave him.

He was lost soon after in a heavy raid upon Cologne. We may ask ourselves: was this then the effect of long range guiltiness as a cause?

No one who knew this young man would say so. He told me of his companions in service, robust and fearless men, caring nothing for tomorrow and with no thought of an afterlife, very unlike himself. He was one of the kindest, gentlest and most lovable characters I have met. In fact, so unfitted did he appear for the task assigned him that I appealed to a higher authority in the hope of having him transferred from it. But it was too late.

We believe in the law of cause and effect. We use it and know its value. But let us beware when and how we apply its doctrine when the innocents, the flower of a generation, go to their graves for a world unworthy of them.

These reflections face us with a thorny problem. Our theories little avail the desolated heart. There are arguments for and against, and after due attention to both I am not sure that our interrogators will still remain unconvinced.

Schopenhauer wrote that *"all great suffering, whether mental or physical, reveals what we deserve: for it could not visit us if we did not deserve it."* For this sweeping statement an acute psychologist called him *"a poisoner and slanderer of life."*

Schopenhauer's statement is very familiar to us. He found it where we ourselves found it, in Eastern literature. We have accepted it as true, not because we have any actual proof of its truth but because it comes from an Eastern source and is implicitly accepted by many. But if it is true we must speak no more of an outraged world and the slaughter of innocents. There are no innocents. Every one of them was guilty and has received his reward.

Not only are men and women of all ranks and culture at a loss to assign a reasonable and just cause for so disastrous an effect on an outraged world; our church dignitaries are in the same position. Some of them however have been as ambitious as the writers mentioned to assign authoritatively a cause. They have been quick to make a case for themselves by placing the blame upon the irreligiousness of the people.

If the former case of philosophy appears untenable, this of religion is more so. The established church in Britain at least has had good innings to date; and if periodical world wars arise because of the irreligiousness of the people, it is to be inferred that the influence of the church on the people has been exceedingly negligible. The late Archbishop of Canterbury in a recent broadcast sadly proclaimed that some 80 per cent of the people of Britain did not bear witness to the Christian faith. This fact, if fact it is, should be far more alarming to the church than to the people. It is not a condemnation of the people, but of the church. It is a plain confession that it has no voice for the growing consciousness of the people.

Nor is it true that even though 80 per cent of the people do not bear witness to the Christian faith, that is, within the church or other religious houses, that therefore they have no religious faith. Such a statement reveals either a distortion of the fact or a complete ignorance of the national mind. If the church has lost its hold upon the minds of 80 per cent of the people, or fails to influence that percentage, then the church has failed in its mission as a mystical body.

We know that the church has so failed. Some of its own leaders have borne witness to its failure out of their own mouths, for it is bound hand and voice by its traditional and obsolete articles. And the people of Britain are less disposed than ever before to subscribe to that bondage or listen to the deadening, orthodoxical, platitudinarian teaching which oozes from it. They demand and will have onward, progressive living, thinking and action.

The reason for the rapidly diminishing influence of the church on the public mind in Britain is that it has shown neither understanding or sympathy with the advancing mind in Britain. Within the past twenty years remarkable advancement has been made in the fields of psychology and psychiatry. A corpus of literature is now available in these sciences of the highest value and significance, and intelligent and thinking persons everywhere have eagerly studied and applied its teachings to a solution of their personal and perplexing problems of mind and conduct.

Acknowledged experts in these sciences have offered to the public a wise and understanding guidance in the way of adjustment to life. They have probed into the world of individual causes so thoroughly, profoundly and revealingly as to make the antiquated church appear in comparison and in fact as whited sepulchres, full of dead men's bones.

The time has passed when the people can be in the least convinced that they are abject sinners, and that their manifold personal aberrations, which the clergy and the laity equally share, are the basic cause of world wars and bloody massacres. I will quote a little from Jung, that master psychologist of world-wide repute, on this subject. It is a sober and damning indictment.

> "I have found," he writes: "that modern man has an ineradicable aversion for traditional opinions and inherited truths. He is a Bolshevist for whom all the spiritual standards and forms of the past have lost their validity, and who therefore wants to experiment in the world of the spirit as the Bolshevist experiments with economics. When confronted with this modern attitude, every ecclesiastical system is in a parlous state, be it Catholic, Protestant, Buddhist or Confucian.

> "Among, these moderns there are of course certain of those denigrating, destructive and perverse natures…, unbalanced eccentrics – who are never satisfied anywhere, and who therefore flock to every new banner, much to the hurt of these movements and undertakings, in the hope of finding something for once which will atone at a low cost for their own insufficiency.

> "It goes without saying that, in my professional work, I have come to know a great many modern men and women, and such pathological pseudo-moderns among them. But I prefer to leave these aside. Those of whom I am thinking are by no means sickly eccentrics, but are most often exceptionally able, courageous and upright persons who have repudiated our traditional truths for honest and decent reasons, and not from wickedness of heart.

> "Every one of them has the feeling that our religious truths have somehow or other grown empty. Either they cannot reconcile the scientific and the religious outlooks, or Christian tenets have lost their authority and their psychological justification. People no longer feel themselves to have been redeemed by the death of Christ; they cannot believe…, they cannot compel themselves to believe…, however happy they may deem the man who has a belief. Sin has for them become something quite relative: what is evil for one, is good for the other. After all, why should not Buddha be in the right, also."

And what have statesmen to offer as a just cause for the wholesale slaughter of innocents? No more than the church, but something far less crude and disquieting. They burn with indignation and resentment against those who wilfully instituted the role of the barbarian and compelled decent peoples to adopt a similar role to avenge it. They do not adopt the miserable subterfuge of the church and openly or tacitly lay the burden of blame and responsibility upon a harmless 80 per cent of the populace which does not choose to wear its heart upon its sleeve and bear witness on the Sabbath to its faith.

The statesmen know, as every intelligent person knows, that we wage war against an evil thing; and their sorrow is no less deep than their indignation that unoffending millions go to their death in furious onslaught to annihilate it. That is kinder, more just, and more compassionate, in my opinion, than in writing a universal epitaph upon these same millions: *"They died for their past blindness and wrongdoing."*

I have sometimes been asked by members why the Order has not made authoritative pronouncements upon the war. No doubt some of these members had this particular problem of cause and effect in connection with world suffering and slaughter in mind, and expected that we should have a definitive statement to offer which would satisfy them.

They no doubt had before them the various solutions of the problem as given by various schools of thought, and felt that we, too, should be at least as oracular as these on so important a matter.

For one thing, it is not within the province of the Order to speculate on world catastrophes. It is observed in "Temple Echoes" in the February *Rosicrucian Digest* that the Rosicrucian Order *"has made and undoubtedly will make few political prophecies."* It might also be added: Nor will it make dogmatic pronouncements on the origin and causes of racial madness, suicide and murder. It is questionable whether any statements so far put forth are not open to severe and honest criticism and likely to do more harm than good by the controversies they promote and the embittered feelings they leave behind them.

Wars and the causes of wars are political issues and fall within the jurisdiction of political discussion and determination. If this is disputed and it is contended that they fall also within the jurisdiction of spiritual and other societies of men, I deny it. Interest in such issues by such societies is granted. They are or should be the interest of all societies and of all men. But wars are decided and waged at the instance of governments, which are none other than political bodies; and while any society of men may speculate and comment, criticise and assign causes for what transpires in the wars decreed by governments, the beginning and the end of them lies in the power and authority of the latter, and what you or I may think or say does not one whit affect the issues.

If this were not so, why have spiritual, esoteric, churchly and other societies of men proved so utterly impotent in the political jurisdictions of nations, whether from within or from without? Indeed, the church in Britain has recently ventured to raise its voice within the precincts of parliament on certain issues of the war, only to be peremptorily reduced to silence and withdrawal of its misguided interference by those with professional experience and far more knowledge of the matters concerned. And I might quote from letters of recent date addressed to a leading organ of the British press. They refer to two ill-timed and presumptuous statements made by the Priest of Rome.

"*Centuries ago,*" says one writer, "*the British people threw over the Pope's domination. We do not desire to be dictated to now by the spiritual head of the Roman Catholics, especially when he advocates a negotiated peace with the enemies of Christianity.*" The other writer, commenting on the Pope's statement that "*a just policy must give to the defeated nation a dignified place,*" writes thus: "*This means Germany. A dignified place! Not if millions of sailors, soldiers and airmen have their way, to say nothing of those bereaved of their loved ones.*"

I welcome the manifest and superior justice in the perspective of these correspondents and deplore the lack of it in the Priest of Rome. I ask you to consider the nature of the controversies likely to have resulted from the above-mentioned letters, or rather from the papal pronouncements quoted in them, and the consequent criticism and resentful feeling, especially in view of the palpable Jesuitry of the Pope during the course of the war and the strong public denunciation of it.

I personally should deprecate very much the Order setting up a political platform and involving itself in questions of government policy and matters which are not within the scope of its constitution. They would deflect its energies from the high and dignified purpose to which it is dedicated; namely, to enable its members to a better understanding of themselves and to live life more scientifically, and to soften and ameliorate and offset much of the suffering of human life.

That purpose is quite comprehensive enough for most of us. It is enough if we assist others who are perplexed and suffer under the world catastrophe to face their particular circumstances with patience and fortitude and become more influential in them.

Several arresting articles have appeared during the past year in the *Rosicrucian Digest*, elaborating this point of view, and very few who have read them will not agree that their influence in the individual life has proved infinitely greater than would a series of abstruse speculations, magisterial pronouncements or political intrusions on the fundamental causes of world upheavals which can but satisfy the intellectually curious or furnish controversial material for debating societies.

So far as my observation of members goes, they are fulfilling this purpose conscientiously and to the best of their ability. This applies not only to members here, but to those I contact from overseas who are in service in Europe. They are practical students, good at heart and bent on greater service. The law of cause and effect is very present to them; their thought and action are based upon it; and nothing would shake their confidence in it, for they have experimental proof of it.

But when we are confronted with the profounder issues of the cause of an outraged world and of untold innocents going to their death to avenge it, let us stand in silence with those who have suffered and lost; or let us confess that we do not know, since it is one of the enigmas of inscrutable destiny before which nations rise and fall, and that we are helpless in the face of it.

Let us not thrust upon them some philosophical or religious platitude which they would never tolerate for their neighbour, much less for themselves. It is better, in such circumstances, to be ignorant than overwise and crush a fellow man with a questionable truth which he cannot accept but would deeply resent and repudiate.

6. The Hour of Trial

Reprinted from the November 1945 edition of the Rosicrucian Digest.

As might be expected, there have been many conflicting views put forth of late by students of philosophy and religion, relative to their attitude toward individual evolution in the face of world events. A prevailing one I would state concisely as follows:

Many of us had worked for the best part of a lifetime toward an ideal of unity, when suddenly with the advent of World War II everything around us went to pieces. It mattered little to what particular school, cult, or society we belonged; all that these had stood for, all that they had done in the name of that ideal, was apparently swallowed up and lost in the tide of a threatened domination of materialism and the common struggle to arrest and overcome it.

Never before had men so deeply questioned the cause and meaning of man's undoing in the face of the good he had striven to do. Strong and good men became silent before the catastrophe of the nations; for try as they would, they could ill-reconcile the obviously irreconcilable factors of the good being trampled upon by the evil. Even the sacred scriptures of the world seemed to have forsaken them. The golden precepts of saints and mystics somehow had not stood the test. The leaders of higher thought and culture have never been so severely interrogated by perplexed and harrowed souls seeking some ray of light, some word of stability, upon which to rest their crumbling faith.

The philosophies of the schools were questioned, but no living word came forth to satisfy. The mysticism of the cloister and the highroad of occultism were alike regarded askance, and the voice of the church had lost its note of reality in the ears of the afflicted and desolate. Indeed, it became evident that a large number who hitherto had but a nebulous faith in a good providence, had lost it.

Now, there is no doubt that this attitude of mind has prevailed among us, and we cannot deny that there has been a reason for it. But does not such a pace of evolution as the present furnish precisely the cardinal test of the intrinsic value of our accumulated knowledge and of our particular belief? Is it not the aim of philosophy to initiate us into the meaning of human existence, its purpose and destiny? To initiate us into the meaning of religion, to imbue us with unswerving faith in a divine government? Of mysticism, to impregnate our consciousness with the continuing presence and leadership of the Christ

Spirit? Of occultism, to establish our whole activity upon the unfailing working and direction of Cosmic laws?

Does any one of these paths of inner experience promise an easy ascent to its luminous summit devoid of questioning, doubt, and many a dark night of the soul? Do they not all hint at or plainly warn us of pitfalls and difficulties for the bravest traveller? Are not the conditions of ascent apt to be overlooked when the eyes are constantly fixed upon the goal, and the hours run smoothly?

The very fact that there have been long intervals of relatively peaceful progress during which nothing sensational or antagonistic had intervened to interrupt the placid measure of contemplative thought, or to unsettle the circumstances of daily living, is liable to unfit for trial those who rest too securely in these intervals of quietude and absence of tension..., those who know little of assault from outward circumstances or from the crises of thought self-induced by the aspiring soul, through which alone the basis of character and action are tested and brought to larger estate.

But when these points of crisis come, as come they must, from without and within, if any real fullness of life is to be attained, then is our philosophy, religious faith, mystical assurance, trust in the Cosmic laws, or whatever of the soul's dedication wherein we have placed complete confidence, brought suddenly to the bar of trial and called upon to face one more of the many minor initiations which stand waiting along the whole path of the aspirant to higher knowledge and insight.

However, there is abundant evidence that those who have a real faith in an overruling wisdom and justice, no matter to what doctrine they claim allegiance, still believe, against all appearances, in the decrees of that wisdom and justice. The reason for this is not far to seek. Their faith is based upon fundamental truths of the inner life as known and demonstrated in the lives of inspired and lofty characters through the ages.

They, too, may be perplexed at times and find it not easy to reconcile the life of the world with the life of the soul, but they never will surrender what they have felt and known in the silence of communion to whatever incongruities and contradictions and tortures of mind and heart the frenzied world may cast against them.

Whatever the appearances may be to the contrary, as seen today in many sections of society, for those who have long meditated the path of wisdom and devotedly followed the instructions of the Masters of life, there is no renunciation of the voice of the soul which has been their guide through the long years of upward striving.

When I consider the lives of those of great and extraordinary attainment on the mystic path, whether of former or of more modern times, I am impressed not only with the works of enlightenment and reform which came from their hands; I am no less impressed by the hard discipline and self-control which really made those works possible.

There is a time in life when we are seized and enamoured by the work of an author who seems to have the immediate right of way to the mind and heart. We meet there with an instant recognition and understanding, and a lucid unfoldment of meaning of that which had been the content of our secret self through the years of aspiration and striving.

It means so much to us that the problems which have shadowed our inward solitary journey, known but to ourselves, sentinels of challenge which we neither could dismiss nor answer and which accompanied us in silence even to the promising threshold of each new day, should be magically brought into the light of a rightful perspective and the menace of their presence be dissipated forever.

We forget that those same problems were also the author's. We forget that they had to be met and challenged by him on the lonely battleground of heart, mind and soul, or they would never have been known for what they were; nor the technique of adjustment formulated which now sheds its light upon our own experience. But later, it may be, we look to the man himself and come to realise that he was what he was and did what he did through accepting the challenge of thought and circumstance and never deviating from the line of approach to the goal he had in view.

If there are some who feel tempted or constrained by adverse opinion, or the pressure of circumstance, to relax the tensity of effort and find repose in an attitude of indifference, I would remind them of the words of high philosophy: *"It belongs to the wise man to direct things."* And the disciple of the Path has learned first of all to direct himself, believing that a disciplined life has its own peculiar influence in directing the tenor of circumstance.

> "What a master is he, therefore," triumphantly declares a Chinese scripture, "who takes hold of the Inner Life, and knows the secret of its hidden springs! In journeyings he fears no danger. In strife, he fears no weapons of war. No power can strike the Inner Life; no power can hold it, no power can penetrate."

From this it is permissible to infer that there is in the aura of those who live in spirit with the Masters of life a magical influence which is stronger than armour of steel. This influence is none other than the kindling fire of the soul irradiating from the temple of the body of man. Indeed, we need not look further than the Christian scripture for a pointer and corroboration of this, although it is not elaborated and technically detailed as in other scriptures:

> "And the Lord whom ye seek, shall suddenly come to the temple..., for he is like a refiner's fire."

As a man ascends the path these pregnant scriptural pronouncements assume a new importance and significance and acquire the dignity of basic principles of mysticism. Not only do they reinforce and justify his early confidence in the path, but they also impress upon him the relative unimportance, the ephemerality, the imposing unreality of so much that discomposes him and threatens to imprison him within the consciousness of space and time.

But if the fire of the soul, the divine afflatus, once has taken possession of the seeker and stamped its rhythm upon the personality, nothing henceforth in the illusionary world of form will have the power to hold him back.

I suggest to those who have reluctantly questioned divine governance before the shock of world events: the path of evolution is still before us; we have a place upon it and a duty to perform. If we turn away from it we but postpone the time and the opportunity. I believe that no greater opportunity is presented to man than at the time of acute crisis and trial. The path of the Great Ones has ever been thus.

Every cycle of life of the advancing man is characterised by a series of rebirths of the soul into the personality. These rebirths are the crises of difficulty and readjustment resulting from a deeper and deeper fusion and blending of soul and personality. It is for us to *"look for the Warrior, and let him fight"*[1] in us.

---

1. From *Light on the Path* (1888) by Mabel Collins.

Section 9:

Selected Correspondence (1932 - 1964)

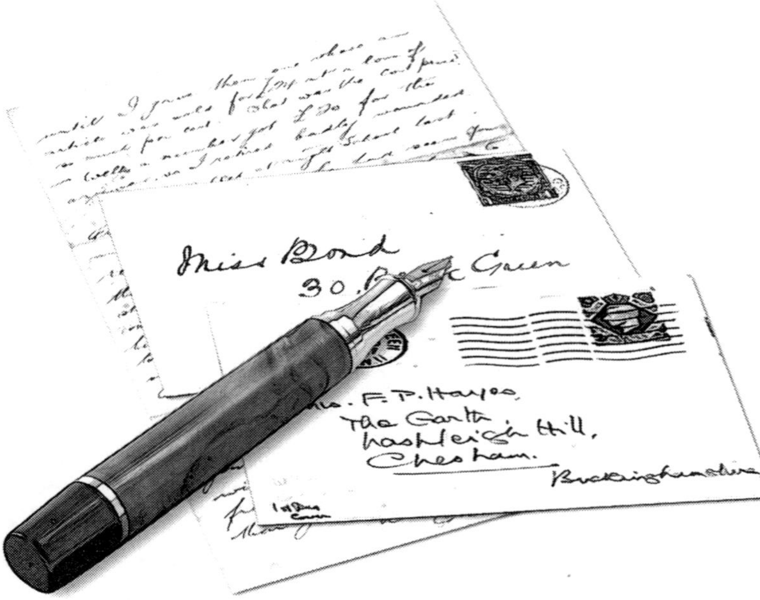

Section 9 - Selected Correspondence (1932 - 1964)

Introduction

This Section has a collection of letters written by Raymund Andrea, in his capacity as Grand Master, to two members of the Rosicrucian Order: Jessie Kenney (1887-1985) and Ellen Kirkpatrick (1901-1990).

The letters are preceded by an address given by Jessie Kenney to the *Francis Bacon Chapter* of the Rosicrucian Order in 1960 in which she praised, among other things, Raymund Andrea's correspondence with members of the Order.

Jessie Kenney was introduced to the Order in 1923 by her sister, the former suffragette leader, Annie Taylor (1879-1953). Around this time, Jessie became the first woman to qualify as a Radio Officer in the merchant navy but she was unable to gain employment as such. At the time of most of the following letters she worked as a stewardess and nurse on cruise liners sailing between England and Australia or America. After World War II she settled in London and served as Master of the *Francis Bacon Chapter* in 1958. More information about Jessie Kenney, including her involvement with the suffragette movement in Edwardian times, can be found on the internet.

Ellen Kirkpatrick joined the Order in 1938. After the War she kept in regular contact with Raymund Andrea and was primarily responsible for disseminating his writings to *Francis Bacon Chapter* and elsewhere in the country. She served as Master of the *Francis Bacon Chapter* in 1964. Some readers may remember her as Ellen Turnbull, for she was widowed in 1968 and later married her Rosicrucian co-worker, Eric Turnbull, after he too was widowed. In 1982 Ellen made a major contribution to *Waiting For The Master*, Francis Bacon Lodge's compilation of Raymund Andrea writings which was issued to commemorate the centenary of his birth. Towards the end of her life Ellen spent several years as a Regional Officer of the Grand Lodge of the Rosicrucian Order.

1. Address to the Francis Bacon Chapter by Jessie Kenney (July 1960)

As we are celebrating the birthday of Grand Master Raymund Andrea today, it is appropriate that this address should be on his leadership, not only of the British Jurisdiction, but of the Chapter group work in London. For it was he that founded it, inspired it and led it through many, many years, which included national crises and the great war of 1939.

He used to send out all monographs to members himself, answer all their letters, and guide them in their work and in their studies. Those who kept in close touch with him were richly rewarded by his unfailing understanding of all their difficulties, not only of their own personal difficulties but of the work they were doing for the Order.

He used to come to London periodically to see his two trusted lieutenants, fratres

Ling and James, as to them he entrusted the group work in London.

During this time he was writing his books which are so well known, not only to us in the British Jurisdiction, but to members all over the world.

In times of stress or difficulty he would send out circular letters to the members of the British Jurisdiction when he felt there was need of a special message or guidance. We have got in our possession some of these letters.

I leave with you at the end of this little address some words that he sent out to us on a Christmas card:

> "May quietness and confidence be yours.
> Beyond the clouds eternal blue endures,
> And life's great providence your place assures."

2. Letter to Jessie Kenney
(24 March 1933)

Dear Miss Kenney,

You may have heard from some source before this that dear Bro. Ling passed away suddenly on the 15th instant. He was taken ill early in the morning with intense pains in the heart, and before a doctor could be fetched he passed away. Thus we lose a loyal worker and a kind friend and beautiful soul. We shall no doubt contact him now in a deeper sense in the reality of soul.

The cremation took place in London on the 18th instant, which I attended, some of the other members being present, and then stayed with the family for the weekend. His children were much distressed, but I think they came to realise that their father's work was finished and he was taken to be prepared for greater work.

I am enclosing you a notice which I have had prepared for Mrs Ling to send to certain relatives and friends, the larger number will be sent by me to those members who either knew Brother Ling personally, or will know him through contact in correspondence for books etc.

I trust you are well and that your present voyage is not too strenuous. I heard recently from Mr Taylor that your sister had made great progress. I have not told her of the passing of Brother Ling, in case the news might unduly shock her.

With my kindest wishes.
    Yours fraternally,
    R Andrea

3. Letter to Jessie Kenney
(11 July 1934)

Dear Miss Kenney,

Thank you for your letter. I had just been thinking about you, as the Imperator will be in London early in September and some of us will be meeting him. But I had an idea that you would be making a voyage and would be away just then. I did not want to mention this to cause you disappointment: on the other hand, I felt I ought to let you know in case you could come to see him. But the date you give for the voyage will find him well on the way back before you return. However, you will probably meet him at San Jose one day.

I send you with pleasure a letter for Grand Master LeBrun. You can be sure of a welcome if you can possibly visit the Lodge, but I would not rush the visit if it is not quite convenient to you.

So you have resurrected something of mine in the journals of long ago! I shall have to disguise my style if this is how I am traced through the years! I did write several articles for the "Theosophist." They all appeared under my name; but the Notes you refer to, I am not guilty of these....

The Lodge, by the way, has another MS of mine, to be a companion book to the other on the Technique. It may be issued this year. If you happen to see Ralph Lewis at the Lodge, you must mention it to him.

I am sending you more lectures for a further three months as I thought you would like to take them with you.

I hope to go on holiday at the end of the month. I feel rather like it, as I have had only a break of a few hours in London since last summer.

I am very glad to hear that your sister is so much better. Please convey my kindest wishes to her. And yourself, I hope the voyage will not be unkind to you but bring new experiences of value and pleasure.

With every good wish.
    Yours fraternally,
    R Andrea

4. Letter to Jessie Kenney
(17 October 1935)

Dear Miss Kenney,

Thank you for your letter with dues. I am sending you lectures for two months..., and some extra ones.

You feel rather sure that you saw my second book on sale abroad, but I have heard nothing of it yet. It may of course be circulating abroad first. I believe this was so last time. However I shall hear in time.

If you find the book has been read abroad, I shall be glad if you get to know the reaction to it, and how that reaction contrasts with that from the former book. It would be interesting to know from what angle it interests, or helps, if at all, and whether there is a demand for that particular line of thought. But do not make this a burden to you: only you will almost certainly meet with the matter in conversation.

Please thank your sister for her letter and dues. I am glad she is well and able to be so helpful to you while you are home. Please thank her for her kind contribution for the Circle which I will remit. I should have been pleased to meet her with you last week. I am sorry the time was short, but I have a lot to do when I am in town and get no peace!

But I am greatly inspired by the kindness and spirit of real service in the London groups. The harmony is perfect; they will take any pains and do anything in the spirit of real sacrifice in the name of love and harmlessness..., and that same spiritual force manifesting everywhere, abroad, in the groups, would produce miracles. That is no exaggeration; that same spirit on a large scale would precipitate.

That is one message you can carry overseas, and tell them to sink their personalities and love each other as souls; because there is no other way. We have to come to that sooner or later, or stay where we are. And in these little books of mine the same note is struck in many tones: to get down to the inner self and understand its workings, thereby understanding the lives of others through personal knowledge, thence understanding the weaknesses and failings of others as our own, thence cultivating compassion, for the sorrows of Karma lie upon us all.

With kindest wishes,
    Yours fraternally,
    R Andrea

5. Letter to Jessie Kenney
(22 June 1936)

Dear Miss Kenney,

I am very pleased to know that you are to talk to the members this week. I am sure they will be most happy and interested, because you have contacted so many of the members abroad and can tell of matters precisely as they are. I hope you will be able to make the members feel the interest there is for the work abroad and also tell them how much their example in this country is really appreciated in the lodges abroad.

Make them feel that no member is alone in this work, however lonely he or she may seem to be, but that there are subtle magnetic bonds between all aspiring souls, that we share each other's knowledge, and sorrows. And sometimes the great pain of life we feel, the "depression" of life, is the actual bearing of the cross of another fellow student..., but only the Master knows that.

Some will need the above thought on Wednesday; that is why I mention it here. Please write me as to the lectures you need in good time.

With kindest wishes.
    Yours fraternally,
    R Andrea

6. Letter to Jessie Kenney
(26 September 1938)

Dear Miss Kenney,

Thank you for your letter with dues. I return your card.

I am sorry that I apparently did not enter in the last supply of lectures you received from me, hence the duplication. I am now sending you two months' supply from the number you mention. Perhaps you can kindly return the others at your convenience.

I was interested to hear of your meeting with the former members. I regret to hear that circumstances have been difficult with them.

I fully sympathise with your comments about affairs abroad. The dictators have been permitted to say and do far more than the wisdom of the world should ever have allowed, and I am inclined to think that the only remedy is a fearful reckoning and that the hour is approaching for it. They both hold their office now by lying, intrigue and infamy, and it is for the rest of the world to give it an answer.

The meetings begin next week at Langham Street and I am sending out notices this week.

With kind regards and every good wish.
    Yours fraternally,
    R Andrea

7. Letter to Jessie Kenney
(25 May 1959)

Dear Miss Kenney,

Thank you for your letter with the enclosure. I am glad to know you are better for your stay in Spain.

It would be interesting if you could write up some of the early days of the London group and I hope some of the older members can help you in this. I regret that I shall not be able to help you much because those early years have become to me much like a past life! I have no details I could supply.

The whole of that period was embodied in personal correspondence with the members, while the contacts were made largely by fratres Ling and James. And all the correspondence of those years went to the war paper shortage. Interesting as it would be to carry out your suggestion, I rather doubt whether sufficient detail would be forthcoming to make it arresting.

I have never kept detailed diaries, so that I have nothing to consult for those years. My time and energy were so occupied with the mounting correspondence and other work in connection with the studies to members, that the entire value of anything I did is only to be found in the lives of those I dealt with. Perhaps that is just as well! I have no objection whatever to your using any quotations you may be able to make from correspondence still in the hands of members from that period.

Of course, I have retained a block of correspondence dating from my first contact with Dr Lewis and subsequent letters on aspects of dealing with the work of my office, as also from the present Imperator, but that is entirely a private correspondence and could not be used in any way.

You are correct regarding frater Ling being the first Master of the London group. I remember urging that office upon him, but he was reluctant about it. But I knew his great value and perfect selflessness and his subsequent service justified completely confidence in him.

And the same can be said of frater James who was a most trustworthy and capable helper to me and others in all kinds of ways. One can only wish they were here today with their quiet confidence and experience. But they are better off.

With kind regards and all best wishes,
    Yours sincerely and fraternally,
    R Andrea

8. Letter to Ellen Kirkpatrick
(9 December 1939)

Dear Mrs. Kirkpatrick,

Thank you for your letter. I note you have now returned home. I am glad to hear of the success in the advertisement order you have had. This is encouraging.

I was interested in your experiences. At the time of the full moon it is quite likely you may have some definite psychic experiences. And I think it quite possible that you may feel the completion of a matter psychically before it is materialised on the objective plane. Seeing that all things originate in the Cosmic, the kind of experience you had is very feasible in suggestion and truth. Whether this particular impression you had about the present war will prove to be true is another matter. But it will be worth while carefully noting for later reference.

With kindest wishes,
    Yours fraternally,
    R Andrea

9. Letter to Ellen Kirkpatrick
(5 June 1950)

Dear Mrs. Kirkpatrick,

I much regret to hear of the trouble and difficulties you have been called upon to face. It is the second great crisis in your life.

It will be poor consolation to say that we grow through crises in life, yet it is the major truth of the path. Indeed, it has been said that, in the case of the true disciple, if life runs smoothly and without incident something is wrong. The meaning of course is, that the increasing tension in a disciple's life should evoke a series of crises, within himself and in circumstances, which indicate, far from failure or regression, but precisely the opposite – that his Karma is coming to birth more quickly in accordance with his demand for growth and opportunity thereby afforded for continual readjustment and deeper experience.

This is a Master's own teaching on this subject and must be accepted, however hard the trial of it. I feel that you can and will do this, because you have the knowledge and insight to do so. I also feel sure that if you seek guidance in the silence the best way will be indicated for you.

I think you will regard this crisis as a major one with rich future consequences. By accepting it in this spirit you really make a claim upon the Master's help, and this can come in most unexpected ways and through unseen channels.

A disciple's life is never a smooth, uneventful one. Status on the path constantly invites a testing of the will and all we know, and by applying all this to the present circumstances you will draw to yourself unfailing good influences.

It would be well to write to San Jose and say that I advised you to seek their help through their Council of Solace, because this group vibration can be potent for your assistance. An airmail letter would reach the Lodge in about four days.

With kind regards and every good wish for the future,
    Yours fraternally,
    R Andrea

10. Letter to Ellen Kirkpatrick
(10 March 1955)

Ellen annotated the letter: "When old age came upon him & he suffered from arthritis."

Dear Mrs. Kirkpatrick,

I thank you for your very kind letter to me. It is true that I have had to curtail activities since Xmas; and I think, as you say, our cruel climate of the past year is mainly responsible. And this particular kind of complaint disables one in many ways and is therefore not easily accepted. However, time takes care of most things sooner or later, if not in the way we wish, then otherwise!

When you refer to the world vibration of our day being against us, that is of course only too true. It is a factor I often referred to in earlier writings, and was perhaps considered pessimistic by the more lighthearted in doing so. But any true "sensitive" would have sensed this during the past 20 years. It has been a challenge to our best efforts all the way along; and those who were not aware of it long since may now, through further study and development, come to realise that the present point of world evolution is directly opposed to them: which means, if they are inwardly enough aware, they will realise that the will is the one factor which will carry them further on the way. From every point of view life today is a direct challenge to the aspirant, whatever his philosophy or religion; and according to his sensitivity will be his suffering under it. I do not refer merely to physical suffering which ills of all kinds may bring. I refer chiefly to mental and spiritual suffering which he must silently face and bear..., it will cost him much to understand and justify it as well.

You recognise this when you refer to the quality of compassion. It is that quality which underlay all my work and my writings of the past. For myself, I have almost forgotten them and should scarcely recognise much that I did write if confronted with it. It was a long, unremitting service to others which somehow had to be done and it fell to my lot to do it. I don't know why. But there was at the heart of all I did the quality of compassion you mention. And it was there, although many did not realise it, because somehow all the problems of others struck right to the heart as personal problems. I seemed to have lived them all previously and suffered under them all. I knew the secret suffering of humanity at first sight. I knew its language instinctively. I recognised its undertones in every voice that came to me, and was only concerned with that.

And now, today, the suffering is deeper and wider. The majority will meet it in its own way, with more excitement and empty worldliness. But for those on the path, it is not well if they do not sense that suffering and develop in themselves compassionate understanding of those who come to them on the path. If they fail in this there is no condemnation or punishment. But should the voice of profound compassion of a Master reach them some day in the silence on the other side and speak but the words, *"Was it nothing to you?"* that will be enough. They will come back with the tones of that voice in their hearts and do just what I have done, and better.

It is a great satisfaction that the work of your Chapter goes steadily forward. It has grown up around a fine ideal and you will never know how much good it has done already in some who needed above all a compassionate understanding of the burden of the heart. For many aspirants will not reveal themselves just because they happen to be members. There must be a far different passport than that. They will only reveal themselves to those whom they instinctively know have travelled the same shadowed ways of former cycles, felt the same disappointments and loss, suffered the same pangs of love and despair, carried secret crosses that no one knew, and know that nothing will be misunderstood, nothing needs to be forgiven, but will have a deep conviction that the same fire has tested them also and made them worthy of their trust.

I am glad to know that your art work continues and hope it may be profitable to you, for I fully appreciate all you say about domestic affairs. It is a daily problem which increases and there is no immediate prospect of better and saner days. For whether we blame science or the heart of man, no one could honestly eulogise the sanity of the nations.

With my kindest regards to you and wishes for Peace Profound,
    Yours sincerely and fraternally,
    R Andrea

11. Extract from letter to Ellen Kirkpatrick
(27 January 1962)

Your letter suggests surprise that a disciple should be liable to ills of any kind. I do not share this view. I think disciples are prone to many ills as they advance to certain stages and are liable to stresses and strains, especially should they be engaged in some discipline under a Master; because in such a case they are deliberately keyed to levels of tension, quite unnatural to them ordinarily, but which result in centre and other intricate adjustments, and when released from that tension some reaction is likely to follow.

That is one reason why I should be inclined to hold a disciple back rather than unduly encourage him and urge him on to what he knows nothing of. Reactions on the real path can be severe and inexplicable and one needs to be able to accept them. I write objectively not personally: I am no humble acceptor. I am a ruthless interrogator of things and events, seen or unseen, which makes me a very poor acceptor!

This applies of course more to disciples of the Eastern tradition who subject themselves to severe discipline, than to those of the R.C. tradition as we know it. They would not face the same kind of tests, as you may easily see by comparing it with some of the textbooks on the subject.

As to your suggestion about disciples being open to attack, there may be something in this. We have read of it but have no proof of it. It is amazing what people accept on mere suggestion or conjecture. The biggest shock they could get would be to see the truth, whereas their belief only lands them in an unseen atmosphere of glamour and mental fog. It would be better to believe nothing without proof and afford an open mind a chance to receive. I believe that is stressed in one of the early monographs.

12. Extract from letter to Ellen Kirkpatrick
(24 July 1962)

Ellen annotated the letter: "Somebody had written that mystical groups share group memories from past incarnations."

The question of group memories of the past can only be a matter of speculation for us. It is not an easily acceptable idea that part of our Self is held back in the Cosmic and only a part of us reincarnated. Personally, I never speculate about this, simply because it is impossible of proof. I think the Self, the indwelling Ego, brings its storied past with it and into those circumstances which will provide what is necessary for further development now, rather than bringing a fraction of itself here and a fraction left behind in a group.

When I mentioned to you that disciples of note are known and in contact with special groups under Master supervision, I had nothing like the above in mind but only that certain disciples intuitionally contact this or that group and receive aid or knowledge as they were fitted for it, but certainly not having access to the whole group content. What disciple could bear that…, the high voltage of senior disciples, one or more of them only deputed to assist him! At this point Ellen annotated the letter thus: *"I had considered whether the Rosicrucians of the past were incarnated now."*

As to the great Rosicrucians of the past, I do not think they are with us now. "Important personalities," yes, plenty of them, but not in the traditional Rosicrucian sense. I look for no outstanding mystics in the present because I think there are none of the type you are thinking of. If there are I doubt if we shall know it or contact them. I think they will be either out of incarnation and waiting for the present chaotic phase of evolution to pass, or, if in incarnation, with their mystical qualities held back within the Self and their present activities focussed upon the scientific aspects of the time. Among them we might find, if we but knew, a character here and there in this or that situation with exceptional powers of insight but with no directly mystical inclination or even belief. But their work would reveal much of the superman in them.

So if you are looking today for the type of mystical genius you refer to, I think you will be disappointed. There is not a hint of him anywhere. Moreover the evolution of today neither deserves him nor would appreciate him. Further, if there really are any "great mystics" about, I imagine they will, having more common sense than compassion, keep well out of the way until the present maelstrom of corrupt nations has gone to its own place and Fate, in a century or two, elects to people the planet with a civilisation worthy of the name.

The history of initiation is a big subject, but I shall willingly read your comments upon it.

13. Extract from letter to Ellen Kirkpatrick
(9 January 1964)

Ellen annotated the letter: "I had been asked to write something for the Bulletin when Master of the Francis Bacon Chapter."

I think the little manual called *The Simple Way of Lao Tsze* might be helpful in suggesting a subject you want to write about. I will just note one of the headings under the title, *The Danger of Strength*.

"Man at his birth is soft and tender; but is rigid and hard at his death. It is the same with everything.

"In growth, trees and plants are pliant and tender; but in death they are withered and tough.

"Thus the hard and the strong have affinity with death; but the soft and the tender are companions of life.

"Therefore he who relies solely on strength will not conquer; a powerful tree invites the axe.

"Thus the place of great strength is below; but gentle softness dwells above."

You will note at once its suggestiveness as opposed to the dynamic will idea which possesses some ambitious students; the idea that a driving will which would impose itself upon others and circumstances defeats itself because such an imposition is contrary to the law of spiritual evolution and this avenges itself upon the personality which uses it. The price it pays for its domination is the opposition of more enlightened students who place their values on a higher level, and in the loss of their sympathy and cooperation. In real mystical development these personality traits have no place simply because they shut the door to the real Path.

This little book of wisdom of the Way could be well recommended to the Chapter members. They will never exhaust the values of it. Their problem will be to realise the values first.

14. Extracts from various letters to Ellen Kirkpatrick

For Francis Bacon Lodge's *1982 publication* "Waiting for the Master," *Ellen Turnbull (formerly Kirkpatrick) contributed these extracts from private letters written to her by Raymund Andrea.*

About natural transition:

"We do miss those who have been with us for so long and I am sure you have had an initiation into loneliness since your husband and your mother passed on,..., not *left* you but only completed a phase of their destined evolution here. We are never really alone but many unseen influences strengthen and guide us if we can be receptive to them.

"You must find *some* comfort in the thought that those who pass at a ripe age do not *leave* those they have known although we appear to lose them, but they know us and spiritually contact and help us, as never possible here."

About personal tragedy:

"I regret very much to know of the present circumstances which are so distressing to you.

"But how little one can say about it, or about life generally. Apart from the cruel onslaught of winter which has added suffering to all, life itself is shot through with the cruellest blows of destiny which can neither be fathomed nor understood. From my early years onward I have watched human suffering, very early in my own home, and it affected me like a laceration of the flesh. Nor has anything, no matter what I have read or written to brace others, in spite of myself, reconciled me to it. Many seem to find a sweet compensation in glibly referring to, 'It's the Law!' but nothing of belief can reconcile others to the unending sweep of cold destiny in human lives, without visible compassion or kindness, or even understanding for those who are stricken by it.

"I get to know through others, who have to minister to these inflictions upon the good and noble, and I am silent. Theories and beliefs are an insult. Even the occult book teachings fade into unreality, and I almost wonder how anything I happen to have written in the past could have helped those they apparently did in the face of an inexplicable evolution.

"So what can I say to you? Only, simply, that I understand your cross: and if the Christ had not endured it in a different and crueller form, I could say nothing. That is the only inward anchor I have in life; and perhaps that is chiefly owing to my dear mother who read it to me nightly before I could understand it, except that the tone in her voice made me feel it was something profoundly wonderful. I never knew then that I should have to live it out. But she had lived it and perhaps foresaw it.

"I shall think much about you and your home and send love and kindest wishes and thoughts...."

Section 10:

The Rosicrucian Digest (1946-1957)

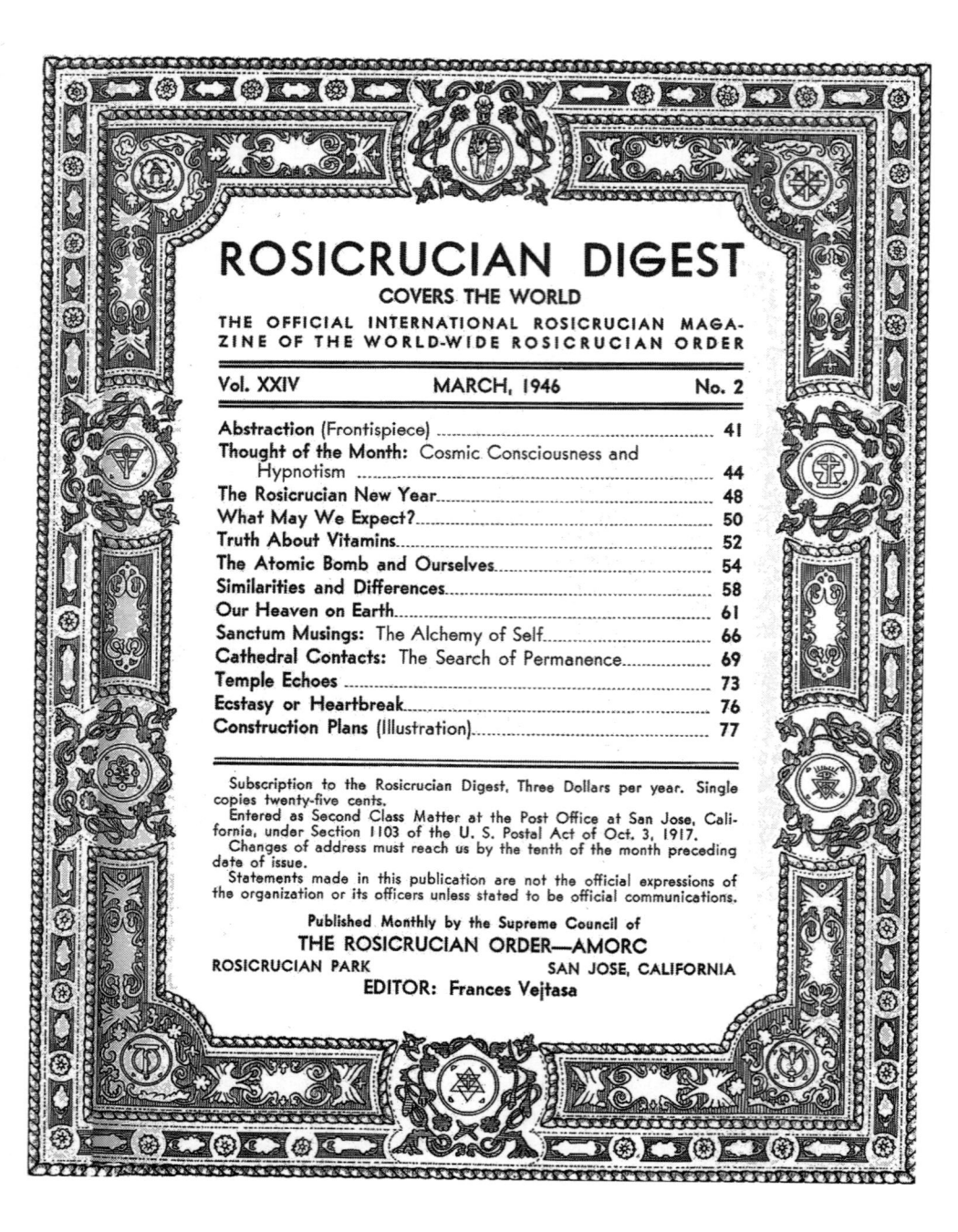

ROSICRUCIAN DIGEST

COVERS THE WORLD

THE OFFICIAL INTERNATIONAL ROSICRUCIAN MAGAZINE OF THE WORLD-WIDE ROSICRUCIAN ORDER

Vol. XXIV	MARCH, 1946	No. 2

Abstraction (Frontispiece)	41
Thought of the Month: Cosmic Consciousness and Hypnotism	44
The Rosicrucian New Year	48
What May We Expect?	50
Truth About Vitamins	52
The Atomic Bomb and Ourselves	54
Similarities and Differences	58
Our Heaven on Earth	61
Sanctum Musings: The Alchemy of Self	66
Cathedral Contacts: The Search of Permanence	69
Temple Echoes	73
Ecstasy or Heartbreak	76
Construction Plans (Illustration)	77

Subscription to the Rosicrucian Digest, Three Dollars per year. Single copies twenty-five cents.

Entered as Second Class Matter at the Post Office at San Jose, California, under Section 1103 of the U. S. Postal Act of Oct. 3, 1917.

Changes of address must reach us by the tenth of the month preceding date of issue.

Statements made in this publication are not the official expressions of the organization or its officers unless stated to be official communications.

Published Monthly by the Supreme Council of
THE ROSICRUCIAN ORDER—AMORC
ROSICRUCIAN PARK   SAN JOSE, CALIFORNIA
EDITOR: Frances Vejtasa

Introduction

If Raymund Andrea's contributions to the *Rosicrucian Digest* increased in the immediate postwar years, this might have been a result of the amalgamation of the two English-speaking jurisdictions of the Rosicrucian Order in 1946 which relieved him of the responsibility of disseminating study material and presumably afforded him more time for writing. (See *In Memoriam*.)

"Rousseau's Response To Life" and "Edgar Allan Poe," which were published in the May 1958 and July 1960 editions respectively of the *Rosicrucian Digest*, have been omitted from this compilation because their contents are included in the readily available *Six Biographical Sketches*[1] by the same author.

1. The Atomic Bomb and Ourselves

Reprinted from the March 1946 edition of the Rosicrucian Digest.

I recently received a letter from a member which opened in this rather dramatic manner:

> "I wish you would write us one of your letters. The discovery of the atomic bomb seems such a tremendous happening."

I do not know why I should be thought qualified to write about the discovery of bombs, atomic or ordinary. I used to hear the latter falling nightly, but the fact and conditions of their discovery had little interest for me.

But it so happened that just before receiving the above letter I had read and marked a comment by the Christian philosopher Jacques Maritain. True, it was written before the war. Had it been written later the tone might have been far more caustic than it is. I will quote the passage:

> "Three centuries of mathematical empiricism have so bent the modern mind to a single interest in the invention of engines for the control of phenomena, a conceptual network, which procures for the mind a certain practical domination over and a deceptive understanding of nature, where thought is not resolved in being but in the sensible itself.
>
> "Thus progressing, not by adding fresh truths to those already acquired, but by the substitution of new engines grown out of date; manipulating things without understanding them; gaining over the real, pettily, patiently, conquests which are always partial, always provisional; acquiring a secret relish for the matter which it seeks to trap, the modern

---

1. *Six Biographical Sketches* is available from the publishers..

335

mind has developed in this lower order of scientific demiurgy, a form of multiple and marvellously specialised sensitiveness, and admirable hunting instincts.

"But, at the same time, it has become miserably enfeebled and defenceless in regard to the proper objects of the intellect which it has basely renounced, and has become incapable of appreciating the universe of rational evidence otherwise than as a system of well-oiled cogs."

I quite agree. We find ourselves caught up in a *"system of well-oiled cogs."* And while the world became hilarious, dumbfounded, and thoroughly frightened by turns at the discovery of the latest (atomic) cog in the system, I confess to being indifferent about it. I saw nothing to be hilarious about, had no reason to be dumbfounded, and as to being frightened, I recalled Emerson's remark to the alarmed Millerite who stopped him in the street one day and informed him that the world would be destroyed in ten days. To this Emerson replied: *"Well, what of it! I don't see but that we shall get along just as well without it."*

In all the world comments I have read on the atomic bomb I have never encountered one approaching the serene and understanding one of Emerson. On the contrary, from high and low, lay and professional, politician and parson, the indication has been that the discovery of the atomic bomb had thoroughly jolted the *"system of well-oiled cogs"* with the fear of personal annihilation. This has struck me as a most unedifying comment upon the times we live in, and I must confess it does not increase my respect for them.

Of course, this cog system has been developing for some considerable time. It was well under way during the first quarter of the century; and Maritain's judgement upon it is far from being merely a disgruntled and caustic one. It is that of a keen-sighted philosopher and profound religionist well able to assess the value of men and circumstances when he confronts them.

Nor is his opinion a novel and sensational one: by no means. The truth of it is perceived only too well and held too widely by sane and enlightened individuals in every country. But it is a crying disgrace that we, at one of the high peaks of so-called civilisation should have to acknowledge it.

This *"tremendous happening"* of the atomic bomb is undoubtedly a triumph of a materialistic age. The masters of materialism concentrated upon the evolution of the genius of destruction; and their dream has materialised in so frightful a form that they themselves *"hover betwixt hope and fear."* And considering the type of humanity which comprises today a formidable percentage of the cog system, and the itching fingers of those whose morbid curiosity craves to discover further diabolical tricks they can make nature perform, there may be, after all, some justification for the anxiety felt by men of compassion and vision as to the goal of a materialistic age if this curiosity reaps further rewards.

Indeed, there is reason for their anxiety for in this pre-eminently scientific and materialistic epoch such an example of supreme concentration and mental cleverness as the atomic bomb discovery sets before the world a prime incentive to countless other aspiring and ambitious individuals in college and laboratory to achieve as much and more and to write their noble names in the roll of fame as masters of destructive art.

For there is no limit to achievement. Infinity lies at both ends. The adept is but an ambitious and aspiring disciple on the path of endless ascension: and the scientist may probe so far in sinister research as to open up a deeper hell than any Atlantean ever plumbed.

The mind is all: it can raise humanity to the presence of God, or lower it through unholy ambition to confederacy with the devil. We have ample evidence of both; and of the latter, in these advanced times, more than ample. The war of the nations has disclosed to us far more of the depths of hell in man than of the divinity of heaven. Nor can it be confuted that the masters of science have been the chief agents in the disclosure.

The atomic bomb was in the making by German scientists long before the end of the European war. Can we deny that our discovery and use of it placed our own scientists in the same category as the former who were frustrated in the attempt? I am not raising the question as to whether it should have been used: I am only interested in the trend of the mind of the age. It may be a logical, even a necessary trend; but it is a pernicious one and still in hot pursuit of more *"devilish enginery"* to excel the first adventure.

Whether these discoveries will be ultimately used to save or slay is another question which the future will decide. In any case, the anxiety and fear expressed by statesmen at the discovery and the doubtful decision to safeguard the secret of it, is a plain indication that human nature is not considered evolved enough to be trusted with it. But as the scientific mind is the same the world over, the attempt of any body of scientists to isolate and claim a monopoly in discovery is ridiculous.

As I write, the Press is voicing the same opinion. What man has found, man will find: what man has demonstrated under the ambitious urge for power, he will demonstrate again. The question remains: To what end will he demonstrate it? The future will also determine this question. The same philosopher, Maritain, wrote fifteen years ago:

> "Imperilled by a degraded civilisation which abandons man to the indetermination of matter, the mind must defend itself at all costs, assert its rights and its essential superiority. It is itself responsible for the evil. It attempted to hold truth captive, affected to disregard what surpasses the level of reason and, finally, reason itself. It is punished by the flesh for having sought to emancipate itself..., by denying their (the senses) existence from the supreme realities which are to be assessed by the measure of God, not man.
>
> "The control of the senses by reason and of reason itself by God is the essential condition of order and peace in the human being, and this can only be achieved through faith and

supernatural love. The first subordination depends in practice upon the second. Adam shattered both: Christ re-established them by His grace and the gifts of His spirit. The error of the modern world and the modern mind consists in the claim to ensure the domination of nature by reason while at the same time refusing the domination of reason by supernature."

This declaration is more true today than when it was written. Truly it refers to our *"degraded civilisation,"* and declares pointedly and accurately that the trend of the modern mind is the cause of it. We feel uncomfortable when the rigid finger of censure points menacingly at the mind of the age, the mind which we worship so boastfully, and declares it to be a common culprit. But if it is a fact, and no honest person can repudiate it, we have to face it.

It is not for us, as mystics, to concern ourselves about the discovery of bombs. At the highest point, the indifference of Emerson has something to teach us. Our concern should be, in the first place, with our own minds. It is for us to make sure that we have not been a causal factor in the degradation of civilisation. I do not see how we can have been if we have taken our studies of the path seriously.

Those who are not serious do not usually waste their time upon these matters. Many of them give their allegiance to politics; and there is always enough degradation in politics to besmirch the honour and dignity of any man. The intellectualists demonstrate to perfection the *"control of the senses by reason,"* the scientists *"claim to ensure the domination of nature by reason,"* and both have to share the responsibility of a chaotic world by *"refusing the domination of reason by supernature."*

It has been left to us, and a comparative few like us, to attempt the control of the senses and reason by supernature, or the superphysical, by the grace of Christ and the gifts of His spirit. That demands an inward strength and courage which it is hopeless to expect from the majority in church or state. We are not disconcerted by this temper of the times. We accept the truth of it. But it is not our responsibility.

Some students seem to think it is pre-eminently their responsibility and are disturbed about it. They might as logically hold themselves responsible for the havoc and desolation caused by the elements when nature demonstrates her superior strength and indifference to man. If, as is sometimes impressed upon us, the world chaos reflects the consciousness of men, we may find this difficult to confute, but I fail to see how any of us who have looked persistently toward a more harmonious world and worked consistently for it, in however small a way, can feel any responsibility for a result so contrary to our mental attitude.

If we do accept responsibility, this is tantamount to a confession that our allegiance to the Christ Spirit and its works is no better than allegiance to the arch criminals of East and West and the pestilential crew which evolution has thrown up around them. That reflection should make us sit up and clear our minds of cant.

Let us preserve the dignity and the equanimity becoming those who can still hold and profess a sound philosophy in a *"system of well-oiled cogs."* But there is a price to be paid for indulging even in that harmless occupation.

The Russian philosopher, Berdyaev, made some pertinent remarks about philosophy in 1938, and the intervening years of war have not qualified the truth of them.

> "The philosopher's situation," he says, "is truly tragic in face of the almost universal hostility directed against him. This hostility has manifested itself in various ways throughout the history of civilisation. Philosophy is, indeed, the most vulnerable part of culture; even its initial premise is incessantly questioned; and every philosopher has, first of all, to justify the validity of his claim to exercise his function. Philosophy is the victim of heterogeneous attacks: religion and science are its avowed enemies. In short, it has never enjoyed the least semblance of popular support; nor does the philosopher ever create the impression that he is satisfying any social demand."

Again:

> "The true philosopher is not satisfied only to apprehend the world; he also desires to modify, to improve, and to regenerate it. How could it be otherwise, since philosophy is essentially concerned with the purpose of our existence, of our destiny? The philosopher has always claimed not only to be inspired by the love of wisdom, but to be the expounder of wisdom itself; so that to renounce wisdom would be to renounce philosophy itself. It is true that philosophy is primarily knowledge, but it is a totalitarian knowledge, one that comprehends all the aspects of human existence. Its essential aim is to discover ways of realising Meaning.

> "Philosophers have sometimes been content to expound a crude empiricism or materialism. But the essential character of a true philosopher is the love of the extra-natural; in this sphere he grapples with the transcendental world and refuses to reconcile himself with any interpretation of knowledge which would restrict his activities to the inferior world. It is the aim of philosophy to investigate beyond the limits of the empirical universe, and thus to penetrate into the intelligible universe, into the transcendental world."

These are the sentiments of an open–minded and independent thinker who sees very well where the tragedy of life arises upon whose shoulders the main responsibility for it rests. We should rejoice to see independent and fearless thinkers state the modern case in plain terms and pass judgement according to the light that is in them. And if I may be so bold as they, I would say that the charge against ourselves and others in the field of mysticism and occultism is that we do not state the case against our *"degraded civilisation"* and the enemies of advanced culture with anything like the same force and conviction as they do.

I know not whether this is due to fear of criticism, or because our philosophy is still with us more a theory than flesh and blood reality which informs our hands, kindles on our tongues, and announces itself in soulful eyes. It is there that our responsibility lies, if it lies anywhere. It lies not in what we are, or in what we belie, but if anything, in what we omit to do.

I have talked with aspirants of many nationalities and I do not question their sincerity in their studies, their desire for progress, or their ambition to succeed in life; but one thing is often lacking in them. There is not sufficient emphasis in their minds upon being of distinct and outstanding service in other lives.

I do not question that they are greatly interested in demonstrating something to themselves; it may be the exercise of some one or other psychic faculty which will be a sign in them of superior ability or achievement, a seizure of special knowledge which will give them, at least in their own eyes, an approved standing on the path. But these are mere rudiments or preliminaries, if they exist at all, in the life of a great soul. They scarcely exist on the mystic way except to be surpassed and almost forgotten as the full meaning of the exact discipline of the path comes to rule the mind.

So long as our studies continue to be the means and end of our effort in life, we may indeed be on the path; but it is still the path on the plain, not the ascension towards the mountaintop of vision and the radiation of the true mystical influence. Our studies should be an incentive and inspiration to the discovery of personal force and its application in the world service. That is their intention, not to narrow the interest and vision to the limits of world achievement, however profitable it may promise to be.

I say this advisedly, not critically: for the limitations of personal interest and ambition are responsible for the *"degraded civilisation"* we face today in the four quarters of the globe. Those limitations are responsible for all we have suffered and shall yet suffer a consequence for the rest of our troubled days.

A world destroyed by the self-blinded consciousness of men is the worst of all possible judgements upon man, and nothing but a new and regenerated consciousness can build a better one. The consciousness that destroyed it still lives and rankles amid the ruins of it, impenitent and awaiting a future hour. And as the wheel of life turns, that hour will assuredly come in the future as it has come in the past unless the peoples of the nations raise themselves on to a higher spiral of consciousness that upon which they are today standing.

This may be strongly objected to by those whose ears are charmed by the deceptive promises which have been voiced by politicians and others since the termination of the war. But no promises will raise the consciousness of men; only an enlightened and understanding mind and the will of man to impose upon himself the hard discipline demanded for inner development will do so. If our influence as professed pioneers on the path of higher culture has been so negligible in the history of our own time, it is not difficult to assess the value of the influence of the rank and file of humanity in it.

One thing is obvious: to make any appreciable impression upon this materialistic age, we shall need to make a far different assessment of our objective in life than hitherto has been the case. Young aspirants will need to be brought rigidly to attention and asked to face up squarely to the hardness and responsibility of the highest soul-personality development, not to the passing success of the hour.

Not that they have to do this. It is a matter of personal choice. But if they do offer themselves for it, they must realise there is not a single easy avenue or short cut to it. It will be the hardest uphill journey they have ever taken.

2. The Sanctity of Work

Reprinted from the August 1947 edition of the Rosicrucian Digest.

The poet Rilke, writing of Rodin [Auguste] the sculptor, said:

"Only his work spoke to him. It spoke to him in the morning when he awakened, and in the evening it sounded in his hands like an instrument that had been laid away."

Could any creative artist wish for a higher tribute to be written of him at the close of his life's full day?

Rilke was a poet of considerable excellence and when he wrote prose he was a poet still, as those who have read his Letters will know; for they have all the colour, music, and pathos that come to the inward eye and ear of the sensitive soul which ponders upon life and the meaning of life, upon nature, and the mystery of human experience.

The poet who would write truly and intimately of life, nature and human experience must leave the surface and lunge into the depths and unfold hidden meanings of things, and reveal traits of character which elude the unquestioning mind and the untrained eye. Rilke was such a poet, and Rodin was for many years his subject.

He lived with the master as his secretary, observed his creations rise day by day from the unformed stone to masterpieces of living art; and if that close association afforded the poet the unique experience of seeing ideas wrought before his eyes into solid and durable material, the master was no doubt equally inspired by the deep insight and appreciative interpretation which the poet brought to the work of his strong and skillful hands.

The work of the many is found outside themselves. They take it up and lay it down as a necessary thing; and the more they can forget it when it is laid aside, the happier they are. That is work, and it brings a necessary remuneration, but it is not the work of a poet, an artist, or a mystic.

All these, in their best type, are creative workers; but they are never outside their

341

work, nor can they ever forget it. They find no real happiness away from it. Work is not an adjunct of their life. It is not merely an occupation. In these creative workers work is the expression of the essential life of the soul, a perfecting in and through the personality of the fine art of creative living.

It was this marked characteristic in Rodin which so forcibly impressed Rilke; and living so long with and thoughtfully observing him, the idea of the dignity and sanctity of work thoroughly gripped the poet and inspired him to write his essay on the sculptor. The essay has much of the classic form of Rodin's own masterpieces. Indeed, in exalting Rodin in language at once sculptural in form and mystical in quality, Rilke is an instance of a poet who, through superior insight and interpretative power, almost forgets his own art in his adoration of the mind and art of another and his desire to reveal the inmost workings of these to the reader. This will be realised by the few quotations I shall give from him.

The quotation at the beginning of this article is a significant and beautiful one. It is a poetical concept of the continuous activity of the mind in creative work. The many do their work, to a chosen few it speaks, as an inspired word. And when a man awakens with the voice of it sounding in his soul and at evening must perforce rest from it, yet carries the vibration of the increasing glory and achievement of it in his hands in repose, how like that experience is to the creative activity of the Master Artist of the universe whose one aim through all the days is the unresting unfoldment of the purpose of evolution. This is supreme concentration, untiring, unrelenting, absorbing all the thought and energy of the man.

"*Rodin once said that he would have to speak for one year in order to recreate one of his works in words.*" That is the criterion of great work which Rodin made peculiarly his own: that of profound thinking, a thinking as strong and vital as his own life blood, which penetrated the inert material under his hand and wrought from it masterpieces of immortal thought.

> "But this young man," writes Rilke, "who worked in the factory at Sèvres was a dreamer whose dream rose in his hands and he began immediately its realisation. He sensed where he had to begin. A quietude which was in him showed him the wise road."[2]

Here already Rodin's deep harmony with Nature revealed itself; that harmony which the poet Georges Rodenbach calls an elemental power. And, indeed, it is an underlying patience in Rodin which renders him so great, a silent, superior forbearance resembling the wonderful patience and kindness of Nature that begins creation with a trifle in order to proceed silently and steadily toward abundant consummation.

Rodin did not presume to create the tree in its full growth. He began with the seed beneath the earth, as it were. And this seed grew downward, sunk deep its roots and anchored them before it began to shoot upward in the form of a young sprout. This

---
2. *Rodin* by R M Rilke, Grey Walls Press, London.

required time, time that lengthened into years. 'One must not hurry,' said Rodin in answer to the urgence of the few friends who gathered about him.

> "At that time the war came and Rodin went to Brussels. He modelled some figures for private houses and several of the groups on the top of Bourse, and also the four large corner figures on the monument erected to Loos, mayor, in the Parc d'Anvers. These were orders which he carried out conscientiously, without allowing his growing personality to speak. His real development took place outside of all this; it was compressed into the free hours of the evening and unfolded itself in the solitary stillness of the nights; and he had to bear this division of his energy for years. He possessed the quiet perseverance of men who are necessary, the strength of those for whom a great work is waiting."

It will be understood that I have chosen this subject of Rodin as presented by Rilke in his essay because of the immense inspiration in it and lessons to be drawn from it.

We live in a time when speed is one of the chief gods of men, and we suffer from the curse which too often accompanies it, superficiality. The factor of speed hypnotises men, and it infects even our students on the path. The short cut to the heights in every sphere is in vogue today. This has one merit: it sharpens the intellect and makes the man feel that he is taking unusual strides in achievement.

Its demerit is far greater and more serious: it confuses and warps the soul and gives the man a false perspective in relation to spiritual advancement. If the soul is timeless, above and beyond the fret and anxiety of time, it will not readily conform to the categories of time we wilfully thrust upon it. These do but blur the prospect of reality, instead of clarifying the vision.

"One must not hurry," says Rodin. Strange words these, at first sight, from a man of superb and restless spirit whose very hands even in repose were moulding thought into articulate figures of beauty and power and adding meaning to Nature's own creations of men and women. But every word of a master mind is precious, a thousand times more precious today, when every lofty soul has its peace and integrity assailed by the voices and purposes of mundane expediency, and the hour of silence has lost its significance.

"He began with the seed beneath the earth, as it were. And this seed grew downward." It is the sin of forgetting the necessity of the silent growth downward of the seed of our ideal that so easily besets us. We think and strive in terms of the fugitive days instead of cultivating an extension of thought over the stern and cumulative experience of the testing years.

That is why our time, for all its boasted achievements, gives us few men of full and completed character whose work shines with the supernatural radiance of enlightenment which will uplift and bless after they are gone. We look in vain for them. It is as if humanity had taken a decisive retrograde step in evolution and the younger generation has for its guides but men of worldly prestige and upon a definitely lower spiral.

The creative artist, the poet of vision, the fervent mystic, has no prestige, is submerged, and has scarcely a name. It is small wonder that we constantly look back to those who have gone and find present consolation in what they were and did. We may incur the censure of living in the past if we do so. But it is far better that we find our inspiration there than follow the blind guides that hold the stage today and who seek to regiment us, one and all, into a soulless army of politicians and economists to build a grand new world for their benefit.

The truth must be said, whether we like it or not. The voice of the world today is blatantly common and unspiritual, and woe to the young aspirant who is seduced by it, conforms to it, and forgets those who have spent their lives, and those who are spending them, for the greater things.

It is not for nothing that our literature points again and again to the great philosophers and mystics who have trodden the way before us. Those characters are a shining lifeline for us in the present maelstrom of materialism. Without them, the idea of evolution and any faith in it, would perish, and we should drift without aim or purpose for anything worthy of even the sleeping Christ in man.

But to return to our theme, this great and silent worker, Rodin. There is so much of inspiration for us in his attitude toward his work and in his strength and patience in pursuing his chosen ideal.

> "There was no haughtiness in him. He pledged himself to a humble and difficult beauty that he could oversee, summon, and direct. The other beauty, the great beauty, had to come when everything was prepared, as animals come to a drinking place in the forest in the late night when nothing foreign is there.

> "For years Rodin walked the roads of life searchingly and humbly as one who felt himself a beginner. No one knew of his struggles; he had no confidants and few friends. Behind the work that provided him with necessities his growing work hid itself awaiting its time. He read a great deal. At this time he might have been seen in the streets of Brussels always with a book in his hand, but perhaps this book was but a pretext for the absorption in himself, in the gigantic task that lay before him.

> "As with all creative people the feeling of having a great work before him was an incitement, something that augmented and concentrated his forces. And if doubts and uncertainties assailed him, or he was possessed of the great impatience of those who rise, or the fear of an early death, or the threat of daily want, all these influences found in him a quiet, erect resistance, a defiance, a strength, and confidence..., all the not-yet-unfurled flags of a great victory.

"Perhaps it was the past that in such moments came to his side, speaking in the voice of the cathedrals that he went to hear again and again. In books, too, he found many thoughts that gave him encouragement. He read for the first time Dante's *Divina Commedia*. It was a revelation. The suffering bodies of another generation passed before him. He gazed into a century the garments of which had been torn off; he saw the great and never-to-be-forgotten judgement of a poet on his age. There were pictures that justified him in his ideas; when he read about the weeping feet of Nicholas the Third, he realised that there *were* such feet, that there was a weeping which was everywhere, over the whole of mankind, and there were tears that came from all pores."

I confess that when I read this searching analysis of the mind of Rodin by Rilke, I feel as deep an intellectual and aesthetic satisfaction in the poet's understanding of it as in the unswerving vision of the master of his life purpose. How much we need this kind of insight into the true greatness of man when it comes, at such far intervals of time! How often in the past has this greatness of man dwelt silently among us and none has acclaimed it. That is sufficient reason, if for no other and personal benefit, why we should if only for brief but constant periods renounce the world atmosphere in which we live and worship in our hearts these supermen of creative genius.

If we do not know how, Rilke can point the way. We should cultivate this habit of entering, by sensitive and appreciative interpretation, into the souls of these men. There is nothing that I know of which will pay richer inner rewards to the aspirant in the years to come as will this living in mind and heart with men of genius through reverent study of their lives and works. And if he is making the kind of progress he should in his studies of the path, the awakening and stimulating influence of those studies should lead him instinctively to a companionship in mind with great souls.

A love for what I have termed the technique of the Masters should lead him to observe in all master minds of creative work the principles and rules, often peculiar to themselves and far from the stereotyped formulae of any school, the pattern, the form and method by which they rose to eminence, and so enrich his own thought and extend his own experience in his particular sphere.

We see in Rodin this steady accumulation of material from many sources, the gathering into himself of an almost unlimited range of inspirational suggestions from the faces and forms of men and women, which he studied with inexhaustible patience.

The reading of Dante, for the first time, for instance, opened up to him a vision of the shadowy forms of another generation suffering under the hand of Karma the sins of former days; and immediately these forms became translated into the all living men and women around him. He saw that the heavy hand of Karma was upon them, too, and the stone he wrought to give them shape became as quivering flesh and blood in his hands expressing all the powers and passions of the hidden soul.

"At last, after years of solitary labour he made the attempt at a step forward with one of his creations. It was a question put before the public. The public answered negatively. And Rodin retired once more for thirteen years. These were the years during which he, still unknown, matured to a master and became the absolute ruler of his own medium, ever working, ever thinking, ever experimenting, uninfluenced by the age that did not participate in him.

"Perhaps the fact that his entire development had taken place in this undisturbed tranquillity gave him later, when men disputed over the value of his work, that powerful certainty. At the moment when they began to doubt him, he doubted himself no longer, all uncertainty lay behind him. His fate depended no more upon the acclamation or the criticism of the people; it was decided at the time they thought to crush it with mockery and hostility. During the period of his growth no strange voice sounded, no praise bewildered, no blame disturbed him.

"As Parsifal grew so his art grew in purity alone with itself and with a great eternal Nature. Only his work spoke to him. It spoke to him in the morning when he awakened, and in the evening it sounded in his hands like an instrument that had been laid away. Hence his work was so invincible. For it came to the world ripe, it did not appear as something unfinished that begged for justification. It came as a reality that had wrought itself into existence, a reality which *is*, which one must acknowledge."

The lesson portrayed so vividly in this passage is that of concentration and patience. For thirteen years the master retires into the solitude of his own mind, with imperturbable faith in his ideal. You may say that one cannot wait in these days of speed and demand: the thing must be done now and receive its recognition.

It is never so with the things that are great. Genius is great; its works are great, and it knows how to wait. Whatever the temptation for achievement and notoriety, we must learn to stand back and nourish the fire of the soul. Rodin did this so perfectly that his work *"sounded in his hands,"* and so became invincible.

If we want these prime lessons of genius focused in one masterpiece of supreme perfection, we may observe Rodin's undraped figure of Hugo in exile. It speaks volumes. The massive and rugged body of the poet seems to partake of the very nature of the granite block upon which it inclines, with which it is incorporated and partly hidden. The fine head rests, heavy with thought, upon one hand, in profound meditation, and in such an attitude that the whole history of the tragedy of genius speaks from it.

No artist can do more than this: to penetrate into and reveal in his art the soul of man and its secret life. For thereby is taught the way of the immortal spirit in the flesh, its struggles in the toils of matter, and the imposition of its will upon the aspiring mind, that it may mirror forth at length in its work the last word of its experience of life conflict.

Moreover, this is exactly applicable to the awakened aspirant on the path; he too must grapple with this same problem of the high ideal of mastering the resources of mind and soul, that he may look with clear and compassionate eye into the soul of men and reveal it to itself.

We call this seership, and of the highest grade. It does not come of crystal gazing or pranayama. Rodin attained to his seership through the blood of the heart; and that is the only way for us. It is a renouncing of the passing and transitory for the enduring values of the informing life.

There are optimists who would have us believe that war stiffens the sinews, enlarges the mind, brings the best out of the youth of the time and plants it on the road to high achievement. I do not agree with them. There is abundant evidence that precisely the opposite is the case. War degrades and demoralises and brings the worst in humanity to the surface. I doubt whether any war has produced such an ebullition of superficiality and slackness of mental and moral fibre, paltry ambitions or none, and a genius for not taking pains, as the war we have just seen.

Authorities in church and state in Britain have publicly testified to it. The idea of the sanctity of work is a theme for derision. But we on the path of a higher culture think and teach otherwise. We hold up these characters possessed with an idea and giving a life's full devotion for it as the only worthwhile example in a world which has lost its bearings. If such characters had not existed in abundance in the past, and many are with us today, I should lose my faith in humanity: for the ideals of men are low.

It is for us to counter to the best of our ability this curse which war has opened upon us. Unless we do so there is no peace for us; life will have lost its beauty, dignity and culture, and we shall have taken that retrograde step in evolution which will brand us for an incarnation with the mark of the many who have gone weakly down with the tide and renounced the hard won and immortal values which every son of genius has striven to fix and establish as a beacon for our guidance to a higher destiny.

The human face, in which is written the story of the beauty of worship, of loving devotion, of fierce ambition, of the mind in adversity, of the spirit rising to supremacy! Rodin has taken all these, and more, for his province. Every line of this human manuscript he scanned inexorably through the years, until he became clairvoyant of types of all conditions and knew just what the hand of destiny had wrought in them.

Rilke has developed this thought with real artistic beauty. I quote him at length here, because it reveals his profound comprehension of the master, and we shall be the better for reading it.

"But he returned to the faces of men with an ever-growing, richer and greater knowledge. He could not look upon their features without thinking of the days that had left their impress upon them, without dwelling upon the army of thoughts that worked incessantly upon a face, as though it could never be finished. From a silent and conscientious observation of life, the mature man, at first groping and experimenting, became more and more sure and audacious in his understanding and interpretation of the script with which the faces were covered. He did not give rein to his imagination, he did not invent, he did not neglect for a moment the hard struggle with his tools. It would have been easy to surmount, as if with wings, these difficulties.

"He walked side by side with his work over the far and distant stretches that had to be covered. Like the ploughman behind his plough. While he traced his furrows, he meditated over his land, the depth of it, the sky above it, the flights of the winds and the fall of the rains; considered all that existed and passed by and returned and ceased not to be. He recognised in all this the eternal, and becoming less and less perplexed by the many things, he perceived the one great thing for which grief was good, and heaviness promised maternity, and pain became beautiful.

"The interpretation of this perception began with the portraits, and from that time penetrated ever deeper into his work. It is the last step, the last cycle in his development. Rodin began slowly and with infinite precaution entered upon this new road. He advanced from surface to surface following Nature's laws. Nature herself pointed out to him, as it were, the places in which he saw more than was visible. He evolved one great simplification out of many confusions as Christ brought unity into the confusion of a guilty people by the revelation of a sublime parable. He fulfilled an intention of nature, completed something that was helpless in its growth. He disclosed the coherences as a clear evening following a misty day unveils the mountains which rise in great waves out of the far distance.

"Full of the vital abundance of his knowledge, he penetrated into the faces of those that lived about him, like a prophet of the future. This intuitive quality gives to his portraits the clear accuracy and at the same time the prophetic greatness which rises to such indescribable perfection in the figures of Victor Hugo and Balzac.

"To create an image meant to Rodin to seek eternity in a countenance, that part of eternity with which the face was allied in the great course of things eternal. Each face that he has modelled he has lifted out of the bondage of the present into the freedom of the future, as one holds a thing up toward the light of the sky in order to understand its purer and simpler forms. Rodin's conception of art was not to beautify or to give a characteristic expression, but to separate the lasting from the transitory, to sit in judgement, to be just.

"His later sculptures of women have a different beauty, more deeply founded and less traditional. Rodin has, for the most part, executed portraits of foreign women, especially American women. There are among these busts some of wonderful craftsmanship, marbles that are like pure and perfect unique cameos, faces whose smiles play softly over the features like veils that seem to rise and fall with every breath; strangely half-closed lips and eyes which seem to look dreamily into the bright effulgence of an everlasting moonlit night. To Rodin the face of a woman seems to be a part of her beautiful body. He conceives the eyes of the face to be eyes of the body, and the mouth the mouth of the body. When he creates both face and body as a whole, the face radiates so vital an expression of life that these portraits of women seem prophetic.

"The portraits of men are different. The essence of a man can be more easily imagined to be concentrated within the limits of his face; there are moments of calm and of inward excitement in which all life seems to have entered into his face. Rodin chooses or rather creates these moments when he models a man's portrait. He searches far back for individuality or character, does not yield to the first impression nor to the second, nor to any of those following. He observes and makes notes; he records almost unnoticeable moments, turnings and semi-turnings of many profiles from many perspectives. He surprises his model in relaxation and in effort, in his habitual as well as in his impulsive expressions; catches expressions which are but suggested. He comprehends transitions, all their phases, knows whence smile comes and why it fades. The face of man is to him like a scene in a drama in which he himself takes part. Nothing that occurs is indifferent to him or escapes him. He does not urge the model to tell him anything, he does not wish to know aught save that which he sees. He sees everything."

There is a note of triumphant finality in this last sentence of Rilke. I do not doubt the assertion as applied to Rodin within the whole sphere of his art. His characters in stone are as perfect as man can hope to make them. These creations impress one with the amazing fullness of experience of the master and his manual dexterity in expressing the most elusive and the most dominating tones of thought and emotion of his subject.

They do not awaken the emotion of beauty so much as the sense of power resulting from deep meditation and willed effort. They are creations of incarnate thought. And the secret of this great art was the one idea which dominated Rodin throughout his life: the sanctity of work. His spirit never slept.

"He was a worker whose only desire was to penetrate with all his forces into the humble and difficult significance of his tools. Therein lay a certain renunciation of Life, but in just this renunciation lay his triumph, for Life entered into his work."

3. The Rejected Gift

Reprinted from the January 1948 edition of the Rosicrucian Digest.

When he was thirty years of age, Zarathustra left his home and went into the mountain, where for ten years he lived in solitude and did not weary of it. Then a change came over his heart, and one morning at dawn he went before the sun and addressed it:

> "Thou great star! What wouldst be thy happiness if thou hadst not those for whom thou shinest!"

Then followed those pregnant words which one of the Old Testament prophets might have spoken:

> "Lo! I am weary of my wisdom, like the bee that hath gathered too much honey; I need hands outstretched to take it."

Why is it that men, a chosen few, write words like these? I imagine that a well-informed literary critic might answer: As the musician, or the artist, so here the poet chants a mournful number under the influence of the poetic mood, but with a veiled glance at his own exaltation and value.

It is a typical academic answer, but no man who says this will be in danger of writing like that. We might expect him to give a similar answer to the Old Testament prophet, when the fire of the Spirit wrung this strophe from him:

> "Therefore I am full of the fury of the Lord, I am weary with holding in. I will pour it out upon the children abroad, and upon the assembly of young men together."

There is little difference between the two utterances, although one came from a blasphemer of religion, as judged by the canon of orthodoxy, and the other, from one of the most inspired writers of the Bible.

There is yet a third utterance, expressing the same pent-up emotion of the poet's heart, that of the psalmist where he says:

> "I was dumb with silence, I held my peace, even from good; and my sorrow was stirred. My heart was hot within me, while I was musing the fire burned: then spake I with my tongue."

There is a superlative beauty and pathos in the compulsatory poetic ejaculations of the heart; and no matter what their source, they are indexes to the mystical truth I unfold here. The wind bloweth where it listeth; and the spirit of inspiration will choose its own vehicle to enlighten and guide all who may read.

I place the words of the prophet and the psalmist alongside those of Zarathustra because all three admit of the same mystical interpretation. Zarathustra had remained for ten years in his mountain retreat in solitary study and contemplation..., then *"he went before the sun and addressed it."*

The period of solitary retirement had done its work. It had not failed him; it had accumulated that fullness of wisdom which no longer permitted him to rest in peace and enjoy it alone. It sought to break the bounds of personal possession and utter itself to the world. He no longer had any pleasure in ruminating what he had found of wisdom during his lengthy meditation. Like the prophet, he was *"weary of holding in."* Like the psalmist, *"while he was musing the fire burned."*

The words of all three are almost identical in declaring what they felt urged to do. Yet, noble and discursive as are the utterances of prophet and psalmist, I feel that the words of Zarathustra have a luminous simplicity which excels both: *"I need hands outstretched to take it."*

The former two tell us what they could do; the latter realises a dire personal need and sends forth a heartfelt petition to the great light of the world for it. Read into the meaning behind the words:

> "I have found in the silence great wisdom, it has become an intolerable burden to me, I petition the rising sun that some may accept and share it with me."

"There is here, below," said Hugo, *"a pontiff, and it is genius."* That is why men, a chosen few, write words like these. Genius is not of the body, nor primarily of the mind, but of the soul. The soul in these men is in the ascendant and has access to the sphere of mystical impression. They have the right of way to the presence of God, and they utter the accents of the divine world because they must. They cannot live to themselves.

No matter how long the season of preparation may be..., and it is sometimes very long..., the time comes when the mounting fire of the heart meets the descending fire of God, the veil of the temple is rent in twain, a crisis of emotion awakens the heart; the voice of the silence breaks the spell of solitary musing and aspiration, and the humble suppliant consecrates his soul upon the altar of service.

This happens in perfection to the chosen few..., to the mystic, the poet, and the prophet; and if we had not the records of their musings, novitiates and utterances, we should be poor indeed. But we have these enshrined in the literature of culture of many centuries. They have been the guide of aspirants in every generation and will ever be so.

The tragedy of recent years, and of today, was and is, that there have been and are so few who have answered that petition of Zarathustra: *"I need hands outstretched to take it."* The voices of the world have been so loud and insistent, the desires of personality so dominant and clamorous, that the innate inspiration of the soul has been smothered, or prostituted to material and purely mental ideals.

All the while, the mystics have been with us. Their researches and experience have been proclaimed and published, and the works and findings of their predecessors have been cited and adduced as testimony in support of their own experience apparently to little purpose. Yet the hope of the immediate future, from the real evolutionary point of view, lies mainly with those of mystical vision, with free, independent, forward-looking individuals, unbound by creed or dogma, unmindful of churchly religion, but possessed of a burning faith in the soul and possibilities of man.

Zarathustra had sought and attained this freedom of soul in solitude; then he came down and looked for those who would accept it and would help to free men from their servitude. The mystics have done this consistently; but the self-sufficient lordly ones of the world and their followers have turned from them and from that which they most needed. The wars of our time are evidence of it.

Instead of retiring to the mountain solitude of the inner life, rulers, statesmen, and people, of narrow and materialistic aims, have pushed this inglorious world at last to the edge of the precipice of disaster. And what they might have learned in the silence and with humility from mystic, prophet, and poet of vision, an iron and knowing fate decrees that the fall and ruin of the idols of men from continent to continent alone shall teach them.

Some who claim insight into national and international Karma have laid the present century martyrdom of man at the door of the impotence of the mystical and religious forces of the nations, their lukewarmness, indifference or apathy, in not exerting themselves to outweigh in influence the impending evil which threatened mankind. I should agree that the religions of the world have failed in this respect..., and those of the East have failed no less conspicuously than those of the West..., and I have more than once expressed an opinion on this leadership.

I should not agree that the mystics, prophets, and spiritual aspirants of the world are likewise culpable, when the church and the people generally have ignored the proffered teaching, inspiration, and guidance of the Zarathustras of the nations.

Let us be just. The Zarathustras have been merely tolerated by the state, never subsidised by it. They have been charitably tolerated as a peculiar and harmless people, instead of an influence of considerable potency and a pronounced asset to any nation. Nor is the church alone guilty of intolerance and indifference to the message of mystic and prophet. An almost incredible attitude is maintained by men of science towards both.

We have been privileged to hear the broadcast opinions of advanced scientists in Britain in response to questions of mystical and psychic import, and the limitations of these men in dealing with such questions give as little hope to the Zarathustras of this generation as the church did in former ones. They publicly discredit the findings of supersensible research and mystic experience, and their academic reputation in the various fields of scientific knowledge and discovery exercises a deleterious influence upon the minds of sincere inquirers who look to them for authoritative guidance.

Therefore, we in the Order are opposed by two representative bodies of belief and opinion, orthodox religion and science, who may be expected to regard us with some suspicion, discredit us with criticism, and attempt to treat us with indifference. In a word, we are beyond the pale of the charmed circle of orthodox religion and materialistic science; the latter even having the unique temerity to declare authoritatively that the case for telepathy has not been proved.

Is it very surprising that civilisation nearly passed out with the world war? Is he a pessimist who sees no indication of a wave of mysticism in the postwar world, when ninety per cent of the people permit this same science and religion to set the frontiers to their thought and discourage all possibility of higher and esoteric enlightenment and insight?

For ourselves, we ignore their frontiers and stand in no need of the encouragement of science or religion, as these representative bodies declare and proclaim them. We have long since taken the measure of both. What value they have we recognise, but we deprecate their influence so far as mystical and esoteric advancement is concerned.

A student of mysticism is occasionally perplexed because, under the incentive of a liberating teaching such as he has received in the Order, the painful limitations of his particular religious attachment are brought into full view.

A young Canadian, on service in Europe during the war, came to see me on this subject. He came of a Catholic family and had spoken, unadvisedly, to his padre about his allegiance to the Order, and asked his opinion. He was persuaded to renounce this allegiance, because the church, the padre insisted, could give him all that the Order could, and all that he needed.

We may dismiss the plain falsehood of the statement. I asked him whether he really wanted the teachings of the Order and if they helped him? He declared that he did want them and could not renounce them. I therefore advised him to follow his own light and let the padre follow his, for the padre had no right or authority to decide for him. This particular case is typical of the attitude of religion and science today, which discourages the seeking and inquiring mind from cultivating a free and expressive creative life.

I do not say that they institute an open campaign of proselytism and range abroad for simple-minded converts. Grounded in tradition, as is the church, dedicated to the intellect and the five senses, as is science, they profess to have the keys of heaven and of this world, and nothing can prevail against them.

But time is moving on: the undercurrents of evolution are gathering momentum; and even if we see no pronounced sign of a forward movement in the direction of higher advancement and demonstration, there is reason for thinking that the impassable frontiers set by religion and science are perceptibly fading in the mist behind us, so much so to some of us that we have long since discounted their existence.

But these frontiers still loom up importantly for many, yet not convincingly as formerly. They are being unceremoniously criticised by inquiring people; and among us are the potential mystics, prophets and poets of tomorrow. The anxious voice of the church calls to them to rescue them from the old damnation: the cold, unspiritual eye of science confronts them to delay their redemption.

Neither gives comfort nor promise of fulfillment to these aspiring personalities. Within those fast frontiers there is no peace for them. But for the existence of schools and fraternities of mysticism and higher culture, they would be like lost souls roaming the highways of a distracted and disillusioned world, where art, beauty, and the true poetry of the mystery of life, and the noblest in man, have been crucified afresh upon a cross of wretchedness, penury, and starvation.

But the same petition goes forth: *"I need outstretched hands to take it."* All through the nightmares of wars of blood, wars of peace, and of the dark night of the soul, throughout the madness and degradation of it all, we have responded to that petition. We accepted the gift in faith and lighted our torch at the source of mystical truth before this century was born; and for half a century we have passed on that light to others..., the handful who would take it.

We came down from the mountain solitude, renouncing many excellent things we would have done for ourselves, and stood before the sun and gave what truth we knew. And it is for those who find no comfort, no guidance, no promise of fulfillment, no enlightenment or panacea for the soul, or no way of spiritual discipline, in the religion and science of today, to accept this gift which points the way to freedom of thought and creative living, and to that true psychological insight into man's soul which will enable them *"to lift a little of the heavy Karma of the world."*

4. The Divine Experiment

Reprinted from the October 1948 edition of the Rosicrucian Digest. *The article was written in response to requests from readers, following an article entitled* "The Imitation of Christ" *by Raymund Andrea, which appeared in the December 1946 edition of the* Rosicrucian Digest.[3]

The lofty theme and influence of Thomas à Kempis in his book *The Imitation of Christ* is another example of how much we are moved by contrasts.

To open this book after closing the forbidding tomes of theology and divinity is to pass into an atmosphere of peace and sanctity where the presence of Christ is an indwelling, directing, and healing power, and not an historical figure formally imposed upon us from without by professional religionists.

It is that willing and easy acceptance of so many persons (because it costs little beyond a subscription) which has given the church its prestige in the world and at the

---

[3]. "The Imitation of Christ" is included in a collection of lectures by the author entitled *The Way Of The Heart* which available from the publisher.

same time has marked its helplessness in all the crises of the evolution of man. Thomas à Kempis, with a pathos peculiarly his own, denotes this same distinction between the man born into the spirit of Christ and the learned divines whose lives he had well studied. In one of his earlier chapters he remarks:

> "Tell me now, where are all those Masters and Doctors, with whom thou wast well acquainted, whilst they lived and flourished in learning? Now others possess their livings and perhaps do scarce ever think of them. In their lifetime they seemed something, but now they are not spoken of. O how quickly passeth away the glory of the world. O that their life had been answerable to their learning! Then had their study and reading been to good purpose?"

Again and again he marks most definitely this distinction between the learned philosopher, the religionist, the orthodox divine, and the mystic: the contemplative, the devotee, secretly and inwardly living in the rich quality of the spiritual influence of Christ. Clear it is to à Kempis that we, at least, cannot fail to see that the man who is considered, in everyday parlance, as a Christian is far removed from what he considers to be a man in Christ.

Concisely, the distinction is here. The average Christian is a believer in exoteric and denominational doctrine; the man in Christ has upon him the sign of the Cross which is revealed in the quality of his inward living. Were there no such distinction, this exhortation to the imitation of Christ would have been superfluous and unnecessary; indeed, it would not have been written. If another such disciple of Christ should write with the same inspired pen "The Repudiation of Christ," it would be a fitting companion to the *Imitation* and be a lasting memorial to the decline of the West and the East in the twentieth century.

Thomas à Kempis was a mystic; his book is one of pure mystical inspiration and has not a compeer in the literature of East or West. It is possible that during his mystical pilgrimage, he passed through all the stages of human experience, from physical debasement, mental unworthiness, and spiritual heedlessness, unto a perfect acceptance of the inward life of Christ revealed to him through his own sufferings.

In the memorable chapter on the Holy Cross we have a series of exhortations to bear the Cross of Christ and to die thereon; we also have impassioned assurances that there is no escape from either if we ever hope to attain Christhood.

It is truly said that we cannot write with strong and irresistible appeal to others of that which we ourselves have not experienced. But it is not always so in the case of a mystical work of this nature; for many who have penned mystical works of undoubted inspirational quality have acknowledged that they themselves have not personally experienced what they had recorded. But I am inclined to think that, judging of the whole tenor of the *Imitation* and especially of this particular and climaxing chapter, à Kempis had lived the book he wrote.

I give this as a personal opinion: for while we have the alleged sayings and admonitions of Christ as recorded by others in scripture, yet it is to à Kempis we must go to have that conception transformed into a living heart contact with Christ as an inwardly sensed spiritual potency of healing and guidance.

The distinction is here again forced upon us between the Christ of Christian belief and the mystical Christ as a spiritual presence within man. Your idea of the Christ in the scripture may be word perfect: to live with Christ as a moving power in the heart is a mystical process and of a totally higher order of experience. Thomas à Kempis' moving portrayal raises the idea of Christ of the scripture to dramatic intensity and appeal as a living entity; he transforms the idea of what Christ said to what Christ can be as an inspirational force in the heart of man.

In the first stanza of the chapter on the Holy Cross, à Kempis says: *"If thou be dead with Him, thou shalt also in like manner live with Him."* Orthodoxly interpreted, this would justify the simple belief that in accepting Christ as the Saviour of the world we are assured of living with Him after transition. But there is no ground sufficient for believing that à Kempis was referring in this and similar passages simply to the status of the disciple of Christ after transition.

For instance, he says:

"In the Cross all doth consist, and in our dying thereon all lieth."

And again, in the same chapter:

"If thou bear the Cross cheerfully, it will bear thee."

And further:

"Nevertheless, this man, thou so many ways afflicted, is not without refreshing comfort, for that he perceiveth very much fruit to grow unto him by the enduring of his own cross."

Clearly, these admonitions and this encouragement have no reference to the disciple's life after transition; nor was à Kempis much concerned with this in his book, but chiefly with living the Christ life here and now; that is, our consciousness would be so raised and enlarged that it would be united with and would partake of the wisdom, glory and peace of the Christ consciousness.

Thomas à Kempis was not a dreamer. He enunciates no soft doctrine, he promises no easy path, he spares neither divine nor philosopher in his spiritual advocacy of Christ. He says plainly and with true mystical authority: the man you are must die if you would live in Christ.

This daily dying must be as sure and certain as a scientific procedure. It must be a secret, inward process which cuts down to the very roots of existence in this world. And it is just because he is this skilful psychologist, who probes to the depths of the heart of man and misses nothing therein which frustrates and damns his own Christhood, that the *Imitation*, known to so many, is acceptable to so few.

Indeed, who reads the *Imitation* today with the devotional humility of the true disciple of Christ? No, it is not because à Kempis was a dreamer and his book beyond the comprehension of intelligent people that it is so rarely encountered or spoken of: it is because the burning words of the saint unsettle the mind, sear the conscience, threaten the strong bulwarks of our materialistic thought and living, and expose too openly the superficiality of the Christianity of our time.

As he approached this chapter of the Holy Cross, he wrote as a fitting prelude to it, severe, censorious, yet pathetic in appeal: *"How few are the lovers of the Cross of Jesus."* It is set in a minor key, as the title foreshadows, and prepares the way for the impressive fugal music of the twelfth chapter.

Pause and contemplate for a moment this noble strain from its third stanza: *"Where shall one be found who is willing to serve God for naught."* It is his searching and just condemnation of man that will repel far more than attract because it opposes the animal in man, whether he be poor and illiterate, learned and a social parasite, or merely religiously respectable.

The gospel of introspection, as presented in the books on yoga, gives us as its basic formula: WHAT AM I? which is an excellent formula for increasing a man's preoccupation with himself, centering his interest in himself, and making him feel very satisfied with himself.

Thomas à Kempis reverses the position. He tells man what he is, makes him very dissatisfied with himself, and focuses his interest upon the Ideal Man he may become. And if he is ready for the first steps on the way, the steady daily contemplation of Christ will quickly awaken the desire to begin to live a sacrificial life in small things. In no long time the habit will become a necessity of his nature and prepare him for greater denials of his mortal selfhood in his daily ministry in whatsoever circumstances.

I knew a man in Christ many years ago who occupied an official position in our Order, to which I elected him, though against his will. I knew it would be a burden to him, but he was so near to Christ in his life that I considered him more worthy of that burden than any other man I knew. He was self-effacing to the last degree, and never counted the cost of his service. Members came to him in trouble and difficulty and went away comforted and heartened. He carried their secret lives in his heart and never failed in his sacred trust. His days were spent in a responsible position in a great city; his nights were devoted exclusively to the work of the Order.

He never spared himself. He took upon himself much of the sad karma of others, and as he served he grew to his task. He had many problems of his own, but those of others were more important. And when he reached that point in his development when it seemed that the full light of the Shekinah would be revealed in him, he passed away suddenly early one morning with his hands crossed over his heart. His life was a benediction and beautiful to the inner eye; and all who knew him still speak of him with reverence and gratitude.

From this reference to a personal friend, whose life was a commentary on the *Imitation*, we may realise what it means to *"die with Christ."*

We are not asked to throw life away so that we may be with Christ. We are to shift our focal centre of living, from the selfhood of the limited interests and action to a higher level of spiritual thinking and intuitional responsiveness to others. I am not an advocate of suffering and self-mortification as a self-imposed discipline to achieve detachment and an indifference to life and all it may bring.

Asceticism is not the way for us. We must live to some purpose. Christ did so, and very fully. It is necessary to have this in mind in reading the *Imitation*. Thomas à Kempis' book is really summed up in one phrase: Bear your cross, willingly and wisely, as Christ bore His.

But bearing the Cross is not a tale of suffering and woe, nor do the words of Christ suggest this, nor does the *Imitation*. In a previous article on the subject I stated: *"If ever the Cross has been laid upon humanity, it has in this century above all others."* That there has been an unprecedented descent of suffering and woe upon humanity is not, I suggest, because of willing and wise bearing of the Cross, but the reverse.

Humanity has been materialistic, selfish, seeking and worshipping false gods; it has been egotistic, strong in self-righteousness, imperialistic, militaristic, and possessing a keen eye to worldly dominion. Humanity has still failed to recognise the meaning of this cross which it has deserved and karmically invoked. There is small evidence that it even seeks the meaning.

If the voice of Christ is sounding in the world today, and I have no doubt that it is, who hears it? Where is the evidence of it? That the influence, power and healing of Christ are in the world today, I am convinced: but they wait, silent and unseen, for man. And if, by a miracle of science, the cross should be lifted from humanity tomorrow and the full tide of teeming prosperity take its place, I believe that science would be the peoples' god, and Christ would still wait.

If the tenor of the *Imitation* inclines the reader to think that its approach to Christ is from the monastic point of view, that does not lessen its truth and practicalness as a mystical guide and inspirational force at the present time. We may allow that the time and environment of à Kempis differed greatly from the present, but that does not weaken one whit its value of applicability today. It is like a soundless voice that has increased in resonance and warning with the years.

The challenge is, either to live in bondage to the earth-bound mortal selfhood, which makes of every passing day a lost opportunity of the soul's unfoldment, or to accept this

Cross of daily dying in the actual terms in which à Kempis presents it.

It is not enough, I repeat, to be merely a respectable Christian, in the commonly accepted sense of the term. The Christianity we know, of yesterday and today, has failed the great ideal. It has proved itself powerless to change the heart of man before and after two world wars, and it rests with politicians, none too sure of themselves, to strive, in the interest of what is called civilisation to offset a major third war.

There is no argument for Christ or an appeal to Him; the argument and appeal are for a secure and comfortable physical and mental existence. A call for spiritual leadership, for men of spiritual vision, for the mystic, the seer, the genuine prophet of God, the man born into the Christ consciousness, is not heard. And if it were, we are so far from this redeemed and elevated consciousness that a call would not be heeded. It would fall upon the ear like the word of an unknown tongue.

It is clear, then, that anything like the Christ man which à Kempis mirrors forth to us, in any sufficient number to be widely influential, cannot be expected in our generation. I forbear to forecast the next. At present it is an ideal for the very few who have lost the savour of life as we know it in the world and are resolved to take the first steps individually, silently, and with inflexible purpose to redeem the time. No hard and fast formula can be given to the aspirant, who finds this purpose rising like a clear light in the mind and subduing all lesser aims, whereby he can feel and know the presence of Christ within him.

The aspirant is in his own place upon the path of evolution, and it is a different place from that of any other aspirant. He may begin his quest with much past concealed power of growth to his credit, and he may not. But I believe that, when the strong desire and the fixed purpose possess him, this is of great promise. This presence of the Christ within is prophetic of rapid advancement because it is very rare among men today.

I do not refer to the outward forms and shows of religion; I refer specifically to the culture of the Christ consciousness, spontaneous, devout, and unceasing. There is no form of outward observance in this; it is an unswerving attitude of the heart and mind which makes a man inwardly holy, no matter what may be his occupation or activity in the world at large.

It is precisely there (within) that the real disciple of Christ dies daily, and no other knows what that living death in Christ may mean to him. The disciple knows, and is content. Christ knew, and no other, and He was content.

The aspirant in our work has many experiments of mental, physical, and psychic culture which ostensibly have no immediate bearing upon this special culture of the Christ consciousness; but they constitute a field of particular cultures of preparing, awakening, and unifying the whole man to a sane and balanced adjustment in the world where he must perforce live and develop and qualify continuously for greater service.

For however great the desire or resolute the purpose of the aspirant, or how singularly he is magnetically attracted by this compelling ideal of à Kempis, the whole way is one of humble forms of service; and it is ever the case that the great ones on the path are those who excel in humility of service.

If the aspirant is now bent upon this divine experiment of indelibly impressing upon his inner life the sign and character of the Holy Cross, what better initiatory process could he engage in than in making this chapter in the *Imitation* his daily contemplation, using other portions of the book as he will to focus attention and meaning upon that climaxing word?

This chapter has a vibration peculiarly its own, and if the soul-personality is prepared for inward ascension there will ensue a response which is real and revealing. He will find that Christ is not a word in scripture, an historical character, variously reported and interpreted, but a living power that rises up within him and descends upon him, a comforting presence and a guiding hand, which he can intimately name in the silence and amid the hard battle of the day, and it will not fail him.

In this name is a magic which exceeds all others in its simplicity and potency, and it awaits the aspirant's dedicated heart and mind to use it with complete confidence and resignation and allow it to shape the course of events in his life to their karmic fulfilment.

Observe those last words: *"to allow them to shape the course of events in his life to their karmic fulfilment."* The Cross of Christ is not a renunciation of life, but the acceptance of it. So many students confuse the issues of philosophy of East and West and allow themselves to be unduly influenced by a foreign interpretation of the meaning and trend of individual evolution.

The Eastern attitude towards life is one of detachment and withdrawal from the experiences of life, and killing at the source of all contacts which involve karmic consequences and eventual forms of personal suffering. And if the *Imitation* inclines the aspirant, because of its noble picture of the Ideal Man, to adopt the idea of the East of self-protective detachment that he may be spared the unpleasant personal contacts of life, then I say that à Kempis has not so taught him.

This is not bearing the Cross of Christ, but a renunciation of it. If he chooses the latter way he retreats from the very conditions of discipline which are essential for attaining Christhood; for, obviously, they who renounce the impact of manifold experiences which are set before them, so that Christhood may be achieved, cannot hope to share in the consciousness of Christ.

Our formula, then, is the steady contemplation of the Christ life, as à Kempis presents it to us, and the realisation of the wonder and beauty and strength of that life. In other words, one is to enter into life upon all planes of activity, fully and completely, as the influence of that contemplation will guide, and is not studiously to avoid its searching discipline for his own peace and security, but make this mental realisation of Christ a standard of judgement and action in the vocation and circumstance to which he is called. Thus, then, will open a secret way of communion between the personality and the Christ which is a light in the soul.

That light may come to be known to the aspirant experimentally in the course of his communion, or for long it may be known only by its beneficent effects, through its guidance, direction, and healing ministration in his life. We know nothing of the private life of à Kempis, but I have no doubt that through his intense contemplation of Christ and his unique exposition of that transcendent character many things were possible to him in the way of demonstration of a miraculous nature.

When we ourselves have proofs of similar manifestations through following his admonitions, we know that our assertions are well based. Life has still its privileges today, although much has gone from it, but I know no greater privilege than to die daily with this supreme Master and, in so dying, to live with Him.

5. The World Shadow

Reprinted from the August 1951 edition of the Rosicrucian Digest.

For the Digest issue of December 1946, I chose as my subject that world-famous classic of devotion *The Imitation of Christ*[4] by Thomas à Kempis. I discussed the book not because I thought that the readers were unacquainted with it, but rather that they might have forgotten or overlooked its value, or that it might be considered not applicable in these years of unrest, disappointment, and pressing objective duties and responsibilities. Many great works have been forgotten, but the letters that reached me in response to that article assured me of the respect and love that Rosicrucians have for the message contained in *The Imitation of Christ*.

But what of those aspirants for truth, and there were and are many, who are troubled with doubts and questionings about this ideal of the Christ life when the whole world is facing and involved in seething turmoil as the Karma of relentless evolution pursues its course and casts a menacing shadow in every direction? Shadows, as ever, are thrown upon the surface of life and things, and they immediately affect us all. It requires trained vision and a stable soul-personality not to be wrongly or unduly influenced by them.

The shadows thrown over the surface of life today are mainly of an ideological and economic nature, but they are so deep and threatening as to obscure entirely, for the majority, the deeper issues and inexorable laws which are working toward the far-off events of spiritual purpose.

It is not that we have forgotten the ideal of the Christ life which we have sought and cherished in our best moments, for this is a kind of magical influence which will never let us go once we have surrendered to it. It is that we cannot reconcile the light of Christ with the shadow of a tormented world. We have come to a point in evolution where the shadow strikes across our path and confuses the senses and the mind, baffles our

---

4. "The Imitation of Christ" is included in a collection of lectures by the author entitled *The Way Of The Heart* which available from the publisher.

efforts, and indeed makes us wonder in which direction we are travelling or whether we are progressing at all.

It sometimes seems as if a *"dark night of the soul,"* that well-known factor in the life of the aspirant on the mystic way, had fallen upon the nations; and whatever reactions there may be against it, however much we may resent it, the "night" must be lived through.

Now, no one can go far in evolution without that shadow of the dark night falling upon him. It looms around and before him and settles within, until it seems that the compassion of Christ had forgotten him.

How many have written to me through the years of this same trial! It is no figment of the imagination. Every mystical teacher testifies to it in some form or other, and there are probably few of us who have not known it. The shadow is of such density that few can see truly or think wisely when it falls, unless they have learned to follow a light within themselves.

The early writers on mystical theology and those prominent in the monastic Orders of former days unfolded very circumstantially in their works the various difficulties and temptations which the novice would inevitably encounter and have to overcome on his way to perfection.

It is true that in accordance with their theological philosophy and belief the difficulties of the way were often attributed to the working of the devil who was ever watchful to oppose the upward striving of the novice by raising up obstacles within his human nature and deflecting him from the hard path of discipline, devotion, and prayer.

Although our philosophy differs much from that of the mystic theologians, the goal of perfection which they had in view differs little from ours. They were possessed with the ideal of Christ and sacrificed everything for it. We have much to learn from them. It is enlightening to note with what particularity and exactness they analysed human nature and revealed its susceptibility to worldly influences, its failings and weaknesses, and how solicitously they instructed the novice by dealing with him patiently but with perseverance and in unfaltering faith never to surrender that ideal.

Therefore the shadow which lengthens before us today raises within us very similar obstacles which confronted the novice of the past. It is the same world with similar problems in a different setting, but a few steps onward in evolution. It is understandable and pardonable if the immediate scene and peculiar shadow conjured by it should fasten the attention of aspirants and cause them to question the Christward direction and the future.

However much the circumstances then differ from those we face now, the novice, aspirant, and mystic of the past had to deal with an enemy within their own selves which assumed reality from their personal reactions to those circumstances, just as we have to deal with the manifold reactions which our response to the shadow produces within ourselves. That the environment of the time and that the conditioning circumstances were different does not alter the crucial fact.

Whatever the environment and circumstances of the past, and some cycles of them were dark enough, they threw the same shadow of doubt, perplexity and fear into the minds and hearts of men and women who were intent upon following those who taught the way; and the more advanced and sensitive types among them suffered the most.

They saw more deeply and felt more keenly, and it was they who wrote most poignantly and searchingly of the various trials which ever beset those who essay to follow the Christ ideal. I know very well that many regard askance the earlier literature on these subjects. They consider it gloomy, perhaps even morbid. I think otherwise.

Our psychologists and psychoanalysts, whatever they may think of the nomenclature those teachers employed, are faced with precisely the same problems and difficulties in human lives, although no doubt these are greatly accentuated by the abnormal stringency of the times. The cure does not lie in their hands; at best it is only a temporary and doubtful relief.

Who of these would enjoin the name of Christ and the following of Christ as a light able to dissipate any shadow that the devil of circumstance casts upon men? Yet this was a sure refuge and the only panacea that the mystics of the past, of whatever persuasion or culture, ultimately found in all their study, vigil, and contact with human lives.

"While reading gives knowledge of doctrine," wrote a saint, *"the name of Christ drives out demons."* No matter what the road..., whether of learned philosophy, mystical theology or asceticism, solitary prayer or retired meditation, or ministry to human hearts in perplexity and anguish and loss..., they all came at last to realise that the potent influence of Christ was a present reality and could be an unfailing solace in all their trials and disciplines of mortal existence.

I said, they came to realise at last, because it is not to be expected that we may enter into the fruits of divine fellowship with Christ in the sense in which mystical writers of all types speak of it, without due preparation for it. So many aspirants expect the fruition and graces of the interior life and higher stages of living before they have lived the earlier ones.

Study of the upward path, of the many approaches to it, is preliminary: then follow its various disciplines, those which you already know and are engaged upon. What we know, however, will not carry us far if it becomes in our hands merely an intellectual exercise to foster an ambition for mental cleverness and exploitation.

There is much we have to renounce in mind and heart on this journey toward the exaltation of soul. It may seem a hard saying, but what becomes of much of that which we have most valued in ourselves, which we have built with strong intent to make the mental edifice a sure refuge from storm and stress, a resistant bulwark against the pain and vicissitudes of life so that nothing may disturb a self-centered peace and happiness, that self-satisfaction, so prevalent among those having the possession of more of the unusual knowledge than others, and the conscious superiority which accompanies it?

All this has to be left behind like some faded memory of childhood. It need not be so, now, if the aspirant does not wish it. He may make his own pace. There is no immediate time limit in life's progress.

If these things, and others of personal value, mean so much to an individual, he can retain them. I only say he cannot carry them with him beyond a certain point; and there is ample time for using and becoming disillusioned by them before he realises their relative insignificance and feels a call to real service. He is safe where he is, so long as he does not invoke more.

But if he has that intensity of soul to any degree commensurate with those who have taken the secret stages to perfection, and is attracted like a magnet to that divine adventure, then the deepening shadows of Karmic trial and discipline will constitute the answer to his petition. That may seem to be another hard saying, but it is familiar on the tongues of the mystics; and since it is true to experience, whether in the past or the present, there is no evading the issue.

Here arise disappointments and questioning in the minds of aspirants of sincere purpose and blameless life. They find it difficult to acquiesce in the justice of this fact of experience, that the more serious effort and purposeful advance made by them should be met with contrary circumstances and unexpected testing of the best within them.

Nevertheless, a definite threshold is crossed at this point, when the aspirant comes under the influence and direction of a will wiser than his own. The very nature of his persistence and progress evokes this higher guidance, the kind of response though unlooked for should be a matter for grateful acceptance.

Why should one fight against his own good? Why after having spent some years upon the basic teaching and experimental technique in moulding the interior life to a fit capacity for the reception, appreciation and serviceable use of higher divine influences, and wider vistas of spiritual achievement open before the soul, should the individual resent, or fear, or retreat from the more exacting conditions which emerge from the silence and solitude around him to challenge his strength and endurance?

The shadows cast by Karma before the soul appear very real and menacing, but they are neither impenetrable nor lasting. It only requires a strong will, a firm step, and an invincible confidence in the invisible guidance which has never failed him to this hour.

Let us make an application of these thoughts, of the individual aspirant, to the collective life of the nations on their way of evolution. It is, I said, as if a Karma of the dark night of the soul had thrown its shadow across the whole world. If then, the aspirant may conclude, the world shadow is the dark night on a large scale, all he has to do is to isolate his infinitesimal fragment of it as a miniature personal tragedy and so evade its full impact.

He can do this, but it will lead him to a dead end in consciousness and experience. It will lead him into a retreat of non-participation, instead of sharing with understanding and compassion in the sorrows and fears of his fellow men and throwing even a glimpse of light into the surrounding darkness.

The world shadow is of such a character, so involving, disturbing and threatening, that none can hope to escape it. The solitary petition of the aspirant for help, guidance, and peace in the hour of inward trial has also become a universal petition of many nations in their fear and perplexity of what the shadow portends.

Multitudes are so obsessed with what it may portend, and are so occupied with the ill effects of it upon every aspect of daily life, that any consideration of underlying causes is ruled out, and this is not limited to the masses only. This applies also to the mentally developed strata of society. The only difference between them is that some sections are more publicly expressive than others.

But all are affected by it. None can escape what is the responsibility of all: and if the aspirant tries to escape, he surrenders his title of discipleship with Christ. He either elects to suffer the world shadow with and for Christ, or denies it.

I want now to introduce another aspect of the present situation to the attention of the aspirant, for I am assuming he is practical, has the courage of his own convictions, and does not fear to express them. I want to state that all classes of society in Britain are publicly expressive, although some more than others. There has been deeper resentment and more bitter criticism directed against officialdom from all sections of the community because of existing economic conditions than ever known before in Britain.

Those who imposed and are responsible for the said conditions have had to swallow the criticism whether they liked it or not, because it has been justified and has emanated from all classes, irrespective of party or belief. The restrictions, controls, and the never ending and mounting sacrifices put upon our people in the name of freedom are bringing them rapidly nearer to the condition of a people subject to invasion by a foreign power. One may suspect that the reason responsible leaders in Britain are so vociferous in assuring us that we are free is that they know full well that we are on the way to losing the rights of a free people.

"*Man is born free,*" said Rousseau, *"and everywhere he is in chains."* We in Britain are aware of this and are giving no uncertain expression to it. We know that the shadow of a war confronts us and the world, and the kind of reaction of millions to this knowledge is not surprising. Their hardships are increased, their ambitions are thwarted, their possibilities of progress and achievement in practically every sphere, except those purely industrial and materialistic, are checked, with the disastrous consequence that apathy and indifference about the future have infected the national life.

But I must say this: it is not the fear of war imminent in the shadow that is responsible for this apathy and indifference and loss of personal initiative and enterprise in our people: it is the steady and increasing governmental deprivation of the rights of the individual, the forcing him into narrower and narrower limits of personal action, the tying of his hands in every field of cultural expression in which he needs encouragement and cooperation.

This condition is what the people of Britain resent today. They have known in the past how to deal with the shadows of war: they will know how to deal with another one; but to deprive them of the means, physically, mentally, and culturally, whereby they live as the sons of nature and of God, is another matter. The virility of man is not sustained on words and promises, empty and unfulfilled; and the time is very near when even politicians will consider how much it profits a nation to increase its wealth and lose its living soul.

With our friends in America the picture is different. I do not think that in America there is more fear of a shadow, such as may portend unavoidable war, than there is here. But I do think that the lowering of standards of life, the curtailing of individual liberty, the debasing of high ideals for which Americans have striven, as well as the blasting of personal enterprise and achievement, and a possible subjecting of all they have and are to the insidious encroachment of the influence and power of one political party or another, is a kind of fear the shadow casts upon their path. And knowing what has happened in Britain, America may well be apprehensive about it. But I do not think that Americans would tolerate it.

My belief is: that if the shadow should threaten to materialise in such a pattern of ignominy, Americans would decide very quickly and unanimously that individual liberty is no less valuable than national liberty; that without the one they might as well be without the other; and that they would set an example to the world in that direction as they have in many others. America would show the world that Lincoln had not spoken in vain.

It may be thought that I am venturing into deep aspects of the shadow; but such aspects confront us all, including those on the mystic path, who can view these matters from a wider and esoteric standpoint. Such persons are faced with the same issues and will be confronted with the same problems, each in his own life and place. But whatever these students of mysticism can do or not do, they should see to it that they are not blinded by the psychological dope which political leaders prepare for them. They should hold fast to the truth and refuse to act the lie.

Whatever the nature of the problems they cannot evade thoughtful participation in them nor responsible decision and action about them under the pretext that such questions are political whilst their aim is spiritual. Is not the liberty of the individual a sacred thing, a freeing of the mind and soul from fetters of the past which have denied individual expression of the truth and a refusal to be bound by them now or in the future? The Rosicrucians have always fought hard enough for the right to express truth, suffered for it, and we now profit by it.

It is not for me to tell the aspirant for truth what he should do or not do in this or that circumstance. He must learn to follow the light within him, born of long championing of the cause of individual liberty of mind and soul, whatever the opposition of circumstances may be..., nor must he fear the incidental suffering which may follow in doing so. For the Masters are not only those who have attained to divine things, but as well those who have suffered them.

No man can so attain without suffering the conditions of attainment; and if his ideal is individual freedom on all planes of life in order that he may live the truth as it was in Christ, and in which alone is freedom, let him view it in the right perspective. Let him give the right value to any who would hinder him..., act according to the truth seen.

6. Thus Spake Zarathustra

Reprinted from the February 1952 edition of the Rosicrucian Digest.

Zarathustra, tired of his mountain solitude, went before the sun and declared that he, too, must *go down* among men, for he had grown weary of his wisdom and needed outstretched hands to take it.

He then began his unique discourses to all manner of people whom he met on his journeyings through many lands. The discourses consist of four series. However, after completing the first series, another inspiration came to Zarathustra, perhaps as unexpected as the first, which had brought him forth from his mountain retreat. He was called back to his solitude.

Prior to that moment he had given lavishly of his wisdom to whosoever would listen to him. Daring, revolutionary, unaccountable words he had spoken, and few must have been those who could accept them. They had a dual meaning and only the wise could rightly interpret them. But he spoke right on the thunder strokes of inspiration as they descended upon him, caring nothing whether he was understood or not, whether praised or blamed.

When the fire of a higher wisdom takes hold upon a man, he cannot argue with it, nor can he mince or dilute it to please or conciliate those who hear it. And considering that a goodly portion of the Scriptures consists of this kind of utterance which people of all nations accept without much question, because it is believed to be inspired, we wonder at the inconsistency of human nature.

Why should today the same spirit of inspiration, when it finds a voice among men, be met with a very different reception? It was so, too, with Zarathustra. For he looked at the people and said in his heart:

> "There they stand. There they laugh. They understand me not. I am not the mouth for these ears."

That happened even during the prologue to his discourses: and he gave twenty-two discourses before his first return to solitude. Years passed, and Zarathustra came again among men and gave a second series of twenty-two discourses. They were as daring and revolutionary as the first series. The concluding discourse of his series is entitled, "The great silence." It tells of the second retirement of Zarathustra to his solitude. I quote from it:

> "What hath happened unto me, my friends? Ye see me troubled, driven forth, unwillingly obedient, ready to go – alas, to go away from you!

> "Yea, once more must Zarathustra retire to his solitude: but unhappily this time doth the bear go back to his cave!
>
> "What hath happened unto me? Who ordereth this? Ah, my angry mistress wisheth it so; she spake unto me. Have I ever told her name to you?
>
> "Yesterday towards evening there spake unto me my great silence: that is the name of my terrible mistress.
>
> "And thus did it happen..., for everything must I tell you, that your heart may not harden against him who suddenly departs!"

And after Zarathustra in his pride had several times questioned and repudiated the peremptory voice of the silence, it was said finally to him:

> "And there was spoken unto me for the last time: 'O Zarathustra, thy fruits are ripe, but thou art not ripe for thy fruits! So must thou go again into solitude: for thou shalt yet become mellow.'"

Again and again this happened to Zarathustra: a wandering among many peoples in divers cities, and a retreating to the mountain and his cave. During this period he gave the third and fourth series of his discourses. Sometimes he gave them to odd characters he met on the way, sometimes to animals that conversed with him, and not infrequently in soliloquy with himself.

Now, whether or not the experience we have so often read of as *"the dark night of the soul"* be indicated in this periodical withdrawal of Zarathustra into the terrifying silence, such an interpretation immediately comes to mind and is impressed upon us. The development of Zarathustra proceeds in alternating cycles of activity and retirement: each period of solitude and silent meditation is followed by one of inspired activity and exhortation of his fellow men. Again the hour of inspiration passes: the message is delivered; and he is called back into the silence of the heart and the lonely communion with the spirit of wisdom.

My readers may know that the book entitled *Thus Spake Zarathustra* was considered by Nietzsche as his greatest work. I have characterised the discourses as daring, revolutionary, and unaccountable; they certainly were and are so to the general reader.

But for those who have travelled a long way over the path of evolution, and are accustomed to the daring and revolutionary in the writings of seers and prophets, these discourses have a decided mystical quality and can be appreciated at their true value. Only a wise man and a seer could have written them.

That he knew he had a mission to fulfil is borne out by the fact that at thirty years of age Nietzsche left his home and spent ten years in mountain solitude and search after the truth of life. He had an extensive knowledge of literature. He had studied exhaustively religions of the East and the West and all the great philosophies.

His strictures on orthodox Christianity are audacious and sometimes profane. So much so, that his bitterest enemies are to be found in Britain, where his books have for a long time been difficult to obtain. Nevertheless, he is a bold and original thinker who is recognised throughout the world today; and it may be noted that nearly every great writer in philosophy, religion, and art quotes him and values his vast erudition and his penetrating insight into every subject he handles.

Nietzsche is not an author to be recommended to every reader. To those of limited intelligence and appreciation some of his work may prove harmful and misleading. To the highly intelligent, albeit of closed mind and orthodox tendencies, he will be rejected as a dangerous and destructive innovator. To the professed religionist he will be anathema and denounced as a betrayer of the soul of man. To those who are witnessing the rapid decline of the West today and then consult his pages, his resounding word will prove so ominous as to make a Christian hate him. To those who seek the truth wherever to be found, who know it to be a two-edged sword which exposes the beauty and ugliness of life with supreme indifference, he can be an inspiration and very much of a guide.

It all depends upon the size and quality of a man's thinking. And it can be said that those who have shown real appreciation of Nietzsche and quoted him the most in their own works, have been precisely those noted for their breadth of vision, depth of learning, and profound understanding of the nature and soul of man.

The nature of the development of Zarathustra is undoubtedly analogous to that phase of evolution known as the *"dark night."* And at once there comes to mind the classical mystical treatise of Saint John of the Cross which deals very fully with the subject. I do not doubt that Nietzsche was well acquainted with this work and made a particular study of it in the course of his omnivorous reading.

For, granted that he was severely critical of certain religious teachings, having discerned in them that which hampered and fettered the mind more than it enlightened, his sharp-sighted intuition exposed the positive and negative phases of these teachings with ruthless indifference and utter disregard of the feelings of those who had been nurtured in them from childhood and rested all their hope of future salvation upon them.

Even so, we do see in the development of Zarathustra something analogous to the doctrine and mystical practice of Saint John of the Cross in his work. St. John comments upon certain imperfections which beset aspirants entering upon the way. Imperfections such as pride, avarice and spiritual sluggishness, anger, envy, and spiritual lukewarmness. He shows why these imperfections assault the aspirant and hinder his progress.

Zarathustra, in his discourses, alludes to the same imperfections with that originality of treatment, fineness of perception and nice discrimination as applied to individual development; as to make us feel that he is one who went into the mountain solitude for good purpose. And that purpose was to get down to the bedrock of truth about himself and life, and record it for the few who had ears to hear it.

But what was the point of this devastating criticism which called forth the bitter hatred and venomous denunciation of those who felt themselves so much better than he? What was his ideal? It was the greater man of the future, the superman.

Now, if you want to bring the worst out of politician or religionist, and men of learning and science, you only need to point to a character that dwarfs and overshadows them. The reception given to Nietzsche's superman proves it.

He thoroughly abhorred some of the sickly sentimental teaching of orthodox Christianity and he treated it mercilessly. Yet, he was seeking all the time the ideal man. At every step he struck hammer blows at the fetters which bound men and held them back from perceiving the truth. And when it is remembered that Christ said: *"The truth shall make you free,"* I do not hesitate to say that the man who dares public opinion and imperils his reputation in a bold and honest search for it, as did Nietzsche, must command the respect of honourable men.

Nietzsche has been condemned because he was a pitiless destroyer of false values. He has been most condemned by those who feared to interrogate those values, who fear any who dare to interrogate them openly, because they have so long lived with them and know that certain worldly prosperity rests upon these values.

He has been condemned by Christian communities because he levelled a bolt with startling effect against the rotten foundations of orthodoxy. Since his day (he died in 1900) those foundations have been subjected to relentless inquiry and criticism from left and right, from within the church and without. And it is interesting to note how scant has been the opposition raised against those declarations of thinking men and women. The fact is that much as we ourselves may recoil from some of the terms of vituperation which Nietzsche permits himself on the subject, we nevertheless find ourselves unable to refute his conclusions.

The condemnation of Nietzsche in Britain has no doubt been enhanced by the fact that the perverted Hitler was known to be interested in his writings. With a characteristic devilish aptitude for twisting good into evil and converting the truth into a lie, Hitler assumed that he himself was the superman of his time; whereas, he was a common murderer.

So the judgement of Nietzsche rests upon a logical fallacy. Hitler studied Nietzsche; Nietzsche taught the superman; Hitler believed himself to be superman; and therefore, Nietzsche was responsible for Hitler.

We have to thank Professor Lichtenberger of France for an unbiased assessment and soundly balanced judgement of Nietzsche. A quotation from his book *The Gospel of Superman* will show at a glance what Nietzsche would have thought of Hitler as an exponent of his superman, had he lived to witness the colossal vanity and impudence of this caricature of the great man of the future:

"Nietzsche's superman was essentially one of those great Initiators who, like Christ or even Buddha or Mahomet, have exercised power over the souls of men. Thus the kind of war that interested Nietzsche was not that which was enacted on the field of battle and which, in its blind fury, indiscriminately attacked wealth, the treasures of art, and the lives and happiness of men. This kind of war might be a fatality, but it was above all a barbarity of which the soul of Nietzsche, so easily moved to compassion, felt more than most men the tragic horror. But the kind of war that fired his enthusiasm was the silent, invisible, mysterious struggle which takes place in the depths of the soul between the great principles that govern human life, and which in the last resort decide the direction evolution will take.

"Material and visible warfare has for its object the hegemony of a people or a race. Spiritual warfare determines what might be called in the widest sense of the word the religious future of mankind. The true disciple of Nietzsche is the man who with all the force of his being aims at the creation of an idea that shall rule mankind, at the triumph of a religious ideal, ancient or modern. The man who is a fanatic in the cause of race or country has no right to connect himself with the name of Nietzsche."

7. Idealism in Practice

Reprinted from the July 1952 edition of the Rosicrucian Digest. *Also published in* "Waiting for the Master" *by* Francis Bacon Lodge *(1982).*

I know that readers will agree that one of the most important features of the *Rosicrucian Digest* is the reprinting of Dr Lewis' articles. That they are as living, instructive, and uplifting as at their first appearance is to be expected, because transcripts of truth, penned under Cosmic direction or inspiration, never lose their original force or value. As surely as they had inspirational value for those who read them years ago, so will they have a like effect upon others who read them today.

There is an innate quality in all writings which come forth under, what I call, the pressure of the burden of Cosmic emotion laid upon the writer who is chosen as a messenger of the truth of the inner life. They differ fundamentally from discourses of a general scientific and philosophical character. These have an academic and informative content of a factual nature; whereas, the former have a moving, inspiriting, and enduring quality which leaves the reader with a permanent impression for good. Moreover, those who have read such writings in the past will find upon reading them again, after a considerable lapse of time, a wealth of meaning which was not apprehended on the first perusal. They perceive possible applications of the truths enunciated which were not before obvious to them and therefore did not make their full impression.

The kind of writings I refer to have a peculiar occult quality: they do not give up their content of wisdom and significance fully on first reading. The mind may understand and acquiesce and pass on, but such writings are not merely a superficial diet for the rational mind. They have a far deeper objective..., the awakening of psychic and spiritual faculties. This requires time, often a long time. However, the awakening goes on silently beyond the frontiers of our mundane life, and the strongest proof we have of this is in the new light and in the quick sympathetic response we experience on rereading the teachings of those who have gone before us on their way in evolution.

Recently, I had occasion to refer to comments by Dr Lewis so far back as 1920 on the work of the higher degrees of the Rosicrucian Order, and the reading of them prompted the above reflections. He directed the mind to a consideration of the value and possible potency of new members entering a lodge of the Order, and offered three points for the serious thought of those who hold responsible offices in lodges. Dr Lewis was not only a thorough master of detail of any subject in hand, he handled his detail prophetically. It is not an unusual thing for a scholar to be a master of detail, but the marshalling of it in unexpected ways and its application to ends which prompt the reader to new thought and action are marks of an original mind. So, when I read these three points regarding new members, written more than 30 years ago, the full significance of them came back to me with singular force. The first point stressed was this:

> "We have noted, often, that unexpected help of the greatest value has come from new members, often unsolicited or without suggestion. On more than one occasion a service or help that has turned the tide in some grave affair of a lodge or of the whole Order, has come from a new member when not hope but expectation was almost gone."

That is a confession indeed, made in deep seriousness, and with a feeling of profound gratitude; for the Imperator at that time was not very far away from the year of the inauguration of the work of the Order in America and was still feeling the heavy weight of the responsibility of a great task which rested mainly upon himself. I sense in his words of grateful acknowledgement the value of the new member and how much that help heartened him in those early days when the Degrees which we know so well were being moulded and adjusted for international use; some of the early Degrees were just then passing into the hands of lodge members while the highest ones were still in preparation for the years to come.

But it was a Karmic decree that when the work became launched, there would come, from near and far, those linked with the Order from past ages, and with the Imperator himself, who would rededicate themselves intuitively through this past association and offer their personality, prestige and knowledge, their appreciation, love and influence, as a manifold gift upon the altar of service to humanity, which the Imperator had proclaimed with all the fervour of a messenger of the hierarchy.

We should not overlook the poignant words, *"when not hope but expectation was almost gone."* They betray the secret anxiety of the master mind who, for all his confidence in himself and the authority behind him, yet stood back from the work of his hands, and looked up and wondered from whence would come just the needed help, although promised..., when it seemed that, if that help did not materialise, so much would remain unfulfilled and the great ideal cherished so devotedly would fade. But the promise was fulfilled; and it has been fulfilled many times during the years since then. But the future is always uncertain, and no matter how luminous and impressive the ideal and the work for it has grown, keen eyes, strong hands, and prophetic minds must ever be watchful, ready to do, and to envisage the morrow, so that nothing shall detract from but more be added to the temple, with all its international ramifications and potencies, which we have cherished, fought for and preserved, through such perilous times.

Dr Lewis' second point is this: *"Do we fully realise the potent power lying dormant in a new member? This should not be mistaken to refer to any financial power of such possible potency."* It is just here that some of the older members have sometimes fallen heavily. The new member, presenting the necessary qualifications, has no doubt been welcomed gladly and courteously, and then been left to himself to find his place and adjust himself in his own way as best he can. Up to a point this is well, but it is not enough.

The long-standing member..., who may be an officer in his lodge..., is far from being in the category of a foreman in a factory who greets the newcomer, indicates his job, and leaves him to it. The new member represents a soul of potential worth, and the prophetic sense of the officer will show its chief act of service in understanding and assessing the evolutionary value of the member on all the planes of his manifesting life. I have seen many new members enter the Order anxiously, yet so diffidently at the first step as to hide the likelihood of any exceptional advancement in them or outstanding service from them, when judged by ordinary standards; but within a short time the spirit of Christ so permeated all they did, that I have had cause to thank the Cosmic for the gift to us. Some of these have finished their journey and gone to their reward, but the memory of them remains: the Order is richer for their service; and their spirit lives with us as a present inspiration and assurance that others will come with secret graces in their hearts and strength in their hands to add new stones to the temple we have been at pains to build and guard through the years.

Dr Lewis was a seer of souls. That is why he could not regard a new member simply as a unit with a number. He made it his business to know the member, as far as was possible from a distance; and when he contacted the member he soon knew the limitations and the possibilities which would sooner or later show themselves. He treated the limitations with kindness and humanity, for he foresaw the struggle of mind and heart which would be needed to overcome them, and the possibilities ripened under his wise guidance and encouragement.

Do you realise, my brothers, how comparatively few there are, even in the realm of studies to which we are dedicated, who possess this rare qualification of the seership of souls? They are few indeed. If it were otherwise we should not witness the whole train of schools, societies and cults of many names, of East and West, exercising so poor an influence in the world today as to be relatively unrecognised and unknown. And recalling what Dr Lewis brought to his contact with members, and what we should endeavour to bring to them today, I cannot do better than quote the famous words of Saint-Martin in one of his letters, as indicating how to equip ourselves with the eminent grace of seership needed to comply with our second point. For, in putting this question to us as to our attitude to the new members, Dr Lewis concealed in it a direct challenge in its simplest form to ourselves. That challenge is *"what capabilities have we evolved in order to deal with the members in the highest sense of proficiency in service?"* The response to us by members possessing strong latent possibilities will depend upon the proficiency of our contact to act as a stimulant to their possibilities. What they need from us is the light of initiation, the revealing word, and the healing hand, and all these are presupposed and comprised in the citation from Saint-Martin. Here it is:

> "The only initiation which I preach and seek with all the ardour of my soul is that by which we may enter into the heart of God and make God's heart enter into us, there to form an indissoluble marriage, which will make us the friend, brother, and spouse of our Divine Redeemer. There is no other mystery to arrive at this holy initiation than to go more and more down into the depths of our being, and not let go until we can bring forth the living, vivifying root, because then all the fruit which we ought to bear, according to our kind, will be produced within us and without us naturally."

The third point suggests how the new members can serve; it briefly notes that for several reasons they are better able to serve with their possibilities than were the new members of the previous years. First, there are more ways, means, and systematised utilities for new members to apply efficiently their possible services. Second, there are more definite, concrete and self-evident needs and channels for such services. Third, there are many advanced members in each lodge and in so many more localities now to guide, suggest to, or assist the new members, or any others, who desire secretly, anonymously, and adequately to render such service to the Order, to a lodge, or to strangers as is easily within their means and consciousness.

Undoubtedly, the possibilities of applied service by the new members have vastly increased since these points were first written. No member needs now to be reminded of the *"definite, concrete and self-evident needs and channels of such service."* They petition him on every hand. But it is the third suggestion which immediately interests me: that there are many advanced members now...

"to guide, suggest to or assist the new member, or any others, who desire secretly, anonymously, and adequately to render such service to the Order, to a lodge, or to strangers, as is easily within their means and consciousness."

I am also particularly interested in one feature of this statement: it does not demand or request: it *suggests* what can be done. I remember the late Imperator very well, for I was in constant contact with him from those earliest years until he passed to higher work, and one of his strongest traits was the wise suggestion to a possible or necessary objective. He did not impose his will or exert undue authority even where he might, for that would have defeated the chief end of development in others. He indicated a way and left it to the initiative, the readiness, of the member or officer to take it. So it is here: *"There are many to guide, to suggest or assist."* If that were so then, how much more is this possible today?

When I look back over 30 years and review the catastrophic events of that period and what they have done to our generation, the cruel burdens they have thrust upon it almost beyond what human beings ever thought they would be able to bear, it requires little imagination to realise what those conditions have done to the mind and heart of humanity. They have crucified both, as surely as Christ was crucified in his day. And anyone who can look into the mind and heart of humanity today and not have pity and compassion for what the world Karma has written there, is but crucifying Christ afresh within his own heart. This must not happen with us. We are called to pity and compassion.

8. The Irredeemable Moment

Reprinted from the May 1954 edition of the Rosicrucian Digest.

Goethe once said: *"Every situation..., nay every moment..., is of infinite worth, for it is a representative of a whole eternity."* A modern writer had the same idea in mind when he referred to the *"sanctity of the present moment."* Statements like these reveal the reflective mind, the kind of mind that pauses long enough and probes deeply enough to seize upon the truth of life and conduct.

Such a person refuses to be torn away from the centre of reality and hurried headlong with the thoughtless and superficial crowd which is carried unheedingly over the surface of life and through the years; only to be awakened abruptly one day by the sting of pain, or loss, or tragedy, and to wonder in his last hours what life has done to him.

This is far from an imaginary picture. It is prevalent on a colossal scale and in the lives of multitudes. Few pause long enough, or are quiet enough in mind, to give to the passing moment its true value.

The majority are so bewitched by the endless round of personal problems and the larger circle of world events..., perplexing, tormenting, and challenging..., that the present moment slips away almost unnoticed in the stream of time; and the present situation falls into a wrong perspective and becomes the victim of a biased judgement. Such persons are subconsciously aware of the passing moment for they have to live in it, but the subsequent effect of their action upon the present situation is the result of chance or fate.

The picture is a real one. I suppose it has been so in every period of society in the past. But the postwar period in which we live bears witness to it beyond any previous one. A thinker now and then becomes a relentless critic of it. He has no remedy for it. There is no remedy whereby the general tone of a nation's thought and action can be magically raised to a level of mental and spiritual sanity which constitutes the ideal of complete manhood.

Many thought that the crucifixion of the war years in Britain would so temper mind and heart that a new manhood, even a spiritual one, would rise from that bitter cross of Karmic chastisement..., and I write that deliberately. They were mistaken.

What we call society, recovering from the merciless blows of the first war, carelessly threw off the shackles of a temporary, more dedicated living and increased its pace with the world as its master. The second war threatened its very life and existence, but it survived, rose from the ashes of destruction and, resuming its former role, tossed ideals to the winds, incurred the censure of religion and culture, ignored both, and gave firmer confirmation to [Oswald] Spengler's prophecy of the decline of the West.

"What concerns us," says Spengler, *"is not what the historical facts which appear at this or that time are, but what they signify, what they point to, by appearing."* That is all very well for those who think in centuries. But it does concern us very much that the facts we are dealing with are what they are. We cannot ignore them. We should not be indifferent to them. On every hand, we see their corrosive influences..., repellent and destructive. What they signify by appearing is another matter. It would require some unpleasant writing even to indicate it.

One fact may be mentioned. World events run to their crisis at a high tempo. This is what blinds so many people to the importance of their individual part in those events, for the present moment is swallowed up so completely that its very existence is almost unheeded.

If our daily reiterated radio news and discussions do partially enlighten the people on world events, they are no less depressing. The distorted views of commentators and half-truths of politicians sketch a picture of the sordid drama which would excite the risibilities of a misanthropist. That the unthinking and a high percentage of the intelligent are alike fascinated by the shifting colours of this bizarre canvas and live mentally in the fog of sensationalism, biased opinion, and half-truth which hovers over them, is a tragedy. It is the main burden of their conversation, hope and faith.

They permit themselves to be hypnotised by a set of "critics," "experts," and nobodies. Men and women who have all the facts of this riotous world at their finger tips, tabulated and pigeonholed with Pelmanlike methodicalness, and who mix the crude colours to their liking and splash about with a little brief authority, the truth, the half-truth, and nothing like the truth to him who will be saved from thinking for himself.

Why, it is a foretaste of purgatory! When Dante was making his dismal way through that region of surprises, one of the spirits cried aloud: *"Rumour and the popular voice they look to, more than truth."* As the crowd was there, so it is here. It must have been a sharp-sighted and courageous spirit that spoke the truth so openly.

There is only one remedy for this absent-mindedness in full consciousness: to turn the light of the silent self just for a moment upon this maelstrom of babel of tongues which would stun us into ineptitude, and observe just what it is doing with us and for us. The present moment should not find us off guard as to its presence or value, and the present situation should not deflect us in judgement and action, to our own undoing and the detriment of others.

If every moment is a fraction in a life cycle, and every situation a revealing of past evolution and a test or liquidation, a challenge or opportunity, then a definite responsibility rests upon us every moment for conducting ourselves wisely and making it master the situation before us. *"A wise man's heart discerns both time and judgement."*

We should shut our ears to the discordant voices of the air and refuse their standard of thought and taste, and their desire to speak for us. A discriminating mind and taste would discern an amazingly small amount of real value or enlightenment in them.

The thought element is often poor and feeble, often destructive. The taste is mediocre in quality, often coarse and vulgar. Our studies should thoroughly disharmonise us with both. If they do not, then we are still under the spell. And so long as we remain under it, it is useless to talk about development, culture or spirituality. The two are sworn enemies of each other.

If a Rosicrucian is not a thinker he has missed his vocation. The initial step for him must be, if the experience of life has not done it for him, to cleanse his mind of rumour and of the popular voice. Nothing will so keep him down and make him subject and a slave to others than respect for the guesswork and the bottomless controversies of these insidious and parroting voices of the air.

By all means let him make a drastic selection from that which is offered him for his passive consumption, to the end that he may be rightly informed and morally elevated, not cajoled or bullied by inconsequential authorities whose value lies in their much speaking, not in their vision.

That is one aspect of the facts as they are. It is not difficult to deduce from them what they signify. Our religion..., such as it is, and our culture, such as it is, have signally failed to cleanse the temple of contaminated air. *"But,"* cries an objector, *"we have a religion: we are a religious people: we have religious broadcasts."*

If these are facts they should be good for something. I fail to see that the nation's taste or the tone of society is raised by them. A consensus of opinion is in the opposite direction. Moreover, I see a marked difference between having a religion and being spiritual. I do not recall that Jesus ever referred to a man's religion. He never desisted stressing the life of the spirit and all that it should mean in the lives of men.

It is perhaps singular that to point the value of these remarks one may instance the example of a high-church dignitary who strongly corroborates them. It will not be amiss to use the sanctity of the present moment to look at our religion since some are so voluble about it. As to our culture, no one should make haste to boast about that.

Recently the transition of Dr W R Inge took place…, the Dean of St Paul's Cathedral from 1911 to 1934. He was a learned and a good man, a Platonist and a mystic; a prolific writer with a caustic pen that chiselled out the truth without fear or favour, sometimes much to the distress of his clerical colleagues. His many contributions to various journals on the signs and affairs of his day formed a body of the most trenchant writings in modern journalism. Whenever he wrote, and whatever he wrote about, he was acutely alive to the present moment and situation. And when the reading public woke sufficiently to grasp the subtle implications contained in his writings, it excused its own guilt and ignorance by nicknaming him *"the gloomy Dean,"* thereby soothing its conscience with that most hazardous of all sedatives: having a religion.

When the noble Dean passed, there was just enough comment to remind the public that he had lived. Had he ascended a high mountain he would have descended in glory and honour and been proclaimed an example to his fellow men. But he ascended a more difficult mountain, with Christ and the mystics in solitude, and the inspiration of his communion is revealed in the truth and beauty of his works. One could fill a book with quotations appropriate to our theme, but one will be quite sufficient:

> "There is no evidence that the historical Christ ever intended to found a new institutional religion. He neither attempted to make a schism in the Jewish Church nor to substitute a new system for it. He placed himself deliberately in the prophetic line, only claiming to sum up the series in Himself. The whole manner of His life and teaching was prophetic. He treated the institutional religion of His people with the independence and indifference of the prophet and mystic; and the hierarchy, which, like other hierarchies, had a sure instinct in discerning a dangerous enemy, was not slow to declare war to the knife against Him.
>
> "Institutional Christianity may be a legitimate and necessary historical development from the original Gospel, but it is something alien to the Gospel itself.... Lovers of peace have not much to hope for from organised religion."

If this is not dangerous doctrine in the mouth of a dignitary of the Church of England, I have yet to learn what is. But the Dean was no common churchman. He was a prophet and a mystic. Because he spoke the truth and refused the role of a hypocrite, obsequiously complying with the vulgar opinions of the times, they (it would be surprising to know what names were among them) nicknamed him *"the gloomy Dean,"* and forgot him. Yet he is far from forgotten. I recall what Hazlitt once said:

> "Conquerors, statesmen and kings live but by their names stamped on the page of history. We have all that Homer or Virgil did, as much as if we had lived at the same time with them. We can hold their works in our hands, or lay them on our pillows, or put them to our lips. Scarcely a trace of what the others did is left upon the earth, so as to be visible to common eyes. The one, the dead authors, are living men, still breathing and moving in their writings. The others, the conquerors of the world, are but the ashes in an urn."

Let us pass on. The moment has become the present hour, and we are very much alive in it. We, in our studies and work, are much in the same case. We are, or should be, thoroughly aware of the present moment, of its value to ourselves, and also of how insignificant and worthless it is to the minds of an overwhelming majority.

There was a time, some years ago, when in a moment of high optimism, I wrote to the effect that the day of mysticism had dawned, that the era of higher culture and endeavour had come. I would not write it today. We can see what tide is flowing now: the flood tide of science, mechanism, and competitive mastery.

"Give me matter and motion," said Descartes, *"and I will construct you the universe."* The spirit of Christ can wait. At present, let us look clearly at it: we are up to our necks in materialism. It is amazing what forms it takes and in what minds. But there it is: the rampant demon of modern times, creating a tottering universe of matter and motion.

And the Church? It is as helpless as I am to call a halt to it or change it. Indeed, the Archbishop of York, in his recent pastoral letter, admonished churchmen to read the Bible! If churchmen need that admonition, the inference is that another war might frighten the masses into reading it.

Have we, as Rosicrucians, a sane and responsible sense of the value of our own time in the midst of this mock show of the advance of civilisation? I know well that my colleagues in Britain have it. They know that any moment may prove to be a unique moment, when enlightenment from a higher source may fall upon a man, or a call come to a higher service for which he has unknowingly prepared himself.

It will never come to the thoughtless and superficial; nor to those who fritter the precious moments away in a weak surrender to the fears and rumours, the trivialities and vulgarities, and the veritable hotchpotch of stewed news and empty gossipry which characterise the radio technique. It would be less than just to lay the onus of censure upon those who provide this kind of fare. It is the demand that lays the curse upon all improper, or questionable, or illicit traffickings in whatever form. So in this instance.

Let the culture of a nation once reach that level of refined tone and taste where decency, truth, and sound instruction become a public demand, and the air would soon become wholesome and fit for a child to breathe. At present the child is living in the same purgatory as the rest, and he is coming to enjoy it. If that is not a straight road to decadence, perhaps someone can tell me where it lies?

These are hard truths, but we must get used to them. The times are hard and vibrant with the threatening tension of harder things to come. If others allow themselves to be rocked into unconsciousness in the cradle of democracy while they are fed with the soft pabulum calculated to keep them docile and amenable, and not to think too seriously, we will have none of it.

We have taken the measure of adolescence and of age and are able to judge what becomes both. But when adolescence continues into ripe age it is time to call a reckoning. Neither prophet nor mystic, and the Rosicrucian is often both, can set a judgement day. He knows it will come and is only solicitous to raise his voice or do what he can to help those who are awake to the issue.

He will then have the satisfaction of knowing that he has lived to some purpose and left firm footprints upon the path of time for those who have the incentive to follow them.

9. Facing the Truth

Reprinted from the April 1956 edition of the Rosicrucian Digest.

If on some occasions I have particularly stressed certain objectionable tendencies of the times in which we live, it would nevertheless be a mistake to regard this as a confession of pessimism.

Were I a pessimist I doubt whether I should have written at all. For the nature of pessimism is to blight and kill; it blunts the edge of the mind, shuts the door to inspiration, and stifles the voice of the spirit. To point to unpleasant facts and indicate tendencies around us which have power to hamper and discourage the aspirant, is not pessimism.

If we have given our allegiance to the articles of truth, that allegiance demands of us to see clearly the false values in life which ignore them, distort our vision, and dethrone those articles in their favour. Moreover, if we have elected to give ourselves to the service of others, I do not consider it wise to appear ignorant of so much in our way of life which might well breed pessimism in those who have to face many untoward circumstances which call for deep faith and courage to overcome them.

Because our philosophy is one of overcoming and progress, no matter what the difficulty, we need not therefore shut our eyes to the fact that among ourselves are many who find the best in themselves put to severe trial in these days when they are called upon, quite unconsciously it may be and through their individual point in evolution, to balance the account of their karma and clear a path for their feet.

But if we are determined not to be pessimists, let us beware that we do not become such radiant optimists through absorbing too much light from sun-gazing, that we distort the truth about ourselves and life, forget the relative value of reason, and flounder as badly as those who profess and call themselves pessimists.

Now, curiously enough, I find myself quite unable to condemn or refute much of the pessimism encountered today. I am not a sun-gazer, much as I appreciate warmth and light. I am inclined to take a level view to the far-off horizon, where I can see what men and women are doing and what is happening to them. And I have no doubt that there is a weight of pessimism brooding over the landscape which only a miracle could lift. It saps the energy and fogs the mind not only of ordinary thinking people, but also of the well-informed and intellectual: for most of them pin their hopes and most of their aspirations to things and circumstances on the mundane ground floor of existence.

They find themselves more and more marshalled and regimented *"for the good of the State."* They are so perplexed and worried with more and more rules and regulations *"for the good of the State,"* and are bewildered with so many decrees and measures *"for the good of the State,"* that it is small wonder then that they doubt whether there is any good in themselves or anything worth hoping for.

I think you will agree with me that not many can play the full-blooded optimist when their hopes and ambitions, aspirations and ideals, are sidetracked and damped in order that generations yet unborn may realise and profit from them. Men are not made of that kind of stuff. They do not feel they were born for retrogression. They have some urge, whatever it may be, for progress; and if that is frustrated and checkmated, you may be very sure that the decline of the West is not the dark vision of a pessimist, but is well under way.

For the heartening of those who believe in and work for the higher possibilities of mankind, it has been affirmed that an expansion goes on over the world in the direction of the mystical and divine that should be a cause for optimism. We do not dispute this, but should like to see evidence of it. The intellectuals appear to be quite ignorant of it, as their pathetic and ineffective controversies in the leading journals of the day plainly show.

They are at a loss what to think. They argue and wrestle and confute one another and demonstrate a commendable skill in the dialectic of the schools. Religion does not satisfy them: it does not stimulate them to individual discovery of self and its powers, but merely on a nebulous future. Philosophy, as they understand it, is a conflict of theories which gives them no firm footing: it exhorts them to be content with their lot, but has no applicable technique how to change it. And science leads them on to a promised land of new but fearsome material revelations: it has no voice for the soul of man. In fact, it is far too clever to trouble about the soul.

Well, if science, philosophy, and religion leave men either spiritually cold or dialectically hot and bothered, with the meaning of life and the possibilities of inner evolution by-passed by those who should be their teachers, what can be expected in the way of inspiration and cooperation from those who imbibe this spiritually negative pabulum and remain as speculative and unconvinced as those who distribute it?

Add to all this the radio talks and commentaries with their pretentious titles from the experts in science, philosophy, and religion, and ask yourselves whether you have even glimpsed a greater light, whether you have been shown a new and secret way to the soul of the universe, or whether you stand where you were, perplexed and questioning still, and needing the wisdom and guidance of the superman?

"*Man is born free,*" said Rousseau, or being interpreted, *"man is born for freedom; and everywhere he is in chains."* But Rousseau was a political theorist, and his classic statement refers to the chains of political bondage.

It is still true that man is born for freedom, and no less true that he is still in chains. But we do not deal here with the political aspect. We know a good deal about it, as much and more than Rousseau did; but that is being dealt with effectively elsewhere, and we shall hear plenty more of it. What perplexes the aspirant today is that he himself is in chains as well as his non-aspiring brother.

I know from long contact with the lives of students of mysticism that the portal of entrance to the larger life often appears more menacing than the broad highway they are trying to leave behind them. This must be so: and it is not surprising that the illusionary mist that dims the threshold should at times instil into the questioning heart of aspirants a pessimism about the things that are, instead of optimism about what can be.

This is what is happening to them. This is the tempter which would turn them back on to the highway they well know and where they have had ample companionship to fortify them in aims and purposes compatible with it.

But once the door is resolutely closed to that and the eyes are fixed on the path of ascent from purely mundane interests to mystical truth, a testing time must ensue. And the more abrupt and determined is this reversal of interest, the stronger is the demand upon the aspirant's will to hold fast to the new rhythm he has set up for himself.

The old ties of the world which have held a man fast for long will not at once fall away and leave him to his new quest for peace. Far from it. He cannot take a pledge to the higher life without having that pledge strongly challenged; and he will be challenged where he is weakest..., and where he is strongest. He alone knows from what level in his nature attacks are likely to come, and he must be prepared for them when and where he least expects.

I doubt whether a single aspirant has not experienced challenges in some form or other. I have observed this trial in the life of every sincere aspirant that I have known. And although I have felt compassion, I knew it was good for them. In some it has been so determined and menacing that they have questioned the validity of their highest ideal. There is no condemnation for that.

Human nature is human, whatever of divinity informs it; and no matter what the religionists say, the fiercest battle for adjustment between the two is featured in the lives of the greatest saints, sages, and mystics of recorded time. Even there, the keenest struggles of the divine in man are not fully seen and can be sympathetically felt only by the few.

How then can we complain if the two-edged sword of destiny touches the heart of life, wounds us where we feel it most, and no more spares the saint than the sinner? For, from a limited point of view, there is no discrimination. They both rise and fall together. And I believe that fact alone has caused as much anguish in the minds of thinking people as any other.

But there are those who feel that, because they have pledged themselves to ascend, the past is therefore miraculously liquidated, the crooked made straight, the imprints and obligations of the incarnations nullified and obliterated having no more power and voice within them, and that the ascent to truth is a prepared and angelic highway.

This idea is as ill-conceived, as unjust, and opposed to fact, as the idea that the watery absolution conferred by a priest's finger upon sinners all and sundry can wipe out the decrees of a presiding and righteous Judgement upon the ways of men. The aspirant who believes his past is blotted out by ignoring the possible consequences of it, is a poor thinker indeed. He knows well enough that if he plays the fool today he will pay for it tomorrow. He would be greatly surprised if it were not so. But he cannot conceive that past lives condition the present one, as the present will determine those to come. And that applies to nations as well as to individuals.

But I believe that comparatively few among Rosicrucian students fall into, or long remain in, this negative attitude. As a general rule one does not feel a call to study until there is a karmic urge to take a step forward in evolution. And it by no means follows that a new student must be a novice. He often has already a good deal of reading and study to his credit which prepare him to enter upon the way of practical experimentation which will consolidate his past knowledge and ensure rapid progress to a life of service. I have known many instances of this: and a very typical one has just reached me in a letter. I will quote from it because of its inspirational character:

> "I cannot resist mentioning the impact that your books, recently read and studied, have had upon me. They tore my soul to pieces. They have a tremendous effect upon me; they not only shake me to the foundations, take possession of my mind, but they have a quality of persuasion and appeal to soul and reason combined that do wonderful things for my personal and soul evolution."

I quote this quite impersonally, because there is a profound lesson in it which can be stimulating and helpful to those who are ready for it. It is not simply the appreciative character of this letter which I note. What arrests my attention is the fact that it comes spontaneously and urgently from the heart. It is an unusual declaration of the inner life. What precisely does it mean?

It means that the writer had suddenly responded to a vibrational level of stated truth of the path which was already hers and awaiting awakening and recognition. In a very real sense it was an initiation for which life and circumstances and study had unconsciously prepared her; and at a propitious karmic moment, and as it were by a single dynamic impulse, a door of inner revelation swung wide and she came face to face with her real self.

That is one of the rich rewards of past effort, of wrestling with life from all angles, of accepted pain and suffering hidden, it may be, in the far past but destined to bear its appointed fruit in this cycle. It shows that we cannot antedate the future. No matter how hard the way, how unpromising, how prone we are at times to yield to the leaden atmosphere of the world around us, this illusionary veil which confronts us must not be taken for reality.

There are forces which would hold us back and keep us down. It is their nature to do so. They have their part in evolution. Every aspirant will be tested and tried by them. We must look beyond this experience and call upon the will to exercise its supremacy, in spite of any opposition, whether of loneliness, of momentary defeat projecting itself from the endless timelessness, whether of personalities or circumstances thwarting the path we have chosen to tread, whether thrown down before us as a challenge to us by friend or foe.

There is a dark and pregnant line in Tacitus which runs thus: *"And those who had not an enemy were destroyed by their friends."* The truth of that is worth bearing in mind, for not a few aspirants have been held back and discouraged by those near to them. What is good enough for them should be so for him; that is the attitude at the bottom of the opposition, criticism and repudiation of old ties.

I have known many such cases, and some of them have been pathetic and cruel. He who holds back his brother from the greater light of the path is the enemy of man: and there is a karmic retribution for that. He who loses a friend in the name of the light will find a greater friend in the hand of his Master. It is only a question of time; and it is time that so often defeats us. Be equal to the trial. Nothing can be lost of value which shall not be recovered later in the greater potency of achievement.

We may have knowledge and experience, but something else is needed – the fire of advancement. There are aspirants who are sometimes brought to a complete standstill in study and purpose: the one thing lacking is the fire of the spirit. Had they called upon that spirit, demanded it in the name of all good, believed in its presence and omnipotency, it would have descended upon them and carried them over the precipice of hopelessness.

There are among us those who have demonstrated this for themselves. They know the aspects of life I refer to and have long since reckoned with them. They have seen through the illusions of life and will never again be dominated by them. The raucous tones of the world do not disturb them, for they have the quiet heart and the seeing mind..., two impregnable ramparts against the damaging and crucifying tendencies of our way of life. They will never surrender what they have fought for and won..., *to help you!*

Do you realise that but for these cultivated types whom karma has mercifully and forcefully and painfully brought to the fore of evolution, there would be not only pessimism but also despair preying upon the vitals of humanity? Are you aware of the secret and impressive influence of those who form the vanguard of evolution? They have not much to show for it: only a life lived determinedly.

But the fire of the heart can make a lightning track across the universe, and those who are not wiser are nevertheless better for it; those who can sense it, awaken and live to some purpose. And today it is purpose, a high purpose and far above the average, that aspirants need to steel them to a new and forward advance. I do not refer to sudden and ill-timed enthusiasms. These are of short duration and soon exact the penalties of the opposites and fade out.

Purpose here means a wisely conceived plan of procedure, a visioned ideal, whether to be fully achieved or not in this cycle, and the accepting with a divine indifference whatever karma decrees of good or ill, knowing well that whatever that purpose precipitates for its swifter achievement is peculiarly ours and has the sanction of law within it.

The fire of the spirit gives indomitable purpose, but it is not for children on the path. It is for tempered souls who will not be deflected from their aim. This temper characterises the few, and always will characterise them.

Nothing in this life is greater or more worthy than the resolving for ourselves to take the measure of these great ones and to belong to them.

10. A Prophet of the Times

Reprinted from the July 1957 edition of the Rosicrucian Digest.

An interesting fact about distinguished men is that often they have been led to their lifework by a so-called chance event. We know that the event is not a chance but destiny, an indication of the direction of karmic influence and of its fulfilment.

Our Rosicrucian studies enable us to realise that the events of our life are prepared during the far backward reaches of time by none other than ourselves; that we have been both the architect and the builder of the selves we are; that we are confronted here and now with a kind of balance sheet of credits and debits as we have drawn it up on all the levels of life experience. It now is for us to wisely adjust so that we ultimately will harmonise completely with the Cosmic intention and purpose.

In saying, as we do, that we are suffering this or that condition under the influence of world karma, we should not overlook the fact that world karma is the collective karma of individuals and that we ourselves may have some responsibility for it. Most of us, looking at the world picture today, have a feeling of incompetency, if not of helplessness, in the face of the rapidly moving events in it.

In early history, life too appeared to be little more than a series of wars, a rise and decline of races, cultures which came to fruition and over which we could have rejoiced had they not vanished as if they had never been.

Yet these histories covering such important periods are in themselves but episodes of their time. In the eyes of the witnesses and writers of them the events loomed so largely, the tragedy and uniqueness fastened their attention so entirely, that all the good and ill of the world seemed to be concentrated into a few years. All that they had seen built up towards an edifice of future and everlasting greatness, the swift hand of not understandable fate tore down and scattered to the four winds. Only the literary records remain as reminders of their one time greatness.

We use these teachers of wisdom to enlighten and interpret our own lives, but forget that much of what they wrote was in just such a time as our own, when the foundations of states and peoples were moving to their end. Indeed, that very fact drew from them under stress and inspiration the word of truth we cherish.

We have lost the fine art of entering into the mind and soul of these powers and peoples that once were. The dignity of those empires of men, their grand effort of life which inspired and fashioned the very word of truth we know, the chronicle of the great ones who saw and lived this truth, we forget.

The same thing is happening today, but we are too localised in vision to see it in proper perspective: races whose foundations are weakening, their grip on survival slackening; others, smitten and bled of their dignity and power by superior forces. We know of all the dire effects arising from such situations, and yet with a characteristic feeling of self-security we believe it could never happen to us.

We can claim no exemption on any ground whatever, neither of pre-eminent goodness, nor of righteousness or superior knowledge, of scientific adroitness or magical manipulation, or of any natural position on the face of the earth. Fate, which we understand as karma, is silent and inexorable. It chooses its time to weigh nations, principalities, and powers in the balance with no less certitude than in the lives of individuals.

If that fact had dominated the minds of past historians, when all they loved and had laboured for was swept away under their hand, they would have had the same facts to relate but they would perforce have lifted their eyes from the then present scene, and in looking backward and forward their grief and bitterness would have been mollified by the universal pageant of their vision.

But the changes they witnessed were so devastating that the range and depth of their genius was focused and magnified within the brief intervals of personal experience. How much indeed do the youth of today in school and college realise of the tragedy and pathos palpitating behind the stern narratives of the passing away of peoples and civilisations, in many respects greater than our own, and who have taught us some of the greatest truths of life?

These reflections have arisen from my rereading that remarkable historical and prophetic survey by Oswald Spengler, *Decline of the West* [1918].

I have referred to the strange way in which many distinguished men have been led to their lifework by a chance event, a happening very often giving no indication of that lifework. It was the event of the Agadir which set Spengler upon his unique task. In 1911 a European international crisis was brought about when the German government sent a gunboat to Agadir in southwest Morocco, to ensure German economic interests in

Morocco.

There were prolonged negotiations between the two countries, and Germany ultimately agreed to forego her claims in exchange for certain portions of French Congo ceded to her.

We may wonder why so relatively unimportant a matter should have been the keynote to Spengler's inspiration. It may well have been neither the right nor the wrong of it, but simply that so much was made of the happening by the parties concerned in contrast with the vast pageant of historical truth which was coming to birth in the historian's mind. It may be that he was so disagreeably impressed by this controversy that he experienced one of those inexplicable psychic impulses to unfold a panorama of historical truth about nations and peoples which would give the West and the East something really important to think about. And he succeeded.

Spengler's first volume appeared in Germany in 1918; the second, in 1922. The work made a profound impression upon the keen and deep-thinking German mind, as it did in America when four years later the first volume translated was made available to the English-speaking world by American publishers.

Little notice however was accorded the book in Britain: while in Germany commentators upon it abounded. They were swift to recognise genius. But original minds like Nietzsche and Spengler receive scant praise in Britain. An effort was made to treat the book with indifference. Any suggestion, for instance, that civilisation in the West could possibly decline was ridiculed and, in Britain, simply could not happen. But much has happened since 1926, and the decline has been augmented.

Thinkers of note in Germany and America acclaimed Spengler and his work. This historical scientist who saw world history as a whole, its meaning and direction, gave to its past epochs their necessary and meaningful existence in the world picture, and saw no less clearly the decline of those of the present and the future. The wealth of learning and observation in this work, which includes the whole world drama of space and time, is unique in historical literature.

For Spengler approaches his subject and deals with it from the vantage point of an ascension of consciousness, from a plateau of vision which links past, present, and future into a comprehensive whole, thereby teaching us to be inclusive and specific, not including all and overlooking much in general terms.

Spengler shows mastery of historical perspective. Phases of history which historians have dismissed as worthy but of briefest mention, or have ignored altogether, he brought to life with a singular emphasis as of personal knowledge: peoples and cultures of which we should have known nothing had not the light of his genius restored them to us.

Spengler introduces in quick succession some startling propositions which no one who is open-minded and has any respect for self re-education can fail to appreciate. But it must be prefaced that a certain preparedness of mind is required in the reader. A closed and self-sufficient mentality will doubtless be repelled by this work. Even such a mind, if it is of any commendable calibre, will not fail to perceive its originality, but it will prove so destructive of existing and cherished landmarks as to be impatiently dismissed. It challenges established opinion, and that is a cardinal sin no matter who the genius may be.

An open-minded reader will gain an unexpected and valuable occult service. The book can clarify his judgement. With increasing clearness of vision and broad-minded judgement a host of individual problems will fall into their place and cease, or at least modify their tyranny.

Here are a some typical instances of the kind of disturbing tremors Spengler initiates throughout his work:

> "The ground of West Europe is treated as a steady pole, a unique patch chosen on the surface of the sphere for no better reason, it seems, than because we live on it..., and great histories of millennial duration and mighty faraway Cultures are made to revolve around this pole in all modesty. It is a quaintly conceived system of sun and planets! We select a single bit of ground as the natural centre of the historical system, and make it the central sun. From it all the events of history receive their real light, from it their importance is judged in *perspective*. But it is in our own West-European conceit alone that this phantom 'world history,' which a breath of scepticism would dissipate, is acted out.

> "It is self-evident that for the Cultures of the West the existence of Athens, Florence or Paris is more important than that of Lo-Yang or Pataliputra. But is it permissible to found a scheme of world-history on estimates of such a sort? If so, then the Chinese historian is quite entitled to frame a world-history in which the Crusades, the Renaissance, Caesar, and Frederick the Great are passed over in silence as insignificant. How, from the morphological point of view, should our 18th Century be more important than any other of the sixty centuries that preceded it?

> "Is it not ridiculous to oppose a 'modern' history of a few centuries, and that history to all intent, localised in West Europe, to an 'ancient' history which covers as many millennia..., incidentally dumping into that 'ancient history' the whole mass of the pre-hellenic cultures, unprobed and unordered, as mere appendix matter? This is no exaggeration. Do we not, for the sake of keeping the hoary scheme, dispose of Egypt, and Babylon..., each as an individual and self-contained history quite equal in the balance to our so-called 'world-history' from Charlemagne to the World-War and well beyond it..., as a *prelude* to classical history? Do we not relegate the vast complexes of Indian and Chinese culture to foot-notes, with a gesture of embarrassment? As for the American cultures, do we not, on the ground that they do not 'fit in' (with what?), entirely ignore them?

> "It is this that is lacking to the Western thinker, the very thinker in whom we might have expected to find it..., insight into the *historically relative* character of his data, which are

expressions of *one specific existence and one only*; knowledge of the necessary limits of their validity; the conviction that his 'unshakable' truths and 'eternal' views are simply true for him and eternal for his world-view; the duty of looking beyond them to find out what the men of other Cultures have with equal certainty evolved out of themselves. That and nothing else will impart completeness to the philosophy of the future, and only through an understanding of the living world shall we understand the symbolism of history."

Those statements are a modest yet revolutionary prelude to nearly a thousand pages of keen observation and profound truth. To review such a work adequately would require a volume in itself, and a competent reviewer. But we can touch upon some of its highlights. For I hold that the very fact that Spengler's work has apparently been neglected tells greatly in his favour.

The work of men of extraordinary insight and outspokenness seldom becomes fully recognised and rightly appraised until centuries after their death. They are charged with a message which is out of tune with the pulse of the day. It is dismissed with a gesture of superiority which makes an understanding mind almost despair of humanity. Spengler had his share of misunderstanding and belittlement from prejudiced and jealous contemporaries. But he finished his work and departed in 1936 at the age of 56.

Spengler contends that every culture has *its own* civilisation, and that such is the inevitable *destiny* of the culture. He contends that civilisations are the most external and artificial states of which a species of developed humanity is capable. But, contrary to our own idea that a civilisation can and should continue to unknown and unbelievable attainments, he takes the reverse view:

"...that civilisations are a conclusion, the thing-become succeeding the thing-becoming, death following life, rigidity following expansion, intellectual age and the stone-built, petrifying world-city following mother-earth and the spiritual childhood of Doric and Gothic. They are an end, irrevocable, yet by inward necessity reached again and again."

When we come to Spengler we have to be prepared for some very startling assertions. He takes a swift and decisive leap beyond the limited horizon of the historians we know. One of the most valuable services he can render us is to shake us free from the static views we hold of nationalism, whether it be our own or that of any other nation.

In Britain we have a traditional national isolationism which, however much it has been rudely disturbed during this century, is as strong as ever it was. Deeply rooted in us and nurtured through several centuries, our views of history and civilisation are precisely those which Spengler challenges. He wrote:

"I hope to show that without exception all great creations and forms in religion, art, politics, social life, economy and science appear, fulfil themselves, and die down *contemporaneously* in all the Cultures; that the inner structure of one corresponds strictly with that of all the others; that there is not a single phenomenon of deep physiognomic importance in the record of one for which we could not find a counterpart in the record of every other; and that this counterpart is to be found under a characteristic form and in a perfectly definite chronological position.

"At the same time, if we are to grasp such homologies of facts, we shall need to have a far deeper insight and a far more critical attitude towards the visible foreground of things than historians have hitherto been wont to display; who amongst them, for instance, would have allowed himself to dream that the counterpart of Protestantism was to be found in the Dionysiac movement, and that English Puritanism was for the West what Islam was for the Arabian world?"

This is as provocative as it is enlightening. Its acceptance requires an open mind; yet, it is only preliminary. But then, he sets out to show that this is exactly so. Are we likely to listen to him, to put the history books aside for a moment and examine the evidence? Or shall we still play the Kant and regard the man of vision as a half-crazed Beethoven? In Spengler's words:

"A man like Kant must always feel himself as superior to a Beethoven as the adult is to the child, but this will not prevent a Beethoven from regarding the 'Critique of Pure Reason' as a pitiable sort of philosophy."

Well, dusty Kant lies in state on the library shelves: the glorious harmonies of Beethoven continue to inspire millions.

Spengler's work is one of the most difficult to quote with any feeling of assurance that one is doing justice to the author, and at the same time is being sufficiently informative to the reader. The author gives the feeling of supreme mastery of his subject, a feeling of extensive and inclusive vision.

A celebrated writer once said that he constantly wondered whence Poe got his literary style. It was entirely his own. The same may be said of Spengler. In the section on "*Music and Plastic*" (chapters 6 and 7…, "The arts of form" and "Act and portrait"), music, painting and architecture are given such unusual associations and applications, as to remind us of Da Vinci, the master of all form.

His style is adapted perfectly to the subject. Indeed, he is considered to have mastered some fifteen sciences and assimilated the whole historical process. He seems to be living among the masters of these arts as a contemporary, with a complete knowledge of their works…, living among them and yet above them, looking down from heightened vision and revealing values they themselves never saw.

Dare I quote a passage of despair from "*Act and portrait*" in connection with which certain aspects of the decline impressed Spengler so profoundly? If it is true we should not be afraid of it. Here it is:

> "The modern artist is a workman, not a creator. He sets unbroken spectrum-colours side by side. The subtle script, the dance of brush-strokes, give way to crude commonplaces, pilings and mixings and daubings of points, squares, broad inorganic masses. The whitewasher's brush and the trowel appear in the painter's equipment; the oil-priming of the canvas is brought into the scheme of execution and in places left bare. It is risky art, meticulous, cold, diseased..., an art for over-developed nerves, but scientific to the last degree, energetic in everything that relates to the conquest of technical obstacles, acutely assertive of programme.
>
> "And the bitter conclusion is that it is all irretrievably over with the arts of form of the West. The crisis of the 19th century was the death-struggle. Like the Apollinian, the Egyptian, and every other, the Faustian art dies of senility, having actualised its inward possibilities and fulfilled its mission within the course of its Culture."

Two chapters in the section on "*Soul-image and Life-feeling*" deal exhaustively with "the form of the soul" and "Buddhism, Stoicism, and Socialism" (chapters 8 and 9). They carry the full weight of Spengler's most fervent thought and cannot be quoted piecemeal with any hope of conveying their intrinsic value. This kind of writing is that of one to whom the full afflatus of inspiration has been given. Such writings are rather for reverent reflection than for quotation and discussion.

I regret that I cannot do Spengler greater justice in this article, having been able to refer only to his first volume. The second invites likewise the deepest study and reflection.

It has been said that he is a dangerous writer to place in the hands of the young. But Spengler did not write his massive work for the young. He wrote it for men and women who are thinking seriously about the trend of our times. For if any problem today should be exercising such minds, we may expect it to be that of our civilisation.

In Spengler's view, civilisations reach a certain maturity and then steadily decline. Now unbiased observers in Britain record that during the past half-century there have been unmistakable symptoms of a decline in our civilisation. We undoubtedly face today a lowered standard of life. It is observable in the manner of approach to and in the handling of the affairs of everyday life, in carelessness and dissipated attention, and in a lamentable indifference to the true values of life. Apathy has become a feature of national life.

In the past, Britain could boast of a selfless devotion to duty, dignity, and courtesy in personal contacts, and a fine quality of craftsmanship in every sphere of execution. It would ill become us to boast of these today. There has never been a period in our national life when government measures and ministers of state, officials in high office and notable personalities, have been so fiercely criticised and subjected to contumely and disrespect with repellent unrestraint. This is regarded as the virtue of freedom of speech and of individual smartness. It has not a decent mental attribute to recommend it.

I have before me a recent press report of the presidential address of a leading lawyer to the Law Society. He said:

> "The common man looked down on the intellectual, or at least regarded him as deserving no particular respect. In these days everyone had a smattering of education. The effect was to make a man believe he was the equal of everyone else in ability and knowledge. A deeper reason was part of the psychological malaise of our days. The majority had power, and standards of value were becoming those of the majority rather than the minority. In consequence there is abroad in society something amounting to envy mixed with hatred of the man of intellect. The tide is running against him."

That is an alarming statement from a recognised authority. It tells profoundly in favour of Spengler's theory. Let us have the patience to observe impartially the significance of it. Many will be disposed to say at once..., this is the day of the common man, a sign that he is coming into his own. They will regard it with complacency, even with satisfaction. They will accept without question, without criticism, the results of this *"coming of age."* I do not regard too favourably the term, the *"common man,"* but it must stand in this connection because it points to a necessary distinction.

The common man is quoted as being in the majority, and we can very well see what such an ill-balance can portend. A medley of facts and ill-assorted fragments of mundane knowledge have so infected the common mind through the press, radio and television, that it assumes a ludicrous and bloated self-importance and looks down upon the professional man and the men of real distinction who have devoted a lifetime of study and application to specialised work and achievement.

Observe the particular terms of the quotation. There we see a civilisation beyond its peak and in rapid decline. If that is a hard statement, I will reinforce it with one from an Eastern seer: *"When the trend of human thought is not toward spirituality, evolution is not accelerated."*

Where is the trend of *spiritual* thought in Britain today? There is a mixed product of religious beliefs which counterfeits the appearance of it. Even the common man has that and we know what he makes of it. There is not a single irresistible trend of mystical and spiritual thought which would arrest public attention in Britain today. One would have to enter a monastery to meet even with a true technique of the science of prayer and its operative effects.

About 400 years ago the Flemish painter Bruegel created that striking picture *The Tower of Babel*. He painted two versions of it within a few years of each other. It is a sardonic masterpiece, full of passion and meaning..., a painter's denunciation hurled across the centuries at the coming pride and presumption of man.

In the first version a vast round tower is seen in process of construction. It rises majestically, tier upon tier, to the clouds of heaven. The busy workmen are seen transporting by machine and ladder massive stones prepared in the quarries below. They work feverishly, appearing and disappearing through the huge doorways and windows. The harbour quay alongside the tower is crowded with shipping bringing material for the great venture. One feels an intense interest and unabated activity throbbing over the whole scene.

At the base of the tower appears Nimrod and his retinue. He surveys with conscious pride and satisfaction the gigantic undertaking. This is the supreme invention of man which will stagger the nations.

In the second version the tower is seen, still uncompleted, but deserted to the last man. An ominous silence broods over landscape and tower. The innumerable windows and entrances are gaping and vacant, as if a mighty wind had swept through the whole and destroyed every living thing in it. From the upper portion of the tower clouds of smoke billow forth, portending its doom.

One cannot contemplate a work of genius like this without thinking of our own times. Painted 400 years ago, it is a moving frontispiece illustration for Spengler's work written but yesterday. It is a warning that man shall not do what he likes with the creation that has been given to him for his highest use and development. That is the lesson of this picture.

What then is the value of Spengler's *Decline of the West*, and what lesson does it teach? The value of the book is that it has made many thinking men and women deeply aware of the trend of the times. And if the will and purpose of the present generation do not harness themselves to right thinking and upward living, Spengler's prophecy of a collapse of civilisation in the year 2200 may prove to be not very wide of the mark.

His book can teach us to look the facts straight in the face, whether we like them or not, and to realise that we are not a privileged and immortal race, but that if we do not use to highest purposes the great stores of knowledge, which have been vouchsafed to us, we shall decline, fade out, and soon be forgotten as other races before us have been forgotten.

Section 11:

The London Rosicrucian (1952 - 1961)

The London Rosicrucian.

Section 11 - The London Rosicrucian (1952 - 1961)

Introduction

The *Francis Bacon Chapter* of the Rosicrucian Order in London, has been the largest affiliated body of the Order in England since its inception in 1947. In 1974 the Chapter was elevated to Lodge status and it is now known as the *Francis Bacon Lodge*. Between 1950 and 1961 the Chapter produced a magazine called *The London Rosicrucian* to which Raymund Andrea contributed some original writings.

1. Recorded Message to the first Rosicrucian Rally in Great Britain - 3 August 1952

Reprinted from the August 1952 edition of The London Rosicrucian *(Volume 2 No. 6).*

This is Raymund Andrea speaking to all Rosicrucian members attending the rally of the Francis Bacon Chapter.

As you will know, Rallies organised by Lodges and Chapters in foreign jurisdictions have been in vogue for some time. The Rosicrucian Rally you are attending today is the first to be held in our jurisdiction. As in the case of the tour recently made to various cities for extending our work, the *Francis Bacon Chapter* must be given the credit for organising the present occasion. Both these events, the tour and the Rally, spring from one motive and one aim. The motive has been to unite members in the various localities.

For many years our members have been receiving Rosicrucian teachings: they have been thinking into it and endeavouring to make their lives conform to that teaching. Now, an inspiring teaching like the Rosicrucian cannot be meditated upon for years without leaving its impress, its sign, its lasting mark upon the individual organism and upon the trend of individual life. Whether we speak of it or not to others, those with whom we associate will undoubtedly come to feel the subtle influence of the teaching in our lives and our attitude and bearing towards other men and women.

It cannot be hidden. Others may not know the source of it, nor be able to explain the why or wherefore of it. But it will be known as an influence for good, making for right living. That is the motive for these events; that they shall demonstrate to a certainty among our members the potent influence which the Rosicrucian teaching carries within itself when expressed in individual lives. Remembering the materialistic times in which we live, every member may well feel a personal responsibility for giving the fullest possible expression to the Rosicrucian Ideal.

The aim has been to encourage members to take action. We expect that members who have been in the Order for years should be good for something. If they are only piling up knowledge of the Path for their own personal satisfaction, as they might the facts of

397

history or science, then that is not action on the Path. Action means that the members multiply their force and influence in other lives.

How they shall do this is not for me or anyone else to direct. You will know as well as I do, that an aspirant of the true type has an auric tension and capacity which acts silently and spontaneously, and that he has some good to impart would be felt by those who are to any degree sensitive to personal atmospheres. When a response takes place then the door of opportunity opens and one can safely ignore politics and economics and speak of higher things. On countless occasions this has happened in the experience of our members. When others have crossed their path they have recognised the footsteps, the voice, the very glance of a troubled and seeking soul. They have taken action, and a swift response has been the answer to an inspired word.

Therefore our members are asked to take action. What is the point of accumulating stores of knowledge and wisdom of the higher life only to allow it to become a dead weight in the mind? It is the property of truth to move us to action. Indeed, it has been said, and I think with some truth, that there is a measure of danger in this self-accumulation of higher truth without adequate expression of it. There should be circulation. That is nature's safeguard on all planes of life.

Granted there should be adequate knowledge and development before these, and our personal experience can be of value to others; but as the fire of the aura and the psychic centres vibrate to a higher rhythm, the Cosmic demand, which has been petitioned for and has been granted to us, should be released in active service. This is the one condition which guarantees our further advancement.

Emerson said *"They who do the thing have the power and they who do not the thing have not the power."* That applies most definitely to development on the Path. The issue is therefore once again clearly before our members and this is a suitable occasion on which to present it. We do not advocate any strained or proselyting methods to urge others to accept our teaching. We want members to be keen, to recognise those who are seeking it.

I do not elaborate this point now because I have dealt more fully with the subject in a special article in the Digest which you may shortly have an opportunity of reading.[1] But I will add this here because some members wonder how they can impress others and attract them to our work. I deprecate anything in the nature of a house-to-house canvass for new members and I know you deprecate it as much as I do, but in business or profession, in fraternal or social contacts, it is there that what we are should exercise its influence and attractive power.

You observe that I adopt a different note on this point because I am referring now to action on the Path and the fact that our studies should speak through us in the language of magnetic attractive influence. Those around us are usually keen enough through long experience to judge of general character. That character is the result of our daily thought, emotions and actions; therefore, if our study and meditation on the Path has been our

---

1. See "Idealism in Practice" in the July 1952 edition of the *Rosicrucian Digest*. Also see Section 10, Chapter 7.

serious occupation for years they should have written their influence deeply into our whole personality and others should not be able to ignore it, whatever interpretation they may place upon it. We can watch for that interpretation on the part of others and correct it if need be, not reject it but invite it and place the key in their hands and let them use it if they will.

I conclude by hoping that this Rally will give members a new incentive to rededicate their lives and service to a remembrance that the Cosmic powers will give their unstinted aid to all their efforts.

2. From the Grand Master's Sanctum

Reprinted from the October 1952 edition of The London Rosicrucian *(Volume 3 No. 1).*

Regarding your enquiry about the brain consciousness, I think you miss the main idea. What are you achieving in your present incarnation with your brain consciousness? You are being urged by your Inner Self to use it in every possible way to enlarge your experience and give that Self a better instrument to work with.

There is reciprocal action here. Versatile brain action gives a multitude of impressions of your personal contact with the objective world which are converted into interior wisdom of the Self life. And the increased activity of that Self compels the brain consciousness to greater world activity in superior incarnations.

It would require a degree of profound insight to put one's finger on the pulse, so to speak, of your individual Karma as it is working out in your life. He who could do so would probably refrain from doing so in accordance with a law which nothing would induce him to infringe – because we must live our own lives and find the path we cannot see by turning upon ourselves.

One view of your present problem is this: you desire higher unfoldment, but from the point of view of world experience there may be certain obstacles to be passed..., mental, temperamental, or physical..., before that experience is so far completed and you pass into your niche. No place can prevent the soul unfolding, and wherever you are your inner aspiration and study can proceed, until the law of attraction brings you into a position which you have fitted yourself to fill.

In the matter of worldly adjustment we are left much to ourselves to find ourselves and our strong points, and use those to live. Our inner mystical life is in a sense a thing entirely apart and concerns a man when he wants to be of real service to his fellowmen, shows this in his vehicles of expression by some special aptitudes, and then gradually trains himself for acceptance at the hands of a Master to carry out some phase of his work.

Nothing, whether of personal contact or congenial circumstances, will take the place in mysticism of study and meditation on its literature. From that study only will come a more comprehensive knowledge of one's self and purpose in life. Even if we are so fortunate as to contact advanced souls in this realm, we should be turned back upon our own study and effort. For it is pre-eminently a field of thought and endeavour in which one has to make his own discoveries.

I do not minimise the value of contact with those whose influence may assist us; but it is too painfully true that everywhere students rush into this or that group, after this or that personality, expecting immediately from others what the law will compel them to find for themselves..., and for this obvious reason: mystical truth cannot be imparted.

You think that adverse circumstances are descending upon you because you are seeking to know yourself and use your forces scientifically. Such a change of circumstances may result through the intense application to a new order of knowledge of yourself and your forces. Yet nothing but good can ultimately transpire from such devotion to the highest culture.

If you travel up a mountain and survey the well-known landscape from that altitude for the first time, your former picture will undoubtedly undergo many modifications. You may see paths you never saw before, observe relationships you never knew to exist; you may be considerably perplexed; but it would be folly to renounce your new knowledge, to turn back, and remain on the paths you knew so well.

The position of the aspirant entering upon the mystical path is analogous to this. Your study and meditation will disturb the equilibrium of your inner life and call for continually fresh adjustments. This does not mean that there would be inevitably sudden and violent changes in your objective sphere; but you would certainly begin to view circumstances and judge them from a new mental ground. And inasmuch as greater knowledge is better and more profitable than less, you cannot be wrong in accepting and using it.

There is another possible result, but I think it would only apply in a case where the aspirant is inwardly well developed generally, is mature in soul, has made good progress on the path in a past life and now resumes his studies where he left off, with a strong inborn bent for attainment, great desire for higher culture and resolution to achieve it.

Such students scarcely ever trouble to count the cost of attainment. They know the cross of circumstances will come upon them; they may be staggering under it already. It matters not: they reached a point in the far past where now in this life they must go on. The voice of that kind of soul sounds out strongly on the inner planes, and in response its past Karma is brought to it swiftly and collectively that it may be worked off as quickly as possible.

Your problem is to ascertain to which category you belong, and I know only one way to do this: to study your constitution in the light of mystical wisdom and through meditation allow your intuition to unfold and instruct you in the light of the increasing knowledge which will come to you.

Adverse circumstances may prove the very best teacher that could be sent you. They may plainly indicate a profitable way of life procedure and inspire you to an inner activity which will disclose a path of usefulness and service in the world.

3. Our Need to Cultivate the Art of Reflection

Originally published as a private letter to members of the Rosicrucian Order in the United Kingdom on 18 December 1940.[2] Reprinted in the December 1952 edition of The London Rosicrucian *and in the June 1996 issue of the* Rosicrucian Beacon.

From time to time a member asks with eager sincerity what he or she can do to help those near or far, who are in dire need of strength, inspiration and comfort. It is a question which we all ask ourselves as the tides of appeal and suffering unceasingly flow in on us. I want to quote the words of a teacher to a pupil which seem to me apposite and illuminating:

> "It is not that you must rush madly out to do. To do: do what you find to do. Desire to do it and even when you have not succeeded in carrying out anything but small duties, some words of warning: your strong desire will strike like a Vulcan upon other ears in the world and suddenly you will find that done that you had longed to be the doer of. Then, rejoice that another has been so fortunate as to make such a meritorious Karma. Thus, like rivers running into unswelling, passive ocean, will your desires enter your heart and help us more specifically to put that admonition into practice."

I am reminded of the words of a disciple of Confucius:

"Every day I examine myself on these three points:

1. In acting on behalf of others, have I always been loyal to their interest?
2. In intercourse with my friends, have I always been true to my word?
3. Have I failed to keep in memory all the precepts that have been handed down to me?"

There is nothing occult or magical in these words of those who have trodden the Way. Indeed, the Way is always like that, simple, direct and applicable to the circumstances of everyday life. The Truth as expressed by the Master of Masters is precisely the same; and all who have spoken before or after him of the truth of the Way, no matter what their height of advancement or their depth of insight, no matter what their race, religion or philosophy, point in the end to acceptance by the pupil of the Karma of his life, of his duty to others in his own place and circumstances, and of doing that duty to the best of

---

2. See Section 7, Chapter 3.

his ability.

Sometimes a member is overzealous for knowledge and power. If he were only master of this or that corpus of literature, if he had this or that power, what might he not do: but neither learning nor power will advance him on the Way. On the contrary, I have known cases where they have proved a snare and deterrent. As to power, few are big enough to use it wisely. How often it leads to pride, self-aggrandisement and ultimately, to disillusionment.

I never think of Christ as a learned man. He was a supremely wise man and His word could touch the compass of the inner life. He was also a Man of Power; but He never used it except to a good end. The careful application of our minds and hands to the task nearest us, with the humble conviction in ourselves that we are doing good, should be more to us and will be infinitely more to others, than all the learning of the scholastic, or the power to do spectacular things.

Knowledge of every kind abounds on every hand. In fact, people have too much knowledge unassimilated, unrelated to and disassociated from the deeper things of the heart and it is a burden and temptation to them. More than ever we need to cultivate the art of reflection, yes, even with the noise of battle in our ears. There is the test for us; and those who have stood this test will one day realise its tremendous value to them. We must continue to stand for the Soul and cherish its values above all that the personality can offer us.

Many of our members have found this secret for themselves and their lives show the dignity and grace, the calm and resolution of it. Let us all endeavour for this, taking the quotations I have given above as a guide and put the knowledge and strength we have derived from our studies into our daily contact with others, no matter how small the deed or apparently trivial the circumstances, no matter how unknown or unacknowledged, for the seeds of wisdom and real power are there and later will be recognised as the foundation stones of the Master character.

4. The Magical Power of Thought

Reprinted from the August and September 1957 edition of The London Rosicrucian.

We have read much in our own teachings and in books of recent years of the power of thought, yet I wonder whether we fully realise its potency for good in our own lives and the lives of others. Note this quotation from a script of occult teaching:

> "Sincere striving for self-perfection is not selfish but has universal significance. The thought of improvement will concern not only oneself. Such a thought carries within itself a flame needed for many kindlings of hearts. As fire will unfailingly ignite when brought into a

place filled with inflammatory substance, so fiery thought pierces the space and infallibly attracts seeking hearts to itself."

Then observe how, in four terse sentences, the power and value of thought arrests the attention: its universal significance, its influence upon others, a living flame needed for awakening the hearts of others, its infallible attractive power upon other responsive hearts.

I am reminded of some who have asked how they can be of service to others when they live in circumscribed conditions, engaged in mundane and homely tasks, study in isolation, and often have difficulty in contacting anyone of similar interests.

The answer is in the quotation above. The body may live to itself, but the mind cannot. The thought of an aspirant, with the fire of the heart's desire for good propelling it, has a magical power of its own which cannot be assessed in words. The winged thought of a Master can impress the waiting and expectant mind of the aspirant without a word spoken or even a hint of his contact. It happens continually. It inspires our minds and directs our hands in solitude and silence, and we should not fail to express our gratitude for it.

If it is of encouragement to the reader, I can testify to the above. For years I thought deeply about the truth of the mystic way, very much alone although active in the affairs of life, but with no contact with others who were likely to appreciate that thought..., rather the reverse.

But from the day I was led to contact the Order I passed at a single step, as it were, into a realisation that *"fiery thought pierces the space and infallibly attracts seeking hearts to itself."* The way had unknowingly been prepared during a period of solitary but insistent affirmation – and petition.

I emphasise the fact of petition. A sincere and directed petition of the heart has great occult value. And when it is made to the Masters with single intent, when an offering is made of oneself as an act of service to them, a response, often very unexpected and in their own time, will come.

But we need to consider well what kind of petition we make to the Cosmic Powers. We are brought to a knowledge of the path not to please ourselves, but for the *"kindling of hearts."* And there must be always preparation for that.

If we seek for response to our petition to do what may be called the spectacular, we shall petition in vain. There have been occasions when some on the path have been chosen to do an unusual piece of work, but only as a result of long preparation and readiness and for a high and definite purpose. It should not be our aim.

If one could do in the world of today one tithe of the works that Christ did before men, he would be torn to pieces by his pseudo friends in the marketplace. We may legitimately aspire to do those works, but the time is not yet; and when the time is ripe we shall need to be strong enough to withstand the powers of darkness which would dethrone the doer.

We may rest in the assurance that the fiery thought of the heart, not the head, will reach and pass beyond the portals of the hierarchy and in a fitting measure will bring a response.

For it is written: *"If ye shall ask in my name..."* I believe that most profoundly.

5. Discipleship on Trial

Reprinted from the April, May and June 1958 edition of The London Rosicrucian.

A member wrote to me recently that my book under the above title had caused a "considerable stir." I was glad to know that, although I am unaware of the nature of the response.[3]

I might have expected some criticism of it from a reader here and there who could not really stomach the plain, undiluted truth, even about the Path. But I have had none. On the contrary, the letters I have received have been extremely understanding and appreciative. It assured me of one undoubted fact; that students are often thinking precisely those things which one has expressed, but for some reason or other the spirit within them has not moved and forced them to declare themselves.

There is one possible reaction to the book which might be foreseen and that is, by some it may be considered to single out individuals or certain student groups for special criticism, belittling them and such efforts as they have made in the way of development. There was no such intention. The subject matter was far too important to me and to all kinds of aspiring minds to circumscribe it to this or that person or group of students.

What then was the intention? The book aimed to be a plain declaration of facts which, in my opinion, brought ourselves..., we of all types of occult, mystical. and spiritual belief and practice..., to the bar of self-examination of what we are, what we have stood for, and what we have done.

It set out to question, maybe to demolish, long-accepted views of our personality value and status, and endeavour to see how and why we ourselves had failed to measure up to that potency and worldwide influence which specialised study and meditation on the cultivation and use of the inward unfoldment of spiritual and occult powers, might have been expected to have equipped us.

The central question I had at heart was that of our discipleship. I used the term in its technical connotation. For discipleship in the occult sense has been the aim of aspirants in most of the recognised groups in the West for nearly a century. Yet it has failed to make any notable and visible impression upon the life of our time. It has failed to influence the national character in any appreciable degree. It has not even been powerful enough to have become a topic of interest or discussion either in the general press, or through the

---

3. *Discipleship on Trial* is available from the publisher.

radio, or in the pulpit, through which channels practically every topic of human interest is thoroughly discussed from every possible angle.

The mind of the nation has devoted itself to the exploration of every avenue of objective research of a materialistic nature. It has dedicated itself to minister in every conceivable way to the public craving for excitement and pleasure and banality of the passing hour. It has not had any interest whatever in, and therefore has never been an example of, a profound research into the life of the soul.

The aim of discipleship was to face that problem of the inner self, to realise its potentialities and declare it to the world. That may be still its aim, but it has failed to justify itself.

Why? Because, in spite of all the many teachings available on it, we have been too limited in vision, too crystallised in our views, too much 19th century in this respect, to realise that discipleship is in reality the next step upward in evolution, and unless it is deliberately and seriously sought, the level of human consciousness will remain what it is, which is nothing to boast of! At the moment it is literally bogged down to a line and waiting with anxiety and trepidation upon scientific and belligerent discoveries, and the prospect of surpassing gladiatorial displays.

But I do not leave the matter there in the book. I had too keen a sense and appreciation of the lifelong efforts of many disciples to write them off as failures and dismiss them. I have known them, and there is everything to be said for them. And I have said it.

No matter how presumptuous to some it may appear, I asked myself whether these advanced individuals, who through the years had proved themselves to have been the most sincere and able servers of the Masters of Life..., had not a rightful claim upon those Masters..., in the name of that same service which the Masters have so insistently inculcated, and which could not be further extended and made potent among men and demonstrated to the world, unless the privileges of higher initiation were conferred upon them.

I asked myself whether such disciples in the West were not entitled to receive that special and individual training at the hands of the Masters, which alone would bestow upon them the power to command public recognition by fortifying them with those abilities of service hitherto not possible to them. It is a petition to those Masters themselves, in the name of these disciples, which is the central thought of the book.

I suggested that the Western disciple needed an applicable technique of a unique nature and different in character from that applicable to the disciple in the East. Yet here, in the West, where humanity has been forced to suffer the cruellest blows under the influence of evil forces, the disciples who sought to do most were left without that super-physical recognition and illumination which might have raised them to be a light to the nation and of paramount service to the groups to which they were allied. They had to stand back in helpless silence.

But to turn to the immediate future. It has been said with some authority that the

Masters shape their plans to a great extent and modify them for future action, according to the response of world disciples..., what the latter can envisage, foresee, and demand for progress.

In a word, hierarchical action springs very much from world disciple reaction. One calls out the other. If one were a preceptor in a school and considering the advancement of certain capable pupils to the university and had to test them for that, when he came to do so he would know at once by the swiftness of their response; their readiness to anticipate his thought; their enunciation of certain factors to be met even before mentioned, what their possibilities were.

That would be the relatively few. The majority would think back over their past lessons and show by their silence their unreadiness for the venture. It was the relatively few I had in mind, of any persuasion, and the purpose of the book was a direct petition to the hierarchy, with which we are esoterically linked, to vouchsafe a necessary and individual technique for disciples in the West beyond anything yet given, who have pledged themselves to specific purposes of service.

It should never be overlooked that we are a functioning group within the hierarchy when out of the body as well as when in the body. We pass back automatically to our functioning in the hierarchy during sleep and associate there. We bring back our best ideas from thence. I do not then consider it amiss if one should take the initiative within our councils there and voice a petition here in concrete terms of requirements and possibilities of those allied with us on the Path.

If the senior members of a group, of all groups, kept that in mind, they might as opportunity afforded, think, aspire, and listen in unity as an impersonal group or groups on the inner side and thereby elicit greater cooperation, wisdom and guidance from the Masters there present, who await a resolute approach to themselves, and an insistent demand for that recognition which would enable them to react and fit disciples for the greater things demanded in the world *now*.

6. Perspectives of Progress

Reprinted from the July, August and September 1958 edition of The London Rosicrucian.

> "You have reached the crucial stage in your development and progress where you are to be used as a special channel for the great Masters."

This statement, which appears in a monograph of one of the higher grades, provides matter for reflection. It can be a statement of fact in the case of some aspirants, and one of promise in the case of others. Whether it is a fact or promise depends upon what has been attained in the way of development during the course of the preceding instruction.

It is a feature of this instruction that the monographs, following one another within very brief intervals, really cover a vast province of inner and psychic development. Indeed, if the instruction which they represent could be assimilated and demonstrated within such brief intervals the result would be spectacular. But such a result could only be expected in the case of those who had made unusual progress in former cycles.

For most of us these high points of the instruction must be regarded as in the nature of a promise. Few flower suddenly in this cycle into the high reaches of the Path. In fact, viewing the world dispassionately, there is a singular dearth of individuals who show any significant signs of such development.

They are not at present in incarnation. That they exist there is no doubt, but they await a propitious time when evolution can accept and profit of their appearance. No one can question how much they are needed, but the Mind of today has not called them forth.

It is no mere conjecture to say they are those of whom the world is not worthy, and would not be recognised and received if they came. Speaking generally in this connection perhaps the remark of an aspirant has much truth in it: that a low order of egos is incarnating in this cycle.

On this assumption, and giving appropriate weight to the comment of a trustworthy critic, *"that England, the most calculative, is the least meditative, of all civilised countries,"* the path of the really esoteric student is far from an easy one. He cannot expect to meet today with much encouragement in his environment in his particular studies. He must be content not to push along the lines too eagerly, expecting too much, but make sure of the steps as he can take with such phases of the instruction as are possible to him.

He must not assess his value or his progress from the ordinary, everyday point of view. For there is a deep truth and of much encouragement in the statement of a Master that, *"a good deal that is unexpected is concealed from the sleeping heart."* Consider that.

Although the aspirant may not enjoy the companionship of great souls in his waking hours, may he not have the felicity and spiritual companionship and help of them when he passes back nightly into their concealed but potent activities in the Cosmic? I often think that if this were not so, the heart would lose its faith and courage to advance amid the depressing currents of our objective life. But it is inspiring to reflect that, although only a part of our life, our waking existence, is fully known to us, our nightly disembodied existence can be vastly important and helpful to us, in that we resume our association with those with whom we have vital links in our studies and aspirations.

If from the hours of sleep we experienced but the gift of physical renewal, the path of life would be difficult indeed for the aspirant. But he returns fortified with the strengthened rhythm and inspiration imparted by those who are in constant contact with him and who work for him in his endeavours to tread the path, and who aid him in the problems of his present Karmic bondage here.

There is truly much concealed from the sleeping heart of a most expected nature, until we have the awakened consciousness of it: but the fact that so much is being done for us unconsciously cannot be overlooked. To remember that we pass nightly from the relative darkness of daily life into the revealing wisdom of unseen personalities and forces can be of the greatest comfort in our mortal sojourn.

Much that we cannot do for ourselves here is done for us there. Our studies and meditation increasingly prepare the way for and make possible the greater assimilation of that light and wisdom, which we petition for and need: and our faithfulness and courage in doing the lesser things possible to us now will surely open the way to revealing to the awakening spirit what is at present eluding the sleeping heart.

7. That Frustration is a Good

Reprinted from the January, February and March 1959 edition of The London Rosicrucian.

It cannot be denied that the occult life is one of many paradoxes. So is everyday life, character and conduct, but these are not so readily accepted.

They are a tempting bait for critics who try to make the most of them. Yet paradoxes and contradictions meet the observer of human life continually. Life does not run smoothly in one direction. It is a challenge to thought and scrutiny, and those incapable of these are the majority who are responsible for most of the misunderstandings and quarrels which beset us.

Observe what a smart critic would make of the above title. I heard one recently deliver an oracular judgement on a book, that the author must be a frustrated person, because the book touched the critic at vulnerable points. Life had presumably been to him a gentle, smoothly flowing stream which had never encountered even a pebble in its course. Presumably his was a tranquil life during which nothing had happened to him, a neutral, pacific existence undisturbed by any untoward circumstance, or in which any opposition of circumstance had softened him up and taught him nothing.

Beware of the passive, self-satisfied critic, or any other individual, who shuns reactions for fear of disturbing his moribund soul and balks at a frustration as from a deadly sin.

I am not eulogising, on the other hand, the individual who hammers his way through life and stirs up all the commotion he can to reach his goal. But there is a marked difference between a passive, accepting, self-consciously non-offensive individual who would not even harm an aggressive mosquito; and a live, positive one who, if need be, will scorch the life out of any frustrations which threaten to defeat him.

You will rarely meet with one of this calibre who had not to overcome a host of frustrations in life. If you look into the lives of men and women who have done things worthwhile in the world, you will find that almost invariably life has done its best to keep them back, thwart their plans, belittle their efforts and throw them down, has done everything in fact to stay their hand and convince them that the goal they envisaged was an impossible one and not for them.

Yet they got there and made the critics wince. Frustrations were their greatest inspiration. They fanned the flame which blazed the trail.

But there is another aspect of this persistency in the face of opposition to be considered by aspirants on the path. In both cases the will comes forcibly into play: but what we have to recognise is, that it is not simply a matter of will or no will which decides the issue for the aspirant. For those on the path it is not enough simply to fight ahead against the frustrations of life for the sake of overcoming difficulty and winning through. We need to ask ourselves why frustrations, often of a very acute and testing kind, beset us when we have keyed ourselves to higher advancement.

We cannot overlook the influence of past cycles upon us. In every department of our lives, in each vehicle which makes up the composite mechanism of the soul, the thinking and emotion of the past have set their mark. Imperfections of the past are here present before our eyes; and it is for us to observe and study the trends, the values and the defects, the facilities and hindrances, the swift response to esoteric and spiritual truth, or the slowness in comprehension of it.

It is not enough to say, "I will:" we must take the measure of ourselves and ask what can be willed, and how, and for what purpose?

So many have been disillusioned on the path just here. They set out with the belief that all things were possible without ever considering dispassionately what kind of instrument is imperative for achieving highly marked goals. And only after the passing of many years do they come to serious terms with themselves and observe in what way and to what extent the past is conditioning their present and make a wise calculation of possibilities within reasonable time limits in the present cycle with such equipment as they have and the opportunities afforded them for improving that equipment and preparing the ground for future attainment.

Ambition is good and awakens the faculties of man, but it cannot take by storm, at will, closely guarded frontiers of the path which require far more than will to pass. It is so often overlooked in placing before ourselves the praiseworthy picture of an ideal esoteric life, the kind and extent of the karmic obligations and tests which will indubitably be precipitated by our own aspiration on the road to that objective.

We shall meet with some of the keenest frustrations life can present to us, and they must be rightly interpreted, not shunned and denied. If we petition for a thing of so great value and ultimate usefulness, we must accept the terms on which alone it can be granted to us. The terms will not be our own. If they were all would be forthright and plain..., and we should lack the very force and ability which constant oppositions are decreed to give.

The exercise of the will in daily life for achievement on the emotional and mental planes is of a different nature from that put forth in esoteric advancement. The same intentness, the same persistency, the same focussing of such energy as one can command, yet the will confined to the level of objective life, to any point within its worldly compass, circumscribed within the limits of material existence, mechanical, not spiritual, self-involved and unprayerful. But for the esoteric the same intentness, persistency, focussed living energy, with thought ever seeking in silence the Christ light in the heart and the overshadowing benediction of the soul. This is the difference.

I do not think that any frustration can be other than good with the mind and heart centred upon the highest we have heard and read and sought through the years. There is a time for all things. If we are confident in our thought and action, we can with patience wait for it. All things must fulfil themselves in time; and that which concerns our highest development will be fulfilled in time.

Through precipitate or hasty procedure we shall but prematurely exhaust powers we need to meet and surpass the frustrations and tests of life. But in facing life with trustfulness and quiet confidence in the outworking of events, we shall give an example of purposefulness and reliability which cannot fail, without any strenuousness on our part.

8. The Tibetan Tragedy

Reprinted from the Summer 1959 edition of The London Rosicrucian.

The exiled Dalai Lama recently gave his first press conference since his arrival in India. I doubt if any Rosicrucian who read the forthright and poignant statement he made at that conference felt other than deep resentment against the Chinese government.

This cruel onslaught upon the greatest stronghold of Buddhistic doctrine and practice in the world, has no parallel in modern times. The wars in the West, although on an infinitely greater scale than this, were also singularly different in character. They had not the supreme ideals of Tibet, neither in theory nor practice. They had their theologies and lip service to Christ: but the dedicated life and devotion of the Tibetan Buddhist was foreign to them.

I was moved to write about this by the photograph of Tibetan victims which appeared in the June *Rosicrucian Digest*, and especially by the heart-searching statement introducing the photograph which ran: *"None of the great nations whose governments are founded upon often-expounded religious ideals have ventured to aid them."*

These great nations watched the Hungarians beaten down by the Russians. Their tears were copious but unseen. They cried aloud for tender conscience's sake, and did nothing. If we have any friends left in Hungary the nations do not deserve them.

The Chinese have beaten down the harmless disciples of Buddha in their sacred temples. The nations neither cried aloud nor did anything. These same nations have sworn before God in church and before man in the street that no nations henceforth should suffer aggression from nation with impunity. They have lied to themselves and to the world.

"The multitude of oppressions" have fallen upon Tibet; and the nations stand afar off, bound by the spell of the aggressors. But what is a small nation of disciples kneeling before the Buddha in comparison with the brave, commercially-driven West? The Dalai Lama at his conference appealed to the world to take some action to help the Tibetan people. He hears daily of the agony and affliction, the cruel deportation and execution of innocent man. If justice and compassion still have any home in the West they are subdued and frustrated by diplomatic caution and selfish personal safety. What nation would risk its prestige, much less its skin, for the love of Buddha or Christ?

These may be thought hard sayings. I make them deliberately because there are countless individuals in all the said nations who endorse them. I merely express what they think and feel. I choose to express their helpless indignation. What a sorry plight we are in when faced with a tragedy of this nature!

It is fitting that we as Rosicrucians should declare ourselves. It is a part of our pledged duty and service. The Rosicrucians never did, and they never will, sit quiet and smother the issues of life and death when their fellowmen are being trodden underfoot by the slayers of goodness, faith and love. We ourselves outwardly can do nothing except express our profound disgust and disapproval of the diplomatic non-action of the nations in giving a free hand to the devilish will of the aggressor upon the harmless disciples of the spiritual kingdom, who in their lives and prayers night and day have sought to bring the light and power of that kingdom upon earth to redeem a frail, erring and sick humanity.

Nor is our protest lost among the silences and inaction of the nations. We know the tremendous power of thought, compassion and petition to the Cosmic Powers, in the name of Buddha and Christ, to move mysteriously and in little expected ways for the halting and downfall of the enemies of the soul of man.

9. Men Learn Most by the Negative Way

Reprinted from the Winter 1959 edition of The London Rosicrucian. *Extracts were published in the Summer 1994 issue of the* Rosicrucian Beacon.

The writings which help us most are not those that simply inform us, but those which hold us up suddenly because they appear to cut right across our personal opinions and beliefs. We English have very settled opinions and beliefs, both right and wrong, and we receive a jolt whenever they are contradicted. Such is the virtue, or the vice, of our insularity, in spite of air planes which toss us about all over the wide world.

Now, to abruptly tell a man who has been mainly battening for years upon the psychology of the schools, which demand, above all things, that he be positive, with a will to domination at all costs at all times, and so become a fiery-eyed magnetic individual whom nobody can approach or influence in any way,..., to tell such a man that he can learn most by the negative way, is enough to make him rage like a tiger. But a saint once said it, and he lived in Christ. That should make a man pause if he has any humility in him. But few in these days know what true humility is; and if they do, their psychology has no room for it.

Positivity has a rightful place in life, but may the gods help the man who is always positive. He may feel very happy and pleased with himself, nevertheless he shuts the door to the realities of life. I remember how that illuminating phrase in the Fama, *"Jesus to me is all,"* impressed me when I first met with it. Perhaps I was trying to be positive at the time, so long ago now, but that devout ejaculation held me up like a flash of lightning. It was so unexpected, a kind of confession I never thought to meet with just there.

And if I said suddenly to a confirmed psychological positivist, *"Jesus to me is all,"* I can imagine how disconcerted he would be. On recovering, he might point to Scripture and remind me that Jesus was positive enough. So he was, but so rightly in time and place, in just the right circumstances, that one scarcely realises his receptiveness to the inspiration of divine wisdom. The influence of Christ was so astounding and unobtrusive, that whereas the positivist is calculated to drive more people from himself than to attract them, those nearest to Jesus could not get near enough, and were ready to die for Him.

When I hear some of our all-knowing positivists over the radio, I am not instructed but repelled, and I fear for them. They need an inoculation of negativity to restore their balance. It is no wonder that the schools for the young breed the same type who fill the air with their strident voices.

Can you think of a voice suddenly emerging from the brassy din..., *"Jesus to me is all?"* A scholar with that humility in him would be sent down and lose his status for life..., among the positivists. But they know no better: and the tragedy to be lamented is, that the really sensitive and so valuable soul is thrust aside and forgotten.

But we know very well what the saint meant when he said a man learns most by the negative way. If we don't, it is time we did. Emerson knew what it meant when he wrote a century ago: *"Let us take our bloated nothingness out of the path of the divine circuits."* I do not think it could be better said. And we might add the words of Boehme to it, *"Only stop thy willing and thinking, thou shalt learn wonderful things from God."* These are the voices which merit attention, not the loud and vulgar broadsides of the *"experts of opinion,"* panting to outstrip one another.

For one thing, these voices mean, to stop running and to learn how to wait. The positive individuals I am thinking of cannot stop and can never wait. For them that would be a criminal neglect of life. Yet how often is the waiting more productive than the running? The positive man is so full of himself, so sure of himself, so capable in himself, that few can teach him anything on earth, much less from heaven. As for being inspired or taught by the Spirit of God, he will never submit to that doctrine until the calamity of life drives him down on his knees.

Another thing is, until a man gets that habit of kneeling in humility before a greater self than himself, he will never know himself or anyone else rightly. In this way of life, which is here called the negative way, a man must willingly surrender himself in act, word and deed with ease and perfect trust at will, that the Cosmic Powers may see and know and use an instrument ready for service.

That is why it is also said that a man must become deaf and dumb on this way if he would have his petitions heard and answered. You see how the way turns a man more and more inward, divests him of the speech and hearing of the positive self, that he may enter a realm of deeper cognition and apprehension and come to the silent interpretation of divine things.

This surrender is an art on the way. A man cannot be both at the same time. He cannot run and hustle and play the positive to the top of his bent and at the same time expect the voices of the silence to unfold to him the secrets of the mysteries of life in a turbulent soul. Hence it is, that he will not have what the negative way can teach him until he learns to *"wait with silence"* and can forget for a term what manner of man he is.

So we approach the profound content of that word of the *Fama Fraternitatis*, *"Jesus to me is all."* It points directly to the way of renunciation, of the surrender of the knowing, active, dogmatic, demanding, psychologising personal self to a quiet, devotional and accepting allegiance to the Master of all Masters, whose aid we shall certainly need tomorrow although we may hurriedly pass by today.

I know this is a fact. The Rosicrucian of the Fama knew it and declared it. We may read the Scripture every day, as millions do, and go our own way, until a time comes, when the Karma of life, mounting to its meridian, strikes upon the heart like a revelation of fire, and we have to pause and surrender the little self to divine guidance. Then the peace of the inner temple where the Master keeps his patient vigil will dawn and we realise the meaning and value of the negative way.

10. Minds: Ancient and Modern

Reprinted from the Spring 1960 edition of The London Rosicrucian.

It is said in the East that *"a man with mind enough can understand the whole world without leaving his study."* This is one of those shock statements which should only be accepted, if accepted at all, with definite qualifications. Not every statement, even of an occult nature, that comes out of the venerable East is fit for literal consumption in the worldly West. The above statement should not be swallowed whole.

We may not be able to contest the belief that an occult adept of a kind, with the best part of the world's evolutionary scheme assimilated and tabulated, may glance over the world at will and be thoroughly posted upon it. But the man who has this inestimable privilege without leaving his study must have travelled far before he settled down comfortably in it.

The same conclusions suggest themselves if we consider the comprehensive and exhaustive systems of thought of many writers of genius, works which have furnished the groundwork of inspiration and enlightenment of students the world over through the centuries. Their range of information has engrossed the minds and provoked the criticism of acute thinkers for the best part of their lives.

Classic examples come to mind. In the field of scholastic philosophy the massive work of Aquinas compels attention, a work of immense compass of intellectual speculation which appears to leave no theological question unconsidered regarding the relation of man to God. And of a very different character, yet containing speculations and conclusions of highest value to the thinker, which have occupied and agitated the minds of students to the present day, and will continue to do so in this transitional stage of mental evolution, is the work of Schopenhauer.

The granite thoughts of these two thinkers and writers fall into position with an ease and precision from which no mortal hand will dislodge them. True, the Roman Church, we know, was swift to adopt Aquinas as her own angelic doctor, and this has done much to fortify her position in the modern world. But we do not need the Roman Church in order to rightly evaluate the work of Aquinas. He belongs to the thinker of every age, and probably more so to those who profess no religion at all than to those who do.

If we look further back and survey the architectonic structures of thought evolved by Plato and Plotinus and others connected with their schools we can see how powerfully their thought influenced these later thinkers. Men of profound meditation and rare insight, grappling with the universal problem with unwearying attention, they set the pace and pattern of intellectual activity for countless students down to our day.

They were far from the ideal man of our quotation. But the point is, they wrestled with their problem from every aspect of its appearance and explained it with a certitude and lucidity which none have surpassed or even approached. They made men think. They turned a brilliant light into the dark recesses of the mind and life. They thought themselves out and inspired lesser men to think themselves out and to observe themselves and life objectively. They did not sit down and expect an understanding of the whole world would be revealed to them.

They were men of a type, of exceptional gifts, flexible mediums of direct inspiration who viewed life from a high vantage point yet who were themselves very close to life. They had studied life profoundly, and the manifold problems which beset millions today and which our psychologists, psychiatrists and psychoanalysts discuss so learnedly and professorially, fell within their prevision and knowledge as a matter of course and prompted them to their best work for the enlightenment of those perplexed and afflicted by them.

Yes, the past gives us an inspiring but sober picture of what men can be and do. But look at today! Maritain, the theologian, said: *"The modern world is blasé; all values have been degraded in it to one dull level of equality by the stale use of custom."* I can accept that statement without any qualifications. It points a sharp contrast with the greatest we know of the distant past. It is true that the works of those I have instanced have been and are an inspiration to many, yet these are the comparatively few as opposed to those who degrade the former values.

Any well-informed listener, for instance, who has heard the inane expositions of some of the rising and vociferous young men in our debating societies of note, will not question this. How many of these young masters of our generation are at sea in their thinking and their speech! One would think that such men as I have referred to had never lived. They have no sheet anchor in the past. They have touched upon it superficially in their textbooks, but it has no weight with them.

Nor has the present much meaning for them; and one may well conjecture what they will be and do in the future. The religionists think they lack the sense of God. That may be true. I should say they lacked the most ordinary common sense. Their strength lies in much speaking. I doubt if there has ever been so much of it to so little purpose.

The art of reflection, the grace and beauty of a quiet inward life within which they can face up to themselves, has no appeal for them. Studies such as our own have no more attraction for them than those of the great masters who have thought for and spoken to them through the centuries.

A member of ours, a clergyman, who lectured in one of our prominent universities on the subject of mysticism, said that he met with an almost total ignorance of the subject among the students. Who is to blame for this: the ignorant students or those who direct their studies and who are mainly concerned to inculcate the primary importance of scientific research as a goal for the immediate future?

Both are to blame: the students, who do not seek beyond the cramping limits of a university education the available mystical literature pointing the way of inner enlightenment; and the authorities, who direct the attention and studies of students into the limiting field of technological and materialistic science as the highest goal for their endeavour. Is it surprising that one so often hears that the young students of our time, within the universities and outside of them, question the very purpose of life, see no meaning in it, entertain doubts even of the value of that they are being taught, and are already, many of them, thoroughgoing skeptics?

With these facts in mind, significant as they are in viewing just one cross section of student life in Britain, what of tomorrow? Among thousands of interested listeners a large number are undoubtedly influenced by these discussions I have mentioned, and many accept them as a guide for themselves, coming from students of their own age.

That is the disquieting thought about it. As for those who disseminate these views of life and feel so clever and elevated in so doing, I would not advise them to immure themselves in their study in the hope of understanding the whole world before leaving it. Time will defeat them.

But I would advise them, even if the spirit of mysticism has no voice for them, to turn again with some reverence to the old masters of thought and mental discipline and remember that they, and men like them, laid the foundation of the best underlying the culture of today; that their thought has permeated so deeply the whole substratum of school and university life, that neither they, nor their preceptors, nor the authorities who dominate both, will be able to get away from the subtle influence of it, even while they may treat it with contempt or indifference.

In the march of events which are crowding upon and challenging these young men, stern alternatives will face them. They will be forced to decide in a not distant future whether they will win the attention and respect of noble souls who have sought steadily and silently for the key to the evolutionary process and aligned themselves with the forces of spiritual advancement which alone holds within its inexorable laws the true destiny of man; or float down the muddy stream of time, wondering still whether life has any meaning, a miserable menace to many of their associates, and an inspiration to none.

11. The Cult of the Average

Reprinted from the Summer 1960 edition of The London Rosicrucian.

The average Britisher would rather fill up a football-pool form than listen to Elgar's *Enigma*. Why this should be so, I cannot tell. It must be something wrong with education. Probably it is the cult of the average: the idea that schools exist in order to make everyone pretty much the same, and that happiness consists in sharing a group life, sweet, humming, undifferentiated, and crowded like bees in a hive.

The critic who says hard things, especially if true, about the average Britisher and suggests that his education has made him average, may be heartily disliked but is worth listening to. This delectable observation cuts deep, and those who feel the thrust need it most.

It is a deliberate, calm, and studied criticism, made without passion or prejudice, by a distinguished authority in classical literature and education. And its value for us is this: it marks precisely a prevailing condition of mind which we should take particular notice of. I make no apology for dealing with topics of this kind and in an uncompromising manner. As Rosicrucians and students of life we should be keenly alive to conditions around us, and where they deserve it we should not fear to pillory them.

If we needed any justification for this attitude, we have but to remember that many of the greatest reforms of the past have been wrought by individuals here and there who had the native fire within them to challenge and hold up to ridicule or condemnation the prevailing practices, deterrent tendencies and unsound standards of their time. And when such individuals have taken an unprecedented stand against a national trend, whether of a physical, mental or moral nature, notwithstanding the obloquy which has usually descended upon them from those who have a personal interest in resisting any reform, they have scarcely opened their mouths than other voices from unexpected quarters have been heard uniting themselves with the original protestants.

Some would, of course, say that if these things are so, why bother about them, why criticise them? That kind of attitude is demoralising: it is weak, undisciplined and banal; and you will find it at its best among so-called esotericists of this or that society who are too self-respecting to open their mouths, or even whisper a word of truth to themselves.

They are the mushy, soft-minded people who will accept anything and question nothing, a kind of home-grown elect, *"sweet, humming, undifferentiated."* But they are much mistaken if they think prevailing conditions around them leave them untouched, untainted, instead of being a perpetual menace to them.

Now the man who will waste his leisure hours trying to win a doubtful fortune out of football-pools rather than upon some form of self-improvement, whether listening to the Enigma or studying the supremely odd enigma of himself, or some other of the thousand enigmas which confront everybody, is a most disgraceful loser, no matter what fortune he wins.

It is the habit of children to note and assimilate the habits of adults with whom they live; and if the habits of the latter are mediocre and trivial, those of the former are not likely to be of an opposite character. Add to this, the type of school education which our critic rightly calls *"the cult of the average,"* and you have more than a hint how the average Britisher becomes.

But is it wrong to be a nonentity in life? No, it is a feature of the time, instilled and encouraged by the radio and television influences upon the mind and heart. Neither is this wrong; but it benumbs, and sinks human nature to a common level of activity and expression until there is no other word in the language to correctly describe it than average.

Indeed, in this respect Britain is more average than it was 20 years ago. Whoever hears of the culture of the soul and the psychic faculties of man? These are enigmas which the average Britisher either scorns or is afraid to think of. There is no entertainment in it, no titillation of the nerves, nothing to increase and fortify his inflated opinion that he is on the top of the world. Yet if the light of the soul struck across his purblind vision, he would fall off his pedestal into an abyss of fear and unbelief; and only his own soul could rescue him.

I am not singular in fully endorsing our critic. Scarcely a week passes without some public criticism in the press or through the radio of the kind of influences which are shaping the present generation. The old discipline which fashioned our greatest men has gone by the board. In its place we have the exhilarating Quiz technique for the education of the young and amusement of the old, *"sweet, humming, undifferentiated."*

If called upon to face another 1939, we can imagine what kind of robust, disciplined opposition we could hope for to meet it. Men of discipline and readiness there would be, but even they have to count upon the stamina of the social order of the time. That is being steadily undermined by laxity, indifference and the absence of high ideals.

It is the prevalence of the cult of the average which deters thousands of promising individuals from attempting to raise the tone and status of life. They fear the ridicule, the circumstances of a change of front.

I once gave to a brilliant scholar, a doctor of philosophy and a minister of the gospel, a book on the Rosicrucian life and teaching. He returned it with the comment that he was too rational to accept it. I gave to a medical man of outstanding ability a book on the psychic life which could have been of peculiar service to him in his practice. He, too, returned it with the comment, that his training in the schools made his acceptance of such a teaching impossible.

Is not the plain truth of this that the schools and universities maintain a closed door against the acceptance, not of the cut and dried and uninspiring theology of the churches, or a creditable knowledge of the physical and mental life of man, but against any encouragement in the direction of mystical research into the mystery and destiny of the inner spiritual man?

The orthodoxy of the theologian and the medical man is the rooted enemy of an experimental knowledge of the spirit of man, and those who have sworn allegiance to it fear what mystical research may reveal, the possible revolutionary mental changes they would have to face in confessing an adherence thereto.

Is this wrong? Yes, profoundly wrong: but the culprit here is the university and training school, not the entrants to them who are compelled to give their allegiance and are bound by a Hippocratic oath, or by the mentally crippling articles of religion forged for their bondage by a set of bishops 400 years ago.

It should be of special interest to us that, notwithstanding this acknowledged flatness and absence of character referred to, there is an increasing number of intellectual and cultured seekers for knowledge who refuse to be mentally bound by the rules and dictates of school, college or church; and many of these would find the Rosicrucian teachings of immediate import and value to them. Comparatively few they may be, but they are well aware of the sinister modern trend. They have no interest in it, nor will they minister to it.

And this growing body of seekers who refuse to be blinded by science and scorn the shackles of authorities which would limit their aspirations, we must seek to contact through every avenue open to us and invite their cooperation in our researches into the laws of the occult and mystical life.

They are ready for and need this research. They believe in real freedom of thought and action. They are as much the avowed enemies of the average as we are: but they wait. They wait to give their allegiance to a high and spiritual ideal, wherein the schools and the churches have failed them.

It should never be forgotten that Rosicrucians, during the various cycles of their activity, have been the first to adopt a pioneering role. May it be more than a hope that among ourselves in this present cycle there will appear some of the same spirit as those of the past. For when we recall the active mental and physical work many of us have engaged in within the Order for the best part of a lifetime, is it encouraging to realise how slight is the impact of it upon every section of the national life?

I know we work as much for the future as for the present, and what has been done cannot be forgotten or lost; but vastly more is needed to offset the insidious rot, no longer hidden but well above the surface, and rouse the average Britisher from his empty self-satisfied importance which a swift turn of fortune would test to the bottom and teach him overnight the value of self-discipline.

12. Anxious Aspirants

Reprinted from the Autumn 1960 edition of The London Rosicrucian.

I know from my experience of members that the question often uppermost in their minds is, "*How much progress am I making in my studies?*"

The reason is obvious. They have carried out a certain number of experiments and exercises given during the work, and narrowly regarding themselves after a few months, they wonder why they are not visibly changed or cannot demonstrate with ease some of the more arresting possibilities mentioned in the course of study.

First of all, let it be said that the Rosicrucian teaching covers a unique field of study not given in books, and prepared by those who were proficients in the science and who knew far more than they gave out. They gave out what the time demanded and warranted and for those whom they knew would have the interest and ability to pursue these studies and so prepare a foundation for the future.

It should not be overlooked that students in different countries have a different psychic background, and this is largely the reason why practical demonstrations among some aspirants exceed those of others. But one of the greatest mistakes of those who feel they have made little progress because they have had little success of a more demonstrable type on the material plane is, that they overlook the fact that they are engaged in an unusual form of development.

While explaining the objective plane of life and seeking to establish aspirants firmly upon it as a necessary foundation, it soon passes inward to the underlying psychic life with a view to making it more active and showing the aspirant how to adjust to it.

Passing from the seen to the unseen is really a long journey, and to expect to traverse it within a definite period is likely to cause disappointment. Think of the many lines of pursuit in life we are willing to repeat under good authority and the time often required before results are obtained. But in the experimental work and exercises of the grades we are dealing with unseen factors of exploration, and the most important of these is that of the etheric centres of activity.

The rhythm of them cannot be changed overnight. There would be great danger if it could be. And there is also such a marked inequality of unfoldment among these centres, nothing approaching a harmonious disposition. One student may record clairvoyant phenomena with facility because of a high condition of unfoldment of the ajna centre: another in whom the rhythm of this centre is dull and slow may obtain no results until its functioning is brought to a high pitch of development.

But the point to note is this: any excessive application to this end is to be guarded against because of possible reactionary consequences. We cannot do just what we like with our etheric centres: in fact, I doubt whether any harmonious development can be expected until the student is far along the path, life has spontaneously accelerated the rhythm of the centres as a whole, and expert guidance is vouchsafed from the inner side.

A similar reasonable kind of attitude should be exercised regarding all inner work. The slowest is the best and the safest. It is not of tremendous importance what a student may see or hear in his foundational work; it is rather how much patience he has to continue that which his reason shows him can be helpful and let specific results come in their good time.

One thing is certain, in some types of concentration and meditation for definite purposes, the architectural lines are being more definitely marked, so to speak, in the psychic self, and the student cannot judge precisely what will be the actual objective results from day to day of this work. If he is observant he may find that certain kinds of development are taking place in directions he least expected. The objective self will be more responsive in ways and circumstances and show forth results where he had not really looked for and expected them.

Nothing is more true of this work than in looking for one thing we often find another of even greater present importance. That spontaneous emergence cannot take place if we close the door to inner processes by demanding this or that kind of result now and no other. The student may really need and be ready for what is immediately given in this way, while the original demand may have to stand in abeyance for some time through causes he cannot foresee.

A further point to be noted is that it is often those students who feel dissatisfaction at certain delayed results who are nevertheless sharpened and alerted to accomplish things in their daily life which they had not intended, or which they had not the confidence hitherto to carry out. The aim is a measure of inner awakening in connection with the circumstances in which we have to move, and no student can estimate merely by certain objective results the truth about that awakening.

But having the goal in view and remembering how success in this or that direction in the studies moves spirally, not step by step open to calculation, there is no ground for disappointment or anxiety. There rather should be expectancy of new disclosures in the student's life and a quick seizure of opportunity and renewed application of interest after reasonable interludes of rest.

The student should be assured that there can be no forcing of issues in his work. Obviously not, for they do not lie fundamentally, in his objective hands; they are wrought out behind the veil, in the psychic sphere of activity.

The operations of that sphere cannot be coerced. It is a sphere of great possibility and expression, but the objective self must know how to adjust to and meet its revelations to him.

13. Advance or Retreat?

Reprinted from the Winter 1960/61 edition of The London Rosicrucian.

There is an aspect of life which the young aspirant sometimes has to face which is not easy for him to deal with, and a few reflections upon it may be of value.

When it becomes known to his family and among his friends that he is a student of the Rosicrucian teachings and practice, he encounters a coldness, or indifference, or criticism of this new departure on his life; and the question is, how shall he meet this kind of opposition to his sincere interest for personal advancement?

Obviously, much will depend upon the temperament of the student. There is often reluctance to become the cause of disharmony and argument within his family, in accepting views of an unorthodox nature. Even the habit of retirement for study and meditation is sometimes cause to awaken suspicion and opposition to that which will prove of the greatest value to him in his daily life and vocation in years to come. But the opposition is there and if little is said he is well aware of the undercurrent of dissatisfaction which exists in those around him.

Yet this is but an early challenge of his resolution to follow a strong leading of his inner self. Religious opinions often work strongly against him here. Has he a right to take a path which opens to freedom of thought and action when faced with an atmosphere of family religious orthodoxy? Undoubtedly he has every right and should not hesitate to exercise it.

It is true that today, when so many views of life and conduct come directly into the family circle through television and radio, this particular type of religious opposition is not so likely to manifest itself as in years gone by when family life and opinion were more circumscribed and a good deal narrower than today. Nevertheless, religious persuasions are not readily changed and the aspirant may well encounter difficulty through them.

Another source of opposition is sometimes through jealousy awakened in religious relatives that the student should be immersed in teachings which promise him unusual knowledge and the fact that it is felt he is gaining advantages and forming associations which are outside the interest of those relatives. This can be a very real trial for the student.

I recall that some time ago a young lady called to see me. She was in tears and obviously distressed. Handing me a parcel containing her books and monographs, she said she could not continue because her husband thought she was mad. That was a pathetic and cruel instance. I have known others but less poignant. But these are extreme types of opposition and I mention them because they do sometimes happen and the student has to take a decision whether to make a deliberate stand against them, or weakly bow to the narrow views and closed minds of those who oppose him.

We hear much today, more than ever before, about the right of the individual to freedom of thought and utterance. Whenever that right is questioned within a student's family circle or outside of it, he should take his stand upon his individual right to recognise the onward march of evolution in thought and expression, and deny emphatically any supposed right of others to curtail his interests and possibilities in pursuing any kind of knowledge and aim which he believes and knows has his highest interests in view.

During the early years of our Rosicrucian activities, the late and the present Imperator and myself encountered many instances of this narrow-minded opposition to our work. They came in many forms of criticisms, denunciations and lying propaganda, contemptible and ludicrous. But they had to be faced as a matter of duty and we faced them with the truths and facts we had long been grounded in.

The critics were silenced and the work went on. But as long as a pioneering work is carried on for the good of humanity, ignoring deeply rooted religious beliefs and certain frontiers of knowledge still held tenaciously in school and university, we may expect critics to rise who will challenge our right to proclaim a knowledge of any higher possibilities of man in advance of their own.

The young aspirant should reflect upon this if he is faced with awkward alternatives regarding his studies. His life is his own to broaden and mature as he will; but to allow the opinions of others to deter and hold him back, is to surrender to an enemy weaker than himself. It will bring him no ultimate credit, but regret that he ignored the voice of his own best self.

There is something eminently stimulating to meet in our Chapter life, as we do, young aspirants, English and foreign, who with little or no encouragement in their daily environment, have pledged themselves with deep sincerity and purpose to its work at the threshold of their life. We understand their lives, problems and difficulties, and seek to fortify them against influences which may cause them anxiety and hinder their progress. We realise, and they will realise in time, that we cannot lend our hand to a nobler work than to impart some of the confidence and knowledge we have gained in our studies to those who are setting out on this voyage of inner discovery.

The student should take advantage of this assistance of the advanced members to the full. There is little in the grasp and thrust of daily life which can bring solace and inspiration compared with that which is derived from periodical communion with the aspirant's own inner self, nothing which will give that nobility and sincerity necessary to cope with the toil of the day.

Indeed, so few in these days seek the inner way, so many are satisfied with an objective and ephemeral attitude towards life, that he will come to view his Chapter contacts and associations as of unique interest and opportunity, as something above and entirely different from the life around him.

It will constitute for him a periodical respite from the everlasting dissension and turmoil which threaten every day of his existence and unfold in his mind a spirit of tranquillity and understanding which will prove the value of his early decision to seek the way, no matter what the temporary difficulties sometimes occasioned by the uninitiated may be.

They have every right to follow what they believe, but they have no right to damp the hopes and frustrate the purpose of the aspirant who one day may blossom into a leading spirit after the Rosicrucian tradition.

14. Birthday Message to Francis Bacon Chapter

Reprinted from the Summer 1961 edition of The London Rosicrucian.

In 1958 Imperator Ralph M Lewis asked all Affiliated Bodies in Great Britain to honour Grand Master Andrea with a special ceremony on the occasion of his birthday each year. This was Andrea's response to the ceremony in 1961.

A member of the London Chapter recently wrote to me to the effect that what helped the officers so much was that I appreciated all they did and never criticised them. It is true, I have always deeply appreciated all that has been done, against many odds at times, and never was disposed to criticise or saw reason for criticism.

I know that a good deal of what I have written has been critical, very much so, but the intention behind it should not be overlooked. I have had the definite intention all through to inspire, awaken attentive thinking, and often placing ideas in a different light than the usually accepted one. If it has been criticism, it has also most definitely been my purpose.

My mission, if I may call it that, was to challenge and agitate and cut across some of the old time accepted thinking about our studies and the path. In that sense I have been directly critical and an intentional destroyer of many accepted and complacent views which I knew meant stagnation instead of advancement and therefore could only prove unhelpful.

There has been no need to criticise those who have worked so conscientiously for the good of the Chapter, since they have realised my intention in writings and have been able critics themselves of what was for its good and what might hinder. There are groups which seem to exist only to continue on a well-worn routine track. There is nothing new, arresting or advancing in them and very little good comes from them.

But the *Francis Bacon Chapter* is an active one, alive, and keen in progressiveness; and other chapters may well take a lesson from it. For myself, I have grown along with it; and what has impressed me through the years most deeply has been the united stability, kindness and affection you have shown me, not simply on an occasion like the present, but always and in so many so directly personal ways. This has been a most potent inspiration to me and I am most grateful for it.

The *Francis Bacon Chapter* came into being on the clear note of service. Had its aim been simply to watch its soul grow, it would have failed. Obviously, because the note of service has always been the Rosicrucian ideal. It was on that note of service that I entered the Order and accepted a peculiar responsibility which I have never had the least inclination to shirk.

That central ideal of service has been the driving force of the Chapter, and you have the satisfaction of realising how much good has been done under its influence.

15. Brains: East and West

Reprinted from the Summer 1961 edition of The London Rosicrucian.

I once asked a lady, who had spent some years in India, why it was that in Britain one never encountered and never heard of a single outstanding character of demonstrable occult attainment; whereas in India to do so was of common occurrence and indeed had been for centuries? And this, by the way, when there has been no lack in Britain of followers of notorious bodies of so-called occultists of many persuasions.

Her reply was brief and to the point: *"We had not the class of brain for it."* Had she said that we lacked brains she would have been wide of the mark. The British do not lack brains, but they are of a very different class from those in the East.

Now, this lady's opinion would not disconcert the British, simply because they have never considered occult development as worth their time and attention. The British brain is materialistic in character, and nearly all their pursuits are likewise in various degrees. It employs itself upon that which is most suitable for it and of a thoroughly practical nature. Science, technology, commerce are the ready tools of the British, and none have surpassed them in the development and use of them.

But what headway has occultism made in Britain? Theosophy, for instance, is a feeble remnant of Eastern philosophy. Anthroposophy is a mixture of Theosophy and German philosophy and has maintained a footing here, and received the attention of some educational authorities because of some practical aspects of it in its application to child welfare and education. While Buddhism is an Eastern doctrine of an esoteric nature whose aim and technique are in some respects repugnant to the worldly West.

Neither of these has any hope of superseding even the orthodox Christian teaching of the West; nor is there any indication that either of them can show anything of the nature of the occult development referred to.

It appears to be literally true that they have not the peculiar type of brain for it. All of them, and innumerable cults besides, chiefly of Eastern origin, have hoisted their flags in Britain through the years in the hope of attracting the interest, if not of the populace, at least of a large section of the intelligentsia; and if the flags still fly scant recognition is given to the followers of them.

The truth is that the remarkable advancement of science and its amazing discoveries have captured not only the popular imagination and the interest of the intelligentsia, and the theories and speculations of the cults have less recognition than ever before. Indeed even theology and the theologians are faced with a challenge which they are ill equipped to meet.

To the thinker the British, and I am thinking only of the British at the moment, present a spectacle of fascinating interest. A gigantic competitive struggle is in progress, even if it be a silent one. Science is striking down frontier after frontier of limitation of thought with alarming rapidity: door after door, flies open before its advance to knowledge of it knows not what. Whether it has interest for the so-called occultist I do not know. It should have because it marks so clearly the advancement of the former and the stagnation of the latter.

Add to this the growing interest and research of the younger generation which is captivated by the modern scientific trend and we have more than a hint of the future. Science is the monarch of British thought: occultism is an importation from the East, revealing no attainments to substantiate its many claims and subsisting mainly upon theories of the unknowable which have been spun out for the West.

Therefore if the brain of the West is not equal in formation and subtlety to that of the East and for that reason cannot demonstrate, and has no hope of demonstrating, the unfoldment of spiritual potentialities and powers which are common to so many Eastern seers of the past and presumably of the present; what chance is there that knowledgeable young men of our day will devote time and energy to the intricate and theoretical expositions of Eastern cults which the Western brain is unable to fathom because of its relative density, and carry to a demonstration in a totally unsuitable environment on the one hand, and in the absence of personal guidance from proficients in acknowledged seership on the other?

These are reflections, not criticisms. Discipleship, in the real sense, and as it has been always known in the East, means acceptance of a promising type of student and a period of personal pupilage under the guidance of a master of occultism until a point of demonstrable efficiency and seership is achieved under that guidance.

In Britain, such a condition and possibility are unknown. Of course, it is open to an objector to say, *"How do you know what demonstrations might be taking place in Britain?"* The answer is: if such are taking place and are of exceptional character, as they should be, or else they are of little value to anyone although they may satisfy the private curiosity of the demonstrator, they should be of unique public interest and be applicable to public needs and ends.

What should we think of an astronomer who after years of patient research kept the stars to himself instead of imparting a knowledge of his discoveries for the enlightenment of his fellowmen? And what should we think of an astronomer who spent years of research with instruments of observation known to be totally inadequate for the observations he wanted to make?

This is the point of the argument. With adequate instruments he is equipped fully to make observations and discoveries which add to mankind's knowledge. He has the class of brain requisite for this and he has the right kind of instruments and can use them. The other fellow lacks both and is a nonentity.

If the brain of the occult investigator in Britain is unsuitable for making discoveries similar to those of the brain of the Eastern seer, what can be expected from his years of research in this direction? We live in a time of unprecedented advancement in every branch of science. Our whole lives are being completely revolutionised by it, little as we may realise it. Yet it is implied that we should be content with the flimsy suggestion that some occult revelations are taking place in occult groups known to none but themselves, adding nothing to the world's knowledge and immediate needs, nothing in administering in an unusual way towards alleviating the eternal pain of humanity.

Whether those in the East who are credited with phenomenal powers of the highest seership employ these powers to any useful purpose, to any practical and compassionate use, is not my business. We have no data on this head..., perhaps there is none. But if those who have them hold them hidden secretly for their diversion or prestige and do not recognise the pressing needs of a humanity as it struggles in ignorance towards the grave, they are not to be envied but pitied more than the believers in occult miracles in Britain who lack the requirements of an occult brain.

The British are safest down upon the earth, or speculating, instrumentally, among the stars. But the ambition to emulate Eastern adepts and seers by following the nebulous teachings of the latter in the current textbooks as we know them, will undoubtedly demonstrate the truth of my friend's remark, that the British have not the brain for transcendental flight operations.

16. Impersonality

Reprinted from the Autumn 1961 edition of The London Rosicrucian.

How often we have used the term "impersonality" in connection with studies of the path and have stressed the need for it? Yet, as with many other terms used through habit or custom, I doubt sometimes if we realise the full significance of them.

This term looks innocent enough and carries a dignified air of its own. It seems to denote a mental and spiritual elevation habitual to the person using it and a directive to others of the highest value; but it should not escape close scrutiny, or criticism, just because some occult authorities make so much of it.

In some of the Eastern teachings impersonality is much insisted upon, as the key to high attainment. It no doubt has its suggested value; but I think it has nevertheless done more harm than good to susceptible and accepting students. Few are ready for anything of the kind, and in striving to be what they are not they cross the borderline of commonsense and do violence to their own nature and disposition, with ill results.

It may be well to assume a virtue which we know we lack, but even virtues need a sound foundation of understanding to give them reality and value. To see little men assuming supermanhood and acting accordingly is not a happy spectacle.

Of course, the term is used in devotional manuals and textbooks to indicate a condition of spiritual aloofness or height which must be striven for if certain spiritual objectives are to be reached. We know from our reading what those objectives are. They are as far beyond the reach of average or advanced students, however well informed they may be, as is levitation by an act of will.

Impersonality is literally a transfer of consciousness from the objective plane of normal functioning upon which we are destined to pass our existence as normal human beings, to a level of functioning which practically ignores the existence and claims of the personality. To a few this blotting out of the one and exaltation to the other may appear a very desirable attainment; but to those who may regard it as a necessary goal of their studies and who endeavour by a forceful approach to satisfy the ambitious craving to belong to a spiritual elect before their time, the imperative need to correct their perspective sooner or later confronts them.

Here, if anywhere, one requires sound sense and the ability to assess one's capabilities. Because impersonality has a lofty spiritual value and an atmosphere of unique detachment about it, does not justify a student to straightway sell all he has in order to grasp it.

I suppose there have been more wrecks on the path of those who from one motive or another have attempted to storm the guarded frontiers of evolution and seize the fruits of impersonality than any other. It is a strange thing that students who in daily and professional life reveal the most commendable qualities of reason, adjustments and mental capacity in their affairs, will sometimes risk all, even their sanity, when working on the path, for the sake of outstripping their fellows in evolution.

We have heard of power complexes. This is one of them, in the spiritual order, and a most dangerous one, which can make a man a far lesser man than he was instead of exalting him.

Some of the Eastern teachings are no doubt responsible for this. It is not the fault of the teachings: it is the fault of those who accept them as the only gospel of the truth for this age and literally follow them. But in time the ambitious and misguided student comes to learn that slaying the personality in order to retreat to a heaven upon earth, is not an easy matter.

The occult books glamour him. Those who write them are often far ahead of him in evolution by virtue of a natural gift and privileged circumstances. They exercise a fascination through the bright prospect of super-attainment if life is but made to conform to suggested formulae.

The human being, however, is not a machine to be accelerated at will and geared to a perpetual tension, with no thought of possible reaction within the personality. The accustomed rhythm of the vehicles involved in the process is easily upset and can produce very unpleasant consequences in those who set an unusual pace for themselves.

We may ask, why do some students set an unusual pace for themselves, what is their motive and what do they expect to get from it? No doubt it is largely due to the sense of urgency of attainment which characterises certain teachings. A student is incited to feel that he has no time to lose and that a future of revelations awaits him.

But time is the arch glamouriser. It misleads the student by its own swift progress and sense of immediacy. A life cycle is usually but a brief period of acquiring a right sense of values and the placing correctly of a few building stones for the future. There is really no urgency about it or any specific demand of nature that phenomenal strides should be made within a cycle. The attempt to realise within one cycle that which sound sense knows full well is the province of many, is one of the pitfalls of the path.

Moreover, the motive has often been the ignoble one of a craving for power and prestige. It invariably fails in its purpose, because the Cosmic Powers know the student rather better than he knows them; and if he thinks he can secretly exploit the watchful guardians for his own doubtful purposes, he is doomed to disappointment. In forcing the issue to grasp much he will find that his neglected personality will demand more and in harder terms.

Is a student sure that the attainment of impersonality, in this higher spiritual sense, will actually bring him what he expects from it? It is obvious that he who sets off on a campaign of speed in order to achieve and know so much apparently more important and valuable than he is conscious of, has not rightly estimated the present needs of his personal self; nor has he regarded what kind of mental and psychic disposition is necessary for the quest. Nature is the best guide in this.

It is observable that some individuals who make rapid and singular progress and attain unusual success in their respective spheres, have done so without stress and strain and to a high degree spontaneously. They have had nature with them and therefore covered the stages of their progress with facility and ease. They are within a sphere in which they operate with understanding and control. This is in marked contrast to those who attempt to invade the citadel of unknown forces and conditions which will exact from them far more than nature has given them, which they have not grown into spontaneously and which will demand exceptional adjustments.

The student may recall the much lauded "Satori" of Zen Buddhism, the so-called simplicity and suddenness of its achievement. He may also recall the prolonged term of extreme self-abnegation and discipline of the few proficients, usually Orientals, who eventually possibly experienced it. In the case of the Western student, that unyielding stress and tension have no justification. They are deplorable and harmful; and should he by chance turn his accustomed world of living and action upside down to realise a doubtful ideal, he does so at his peril.

So with he who, under the glamour of textbooks, would depreciate the self he is and somewhat knows, and upon which his whole life activities and contacts depend; turns his back upon the region of sanity wherein he is a helpful and useful being, to grasp a dreamland experience in which he has neither the ability of interpretation or power of control; but rather a confusion of vision and discomposed faculties to face the realities of his personal life.

I sometimes wonder whether a student who labours under this delusion of inevitable speed in development, realises the necessity for a fullness of personality as an imperative condition for dealing adequately with higher vibrational levels of understanding and adjustment.

To be a consciously full and widely informed personality should be his chief guidance here. His rearing should be catholic, his experience mature. He should be able to meet the many claims of life experience from all aspects of his threefold nature, and his contacts with others should bear the impress of this. He should evoke the many meanings of the Karma of his present position and response in daily life, not make strenuous efforts to enter into the hidden highways of spiritual contact and aloofness without the long, arduous and needed preparation which fall to the lot of very few at this point of evolution.

There is much against him and not with him for a safe journey. This is for him, at the right time, when the personality has reached its fullness of experience, giving itself fully in a life of service, and can trust serenely to the Cosmic Powers to reveal to him the kind of responsibility and higher service they have proved him to be capable of.

There is no danger and everything to be gained by trusting those Powers to work in his behalf and for his advancement. To attempt to force the doors of revelation is fraught with danger.

Section 12:

Writings of Unspecified Date

ISSN 0966-33X

Published quarterly by the
English speaking jurisdiction
for Europe and Africa of the
ROSICRUCIAN ORDER, A.M.O.R.C.
P.O. BOX 35
CROWBOROUGH,
EAST SUSSEX TN6 1ZX
ENGLAND

Tel: 01892-653197
Fax: 01892-667432

Official Magazine of the
Rosicrucian Order, AMORC
(Europe and Africa)

Issued free to members as an
incidence of membership

EDITORIAL BOARD

Editor:
Ken Alexander

Assistant Editor:
Jack Belcher

Production:
Trudy Prudden

Statements made in this publication are not the official expressions of the organisation or its officers unless declared to be official communications.

All material in the Rosicrucian Beacon is copyright and may not be reproduced in any form without the prior consent of the publishers and individual contributors.

Changes of address must reach us by the first of the month preceeding publication.

Rosicrucian Beacon
September 1996
Vol 5 No.4

CONTENTS

4   Grand Master's Message
5   A Word of Encouragement - by Raymund Andrea
6   The Flaming Pioneers - by Sri Aurobindo
7   Metaphysics: A Personal Awakening - by Larry Claassen
10 Myths and Legends (Part 1) - by Dany Dalmia
14 The Gems which Fall from my Books - by the Editor
15 What Are We Here For? (part 3) - by H K Challoner
17 Frankenstein - Myth or Prophesy? - by Fr Paul Whinfield
19 An Early Morning Walk - by Fr Larry Kee
20 Readers' Letters
23 Bacon's Open Secret - by J. C. Belcher, C.Eng. FRC
28 We Come to this Sacred Place - by Fr Harold P. Stevens
29 Out of This World - by Divinator
31 The Mind and The Mystery of the Soul - by Rev. J. T. Ferrier
33 Poems: - Night and Day - by Roland Northover
     My Wish for You - by Sr Cecilia Hawkins
     Autumn Scene - by Sr Sheila Chung
34 Mindquest - Your Personal Healing Power - by G Buletza Jr. Ph.D.
37 Interpretation of Truth - by E. Suthers Mitchell, M.A.
38 Life, some days, is just a Galaxy of Troubles - by R. Baker
40 Healing - by Dr. Alec Forbes M.A. DM. FRCP

COVER PAGES

Outer Cover: *The Traveller* - Keith English Collection
Inside Front Cover: *The Cornish Pronaos Mystical Weekend*
Inside Back Cover: *The Traveller* - poem by Jodieanne English

The Rosicrucian Beacon -- September 1996   [3]

Introduction

The first two of these articles were carried by the *Rosicrucian Beacon*[1] but no indication of their initial publication was given. The source of the last two items is also unknown. *A Word To The Neophyte* was found among the papers of the late Ellen Turnbull, while *The Unseen Influences Of Our Rosicrucian Studies* was issued to affiliated bodies of the Rosicrucian Order in June 1983 by the then Grand Master, Robert E Daniels.

1. A Word of Encouragement

Reprinted from the September 1996 issue of the Rosicrucian Beacon. *The source and date of original publication are unknown.*

No matter what point we may have reached in our group or individual studies in the Order, obstacles of one kind or another run unexpectedly across our path. We must accept these with an understanding mind and firm resolve not to be diverted from our objective. Our first duty is just where the immediate attention is demanded. The persistent doing of that which faces us at the moment on our particular path is the key to inner growth. Not to be distracted by untoward events, that is the best exercise in concentration.

Our knowledge of the Path of Karma assures us that every experience has its personal lesson and meaning for us, and those on the inner side of life who control and adjust our karma know just how and where the cross of circumstance must be laid in order to bring forth in us the finest product of development and so free us for greater service. We trust them.

Under the influence of our studies there is so much that can be done and if we are patient the way will be shown how to do it. We must be willing to wait for results to grow naturally and not try to force issues. There are different phases of experiences which are necessary and right for us and our best wisdom is to work quietly through them. Think for a moment. If the nature of the whole Path was one of uniform progress and non-event, how would any depth of wisdom be attained? However, it is far from that and we come to see that it is only through going steadily onward in spite of any or all opposition that we come to a true understanding of ourselves and unfold the best in us.

I know that some aspirants are inclined to reproach themselves because they are unable to do all, from the ideal point of view they feel they should. But even the Masters and Servants of Karmic Law cannot do all they would like to do for us. Every stage of the Path has its own limitations and its Laws which compel obedience. But if we do all that lies directly in our path it is enough. At every stage of it there faces us the challenge to serve.

---

1. Several other pieces in this volume were reprinted in issues of the *Rosicrucian Beacon* between 1993 and 2002.

If we do not accept and comply with it we do not expect to attain to the companionship of great Souls who are the greatest Servants of all.

Others are prone to emphasise the antagonism, the apparent antagonism they feel between their studies and everyday environment. Their increasing psychic sensitivity is responsible for this and is really a sign of advancement. It should not retard their progress but confirm their resolution. One of the difficulties experienced in this gradual raising of their vibrations is they feel less harmoniously attuned with those who still function upon the former lower level.

It is not unreasonable for us to fight such conditions which confront us and which we have precipitated through our own efforts. We must look to ourselves for strength to meet and use any discomfort, disagreements or criticisms which may fall to our lot in our quest, ever remembering that this is the way of advancement. Let us not antagonise minor circumstances but be swift to see the point of right adjustment.

It matters nothing if we are not understood and our attitude regarded as just weakness. Opposition will fall away of itself if we can learn a wise detachment. Some personalities are such that one must mentally fence them off, study them dispassionately and refuse to yield to their vibration. It is identification with other personalities which gives pain but is this not necessary if we are to serve them? Here we face an occult paradox. It is a necessity in our lives of service; but at a certain stage of inward growth we WILL to contact or not, as the occasion demands.

2. Human Identification

Reprinted from the December 1997 issue of the Rosicrucian Beacon. *The source and date of original publication are unknown.*

Those who read my last article [in the September 1997 issue of the Beacon] will have noticed that I wrote "Towards the Ideal," not attaining it.[2] I always use the term ideal with some reluctance because it can often prove to be an elusive one. In referring to the ideal in anything we are contemplating a conception of something in its highest perfection, a standard of perfection, beauty of excellence believed to be capable of realisation or attainment. But we do not need to be reminded that there are enough crosscurrents of thought, impulses and influences which we have to face daily which are sometimes strong and insistent enough to dim the shine of the ideals we enthusiastically set up. This has always been so and always will be while we are in a world so unidealistic in character and purpose.

I know there are some who turn away from this kind of reflection, not because they disbelieve it but because they are afraid of it. But we are not children requiring to

---
2. This article appears in Section 13.

be kept amused in an atmosphere of illusion. We are out to understand the path of life, life as it is here and now, and what life is doing to us. I have often written not simply to express my own views and opinions but because of a certain degree of sensitivity I possess, I know that I am sensing the minds and feelings of others in their daily lives and I know that the problems I see and feel are also theirs. And if any student believes he can make much progress on the inward way and can remain intact and safely enclosed within his own skin and register nothing of what is happening around and within his fellowmen, he is ill-informed indeed. His objective in this quest is not to live merely within the limits of himself, shut up and mentally and spiritually protected to his personal satisfaction, but to be a highly sensitised organism through which the thought, action and suffering of humanity can teach him the truth of mortal existence.

Those who have read Renan's, *Life of Jesus*, may remember that whilst treating the Master as a transcendent example of compassion and love, of wisdom and clairvoyance, and of unimpeachable probity of speech and action, this writer brought him down from a pedestal of isolation and unapproachable divinity to the common level of companionship with men and women, even to the sharing in the emotional and mental interplay of their manifold circumstances. And the problem of some aspirants is, not by any means to descend from a pedestal of divinity, but rather to release from a relative intellectual isolation and fixity self-constituted barriers which prohibit a sympathetic sharing in aspects of human life, which are actually awaiting their participation in them.

It is, therefore, not a faraway ideal life which should claim our attention, but something far more humble and necessary, a forgetting of personal importance, whether of intellectual or spiritual values, and giving unobstructed permission, within reason, to the interplay of life upon all levels in human units. The aim is a prompt recognition of, and reaction to, the meaning and need of the multifarious life which will release them and ourselves from the bondage of self and give full expression to the soul.

Our objective should not be height, but light, expressing the light we have, not hiding it. Self-development is not the keynote now, but expression of self. Aspiration on the path should mean the generation of love force which can lighten the darkness of many a life, known and unknown to us, by its beauty and influence in radiation, its potency and attractiveness. And all the while we seek the presence of a Master hand: for we are yet unborn. There are shadows upon us as surely as upon the veriest tyro, the only difference being that we recognise them and know the cause. This really constitutes the tension of our novitiate. We have knowledge of the cause and have not yet overcome its inhibiting effects. The tension is greater in the mature life because the habit arising from ability and experience to definitely lay hold of causes and shift them at will is strong in us.

But this ability loses some of its effectiveness in Chapter aspiration and achievement because we wait for each other. Some are before, some behind, a given stage but it is scarcely within our power to determine which. That should eliminate the possibility of self-satisfaction. The most brilliant may be last and the least so first. I have known the self-forgetting love of an aspirant humiliate the brilliancy of his teacher; and the preceptor has learned a pregnant lesson from his pupil. It is lessons of this nature that can continually break in upon a group of aspirants. Sometimes they break in so unexpectedly and so plainly falsify our past and rooted values, that we are constantly faced with alternatives which cannot be ignored. The imposition of them comes through personalities and circumstances, but the lessons themselves arise from the meeting point within the soul and personality, the old rhythm and the new. It is as if a hand were laid softly but firmly upon the heart in unmistakable and compulsive guidance. Have you realised that the autobiography of a Chapter might prove far more interesting and revealing than that of an individual?

3. A Word to the Neophyte

The source and date of original publication are unknown.

I know from experience what the first thought of many a neophyte or aspirant entering a lodge of our Order is, what he or she hopes to get from it in the way of knowledge or inspiration. This may naturally be the first thought, but others should accompany it.

Obviously the aspirant enters the lodge in the hope of increasing knowledge and sharing in the inspirational life within it. That is one aspect of group cooperation, necessary and legitimate.

But there is another aspect of group contact which is no less important. What can the aspirant bring in to the group? He does not come in as a mental and emotional nonentity seeking initiation into emotion and thought like an infant entering the first classroom. He comes in as a responsible individual of some development, at least along the usual educational lines, with the purpose of adding to this general culture, a psychological and mystical understanding which will enable him to attain a dignity and status on the path of evolution and power of accomplishment in life far in advance of merely academic training. But he cannot receive this new understanding unless he brings a certain preparedness of mind and heart with him.

What the entrant does often overlook is the fact that, as surely as the group vibration will influence him, so will his individual vibration influence the group. No one can ally himself with an ordinary group of thinking people without this interplay of forces, one upon the other. But to ally oneself with a mystical and psychic group of progressive minds without fully appreciating this fact of the interaction of individual and group vibrational influence, is to invite disillusionment, disappointment and trouble.

He must understand that the group that he enters has a strong and stable vibration of its own as the result of concerted study and meditation, like a light radiating from a focal centre; and the effect of that radiation upon the entrant may be inspiring or disturbing..., contingent upon his preparedness to receive, interpret and assimilate it or not.

If there is not a certain preparedness in the entrant of an open mind and attitude of tolerance in accepting and reflecting upon the new truths and unusual practices given in the group until he can make them entirely his own and so fuse his interest and purpose with that of the group, then we are likely to see in no long time the impatient critic, the skeptical interrogator, the assertor of his own accumulated knowledge as the only sure criterion of judgement.

This is not a stretch of the imagination. It has happened again and again among neophytes entering upon lodge work. It is not easy for them to accept that warning, which is also a severe test: *"Stand ready to abandon all thou hast learned!"*

I do not say that the entrant has to face so complete a test of character and selflessness at the outset; there is time for that later on. But if he has a sincere desire not only to profit of the group he enters, but to be a helpful force and influence to others in it, he must show that stability of character and willingness to be instructed which the above warning plainly demands.

He must remember that the group exists to serve him: that those who supervise it have pledged themselves to a life of service and therefore will not fail him. Is it then too much to ask that the neophyte should recognise this and make an honest endeavour to comply with the few simple rules of conduct and procedure which this first crossing of a threshold to larger life and concerted action impose upon him?

4. The Unseen Influences of our Rosicrucian Studies

Reissued by Grand Master Robert E Daniels *in his* Monthly Message *for June 1983. The source and date of original publication are unknown.*

What do we envisage for the young members attending this or other affiliated bodies? A life of definite usefulness under the Rosicrucian guidance.

We can regard them as a group of eager recruits willing to qualify under a self-imposed discipline for positions of authority as real servers. For we may be assured that the hierarchy of Masters is not standing still. Its entire personnel is alert and vitally active, well aware of and directly interested in all aspirants who are seeking and following the path in any of its many stages. They are all within the vision of the hierarchy and will receive help and guidance if they demand it and resolve through meditation and service to attune their lives to the rhythm and aims of the hierarchy.

It is an illusion if they think that their faithful and humble efforts, at whatever stage they may be, can count for little because the higher reaches of the Path appear far beyond them. The humblest aspirant, because of his life and service, may be of exceptional promise in the eyes of the hierarchy, and a few years of special effort will bring him an enlarged consciousness and an inner assurance of recognition. Like nature, the revelations of the Path are many and unpredictable. They come, not when actually seeking them, but when the mind and heart are made ready for them.

This is my word of encouragement for the young aspirant. The world outside will give him no such encouragement. It will leave him to his own dreams and aspirations, and it is up to him to take speedy means to materialise them under the watchful care of those ready to help him.

And what of ourselves, the older members and officers, who serve in their various capacities in the work of the group? I think of them with admiration and deep appreciation because of the labours and responsibilities they accept so willingly and so ably discharge. But what urges and sustains them in this task? Fundamentally, and deep within, they sense and know the ever-present sorrow and suffering of humanity. That is the keynote to all their labours.

Among humanity there is a prevailing mental chaos, a reaching out for it knows not what; a stumbling, a bewilderment from the onslaught of opinion, towards an unknown goal of mental achievement. We are aware of this because we have to live with it. So much the harder is the task. It calls for courage, perseverance and untiring application; and the influence of our hierarchal contact alone sustains and guides us. In a word, we have to make our way within a kind of circumscribed circle of upward aspiration. We cannot get much help from outside it. We have to look upward and draw more and more upon the inspiration of the hierarchy and its readiness to respond to us.

Nor must we forget that we believe in the cooperation of those who have gone before us. They left their work here unfinished, and only to see more clearly beyond the veil and to cooperate more understandingly and helpfully in the greater things they wished to do and to which we are dedicated. It would be a sorry thought to think that when the book of knowledge was closed for them here, it would not be opened for them to continue their advancement with the greater souls in the Cosmic to whom they belong. They have made contacts which we, within our present limitations, are unable to make, or only at times quite unknowingly. We know that at certain stages of the Path we have to travel alone; but that aloneness is an incident of our sojourn here.

There is no aloneness on the other side. We work in closer association than is possible here; and as we each seek here to lift some of the burden of life from human hearts, so shall we do it there collectively and more effectively. It is a chastening and inspiring thought that the doubts and illusions which hinder and perplex us will fall away beyond the veil and we shall know, with our departed brothers, what the Hierarchal Beings have done for us through all the vicissitudes of life. We must hold on to that thought, and most when life seems to close down upon us in its many changing moods and challenges our faith in unseen help and direction.

Unseen influences are ever with us, whether waking or sleeping; in moments of abstraction we are well aware of them; but to interpret the nature and significance of them calls for a degree of intuitional sensitivity which has to be cultured for. Yet we have gone a good way towards this objective in our studies and especially in our practice. We have reached a stage when our combined concentrated thought affects very strongly those we seek to help in difficulty or illness.

Here we touch the very heart of the Rosicrucian life. The burden of sorrow often descends upon us through this very act of alleviating the distress of other souls. You may remember the scripture which refers to the disciple's lifting a little of the heavy karma of the world. That lifting means that we are actually taking upon ourselves something of the burden of souls who await deliverance each in its own way; and by reason of our development and willingness to see and accept this, we are made the instruments of blessing and redemption, through our deliberate effort, but often enough quite unknown to us.

You will not consider these reflections as of a too introspective character. They are of the very nature of our studies and arise naturally from the habit we have cultivated of feeling and seeing below the surface of life and of applying our findings to the problems which beset ourselves and others. We do not believe with some that we have done well and all that is needed if we merely read or listen to teachings of the Path. They have to be transfused into the blood of the heart and issue forth as the realised truth of life. Our studies teach us to interrogate life in all its aspects: then we reverse the process and look inward in silent contemplation and receive the deeper truths which only await recognition.

We shall come to realise more and more the effect of the spiral process of development which operates in our lives. This takes place very much unknown to us as we pass on through the years. The foundation having been truly laid, the interrogation of life under the guidance of our studies; and the inward contemplation to receive the unfolding truth of them, coupled with the silent passage of time, reveal the changes wrought by our spiral development most clearly in the consciousness that we have outgrown the former more limited selfhood, have a new scale of values, and an assured and confident approach towards all that life decrees for us.

The decrees of life bring surprise and change, so different from what we expected, so often opposed to so much we hoped for and felt sure of. Yet it is much if we are able to meet all eventualities with insight and composure, for that is perhaps the surest sign of real inner advancement.

Our life in the affiliated body has brought us a long way from the early years of self-development of the aspirant to the expanded outlook of mature consciousness, where the true spirit of self-sacrifice asserts its right over us. We must not regret or refuse this, no matter what it demands from us, or what it elects to do with us.

We may not be known of men in the busy life of the world, but if the sacrificial spirit reigns in our heart, every step of the way is foreseen and known on the inner side, and nothing can prevail against it.

Section 13:

Francis Bacon Chapter Bulletin (1963 - 1973)

Francis Bacon Chapter

LONDON ENGLAND

Bulletin

XXII Year

AMORC

WINTER
JAN. 1970

In sending you this Dove-grey cover, may it
speak to you in accents tender of that emotion
symbolized by this beautiful bird

Section 13 - Francis Bacon Chapter Bulletin (1963 - 1973)

Introduction

After *The London Rosicrucian* (see Section 11) the *Francis Bacon Chapter* published a quarterly bulletin which also carried specially prepared pieces by Raymund Andrea. These are his last known writings, the latest of which – from two years before his passing…, is separated from his earliest known piece, *The Occult Life*, by 54 years.

1. Seeking Ourselves

Reprinted from the November 1963 edition of the Francis Bacon Chapter Bulletin.

When Heraclitus said, *"I sought for myself,"* he pronounced one of the most pregnant of maxims and, as far as the mystic is concerned, a directive for all time. For no student of the path is fully alive to the meaning of his quest until he comes to a decision to seek for himself.

It does not matter what teachings are put into his hands, or what teachers he may have had, he will find himself eventually faced with precisely this same injunction of the Greek philosopher of 500 BC.

It is astonishing to think how much the ancients gave us of the inward truth of life and self, and how little generation after generation seems to have profited of it. I suppose it is because they wrote so long ago, that the very ancientness of their teaching would seem to have little application for the present day, hypnotised as it is by the discoveries and expediencies of science over the whole field of exoteric life.

For ourselves, we regard those early pioneers of thought with reverence. And those who have reached a certain stage in our studies know that they proceed alone from that point. Not that further teaching is withheld from them and unseen help, but that an aspirant has to turn to himself in order to implement the instruction he has received; and he comes to realise what it means to seek within himself the way to the Master.

For there are definite stages of the path at which the aspirant must find his own way. Real inner development does not consist in merely adding knowledge to knowledge from sources of instruction. It comes from a deep and sincere understanding and application of what is given, to life and action in the world. He must deliberately test himself out in life and circumstance, and learn lessons which can be learned in no other way.

The same principle applies in any art or science. A time comes when the student has to turn back from the textbooks of accumulated facts and prove their value in his own life through meditation and experimentation.

Heraclitus enunciates the same truth in his own way when he says: *"Travel over every road, we cannot discover the frontiers of the soul…, it has so deep a logos."* The *"frontiers of the soul"* are not in the diversities of instruction, but within; and the purpose of instruction is to enlighten and strengthen us sufficiently to research inwardly to the frontiers of the inner self, to endeavour to know our individual mission in life, and pledge ourselves to a devoted service.

I know this appears to some very much merely as a hopeful ideal within the world picture which confronts us today. But we cannot ignore it if we mean to move onward and upward. I know too, that to hold and nurture this ideal against so much opposition which would deflect us from it brings us to trial in many ways and sometimes makes the path harder. But all advancement has its price, and this is a peculiarly keen and personal one.

Yet there is a reward for every spiral of the way trodden with steadfast purpose and compassion. For every aspirant each spiral has a different history and individual karma which, if accepted in the silence and soul of prayer, brings deeper and deeper realisation that we draw nearer and nearer to the world of the Master.

Seeking oneself in the truest sense means entering more and more into a life of selflessness, a loosening of bonds that hold us back, and to achieve that, it is wonderful indeed if we can surrender to the fire on the secret altar of the heart.

2. Towards the Ideal

Reprinted from the September 1997 issue of the Rosicrucian Beacon *which gave the original publication as a* Francis Bacon Chapter Bulletin *from 1965.*

It should be possible to regard a Chapter, in its supervising and working capacity, as an active centre comprised of high tension units radiating an example worthy of imitation by members sympathetically drawn to and needing the expressive quality of those units. A high tension unit inevitably draws others to its sphere and directly that power begins to operate the unit recognises and accepts a responsibility to those unseen Forces which have been silently instrumental in shaping its destiny to specific ends.

In some instances, in spite of our profession and allegiance, this idea of destiny is not accepted with much grace. I think it quite consistent with a good deal of esoteric development that the very circumstances which have brought about a desirable consummation should have been strongly resented. I have resented many; but that fact has never acted as a deterrent to continuous aspiration and progress. On the contrary, the result has been that, underlying all the strong emotion of seeming injustice and the phase of evolution not fully understood, there has evolved an immovable faith in, and affection for, the Master guidance which so patiently awaits its time. That attitude I believe to be a necessary one and the units in an official group who have it will possess a vibratory quality which is bound to make its presence felt for good.

Individual as these official units are, operating within a Chapter, yet etherically they should be firmly united and be one in conscious purpose. What should be the constituent elements of that alert and intentional and mutual assimilation? Perhaps, ideally put: a mature knowledge of personality, both quiescent and active; a clear idea of its present limitations which act as hindrances to more extended service; a ready ability of adaptation to others in assessing their personal needs and swift and positive ministration to those needs from an intuitional evolutionary standpoint; a persistent personality aspiration to quickly measure up to the vibration and knowledge resulting from study and meditation. These main elements, which yet comprise many lesser ones, will not characterise all the units in equal measure but they should be recognised as essential for the far reaches of the Rosicrucian path and be in process of perfecting.

Now, the quality of the attractive force of the official life of a chapter will be determined by the strength and skilful use of these elements: and the basic tone of this quality I denote as sincerity and all that the word implies. Without that, little real good can be accomplished. In our chapter I know that we have it.

But to gauge the effect and value of a Chapter in action, it is necessary to regard keenly and sympathetically the effect of the unit in action. In one sense we cannot expect a Chapter to effect what the individual unit cannot. I grant that the collective force may do in some respects what the unit alone is powerless to do; but for that collective force to be at full potency demands its degree of full potency in every official unit. That is what the unit has to work for. I had almost said, the unit must aim at carrying the potency of the chapter in itself at will.

These points will no doubt cause reflection, possibly some dissent. But it will be understood that I am referring here not to a chapter in assembly but to the active heart centre of the Chapter, to the body of selected officers who study with all seriousness the work to which they have dedicated themselves, who can be relied upon not to abuse their authority and whose aim is to penetrate more deeply into the mystical life of insight as set forth in our (Rosicrucian) teaching.

I know it is easier to write these things than to demonstrate them as we would wish, because, whether we admit it or not, life presses upon us from many sides, demanding time, attention and care. We cannot ignore them. We have to meet them. Indeed, they often confront us with opposing aspects whose very purpose seems to threaten our resolution and persistence. Yet, let it be so. The spiritual fire of the heart was not implanted within us for nothing. It is equal to emergencies and will not fail when we petition for its help and guidance.

3. Loneliness

Reprinted from the July, August and September 1965 edition of the Francis Bacon Chapter Bulletin. *Also published in* "Waiting For The Master" *by* Francis Bacon Lodge *(1982).*

It is stated in one of our higher grades that a time comes when each seeker who travels the path must travel alone. This is undoubtedly true: but there are many kinds of loneliness. It does not mean isolation from others, whether our friends or family; but that, dependent upon the sincerity and strength of demand of the student, the time does come when he and his interior development are solitary companions. But a very common phase of his loneliness does arise within the sphere of family relationships.

For instance, as the student pursues his studies and is intent upon progress, the new knowledge he acquires soon brings him at cross-purposes with the orthodox views of others and sometimes throws him out of sympathy with family and friends. He must assure himself that this parting of the ways cannot be evaded. How can he take a new road and still travel upon the old one? A live student in search of knowledge for the service of man will soon settle this question for himself. He finds that in his immediate circle he is alone in this quest and therefore must take the consequences and not mind being considered an innovator or something worse.

Progress means that he cannot stay where he was; and to move on to new ground means change within and without. I am thinking now not so much of those who fully understand, for life will have already taught them this, but of those who are hesitating at the parting of the ways. I know it is a hard choice, between the personality and the soul. But those who are in a sense left behind often come to see and realise, though they cannot understand, that the force of good is operative in the one engaged in the quest and should not be thwarted. It is well if that kind of adjustment can be made. The world and all it stands for likes you to go its way: it does not like higher and steeper roads, but smooth and well-worn ones. And if you go against its wishes it will leave you alone.

But the quotation above refers most definitely to inner and higher ascension. There are other phases of it, but from whatever cause it comes it should not deter us. We should deal with it rather wilfully, as we have to deal with obstacles in temperament and hindrances of character. We do not succumb before these. We know that as we approach doggedly step by step higher potencies on the path, these will pass away or cease to trouble us. This is exactly what our individual studies should do, free us more and more for perfected action.

Yet here arises the very cause which often affects our relationships and makes us appear different in the eyes of others: the tendency of the personality to feel less assertive as the inner life increases in volume. You remember the scripture: *The power of the disciple is such as to make him appear as nothing in the eyes of men.*

We know what it means; but it is a hard saying for a novice to swallow, and a good deal harder for those connected with him. But there it is. The truth is like that: it runs contrary to illusion and compels the student along a new road. The ordinary worldly assertiveness of the personality passes away almost imperceptibly to the student himself: for if he stands back with a deeper understanding where others rush forward with much less, there is his departure from an accepted standard and a certain phase of loneliness or isolation follows.

Is the student strong enough, well informed enough, reflective enough, to regard phases of loneliness arising from changes in himself with insight and placidity? Because if he cannot adjust himself to these periods of individual evolution, peculiar to himself, it is safe to say he will not progress very quickly on a new road. For there, it is the personal force and initiative of the student, in his own individual life, which means everything, whatever the world has to say about it. Some of us know full well, that every stage of the path hitherto has been a cold-blooded tenacity in the face of factors which have daunted many. We were early convinced that loneliness played a good part in it; and it will play a part in your journey, the sooner the more deadly in earnest you are.

The Bible can teach us more profoundly upon this subject than any other writing, if we are ready for it. There is a solitary verse which ever echoes in my memory. It is the voice of the Master, saying: *"Whom shall I send, and who will go for us?"* Then said I: *"Here am I; send me."*

There you have the immediate response of the disciple who had travelled the path of loneliness or he could never have had the courage and initiative to make the response to a high call and undertake so momentous a mission. He had found his readiness by going up into the mountain, to pray, alone. It is that praying alone, the periodical reverent meditation, not on the mountain top out there, but within himself at the high peak of spiritual light and inspiration, where loneliness will lose itself and vanish in the presence of Divine companionship.

4. Mind Quest and Soul Vision

Reprinted from the October, November and December 1965 edition of the Francis Bacon Chapter Bulletin.

As a contrast to our habit of considering what we shall write tomorrow, it is interesting to look back sometimes and note what we wrote yesterday. I have been doing that and noting what I wrote many years ago on the subject of service.

I recalled a point of importance: that for a long time before, shall I say, I served on the path, I was more interested about my own progress and the possibility of contacting Masters upon it. But entering upon the active work of the Order, the first and necessary injunction I received was, to be a servant. On first sight that did not appear to be a very inviting proposition; but in fact, it is the key to all subsequent and greater progress you will make on the path of attainment. So many things appear more attractive than this and far more rewarding now. They appear to be; but on the path time will shatter that illusion.

Today this illusion is more dominant than in the past because, in spite of the growth of general knowledge on every subject, life is far more superficial. True, there is an aggressive intensity of effort over the whole field of life, but for self, except for a certain growth of humaneness discernible in it. The educational processes in vogue today, in school, university and group, are a constant stimulus to the mental life; and while half of those who feel and react in the mass to some degree to it, they do not know where they are going or what they can do. In a word, they really need re-education. And most of the others have nothing but a worldly aim and feel that the end of life is to grasp and hold, under a violent ambition to overtake and dominate.

Well, they are right for as far as they can see, but with that type of mentality the path would only prove a dead end to them. It would prove more disappointing than keeping to the road they are on, because that road ever and only can promise certain doubtful rewards of the passing moment. The other is absolutely opposed to it. I know that some have tried to grasp the rewards of both at the same time, but they have failed and are forgotten. The forgetting is not a tragedy, but there is regret that a capable service in their hands could have been a blessing to others and done honour to themselves.

Those who have gone a long way with us in the work are reminded in it that the time comes when they should give practical advice to others less advanced than themselves, even to the instruction of classes of students, and so make their knowledge definitely useful; not to continue amassing knowledge and instruction merely for personal use, but to make their influence effective in other lives. That means again, cultivating the habit of wise self-expression. We do express ourselves and well enough upon the ordinary levels of life, about our educational prospects and our social achievements.

I am generalising, because in the Order we know we are there for purposes far beyond the ordinary and the horizon of the average. We are but a small minority, it is true, but it should count. The majority we can never hope to impress; and, I admit, you cannot express yourself freely even when you want to.

But if the few are with us rather than the many, we should be all the more ready to answer the enquiry of young men of university and school who find nothing in the church or anywhere else to which they can safely anchor and look with some promise for the cultivation and exercise of the innate powers of the soul, so easily submerged and neglected amid the perplexing and demoralising influences of modern life. Neither school nor university can do that for them. Their mental quest is one of facts and many fancies. The soul is out of bounds.

I recently talked with one of these brilliant young men from the university, engaged upon various kinds of research, a man of degrees and expectation. He had medicine, hypnotism, psychology and psychiatry, and an imposing framework of sciences to his credit; but they had failed him. Life had come down upon him and he was feeling the burden of it. He came to me for "direction," a term I told him I much disliked, for obvious reasons, so he qualified it with "hints."

He had never studied the massive psychology of [William] James, but the latter's study of religious and mystical experiences had much interested him. Now there was the turn of the tide; so we rose above the abyss of manifold theories and speculations and talked of the soul.

This is the kind of service we are advocating here. It must get down to the man himself and not be entranced and put off with the muster of theories and speculations, however pretentious or formidable they may appear, and which dazzle and frustrate him. These are infinite and are applauded everywhere. But how often do you hear a word of wisdom concerning the soul of man?

5. The Critical Decision

Reprinted from the January, February and March 1966 edition of the Francis Bacon Chapter Bulletin. *Also published in* "Waiting For The Master" *by Francis Bacon Lodge (1982).*

I have sometimes observed in a student a particular problem which causes him much self-questioning. The increasing interest in his studies, demanding daily periods of experiment and meditation, means an increasing demand upon his time and leisure, in addition to claims upon time and attention of a professional, business or personal nature. There is a strong call in the mental life to excel in various departments of activity, very possibly because in the far past he has excelled and played a master part in them; and he fears to be disloyal to the mind and its law of evolution in neglecting any opportunity of continuing those earlier activities. His problem is what should be pursued and what should be renounced. There are so many things he feels he could be and do did circumstances permit. It is not merely a matter of worldly ambition: it is rather the 'flower of the mind,' from the past, comes back to him under the impetus of his higher training. It comes back, seeking a more perfected expression.

This is no child's problem to certain individuals. It is a matter for wise decision; for there is a keen consciousness that many things one could do, for which the ripe faculty exists, have to take a subordinate place in the student's life if the higher stages of the path are to be taken.

The conflict between what one would do and can do is a common one, and the advancing student feels this most keenly. It often, but not always, arises in having to make a decisive choice between the mental and the mystical; but if the mystical life has been studied and understood and its value and influence deeply experienced, the choice should not be a difficult one to make. And for this reason: in the latter study the aim and interest are constantly shifting their ground from a consideration chiefly for himself and a consideration of his value and influence in other lives. If this is not so it should be so. Now some of the avenues of activity one would develop, it is fully recognised, would give satisfaction and happiness to himself, not to others. But a serious student on the path should feel the necessity in his advance to reverse that, in that he comes more and more to feel that his life is no longer a matter for his own personal satisfaction but for raising the level of thought and aspiration in other lives.

The mystical life is not one for the execution of mental gymnastics, but for a deepening of the life of the heart and all that means, in meeting increasingly the needs of burdened hearts and anxious minds, seeking liberation from self. It may take some time to come to that decision, but I have found that those who have had much contact with seekers sincerely trying to find the way to a higher cultural level soon arrive at the decision that, for them, whatever the voices of lesser souls may suggest, the decision is willingly and finally made.

There is such a thing as renunciation on the mystical path and, while this does not call for suppressing or ignoring the insistent memories of past attainments which would reassert themselves and add beauty and depth to the personal life, nevertheless the devotion of the mystic is a precious thing and his possible achievements in the present brief cycle were never more needed and should decide the issue for him. I have known of many who have made that decision. I have never known any who regretted it.

On the question of dedication and devotion I have a case in mind bearing directly upon it. It is from a rather different approach than the above, but stresses a point worthy of reflection. It concerned the pupil of a Master, not haunted by past ambitious memories of achievements seeking to reassert themselves and therefore conflicting with his allegiance to the Master; but a pupil lamenting the fact that the discharge of so many common duties of life held him back from complete absorption in the Master life. The gentle admonition and encouragement of the Master was this:

> "What better cause for reward, what better discipline, than the daily and hourly performance of duty! The man or woman who is placed by Karma in the midst of small, plain duties and sacrifices and loving kindnesses, will, through these faithfully fulfilled, rise to the larger measure of duty, sacrifice and charity to all humanity. Be not discouraged that your practices fall below your aspirations."

6. The Word of the Prophet

Reprinted from the April, May and June 1967 edition of the Francis Bacon Chapter Bulletin.

The Koran, referring to those who believe not the word of the prophet, says:

> "But most of them have no understanding. This present life is nothing but a diversion and a sport: surely, the Last Abode is life, did they but know."

This is one of those ominous and pathetic contrasts to be met with in all spiritual writings. They are so personal and penetrating that no one can fail to note them, however quickly he may pass them by. They are passed by in our time as in the day of Mohammed, because they are revolutionary, and neither the ignorant nor the intellectually arrogant can stand them. How far the brave and knowing ones would admit that life is but a diversion and a sport, we do not know. We only know that they think and act as if it were.

We may interpret the "Last Abode" in other terms than the Koran, but we can be sure that the "Life" referred to will present to us far other problems than this one and lessons of a kind not to be passed by or evaded. If it were not so, I fail to see the value of the instruction and discipline and the many self-sacrifices to which so many deliberately dedicate themselves, with little prospect of present recognition or reward.

But this attitude to life, and we see plenty of it around us, is nothing new. Every revealer and every revelation, before and after Mohammed, has had to face the same crass criticism, the same superficial disbelief. They have always been a prominent feature of the evolutionary pattern, and no prophet would quite realise the nature and value of his mission without them.

The Koran opens with a stern warning of the chastisement of God; and a newcomer to the scripture may be struck by the reiterated insistence of the prophet on its inescapability. Although every chapter is introduced, *"In the name of God, the Merciful, the Compassionate,"* this note of chastisement, in various forms, persists throughout his prophecy and gives a kind of dramatic emphasis to the vivid pictures of rewards and punishments, with many stories from the Bible and the Apocrypha.

It is said that the prophet comes when he is needed. I think he also comes before his time. For while the religious communities in the West argue fervently their respective views, even to the union of the English and Romish churches, Mohammed was pursuing his ideal of uniting the three chief religions in his country..., Judaism, Christianity and Heathenism..., before A.D. 632, the date of his death.

But the word of another Christ or Mohammed, preaching peace or a sword, whatever the promised good, unless it were a materialistic one, would raise the fire in our humanity ill-disposed to accept it. Humans still would not understand. If diversion and sport did not feature mainly in their way of life, never would spiritual vision have any meaning for them, or even a modified higher culture which would lead to it.

7. Master and Members

Reprinted from the July, August and September 1967 edition of the Francis Bacon Chapter Bulletin.

The office of Master in a Chapter carries with it a particular responsibility; I had almost said a burden. He is chosen for this office because of approved past good service in the Chapter and a strong desire to extend the values of it in the lives of those who attend it.

But it seems sometimes to me that in some cases the members of a Chapter are inclined to place the main weight for its progress upon the Master. They turn the focus of attention mainly upon him, instead of largely upon themselves.

This was put to me recently by the Master of a Chapter who felt that perhaps he himself, through being unduly ambitious for the Chapter's progress and anxious to evoke more interest and enthusiasm from the Members, was expecting too much from them. I did not think so. It is right that the Master should be ambitious for the Chapter's progress and to inspire the members with an enthusiasm for it.

Now, a point to consider might be that the Master is not a miracle worker: he cannot raise the Members at a word beyond their existing selves, nor can he make them think and feel in precisely the way he does. He can do much to inspire and hearten them in their daily lives, if he is a knowledgeable man with a full sense of the importance of his office.

This suggests a very important point for further consideration; to what extent is the Master a knowledgeable man? Because to be of real value to those looking to him for guidance in this work, he needs definite qualifications empowering him to this end. Authority does not need to talk down to others, but it does mean ability to intellectually meet them and commune with them on the level of their own approach to him. The higher the level of approach the stronger the test and the better for him.

Is it then too much to ask Members, on their part, to read widely and think deeply about their studies, so as to interrogate wisely and endeavour to express themselves understandingly to and with their Fellow Members; and so to enjoy to the full the kind of communion we expect to find in those who are seeking together light on the path of life? For this is the goal which invites all of us.

8. The Potency of the Word

Reprinted from the October, November and December 1967, and the January, February and March 1968 editions of the Francis Bacon Chapter Bulletin.

The *Bhagavad Gita* will be well-known to many students of the mystical life. It has been called *"the Study of adepts."* This might well be so, for discipleship and adeptship are the burden of it. And for the disciple, it is a classic which, together with the *Dhamma Pada* and *Light On The Path*, has a devotional direction on the path which is unsurpassed.

The direct and luminous teaching of the Gita revolves around the perplexed and aspiring character of Arjuna. And remembering that, for many of us, much of our lives has been deeply affected by the prevailing atmosphere, near or far, of problems arising from the stupidities of war and threatenings of war, the Gita strikes home to the very heart of the facts concerning the thought and action of the aspirant to peace and compassion.

What is so impressive about this scripture in which Krishna imparts the rarest teaching to the disciple, is the magical effect it had upon Arjuna; for at the close of its 18 discourses the latter is a completely changed man, who can say: *"Destroyed is my delusion. I have gained knowledge through thy grace, O immutable one. I am firm, my doubts have fled away."*

There is a quality of unusual strength in the character of Arjuna: his mental alertness. I note it because it is the characteristic mark of a real aspirant. And on this path he must be clear-minded and observant, refusing to act with half closed eyes and from partial information; so that the judicious exercise of a right curiosity born of the quality of alertness is indispensable for progress. In Arjuna we have a disciple ready to interrogate the truth, subject every statement to a close scrutiny, and requiring it to satisfy fully reason and intuition.

It is interesting to note the compelling influence of the virile wisdom of Krishna upon his disciple. It acts as an awakener, not an anesthetic. He realises at once that the theory he has been resting upon is inadequate for his purpose. He seeks a righteous demonstration in his own life: how to reconcile action with contemplation. He has been given knowledge of the path to peace by the way of concentration and self-mastery and a renunciation of attachments. How then could he engage in violent action which lay right in his path and withal follow this science of peace?

This is the problem which confronts, in various ways, every disciple: the opposites on the path. Inner peace is only to be found on the path of duty. Those who study the Gita and other Eastern scriptures often enough find themselves face to face with this problem of the opposites.

The contemplative and reposeful life of the mystic has a powerful fascination for them, especially today when practically the whole of life is set against it. I regard this as one of the most disturbing phases of the path. Contemplation comes to be considered the main thing, the one requirement for the attainment of peace and stability; but the voice of the world denies it, ridicules the very idea of it, acts contrary to it, and threatens again and again through its influence to throw the aspirant's life into confusion.

To meet successfully the exigencies of ordinary everyday life, a certain tone or quality is necessary in the aspirant. This quality has to be raised to a far greater strength and capacity for attaining the mystic path. It is the new and unexpected that test us severely in daily life, yet every such occasion may prove one of valuable self-discovery, if keen introspection follows the circumstance.

It was just here that Arjuna initially failed. The veil was rent suddenly and the revelation of it stunned him. He had not touched deeply enough the essence of life. Concentration, self mastery and renunciation had only done half their work.

The immediate result was, that the self-revealing wisdom of Krishna loosened his hold of the centre within and brought him instantly to the surface of the personality life.

You will remember that I mentioned his mental alertness, his readiness for instruction. That alone saved him. His momentary surprise passes and he challenges the omniscience of the Great Master himself with the demand: *"Tell me with certainty the one way."* Nor did the Sage resent the disciple's challenge. It assured him of the strength and intensity of his aspiration and purpose.

Perhaps nowhere in life, in order to attain a complete success, is a longer and more careful preparation essential as that to meet the test which came to Arjuna. It is so manifestly different from the struggle in the outside world. Here within, we take our quick life into our own hands and, in full consciousness and with deliberate purpose, pass it through the furnace kindled by our own aspiration.

And the secret of success in it is to kindle this fire so powerfully that before the trial comes the whole personality shall be permeated with its intensity, that the preparation shall be so true, intense and vital, so fashioned after the Master's own heart, that we pass over to the new condition as naturally and joyfully as the blossom suddenly expands into maturity.

9. Mystical Neophytism

Reprinted from the April-June 1968 through to July-September 1969 editions of the Francis Bacon Chapter Bulletin.

Entering upon the mystical studies of our work means to a neophyte a new departure in life. He sometimes regards it as just another interest, a mental experiment, like many others he has experienced; but he soon finds that he cannot simply fall into line and follow the beaten track he knows. He has to strike out for himself and sometimes against adverse currents. He cannot make headway by leaning upon the past: he must cultivate a present strength of his own. He must have courage and initiative to use confidently that which is offered him.

The first discovery he makes is, that the studies initiate him into a very different world of thinking from the one he is familiar with; that he needs humility and patience to recognise and accept this fact. He has to accept a curriculum of study and meditation which turns his attention inward upon himself, his constitution, and his possibilities as a spiritual and psychic being; and much of this proceeds along avenues of thought very much opposed in principle and promise to that he is accustomed to.

The firmer his adherence to a worldly standard of knowledge and achievement, the greater the difficulty will he experience in adjusting to the new scale of values with which the mystical life confronts him.

It is well to remember that the mystical life, no matter what the way of approach to it may be, offers the only hope of advancing beyond accepted standards of thought and action, even those of the latest scientific genius, unless he consciously concerns himself with the soul factors, latent because unrecognised, in the background of his activities. There does await him a new world of thought, emotion and action, but its existence has to be believed in and striven for over a long period.

Through conscious soul training he will raise his activities into a new dimension. Literature, art and science will reveal to a deeper perception new meanings and relationships. Whatever he has and prizes deeply can be recreated and become a thing of greater beauty and value in the light of the soul. Nothing of past value is lost: much is added to it. What he has striven for through the years need not be renounced. The only change that faces him will be, that all his acquirements on the plane of mind will be rightly appraised and its power of service and usefulness increased through a comprehension of the laws of higher evolution.

The neophyte will realise that creations of art and discoveries of science originate in the minds of exceptional men and are the offspring of inspiration and if he ever hopes even to approach them and correctly appreciate them, he must approach them from a higher level than that of the everyday world. These creators work from within the world of mystical forces, and to that world the neophyte must look to gain any real understanding of them.

The finest things in life are wrought out in a hard school with its own distinctive laws which await the neophyte's discovery in his studies and meditations.

It will be noted that I write chiefly with the neophyte in our studies in mind. Those students of mature age and advancement in the work will scarcely need this kind of encouragement. They realise the value of their effort and progress on the path. Their outlook and grasp in their various life activities have been widened and strengthened through the discipline of the period of training.

This discipline may at first have been strange to them and perhaps seemed to promise little, but their keenness and desire for knowledge and attainment quickly surmounted any initial difficulty. In some cases a long mental habit had crystallised them somewhat within the confines of the intellect; but under the new direction of thought and the emergence of the higher possibilities of soul development, the influence of an expanded consciousness spread over the whole life.

To feel himself destined at no distant time to take his place among those who have the ability to exercise a special influence in chapter life, should be an inspiration to the ambitious aspirant. In this new venture the established rhythm of life may have to give place to the new, and if the neophyte experiences temporary unsettlement in his personal life, that is but an indication of his growth and advancement and calls for understanding and adjustment.

Changes must follow increasing knowledge in any sphere, and in these days of many necessary and compulsory adjustments in circumstances generally, should cause no surprise on our journey along the way.

Some aspirants are tried just here. They desire advancement and their very attitude compels it; and straightway they find themselves in the midst of a personal battlefield with opposing influences of various kinds confronting them. It is well for them if they recognise and fully accept the situation in the name of progress and service. Some do look back and stand in doubt. But there is the test for the volunteer. If he realises that this little revolution in his personal life is precisely the time for wise action, an ascent in consciousness will be made and new strength will be his.

Hitherto all was understood: the aspirant was at relative peace with himself. He was sure of his strength, because no unknown element had tested it. Confined views directed to personal ends have an alluring and delusive strength of their own, often overconfident and intolerant; and when the narrow barriers, which alone support him, are removed through the aspirant's own efforts to transcend them, the resulting experience may not be a very stimulating one.

This however is but a phase of the biography of the personal self. From that point he seeks to unfold the biography of the spiritual man.

I suggested that many preliminary and incidental difficulties of the aspirant are but a phase of the biography of the personal self, and that he should now look onward and unfold the biography of the psychic and spiritual man. This is where some of the ordinary motives for action will gradually change: he has to think in terms of others as well as of himself.

The neophyte, and sometimes those more advanced, when it is suggested that they exert their influence in other lives, think for them, and extend their knowledge to them, fail to see any connection between self-development and interest in the development of others. Because the Masters of life are referred to as the servants of men, they think the law of service does not apply until they themselves are well advanced in the grades of study.

This is a mistake; but it is understandable because many systems of higher education do not appraise in any way or advocate the importance of service but, with the idea of personal power as the sole objective, concentrate mainly upon that.

This may be legitimate and possible and promises results within a very limited sphere. But it relegates the essential inner self to the background and its true values and possibilities remain an undiscovered territory; whereas an ascension of consciousness is the aim for the aspirant, in devotion to high purpose and making that a visible and active force in his environment.

He should not merely live in his environment, but make himself felt in it. It is only then that the soul life asserts its deeper nature and the aspirant begins to unfold the biography of the inner and invisible man.

The central aim and attractive force of the Rosicrucian ideal has always been service. The Master is perfected in service, and there can be no intimate association or mystical contact with him in his world work until the neophyte has through long probation learned to serve efficiently.

It is the mood of self-involvement, the concentrated interest upon self, destined to bring no abiding satisfaction nor lasting peace, which neither fulfills the purpose of life nor reveals in expression the true dignity of man..., it is these ephemeralities of the personal biography during the mystical venture which have to go, gradually, silently and almost imperceptibly.

The injunction, which we so often meet with in writings on the mystical life, that the neophyte must learn through long probation to serve efficiently, is sometimes given a too narrow interpretation. He is prone to limit the kind of service he is to render and think that every effort for others must necessarily be of an exceptional nature.

But fortunately, today the neophyte, whose knowledge and perspective in life should be constantly increasing in depth and vision, is being enlightened through the very experiences of swiftly moving life itself, and we expect him to manifest a proper sense of humility in his approach to and use of his studies. For, to tell the truth, it is a long journey which lies between the average student and the Master. And remembering the inspiring example of the reality and self-effacement which the Master can afford him, the neophyte comes in time to assess more accurately the distance between the two.

A Master gave a hint of this to an aspirant who expected too much on his own terms, a kind of service befitting his age and personal dignity: *"But what better cause for reward, what better discipline, than the daily and hourly performance of duty?"* This turns the neophyte decisively back to first principles, to the place where he now stands; and he is bidden to be productive in that place, in those circumstances. That may not appear very attractive to the beginner, if he looks for and expects something important and unusual at the outset, something different from the life duty of the average man.

If the demand for service carries with it too strong an idea of self-effacement, it is not the idea which is wrong or irrelevant, but the conception of the neophyte of the task before him. For the law pertaining to the inner way of development is just as exacting as in the outside world; and that law, simply interpreted, is that there is a price to be paid for advancement, as in any other sphere of culture.

It is during the years of service that the neophyte is engaged upon the building of the structure of his inner life and writing, invisibly, the biography of the soul. Every true act of service is a building stone in the erection of the character he is to become on the path. He is apt to overlook that. In lifting, or attempting to lift, the burden of other souls, of whatever nature it may be, from that of the most ordinary nature to that of the most hidden and spiritual, there ensues a refinement and intensifying of his own vibrational quality, a gradual accession in insight, an enhancement of the growth of the soul.

It is often surprising to note how backward a neophyte can be in recognising the differences in mental outlook and the values arising from them when the attention and interest are periodically focused upon these slight changes taking place within his consciousness and expressive life. He may carry out various exercises and experiments and pass from one to another, yet overlook, through lack of proper introspection, how these external acts are gradually changing the tenor of his everyday life. More often than not others notice these changes more quickly than he does.

But this ever increasing sensitivity must be sought for and cultivated at every step of the way. It is a sure sign of inward progress. The biography of the inner man is being written and if it is written with strong intention and purpose, the outer, acting, personal man will reveal its content in stronger colour and vibrational force. He should realise this too: for others will often do so, and confront him with it, for good or ill.

The ill may only amount to an attitude of criticism on the part of some who observe a different approach to them and to life; but a certain indifference should enable him to surmount any petty criticism in the interest of his own development. His task is to forge ahead and display initiative in his progress until the character of the soul life is such that he can trust implicitly in its guidance, assert its influence in his personal life, and prove his value and ability to radiate light and leading in his environment.

I intimated that, often quite unconsciously to himself, the neophyte who is making steady progress in increasing the content and strength of his inner life, will soon be aware of a new influence upon others in his environment. There is no magic about this: it is simply a response to the law of cause and effect, that the firm intention of the centralised will must declare itself.

Let us go a little deeper into this and base it upon the statement that *"the heart contacts all the sensations of the Cosmos."* I think few of us realise the depth of meaning in that pregnant sentence, but we can try to read a little of it. Some of the deepest truths of mysticism come to us in the guise of simplicity and they mean precious little to the busy intellect.

That is a fact to be noted: when the heart would declare itself it is time for the intellect to retire. Both cannot speak at once. And paradoxically, there are occasions when we need to descend from the intellect and ascend from the heart. No neophyte can hope to realise that the heart contacts all the sensations of the Cosmos. He can only take slow steps towards it. The cultivated heart life of the adept can sense all without hindrance; but to realise such a range of contacts the heart must be open and sensitive to impressions far beyond the level of the physical, mental and psychic levels of existence.

Nevertheless, that is the work which the neophyte is embarked upon, little as he may realise it: a gradual extension of the radiation of his sensitive inner nature in order that he may respond more readily to impressions of the surrounding Cosmic life which continually impinge upon the sensitive heart.

We do not like to pass a critical word upon the intellect: we owe it so much. But there is no doubt that during our progress on the way it can distort the vision with many and subtle illusions. That is why the habit of inner silence is so much enjoined upon us. The intellect is a speech maker: it loves to be heard: it talks incessantly; but only too often at the expense of the heart.

All this has to be changed; and the choice is, between the most limited range of the intellect and the ever widening horizon of the sensations, the impressions, of the Cosmos. I will repeat here the scriptural passage on the heart made in a recording some years ago:

> "To behold with the eyes of the heart; to listen with the ears of the heart to the roar of the world; to peer into the future with the comprehension of the heart; to remember the cumulations of the past through the heart; thus must one impetuously advance upon the path of ascent."

10. Mystical Ascension

The following extract is selected and compiled from material originally appearing in 10 parts in editions of the Francis Bacon Chapter Bulletin *from October-December 1969 to January-March 1972.*

There is a point in the mystical ascension where one meets with the unexpected in life and circumstance. It is the unexpected which often defeats us, chiefly through the influences of long established habits of thought and action which we are reluctant to change.

Yet this kind of reversal of ourselves is imperative for progress and must come; and I think it will more definitely and swiftly come at the present time when the whole world around us is facing the unexpected and is not a little bewildered by it.

Those of us who can look back even for 30 years can bear witness, certainly not of the transformation of man of the kind I have referred to, but undoubtedly a transformation within the range of their circumstances; while the younger student, who can look back but for a few years may honestly feel perplexed and question where life is leading him. But right here is the challenge to him, should he find his way lonely because of the fewness of others like-minded and with similar aims, and is, therefore, inclined to turn back and seek the shelter, such as it is, of an uninterested majority, and so ease him somewhat of the burden of being himself.

But the unprecedented rapidity of changes in the world consciousness need not dismay, even if they perplex, the aspirant to higher vision. He may experience some difficulty in adjusting to them. They will work strongly and self-righteously to maintain the ascendancy over him in thought and action. They will, directly or covertly, persuade a relinquishing of the uncertainties of the future for the immediately and curiously satisfying, to such an extent that he feels himself here and now in the midst of a battleground of his own inner life.

What then? So far from feeling a sense of defeat, he should welcome these reactions which are an inevitable response to his silent efforts to contact the life of the soul. He has demanded this and the response comes in the form of sundry tests and hindrances within and without which will prove his strength of character and fitness to advance. Why fear it!

Some students are not too happy when they learn that their efforts on the path seem to initiate circumstances which test their quality in some respects and make life a little harder for them. They should recall the first intention they had in mind when inviting invisible forces and influences.

They sought knowledge and enlarged consciousness for the purpose, it is assumed, of doing better work in the world and to be increasingly helpful to their fellowmen. Without such a purpose the search is lacking in its basic conditions for advancement and cannot be expected to yield any mystical values.

One thing is certain if the young student sets out with this definite purpose in mind: at no stage of the upward path will life continue at an even pace and afford him nothing but a mounting series of self-satisfactions. To voice this purpose in the heart with a resolution to pursue it, is a challenge to those forces which will test him. And it is to be noted that at this crucial point of evolution, when human beings are literally facing the bar of inner judgement, the student who means to advance will be the first to be singled out for trial.

If this seems unjust, reflect for a moment. So long as a man is satisfied with life as it comes and ignores its deeper issues, why should the Masters of life and those who serve them spend their time and hard earned development on those who deny and repudiate all they stand for and are well content on their chosen level of life? No, let them sleep out their incarnation, and when they wake up in a later one, with the haunting memory of wasted years and life unfulfilled, the Masters may turn an eye upon them.

And when that happens what is to be expected? An inner conflict between the present and the past inevitably follows, the rhythms of the past persist in endeavouring to maintain an ascendency over the present, and the more determined the type of student to compel the change the keener the struggle and the sense of manifold frustrations projected by Karmic forces against him.

This is what I mean by facing the bar of inner judgement. On a first reading it may appear a fine-spun theory; but it is only a matter of time when he will feel it transformed into a hard reality.

Therefore to have been called to the higher life with a sense of urgency is the greatest gift and the Karma he is called upon to face is indeed a directive for the present hour.

Our lot has fallen within a period when the Cosmic Powers seem to be engaged in liquidating a heavy bulk of Karma which the nations in their blindness in the past stored up for themselves in thought and action. Which means, I suppose, that, as a nation, we have asked for our share in it and the law of compensation is fulfilling itself.

The thoughtful student will observe, that as he seems to climb up in his mystical studies and glimpse the outworking of the inner law he is forced to descend upon the lower level of the outer self and face conditions which he thought would no longer claim his attention; in a word, his rising in consciousness on to a higher level of functioning, brings an inevitable reaction of descent on to the former level. In the general mystical language of the schools, the law of Karma makes us pay for our apparent advance by certain penalties in circumstance.

I am not competent to expatiate on Karma and its intricate manifestations; nor will the student find it possible to do so. He will do one of two things: either resent much that happens to him, apparently under Karmic decree, or accept the fact that life in its onward movement, imposes the same trials of circumstances upon him as upon everyone else.

What puzzles the student, who is fully aware of this, is how to avoid the reactionary effect of life on the path. He quotes to me from one of the occult devotional manuals:

> "He who would escape from the bondage of Karma must raise his individuality out of the shadow into the shine. He simply lifts himself out of the region in which Karma operates."

I agree with him: that is the theory of it. It is sound doctrine; but it gives him but a misty outline and the substance which comprises his act of living is passed over. I know, as he does, that if I climb yonder mountain I shall be rewarded with a breathtaking prospect below; but what are his chances of reaching the top? The answer is, in these circumstances of ours, riddled with doubts and perplexities, and its slow, often unthankful responses, there is little to encourage him of any certainty that he will get above the operative level of Karma.

There is one thing the student must steel himself against. The shining prospect reflected from the book captures the imagination and appears to promise easy conquest; but his individual circumstances will not harmonise with them. From the book to the world outside is but a short distance, but the unexpectedness of the intervening steps will demand all the faith and courage a good man can summon. And it is those steps which will call for his most exacting attention and interpretation, even to forgetting the bright prospect of the mountain top for a long time.

Where do our thoughts lead us as we meditate step by step in this inward way? For one thing, we shall note that however much regard we come to have for the contemplative life, we are again and again sadly disturbed by outward events which add a burden to the way; and when we think of the classical mystical writers of earlier times, with their insistence upon retirement and absolute absorption in their studies, we feel that the mysticism of today cannot be as it was in the past. Its character has not changed, but the environment today in which it must be exercised is crudely different. The very idea of contemplation and recollection, which was enjoined upon the neophyte by the early mystics, is practically forgotten before the impact of the strong tide of materialistic tendencies which threaten to engulf all.

With so many external influences trying their best to call us away from our central aim, we need more than ever that habit of recollection which the early writers insisted upon; which is far other and more important than merely a memory exercise. On the contrary, recollection has the virtue and value of a peculiar and distinctive nature. We should pause and consider what recollection, in the mystical sense, really is. In dealing with the mystics we have to get away from the usual academic and intellectual definitions of the schools. They only leave us standing where we were upon the surface of life, whereas the recollection we are considering ignores the surface and passes beyond it.

When I wrote recently that the student must be big enough to know immediately that he needs to tread softly and approach life quietly, with humility and refined insight, I was really touching upon the approach to inner recollection. We can see at a glance that there is nothing like that around us today. What then? We must create it within ourselves.

In the words of Dionysius:

> "For the higher we soar in contemplation the more limited become our expressions of that which is purely intelligible; even as now, when plunging into the Darkness which is above the intellect, we pass not merely into brevity of speech, but even into absolute Silence, of thoughts as well as of words."

The impression made by this quotation may be that of retirement from the world of phenomena and of complete self-effacement. But the quotation gives only one aspect of a profound truth. There is a reverse aspect to everything: this is certainly so in regard to mystical and occult truth. To fail to recognise this is the cause of much misunderstanding, and we need to watch for these two aspects of truth whenever we encounter a statement which seems perplexing. Offhand and swift judgement will not help us here.

There are two aspects to this quotation, two levels of consciousness, subjective and objective. On returning to objective consciousness from contact with the subjective, we have to adjust to the life of everyday; and if I say, to the anxiety-dream of the world, we shall not be far wrong. This anxiety-dream is real enough to most of us.

The mystic loves his retirement and peace and quietness, although that, too, has much of the quality of dream. But it is within the objective life that we come face to face with the anxiety-dream which inflicts itself upon the majority of people today. Yet it is what Karmic law has decreed for us, and we fulfil our part if we remember always that life to most people is a constant stream of anxiety moments presented to us, and the challenge and test for us is in giving all that we receive in the silence to compassionate thought and helpfulness to our fellowmen.

We do not rest with contented mind and heart in what we receive of Cosmic grace and turn away from this anxiety-dream pervading the world. Do not ask me, what anxiety? You have an aloof overall picture of it in the press and radio daily. And it is here that the mystic has to step down from on high and through his seership see and know the anxiety-dream there before him invading men and women in mind and heart. To pass it by, to ignore it, to try to forget it is to retreat to a silence which no mystic need be proud of.

This is where our retreat and contemplation should lead us, right down to the emotional and mental chaos which visibly and invisibly surrounds us. If we say we do not see it or sense it; that is a plain confession that the contemplative life has not taught us its chief lesson: we have not evolved to spiritual sensitivity, to the refined touch of the soul's presence and leading within us; and without that we are still but neophytes.

11. The Problem of the Neophyte

Reprinted from the July to September 1972 edition of the Francis Bacon Chapter Bulletin.

There is a curious trait of character which has often been met with in those who first enter upon lodge work within the Order. They declare that they seek new knowledge and instruction, yet after having taken the first steps on the path to the new teaching, they find that it clashes, or appears to clash, with their previous knowledge and training. In a word, they want new instruction, but on their own terms. They want nothing that will disturb those aspects of truth they already know, or to have them questioned in any way. The new knowledge they seek must conform to what they already know; if it does not, then the new knowledge is suspected and they become destructively critical.

This is a singular attitude of mind. A specialised training given to one upon his own terms is an absurdity. Why seek authoritative instruction and influence if he is so sure of himself that his own methods of procedure are to be the criterion of future progress?

Now it is just here that the first act of self-surrender must take place. An aspirant should have no voice when his preceptor speaks. Even in the school of everyday life common courtesy requires this act of grace from its pupils; how much more so when the comprehensive life of the inner man is the subject of study? Surely it is wisdom and an act of proper humility to render obedience to a new voice which can teach the way in which the highest service can be rendered.

There can be really no bargaining in this matter. The personality must, to some extent, lose ground when the aspirant passes within the group rhythm of a lodge. It is the one condition upon which the power of the group can be fully evolved and applied. Instances have occurred where individuals have accepted lodge invitation, yet when the multiplied group power has come to them in but a preliminary and testing measure, they have, with unpurified motive, grasped it and reverted to its individual assertion, thereby denying the very cooperativeness that gave it birth and so forfeiting the right and ability to exercise it. These are they who have fallen into forgetfulness of the word of scripture they have long known *"...that the power which the disciple shall covet is that which shall make him appear as nothing in the eyes of man."*

It is well if the aspirant has through the years learned in spirit and in truth the nobility and beauty of self-effacement. It cannot be taught. Mysticism can fail, and often has lamentably failed, to instil it into the heart. The multiplied power to which each member in a group has access should produce in him something akin to creative genius. It is a power to use individually, but to corporate ends.

In lodge work the emphasis is shifted from individual to group importance. This provides the greatest test that can be conceived of true impersonality in the aspirant. That some retreat after acceptance of the conditions involved is no matter for surprise. Modern life has emphasised the importance of personal and individual power beyond anything hitherto known, and it is small wonder that many an aspirant should be swept into the vortex of this compelling influence.

It may be no exaggeration to say that, all circumstances considered, mystical teaching today for a large percentage of seekers, has promised little more than an augmented personality potency to cope with life; and until that potency reveals to them its fundamental insecurity, will they be likely to accept with chastened mind and heart, the idea of surrender of personality which group amalgamation demands.

When once the position is accepted that Rosicrucianism must be cooperative, that this is a decree of those who alone can bring them safely to their goal, a strong barrier to advancement will be removed.

12. The Time for Decision

Reprinted from the October to December 1972 edition of the Francis Bacon Chapter Bulletin.

The acquirement of knowledge by the aspirant is not so difficult a problem to him as is the wise use of it. The accumulation of facts and principles proceeds apace in the course of his studies, but in time he becomes self-reflective and looks to himself for a special kind of higher leading in the course of his instruction. He decides that it must prove its value from within himself, that the purpose of all expansion of consciousness is to invoke guidance from higher levels that he not remain at the mercy of the everyday mundane traffic of life we all have to indulge in. If the instruction does not inspire and raise him above this routine level, he misses its aim.

Today the world race of the nations is with us. One nation outdistances its competitors in some respects, and just as surely in other respects and in different ways falls behind them. None can ultimately defeat cyclic law. There is no superman nation today. So swift is the race that illusion blinds the eyes of the keenest. The mantle of superiority which appears to enrobe one nation for a day is snatched violently by another, while the race continues around the spectral dial of the planet with mounting velocity.

These may well be the reflections of the student as he surveys the unrolling panorama around him. He has already looked to the world for the guidance he needs, and not finding it, he thinks it time to look within for it. He sees now that if he refuses or neglects that, he might as well join in the world's race and share its illusions.

Many have done so, both young and mature in years and of able mind, because the speed and overpowering direction of external life glamoured them; and it asks a good deal of patience and not a little application to get on spiritual terms with the indwelling Self and win its confidence to the extent of becoming a sure guidance for them. And if ever they have needed that guidance, they need it today.

13. Reading and Being

Reprinted from the January to March 1973 edition of the Francis Bacon Chapter Bulletin.

> *"There is nothing more sublime than contemplation as we find it in books; nothing more beautiful or grander than passive prayer in theory. But in practice, there is nothing more humiliating, more crucifying."*

This pungent quotation comes from a French mystical writer of long ago, and it is as applicable today as when it was written. If there is a touch of cynicism in it, that is pardonable. The reception it would probably get today would be one of supercilious indifference and deserve more than cynicism.

But note how well chosen his words are, and what they signify. It is surprising what a world of meaning can be hidden in a sentence, waiting for interpretation. Who would imagine that the writer was marking the difference between reading and being! The weight of his sentence falls upon being as contrasted with reading about it: and the fact of being should mean all to the mystic.

Note again how two worlds of feeling are clearly marked in the quotation: one of beauty and grandeur, even sublimity; and the other of deep gravity and pain. It is a theme for serious reflection. For one thing, we make too much pain for ourselves through expecting too much rejoicing from our reading. Many students take the written word as the particular truth from which there is no appeal, instead of reflecting upon its value or non-value as applied to the act of living, the actual day and experience they are passing through. But life will not be shelved and glossed over like that. It is a stern and silent taskmaster which misses nothing.

It has been said that a writer puts himself into his book; but that is only a half-truth. A writer cannot put himself wholly into his book. He gives us but the contours and the shadows of what is passing within him. One of the most surprising happenings would be, if a writer could really put himself into his book: it would prove a staggering experience for the reader. We are fortunate in receiving what he can impart to us and should not expect the impossible.

Now, when the wheel of life, ever moving on to completer knowledge, brings phases of experience the student looked not for which lower the temperature of the written word, he either stagnates or revises his thinking. *"But in practice,"* says the quotation, the true colours of life manifest themselves. And why? Because the life of the truly mystical and spiritual aspirant, inwardly, is compelled sooner or later to live in the shadow of the Cross. That is why the quotation changes its note from happy rejoicing to solemn reflection. From then on the pain of life will teach and culture him. Nothing less will do it; and *"nothing is more humiliating"* to mortal man. Need we add *"more crucifying?"* This is a hard word. It suggests the extremity of feeling and pain applying to all the planes of existence; and the more refined the recipient the more pronounced the feeling: and that is why so many turn from it.

Yet feeling becomes increasingly acute as consciousness passes upward and functions upon the higher levels of life. We experience pain through disharmony on the physical plane, maladjustment on the mental plane, and cosmic cognition on the plane of spirit. Cosmic cognition acquaints us with the collective pain of humanity. Only the Great Master knows experimentally that crucifixion; and when at some time during the incarnations the student comes to know it, its name will be changed.

In Memoriam

Raymund Andrea (1882-1975)

In Memoriam

The Rosicrucian Digest September 1975

Raymund Andrea, Grand Master Emeritus of Great Britain, passed through transition, experiencing the *Great Initiation* into the hereafter in his home in Bristol, England, on Tuesday, 22 July, 1975. He had served the Rosicrucian Order as Grand Master unostentatiously and we very much doubt that he would even want a simple eulogy at this time. However, in justice to all those members of long standing who know of the inspiration and counselling which he gave them and who feel greatly indebted to him, we feel that this is necessary. Due to the long retirement of Raymund Andrea, having reached the very advanced age of 93, he had almost become a legend to the more recent members of the Order.

Rosicrucian activity, at least in an organised form, was inactive in Great Britain in the early part of this century. There was an interest in the doctrines of the Order but no means of obtaining the teachings. Raymund Andrea however, had received the teachings of the Order through his intimate association and friendship with Dr H Spencer Lewis, Imperator of the Rosicrucian Order in America. Consequently, realising the need for renewing the work in Great Britain, in 1921 Dr Lewis issued a Charter of Authority to Raymund Andrea as Grand Master of Great Britain. This of course required certain preparation, and instructions were forwarded to him by the Imperator.

There were no funds available to start this great work at the beginning. The Rosicrucian Order in America was still in its incipient state in its Second Cycle with no great material resources at the time. Dr Lewis provided Grand Master Andrea with all the rituals and teachings which had been translated from the older European works and which had been modernised. Single-handedly, except for the loving assistance of his wife, Andrea began his great labours. He preferred solitude and felt that his greatest good could be accomplished in writing and counselling by correspondence and occasionally personally meeting with members. He was a scholar and primarily an introvert, burdened by considerable routine work in the dissemination of the teachings because of the relatively small membership to provide support for extensive activities.

Then came the great holocaust of World War II. The city of Bristol in which Andrea resided was one of the most badly bombed cities in England. It became impossible for members to receive monographs because of Andrea's inability to obtain supplies and also because of the health of his wife and himself as the result of the incessant bombings. In 1939 the Supreme Grand Lodge in San Jose, California, wrote to Andrea, offering to continue dissemination of the studies of the Order to members in Britain. This the Rosicrucian Order did for the entire period of the war without monetary assistance.

Almost immediately at the conclusion of the war, the incumbent Imperator [Ralph M Lewis] arranged to meet with Andrea in England. The city was very much destroyed and Andrea, obviously exhausted by the ordeal, was still unable to obtain the necessary materials to continue to serve the British membership. It was therefore decided in 1946 that the two great English-speaking jurisdictions of the Rosicrucian Order should amalgamate into one. Consequently, the studies were then disseminated from the American facilities which had so increased as to be able to provide adequate services. Raymund Andrea continued his writings and the Rosicrucian Order in San Jose published and distributed his books. He kept up his great service of counselling members by correspondence, and personally whenever possible, until the time of his retirement.

There was a great rapport between Raymund Andrea and Dr H Spencer Lewis. Dr Lewis many times referred to Andrea as exemplifying the modern mystic. During any leisure moments that Andrea had, which were few, he found enjoyment in his love and knowledge of music; and the harmony of music manifested in other forms as in his writings and in his personal life.

A Memorial Service was held for Raymund Andrea in the Francis Bacon Lodge in London on August 14. Present were the Imperator, Ralph M. Lewis; Raymond Bernard, Supreme Legate of Europe; and other dignitaries of the Rosicrucian Order.

Alphabetical List of Selected Writings and Letters

Alphabetical List of Selected Writings and Letters

Address to the Francis Bacon Chapter by Jessie Kenney (July 1960)	319
Advance or Retreat?	421
Ambition or Stagnation	300
Anxious Aspirants	419
Are We Abnormal?	202
Atomic Bomb and Ourselves, The	335
Biography of Raymund Andrea (21 July 1882 - 22 July 1975)	13
Birthday Message to Francis Bacon Chapter	423
Brains: East and West	424
Bulwer-Lytton	141
Comte de Gabalis, The	70
Comte de St Germain, The	115
Crises In Development	246
Critical Decision, The	449
Cult of the Average, The	416
Dark Night of the Soul, The	208
Discipleship on Trial	404
Divine Experiment, The	354
Extract from letter Ellen Kirkpatrick (27 January 1962)	328
Extract from letter to Ellen Kirkpatrick (24 July 1962)	328
Extract from letter to Ellen Kirkpatrick (9 January 1964)	329
Extracts from various letters to Ellen Kirkpatrick	330
Facing the Truth	380
From the Grand Master's Sanctum	399
Future of Occultism, The	28
Guiding Hand, The	229
Hour of Trial, The	313
Human Identification	434
Idealism in Practice	371
Impersonality	427
Irredeemable Moment, The	375
Lafcadio Hearn's "Karma"	161
Letter to Ellen Kirkpatrick (9 December 1939)	325
Letter to Ellen Kirkpatrick (5 June 1950)	325
Letter to Ellen Kirkpatrick (10 March 1955)	326
Letter to Jessie Kenney (24 March 1933)	320
Letter to Jessie Kenney (11 July 1934)	321
Letter to Jessie Kenney (17 October 1935)	321

Letter to Jessie Kenney (22 June 1936)...322
Letter to Jessie Kenney (26 September 1938)......................................323
Letter to Jessie Kenney (25 May 1959)..324
Letter to Members (28 August 1940)...254
Letter to Members (18 December 1940)...256
Letter to Members (3 April 1941)...258
Letter to Members (4 August 1941)..260
Letter to Members (18 December 1941)...262
Letter to Members (10 June 1942)..265
Letter to Members (20 April 1943)...271
Letter to Members (Christmas 1931)..253
Letter to Members (December 1942)...266
Letter to Members (December 1943)...273
Letter to Members (December 1944)...277
Letter to Members (December 1945)...283
Light of the Soul, The..54
Lodge Masters and Activities...216
Loneliness...446
Love's Apotheosis...200
Magical Power of Thought, The..402
Master and Members..452
Men Learn Most by the Negative Way..411
Message from the Grand Master of Great Britain, A............................298
Mind Quest and Soul Vision..447
Minds: Ancient and Modern..413
Mystical Ascension..459
Mystical Neophytism..454
Mystical Novitiate, The..232
Novitiate, The...39
Occult Initiative..168
Occult Life, The..21
Occultist and His Critics, The...32
On The Mystic Path..237
Our Need to Cultivate the Art of Reflection...401
Pain of Development, The...30
Paracelsus, the Rosicrucian..193
Perspectives of Progress..406
Potency of the Word, The..453
Problem of the Neophyte, The..463
Prophet of the Times, A...385

Alphabetical List of Selected Writings and Letters

Raymund Lully, The Eminent Rosicrucian Master 129
Reading and Being 465
Recorded Message to the first Rosicrucian Rally in Great Britain - 3 August 1952 397
Reflections on the Third Temple (Postulant) Grade: Article 1 85
Reflections on the Third Temple (Postulant) Grade: Article 2 93
Reflections on the Third Temple (Postulant) Grade: Article 3 96
Reflections on the Third Temple (Postulant) Grade: Article 4 100
Rejected Gift, The 350
Roger Bacon, The Rosicrucian 172
Rosicrucian Manual: An Appreciation, The 84
Rosicrucian Order and Cooperation, The 136
Rosicrucian Order in Great Britain, The 59
Rosicrucian Order, Past and Present, The 111
Rosicrucian Technique: A Word to the Critics, The 219
Rosicrucians and World Affairs 289
Sanctity of Work, The 341
Science of Death, The 50
Science of Seership, The 213
Section 1: Early Writings of Herbert Adams 19
Section 2: The Mystic Triangle (1927) 57
Section 3: The Mystic Triangle (1928) 91
Section 4: The Mystic Triangle (1929) 139
Section 5: The Rosicrucian Digest (1929-1935) 187
Section 6: The Modern Mystic and Monthly Science Review (1937-1938) 227
Section 7: Messages to Members (1931-1945) 251
Section 8: The Rosicrucian Digest (1939-1945) 287
Section 9: Selected Correspondence (1932-1964) 317
Section 10: The Rosicrucian Digest (1946-1957) 333
Section 11: The London Rosicrucian (1952-1961) 395
Section 12: Writings of Unspecified Date 431
Section 13: Francis Bacon Chapter Bulletin (1963-1973) 441
Seeking Ourselves 443
Self-Knowledge 46
Spiritualism, the Church and Ourselves 65
Task for Rosicrucians, A 293
Technique of the Disciple, The 223
Technique of the Master (1927), The 77
Technique of the Master (1929), The 150
That Frustration is a Good 408
Theosophical World Teacher, The 62

Theosophy and Anti-Christianity 36
Three Wise Men, The 240
Three Years in Tibet 121
Thus Spake Zarathustra 367
Tibetan Messenger, The 42
Tibetan Tragedy, The 410
Time for Decision, The 464
To me Jesus is all in all 189
Towards the Ideal 444
Unseen Influences of our Rosicrucian Studies, The 437
Wagner and Occultism 25
Waiting for the Master 156
White Brother, The 178
Word of Encouragement, A 433
Word of the Prophet, The 451
Word to the Neophyte, A 436
World Catastrophe and Responsibility 306
World Shadow, The 361
Yone Noguchi, Poet and Mystic 105

Index

Index

A

Abbe Villars 72–73, 75–76
Adams, Clara 14
Adams, Herbert (Raymund Andrea) 11–17, 21, 43
    Bristol (hometown) 13, 469
Agrippa, Cornelius 198–199
à Kempis, Thomas 354–361
    Imitation of Christ, The 238, 354–361
Alchemy 195
Ambrosiana Library at Milan 120
America(n) 15, 93, 209, 265, 267, 271, 372, 469–470
    alignment of purpose 294–296
    alliance of thought 260–261
    Bailey, Alice 43
    Hearn, Lafcadio 161–162
    Lincoln, Abraham 366
    Noguchi, Yone 105–109
    Spengler, Oswald 387–388
    the Order and Cooperation 137–138
    Theosophy 62–63, 65
    world affairs 289–293
    world shadow 366
American Rosae Crucis, The 59
Andrea, Raymund
    Is America Neutral? (review).
        See Imperator
    Science of Seership (review). *See* Hodson, Geoffrey (Theosophist)
Andrea, Raymund (Books)
    Discipleship on Trial 16, 404–406
    The Disciple and Shamballa 16
    The Mystic Way 11, 15, 229
    The Technique of the Disciple 11, 15, 223–225
    The Technique of the Master 11, 15, 221, 223–224. *See also* Contents

The Way of the Heart 11
Waiting For The Master 11, 13
Anthroposophy 425
Apocrypha, The 451
Aquinas, Thomas 414
Archbishop of
    Canterbury 309
    York 379
Aristotle 175
Athens 388
Atlantis 55
Austria
    Rosicrucians of 120–121

B

Babylon 388
Bacon, Francis 50, 88, 99, 170, 215, 229, 300, 302–304
Bacon, Roger 14, 172–178, 219
    and Clement IV 174–175, 177
    and Oxford 173–176
    and Paris 173–175
    born in Somerset 173
    British Academy (subject of lecture) 173
    Dr Little (lecture on) 173–176
Bailey, Alice 42–44, 54–55
    Light of the Soul 54
    Tibetan Teacher 42, 44–45, 54–55
Balzac, Honoré de 348
Barbary [Coast] 133–134
Barker, A T (Theosophist) 62
Beethoven, Ludwig von 390
Berdyaev, Nikolai (philosopher) 339
Bernard, Raymond 16, 470
Besant, Annie 62
Bhagavad Gita 46, 48, 54, 453
Bible, The 21, 35, 175, 350, 379, 451

and Roger Bacon 177
Bibles of humanity 29, 100
for Rosicrucians 98, 447
influenced Paracelsus 194
misuse of 138
Blavatsky, Helena 32, 36–38, 43, 62, 95, 104, 196
   HPB (initials) 43–45, 54–55, 62–63, 142
   Mahatma and Blavatsky Letters 62
      in the Morning Post 62
   on Comte de St. Germain 116, 120
   The Secret Doctrine 44, 181
   Voice of the Silence 54
Boehme, Jacob 199, 412
Bonaventura (Franciscan Order) 174
Bossuet, Jacques Bénigne (orator) 97
Brother(hood) 55, 71, 116, 171, 291
   Brotherhood in India 142
   Brotherhood of Masters 36, 56, 115
   Brother M 178
   Brother Serapis 150, 153
   Brothers of the Shadow 82
   Eastern Brotherhood 63, 150
   Egyptian Brotherhood 153
   Frater James 320, 324
   Frater Ling 320, 324
   Rosicrucian Brotherhood 59–61, 70, 150
   Temple of the Brotherhood 71
   Tibetan Brother 54
   White Brotherhood 210, 244
   White Brother, The 178–184
Bruegel, Pieter (Flemish artist) 392
   The Tower of Babel 392
Brunton, Paul (mystic) 21
Buddha 25–26, 28, 40, 50, 102–105, 109–110, 125–129, 202, 310, 371, 410–411
   and Wagner 211
Buddhism 108–110, 121–129, 162, 310, 425
   and Oswald Spengler 391
   and Rosicrucians 279

and Tibetan invasion 410
Zen Buddhism 102, 107, 109, 429
Bulwer-Lytton, Edward 70, 76, 116, 141–150
   and Chauncey Hare Townshend 143
   and Paris 144–145
   and Rosina Wheeler 144–148
   at Bath 145
   at Bristol 145
   at Cambridge 142–143
   at Cheltenham 145
   at Ealing 142
   at Versailles 144–145
   buried in Westminster Abbey 150
   House of Commons 144, 146–147, 149
   in France 144–145
   military service 144
   Zanoni (character) 116, 169
   Zanoni (novel) 70–71, 121, 141–142, 149

C

Caesar, Julius 388
Cagliostro, Alessandro 120
California 15, 62–63, 105–107, 265, 469
Canada 308
Carlyle, Thomas (quotation) 119
Cathedral
   of the Soul 295
   St. Paul's 378
China 106, 117, 122
   and Tibet 410–411
   culture 388
   language and texts 122, 315
Christmas 15, 240, 245
   Christmas card quotation 320
   in letters to members 253–286
Churchill, Winston 270
Church (The) 28–29, 35, 38, 55, 70, 98, 103, 111, 132, 134, 137–138, 175, 177, 196, 230–231, 243, 291, 347, 352–354, 370, 448

Index

and Rosicrucians 418–419
and Spiritualism 65–67
failure of 309–311, 313, 378–379
of England 67, 378, 451
of Rome 67, 130, 174–178, 194, 414, 451
Collins, Mabel
    Light on the Path 54, 300–301, 453
        quotation from 239, 316
Comte de Gabalis, The 70–77, 141
    Comte de Gabalis (book) 182
        Invocation to the Flame (quote) 71
Comte de St Germain, The 115–121, 141
    and Freemasonry 119–120
    and Mesmer 120
    and Paris 118–120
    and Russia 116, 118
    and St. Martin 120
    and the Shah of Persia 117
    at court of Louis XV 117
    Countess v Georgy comment 117
    Graffer, Franz (quote) 120
    in India 117–118, 122
    in Vienna 118, 120–121
    Jacobite Revolution (spying) 117
    Karl Cobenzl letter 118
    warnings to Marie-Antoinette 119
Confucius
    quote from disciple 257, 401
Cooper-Oakley, Mrs (writer) 116
Corelli, Marie (writer) 138
Crusades, The 388

D

d'Adhemar, Madame 117, 119
Dalai Lama, The 127–128, 410–411
Daniels, Robert E 433, 437
Dante Alighieri 345, 377
    Divina Commedia 345
Da Vinci, Leonardo 390
Descartes, René (quote) 379

Dhamma Pada (Buddhist work) 453
Dharuma (Hindu monk) 102
Dionysius (quote) 462
Douay (English convent) 174
Doyle, Sir Arthur Conan 68
    Pheneas Speaks 68

E

Emerson, Ralph Waldo 295, 336, 338, 398, 412
Erasmus (humanist scholar) 196

F

Fama Fraternitatis 103, 191, 238, 412–413
France 119–120, 195
Franciscan Order, The 173–176
    in Great Britain 174
    in Ireland 174
Frederick the Great 388
Freemasonry. *See* Comte de St Germain, The

G

Gasquet, Cardinal 178
Germany 193, 293, 308, 312
    and Oswald Spengler 387
    Letter to members (Dec 1942) 266–271
Gibbon, Edward (historian) 144
Goethe, Johann Wolfgang von 145, 229, 375
Gould Dr. *See* Hearn, Lafcadio

H

Hartmann, Franz 21, 196
Hazlitt, William (writer) 379
Hearn, Lafcadio (writer) 121, 161–167
    and New York 161
    and Poe 162
    influence of Dr Gould 162
    in Japan 121
    Lippincott's Magazine 161
Heindel, Max 63

Helmont, Jan Baptista van (chemist) 199
Heraclitus (philosopher) 443
Hitler, Adolf 370
Hodson, Geoffrey (Theosophist) 213
   Science of Seership 213–216
Hugo, Victor (writer/poet) 346, 348, 351
Hungary 120, 410
Huxley, Aldous (novelist) 246–248
   Grey Eminence (quote) 246
   life of Father Joseph 246–247

I

Imperator
   H S Lewis 13–15, 64, 95, 111, 174, 219–220, 296, 321, 324, 371–375
      Andrea's letter to 220
      Charter of Authority to Andrea 469
      Is America Neutral? (article review) 289–292
   outside opposition to work 422
   R M Lewis 15–16, 321, 324, 469–470
      honouring Andrea 423
      praising Andrea 298
India 117–118, 122, 142
   and Dalai Lama 410
   culture 388
Inge, Dr W R (Platonist/mystic) 378
Isaiah, Book of 98
Italy 193, 195

J

James, William (psychologist) 449
Japan 106, 108, 121–125, 128–129, 161–162
Johnston, Charles (publisher) 54
Jung, Karl (quote) 310

K

Kabala 195, 199
Kant, Immanuel (philosopher) 390
Kawaguchi, Ekai (Japanese priest) 122–129

   and Nepal 122, 124–125, 129
   Aphorisms of the White Lotus 122
   at Benares 122
   at Shigatze and Lhasa 127
   in Calcutta 124–125
   in Kyoto 122
   in Lhasa 127
   in Singapore 123
   Three Years in Tibet 121–122
Kenney, Jessie 253, 319–324
   and Annie Taylor (suffragette) 319
   and London 319–324
   Grand Master LeBrun 321
Kirkpatrick, Ellen 319, 325–331
   as Ellen Turnbull 16, 319, 330, 433
Koran, The 451
Krishnamurti 62–65, 137

L

Lao Tsze
   Simple Way of Lao Tsze, The (quote) 329
Leadbeater, Charles (Theosophist) 62
LeBrun, Grand Master. *See* Kenney, Jessie
Lemuria 55
Liverpool 130, 265
Lodge, Sir Oliver 68–69
London 179–180
   and Bulwer Lytton 146–147
   and Comte de St Germain 118
   and Jessie Kenney 319–324
   Andrea's memorial service 470
   and Tagore 275
   Occult Review published 21
   RML meets with Andrea 15
   the cafes of Soho 181
   Theosophical Society 36
   Yone Noguchi 108–109
London Chapter 423
London Rosicrucian, The 397–429, 443
Loneliness

Andrea article 446
on the Path 32, 87, 160–161, 192, 207, 384
Lully, Raymond 129–136
  and Paris 133–134
  and Pope Boniface VIII 134
  and the Moors 133–134
  Artis demonstrativae 133
  Art of Finding Truth 133
  at Genoa 133
  at Montpellier 133
  at Pisa 135
  Council of Vienne 135
  Hill of Randa 132
  in Famagusta 134
  in Naples 134
  in Sicily 136
  in Tunis 133–136
  Mallorca 130–136
  Peers, E Allison (researcher) 130
  received in Limisso 134
Luther, Martin 194, 196
Lytton, Lord. *See* Bulwer-Lytton, Edward

M

Maritain, Jacques (philosopher) 335–337, 415
Master Kut-Hu-Mi 77–78
Master Morya 178
Mesmerism 143
  Mesmer, Franz Anton. *See* Comte de St Germain, The
Millerite 336
  Miller Joaquin. *See* Noguchi, Yone
Mirandola, Pico della (Renaissance philosopher) 194
Modern Mystic and Monthly Science Review. *See* Contents
Mohammed(an) 175, 451
Morocco 386
Munich (agreement) 292

Mystic Triangle, The. *See* Contents

N

Nietzsche, Friedrich 368–371, 387
  Professor Lichtenberger 370
Noguchi, Yone (Japanese poet) 102, 105–110
  and Poe 107
  at the Yosemite Valley 107
  From the Eastern Sea 109
  in California 105–107
  in Chicago 107–108
  in San Francisco 105–106, 109
  Japanese Temple of Silence 102, 108
  leaves Tokyo 105
  Markino, Yoshio (artist friend) 108
  Miller, Joaquin (poet) 106–109
  Monologues of a Homeless Snail 109
  On the Heights 107
  Story of Yone Noguchi, The (1914) 105
  The Lark (magazine) 107
  The Pilgrimage 109

O

Occult Review, The. *See* Contents; *See also* London
  Ralph Shirley (editor) 42

P

Paracelsus 193–199
  alchemy 195, 197
  among Turks and Tartars 195
  and the Kabala 195, 199
  and the Netherlands 195
  at Basel 196–198
  at Beratzhausen 198
  at Nuremberg 198
  at Strasburg 197
  death at Salzburg 199
  Dr Franz Strunz (on Paracelsus) 197

flight from Prussia, Lithuania and Poland 196
healed Markgrave of Baden 196
healing at Colmar 198
heals the publisher Froben 196
in Appenzell 198
in England 195
in Schwatz 195
Leipzig, Medical Faculty of 198
meets with Erasmus (humanist) 196
no truth in Europe 195
Professor Strunz (quote) 199
Prognostications 198
pupil of Trithemius 194
Universities spurned 195
Paris 388. *See also* Bacon, Roger; *See also* Bulwer-Lytton, Edward; *See also* Comte de St Germain, The; *See also* Lully, Raymond
Parsifal 346
Pascal, Blaise 229
Plato 36, 414
  neo-platonism 199
Plotinus (Neo-Platonist) 414
Poe, Edgar Allen 229, 335, 390. *See also* Hearn, Lafcadio; *See also* Noguchi, Yone
Poland 196, 306
Pope 312
  Boniface VIII 134. *See also* Lully, Raymond
  Clement IV 174–175, 177. *See also* Bacon, Roger
  Clement V 135

R

Rakoczi, Master 116
Renaissance, The 193, 199, 388
Renan, Ernest (writer)
  Life of Jesus 435

Richelieu, Cardinal 246
Rilke, Rainer Maria (poet) 341–344, 347–349
Rodenbach, Georges (poet) 342
Rodin, Auguste (sculptor) 341–349
  Brussels (in) 343–344
Rome 174–175, 194
Rosicrucian Beacon 189
  reprinted articles 21–32, 42–49, 200–202, 240–245, 401–402, 411–413, 433–436, 444–445
Rosicrucian Code of Life 84–85
Rosicrucian Digest 12–15, 21, 59, 410. *See also* Contents
  in memoriam Sep.1975 469
  reprinted article 246–250
Rosicrucian Forum 13, 168
Rosicrucian Manual 84–85, 112–114
Rousseau, Jean-Jacques 229, 335, 365, 382
Russia 116, 118, 306, 410

S

Saint
  Francis 131, 174
  Jerome 177
  John 369
  Paul 34
  Thomas 238
Saint-Martin, Louis Claude de 120, 229
  quotation 374
San Jose 15, 321, 326, 469–470
Savonarola, Girolamo (Dominican reformer) 194
Schopenhauer, Arthur (philosopher) 309, 414
Shakespeare, William 99
Six Biographical Sketches 16, 229, 335
Spain 195, 324
Spengler, Oswald (historian and philosopher) 376, 386–393
  Decline of the West 386, 393
  Music and Plastic 390

Index

Spiritualism 35, 61, 65–70, 137, 181, 213
Steiner, Rudolf 63, 69, 193
    quotation 198
    sarcasm from Evelyn Underhill 193
Stoddart, Miss A M 193
    of the life of Paracelsus 193
Stoicism (a philosophy) 175, 391
Sutras, The 54–55

T

Tacitus (Classic historian) 268, 384
Tagore, Rabindranath (Indian poet) 274–276
    Gitanjali (Song Offerings) 274
Tennyson, Lord Alfred 142
    line of verse 22
Theosophical Society, The 21, 36–39, 43, 103, 181, 214
    Herald of the Star 62
    The Theosophist 21. *See also* Contents
Theosophy 13, 36, 45, 62–63, 94, 151, 169, 181, 209, 219–220, 424–425
Tibet 122–123, 127, 410–411. *See also* Bailey, Alice
    Book of the Dead (Bardo Thodol) 50–54
    Buddhism 122, 124, 128, 410
    language 122, 124–125
Trismosin, Solomon
    Splendour Solis (alchemical treatise) 194
Turnbull, Eric 319

U

Underhill, Evelyn (writer) 193, 199

V

Vansittart, Sir Robert
    Black Record (booklet) 268

W

Wagner, Richard 25–28, 211–212
    letters to Mathilde Wesendonck 25

Waite, Arthur Edward 21, 129–130, 136
Whitman, Walt (essayist) 302
World War 15, 248, 253, 309–310, 313, 319, 353, 388, 469

Y

Yoga 49–55, 88, 357

Z

Zarathustra (Zoroaster) 350–352, 367–369

The Rosicrucian Order

The Rosicrucian Order®

Several references are made in this book to the Rosicrucian Order. Therefore, anticipating questions you may have, we would like to take this opportunity to explain the purpose of the Rosicrucian Order and how you may learn more about it.

Some organisations have in their titles words such as Rosicrucian, Rose-Cross, Rosy-Cross, Rozenkreutz or words similar to them, but such organisations have nothing to do with the Rosicrucian Order itself. There is only one universal Rosicrucian Order in the world today, united in 17 language jurisdictions under the direction of a single governing body called the *Supreme Grand Lodge of the Ancient and Mystical Order Rosae Crucis*.

The Rosicrucian Order uses modern educational tools to bring out the highest qualities of human goodness and sanctity in all who seek a change for the better. For those who seek a deeper meaning and transcendent purpose in life, the Order teaches highly effective techniques to enable people to experience their innate spirituality in the broadest, most tolerant and universal manner possible. The pursuit of mystical wisdom and experience is regarded as the most important of all human endeavours, and those who have the courage, patience and fortitude to seek it out, regardless of the occasional challenges this involves, will find within this Order of mystics, a warm and loving spiritual home.

With membership of the Rosicrucian Order coming from widely diverse social, political and religious strata and spanning virtually every country in the world, the Order retains the ancient traditions, teachings, principles and practical helpfulness of the original Rosicrucian fraternity as founded centuries ago. It is known throughout the world as the Ancient and Mystical Order Rosae Crucis, which is abbreviated as AMORC. The publishers of this book, *The Rosicrucian Collection*®, is a wholly owned subsidiary of the English Grand Lodge of the Rosicrucian Order for Europe, the Middle East and Africa, and is located at...

Greenwood Gate, Blackhill, Crowborough
TN6 1XE, United Kingdom
Tel: +44-(0)1892-653197
Fax: +44-(0)1892-667432
Email: sales@amorc.org.uk

If you wish to know more about the Rosicrucian Order, please read on, or visit our international website at *www.amorc.org* and choose your language and region preference.

Rosicrucians and Mysticism

The Rosicrucian Order uses the word "Mystical" in its official title, and for good reason. For mysticism, especially in its present-day form, far from dealing with weird or strange phenomena, is a modern, personal discipline which, when correctly applied to daily situations, opens us to a satisfying understanding of many of those things that remain beyond the realm of modern science. Call it metaphysics if you will, but mysticism goes far beyond even that, for it has the potential of leading you to a state of personal accomplishment, happiness and peace beyond your greatest expectations.

Mysticism is not merely a matter of gaining intellectual knowledge; there are many excellent colleges and universities that serve you best in that area. It requires no arduous academic training, no formulas, names or dates to learn by rote; and there are no exams other than those that life itself compels you to pass. Mysticism does however require sincerity of purpose and dedicated work on the improvement of your self. In one respect, the discipline of mysticism attempts to establish a conscious link between yourself and a certain source of knowledge that lies beyond the limits of the known universe and the present state of science. In another respect, and one that has been spoken of eloquently within widely diverse religious and philosophical systems over thousands of years, mysticism seeks to unite the whole life experience of the individual with what each of those religions and philosophies conceived as the sole God of all that is, or the source of all that is good.

That a source of wisdom and inspiration actually exists beyond the range of normal human intellect has been attested to by many of the greatest minds the world has produced in the past, and continues to be eloquently spoken of by some of the greatest thinkers of our own era. And this source of wisdom, in a nutshell, is what mysticism seeks to unite you with.

Through a study and application of the principles taught by the Rosicrucian Order, you can relatively easily learn to recognise and respond to a source of infallible wisdom which already exists within your own being. You can learn to seek guidance from this source which with purpose, intelligence and clarity seems to originate from the greatest depths of your very own being. What could be more satisfying than discovering in your own time, at your own pace and on your own initiative, new and exciting truths that have immediate, practical use in your life?

This inner guidance has variously been called the "still, small voice within," the "Inner Self," or the "Master Within." In most cultures there is a name for it, for in every human being there is a recognisable deeper nature or personality of almost unbelievable potential, a nature of considerable sophistication, refinement and capacity for development; and you too have this potential just waiting to be released. Your "inner sanctity" plays its part constantly in guiding and urging you to do what you know to be right for yourself, your loved ones, and even for those you care very little about.

In developing your awareness of this inner life, you soon learn of the inherent error of relying exclusively on your objective senses and thought processes when coming to decisions that have an important impact on your life. There is a different, more refined, sophisticated and accurate method of getting precisely the answers you want, when you want; and the Rosicrucian Order assists people through its system of weekly home study lessons, how to accomplish this.

On a purely practical level, the study and application of mystical techniques lead to the development of a more mature and integrated personality, greater success in your daily activities, and a growing feeling of happiness and peace in your personal life. Although the benefits of being a Rosicrucian are also of a deeper and more transcendental nature, if peace and happiness were the only things that entered your life in abundance, would it not still be worth your while pursuing such a path?

The Rosicrucian techniques of self-development include specific and highly effective methods of concentration, visualisation, contemplation and meditation, to mention but a few; and a proper study and application of these techniques can provide you with exceedingly powerful tools to help you shape your life at all levels, whether physical, mental, psychic or spiritual.

If you are seeking a new path in life, or simply wish to know more about your options, why not investigate further. Contact us, requesting our free introductory booklet entitled *The Mastery of Life*. In it, you will get a better idea of who we are, where we come from and what you can gain by allowing the Rosicrucian Order to assist you in creating your own customised path of inner development.

Other Books by Raymund Andrea

Raymund Andrea wrote extensively for over 50 years. Here is a selection of other titles by this author available through *The Rosicrucian Collection*.

The Technique of the Master

The Technique of the Disciple

The Disciple and Shamballa

Discipleship on Trial

The Mystic Way

The Way of the Heart

Six Eminent Mystics

Other Books from The Rosicrucian Collection

Rosicrucian History and Mysteries
by Christian Rebisse

For centuries, mystery has surrounded the brief flowering of religious tolerance and intellectual achievement that the early 17th Century Rosicrucians ushered in with the publication of three manifestos between 1614 and 1616: the *Fama Fraternitatis* (Fame of the Fraternity), the *Confessio Fraternitatis* (Confession of the Fraternity) and the *Chymical Wedding of Christian Rosenkreuz*.

Leading lights in the academic and religious worlds of 1614 were shaken to the core, and some were deeply moved to action by these publications which appeared at yearly intervals and which in due course led to far reaching changes throughout Europe, and later in the New World of the Americas.

Having been branded for centuries as a secret society of occultists, witches and wizards by uninformed and jealous people, the Rosicrucian Order is one of the most enigmatic and yet most open of the handful of true initiatic Orders still in existence. By retracing its mysterious origins, this book attempts to place the Rosicrucian stream of intellectual and spiritual philosophy in an historical context by outlining the most important people and events that led to the genesis of the Western branch of esoteric spirituality and ultimately led to the establishment of the Rosicrucian Order itself.

Numerous movements which have sprung directly or indirectly from the Rosicrucian tradition are detailed, and a particular place of pre-eminence is given at the end of this book to the most important modern-day torchbearer of Rosicrucian thought and practice, the Ancient and Mystical Order Rosae Crucis.

Besides the meticulously researched historical facts, this richly illustrated work invites us to discover the "way" or "path" that past and present Rosicrucians have attempted, and continue to attempt, to discover every day. That path is like an inner thread leading people on to a realisation of the great natural sanctity which lies dormant within all human beings, and which has the huge potential of bringing all nations together in permanent peace.

For anyone interested in the broader aspects of the Western esoteric movement, and who seek a path of discovery to their own innate spirituality, this book is a good place to start.

Other Books from The Rosicrucian Collection

Practical Mysticism
by Edward Lee

To many, the word *Mysticism* conjures up images of dangerous occult practices, weird rituals and unsavoury characters. But nothing could be further from the truth; for mysticism lies at the very heart of all major religions and is the driving force behind mankind's eternal quest for transcendent meaning to some of the greatest questions of all time: What are we? Why are we here? Is there a "higher purpose" to our lives? Have we lived before and will we live again?

In *Practical Mysticism*, author Edward Lee presents a frequently asked questions primer specifically on the *practical* issues relating to mysticism, and discusses many searching issues. In his capacity as an official representative of the Rosicrucian Order AMORC for over thirty years, the author has addressed these topics many times and often in the context of fiercely competing world views.

Among the many pertinent subjects covered are reincarnation, karma, the role of freedom in our lives, how (and how *not*) to give advice to others, how to set a good example for others to follow, how to solve daily problems, how to effectively concentrate, how to visualise whatever you want, and how to meditate whenever you choose, rather than having to wait for the "right mood," and how to make a success of anything you set your hand to.

In these chapters you will find sane, practical advice on how to lead not the life of a dreamer but the life of a practical, modern, competent person who has the added advantage of being an aspiring mystic as well. This is a valuable "how-to" guide for applying mystical principles in improving your life. *Practical Mysticism* has universal appeal because, as the author points out, during his many years of answering correspondence about Rosicrucian teachings he came to realise that his answers and comments were relevant not only to students of mysticism, but to everyone seeking to better their lives.

ABOUT THE AUTHOR

Edward Lee is a long time Rosicrucian who for many years served the Rosicrucian Order AMORC in the field of mystical instruction and research. Although now retired, he has continued as a Rose-Croix University instructor, delivering seminars on topics related to mysticism. A graduate of the American Academy of Dramatic Arts in New York, the author has also worked as a professional actor and radio announcer for many years.

Other Books from The Rosicrucian Collection

Self Mastery | and Fate
with the Cycles of Life

by H Spencer Lewis

In the hustle and bustle of modern life, wouldn't it really be something if we could always be in the right place at the right time, always have that slight edge that makes the difference between success and failure?

This book provides just such a guide. Simple, easy to understand, and based on an ancient system of periodicity and natural laws, the *System of 7* explained in this book is built upon self evident truths that can easily be demonstrated for yourself. Far from pandering to some unmoveable "fate," as many divinatory systems do, this system supports our privilege to choose and decide on everything for ourselves. Free will is the central thread running through this seminal work.

By understanding the qualities associated with the binary and septenary periods of the cycles explained by the author, you will soon be planning and tracking according to the *System of 7*, every day, week, month and year, thereby allowing you to take charge and gain control of your personal happiness, health and prosperity. The cycles include:

- Personal and business periods.
- Health and disease periods.
- Daily fortunate periods.
- Inner soul character.
- Business opportunities.
- Special fitness for success.

These cycles are not based on astrology, fortune telling or any other form of divination. And you don't need mathematics or complicated charts to put them to good use. Once you have become familiar with the system and have learnt to apply it in a practical, useful manner in your personal life, you will escape the overrated clutches of so called "fate" and develop a mastery of all the affairs of your life.

ABOUT THE AUTHOR

Dr H Spencer Lewis wrote several books including *The Mystical Life of Jesus*, *The Secret Doctrines of Jesus*, *Mansions of the Soul*, *Mental Poisoning* and others. Up to his death in 1939, he served as Imperator of the Rosicrucian Order AMORC. For decades, students of mysticism and philosophy have been fascinated by his timeless writings. His simple, straighforward style reveals a keen insight into the age-old mysteries of life.

Other Books from The Rosicrucian Collection

The Rosicrucian Manifestos
Edited by Paul Goodall

At the start of the 17th Century, the reign of Elizabeth I was coming to an end. England was a prosperous nation and the leading lights of literature, science and the arts were making their marks on society. Francis Bacon, Robert Fludd, John Dee and William Shakespeare are but a few from this latter part of the Renaissance period. In Europe too, notably in the German speaking Protestant states, hopes for a new age of enlightenment were high. Into this milieu of hope and expectation arose three unique manifestos, the *Fama Fraternitatis* (1614), the *Confessio Fraternitatis* (1615) and the *Chymical Wedding* (1616), causing great interest in academic and literary circles and deep consternation amongst the Catholic clergy. They all espoused in their individually unique way one dynamic message, and that was the need for a universal reformation of ideas and outlook embracing the arts and sciences, but particularly religion.

Unfortunately, the hoped for universal reformation that was to bring about a utopian society did not materialise in the early 17th century despite the attention that the Manifestos received. But the spirit of the Rosicrucian Order lived on, simmering as an undercurrent while the forces of the later Enlightenment and religious authority battled it out. As the 19th turned into the 20th century, a new wave of interest in esotericism had been gaining momentum and the Rosicrucian Order publicly opened up its membership once again.

In 2001, the Rosicrucian Order AMORC, concerned about world events, produced a fourth manifesto, the *Positio Fraternitatis Rosae Crucis* which addresses the critical issues of the modern world. At its heart is a cry for a spiritual re-awakening of mankind. With Love at its centre, it is anticipated that this Rosicrucian utopia will have far reaching effects impinging on every aspect of human existence for the general amelioration of mankind.

ABOUT THE EDITOR

Paul Goodall is a long standing Rosicrucian who for many years has served the Rosicrucian Order AMORC. As the author of many informative articles relating to Rosicrucianism and Hermetic studies, he has edited and produced several books, and is currently co-editor of the Rosicrucian Beacon magazine and editor of the Rosicrucian Heritage of West Africa. Paul is married and lives in Portadown, Northern Ireland.